Encyclopedia
of South Africa

Editorial Advisory Board

R. Hunt Davis Jr.
University of Florida

Sandra Klopper
Stellenbosch University

Peter Limb
Michigan State University

Zine Magubane
Boston College

Dominique Malaquais
Centre d'Etudes des Mondes Africains and
Centre National de la Recherche Scientifique

Shula Marks
School of Oriental and African Studies,
University of London

N. Barney Pityana
College of the Transfiguration

Encyclopedia of South Africa

EDITED BY
KRISTA JOHNSON
SEAN JACOBS

LYNNE
RIENNER
PUBLISHERS

BOULDER
LONDON

Published in the United States of America in 2011 by
Lynne Rienner Publishers, Inc.
1800 30th Street, Boulder, Colorado 80301
www.rienner.com

and in the United Kingdom by
Lynne Rienner Publishers, Inc.
3 Henrietta Street, Covent Garden, London WC2E 8LU

© 2011 by Lynne Rienner Publishers, Inc. All rights reserved

Library of Congress Cataloging-in-Publication Data
Encyclopedia of South Africa / Krista Johnson and Sean Jacobs, editors.
    p. cm.
  Includes bibliographical references and index.
  ISBN 978-1-58826-749-8 (hardcover : alk. paper)
  1. South Africa—Encyclopedias. I. Johnson, Krista. II. Jacobs, Sean.
  DT1714.E53 2011
  968.003—dc22
                                      2011020125

British Cataloguing in Publication Data
A Cataloguing in Publication record for this book
is available from the British Library.

Printed and bound in the United States of America

The paper used in this publication meets the requirements
of the American National Standard for Permanence of
Paper for Printed Library Materials Z39.48-1992.

5 4 3 2 1

Contents

Preface		vii
Map of South Africa		viii

Encyclopedia of South Africa 1

Appendix 1	Chronology	325
Appendix 2	Heads of State Since 1910	331
Appendix 3	Government Structures	333
Appendix 4	Provinces and Major Cities	335
Appendix 5	Political Parties in the April 2009 National Elections	337
Appendix 6	Key Racial and Apartheid Legislation, 1856–1967	339

List of Acronyms	343
The Contributors	345
Index	349
About the Book	373

PREFACE

The *Encyclopedia of South Africa*—the result of a long-term collaboration among an international group of scholars—was designed to broadly cover South Africa's history, government and politics, law, society and culture, economy, infrastructure, demography, environment, and more, from the era of human origins to the present.

To be as comprehensive as possible, we have interspersed the substantive entries with numerous "blind entries" that reflect variations of a word or phrase for which the user might be searching (such as acronyms and alternate spellings). Entries also include extensive cross-references to other entries, and bibliographies point to sources for further research. The comprehensive index offers access to the information at the most detailed level.

* * *

A note on terminology: Terminology referring to racial classifications in South Africa has fluctuated over time. The Population Registration Act of 1950 specified "Whites," "Coloureds" (mixed race), "Blacks" (also referred to as "Natives," "Africans," and "Bantu"), and later, "Asians," the latter applying primarily to those from the Indian subcontinent (see Appendix 6). With the advent of the Black Consciousness Movement in the 1960s, "black" became a politically correct label uniting all people of color in South Africa. But that usage of "black" has been challenged—applied by some only to native Africans and by others to the larger category of all "nonwhites."

"Coloured" is still used, but the trend is toward no longer capitalizing the word. Throughout this encyclopedia, we have adopted the South African usage of "coloured." (For more on the issue, see the entry "Coloured People.")

* * *

We would like to thank those who helped to make this encyclopedia possible. The members of the Advisory Board gave invaluable help. We are particularly grateful to them and to the contributors for their careful work. Our efforts were greatly aided by Jau-Yon Chen and Adam Esrig. Krista Johnson would like to acknowledge the support of Howard University through a New Faculty Grant awarded in 2009. We also wish to thank Lynne Rienner and Shena Redmond at Lynne Rienner Publishers for seeing this project through to completion.

—*Krista Johnson*
Sean Jacobs

South Africa

Abdurahman, Abdullah (1872–1940)

Abdullah Abdurahman, a politician and a physician, was born in the town of Wellington into a relatively affluent CAPE MALAY family. He received his medical training in Glasgow, Scotland, qualifying as a doctor in 1893, but received his early education in Wellington and then in CAPE TOWN where he set up his medical practice upon returning to South Africa.

In 1904, Abdurahman was elected Cape Town's first COLOURED city councilor, and he remained a councilor almost without interruption until his death. He worked to improve the conditions of the coloured community, especially within the field of education, and helped set up the first secondary schools for coloured children in Cape Town. But much of his political work was directed through the African Political Organization (APO), of which he was elected president in 1905. The APO's goal was to fight the increasing racial oppression in the country, initially only on behalf of non-African coloureds. Before the creation of the UNION OF SOUTH AFRICA in 1910, Abdurahman unsuccessfully led two delegations to London to secure franchise rights for coloureds. (In the Union of South Africa, coloured males in the Cape Province who met certain income, property, and education standards were granted the right to vote.) Later, between 1927 and 1934, Abdurahman and the APO started working more closely with black African political leaders in an attempt to create a united front. However, little came of this, and some contemporary commentators regard the APO's position as being too accommodating to the white authorities. By the late 1930s, other political parties, such as the more radical National Liberation League, had surpassed the APO in prominence, leaving Abdurahman and his party with a mixed political legacy. Nonetheless, Abdurahman was clearly a powerful politician and popular among the non-European community.

Achmat, Abdurazzack (Zackie) (1962–)

Founder and president of the AIDS activist group the TREATMENT ACTION CAMPAIGN, Abdurazzack (Zackie) Achmat was a child activist in his native CAPE TOWN (he was arrested numerous times between 1976 and 1980) and a gay rights activist in JOHANNESBURG in the late 1980s and the early 1990s. Raised in a Muslim COLOURED family, Achmat studied at the University of the Western Cape where he received his bachelor's degree in English in 1993. He is a member of the AFRICAN NATIONAL CONGRESS but has publicly clashed with the political party's hierarchy, particularly with former South African president THABO MBEKI, over the government's AIDS policies. Openly gay and HIV-positive, Achmat helped found the National Coalition for Gay and Lesbian Equality in 1994 and advocated for laws and policies forbidding discrimination based on sexual orientation in the postapartheid dispensation. In 1998, he helped found the Treatment Action Campaign, initially aimed at advocating for affordable and accessible antiretroviral drugs (ARV) for people living with AIDS. He himself has succumbed to numerous AIDS-related illnesses and must take ARV drugs. In January 2008, he married his partner Dallie Weyers (South Africa legalized gay marriage in December 2006). Achmat was nominated for the Nobel Peace Prize in 2004.

See also TREATMENT ACTION CAMPAIGN

Act of Union
See SOUTH AFRICA ACT

Adams College
Adams College was a mission school established by US missionary Dr. Newton Adams in 1853 in present-day KwaZulu-Natal Province. It is the second oldest school, after Lovedale, established to educate black South Africans. Originally named Amanzimtoti Insitute, this school inspired many Africans to attain higher levels of education and boasts many famous alumni, including Chief ALBERT LUTHULI, Chief MANGOSUTHU BUTHELEZI, and Dr. Nkosasana Zuma. Like so many great schools during the APARTHEID era, Adams College suffered the impact of racism and segregation but has experienced a revival in the postapartheid era. With the passage of the BANTU EDUCATION Act in 1953, the college was renamed the Amanzimtoti Zulu Training School but was named Adams College again with the demise of apartheid. Z. K. MATTHEWS became the first black head of the school in 1925, and prominent political leaders including Luthuli and GOVAN MBEKI were teachers at the college for a period of time. The school continues to operate today.

Affirmative Action
Also referred to as "employment equity," named for the Employment Equity Act passed in 1998, affirmative action is integrally connected with the government's broader policy of BLACK ECONOMIC EMPOWERMENT (BEE). Against a background of racial disparities in skilled jobs inherited from APARTHEID, the law is designed to ensure that designated groups defined as black people (meaning Africans, COLOUREDS, and INDIANS), women, and people with disabilities have equal opportunities for employment. The policy has been vigorously applied in the public sector, though less vigorously by private businesses. Businesses with more than fifty employees and with an annual turnover defined in the Employment Equity Act are subject to the legislation. The law requires that employers draw up an equity plan, achieve certain quotas and specific outcomes, and submit reports to the Department of Labor. Critics of affirmative action argue that it has benefited a small group of well-connected black businesspeople and has excluded coloureds and Indians among its beneficiaries. White critics claim it amounts to "reverse racism." In turn, proponents of affirmative action argue that forty years of apartheid rule can be considered de facto affirmative action for whites and that the postapartheid government has an obligation to redress some of the past imbalances.

See also BLACK ECONOMIC EMPOWERMENT

African National Congress
In the years following the 1994 democratic transition, the African National Congress (ANC) has dominated South African politics. The legitimacy and popularity of the movement has its more immediate origins in securing black majority rule in 1994, but its deeper genesis lies in the ANC's long history of resistance to white rule, both legally until 1960 and underground and in exile until 1990.

The Formative Years (1912–1940)
The ANC was founded in 1912 as the South African Native National Congress (it became the ANC in 1923) at a convention in BLOEMFONTEIN called by Pixley Seme, a political activist, lawyer, and journalist who had been educated in Britain and the United States. The formation of the ANC was prompted by the 1909 SOUTH AFRICA ACT of Union that largely excluded blacks from political franchise. (In the Cape, some African and COLOURED males could vote as part of a qualified franchise.) Provincial congresses had emerged over the previous decade, and, in 1912, these were united under the leadership of JOHN DUBE (president) and SOLOMON PLAATJE (secretary). Founder Seme, who was partly influenced by his studies in the United States at Columbia University where he gained some appreciation of the US structures of government, notably Congress, emphasized national unity over ethnic-regional divisions, and this remained a central policy.

The period of ANC formation saw diverse ideological currents among Africans: from Christianity, British empire loyalism, and liberalism to nascent AFRICAN NATIONALISM; the ANC did not adopt the latter until the 1940s, but its influence gradually spread. The nature of power in a white settler society created a deeply ambiguous context in which African political culture developed. ANC leaders were largely drawn from the mission-educated, Christianized black elite. However, given the nature of settler rule, this was a powerless elite, and the ANC had to seek support from a wide range of social strata.

The early ANC had a checkered history. In its first decade, it was clearly the major African political organization, submitting petitions against the NATIVES' LAND ACT OF 1913 and other discriminatory legislation, with Plaatje as an eloquent publicist, and sending delegations to Britain in a vain but principled appeal for intervention. From 1918 to 1920, the Transvaal branch supported mass worker and anti–PASS LAWS demonstrations. This radicalism came to an end in the 1920s when the ANC was eclipsed by the populist INDUSTRIAL AND COMMERCIAL WORKERS UNION (ICU), while ANC members diverted energy into the liberal Joint Councils, largely white-initiated and -dominated groups supportive of interracial cooperation. Another short period of ANC radicalism under President J. T. Gumede ended in 1930 when Seme assumed the presidency, ushering in a period of profound stagnation.

At the provincial level, ANC politics were complex. While most members were urban based, a House of Chiefs was modeled on the British House of Lords, and ethnic politics were not entirely absent. In Natal, A. W. G. CHAMPION forged ties between the ICU and ANC, but the ANC in Natal was split. There also were rival branches in the Cape Province, with Western Cape ANC president James Thaele espousing radical GARVEYISM and James Calata in the Eastern Cape pursuing a moderate path. Nationally, the ANC remained weak and lacked strong media outlets. The Transvaal ANC's organ, *Abantu-Batho*, became the national medium but was defunct by the early 1930s, and the ANC never developed a strong, permanent newspaper.

In its first three decades, the ANC remained small, with limited mass appeal. Provincial structures were loosely structured and poorly financed. Estimates of nationwide membership vary from 1,000 to 4,000 in the interwar years, though an interlocking of membership with grassroots, community-based Advisory and Vigilance associations gave it wider, indirect support. Nevertheless, the ANC lacked a mass membership. Leaders were overwhelmingly male and middle class, and women lacked full membership rights before 1943. Yet, some activists remained deeply concerned at the harsh conditions of most Africans, while the Bantu Women's League (founded in 1918, which in 1948 became the ANC Women's League) under Charlotte Maxeke worked with some ANC leaders, though it did not affiliate with the ANC until 1931.

In the mid-1930s, African politics were reignited by the discriminatory J. B. M. HERTZOG Bills. By the end of the decade, the ANC began to reorganize under Secretary Calata. In December 1940, the ANC elected A. B. Xuma as president. In addition to espousing African nationalist and liberal philosophies, Xuma oversaw the ANC's steady growth to a more centralized, financially viable body. Membership grew from 1,000 in the 1930s to

5,500 by 1947. Xuma's reforms included abolition of the elitist Upper House and equality for women, confirmed in a new 1943 ANC constitution and the 1948 formation of the AFRICAN NATIONAL CONGRESS WOMEN'S LEAGUE. Xuma led a committee that coauthored *Africans' Claims in South Africa* (1943), calling for African self-determination. He forged an alliance with the SOUTH AFRICAN INDIAN CONGRESS, and ties with African labor unions were strengthened by the work of ANC communists such as J. B. Marks and Moses Kotane.

Years of Growth and Protest (1940–1960)

The growth of African nationalism was seen in the 1944 formation by ANTON LEMBEDE, WALTER SISULU, NELSON MANDELA, and OLIVER TAMBO of the AFRICAN NATIONAL CONGRESS YOUTH LEAGUE, which undermined Xuma's moderate position after the NATIONAL PARTY's victory in the 1948 elections, and its brutal promotion of APARTHEID pushed the ANC to adopt in 1949 a radical Program of Action endorsing direct action by boycotts and strikes.

The DEFIANCE CAMPAIGNS of the 1950s saw the ANC develop into a mass movement; the 1952 protests boosted numbers from 20,000 to 100,000. Now, its constituency was truly national with great strength among urban workers, as in PORT ELIZABETH. The ANC supported campaigns against forced removals of blacks from areas designated for whites and BANTU EDUCATION, if ineffectively. Mandela emerged as the powerhouse behind the campaigns, and, with African liberation on the continent imminent, the ANC was buoyed, posing a real challenge to PRETORIA, which intensified repression. The ANC fought back by forging the Congress Alliance with INDIAN, coloured, and white progressives and, in 1955, by hosting the Congress of the People that adopted the FREEDOM CHARTER to embody aspirations of all South Africans; it became a central ANC policy document. These wider alliances prompted a 1959 split spawning the PAN AFRICANIST CONGRESS. The state continued to harass ANC leaders, many of whom were on trial from 1956 to 1961 in the TREASON TRIAL.

For much of the 1950s, ALBERT LUTHULI was the ANC president. The first African awarded the Nobel Peace Prize, he remained a committed Christian and a firm proponent of the African nationalist and liberal ideas of an ANC that emphasized majority rule by constitutional means. This peaceful avenue, however, was closed when the government banned the ANC in 1960, leading it to resort to armed struggle and exile.

Exile Years (1960–1990)

After the ANC's outlawing in 1960, Mandela and communist leader JOE SLOVO founded Umkhonto we Sizwe (translated as Spear of the Nation and also referred to as MK), the people's army. MK was an integral part of the liberation movement led by the ANC but technically separate due to risk of repression. Following the arrest of much of the ANC leadership and their banishment after the RIVONIA TRIAL to ROBBEN ISLAND, the focus of ANC's work shifted to exile. This does not mean it ceased to have influence inside South Africa—on Robben Island, Mandela, GOVAN MBEKI, and other ANC leaders educated a new generation of freedom fighters from the 1976 SOWETO STUDENT UPRISING who were sent to the island, and underground structures persisted—but the ANC was now illegal, as its machine was smashed. The vacuum in black politics was filled in the late 1960s and 1970s by the BLACK CONSCIOUSNESS MOVEMENT and labor unions, and in the 1980s by the UNITED DEMOCRATIC FRONT (UDF), which aligned with the ANC.

MK continued to operate, now from exile. Sabotage of the early 1960s directed primarily against apartheid military sites and strategic economic and energy positions developed into wider military campaigns from forward bases in the FRONTLINE STATES. In 1982, the ANC was pressured to leave Mozambique, which had been a main base of operations for them, but MK continued to implement effective special operations, notably symbolic attacks on the headquarters of Pretoria's army and the Sasol oil refinery. The ANC, however, continued to view armed struggle as only one pillar of a strategy that also included politics and international solidarity.

Tambo became the chief leader in exile as the ANC constructed important bases in the Frontline States, notably Tanzania and Zambia, and in

Mozambique after 1975. A major ANC office was located in Britain, which hosted a significant number of exiles. The ANC launched a major diplomatic initiative by opening offices from India and the United States to the Pacific. Many leaders were prominent in diplomatic and solidarity work. In the 1960s, important foundation work was done by Tambo and Robert Resha, with ANC publications such as *Sechaba* founded to unite and educate widely dispersed members. Others active in exile included Johnny Makatini in New York, ANC India chief representative Mendi Msimang, Edwin Funde in Australasia, writer ALEX LA GUMA in Cuba, Alfred Nzo, Ruth Mompati, and FRENE NOSHIR GINWALA.

In Tanzania, the ANC's Solomon Mahlangu Freedom College educated the 1976 SOWETO STUDENT UPRISING youth streaming out of South Africa. The ANC in exile worked closely with the South African Congress of Trade Unions and recreated its military, women's, youth, and religious structures through the work of people such as Slovo, Andrew Masondo, Mavis Nhlapo, Gertrude Shope, and Father Michael Lapsley. After the ANC's 1969 Morogoro Conference, whites were permitted to join the ANC, with Slovo serving on its Revolutionary Council and other progressive whites, including Jack Simons, Ray Alexander, and Albie Sachs, prominent in exile structures.

Exile was a lonely, isolating experience, accompanied by assassinations orchestrated by Pretoria (Joe Gqabi in Harare and Dulcie September in Paris) and occasional dissent, as in MK camps in Angola. The ANC sought to overcome the alienation of exile by creating cultural formations such as the musical troupe Amandla! By the mid-1980s, the ANC's diplomatic strategy was working, with sectors of white South African society willing to negotiate and more countries recognizing the ANC as a legitimate representative of the South African people rather than Pretoria. The ANC had become a government-in-waiting.

Transformation and Rule (1990–)

With financial sanctions biting, the Cold War over, and intense internal opposition, the apartheid regime unbanned the ANC and released Mandela in February of 1990. The ANC quickly and effectively reestablished its structures inside the country, successfully navigating a complex and dangerous transition period fraught with political violence from the state and from political rivals such as INKATHA FREEDOM PARTY (IFP), as seen in the 1992 Boipatong Massacre, for instance, where IFP members attacked the resident of an informal settlement south of Johannesburg, killing forty-five people. Eager to open up space for negotiations, the ANC suspended armed struggles in mid-1990, encouraged lifting of sports sanctions banning South African athletes and sports teams from competing in international competitions, and entered negotiations in 1991. In CONVENTION FOR A DEMOCRATIC SOUTH AFRICA (CODESA) negotiations, the ANC succeeded in gaining agreement for democratic elections, which it won convincingly in 1994 (receiving 62.6 percent of the vote) and again in 1999, 2004, and 2009—so much so that commentators were worried that the ANC's transition from a liberation movement to a more conventional political party had been accompanied by shift to a "one-party dominant party" situation. This electoral dominance was underlined when the ANC later won provincial elections in KwaZulu-Natal and the Western Cape, taking over seats previously held by other parties. The ANC's return from exile also saw tensions with ex-UDF forces over the level of democratic inner-party practices.

The Mandela administration (1994–1999) achieved impressive advances in reconciliation, housing, electrification of black townships, and economic stability. Mandela endorsed the TRUTH AND RECONCILIATION COMMISSION, formed in 1995, as a way to heal a nation divided under apartheid. Yet, while apartheid was dead, elements of its socioeconomic legacy persisted to limit the impact of ANC policies. Government sought first to boost domestic accumulation and social equality in the RECONSTRUCTION AND DEVELOPMENT PROGRAM but, in 1997, jettisoned its prosocialist policies to introduce the capital-friendly GROWTH, EMPLOYMENT, AND REDISTRIBUTION STRATEGY.

THABO MBEKI's administration (1999–2008) continued Mandela's economic policies but also failed to solve high black unemployment and inequality. Mbeki adopted a controversial and widely derided position on HIV/AIDS, avoiding proven medical treatment. Like Mandela, Mbeki played an active role in African affairs, including conflict resolution. He encouraged black pride through the concept of AFRICAN RENAISSANCE and African economic empowerment through New Partnership for African Development, returning the ANC to a strongly African nationalist ideology, underlining that the ANC's abandonment of most of its radical programs echoed processes in other postcolonial African countries. The ANC Youth League and the ANC Women's League remain important constituents, while the alliance with the CONGRESS OF SOUTH AFRICAN TRADE UNIONS and the SOUTH AFRICAN COMMUNIST PARTY persists despite recent serious tensions over economic policy and internal democracy.

By 2006, rising labor and internal ANC dissatisfaction with Mbeki's overly centralized rule widened deep fissures, resulting in Mbeki's replacement by the controversial JACOB ZUMA as ANC President in 2007, and then by Kgalema Motlanthe as state president in September 2008. A breakaway Congress of the People (COPE) party later that year was the first major ANC split since 1959. In 2009 elections, COPE had difficulty establishing a separate platform, receiving only 7.4 percent of the vote, and while the ANC's majority weakened nationwide from 69.69 percent to 65.9 percent, it increased in KwaZulu-Natal. In municipal elections in May 2011, the ANC slipped to 61 percent, with COPE falling to only 2.1 percent, and with some areas reporting higher abstention rates. Zuma's assumption of the state presidency from May 2009 has not seen major policy changes. The government continues to struggle to find solutions to massive deindustrialization and unemployment—the economy revived only partially by staging the 2010 soccer World Cup—as well as rising xenophobia and dissatisfaction over the slow pace of land reform.

Notwithstanding these problems, the ANC remains Africa's oldest nationalist body with outstanding achievements, not least of which are the ending of apartheid, establishment of democracy, and the winning of three consecutive elections.

See also ARMED STRUGGLE; DEMOCRATIC POLITICS SINCE 1994; FREEDOM CHARTER; GOVERNMENT STRUCTURES; NELSON MANDELA; THABO MBEKI; SOL PLAATJE; OLIVER TAMBO; JACOB ZUMA

Bibliography
Benson, Mary. *The African Patriots: The Story of the African National Congress of South Africa.* London: Faber, 1963.
Dubow, Saul. *The African National Congress.* Stroud, UK: Sutton, 2000.
Gumede, William Mervin. *Thabo Mbeki and the Battle for the Soul of the ANC.* Cape Town, South Africa: Zebra Press, 2005.
Holland, Heidi. *The Struggle: A History of the African National Congress.* New York: Braziller, 1990.
Johns, Sheridan, and R. Hunt Davis, Jr., eds. *Mandela, Tambo and the ANC: The Struggle Against Apartheid.* New York: Oxford University Press, 1991.
Karis, Thomas, Gwendolen Carter, and Gail Gerhart. *From Protest to Challenge: A Documentary History of African Politics in South Africa.* 6 vols. Stanford, CA: Hoover Institution Press, 1972–1977; Bloomington: Indiana University Press, 1997, 2010.
Lodge, Tom. *Black Politics in South Africa Since 1945.* Johannesburg, South Africa: Ravan, 1983.
Mandela, Nelson. *Long Walk to Freedom: The Autobiography of Nelson Mandela.* Boston: Little, Brown, 1994.
McKinley, Dale T. *The ANC and the Liberation Struggle: A Critical Political Biography.* Chicago: Pluto Press, 1997.
Meli, Francis. *A History of the ANC: South Africa Belongs to Us.* Bloomington: Indiana University Press, 1989.
Odendaal, André. *Vukani Bantu! The Beginning of Black Protest Politics in South Africa to 1912.* Cape Town, South Africa: David Philip, 1984.
Rantete, Johannes. *The African National Congress and the Negotiated Settlement in South Africa.* Pretoria, South Africa: Van Schaik, 1998.
Suttner, Raymond, and Jeremy Cronin. *30 Years of the Freedom Charter.* Johannesburg, South Africa: Ravan Press, 1986.
Walshe, Peter. *The Rise of African Nationalism in South Africa: The African National Congress, 1912–1952.* Berkeley: University of California Press, 1971.

—*Peter Limb*

African National Congress Women's League

Five years after women were admitted to the AFRICAN NATIONAL CONGRESS (ANC), they established a branch in 1948. The African National Congress Women's League's major campaigns were the 1952 DEFIANCE CAMPAIGN and a mass women's march in conjunction with other women's groups in Pretoria on August 9, 1956, protesting government repression (celebrated as Women's Day in South Africa after APARTHEID). After 1994, it declined in influence. Some of its prominent members and leaders include LILLIAN NGOYI (the first woman elected to the ANC's National Executive Committee in 1956), ALBERTINA SISULU, and WINNIE MANDELA.

See also AFRICAN NATIONAL CONGRESS; WINNIE MANDELA; LILLIAN NGOYI

African National Congress Youth League

The African National Congress Youth League (ANCYL) was founded in 1944 by ANTON LEMBEDE, Ashby Peter Mda, NELSON MANDELA, WALTER SISULU, and OLIVER TAMBO as the youth wing of the AFRICAN NATIONAL CONGRESS. It marked the rise of a new generation of leadership of South Africa's African population that was more radical and confrontational than its predecessors.

The ANCYL developed its own manifesto in 1944, and its Program of Action was adopted by the ANC in 1949, signaling the Youth League's increasing control over the entire organization. This was in part due to the leadership of Mandela, who was elected national secretary of the Youth League in 1948. A year later, he and other founding members of the ANCYL were elected to the National Executive Committee of the ANC. The Youth League mobilized mass protests and called for civil disobedience and strikes against racial discrimination and the newly implemented APARTHEID system. It was under the leadership of many Youth League founders that the ANC launched DEFIANCE CAMPAIGNS in the 1950s, invigorating the ANC and expanding the movement dramatically.

In 1959, many ANCYL members broke away to form the rival PAN AFRICANIST CONGRESS. After 1960, when many of the liberation movements were banned by the government, the Youth League continued its activities underground during the remainder of the apartheid years. In 1990, President F. W. DE KLERK legalized the ANC and its associated organizations including the Youth League. After many years in exile, the ANCYL was rebuilt inside South Africa with the main objective of mobilizing all sectors of youth into active participation in the struggle to secure democracy.

See also AFRICAN NATIONAL CONGRESS; APARTHEID; ANTON LEMBEDE; NELSON MANDELA; WALTER SISULU; OLIVER TAMBO

African Nationalism

See POLITICAL CULTURES AND IDEOLOGIES

African Renaissance

THABO MBEKI, president of South Africa from 1999 to 2008, popularized the idea of an African Renaissance after South Africa's democratic ELECTIONS in 1994. This concept calls on African people and nations to be the key drivers of change and development on the African continent as opposed to having Western nations set and push the agenda. Key elements of the African Renaissance include social cohesion, democracy, economic rebuilding and growth, and the establishment of Africa as a significant player in geopolitical affairs. Although this term's popularity has waned in the past decade, it continues to be a significant part of the South African intellectual agenda after APARTHEID.

Among other things, the African Renaissance is a philosophical and political movement aimed at ending the violence, elitism, corruption, and poverty that plague the African continent and replacing them with a more just and equitable order. Thus, the African Renaissance agenda encourages education and the reversal of the "brain drain" of African intellectuals, and urges Africans to take pride in their heritage as well as to take charge of their lives.

Undergirded by a pan-Africanist ideology, the goals of the African Renaissance have been taken up by a new generation of African leaders, including President Yoweri Museveni of Uganda and President Paul Kagame of Rwanda. Together with President Mbeki, as well as other African leaders, they have sought to transform the African Renaissance vision into a practical reality through such projects as the creation of the AFRICAN UNION (that replaced the old and relatively ineffective Organization of African Unity), the New Partnership for African Development, and the Millennium Africa Programme that seek to define a new relationship between Africa and the West based on partnership and on Africans taking ownership and responsibility for the continent's economic development.

The African Renaissance has also drawn criticism from some circles, as some see the concept as utopian and impractical given the prevalence of conflict and war in many parts of Africa. Others suggest that it is a South African project aimed at spreading the country's dominance throughout the continent. The project has also been accused of conforming to the dictates of neoliberal globalization and thus promoting the interests of the West over those of Africa.

African Union

Established in 2001, the African Union (AU) is a continental organization composed of fifty-three African member countries, covering the entire continent except for Morocco (which opposes the membership of Western Sahara in the AU). It succeeds the amalgamated African Economic Community and the Organization of African Unity and has the expressed goal of uniting and integrating the African continent. Eventually, the AU aims to have a single currency (the Afro) and a single integrated defense force, as well as other institutions of state, including a cabinet for the AU heads of state. Inspired by the vision of an AFRICAN RENAISSANCE, the AU works to secure democracy, human rights, and sustainable economic development for the continent. South Africa played a founding role in the AU, and South African president THABO MBEKI was the organization's first president.

Afrikaner(s)

Afrikaner is both a self-identity (equal to an ethnic identity) as well as a political identity among a significant portion of South Africa's white population forged in the nineteenth and twentieth centuries. The identity became synonymous with the policy of APARTHEID, the South African state, and the NATIONAL PARTY. The term *Afrikaners* was first used in the early eighteenth century to refer to whites of a variety of European heritages. However, it was not until the mid-twentieth century that it was used exclusively to refer to white Afrikaans speakers (a significant proportion of COLOURED PEOPLE and a smaller group of black South Africans also speak Afrikaans). By the early twentieth century, there were significant economic and social differences among Afrikaans speakers. In recent decades, the link between an Afrikaner nationalist identity, regime, and state, which characterized the years of apartheid government as well as sustained a balance of ethnic, racial, and class forces, has fractured.

The group identity of Afrikaners has fluctuated considerably over time but was most coherent during the apartheid era when an organizational axis of the state and the National Party offered systematic access to the ear, agency, and largesse of the government. Indeed, with the onset of democratic, majority rule in 1994, many suggested a bleak future for Afrikanerdom under an AFRICAN NATIONAL CONGRESS (ANC) government perceived to be broadly opposed to Afrikaner interests. In spite of the recent and marked increase in white poverty levels, it is evident that the Afrikaner minority still retains a substantial material and cultural inheritance accrued during the apartheid era. While some Afrikaners feel increasingly marginalized in this new order, others are thriving in the new South Africa.

Racial hierarchies were present from the foundation of the Dutch CAPE COLONY in the seventeenth century and were gradually transformed into a hierarchy of legal status groups based on race that established the basis for a racial order, with whites being viewed as superior and blacks being viewed as inferior. The extension of British control over the colony during the nineteenth century increased with the prohibition of the slave trade during 1807 and, more significantly, a battery of legislation from 1828 onward that served to weaken the colonialists' authority over their native workers. Nonetheless, relations between the different frontier communities established further into the interior of South Africa and settlers were at times harmonious.

The discovery of diamonds and gold in 1867 and 1886, respectively, signaled the advent of modern capitalism in South Africa and an era characterized by fundamental societal change. Thereafter, development by different racial groupings progressed unevenly, with English-speaking white capitalist entrepreneurs fast accumulating wealth and power, and the African population being transformed into a poor proletariat, and this more broadly contributed to the fractured class and ethnic awareness upon which an Afrikaner nationalist identity would be founded. It also shaped perceptions among Dutch-Afrikaner professionals that a significant section of their group was faced with economic and cultural degeneration. Thus, in 1875, the Genootskap van Regte Afrikaners (Fellowship of True Afrikaners) was established to champion the cause of the Afrikaans language. The Afrikaner BROEDERBOND, which was founded in 1918 and comprised a middle class and urban-orientated elite, formulated similar strategies ensuring that Afrikaans was recognized as an official, exclusively racially defined language alongside English in 1925.

It was not until the National Party's 1948 electoral victory that the highly successful and rapid socioeconomic transformation of the status of the majority of Afrikaners properly began. Apartheid provided an ideological axis for this nationalist order, and in the decades that followed, the broad social coalition that had sustained the rise to power was continually refashioned. From the start, contradictions were apparent both within the nationalist alliance and apartheid itself. These came to a head with efforts to reform apartheid in the form of the vicious *broedertwis* (divisions between brothers), which centered upon the changing composition of the Afrikaner *volk* (an ethnic group or a people) during the early 1980s.

The emergence of the Conservative Party, which followed the National Party's split in March 1982, shattered any semblance of political unity among the *volk*. In particular, the rise of an urbanized managerial middle class and a relatively independent group of capitalists in the commercial and financial sectors led them to begin to side with their white English-speaking class counterparts as economic growth began to conflict with a nationalist identity.

National Party attempts at liberalizing the economy during the late 1980s meant that the government and its business allies began the political transition to majoritarian liberal democracy in 1994 with considerable confidence. Indeed, these efforts bore fruit during the bilateral negotiations between the then National Party government and the ANC, and during the transition process itself, 1990 to 1994, as domestic business elites helped to secure a favorable transition characterized by a successful macroeconomic compromise among policy elites. The fact that the dramatic political transition to majoritarian, democratic rule and the adoption of a new constitution was not matched by significant economic restructuring has meant that the postapartheid growth path and distributive regime have maintained overall levels of inequality, including most importantly those related to the distribution of economic power; of property and land; economic, entrepreneurial, and educational opportunities and experience; and the share of income and per capita income of the different population groups. Nonetheless, the white population's share of total income has declined from a high point in the 1970s. According to the South African Institute of Race Relations, white household incomes increased by 67 percent between 1995 and 2004, while African household incomes were only 24 percent of whites in 2004, and a mere 1 percent higher than in 1995.

The end of apartheid also meant the end of Afrikaner political control, but white Afrikaans speakers remain important in postapartheid South Africa due to their longstanding economic and cultural influence built up during the decades of apartheid. During 2010, the white population formed 9.2 percent of the total population; however, Afrikaans and English speakers comprised 13.35 percent and 8.2 percent of the total population respectively, as the majority of Afrikaans speakers today are not white. Most striking has been the manner in which Afrikaner groupings have adapted to the loss of political power while also experiencing a substantial rise in economic influence. Since the end of minority rule, there has been an acceleration in ethnic affiliations centered upon the characteristics of culture, descent, and language, and the range of identification among Afrikaans speakers is considerable. A large section of the coloured community, black Afrikaans speakers, and *verloopte* (walked away) Afrikaners remain outside of any established community.

A resurgence of group-based politics among Afrikaners has placed the legitimacy of minority cultural rights, including most prominently language rights (the *taaldebat*), at the top of the group's cultural agenda. Tensions between the ANC government's goal of increasing diversity and addressing past inequities through the widening of access in the higher education sector on the one hand and the survival of Afrikaans as an academic language with higher functions have come to center upon the historically Afrikaans-speaking University of STELLENBOSCH in an ongoing and high-profile public debate. The unique population and language demographics of the Western Cape Province, where the University of Stellenbosch is located, as well as the insistence of the vocal *taalstryders* has made this a test case for the self-styled guardians of the Afrikaners' language and culture. Interestingly, the Afrikaans-speaking universities have been at the forefront of radical transformation in higher education, to address the racial imbalances in access and the critical need to educate growing numbers of black South Africans to take up skilled and leadership positions within the economy. Among the younger generation, a wider cultural revival has seen Afrikaans literature and music flourish over the past decade to encompass many voices, which range from Bok van Blerk's controversial and nostalgic elegy to Koos de la Rey during 2007 to more mainstream and traditional genres.

Much of the dialogue among Afrikaans intellectuals during the postapartheid period has focused upon disputes over perceptions of marginalization, entitlement, and belonging, and the prospects of divorcing Afrikanerness, characteristically expressed in terms of cultural attributes and less frequently descent, from Afrikaner nationalism, a political project. These perceptions have struck a chord with the 100,000 blue- and white-collar, predominantly white members of the trade union Solidarity, which campaigns against government policies, including AFFIRMATIVE ACTION and empowerment initiatives. Nonetheless, the Afrikaans business elite and the middle class remain key to both the national economy and success of the government's empowerment initiatives. Paradoxically, the enrichment of these constituencies has ensured that class and even race constitute significant divisions among the grouping. It is too early to identify the extent of the transformation that is occurring among the Afrikaner grouping today, but it is clear that Afrikanerness and being an Afrikaner have a diversity of meanings in postapartheid South Africa.

See also AFRIKANER WEERSTANDSBEWEGING; ANGLO-BOER WAR; APARTHEID; BOER REPUBLICS; BROEDERBOND; F. W. DE KLERK; POLITICAL CULTURES AND IDEOLOGIES; H. F. VERWOERD

Bibliography

Davies, Rebecca. *Afrikaners in the New South Africa: Identity Politics in a Globalised Economy.* London: I. B. Tauris, 2008.

Giliomee, Hermann. *The Afrikaners: Biography of a People.* Cape Town, South Africa: Tafelberg, 2003.

O'Meara, Dan. *Volkskapitalisme: Class, Capital and Ideology in the Development of Afrikaner Nationalism, 1934–1948.* Cambridge, UK: Cambridge University Press, 1983.

———. *Forty Lost Years: The Apartheid State and the Politics of the National Party, 1948–1994.* Randburg, South Africa: Ravan Press, 1996.

South African Institute of Race Relations (SAIRR). *2004/05 South African Survey.* Braamfontein: SAIRR, 2006.

Seekings, Jeremy, and Nicoli Nattrass. *Class, Race, and Inequality in South Africa.* Scottsville, South Africa: University of KwaZulu-Natal Press, 2006.

Terreblanche, Solomon. *A History of Inequality in South Africa, 1652–2002.* Pietermartizburg,

South Africa: University of KwaZulu-Natal Press, 2002.

—*Rebecca Davies*

Afrikaner Nationalism
See POLITICAL CULTURES AND IDEOLOGIES

Afrikaner Weerstandsbeweging

The Afrikaner Weerstandsbeweging (AWB), meaning Afrikaner Resistance Movement, is a political and paramilitary group committed to the restoration of an independent AFRIKANER republic, or "Boerestaat," within South Africa. At the height of the movement in the 1990s, during the negotiations for a new democratic dispensation, the AWB boasted a following of 70,000 members and received much domestic and international publicity as a white extremist group.

Founded in 1973 by EUGENE TERRE BLANCHE, the AWB from its inception opposed the reform of APARTHEID laws and the so-called liberalizing influences within the ruling NATIONAL PARTY. The targets of AWB violence, particularly during the State of Emergency from 1984 to 1986, were often unarmed blacks. It especially opposed liberation movements such as the AFRICAN NATIONAL CONGRESS in which members of the SOUTH AFRICAN COMMUNIST PARTY played an important role. Terre Blanche was a flamboyant orator and forceful personality, and at the AWB's height was able to convert several thousand white South Africans to his cause. The group was responsible for disrupting the formal talks between the apartheid government and the ANC and other key black liberation movements being held at the Kempton Park Conference Center just outside of JOHANNESBURG when AWB members drove an armored car through the glass front of the building, threatened delegates, and pasted slogans on the walls. The AWB was also behind the failed attempt to defend the dictatorial government of Lucas Mangope in the homeland of Bophuthatswana, which led to many innocent civilian deaths.

In 2001, Terre Blanche was sentenced to six years in prison for assaulting a gas station worker and the attempted murder of a security guard and former employee of his. He was released in June 2004 after serving three years. During his time in prison, he became a born-again Christian, claimed he had moderated many of his more racist views, and preached reconciliation as "prescribed by God." In 2010, Terre Blanche was beaten to death on his farm by two black farmworkers after a dispute over wages.

AIDS

Initially identified in the United States as early as 1981, AIDS was first reported in South Africa in 1982. As was the case in the developed world, the early South African epidemic was concentrated mainly among gay men, blood transfusion recipients, and hemophiliacs. But in the early to mid-1990s, it became clear that the epidemic had become generalized, with various studies confirming that HIV had already entered the general population by 1989. The 2010 data suggest that over 700 people were dying of AIDS-related illnesses—and even more became newly infected—each day.

With more than five million people estimated to be living with HIV and general prevalence levels that only started to stabilize from 2005 to 2009, South Africa's epidemic remains one of the country's most pressing challenges. But while the absolute numbers are disturbing, the unequal distribution of the epidemic is alarming. For example, prevalence levels among females are significantly higher than among males, being 2.7 times higher in the 15–19 age group. HIV prevalence peaks at 32.7 percent among women in the 25–29 age group. Among men, a lower peak—25.8 percent—is reached more gradually and a few years later.

Geography, socioeconomic status, and race also have an impact on vulnerability to HIV infection. Prevalence is greatest in KwaZulu-Natal, being more than four times higher than in the Western Cape. Furthermore, those living in urban informal settlements, where proper housing, sanitation, and electricity is scarce, are most at risk of infection, with prevalence in this group being 50 percent higher than among those living in similar conditions in rural areas. Although epidemic levels are observed among all groups, black Africans are disproportionately affected—with the Human Sciences Research Council noting that "race is an important epidemiological variable because it embodies socio-economic contexts that influence risk of HIV infection."

Prevalence levels only tell part of the story. The large number of people living with HIV/AIDS (PLWHA) is accompanied by a crisis of AIDS-related deaths, reflected in dramatic changes in the country's mortality profile. Between 1997 and 2004, for example, death rates for women age 20 to 39 more than tripled. In the same period, deaths for men between 30 and 44 more than doubled. For women, deaths peaked at age 30 to 34; for men, they peaked at a relatively lower level somewhat later.

At the same time, AIDS-related deaths among PLWHA in the developed world started to fall dramatically. A medical breakthrough in 1996 showed that combinations of antiretroviral (ARV) medicines could control the replication of HIV, reducing levels of the virus in the blood to undetectable levels and allowing the damaged immune system to recover. Among those with access to the new combination therapies, HIV infection was transformed from an automatic death sentence to a chronic but manageable medical condition.

In the context of unacceptably high prevalence rates and seemingly avoidable deaths, how does one assess the country's response to the epidemic? One way is to consider the manner in and the extent to which the legal and policy framework has been developed and used to limit and/or protect the rights of PLWHA and those at risk of HIV infection. Another is to evaluate public sector, civil society, and business interventions aimed at preventing and treating HIV infection and providing care and support for PLWHA and their families.

Responding to the Epidemic: The Early Years
As was the norm internationally, South Africa's initial response lacked humanity and insight. The first reported AIDS-related deaths were described as isolated cases, with the APARTHEID government assuring the public that there was no need to panic as only gay men were considered to be at high risk. In 1987, regulations provided for foreign nationals with HIV to be denied entry to and/or to be deported from the country. A year later, 1,000 foreign mine workers with HIV were repatriated after their contracts were not renewed. Two years earlier, a survey found a 0.02 percent prevalence of HIV among South African mine workers, with a significantly higher prevalence of 3.76 percent among mine workers from Malawi.

The early 1990s witnessed a significant shift. Shortly after its unbanning in February 1990, the still-exiled AFRICAN NATIONAL CONGRESS (ANC) hosted a health conference in Maputo that recognized the need to prioritize HIV prevention. CHRIS HANI, a senior SOUTH AFRICAN COMMUNIST PARTY and ANC leader who was assassinated three years later, warned against "allow[ing] the AIDS epidemic to ruin the realization of our dreams." Noting that "statistics indicate that we are still at the beginning of the AIDS epidemic in our country," Hani predicted that, if left "unattended," the epidemic would "result in untold damage and suffering." Soon thereafter, the ANC worked closely with the then Department of Health (DoH) to set up the National AIDS Convention of South Africa (NACOSA), an umbrella body to coordinate the country's response. In late 1993, just seven months before South Africa's first democratic elections and the adoption of its first Bill of Rights, the country's highest court (at the time) recognized the right of PLWHA to medical confidentiality. But at the same time, HIV prevalence among antenatal clinic attendees mushroomed—from an estimated 0.7 percent in 1990 to 7.6 percent in 1994.

Within months of President NELSON MANDELA's government taking office, the NACOSA AIDS Plan—which included a focus on law and human rights—was adopted as official policy. A new HIV/AIDS directorate in the Department of Health sought and received assistance from the then Wits University–based AIDS Law Project—now SECTION27—on the implementation of a rights-based approach. Numerous court decisions and legislative developments gave substance to the new constitutional protections against unfair discrimination and unjustifiable limitations of the right to privacy.

The rumblings of dissatisfaction, however, had also begun. In 1996, the Department of Health's funding of a musical production—with deeply flawed HIV prevention messages—came under fire, primarily because public sector tender processes had not been followed. This was followed shortly thereafter by the Virodene scandal, which saw official cabinet support for an alleged cure for AIDS—later determined to be a toxic industrial solvent—that had been tested on human subjects without the approval of the relevant medicine regulatory authority.

Mandela, who—like former US president Bill Clinton—became increasingly outspoken on HIV/AIDS after leaving office, has admitted that he could and should have done more when in power. It was during his presidency that highly active ARV therapy became the standard of care in the developed world; when research proved that ARV medicines were effective in preventing mother-to-child transmission of HIV; when Gugu Dlamini was stoned and stabbed to death shortly after publicly disclosing her HIV status, accused of shaming her community near Durban; and when ZACKIE ACHMAT, Mark Heywood, and others formed the TREATMENT ACTION CAMPAIGN (TAC). These developments were to set the scene for the heightened conflict between civil society and the post-Mandela government.

Denialism Rears Its Ugly Head
In a speech delivered in Parliament in October 1999, just six months after coming into office, former president THABO MBEKI began his public questioning of the causal link between HIV and AIDS. Early the following year, he established an international AIDS advisory panel tasked with—among other things—advising him on whether, in fact, HIV causes AIDS. The panel, composed of equal numbers of orthodox scientists and denialists, reached a predictable deadlock.

The evidence shows that Mbeki supported the position of the denialists and that powerful elements of denialism continued to bedevil the country's response to the epidemic throughout his presidency. A 2008 study published by researchers at Harvard University conservatively estimates the cost of denial in South Africa at over 330,000 lives.

Yet despite his views, the first term of the Mbeki presidency also saw significant legal and policy developments. Numerous statutes and regulations expanded the rights of PLWHA, with a host of legal actions and court judgments addressing issues such as unfair discrimination in the workplace, access to essential medicines, and the state's obligation to implement a comprehensive program to prevent transmission of HIV from mother-to-child. By April 2002, the cabinet had recognized—albeit reluctantly—the role of ARV medicines in the prevention and treatment of HIV infection.

Largely as a result of the civil society campaign for the public provision of ARV treatment, which was spearheaded by TAC, the cabinet later agreed to develop—and subsequently adopted in November 2003—the Operational Plan for Comprehensive HIV and AIDS Care, Management, and Treatment for South Africa. But it would take the threat of further litigation some four months later before the plan was implemented and the state started to provide ARV treatment to public health system users.

According to the Joint United Nations Programme on HIV and AIDS (UNAIDS), more PLWHA in South Africa are said to be accessing ARV treatment—in the public and private sectors collectively—than in any other country. But absolute numbers only tell part of the story. South Africa's treatment gap—the difference between those who have and those who need—still remains large. According to official figures, public sector coverage was 56 percent by the end of November 2009. With new ARV treatment guidelines that came into effect in April 2010, which contemplate much earlier initiation of ARV treatment for infants, pregnant women, and those who are also infected with tuberculosis, the treatment gap will have dropped significantly.

In the area of prevention, policy interventions that previously had a limited impact are finally giving way to more comprehensive programs. While the discredited ABC approach—abstain, be faithful, and condomize—officially remains in place, it is now being supplemented by a range of new interventions. These include an ambitious HIV Counseling and Testing campaign, which aims to have fifteen million South Africans tested for HIV by the end of 2011, and the introduction of free voluntary medical male circumcision services.

At the intersection of treatment and prevention lies mother-to-child transmission prevention services. While countries such as Thailand and Uganda have long abandoned suboptimal protocols, South Africa was slow to develop its program in line with international guidelines. In response to civil society pressure, the protocol was first amended in 2008 to introduce a more effective protocol that nevertheless still fell short of globally acceptable standards. By April 2010, however, the program had developed to the point where it fully recognized the centrality of maternal health, offering pregnant women options that placed their health needs at its center. According to scientific consensus, this is best for both mother and child.

Broader Impact of the Country's Response
Notwithstanding its negative impact, the AIDS epidemic has managed to place health and other socioeconomic entitlements on the political agenda. It has reinvigorated civil society, allowing for mobilization and action across class lines. TAC, for example, has been able to pull organized labor, the faith-based sector, academics, and health care providers together. Many unemployed people have been trained in treatment literacy, being both willing and able to assist in the provision of public health care services. Well supported by legal groups such as SECTION27 and the Legal Resources Centre, TAC has also made creative use of the law to compel a reluctant state—as well as numerous drug companies—into action.

The impact of these positive developments in South Africa has been felt beyond the country's borders. TAC's leadership at the International AIDS Conference in Durban in 2000 forever changed the relationship between the prevention and treatment of HIV infection. Before, the two were pitted against each other. Although a significant global treatment gap still exists, by the middle of 2010 an estimated three million PLWHA were accessing ARV treatment in the developing world. Without Durban, this would not have been possible.

Furthermore, South Africa's united stand against the multinational pharmaceutical industry in 2001—which saw TAC and the state on the same side—paved the way for a groundbreaking agreement on patents and public health at the World Trade Organization's Doha, Qatar, meeting in November of that year. The prices of many ARV medicines, integral to any comprehensive HIV/AIDS program, have plummeted since then. Whereas in 2001 it cost US$727 to treat an adult in a developing country for one year with a standard triple ARV first-line regimen, for countries that have chosen to exercise their rights to access generic medicines, the same treatment can be provided in 2011 for as low as US$61.

Mbeki Leaves Office
On September 25, 2008, KGALEMA MOTLANTHE replaced Thabo Mbeki as president of the Republic of South Africa. While Mbeki had continued—right until the end of his administration—to deny the existence of any crisis, with Manto Tshabalala-Msimang—his health minister—remaining steadfast in her refusal to concede the inadequacy of her department's performance, others in senior positions in government had already started to take action in late 2006.

Working in collaboration with all sectors of civil society, these partners in government finalized and the cabinet adopted the National HIV and AIDS and STI Strategic Plan for South Africa, 2007–2011 (NSP) in early May 2007. In addition to setting clear targets and time frames and allocating responsibility for the implementation of a range of prevention, treatment, and other key interventions, the NSP contemplates transforming the South African National AIDS Council into a truly consultative body that delivers on its mandate as the country's leading advisory and oversight structure on the epidemic.

A cabinet reshuffle following Mbeki's departure saw the appointment of Barbara Hogan—a well-respected and independent-minded member of Parliament—as the new minister of health. Addressing an international conference only a few weeks after taking office, Hogan acknowledged the causal link between HIV and AIDS, recognized the depth and severity of the crisis, and committed the government to achieving the NSP targets. But a budgetary and management crisis in the Free State Province in late 2008 cast doubt on the sustainability of the national ARV treatment program and Hogan's ability to rehabilitate and reinvigorate her department.

Shortly after coming into office in May 2009, President JACOB ZUMA appointed Aaron Motsoaledi—a medical doctor—as his new minister of health. Dr. Molefi Sefularo, Hogan's competent deputy, retained his position. But so too did Thami Mseleku, Tshabalala-Msimang's trusted director-general, who was only removed from office in September 2009. His removal paved the way for a scaling up of the NSP's implementation, the introduction of new ARV treatment and prevention protocols, and the rebuilding of relationships between government and civil society.

The Eighteenth International AIDS Conference held in Vienna in July 2010 signaled the completion of South Africa's return to an evidence-based response to the epidemic. Both Motlanthe and Motsoaledi addressed plenary sessions of the meeting, with the latter receiving a standing ovation. While there is reason to be hopeful, much of the damage caused by Mbeki's decade of denialism remains. It will take sustained effort from all, accompanied by the allocation of significant financial resources, to turn the epidemic around.

See also HEALTH; THABO MBEKI

Bibliography

Abdool Karim, Salim S., and Cheryl Baxter. "Introduction." In *HIV/AIDS in South Africa,* 2nd ed. Edited by Salim S. Abdool Karim and Quarraisha Abdool Karim. Cape Town, South Africa: Cambridge University Press, 2010.

AIDS Law Project. *Antiretroviral Treatment Moratorium in the Free State: November 2008—February 2009.* http://www.tac.org.za/community/node/2491, 2009.

Barrett-Grant, Kitty, Derrick Fine, Mark Heywood, and Ann Strode, eds. *HIV/AIDS and the Law: A Resource Manual,* 3rd ed. Johannesburg, South Africa: AIDS Law Project, 2003.

Berger, Jonathan. "Litigating for Social Justice in Post-Apartheid South Africa: A Focus on Health and Education." In *Courting Social Justice: Judicial Enforcement of Social and Economic Rights in the Developing World,* 38–99. Edited by Varun Gauri and Daniel M. Brinks. New York: Cambridge University Press, 2008.

Cameron, Edwin. *Witness to AIDS.* Cape Town, South Africa: Tafelberg Publishers, 2005.

Cameron, Edwin, and Jonathan Berger. "Patents and Public Health: Principle, Politics and Paradox." *Proceedings of the British Academy* 131 (2005): 331–369.

Campaign for Access to Essential Medicines, Médecins Sans Frontières. *Untangling the Web of ARV Price Reductions,* 11th ed. Geneva: Médecins Sans Frontières, 2008.

Chigwedere, Pride, George R. Seage III, Sofia Gruskin, Tun-Hou Lee, and M. Essex. "Estimating the Lost Benefits of Antiretroviral Drug Use in South Africa." *Journal of Acquired Immune Deficiency Syndromes* 49 (2008): 410–415.

Government of the Republic of South Africa. *Country Progress Report on the Declaration of Commitment on HIV/AIDS.* Pretoria, South Africa: Government Printer, 2010.

———. *HIV and AIDS and STI Strategic Plan for South Africa, 2007–2011.* Pretoria, South Africa: Government Printer, 2007.

Heywood, Mark. "The Achilles Heel? The Impact of HIV/AIDS on Democracy in South Africa." In *HIV/AIDS in South Africa,* 371–383. Edited by Salim S. Abdool Karim and Quarraisha Abdool Karim. Cape Town, South Africa: Cambridge University Press, 2005.

———. "South Africa's Treatment Action Campaign (TAC): Combining Law and Social Mobilization to Realize the Right to Health." *Journal of Human Rights Practice* 1 (2009): 14–36.

Hogan, Barbara. "Speech by the Minister of Health Ms Barbara Hogan at the HIV Vaccine Research Conference, Cape Town International Convention Centre, 13 October 2008." http://www.tac.org.za/community/node/2421, 2008.

Kapczynski, Amy, and Jonathan Berger. "The Story of the TAC Case: The Potential and Limits of Socio-Economic Rights Litigation in South Africa." In *Human Rights Advocacy Stories,* 43–79. Edited by Deena R. Hurwitz and Margaret L. Satterthwaite. New York: Foundation Press, 2008.

Shisana, O., T. Rehle, L. Simbayi, W. Parker, K. Zuma, A. Bhana, C. Connolly, S. Jooste, et al. *South African National HIV Prevalence, HIV Incidence, Behaviour and Communication Survey, 2005.* Pretoria, South Africa: Human Sciences Research Council Press, 2005.

Shisana O., T. Rehle, L. Simbayi, K. Zuma, S. Jooste, V. Pillay-van-Wyk, N. Mbelle, J. van

Zyl, et al. *South African National HIV Prevalence, Incidence, Behaviour and Communication Survey 2008: A Turning Tide Among Teenagers?* Cape Town, South Africa: Human Sciences Research Council Press, 2009.

Statistics South Africa. *Mid-year Population Estimates, 2010.* Pretoria, South Africa: Statistics South Africa, 2010.

UNAIDS. *Outlook Report 2010.* Geneva: UNAIDS, 2010.

—Jonathan Berger

All-African Convention

The All-African Convention (AAC) was founded by Professor DAVIDSON DON TENGO JABAVU in 1935 in response to President J. B. M. HERTZOG's Native Bills, which were intended to increase the percentage of land allocated to native reserves from 6 percent to 13 percent, but also to disenfranchise black Africans and prevent them from owning land outside of the reserves. The convention brought together the entire spectrum of opposition to the white government and included a number of leaders and provincial bodies of the AFRICAN NATIONAL CONGRESS (ANC). Given the overlap in membership, the relationship between the AAC and the ANC was always an issue, with the AAC offering somewhat of an alternative to the ANC at the time. As the AAC turned more militant, it later partnered with COLOURED and INDIAN organizations to form the NON-EUROPEAN UNITY MOVEMENT to reject cooperation with the government and push for full rights for all black South Africans. The AAC itself was short-lived; by the 1950s, its following had waned and some of its members joined the ANC or the SOUTH AFRICAN COMMUNIST PARTY.

See also AFRICAN NATIONAL CONGRESS; DAVIDSON JABAVU

ANC

See AFRICAN NATIONAL CONGRESS

Anglo-Boer War

The discovery of gold on the Witwatersrand (literally white water ridge), the area surrounding Johannesburg, in 1886 made the Transvaal—until then a struggling independent BOER REPUBLIC—potentially a political and economic threat to British supremacy in southern Africa. This was at a time when Britain, which had gained CAPE COLONY and NATAL along the coast in the first half of the nineteenth century, was engaged in the scramble for African colonies with France and Germany.

In 1896, the Jameson Raid, a scheme devised by CECIL RHODES, the prime minister of the CAPE COLONY, to overthrow the Transvaal government under President PAUL KRUGER, failed abysmally. This caused AFRIKANER NATIONALISM to flare up throughout South Africa. Although Kruger was only interested in preserving the independence of the Transvaal, the British colonial secretary, Sir Joseph Chamberlain, and the British high commissioner in South Africa, Sir Alfred Milner, believed that the Transvaal was pressing for a united South Africa under AFRIKANER rule. Milner, a self-acknowledged race patriot, resolved that if the Transvaal refused to grant the right to vote to foreign mine workers and other foreigners who came because of the mines (Uitlanders)—mostly British—war would be the only way to facilitate the development of the British gold mining industry in the Transvaal and to eliminate the BOER oligarchy, which allegedly threatened British supremacy. In this way, Milner became involved in the Transvaal's domestic issues, stirring up agitation, which, if successful, would ensure a British majority in the Boer state. In the diplomatic tussle that followed, Kruger refused to budge on the issue of the vote, despite a meeting with Milner in spring 1899 in BLOEMFONTEIN, the capital of the other Boer republic. A political deadlock was reached.

Beginning of War

On October 11, 1899, the Anglo-Boer War broke out after Britain rejected the Transvaal ultimatum demanding that all disputes between the two states be settled by arbitration; that British troops on the borders of the Orange Free State and Transvaal be withdrawn; and that troops from all over the British empire bound for southern Africa by sea from Britain should not be permitted to disembark at the ports of the Cape Colony and Natal.

The Orange Free State joined the Transvaal in terms of the military alliance signed between the two Boer republics in 1897. As the war progressed, the British Army was reinforced by volunteer contingents from Canada, Australia, New Zealand, the Cape Colony, and Natal.

The first five months of the war was a set-piece battle phase. The Boers besieged Ladysmith in Natal and KIMBERLEY and Mafeking (the black town was called Mafikeng before the British annexation in 1885, but the British called the white town that developed there Mafeking, a name that stuck until after 1994 when it was again renamed Mafikeng) in the Cape Colony, while the British forces strove to relieve their beleaguered garrisons in these towns—Lord Paul Methuen in the west and General Redvers Buller in Natal. From their camouflaged positions, the Boers scored impressive victories at Stormberg and Magersfontein in the Cape Colony, and Colenso in Natal in mid-December 1899 (called "Black Week" in Britain) and Spioenkop in Natal in January 1900. But, by February 1900, there was a dramatic change in fortunes. Kimberley and Ladysmith were relieved, and the Boer general Piet Cronjé surrendered at Paardeberg in the Orange Free State with 4,000 burghers who were Boer civilians. All the Boer fronts collapsed under British pressure.

The next six months' time was a period of great confusion for the Boers. Everywhere, they were compelled to retreat. On March 13, 1900, Lord Frederick Roberts, the British commander-in-chief, occupied Bloemfontein, and on June 5, 1900, he took Pretoria, the capital of the Transvaal. He then annexed the Orange Free State on May 24, 1900, and the Transvaal on September 1, 1900.

Lured by British promises of peace and protection, many Boer civilians surrendered and were called *hendsoppers* (having "hands up"). By the end of the war, they totaled no fewer than 20,000 men—about a third of the original Boer force. (Another third of the Boers were taken prisoners of war, and the last third were call "bitter-enders" for having stayed in the field until the end of the war.) In the last six months of the war, about 5,400 of these *hendsoppers* joined the British Army as collaborators (known as "joiners").

Meanwhile, there was a revival in the Boer military effort. In the Orange Free State, General Christiaan de Wet led the recovery of Boer resistance with surprise attacks on Roberts's vulnerable line of communication. After Roberts had dispersed the Transvaal forces in the last pitched battle of the war at Bergendal (Dalmanutha) in the eastern Transvaal in August of 1900, General Louis Botha, like De Wet in the Free State and General Koos de la Rey in the western Transvaal, applied guerrilla tactics by swiftly gathering his scattered commandos, attacking isolated British columns, and then disappearing into thin air. In this way, the resistance of about 20,000 Boer bitter-enders was to continue for almost two years—in what became known as the guerrilla phase of the war.

Lord Horation Kitchener, successor to Roberts, adopted a threefold strategy to end the war. First, he continued to implement Roberts's scorched earth policy. The Boer republics were deliberately and systematically devastated, with towns and thousands of farmsteads burned or ravaged. This onslaught on the Boer means of survival was exacerbated by a destruction of their food supplies, including livestock and crops.

Second, Roberts's concentration camp system was expanded. Boer civilians, especially women and children whose houses had been burned, were forcibly confined to camps. In Kitchener's view, this meant that burghers on commando (that is, in the field) would no longer be able to obtain food from women on the farms and would have to surrender to reunite their families. Black people, too, were taken to concentration camps, partly to deprive the burghers of another source of food as they had been providing the Boers, voluntarily or involuntarily, with their own supplies. The bad administration of the camps led to poor quality food, unhygienic conditions, and inadequate and inefficient medical arrangements, all of which meant that civilians suffered terribly. Eventually, 26,000 Boer women and children, 2,000 Boer men, and at least 20,000 black people died in these British camps.

Third, Kitchener launched his military drives. This was a method of trapping commandos against lines of blockhouses that were constructed in a network across the entire theater of war, for, by 1901, the Boers had moved deep into the Cape Colony to spread the war over a larger area and incite colonial Boers into rebellion.

In the long run, Kitchener's strategy was effective. Despite some resounding Boer victories—for example, at Nooitgedacht, Bakenlaagte, and Tweebosch in the Transvaal and Groenkop in the Orange Free State—fifty-four out of sixty Boer delegates at Vereeniging in the Transvaal decided on May 31, 1902, to submit to the unfavorable British peace terms. The Transvaal and the (by this time) Orange River Colony became crown colonies of the British Empire. The Boers had lost their independence.

African Participation

Although both the Boer and British leaders initially believed that the war should be "a white man's war," Africans played an important part too, and, as has been seen, suffered severely. From the beginning of hostilities, both warring parties employed Africans in noncombatant roles. About 10,000 *agterryers* (black henchmen, or literally after-riders) accompanied the Boers to perform camp duties on commando. A very small number of them unofficially took up arms on the Boer side. In the British Army, at least 14,000 Africans operated as wagon drivers, and, increasingly, Africans were employed in combatant roles as spies, guides, and eventually as soldiers. Under Kitchener's command, they were armed for self-defense against the Boers, who summarily executed them when captured. By the end of the war, there were probably 30,000 armed Africans in the British Army. Moreover, African communities drove Boer commandos and families from large areas in the Transvaal, curtailing Boer operations and thus contributing to the Boer acceptance of the peace terms.

Outcome of the War

The imperial policy promoted by Milner, including rigorous Anglicization efforts, failed soon after the war and merely fanned Afrikaner nationalism.

The war devastated the Afrikaners both economically and psychologically; it also increased the number of poor whites who had been emerging before the war, and accelerated urbanization as *bywoners* (landless Afrikaners) flocked to the gold mines of the Witwatersrand to eke out a living. In the course of the twentieth century, the Afrikaners gradually came to dominate South African politics, and they resolved to become independent of the British sphere of influence. This shaped them as race patriots and gave rise to an aggressive nationalism that promoted Afrikaner aspirations to attain self-determination and predominance in South Africa. This, together with a fear of the African majority, helps explain the implementation of the APARTHEID policy. With the formation of the Republic of South Africa in 1961, the Peace of Vereeniging seemed, in a certain sense, to be avenged.

Africans were equally devastated by the war, with similar results as far as poverty and urbanization. Moreover, their occupation of Boer-owned land was not recognized nor did they receive an extension of the qualified franchise that was practiced in the Cape Colony and Natal (meaning that an African male who owned land and paid a certain amount of taxes could vote in these British colonies).

Historiography

Although the debate on the causes of the war soon became a favored topic for historians, the military course of the conflict, the role of prominent commanders, and the political aspects were the focus of research until the 1970s. These themes have by no means been exhausted, but historians have since begun to consider other aspects of the war, thus dramatically broadening our view. The emphasis has shifted to war and society—the fate and vicissitudes of ordinary soldiers and civilians in wartime. The Anglo-Boer War is now seen as a total South African war in which all groups participated and which affected all the inhabitants of the country—hence the designation "South African War" by many modern historians.

The new approach places particular emphasis on the circumstances, role, and suffering of Africans during the war, showing that they saw the conflict as an opportunity to regain the territory lost to the Boers when the latter entered their territory and defeated them in the second half of the nineteenth century through such battles as the BATTLE OF BLOOD RIVER.

In the first half of the twentieth century, Afrikaner historiography focused on the suffering of the Boer women and children in the concentration camps; this gave Afrikaner nationalist leaders in the period from 1930 to 1960 the opportunity to promote Afrikaner nationalism. Recent Afrikaner research is more balanced and tends to emphasize the social aspects of the Boer experience.

See also SOUTH AFRICA ACT; BRITISH IMPERIALISM AND SETTLER COLONIALISM (1870–1910); SOL PLAATJE; J. C. SMUTS

Bibliography

Amery, Leopold Stennett, ed. *The Times History of the War in South Africa*. 7 vols. London: Sampson Low, Marston, 1902.

Cuthbertson, Greg, Albert Grundlingh, and Mary-Lynn Suttie, eds. *Writing a Wider War: Rethinking Gender, Race, and Identity in the South African War, 1899–1902*. Athens: Ohio University Press, 2002.

Denoon, Donald. *A Grand Illusion: The Failure of Imperial Policy in the Transvaal Colony During the Period of Reconstruction, 1900–1905*. London: Longman, 1973.

Farwell, Byron. *The Great Anglo-Boer War*. New York: Harper and Row, 1976.

Gooch, John, ed. *The Boer War: Direction, Experience, and Image*. London: Frank Cass, 2000.

Grundlingh, Albert. *The Dynamics of Treason: Boer Collaboration in the South African War of 1899–1902*. Pretoria, South Africa: Protea Book House, 2006.

Judd, Denis, and Keith Surridge. *The Boer War*. Basingstoke, UK: Palgrave Macmillan, 2003.

Lowry, Donal, ed. *The South African War Reappraised*. Manchester, UK: Manchester University Press, 2000.

Maurice, Frederick, and Maurice H. Grant, eds. *History of the War in South Africa, 1899–1902*. 4 vols. London: Hurst and Blackett, 1907.

Nasson, Bill. *War for South Africa: The Anglo-Boer War, 1899–1902*. Cape Town, South Africa: Tafelberg, 2010 (revised edition of *The South African War, 1899–1902*. London: Arnold, 1999).

Pakenham, Thomas. *The Boer War*. London: Weidenfeld and Nicolson, 1979.

Pretorius, Fransjohan. *The Anglo-Boer War, 1899–1902*. Cape Town, South Africa: Struik, 1999.

Smith, Iain R. *The Origins of the South African War, 1899–1902*. London: Longman, 1996.

Warwick, Peter. *Black People and the South African War, 1899–1902*. Cambridge, UK: Cambridge University Press, 1983.

—*Fransjohan Pretorius*

Anglo-Zulu War

The Anglo-Zulu War was fought in 1879 between Great Britain and the ZULU Kingdom. While the origins of the war are many and complex, the outcome was the defeat of the Zulus, the end of the independent Zulu Kingdom, and its division into smaller tribal units that has had a lasting impact on the social and political landscape of the region that now comprises the KwaZulu-Natal Province.

By most accounts, the war was provoked by an unwarranted act of aggression on the part of the British. In the 1870s, Britain had adopted a forward policy in the region, aimed at uniting the entire territory, including British and BOER colonies as well as the independent Zulu Kingdom. British high commissioner Sir Henry Bartle Frere provoked a fight with Zulu king CETSHWAYO, with the expectation that the Zulu army would be no match for the British. British troops invaded Zululand but were quickly defeated at Isandlwana Mountain. In one of the worst disasters of the colonial era, over 1,300 British troops and their African allies were killed. But, the success at Isandlwana exhausted the Zulu army, and they were unable to mount an effective defense against the invading British. The British army based in Natal regrouped with the help of troops from other British colonies and advanced toward the Zulu capital of Ulundi, the site of this war's last great battle. The Zulu army was defeated, King Cetshwayo was captured and sent into exile in CAPE TOWN, and Zululand was divided among thirteen pro-British chiefs, a move that led to a decade of destructive civil war and whose legacy continues to the present through ethnic and political tensions.

See also BRITISH IMPERIALISM AND SETTLER COLONIALISM (1870–1910); CETSHWAYO; NATAL; ZULU

Anthropology
See PALEOANTHROPOLOGY

Apartheid

An Afrikaans word, *apartheid* (apartness) (pronounced *apart-hate*) was the name given to the broad array of discriminatory laws and policies adopted by the NATIONAL PARTY to secure white supremacy in South Africa after 1948. During the first two and a half decades of National Party rule, Prime Ministers D. F. MALAN, Johannes G. Strijdom, HENDRIK VERWOERD, and John Vorster constructed a vast edifice of apartheid laws and repressive mechanisms to contain antiapartheid opposition. In its final decade and a half in power, the National Party under P. W. Botha and F. W. DE KLERK tried to dilute apartheid in order to counteract domestic and foreign criticisms. Ultimately, apartheid was abandoned under pressure from black resistance and hostile world opinion, both of which threatened to cripple South Africa's economy.

Apartheid to 1948

Apartheid laws and policies were buttressed by an ideology with philosophical roots in Europe and by a long tradition of racist colonial attitudes. Although the word first gained notoriety as a National Party campaign slogan in the general election of May 1948, apartheid's main ideological features took shape in the 1930s and 1940s as a by-product of emerging doctrines of AFRIKANER NATIONALISM. Nationalist intellectuals at that time were influenced by Johann Gottfried von Herder and Johann Gottlieb Fichte, eighteenth-century German nationalist thinkers, as well as by the nineteenth-century Dutch neo-Calvinist theologian Abraham Kuyper. Centered in the AFRIKANER BROEDERBOND, these intellectuals disseminated their ideas through the DUTCH REFORMED CHURCH and the Afrikaans press and universities, popularizing the central concept of the *volk* (an ethnic group or a people) as the fundamental building block of all societies. Propounding a quasi-religious doctrine of Christian nationalism, they asserted that public rights and duties were not primarily an individual matter but belonged collectively to "peoples," each of which was justified in seeking autonomy and political self-determination as its highest goal. Since individuals could find their highest fulfillment only as part of a *volk*, it followed that churches, schools, and families were duty bound to inculcate this sacred *volk* identity in each new generation.

Apartheid ideology held that the destiny willed by God for the Afrikaner *volk* was also the correct path for other peoples defined by common language, culture, and historical experience—including Africans. Contrary to the liberal belief that Africans should be encouraged to assimilate European culture, apartheid stood for the greatest possible segregation of Africans in order that they might pursue the unhindered development of their own God-given destinies as ethnic nations. As National Party policy unfolded after 1948, this idealistic do-unto-others vision convinced many Afrikaners that apartheid was grounded in moral principles, even if these might not be fully realized in practice.

In the two decades before 1948, apartheid ideology coexisted with an increasingly virulent racism among South African whites. Inspired by the rise of Nazism and fed by the pseudoscientific literature of eugenics then being produced in the United States and Britain, South African eugenicists popularized a theory of biological determinism that cast the Afrikaner *volk* as a special breed threatened by degradation through genetic mixing with other races. A pledge to prevent this degradation became an important plank in the National Party's election platform from 1948 onward, with laws against interracial sex and marriage prioritized in the party's legislative program of 1949–1950.

Academic Dan O'Meara has argued that, in embracing apartheid, the Nationalists united the Afrikaner electorate through appeals that aligned working-class voters with the economic interests of emerging Afrikaner capital. White workers, especially the many thousands of rural-born, low-skilled Afrikaners who had migrated to towns during the Great Depression and World War II, saw in apartheid a promise of expanded job reservation laws that would protect them against competition from cheaper African labor. Aspiring Afrikaner businessmen could be confident that new laws controlling the mobility of African labor would guarantee a reliable stream of docile and low-paid workers to commerce and industry once the needs of white workers were met. Most importantly, white commercial farmers saw in apartheid a guarantee that tighter PASS LAWS would control the townward movement of Africans, by requiring that all Africans carry a pass book and that only approved Africans could come to the urban areas for work, and thus ensure a steady supply of farm workers without any increase in wages. Academic Deborah Posel questions this picture of a party brought together around the interests of Afrikaner capital and points to fundamental contradictions between apartheid's promises of political segregation, economic integration, and permanent white supremacy in "white" areas where blacks for practical reasons would always be a majority. Far from launching its new policy of apartheid as a coherent grand design for the future, Posel argues, the National Party proceeded from the start with an ambiguous plan that tried to straddle conflicting views about the future of African urbanization and migratory labor.

Apartheid Legislation
To give substance to the pledge that whites would be supreme in their own areas and that other people, under white direction, would be appropriately compartmentalized elsewhere, the South African Parliament in the 1950s passed a series of segregation laws, starting with the Population Registration and Group Areas Acts in 1950. The first of these laws required every citizen to have a racial classification, while the second required all towns and cities to be zoned by race, reserving the best residential and commercial areas for whites and pushing everyone else out to the peripheries. Particular attention was given to removing INDIAN shops from prime areas coveted by aspiring Afrikaner entrepreneurs. In inner-city CAPE TOWN, the picturesque DISTRICT SIX, occupied mainly by COLOUREDS, was demolished block by block and rezoned for whites. The 1953 Separate Amenities Act provided legal sanction for the provision of separate (and better) facilities for whites in transport services, office buildings, elevators, museums, restaurants, and the like. Even park benches were inscribed with *blankes* (whites) and *nie-blankes* (nonwhites) signs. Sports teams and facilities were also rigidly segregated for almost three decades, despite South Africa's exclusion from international competition as a consequence.

The BANTU EDUCATION Act (1953) brought all African schools under state control, clearing the way to impose dumbed-down curricula and to segregate school children according to language group, hypothetically to facilitate each group's "separate development" as a *volk*. In 1959, the Extension of University Education Act restricted existing universities to whites only and launched the construction of ethnically segregated state universities (later dubbed "bush colleges") for blacks. A decade later, these tightly controlled institutions spawned the South African Students' Organisation with its militant antiapartheid ideology of solidarity among all nonwhites, who were now collectively rechristened "blacks."

Apartheid laws of an overtly political kind were designed to weaken the National Party's enemies, silence its critics, and bolster its parliamentary majority. The Suppression of Communism Act (1950) banned the SOUTH AFRICAN COMMUNIST PARTY and established procedures for gagging and restricting individuals alleged to be furthering its aims. The AFRICAN NATIONAL CONGRESS (ANC) and the PAN AFRICANIST CONGRESS were similarly suppressed by the Unlawful Organizations Act (1960). When the ANC experimented with passive resistance in 1952, a new law was passed to make civil disobedience itself a crime punishable by imprisonment, fines, and/or flogging. The Senate Act of 1956 led to the removal of coloured voters in the Cape from the common voters' roll, placing them on a segregated roll and depriving the opposition United Party of their votes. In 1968, the Liberal Party disbanded when the Prohibition of Political Interference Act banned multiracial political parties. The Affected Organizations Act (1974) enabled the minister of justice to prohibit any organization from receiving foreign funds.

From the early 1960s, a series of harsh security laws made imprisonment for political offenses increasingly common. Acts of sabotage

Sign in Durban that states the beach is for whites only under apartheid laws.
The languages are English, Afrikaans, and Zulu.

brought stiff penalties after 1962, and, from the following year, torture became routine when a new measure was introduced enabling police to detain suspected political offenders or witnesses for up to ninety days without charge or access to a lawyer. Habeas corpus was dispensed with altogether when the Terrorism Act of 1967 provided for indefinite detention without charge. In the 1970s and 1980s, the state conducted hundreds of political trials. The accused of all races sat side by side in the dock, but, when convicted, they went to segregated prison cells and, when hung, to segregated cemeteries.

A further set of apartheid laws and policies addressed the administration and development of the various supposed "Bantu nations." Whites of all ethnicities, under the leadership of the Afrikaner *volk*, were seen as one nation, but Africans were said to comprise ten nations, each with a designated geographical homeland, or BANTUSTAN. The Bantu Authorities Act of 1951 began the process of inventing these entities, and with the 1959 Promotion of Bantu Self-Government Act, Hendrik Verwoerd put the world on notice that these emerging nations, as in the rest of Africa, were eventually to be "decolonized." Starting with the Transkei in 1976, four were eventually granted nominal independence. The reality, however, was that the bantustans were never viable political entities and relied heavily on the apartheid government financially and otherwise. Rural Africans living on freehold farms purchased by their forebears before the 1913 NATIVES' LAND ACT were systematically forced from these "black spots" into the bantustans as part of the nation-building exercise. In the meantime, coloureds and Indians, who had no territorial homelands, were nevertheless put on a path to racial self-determination through the establishment in the late 1960s of two national advisory bodies, the Coloured Persons' Representative Council and the South African Indian Council. Like the bantustans, however, these achieved no more than paltry popular recognition inside South Africa and won no praise for apartheid abroad. Critics often pointed to the wasteful cost of employing thousands of bureaucrats to administer apartheid's multifarious laws and regulations. For the National Party, however, these jobs were a valuable form of patronage, helping to secure the loyalty of thousands of Afrikaner voters.

Apartheid After 1976
Notwithstanding the National Party's continuing electoral strength, the SOWETO STUDENT UPRISING of 1976–1977 caused *verligte* (enlightened) Afrikaners to question the government's reliance on old-style apartheid in light of changing economic and political conditions. Radical academics like Dan O'Meara had long argued that apartheid and advanced industrial capitalism were compatible, while liberals like Merle Lipton maintained that capitalists would eventually find apartheid too inefficient and unwieldy. By the 1980s, the weight of evidence was tilting toward the latter view. African attitudes were hardening. POLITICAL VIOLENCE provoked growing pressure for international sanctions. As the bargaining power of skilled African workers increased, the logic of recognizing black trade unions became irrefutable. To dilute apartheid and win foreign approval, the National Party introduced separate coloured and Indian houses of parliament. Although conservative foreign governments hailed this as "a step in the right direction" by PRETORIA, opposition groups in South Africa, galvanized by the new multiracial UNITED DEMOCRATIC FRONT, seized on the first elections to the tricameral parliament in 1984 to mount a massive show of resistance.

Turmoil in the black townships, protest strikes, and industrial disputes built to a crescendo over the following two years, plunging the Botha government into a prolonged crisis of indecision. The pass laws became unenforceable and were repealed in 1986, along with the prohibition on mixed marriages. Shantytowns mushroomed as rural poverty accelerated the migration of Africans to towns. The National Party acquiesced as all-white universities accepted growing numbers of black students and private high schools began to integrate. Municipalities began to drop petty segregation in public places, and residentially integrated "grey areas" gradually spread in major cities in defiance of the Group Areas Act.

These derelictions from the old apartheid order were denounced by the Conservative Party, a 1982 right-wing breakaway of working-class Afrikaners from the National Party. The National Party, no longer bound by the outmoded tenets and tactics of Afrikaner nationalism, held onto power by attracting English-speaking voters to whom there was nothing sacred about apartheid per se as long as white dominance was maintained. Eventually, however, P. W. Botha's faltering leadership led his own cabinet to oust him in August 1989. Under his successor, F. W. de Klerk, a rapid change of course was effected, leading to the repeal of all but a handful of apartheid laws by 1991. Initially prepared to concede only that apartheid was a noble experiment that failed, de Klerk in later years has spoken for many whites in regretting the centuries of injustice suffered by blacks.

See also AFRICAN NATIONAL CONGRESS; AFRIKANER NATIONALISM; APPENDIX 1; BANTU EDUCATION; BANTUSTANS; F. W. DE KLERK; NELSON MANDELA; NATIONAL PARTY; H. F. VERWOERD

Bibliography

Cock, Jacklyn. *Maids and Madams: A Study in the Politics of Exploitation*. Johannesburg, South Africa: Ravan Press, 1980.

Dubow, Saul. *Scientific Racism in Modern South Africa*. Cambridge: Cambridge University Press, 1995.

Giliomee, Hermann. *The Afrikaners: Biography of a People*. Cape Town, South Africa: Tafelberg, 2003.

Giliomee, Hermann, and Lawrence Schlemmer, eds. *Up Against the Fences: Poverty, Passes and Privilege in South Africa*. Cape Town, South Africa: David Philip, 1985.

Lemon, Anthony, ed. *Homes Apart: South Africa's Segregated Cities*. Bloomington: Indiana University Press, 1991.

Lipton, Merle. *Capitalism and Apartheid: South Africa, 1910–84*. Totowa, NJ: Rowman and Allanheld, 1985.

O'Meara, Dan. *Forty Lost Years: The Apartheid State and the Politics of the National Party, 1948–1994*. Athens: Ohio University Press, 1997.

Omond, Roger. *The Apartheid Handbook*, 2nd ed. New York: Penguin Books, 1986.

Posel, Deborah. *The Making of Apartheid, 1948–1961: Conflict and Compromise*. Oxford: Clarendon Press, 1991.

Smith, David M., ed. *Living Under Apartheid: Aspects of Urbanization and Social Change in South Africa*. London: George Allen and Unwin, 1982.

Swilling, Mark, Richard Humphries, and Khehla Shubane, eds. *Apartheid City in Transition*. Cape Town, South Africa: Oxford University Press, 1991.

Welsh, David. *The Rise and Fall of Apartheid: From Racial Domination to Majority Rule*. Johannesburg, South Africa: Jonathan Ball, 2010.

—Gail Gerhart

Armed Struggle

The armed struggle that originated during the early 1960s by blacks against the APARTHEID regime arose from the long history of nonviolent opposition to injustice. In the decade before the turn to violent tactics, some within the AFRICAN NATIONAL CONGRESS (ANC)—as well as many people outside of the organization—were beginning to doubt the effectiveness of nonviolent protest, particularly against a state willing to use deadly force to suppress peaceful opposition from the black majority. The 1960 SHARPEVILLE MASSACRE, in which police killed at least sixty-nine people who had been protesting PASS LAWS, reinforced an argument that had been gaining ground within the ANC and within the rival PAN AFRICANIST CONGRESS (PAC) that organized opposition movements would have to adopt the strategic use of violence to counter the state's violence.

Strategic Use of Violence

Nonviolence was a tactic born out of the military conquest of African chiefdoms and kingdoms primarily by the British in the late nineteenth and early twentieth centuries. Many Africans believed it would be futile to attempt further armed struggle and instead looked to the limited parliamentary means available to them to make their political voices heard.

By the late 1950s, however, politically engaged Africans were changing their analysis. The NATIONAL PARTY state (first elected in 1948) had tightened existing segregationist legislation and was enacting the more stringent laws that became apartheid. A new generation of African leaders who had come to power in the ANC was ideologically committed to a more activist stance. This activism initially led to a broader use of Gandhian passive resistance (*satyagraha*), but as the state refused to make concessions and instead stepped up its enforcement of segregationist laws (and then banned the ANC—the most important cause), some ANC leaders, including NELSON MANDELA, drew up plans for the limited use of violence. In addition, some ANC members, notably ROBERT SOBUKWE, earlier broke away from the ANC to form the rival PAC partly because of a growing frustration with what they characterized as the ANC's "go-slow" tactics.

In the 1950s, antistate violence had already erupted in several BANTUSTANS of South Africa. Originating from the deteriorating economic and social conditions in the countryside, the insurrections were not controlled by either the ANC or the PAC. The organizations' leaders, however, saw the rebellions as both a hopeful sign that people were willing to resist the state openly and that political organizations needed to prepare for some form of armed struggle to remain relevant to the larger African population. In 1960, the state banned the ANC and the PAC, making it illegal for them to pursue their objectives peacefully and making it necessary to develop underground networks.

Both the ANC and PAC launched quasi-autonomous wings to promote the armed struggle. The ANC's wing, Umkhonto we Sizwe (Spear of the Nation), was better organized and better funded and unleashed its first sabotage campaign on December 16, 1961, with attacks on various state installations. PAC's wing, Poqo (Ourselves Alone or Pure), initiated its campaign of violence with an attack on the police station in Paarl in November 1962, which resulted in the deaths of five Africans and two whites.

The South African state responded with legislation effectively categorizing all dissent—peaceful or not—as treason punishable by the death penalty and aggressively infiltrated African organizations. New laws granted sweeping powers to the police to detain and torture people suspected of promoting armed resistance. In 1963, most of the Umkhonto we Sizwe's High Command were arrested in a raid and subsequently tried for making preparations for sabotage and guerrilla warfare, and furthering the aims of communism (the RIVONIA TRIAL). By the late 1960s, most ANC and PAC leaders were either in exile or in prison serving life sentences.

Banned within South Africa, the ANC and PAC established training camps for guerrillas beyond South Africa's borders. The ANC, relying on its alliance with the SOUTH AFRICAN COMMUNIST PARTY, developed contacts with the Soviet Union, which provided guerrilla training and arms. The ANC later established training camps in MOZAMBIQUE and Angola after the Portuguese colonial regime collapsed in 1975. However, through the early 1970s, successful acts of sabotage were relatively few within South Africa. The apartheid state defined sabotage in such sweeping terms in the 1962 General Law Amendment Act (known as the Sabotage Act), however, that political activists continued to be convicted of sabotage even if they had not committed any acts of violence. By the late 1960s, the state's repression had rendered the PAC's armed wing, Poqo, and the ANC's Umkhonto we Sizwe (MK) largely irrelevant as significant threats within South Africa. MK guerrillas did, however, fight in conflicts in neighboring states, including the "bush war" in Southern Rhodesia (now ZIMBABWE) in which MK fighters operated alongside guerrillas from Joshua Nkomo's Zimbabwe African People's Union (ZAPU). This regional engagement of MK in independence struggles in other countries—which mirrored the actions of the apartheid state's military in shoring up other white supremacist regimes in the region—posed a threat of military invasion into South Africa by armed and experienced guerrillas.

The 1970s saw the broader politicization of the South African population with the BLACK CONSCIOUSNESS MOVEMENT, headed by STEVE BIKO. Politicization led to the creation of a number of organizations whose members expressed political opinions at odds with the apartheid regime, sometimes in very confrontational terms. The state responded to all criticism by Africans, whether they were leading organized resistance or not, with harsh reprisals, including detention without trial, increasingly draconian legislation that criminalized all forms of dissent, and with the deployment of death squads, which in combination with infiltrators inside African organizations, kidnapped and murdered African resistance leaders inside and outside South Africa. The brutal suppression of the SOWETO STUDENT UPRISING in June 1976, in particular, pushed several thousand young South Africans into exile, many in search of guerrilla training.

The ANC initially found it difficult to integrate the large number of new recruits into their guerrilla training operations. There were numerous cases of abuse of recruits, some of whom were suspected of being informers for the South African security police and some of whom were merely critical of the ANC's operational failures. CHRIS HANI, who became a charismatic leader of Umkhonto we Sizwe in the 1980s, was sentenced to death by Umkhonto's High Command in 1969 for submitting one such critical report. The ANC political leaders quickly reversed his death sentence, but the episode was indicative of some of the problems faced by the organization in exile. Yet, despite operational problems, the number of successful acts of sabotage undertaken by Umkhonto increased over the years 1977–1983 with attacks on police stations, a state-owned oil refinery, and notably the Koeberg nuclear power plant outside CAPE TOWN.

Development of a Broader Armed Uprising
The founding of the UNITED DEMOCRATIC FRONT in South Africa in 1983 by political activists sympathetic to the ANC marked a turning point. The front, although committed to peaceful methods, developed political networks and created momentum for change. The uprising that flared in late 1984 and then spread into a conflagration through 1986 pitted African youths (many of whom were not trained guerrillas) against the well-armed state. Increasing numbers of trained guerrillas infiltrated from the neighboring FRONTLINE STATES into South Africa as well, and the number of clashes with the state's armed forces soared. Violent resistance was no longer limited to acts of sabotage, as youths confronted armored personnel carriers and police with rifles, and guerrillas planted land mines on rural roads used by white commandos and attacked military bases and government offices. Violence also spread beyond urban areas and black townships into the countryside where the state found it difficult to maintain control. While the armed struggle never scored a decisive victory against the South African military, it contributed to fomenting resistance inside South Africa, and to destroying confidence in the state both at home and abroad.

Continuing Violence After Suspension of Armed Struggle
The unbanning of the ANC and PAC and their armed wings in February 1990 effectively suspended the formal armed struggle. Political violence continued, however, even after the first universal suffrage election in April 1994. Some of this violence was fomented by elements of the National Party government to raise questions about the ANC's ability to control its cadres and ultimately to govern. Different political and ethnic groups within the African population also fought each other as they tried to position themselves for political advantage in the coming postapartheid state. With the election of the ANC to power in 1994, the postapartheid state was successful in defusing some of these conflicts and worked to integrate former antiapartheid guerrillas into the South African military.

See also AFRICAN NATIONAL CONGRESS; CHRIS HANI; PAN AFRICANIST CONGRESS; JOE SLOVO; TREASON TRIAL

Bibliography
Adam, Heribert, and Kogila Moodley. "Political Violence, 'Tribalism' and Inkatha." *Journal of Modern African Studies* 30 (1992): 485–510.

Barrell, Howard. "The Turn to the Masses: The African National Congress' Strategic Review of 1978–1979." *Journal of Southern African Studies* 18, no. 1 (1991): 64–92.

Bopela, Thula, and Daluxolo Luthuli. *Umkhonto we Sizwe: Fighting for a Divided People*. Alberton, South Africa: Galago, 2005.

Bundy, Colin. "Land and Liberation: South African Liberation Movements and the Agrarian Ques-

tion, 1920–1960." *Review of African Political Economy* 29 (1994): 14–29.
Carter, Charles. "Community and Conflict: The Alexandra Rebellion of 1986." *Journal of Southern African Studies* 18 (1992): 115–142.
Delius, Peter. "Migrant Organisation, the Communist Party, the ANC, and the Sekhukhuneland Revolt, 1940–1958." In *Apartheid's Genesis, 1935–1962*. Edited by P. Bonner, P. Delius, and D. Posel, 126–159. Johannesburg, South Africa: Ravan Press, 1993.
Ellis, Stephen. "Mbokodo: Security in ANC Camps, 1961–1990." *African Affairs* 93, no. 371 (1994): 279–298.
Frankel, Philip. *An Ordinary Atrocity: Sharpeville and Its Massacre*. New Haven, CT: Yale University Press, 2001.
Gerhart, Gail. *Black Power in South Africa*. Berkeley: University of California Press, 1978.
Hani, Chris. "25 Years of Armed Struggle: Army Commissar Chris Hani Speaks." *Sechaba* (December 1986): 10–18.
Johns, Sheridan, and R. Hunt Davis. *Mandela, Tambo, and the African National Congress*. New York: Oxford University Press, 1991.
Karis, Thomas, Gwendolyn Carter, and Gail Gerhart. *From Protest to Challenge: A Documentary History of African Politics in South Africa, 1882–1990*. 6 vols. Stanford, CA: Hoover Institution Press, 1972–1977; Bloomington: Indiana University Press, 1997, 2010.
Lodge, Tom. *Black Politics in South Africa Since 1945*. Johannesburg, South Africa: Ravan Press, 1984.
———. "The Poqo Insurrection, 1961–1968." In *Resistance and Ideology in Settler Societies*. Edited by J. Lonsdale, 179–222. Johannesburg, South Africa: Ravan Press, 1986.
Mbeki, Govan. *South Africa: The Peasants Revolt*. Harmondsworth, UK: Penguin, 1963.
Nicholson, Christopher. *Permanent Removal: Who Killed the Cradock Four?* Johannesburg, South Africa: Wits University Press, 2004.
Orkin, Mark. "'Democracy Knows No Colour': Rationales for Guerrilla Involvement Among Black South Africans." *Journal of Southern African Studies* 18, no. 3 (1992): 642–669.
Redding, Sean. "Government Witchcraft: Taxation, the Supernatural, and the Mpondo Revolt in the Transkei, South Africa, 1955–1963." *African Affairs* 95 (1996): 555–579.
Sitas, Ari. "The Making of the 'Comrades' Movement in Natal, 1985–1991." *Journal of Southern African Studies* 18 (1992): 629–641.
Van Kessel, Ineke. "'From Confusion to Lusaka': The Youth Revolt in Sekhukhuneland." *Journal of Southern African Studies* 19 (1993): 593–614.
Williams, Rocky. "The Other Armies: A Brief Historical Overview of Umkhonto we Sizwe (MK), 1961–1994." *Military History Journal* 11, no. 5 (2000): 1–17.

—Sean Redding

Azania

Azania was the name used in place of South Africa by members and supporters of the PAN AFRICANIST CONGRESS (PAC) and the BLACK CONSCIOUSNESS MOVEMENT. Historically, Azania referred to the East African Coast. From the late 1960s through the early 1980s, the term was popular among groups fighting APARTHEID and appeared in the names of groups such as the Azanian People's Organization and the Pan Africanist Congress of Azania. At the time of the democratic transition in 1994, some proposed changing the name of the country from South Africa to Azania, but this never had broad support among the public, and the dominant AFRICAN NATIONAL CONGRESS party identified the name with its rival party, the PAC.

B

Baartman, Sara/Saartjie (1770s–1815)

Sara, or Saartjie, Baartman has become a symbol of the objectification, exploitation, and humiliation experienced by black people under the colonial and APARTHEID systems. Born into a KHOIKHOI family in the 1770s in the Eastern Cape (she was long believed to have been born in 1789, but new research contradicts this), Baartman's original name is unknown. Historical accounts differ about many details of her life, but it is confirmed that, in 1810, she traveled with British ship doctor William Dunlop from CAPE TOWN to London. She reputedly was promised high wages by Dr. Dunlop if she allowed spectators to view her body, which was considered unusual in shape by most Europeans. Baartman had unusually large buttocks and genitals, and Europeans arrogantly displayed her as a scientific freak show to confirm their perceptions of their own superiority over darker races, and the hypersexual, inferior nature of Africans in particular. Indeed the cultural context of Baartman's exploitation was heavily influenced by debates within European society at the time on race and sex, a hierarchy of human forms, and later on racialized science.

After learning of her public display, the African Association, an abolitionist benevolent society, unsuccessfully petitioned the British government for her release, citing the Slave Trade Act of 1807. In the ensuing trial, the London court ruled that she had wittingly entered into a contract with the doctor to share in his profits.

In 1814, Baartman was taken to Paris and exhibited by an animal trainer in a traveling circus for fifteen months. Records indicate that she was sometimes displayed in a cage and was not cooperative with ogling onlookers who requested to see her genitalia. Referred to as "the Hottentot Venus," she captured the attention of French naturalists who created "scientific" paintings of her. Noted anatomist Georges Cuvier used his studies of Baartman to prop up his pseudoscientific ideology of racism, premised on the belief that Europeans were superior to all other races.

Sara Baartman died of illness in Paris on December 19, 1815. Some historians believe she was forced to turn to prostitution in her final years. After her death, Cuvier made a plaster cast of Baartman's body and then dissected her. He preserved her skeleton, brain, and genitalia, which were displayed in the Musee de l'Homme in Paris until the mid-1970s when they were moved to storage.

Calls for her repatriation date back to the early 1940s and were repeated by newly elected president NELSON MANDELA in the 1990s. Only after extensive lobbying and debate did the French National Assembly pass an act in 2002 guaranteeing the return of her body parts. On Women's Day, August 9, 2002, a ceremony officiated by then president THABO MBEKI was held in her honor, and Baartman was reburied near the Gamtoos River of her childhood. Her gravesite has been designated a national heritage site.

Bibliography
Crais, Clifton, and Pamela Scully. *Sara Baartman and the Hottentot Venus: A Ghost Story and a Biography.* Princeton, NJ: Princeton University Press, 2008.

Bambatha Rebellion

The Bambatha Rebellion of 1906 is regarded by many as the beginning of the struggle against white domination in South Africa and the precursor to the nationalist movements' armed opposition that formed as part of the struggle against APARTHEID.

The immediate roots of the rebellion lay in the colonial administration's attempts to extract a poll tax from unmarried African males over the age of eighteen. Many ZULU refused to pay the tax and were subsequently punished by the British authorities. As black discontent spread and white fears grew with sporadic clashes between black ethnic groups and white tax collectors in Natal, a chief named Bambatha kaMancinza of the small but influential Zondi chiefdom was targeted as the main culprit. When it came time for his people to pay the taxes, they not only refused but resisted. The colonial authorities interpreted this protest as a rebellion that must be put down with force. After Bambatha temporarily fled to consult Zulu king Dinizulu, the British ousted him as chief and replaced him with his uncle who was more supportive of the colonial authorities. In response, Bambatha mobilized a large following and proceeded to launch guerrilla attacks on the colonial town of Greytown. The battle that ensued brought heavy casualties to the Zulu—between 3,000 and 4,000 (some of whom died fighting on the side of the Natal government). More than 7,000 were imprisoned and 4,000 flogged. Bambatha was killed and beheaded during the battle. King Dinizulu was arrested and sentenced to four years imprisonment for treason.

See also ARMED STRUGGLE; BRITISH IMPERIALISM AND SETTLER COLONIALISM (1870–1910)

Bantu Education

This separate educational system for Africans was officially established in 1953 with the Bantu Education Act (Act No. 47). Written by APARTHEID architect and minister of native affairs HENDRIK VERWOERD, the act enforced racial segregation for all schools. It established an Education Department for Africans in the Department of Native Affairs tasked with developing a new curriculum suited to "the nature and requirements of the black people." Quoted in Nancy Clark and William Worger's 2004 book, Verwoerd is attributed as saying that Africans had "no place" in the European community "above the level of certain forms of labor" and should not be "misled" into developing "expectations in life which circumstances in South Africa do not allow to be fulfilled."

The new law led to meager and thinly spread government resources for black educational institutions, which were to be funded primarily from direct taxes paid "by Africans themselves." When the law passed, 90 percent of African schools were state-supported mission schools. Most closed to avoid discriminatory mandates of the apartheid state.

The Bantu Education Act enabled much greater administrative control and surveillance by the state than before. Schools were required to register with the Bantu Education Department, which now controlled teacher training, hiring, and curriculum development. Teachers and administrators seen as subversive were removed.

In keeping with the aims of Christian national education, a key component of early AFRIKANER NATIONALISM, it was hoped that Africans schooled in the Bantu education system would maintain their separate Bantu culture and either remain in the state-designated "homelands" or work as manual laborers for Europeans. The system called for mother tongue instruction at the primary level, which served to further fragment the African population into distinct and separate groups, in accordance with homeland policies and later zoning laws.

In 1954, the AFRICAN NATIONAL CONGRESS called for a boycott of all Bantu education schools and proposed alternative informal education for African children. The boycott campaign failed to gain momentum, however, as funds were limited and participating teachers were threatened with blacklisting by the state.

In 1959, the Extension of University Education Act placed similar demands on institutions of higher education in calling for the establishment of new, ethnically based institutions for blacks and separate universities for COLOUREDS and INDIANS. For black students who could no longer attend white universities, the options at the time were few, including the UNIVERSITY OF FORT HARE, a state-controlled institution designated for XHOSA people; the University of Natal medical school (open to Indian, black, and coloured students only); and the University of South Africa, a correspondence institution.

Students in the new system grew increasingly resentful of the inferior education they were receiving and increasingly organized in their resistance. In 1969, the black South African Student Organization was formed. Students' Representative Councils became a major site of organized youth resistance, which came to a head on June 16, 1976, in the SOWETO STUDENT UPRISING. On this day, thousands of schoolchildren gathered to protest the imposition of Afrikaans as the language of instruction and the Bantu education system more generally. They were met by police in armored cars, who sealed off Soweto township and opened fire on the students. Mass protests spread across the country and the world. "Liberation Now, Education Later!" became a rallying cry for black South African youth who played an increasingly crucial role in mass politics and popular protest.

In 1979, the Congress of South African Students (COSAS) was formed. Throughout the 1980s, few African schools were functioning due to the increasing pressure to boycott them. In 1985, a state of emergency was declared, and COSAS was banned. The Soweto Parents Crisis Committee was formed, followed by the NATIONAL EDUCATION CRISIS COMMITTEE in the following year. These groups and others became part of the growing Movement for People's Education. The movement had a more democratic and participatory vision involving greater student and parent participation, and fighting for a liberation that would only be realized some ten years later.

In 1995, with the end of apartheid and the beginning of democratic, black-majority rule, a single educational system for all South Africans was introduced, but the legacy of educational inequalities continues today.

See also APARTHEID; EDUCATION

Bibliography
Clark, Nancy, and William Worger. *South Africa: The Rise and Fall of Apartheid.* Harlow, UK: Longman Publishers, 2004.

Bantustan(s)

Although indirect rule over "Native Reserves" predated APARTHEID, the NATIONAL PARTY reorganized the reserves into ethnically defined, self-governing African homelands, or bantustans. The Bantu Authorities Act (1951) consolidated and generalized the existing hierarchy of chiefly authorities administering customary law in the scattered reserves. Building on the proposals of the government-appointed Tomlinson Commission (1955) that was tasked with assessing the viability of independent bantustans, the Promotion of Bantu Self-Government Act (1959) introduced the policy of separate development by creating legal ethnic categories for Africans, amalgamating the reserves into eight (eventually ten) ethnically defined bantustans, and encouraging the eventual "independence" of the bantustans. Later, the Bantu Homelands Citizenship Act (1970) stripped Africans of their South African citizenship and assigned them citizenship in one of the bantustans on the basis of their legally designated ethnicity.

The ten bantustans (and their ethnic groups) were: Bophuthatswana (TSWANA), Ciskei (XHOSA), Gazankulu (TSONGA/Shangaan), KaNgwane (SWAZI),

KwaNdebele (NDEBELE), KwaZulu (ZULU), Lebowa (North SOTHO), QwaQwa (South Sotho), Transkei (Xhosa), and Venda (VENDA).

Separate development and the bantustan strategy emerged in response to mounting anticolonial resistance, growing international isolation of the apartheid state, and the rapid urbanization of black South Africans due to the mechanization of agriculture, industrial demands for semiskilled labor, and the economic decline of the reserves. The new strategy reinforced indirect rule with nominal independence, intensified forced removals to the bantustans to counter urbanization, and secured migrant labor while stabilizing an urban working class.

After 1960, the South African government stopped constructing African townships on the outskirts of white cities and instead built them inside the bantustans. The bantustans became dumping grounds for South Africa's "surplus population," that is, those deemed unnecessary for the maintenance of white South African society. From 1960 to 1983, at least 3.5 million Africans were forcibly removed from urban areas, white farms, informal settlements, "black spots" in white-designated areas, and lands excised from the bantustans. Additionally, hundreds of thousands were annually deported to the bantustans for PASS LAW violations. While only 39.7 percent of Africans lived on reserves in 1950, 52.7 percent lived in bantustans in 1980.

The bantustans suffered from high rates of overcrowding, unemployment, undernourishment, tuberculosis, child mortality, overgrazing, and environmental degradation. Workers employed in South Africa provided 75 percent of the annual income to the bantustans, despite the South African government's efforts to decentralize industry to the bantustans and to promote agriculture through improvement schemes and forced villagization. In the 1970s, the South African government proposed consolidating the bantustans, most of which incorporated multiple enclaves separated by white-controlled territory. Through land swaps and forced removals, Bophuthatswana was reduced from nineteen to six enclaves and KwaZulu from forty-eight to ten.

The ideal bantustan was the Transkei, which became a self-governing territory in 1963 and a supposed "independent" state in 1976. Bophuthatswana (1977), Venda (1979), and Ciskei (1981) followed suit, but the other six never proceeded beyond the status of self-governing territories. The devolution of political authority increased the administrative and repressive powers of the governing chiefs, but their autonomy was severely constrained. The bantustans were heavily dependent on financial assistance from the South African government, which retained the right to approve or veto legislation and appointed white officials to run the bantustan administrations. The bantustans were never internationally recognized as independent states.

With the demise of apartheid and the introduction of democratic, black-majority rule, the CONSTITUTION of the Republic of South Africa Act (1993) abolished the bantustans and restored South African citizenship to their residents.

See also APARTHEID

Battle of Blood River

The Battle of Blood River occurred on December 16, 1838, between the ZULU and the AFRIKANER Voortrekkers (that is, pioneers), who, as part of the GREAT TREK out of the British CAPE COLONY, sought new land to settle and graze. The Voortrekkers had previously suffered a number of catastrophic defeats at the hands of the Zulu. But, at the Battle of Blood River, a relatively small group of 470 Voortrekkers, led by Andries Pretorius, defeated a Zulu army of approximately 10,000 on the banks of the Ncome River in present-day KwaZulu-Natal Province. Over 3,000 Zulu were killed, turning the Ncome River red, while the Voortrekkers purportedly suffered no fatalities. Thus, the event has become a central trope in the construction of AFRIKANER NATIONALISM, identity, and history. The Voortrekkers credited their victory that day to divine intervention, not technological superiority, and took it as a clear indication of their right to exist.

The battle was initiated as a retaliatory attack by the Voortrekkers. Upon confronting the Zulu army, the Voortrekkers assembled their wagons into a *laager* (circular formation) and used cannons and muskets against the Zulu *assagis* (a short stabbing spear that is effective only at close contact). The Zulu eventually fled.

The defeat propelled the Zulu Kingdom into political strife and turmoil. The battle also became the main historical event undergirding APARTHEID'S vision of an exclusivist Afrikaner nationalist identity and inculcating a sense of having a unique history and place in Africa, and thereby legitimizing white supremacy in South Africa.

See also GREAT TREK; ZULU

BCM
See BLACK CONSCIOUSNESS MOVEMENT

BEE
See BLACK ECONOMIC EMPOWERMENT

Biko, Steve Bantu (1946–1977)

Founder and martyr of the BLACK CONSCIOUSNESS MOVEMENT (BCM), Steve Biko was born on December 18, 1946, in King Williamstown in the Eastern Cape Province. The youngest in his family, Biko from an early age was a student activist and became involved in political movements against APARTHEID. He was expelled from his first school, LOVEDALE, and finished his studies at a Roman Catholic boarding school in NATAL. He then enrolled at the University of Natal Medical School and quickly became involved in the National Union of South African Students (NUSAS). For Biko, NUSAS was too dominated by white liberals and failed to address many black students' needs. He resigned and founded his own organization, the South African Student Organization.

In 1972, Biko help found the Black People's Convention (BPC), a coalition of about seventy black consciousness organizations, and became the group's first president. After being expelled from medical school, he devoted all of his time and energies to the BPC's work. In 1973, Biko was banned by the apartheid government and confined to King Williamstown. He continued his black consciousness and antiapartheid work in spite of harsh state repression. Although Biko's activities were curtailed, his ideas on black consciousness were pivotal in organizing the 1976 SOWETO STUDENT UPRISING. At the time, the AFRICAN NATIONAL CONGRESS and its leaders were not supportive of Biko or the BCM, viewing him as a threat to their dominance in the antiapartheid struggle. Since then, however, the ANC and other antiapartheid groups have recognized Biko as one of the most formidable antiapartheid figures.

Between August 1975 and September 1977, Biko was detained and interrogated by the apartheid police four times. He was last detained on August 21, 1977, by the Eastern Cape police. On September 7, he sustained severe head injuries during interrogation. Instead of providing medical treatment, the police chained Biko to a window grille for one day. On September 11, after falling into a semiconsciousness state, he was loaded into a truck, stripped naked, and taken 1,200 miles to a hospital in Pretoria where he died shortly after his arrival. The police suggested that Biko had died of a hunger strike, but it was later confirmed that he had died of multiple head injuries, which caused severe brain damage. The cause and circumstances surrounding Biko's death created an international outcry, and he became a martyr and symbol of black resistance in South Africa and beyond.

Through his writings (his most famous book was *I Write What I Like*) and his activism, Biko sought to empower blacks by restoring African consciousness and pride. He inspired a new, young generation of black South Africans at the forefront of the struggle for democratic change. Biko's wife, Ntsiki Mashalaba, was also a black consciousness activist, and the couple had two children together. Biko also had two children with Dr. Mamphela Ramphele, another prominent black consciousness activist and subsequent vice chancellor of the University of Cape Town.

See also BLACK CONSCIOUSNESS MOVEMENT; POPULAR POLITICS

Bill of Rights

The Bill of Rights, contained in Chapter 2 of the 1996 South African CONSTITUTION, incorporates civil and political rights as well as social, economic, and cultural rights. These rights are equal and mutually supportive but impose different obligations on the state.

The civil and political rights provisions (Sections 9–23) grant rights to life, equality, privacy, and freedom of expression, assembly, association, and movement. Prompt and fair treatment under the law is also guaranteed (Section 35). Except for specified reasons of public security, these rights cannot be infringed by the state.

The Bill of Rights outlines extensive social, economic, and cultural rights that the state must work toward realizing as well, including the right to housing, health care, food, water, and social security (Sections 26–27). The Constitution incorporates the right to property (Section 25), education (Section 29), a clean environment (Section 24), and special protections for children's rights. Language and culture rights are granted (Sections 30–31) as long as they are not exercised in a way that would violate the other rights. The Bill of Rights can be changed only if two-thirds of National Assembly members vote in favor of the change, plus at least six provinces in the National Council of Provinces.

Background
Prior to 1993, South Africa's constitutions offered only whites full citizenship and contained no specific rights protections. Instead of the Constitution, PARLIAMENT reigned supreme. Under white minority rule, black South Africans in particular suffered widespread rights violations, including freedom of expression, assembly, movement, equal treatment under the law, and property and cultural rights, but no one who opposed the government was immune from civil and political rights infringements.

Until the 1980s, the main advocates of a Bill of Rights were English-speaking, white liberals, including liberal parties in parliamentary opposition. The Democratic Party and Lawyers for Human Rights remained strong advocates of a Bill of Rights in the interim Constitution that was drafted during the DEMOCRATIC TRANSITION and would bind citizens and the government in the new democratic dispensation.

By the late 1980s, the AFRIKANER-led NATIONAL PARTY (NP) and the AFRICAN NATIONAL CONGRESS (ANC) also supported a Bill of Rights. The National Party shifted from strong opposition to champions of constitutional civil, political, and property rights and, in 1993, published a Bill of Rights draft with extensive political, civil, and property rights. The ANC had long demanded equal civil, political, social, and economic rights for all. In the 1980s, Albie Sachs—a prominent activist, antiapartheid lawyer, and friend of the ANC—emerged as a champion of a constitutional Bill of Rights, including social and economic rights, though he and others were concerned it could be used to maintain inequality under majority rule. Reflecting these concerns, activist lawyers and ANC members Dullah Omar and Kader Asmal argued that rights provisions should be determined after majority rule. While the debate over the role of a Bill of Rights and its content continued to unfold within the ANC, the party eventually agreed that the interim Constitution needed to protect civil and political rights for election campaigning, but other rights guarantees should be decided by a democratically elected government.

In 1993, the constitutional negotiators created a technical committee on fundamental human rights. Their priority was rights directly relevant to the 1994 national general election. The result was Chapter 3 (Fundamental Rights) of the Interim Constitution (1993), which incorporated extensive civil and political rights as well as property and collective bargaining rights but only a limited set of social and economic rights.

The drafting of the 1996 Constitution began after the 1994 election. The Constitution had to adhere to the thirty-four constitutional principles agreed to by the two main parties—the ANC and the NP at the time of the political negotiations—one of which was a Bill of Rights. The Constitutional Assembly, comprising the 400 elected members of the National Assembly and ninety members of the National Council of Provinces, widely consulted the public. Committees of experts examined other constitutions and conducted independent research. The resulting Bill of Rights established extensive social, economic, and cultural rights, and strengthened civil and political rights, making it one of the most progressive and comprehensive ones in the world.

Implementing the Bill of Rights

In accordance with the Bill of Rights, the postapartheid government signed and ratified most major international human rights treaties and dismantled many pieces of APARTHEID-era legislation. However, the high levels of poverty and violence in the country meant that many South Africans could not yet fully enjoy their constitutional rights. Financial and other constraints have made it difficult for the postapartheid state to guarantee the right to health, for example.

Also in accordance with the Bill of Rights, in 1995, the TRUTH AND RECONCILIATION COMMISSION was created to investigate human rights violations during apartheid. Its 1998 report confirmed widespread abuses by state officials. The commission offered amnesty to petitioners who fully disclosed their roles and granted restitution to some victims. In addition, several permanent institutions help protect and promote human rights. The Constitutional Court, composed of eleven members, is the final appeal court in constitutional matters. The Public Protector protects individuals from rights violations by the state, responding to complaints by investigating and recommending corrective action. The Commission for Gender Equality advises Parliament and other legislatures when laws or proposed legislation affect gender equality. It can receive and investigate complaints of gender-based discrimination. The Commission for Human Rights monitors the overall human rights situation and educates the public on these issues. It also can investigate and seek redress when human rights have been violated.

See also CONSTITUTION

Bibliography

Klug, Heinz. *Constituting Democracy: Law, Globalism and South Africa's Political Reconstruction.* Cambridge, UK: Cambridge University Press, 2000.

Sachs, Albie. *Protecting Human Rights in a New South Africa.* Cape Town: Oxford University Press, 1990.

—*Carolyn Bassett*

Black Consciousness Movement

The Black Consciousness Movement (BCM) emerged in the mid-1960s in response to the political vacuum left by the banning and decimation of the major groups fighting APARTHEID, such as the AFRICAN NATIONAL CONGRESS (ANC) and the PAN AFRICANIST CONGRESS. This movement is most closely associated with STEVE BIKO, a leading student activist and martyr of the antiapartheid movement. Biko began espousing black consciousness ideals in medical school after he resigned from the National Union of South African Students, a predominantly white liberal organization, and formed the South African Student Organization (SASO). The BCM was given further organizational structure with the formation of the nonstudent group the Black People's Convention, organized by Biko and other black consciousness leaders. The BCM concerned itself not only with political liberation but also with reclaiming African identity and blackness and with challenging the white monopoly on knowledge production. Part of BCM's insight was in understanding that black liberation required not only structural political changes but also a psychological transformation in the minds of black people themselves.

Most importantly, the BCM defined black to include all people of color in South Africa, which served to bring together African, COLOURED, and INDIAN antiapartheid groups. Indeed, the BCM played an important role in not only challenging apartheid racial categories, but in pushing the coloured and Indian communities to redefine and reclaim their identities.

As a philosophy, two stages were outlined by Biko for restoring African consciousness: physical liberation and psychological liberation. For the BCM, an important component of psychological liberation was the insistence that blacks be the leaders of black liberation movements, a clear rejection of the nonracial approach to political struggle later adopted by other liberation movements such as the ANC. In addition, through its Black Community Projects, the BCM built schools and day-care centers, and organized community medical clinics and adult literacy classes, as well as black "consciousness" classes for the black community.

The BCM also staged political protests and rallies, with many of its members incurring the wrath of the apartheid state. In 1973, both SASO and the Black People's Convention were banned, and many of their leaders were detained or arrested. The prominent trials of the Pretoria Twelve and the SASO Nine, in which prominent black consciousness activists were on trial for attempting to overthrow the state, provided a platform on which to explain the black consciousness philosophy and served to further strengthen and grow the movement. The BCM was a leading force behind the SOWETO STUDENT UPRISING of 1976, which began in part in response to the demand that black students be taught some of their classes in the Afrikaans language. The apartheid state's efforts to define South African national identity in line with AFRIKANER identity was seen as a direct threat to the BCM and its principles. After 1976, the police cracked down on BCM leaders and organizations. In 1977, Biko died from serious head injuries while in police custody. However, the BCM lived on, most notably with the formation of new organizations such as the Azanian People's Organization. (Azania was an alternative name for South Africa used by many black African nationalists and BCM activists.) Organizationally, the movement weakened and declined in prominence, but its legacy has been the dissemination of its ideas and principles throughout many black political organizations. As a philosophy, its presence in South African politics continues today.

See also STEVE BIKO; POLITICAL CULTURES AND IDEOLOGIES; SOWETO STUDENT UPRISING

Black Economic Empowerment

Black Economic Empowerment (BEE) is a program instituted by the AFRICAN NATIONAL CONGRESS–led government after APARTHEID in an attempt to address the socioeconomic inequalities of the past. It seeks to provide economic opportunities, including skills development, ownership, management, preferential procurement, and employment equity to previously disadvantaged groups including black Africans, COLOUREDS, and INDIANS. The program also extends to women and to the physically challenged of all races. Responding to the fact that in 1994 the overwhelming majority of businesses were owned by whites who made up only 10 percent of the country's population, the BEE policy is more than simply a moral imperative. The idea behind BEE is that South Africa can only prosper economically when wealth is shared more evenly, when the productive capacities of all South Africans are utilized, and when the needs of all South Africans are met.

With the passage of the Black Economic Empowerment Act of 2003, concrete measures were put into place to promote the development and acquisition of businesses by historically disadvantaged black South Africans. For example, quotas for black employment have been instituted for medium-sized and large businesses, as have quotas for black ownership in key economic sectors, including mining, financial services, information technology, agriculture, and tourism. In addition, codes of good practice have been instituted for many companies, and businesses are now rated based on various scorecards and criteria, including ownership, management, employment equity, and skills development. In this regard, BEE goes much further than most affirmative-action programs in other countries.

The BEE policy has been criticized as a program for enriching a few blacks at the expense of the rest. Critics point to the fact that levels of inequality between the rich and the poor have not changed since the DEMOCRATIC TRANSITION. They argue that rather than focus on transferring the ownership of a few companies to a few black businessmen, the government should be targeting secondary and tertiary education, providing the foundation for blacks to compete equally with their white counterparts in the workforce.

See also ECONOMY

Bloemfontein

Founded in 1846 as an outpost in the Transoranje region as part of British colonial expansion into the South African interior on land already settled by white Voortrekkers (pioneers), as well as indigenous SOTHO and GRIQUA people, the city of Bloemfontein later became the capital of the

AFRIKANER republic, the Orange Free State republic (1852–1898). Like most South African cities, Bloemfontein is still heavily racially segregated. It later became the capital of the Orange Free State Province once South Africa became a union (1910–1994) and of the Free State Province after the 1994 democratic elections. The city also serves as the seat of the Supreme Court of Appeal, the highest court in the country except in constitutional matters. In 2000, the city was integrated, along with nearby Botshabelo (twenty miles outside the city) and Thaba Nchu (a farther six miles), into the Manguang Local Municipality. Manguang is also the Sotho name for Bloemfontein.

Located in the center of South Africa, the city spans 163 square miles and has an official population of 850,000 people. Noted South Africans who were born in Bloemfontein include the writer J.R.R. Tolkien, the track and field athlete Zola Budd, and the disgraced cricket captain Hansie Cronje. Both the AFRICAN NATIONAL CONGRESS (1912) and the NATIONAL PARTY (1914) were founded in Bloemfontein.

See also APPENDIX 4: PROVINCES AND MAJOR CITIES

Boer(s)
See AFRIKANER(S)

Boer Republics

The Boer republics were independent states established as early as 1795 by the Dutch-speaking BOERS who migrated from the CAPE COLONY, later known as AFRIKANERS. When Britain took over as the colonial power of the Cape, the Boers escaped their administrative control by embarking on what has come to be known as the GREAT TREK of 1835 into the heartland of South Africa to find new land to settle and a new supply of African forced labor. However, states were also established by other population groups, most notably the GRIQUA, a subgroup of South Africa's heterogeneous and multiracial COLOURED people who established Griqualand West and Griqualand East.

The Boers, or Voortrekkers, were semi-nomadic, pastoral farmers. In their search for land, they often came into conflict with many indigenous tribes but were able to defeat many of them, given their superior weaponry, and establish independent republics. For example, the NATAL Republic was established in 1839 after the famous defeat of the ZULU army by the Boers in the BATTLE OF BLOOD RIVER. But, many of the Boer republics were in fact mini-states and short lived. The Natal Republic soon became the British-controlled colony of Natal. The Transvaal (South African Republic or Zuid-Afrikaansche Republiek) and the Orange Free State, however, developed into successful independent countries that were recognized not only by Britain and the Netherlands but also by France, Germany, Belgium, and the United States. In these two states, the Boers established a republican form of government, with the creation of a constitution and an elected governing body.

However, when diamonds were found in 1867 along the Vaal River and gold was discovered in 1886 on the Witwatersrand hills in the Transvaal Republic, the British renewed their interests in acquiring the two functioning Boer Republics. British and German fortune seekers flooded into the Transvaal Republic, eventually even outnumbering the Afrikaners. Tensions between the two Boer republics and Britain eventually led to the ANGLO-BOER WAR, which brought the defeat of the Afrikaners and the end of independence for the Boer republics.

Boesak, Allan Aubrey (1945–)

Reverend Allan Aubrey Boesak is a cleric in the South African DUTCH REFORMED CHURCH and was a leading liberation theologian and activist against APARTHEID in the 1970s and 1980s. Born to Christian parents who were classified as COLOURED, Boesak was drawn to preaching from an early age. He first pursued his theological studies at the University of the Western Cape and was ordained in the Dutch Reformed Mission Church (the coloured affiliate of the white Dutch Reformed Church) in 1968. After studying in the Netherlands and the United States, he returned to South Africa and became politically active in the BLACK CONSCIOUSNESS MOVEMENT and began teaching and preaching while organizing opposition to apartheid in CAPE TOWN. Boesak played a key role in exposing the relationship between apartheid and the white Dutch Reformed Church and articulating a South African variant of liberation theology. The Dutch Reformed Church provided the religious justification for much of the racist policies of apartheid, such as the prohibition of interracial marriages and the moral justification for separate development for the racial groups.

In 1982, Boesak was elected president of the World Alliance of Reformed Churches and persuaded the organization to suspend the membership of white South African churches. In 1983, he was one of the founding members of the UNITED DEMOCRATIC FRONT (UDF), a multiracial coalition of many antiapartheid organizations, which was the umbrella body for many of the political protests and demonstrations that took place in the 1980s and played a significant role in the demise of apartheid.

When the UDF was disbanded, following the unbanning of the AFRICAN NATIONAL CONGRESS (ANC), Boesak became a leading figure in its Western Cape affiliate. He was the ANC candidate for premier of the Western Cape Province in 1994. However, that same year, he was accused of misappropriating money that was donated to his charity, Foundation for Peace and Justice. In 1999, he was subsequently convicted of theft and fraud and ended up serving one year of a three-year sentence. In 2005, Boesak was granted a pardon from President THABO MBEKI and returned to the pulpit.

Boesak is the author of several books, including *The Finger of God: Sermons on Faith and Socio-Political Responsibility* (1982) and *Black and Reformed: Apartheid, Liberation, and the Calvinist Tradition* (1984).

See also UNITED DEMOCRATIC FRONT

Breytenbach, Breyten (1939–)

Born in Bonnievale, Western Cape Province, in 1939, poet and activist Breyten Breytenbach gained Afrikaans literary praise after the publication of two major works in 1964, including *Die Ysterkoei Moet Sweet* and *Katastrofes*. His outspoken nature and opposition to the APARTHEID government contributed to his imprisonment, exile, and dedication to art as a form of activism.

In 1959, Breytenbach left his studies at the University of CAPE TOWN to explore Europe, where he began his writing and painting career. While in France, he married a French woman of Vietnamese descent, Yolande Ngo Thi Hoang, in 1962. Based on the restrictions of the Mixed Marriages Act and the Immorality Act, she was denied a South African passport. After the government relented and issued the passport, the couple was finally able to visit South Africa in 1972. The public refusal of the passport placed Breytenbach in the national spotlight, raising awareness of dissent and intellectual reflection about apartheid in the AFRIKANER community.

While in France, he began covert operations in the freedom struggle as a founding member of Okhela, an exiled resistance group. In 1975, with a fraudulent French passport, he returned to South Africa to recruit representatives of trade unions into Okhela. After being arrested, Breytenbach served seven years of a nine-year sentence under the Terrorism Act. Upon his release in 1982, he returned to France and resumed his activities as a writer and as an antiapartheid activist.

His writing and artwork reflect autobiographical accounts of his life as an intellectual straddling different nationalities and identities. Such reflections are included in *A Season of Paradise* (1980), *The True Confessions of an Albino Terrorist* (1984), and many works of poetry, prose, and essays. Much of his work is translated from Afrikaans into English.

See also LITERATURE

British Imperialism and Settler Colonialism (1795–1870)

British imperialism in South Africa has been the subject of a considerable amount of literature. Criticized in the settler historiography of the nineteenth century as "negrophile," the "imperial factor" in South Africa received a more favorable press from liberal historians in the first half of the twentieth century, who saw British intervention as a reluctant but nonetheless important counter to the aggressive racism of settler colonialism. More recent judgments, grounded in a greater appreciation of the part played by imperialism in the conquest and exploitation of African societies, its destructive impact on the fabric of African life, and its crucial role in the construction of South Africa's racial order, have been less forgiving.

These generalizations need, however, to be tempered by an appreciation of the ambiguities of imperialism and diversity of motives and actions of its agents; tensions existed between the liberal paternalism of early humanitarians, as evidenced in the antislavery movement or the campaign to ameliorate the condition of the laboring poor on the one hand, and the prosettler belligerence of many local officers on the other. The result for much of the period was vacillation between social and economic assimilation supported by colonial and imperial merchant capital and humanitarian officials, and military conquest and expropriation favored by the military, speculators, and land- and labor-hungry settlers. Often seen as agents of imperialism, missionaries, who came to South Africa from a variety of denominations and in increasing numbers starting in the 1790s, were equally divided, despite their common objective of converting the "heathen." The three Cs of colonialism—conquest, CHRISTIANITY, and commerce—were to transform the lives and identities of all South Africa's inhabitants.

Yet, British imperialism and settler colonialism were neither monolithic nor all powerful, even at the CAPE COLONY, the earliest and largest of the two British colonies in this period. Nor were the indigenous peoples of southern Africa simply the hapless victims of British ruthless machinations. At key moments, they enlisted often unwitting imperial allies to fight their more local battles, and early nationalists, both black and white, used the liberal language of empire for their own purposes.

The British at the Cape: The Early Years

The DUTCH EAST INDIA COMPANY's settlement at the Cape of Good Hope first passed into British hands in 1795 after the Napoleonic conquest of the Netherlands. This occupation was brief although the problems faced by the first British administration (1795–1803) and by the Batavian Republic (as the Netherlands was known under Napoleonic sway) that followed (1803–1806) presaged the problems that were to preoccupy the British when they took over the Cape with the resumption of hostilities with France in 1806; British control of the Cape was formally ratified in 1814. Although not immediately apparent, the substitution of British for Dutch rule at the Cape was no mere switch in nationality but the supplanting of a mercantile company by an imperial state already undergoing the complex economic and social changes of its industrial revolution. By the 1790s, humanitarian enlightenment and evangelical enthusiasm were its ideological companions, although initially, this too was far from clear as a series of military governors held sway at the Cape. Ineluctably, the capitalist transformation of the Cape Colony had begun.

Strategically important on the sea route to Asia, the late-eighteenth-century Cape Colony was a sprawling and troubled possession in which some 22,000 burghers (European citizens) constituted a master class. The vineyards and wheat fields crucial to the economy of the western part of the Cape Colony depended on the labor of some 25,000 slaves drawn from a wide arc around the Indian Ocean; to the north and east, pastoral farming, based on a labor force of largely indigenous KHOIKHOI and SAN (or Khoisan, as the two related ethnic groups are often called collectively), necessitated large tracts of land especially in the more arid regions. By the end of the century, however, settler expansion had come up against a double barrier: the fierce resistance of Khoisan on the colonial north and northeast mountains frontiers and densely settled XHOSA people living in the summer rainfall area beyond the Great Fish River, whose economy was equally dependent on cattle.

Once the British took over the colony, their first tasks were to find collaborators to serve in the administration and develop the economy. In so doing, they were guided by the overarching imperative of imperial rule: if the colony could not produce economic benefits through the production of raw materials and the purchase of British manufactures, at least it should not be a burden on the British treasury. For the military governors who were appointed to the Cape, this meant sustaining the existing social order through an alliance with men of wealth and standing among the burghers in CAPE TOWN and its environs. In the 1820s, increasing pressure from humanitarians in Britain and missionaries in the Cape led to some improvement in the lives of slaves and Khoikhoi laborers. Yet, the reforms left existing power and property relations largely unchanged, with whites controlling all of the land. Moreover, the racial and class domination that characterized social relations at the Cape at the end of the eighteenth century spread with the dispersal of white settlement in South Africa and remained largely intact until minerals were discovered in the interior in the last third of the century.

Until the 1820s, when the advent of some 4,000 British settlers in the eastern part of the Cape Colony provided an alternative, the British authorities retained existing administrative and legal practices, leaving in office Dutch *landdrosts* (magistrates) and *heemraden* (local officials) as district commandants in the army. Together with British recognition of the Dutch language, the revitalization of Dutch high culture, freedom of worship (first established by the Batavians), and increased access to the British market for Cape wine, this served to reconcile the wealthier Dutch farmers and officials to imperial rule. Many Cape-born officials of the Dutch East India Company transferred their allegiance to the British, increasingly adopted English styles, spoke English, and allowed intermarriage with English officers and officials.

Not all the Cape Dutch settlers acquiesced in British rule so readily. In the vast Graaff-Reinet District, rebellion had rumbled even before the British arrived. In 1799, troops were sent from the Cape to subdue its unruly burghers but also to remove the Xhosa, who had begun to contest the grazing land in its southeast corner known as the Zuurveld. The arrival of the British on the colonial frontier was greeted with enthusiasm by the laboring Khoisan who believed their oppression at an end. They deserted the farms en masse with their masters' horses and guns, hoping to regain lost lands. When their hopes were dashed, they joined the western Xhosa, whom the British had failed to dislodge in the colony's third frontier war, which lasted until 1802 and confronted the colony with its gravest threat since its founding. Although the Khoisan were driven back to the farms by 1803, the Xhosa and their allies were only pushed out of the Zuurveld in 1812, with the appearance of British troops on the frontier. For the first but not the last time, the balance of power was tipped against an African people by the British army.

In all, there were nine major wars between the Xhosa and the Cape Colony between 1779 and 1889. Often precipitated by drought and crop failure, unequal exchange of goods and services, or particularly harsh treatment, the wars were punctuated by intermittent skirmishing and mutual cattle raiding. Underlying this hundred-year conflict were the expansion of white settlers into African lands; black-white competition over grazing, water, and cattle; and the incessant demand of the colonists for labor. War was not infrequently provoked by colonists with an eye on war profits and grazing land for the sheep that were the Cape's most profitable commodity from the 1830s until the discovery of diamonds in 1868, while black captives were always a useful windfall for the labor market. Despite the Colonial Office's ambivalence about white settler expansionism, the recall on occasion of an overly supportive governor, and even the sporadic withdrawal from annexed territory, the colonial frontier marched ineluctably east- and northward. Despite its concern to control expenditure, the British government was almost always dragged in to defend white colonial subjects, protect their property, and satisfy their call for (cheap, black) labor.

The 1820 Settlers

Pressures on the eastern frontier were further exacerbated by the arrival of around 4,000 government-sponsored British immigrants in 1820, a critical moment in the colony's Anglicization. The scheme was designed to relieve unemployment and defuse radicalization in post-Napoleonic Britain as well as to provide a buffer of small-scale farmers between the colony and the Xhosa. It proved a dismal failure, as few of the would-be settlers had farming experience. Within a short time, the majority of the immigrants had drifted to the eastern Cape towns, while the more adventurous turned to trading and hunting in the colonial hinterland. Mostly enterprising men in search of opportunity, the more educated brought with them the ideology of respectability and progress, which was characteristic of the British middle class, as well as a lively curiosity about the world they were entering. They also brought well-honed beliefs about the rights of the free-born Englishman and supported efforts to attain freedom of the press and more representative institutions in the colony, although executive power remained the governor's prerogative for another thirty years.

The presence of a substantial body of British settlers on the eastern frontier further complicated the issues confronting the British government at the Cape: how to regulate the colony's often brutal labor regime in the interests of stability and how to resolve conflict on the eastern frontier without increasing expenditure. For the most part, however, the British authorities supported masters against servants and settlers against indigenous peoples, despite humanitarian and missionary lobbying.

Hottentot Codes and the Abolition of Slavery

The abolition of the slave trade in the British Empire, including the Cape Colony, in 1807 intensified the pressures on the Khoikhoi (called Hottentots by the settlers) who, in the absence of foreign slaves, had been forced at the end of the 1799–1802 uprising to return to work on settler farms, usually for minimal or no wages. Most British governors recognized the need for legal regulation to curb the endemic violence of the master-servant relationship. The Hottentot Codes, passed by the British in 1809, 1811, and 1819 for use in the Cape Colony, had a dual purpose. On the one hand, they enforced contractual relations between colonists and Khoikhoi and immobilized Khoikhoi laborers on the farms through a pass system and the apprenticeship of their children to their eighteenth year. On the other hand, conditions of service were laid down, and circuit courts were established enabling rural laborers to complain of ill treatment to the authorities. An attempt by the 1812 Circuit Court to investigate some 200 complaints of ill treatment outraged the frontier whites, though few complaints succeeded. In the 1820s, a series of laws strengthened legal protection for slaves, and considerable numbers of slaves brought such complaints to official attention.

The increased influence of humanitarians in London, and their belief in the efficacy of well-treated and "free" labor was also reflected in Ordinance 50, passed in 1828, which abolished the PASS LAWS, prohibited the indenture of children or the withholding of workers' wages, provided for regulated contracts, and gave the Khoisan equal access to the courts. Six years later, the British Parliament proclaimed the emancipation of slaves in the British Empire after a four-year apprenticeship. Despite Ordinance 50 and emancipation, however, in the absence of land or the resources to work it, the majority of slaves and Khoisan remained on the white farms in servile conditions, although some moved to mission stations or towns. Inadequate as these laws were to transform the lives of the laboring poor, the intervention of the missionaries and humanitarians was anathema in the Eastern Cape, where settlers complained bitterly of black vagrancy and cattle theft.

The Mfecane/Difiqane

Colonial fears of African vagrancy and cattle theft increased from the mid-1820s as news of disorder beyond the colony's borders first reached the British authorities at the Cape through a mist of rumor and misinformation. Known conventionally as the MFECANE or *Difiqane* (most commonly translated into English as "the crushing" or "the scattering") until comparatively recently, the turmoil beyond the colony was attributed solely to the evil genius of SHAKA, who became king of the small ZULU chiefdom in 1818. Most historians now believe this greatly exaggerates the role of Shaka in the region's turbulence and conflates several separate cycles of violence intensified, if not generated, by the activities of Europeans and their surrogates in the hinterland of the Cape and Delagoa Bay from the late eighteenth century. These came together with explosive effect in the severe drought of the early 1820s.

Increasing numbers of often desperate and starving African refugees entered the colony from the 1823 Battle at Dithakong to the north and raids on the Thembu chiefdoms to the northeast. They were viewed as a security threat as well as a welcome source of labor for the chronically labor-hungry eastern Cape. This was recognized in Ordinance 49 of 1828, which allowed Africans from beyond the boundaries of the colony to seek work, provided they carried official passes. So concerned were the British with the potential military threat, however, that in 1828, at Mbholompo well into the Transkei, imperial troops backed Xhosa, Thembu, and Mpondo chiefs in attacking Ngwane refugees, whom the British mistook for Zulu.

The War of Hintsa

Closer to home, tensions between the colonists in the eastern districts and the western Xhosa also mounted, as Xhosa loss of land and cattle to settlers and speculators led to a cycle of violence and counterviolence—as well as a battle of words between missionary and humanitarian supporters of the Xhosa and the settlers. At the end of 1834, the fifth Xhosa frontier war erupted, which many recent historians believe marked a turning point in white-black relations in the Eastern Cape, as British settler attitudes toward Africans hardened. At stake were two competing visions of the future: continued settler expansion and land speculation backed by the imperial army or the assimilation of African peasants producing for the market and purchasing British goods. Neither vision left room for the continued independence of African society.

The war was portrayed by the colonists and their apologists as an unprovoked attack, masterminded by the titular paramount of all the Xhosa, Chief Hintsa of the Gcaleka clan, who at that time lived well beyond the colonial frontiers. In essence, however, the war represented a last-ditch effort by a section of the western Xhosa to prevent further seizures of their land. The governor, Sir Benjamin D'Urban, and his military commandant, Sir Harry Smith, carried out an attack into the Xhosa heartlands against Hintsa, who had previously played no direct role in the confrontations between the virtually autonomous western Xhosa and the settlers. Hintsa was captured, publicly humiliated, and brutally shot, his corpse mutilated as the troops ravaged African lands, looted cattle, burnt homesteads, and captured Xhosa women and children. Smith and D'Urban took the opportunity to bring into the colony some 1,000 MFENGU, allegedly African refugees from the Mfecane held against their will by the western Xhosa, together with 22,000 head of Gcaleka cattle. Gcaleka lands were annexed as Queen Adelaide Province. The Mfengu were to prove valuable soldiers and collaborators for the British. Among the Xhosa, the war became known as the War of Hintsa; the treachery of the king's death haunted Xhosa-British relations throughout the nineteenth century.

The Province of Queen Adelaide was short-lived. To the fury of BOER and British settlers alike, the British colonial secretary Lord Glenelg rescinded its creation, recalled D'Urban, and appointed an official enquiry into Hintsa's death. This marked the high point of British liberal intervention in South Africa. Following the war, colonial officials attempted to enlist independent African chiefs beyond the Fish River to maintain law and order, a policy already adopted in relation to GRIQUA chief Andries Waterboer to the north. This so-called treaty system was short-lived, however. Among the Xhosa, it was completely destroyed with the particularly vicious seventh frontier war (the War of the Axe), which ended with the British annexation of all the land between the Fish and Kei rivers as the districts of Victoria East and British Kaffraria.

The Great Trek

In the frontier districts specifically, Boer grievances against British rule had also accumulated since the mid-1820s: the Anglicization of the courts, local administration, and currency; the refusal of the British government to entertain antivagrancy legislation; and the inadequate and botched compensation granted by the British for the emancipation of their slaves all incensed frontier farmers. Already suffering land shortage, their temper was not improved when the government decided to implement its reform of the Cape's land tenure system, which introduced more of a free market system and led to an escalation of land values. Huge tracts were engrossed by wealthier Western Cape burghers, making it more difficult for those without capital to acquire farms. Recurrent droughts in the 1820s and the Xhosa block to settler expansion eastward had already persuaded some to move north across the Karoo region in the wake of earlier Griqua, Baster, and Oorlam pioneers of the Cape's northern hinterland. In 1824, the northern frontier had reached the Orange and Stormspruit rivers—by which time many pastoral farmers had trekked well beyond it. A record number of bankruptcies in 1834 and the increasing insecurity that culminated in the War of Hintsa caused more families to move out of the colony. Even before the retrocession of the Province of Queen Adelaide further inflamed settler opinion, reconnaissance parties had been sent to explore the possibilities of settlement beyond the frontier. They returned with glowing reports of an allegedly "empty" land. Between December 1833 and 1840, approximately 6,000 to 10,000 AFRIKANERS left the Cape Colony in a movement that subsequently became known as the GREAT TREK. Unlike the earlier drift of cattle farmers beyond the settled areas of the colony in search of land and water, most of whom had no desire to lose their access to British markets and protection, this movement was highly politicized. For many, it was an alternative to outright—but futile—rebellion. They left the Cape with little by way of a constitutional agenda but with a strong sense of color, class, and community. Organized in a number of parties, they usually consisted of a prominent and relatively affluent leader and his family and friends, as well as their Khoisan laborers, former slaves, and white dependents and clients. The emigrant farmers, as they were known at the time, or Voortrekkers (pioneers) as they were termed by subsequent Afrikaner nationalists, made their way north and east of the Cape, where they established a series of republics that dramatically expanded white settlement in South Africa. Although this was made possible because the Mfecane had dislodged many of the indigenous ethnic groups that had lived there historically, it was the divisive nature of these wars that enabled the trekkers to establish themselves by forming alliances with local people. Independent African allies, equally anxious to defeat the Zulu and NDEBELE conquest states, were crucial to the Boer victory in battle and their ability to establish themselves temporarily in NATAL and more permanently in the interior.

Contrary to an older liberal narrative, which construes the Voortrekkers as archaic and anarchic, and an Afrikaner nationalist historiography, which portrays them as heroic pioneers entering virgin territory, the emigrant settlers, as they were known at the time, were dependent on continued links with the world economy, while they followed the trails of earlier hunters, traders, and missionaries guided by Africans in the interior. The Boer republics were dependent on access to—and speculation in—land. Christianity and literacy were crucial to their self-image, and trade—especially but not only in arms and ammunition—was even more crucial to their survival; they were soon to find it difficult to sustain these through purely internal resources. Even those trekker leaders most determined to escape British influence sought an outlet to the sea and made their way to Port Natal (where a small number of British traders, hunters, and missionaries had settled since 1824) or hoped to reach an accommodation with the Portuguese at Delagoa Bay (now Maputo). Part of the expansion of Europe and its land colonization schemes, they were harbingers of colonial capitalism and not anachronistic relics of an earlier age.

Yet, the republics that the trekker parties established in Natal and north of the Vaal River were fragile; the Orange Free State republic with its enclave of British merchants and strong ties to the Cape economy had greater stability. Despite the need for unity, the citizens of the little republics established north of the Vaal were reluctant to assist their neighbors as their dissensions had escalated into civil war. Their administrations were weak and their finances were chaotic. Initially, guns, horses, and ox wagons gave the Boers an advantage over Africans armed only with spears and *assagis*, but in the longer term, they were unable to establish their rule over the larger African chiefdoms.

Trekker states were premised on—and undermined by—their expropriation and exploitation of the African inhabitants of the lands they entered, which brought the trekkers once more into conflict with the British. Initially, the latter did not attempt to prevent Boer emigration beyond passing the Cape of Good Hope Punishment Act (1836), which held them liable to the Cape courts for all crimes committed south of 25-degrees latitude, well beyond the boundaries of the Cape Colony. When, in 1840, the Zulu king, Mpande, granted the trekker Republic of Natalia the land between the Thukela and Mzimvubu rivers, the Boers gained control over Port Natal. Concerned lest the sea route to India fall into the hands of a hostile power and apprehensive that Boer policies would revive disorder on its eastern frontier, the British occupied Port Natal in 1838 and, after a brief military incursion, annexed the republic in 1843 as an "autonomous" district of the Cape Colony.

British Annexation of the Lands North of the Orange River

Despite British endeavors to win over the Boers in Natal, by 1848 most had joined their confreres on the southern *highveld* (plateau) in the Orange Free State republic, where the expansion of merino sheep farming in the 1840s had created a mini-boom—and had increased conflict over grazing land with local African communities. In 1845, in response to appeals from the indigenous groups in the area—the Griqua, under Captain Adam Kok III and the SOTHO under King MOSHOESHOE, with whom the British had signed treaties in 1843—the Cape governor sent troops against the Boers and defeated them. This was the first time the British had intervened beyond Orange River, and it proved the prelude to the annexation in 1848 of the whole of the area claimed by the Boer republics north of the Orange by Sir Harry Smith who had returned to the Cape as governor and high commissioner the previous year. Although Smith initially recognized Moshoeshoe's land claims, his main concern was to conciliate the Boers and open the arable land in the Orange River Sovereignty to white farmers. In 1849, the British residents in BLOEMFONTEIN redrew the boundaries in the fertile Caledon Valley, allocating most of it to white farmers, and in 1851, Smith led a combined force of colonial troops, and Moshoeshoe's Sotho and Griqua opponents against the king, who was reinforcing his power over the chiefdoms in the Caledon Valley. The British attack ended in disaster, however, and contributed to the recall of Smith, who was seen as the source of disorder in South Africa. His successor concluded peace with Moshoeshoe in 1852.

While the annexation of Natal had clear strategic merit, the British government had little interest in contested land beyond the Orange River, which at that time had few resources other than the wool already destined for Cape and British markets. The 1852 and 1854 conventions between the British and the Boers returned sovereignty to the Boer republics north of the Vaal and Orange rivers, respectively, and abrogated all of Britain's alliances with African chiefs. More importantly, they also prohibited the sale of firearms to Africans, who were beginning to use them with devastating effect. Over the next decade, Moshoeshoe consolidated his hold over his mountain kingdom, although the Sotho-Boer friction over land continued, erupting into war with the Transvaal Republic and the Free State in 1865. Despite a valiant defense, Moshoeshoe appealed for British protection, which was granted in 1868, and his much reduced realm was incorporated into the Cape Colony three years later.

The War of Mlanjeni

British repudiation of Smith's policies of divide-and-rule and the use of African groups to wage conflict against other African groups also resulted from renewed turmoil on the eastern frontier. Despite Smith's assurances that he had "settled" the Cape's eastern frontier after the 1846–1847 war, conflict erupted once more in 1850. The 1850–1853 War of Mlanjeni, the eighth frontier war between the British and the Xhosa, was devastating for both sides: it was the longest and most formidable black-white conflict anywhere in southern Africa in the nineteenth or twentieth century. It cost the British taxpayers some £2 million to £3 million. The cost to the Xhosa and the mostly Christian, coloured inhabitants of the Kat River settlement who joined them was far higher.

Some 16,000 Xhosa were killed, their cattle confiscated, and their crops deliberately destroyed, while the Kat River rebels lost their lands to white settlers and saw their leaders publicly executed.

More Xhosa cattle died in the lung sickness epizootic, which ravaged African herds after the war, while Sir George Grey, the Cape governor, deliberately undermined chiefly powers and planted British and German settlers on confiscated Xhosa lands. When Xhosa crops also failed, the millennial visions of a young girl, NONGQAWUSE, found ready soil among a starving people, many of whom killed their remaining cattle for food to stave off further infection or as a last resort in response to Nongqawuse's prophecies. By the end of 1857, the western Xhosa had been totally dispossessed, and thousands died of hunger or poured into the colony in search of food and work. A final frontier war, or Xhosa war, from 1877 to 1878 simply put a seal on the existing reality. By then, the western Xhosa and Khoisan had lost their lands, their livelihoods, and their independence, and most had been reduced to laborers on settler farms, towns, and mines.

Representative Institutions at the Cape

By the 1840s, both English and Dutch speakers in the Cape were increasingly disaffected with their lack of access to decisionmaking in the colony. By the end of the decade, this had fused with colony-wide agitation both against British policies on the eastern frontier and against imperial attempts to ship British convicts to Cape Town, opposition to which had brought the government to a standstill. The anticonvict agitation led to a broader alliance when COLOUREDS—as the Khoisan and emancipated slaves were now coming to be called—in Cape Town and on the missions joined the opposition. This was all the more formidable as rebellion was also rumored among coloureds in the rural western Cape, while on the eastern frontier, the coloured inhabitants of the Kat River, who were being expelled from their lands, had joined the Xhosa in the War of Mlanjeni. In the demand for representative institutions, these supposedly dangerous classes had to be accommodated.

From the 1820s onward, settler demands for representative institutions had been refused by the British on the grounds that enfranchised colonists were likely to use their vote to oppress indigenous peoples. Now, therefore, liberal opinion in the Western Cape was for the enfranchisement of all—regardless of color—including those who had little property and low wages. Liberal values may initially have been a British transplant at the Cape; nevertheless, by mid-century, some members of the Cape Dutch elite were using the language of universal human rights, usually regarded as the prerogative of British humanitarians. This reflected their stake in a low electoral qualification, which would enfranchise their poorer brethren. Once achieved, however, a degree of cynicism entered in relation to electoral politics in general, and the votes of coloureds, many of them indentured farm workers, were frequently determined by their white masters.

Liberalism at the Cape was, as elsewhere, the ideology of the propertied, and it underpinned their demands for political representation, equality before the law, the abolition of mercantilism, and a free market in labor; it was not about abolishing the class and racial distinctions between masters and servants or recognizing cultural difference. Ambiguous and limited, liberalism at the Cape was always a minority belief although it had Afrikaner and British adherents; its most articulate and outspoken antagonists were the English-speaking settlers of the Eastern Cape and Natal, who believed that the CAPE FRANCHISE was an unmitigated disaster. Nevertheless, the nonracial vote differentiated the Cape's political system from that of its neighbors and gave black residents a different constitutional framework within which to operate. Although colonial politicians, who had achieved self-government in 1872, raised the franchise qualifications in 1887, by the early twentieth century, African voters held the balance in fourteen Cape constituencies.

Colonial Rule in Natal

The largely British colonists in Natal who had settled there from the 1820s were granted representative institutions in 1864. However, property qualifications for its franchise were high, while the hurdles confronting Africans—which included their exemption from the provisions of customary law—were so formidable that only six had qualified for the vote by the turn of the century.

With the British annexation of Natal and the departure of the trekkers, absentee land speculators and merchants bought vast tracts of land in the new colony, hoping to profit from future immigration. Although, with British rule, large numbers of Africans returned from their war-time dispersal, the anticipated British immigration was slow in coming. Renting land to Africans, most of whom already had claim to the land, proved a profitable alternative.

Between 1846 and 1864, Theophilus Shepstone, who was appointed diplomatic agent to the native tribes (later secretary for native affairs), set aside eight reserves for the sole occupation of Africans, some one-eighth of Natal's land area. Large tracts were also set aside as mission reserves. In the absence of administrative or financial resources, Shepstone reconstituted Africans on the reserves into "tribes," which were governed through chiefs authorized by the government. African customary law, codified by Shepstone, was recognized insofar as it was not "repugnant" to "civilized" practice, and the British governor took the position of "supreme chief," with autocratic powers resembling those of the Zulu kings. After Zululand's annexation by the British in 1887 and its incorporation by Natal in 1897, similar policies were applied north of the Thukela River, now part of the colony.

Greatly outnumbered by Africans, Natal settlers nevertheless complained bitterly of labor shortages and held Shepstone's policies responsible. They constantly demanded—unsuccessfully—that he raise African taxation, reduce the size of the reserves, and abolish polygyny. So long as they had access to land, Africans had little need to work on the white-owned sugar plantations that had become the most important sector of the colonial economy by the 1860s. As a result, indentured laborers were brought to Natal from India and Mozambique. Initially, rural Africans in Natal appear to have acquiesced in colonial rule, not least because Shepstone was responsive to their needs. As Africans moved into the white urban areas, however, their movements were controlled by passes, similar to those in the Cape Colony, and they were legally bound to conform to European dress and decorum. By the 1860s, petitions to the British government from Africans on the mission reserves appealing for equality before the law signaled the emergence of literate and articulate Christian—or *kholwa*—communities on the reserves who found Shepstone's policies increasingly irksome.

The first distinctive policies to govern large numbers of Africans within a colony of settlement, Shepstone's indirect rule in segregated reserves prefigured much later imperial and, indeed, apartheid practice. For the most part, however, his accommodation with chiefs saved Africans and colonists in Natal the cruel warfare that savaged the Eastern Cape in the nineteenth century and earned him an enviable reputation as an African administrator. All this was to unravel in the 1870s.

In 1867, alluvial diamonds were discovered near the confluence of the Vaal and Harts rivers, followed by even richer finds at Bultfontein and Colesburg Kopje (later KIMBERLEY). A prolonged contest for land among the Orange Free State, Griqua, and TSWANA chiefs ended in 1871 when the British annexed the diamond fields as the new colony of Griqualand West, signaling renewed imperial intervention in the subcontinent. As fortune seekers from every corner of the globe made their way to the diamond fields, a turbulent new era in the history of South Africa had begun.

—*Shula Marks*

British Imperialism and Settler Colonialism (1870–1910)

The mineral discoveries that launched its industrial revolution between the late 1860s and 1910 were crucial in the shaping of modern South Africa and brought with them renewed imperial intervention in the southern African region. The era was framed at its beginning by Britain's annexation of the disputed diamondiferous region in 1871 as the Crown Colony of Griqualand West and at its end by the unification of the former AFRIKANER republics, British colonies, and African territories. It was punctuated by the South

African War of 1899–1902, which brought all the former colonies and republics under British control, accelerated processes of modernization, and invigorated a sense of pan–South African identity among both blacks and whites.

The Discovery of Diamonds
The first diamond was discovered by chance at the appropriately named Hopetown and was followed by the more spectacular finds in nearby KIMBERLEY. Fortune seekers flooded to the diamond field from within southern Africa and without. Five years later, Kimberley had become the largest producer of diamonds in the world and South Africa's second largest city. With the influx of population and capital, economic activity increased dramatically all over South Africa. New towns, railways, roads, and harbors were built, and new markets opened for agriculture. All over South Africa, the pressure on African lands threatened confrontation between blacks and whites, and the demand for labor was insatiable, as employers competed for workers at almost any price. At the same time, the continued independence of powerful and self-sufficient African kingdoms was seen as an obstacle to the transformation of their subjects into tractable workers. As tensions mounted, the lure of firearms led many chiefs to send groups of men to the mines to earn money to buy the guns that were readily available in Kimberley. For both blacks and whites, the arming of African peoples at the very moment that fresh encroachment was being made on their lands was highly charged. All over South Africa, it was believed that African rulers under the leadership of CETSHWAYO, king of the ZULU, were conspiring "to drive whites into the sea."

Carnarvon's Attempted Confederation of South Africa
As early as 1873, the issue of firearms in African hands had led to a skirmish with momentous consequences in NATAL when the Hlubi chief Langalibalele failed to register the guns his people had earned in Kimberley, as required by Secretary for Native Affairs Theophilus Shepstone. Summoned to Pietermaritzburg, Langalibalele feared the worst and fled to Lesotho, pursued by Natal volunteers. An accidental clash, in which four white Natalians were killed, resulted in the dispatch of British reinforcements and a savage campaign against the Hlubi and their allies. Langalibalele was captured, tried, and sentenced to life imprisonment on ROBBEN ISLAND. The travesties of his trial led Lord Carnarvon, the British colonial secretary between 1874 and 1878, to recall the governor, mitigate Langalibalele's sentence, and send Sir Garnet Wolseley, Britain's leading soldier, to Natal as a special commissioner.

This episode was a prelude to the turbulent decade that followed. The 1870s and early 1880s were characterized by unprecedented African resistance to colonial encroachment across a vast swath of territory, their hopes kindled by their access to arms. In area after area, chiefdoms were destabilized as new bases of power began to emerge. Civil wars wracked many communities as land-hungry farmers; profiteering, mainly British, concessionaires; "freebooting" mercenaries; and colonial officials found and manipulated the social fault lines in unraveling chiefdoms, from the TSWANA and GRIQUA on the southwestern *highveld,* to the Mpondo on the Transkeian south coast, the Zulu Kingdom north of the Tugela River, and the PEDI in the northeastern Transvaal (now Mpumulanga). The immediate precipitants of war differed in each case, but underlying most conflicts were intensified pressure on African land and labor, the undermining of chiefly authority, and the imposition of a new bureaucratic colonial order. Carnarvon's ambition to bring the South African republics, colonies, and independent African kingdoms, by persuasion if possible and by force if not, into a single federation compounded the warfare. It led not only to the annexation of the South African Republic (known informally as the Transvaal Republic) but also to the defeat of most of the remaining independent African states by the British army.

To Carnarvon, who had piloted the Canadian federation, the merit of a self-governing, united South Africa within the British Empire seemed the cheapest and most effective way of securing metropolitan and imperial interests. His imperial vision was expansive and chimed well with Prime Minister Benjamin Disraeli's proactive approach

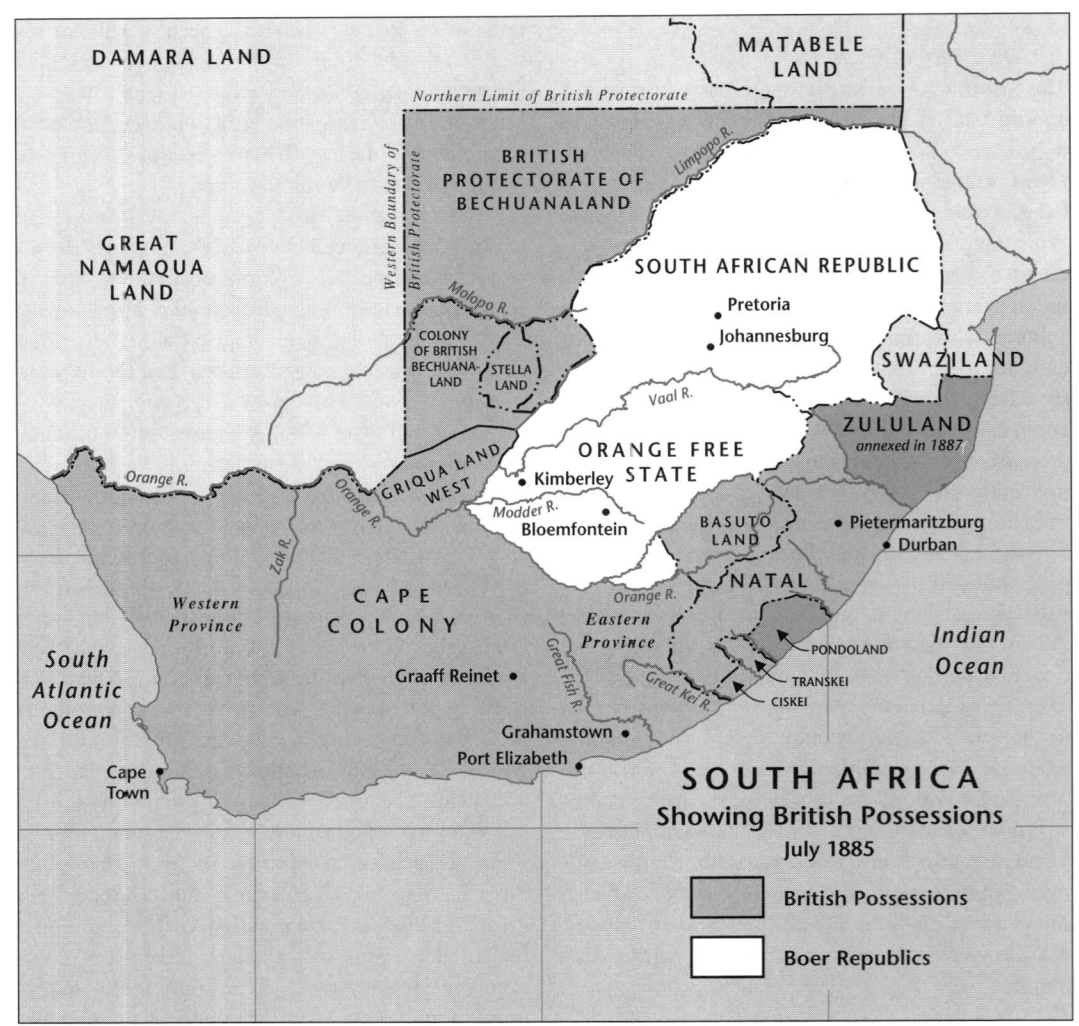

to empire, at a time when Britain faced increasing competition for global markets and raw materials.

The problem, which was to prove insoluble in this period, was how to persuade or cajole the British settler polities to agree to submerge their local sovereignties. The confederation's success depended on the CAPE COLONY, the most populous and economically advanced state in the region, but the Cape cabinet was hostile from the outset, and Carnarvon's subsequent actions simply increased their suspicions. For the British, the Langalibalele affray seemed to point to a way out: Wolseley was instructed to cajole the Natalians to revert to Crown Colony status. His success—and the advice of Shepstone then in London—persuaded Carnarvon that he could achieve his ends through force, elsewhere in the more established Cape Colony, for example, or the republics controlled by Afrikaners. The award in 1875 of the disputed territory of Delagoa Bay (now Maputo) to Portugal rather than Britain, which gave the Transvaal Republic access to the sea through a port beyond British control, and news that the Transvaal president was seeking investment for his Transvaal–Delagoa Bay railway added urgency to Carnarvon's schemes. When news of the republic's humiliating defeat at the hands of the powerful Pedi Kingdom reached London in August 1876, Carnarvon secretly instructed Shepstone to go to the Transvaal and annex it, with local consent if possible, by force if not. Sir Bartle Frere, a well-known humanitarian, who shared Carnarvon's expansive view of empire, was appointed high commissioner of South Africa. Once there, Frere quickly determined that independent African polities were a major obstacle to the confederation and had to be crushed.

In April 1877, Shepstone annexed the Boer Transvaal Republic in the name of Britain. He was urged on by the small English-speaking community and by the Cape and Natal merchants who hoped for a boom in land prices with a British takeover. The Transvaal treasury was bankrupt and its president unpopular. Land speculation and the allocation of huge farms to government officials meant that, by 1877, the sale of land had all but ceased. As in the past, the solution was encroachment on African lands, but this had become a more hazardous expedient as Boer failure to defeat the Pedi and the conflict brewing on the Zulu border had revealed.

For the most part, the burghers (the Afrikaner citizens) waited to see what the imposition of British rule meant. They soon found out. Shepstone governed the Transvaal autocratically as a Crown Colony; his first priority was to make it pay for its own administration. No longer able to simply extort taxes from Africans through random raiding as the Transvaal Republic had done, Shepstone attempted to tax the white population. In an attempt to ward off his increasing unpopularity, Shepstone now backed BOER claims to Zulu lands, which he had formerly dismissed.

The End of African Independence
Despite a commission of inquiry appointed by the governor of Natal, which fully supported the Zulu case, Frere and Shepstone now set out to foment war with the Zulu, which broke out at the beginning of 1879. Despite early spectacular victories, faced with mass starvation, the Zulu were eventually forced to sue for peace from Wolseley, who took command of the British army after the Battle of Ulundi. The British withdrew, having sent Cetshwayo into exile. The kingdom, divided into no fewer than thirteen warring chiefs, rapidly descended into chaos. In the hope of restoring peace, in 1883, the British returned the king to a kingdom that had been severely truncated by Natal officials. The civil war that ensued between the Zulu royal family's followers and their enemies marked the kingdom's true destruction.

From Zululand, Wolseley next marched against the Pedi who had continued to resist Transvaal jurisdiction. This time, they were comprehensively crushed. Their chief, Sekhukhune, was captured and imprisoned. Far from reconciling the Boers to British rule, however, the British defeat of their powerful Zulu and Pedi enemies encouraged Boer resistance. Led by PAUL KRUGER, former commandant-general of the South African Republics, the Boers defeated British troops at the Battle of Majuba in 1881. The Liberals, now in power in Britain, withdrew from the Transvaal, while attempting to retain a vague British "suzerainty" over the republic. The Boers were left to consolidate their rule through a familiar combination of force and intervention in chiefly politics. Several of the less powerful African polities in the Transvaal were conquered by Boer commandos, although the VENDA in the Soutpansberg, who like the Pedi had temporarily reversed Afrikaner expansion in the 1860s, were only finally conquered in 1898, when their chief was driven across the Limpopo River. On the republic's western flank, Tswana chiefdoms also experienced continued Boer expansion, which only ended when the British proclaimed a protectorate over the land north of the Molopo River in 1884 and then annexed the territory to its south as British Bechuanaland in 1885. Continued Transvaal incursions into Zululand and the intervention of Natal officials powerfully shaped the civil wars that ended in 1888 with the exile and imprisonment on St. Helena of Dinuzulu, Cetshwayo's son and heir; the creation of a Crown Colony in Zululand (minus the New Republic claimed by South Africa); and its incorporation in 1897 by Natal, which had achieved self-government in 1893. For Africans all over southern Africa, the wars of the 1870s and 1880s caused a great crisis of commitment. They were not simply fought between black and white; everywhere, "loyal African levies" assisted colonial and imperial forces—most notably, but not exclusively, the MFENGU in the Eastern Cape and the SWAZI against the Pedi in the eastern Transvaal. In these, as in other cases, ancient enmities overrode any necessity for unity against settler expansion, while on occasion, as in the case of the Swazi, strategic collaboration could ensure a protected status under imperial rather than colonial rule. At the same time, in the Eastern Cape and Natal, many mission converts who had hitherto supported imperial armies now turned to resisting colonialism with the pen rather than the sword and created new political organizations.

As they lost their independence, Africans found themselves disarmed and taxed by British troops and administrators, and initially many were able to increase their agricultural production, making use of the wages earned on the mines to purchase plows, seeds, and fertilizer. In the long run, however, the majority of young men were forced into less discretionary forms of wage labor on white-owned mines and farms. Despite the extent of the upheavals, Africans were not uprooted from their lands in vast numbers, although almost everywhere some land was lost and people were forced into the labor market. The intervention of the British, aware of the costly resistance that could be provoked by large-scale expropriation, meant that in Zululand, the Eastern Cape, and the Basutoland and Bechuanaland protectorates (in which Africans were brought under British rule but their chiefs retained some autonomy), most Africans retained their already truncated lands. Elsewhere, "locations," which were the precursors to African labor reserves, on the models of the Eastern Cape and Natal reserves were set aside. They became the basis of the migrant labor system, which characterized South Africa's political economy in the twentieth century.

Race and Class in Kimberley and on the Witwatersrand

Kimberley was the crucible of South Africa's industrial revolution. It was built on the expropriation of its original inhabitants, the bitterness of the ousted Boer republics, and the unrealizable expectations of thousands of overoptimistic prospectors. It also saw the establishment of the world's first monopoly over the production and sale of diamonds. Here, the relationship between race and class was first fought out in an urban, industrial setting, and new class, racial, and ethnic identities forged; here, too, a new racial hierarchy evolved in which whites came to own the mines and machinery and to serve as overseers and skilled workers, while supposedly unskilled black men labored for a fraction of the pay. In Kimberley, under direct British rule and at the behest of largely British capital, the nexus of institutions that came to characterize South Africa's towns— the urban location, migrant labor system, closed compounds inhabited by only mine workers, and PASS LAWS—was brought into being and the contours of its industrial environment were first discernible.

The industrialization and social change set in motion in Kimberley were greatly accelerated after 1886 when, nearly twenty years after the opening of the first outcrop mines in the eastern

Transvaal, extensive seams of deep-level gold were discovered in the Witwatersrand hills, also known as the Rand. A new market for agricultural produce, more efficient transport, and a host of ancillary industries all sprang up in the wake of the gold discoveries. By the end of the century, the South African Republic had become the world's largest single supplier of gold and the pivot of the southern African political economy. Increasingly, its alliances were with Mozambique and the coastal colony of Natal, while the Orange Free State was also drawn into the Transvaal's orbit. The Cape Colony, the oldest, wealthiest, and most populous of the southern African territories, found itself sidelined—in part a result of its own parochialism.

The demand for black labor was incessant and insatiable. Initially, this gave black miners a degree of bargaining power, similar to that in 1870s Kimberley. At the outset, wages were high—and paid for the newly imposed taxes, as well as for the seed, fertilizer, and plows—which supported a burgeoning African peasantry. The balance changed in the mid-1890s, however, as the rinderpest epizootic and the conquest of Gugunyane's Soshangane kingdom in southern Mozambique forced large numbers of black men into the colonial labor markets. Within a decade, some 100,000 Africans were making their way to the Rand mines annually, leaving their wives behind in southern Africa's rural hinterland where female agricultural labor not only provided a crucial subsidy to miners' wages that were increasingly inadequate to support their families but also constituted a form of insurance for the migrants that their patrimony would be there on their return. Unlike in Kimberley, however, class interests on the Rand precluded the total incarceration of black workers, as a host of small-scale white entrepreneurs became dependent on black customers.

As in Kimberley, fortune seekers from all over the world flocked to the Rand, among them skilled miners from the hard-rock mining frontiers of the world, bringing their own understandings of class and race. From the outset, there were tensions between mine owners and white workers. On the Rand, the ore was poor and the seams ran deep, making its exploitation costly and difficult, while the fixed price of gold meant costs could not be passed on to consumers. Mine owners complained bitterly that South Africa's railway and dynamite concessions further increased their costs. Labor was the one area where costs could be forced down. Kimberley had already shown that the magnates' control of the state, the compound system, labor migrancy, pass laws, and access to land in the reserves, which contributed to the support of their families, ensured that black labor was both cheaper and more easily controlled than its white counterpart. This gave mine owners every incentive to substitute black labor for white miners, as the latter were well aware. Yet, in the 1890s, skilled miners could only be attracted to the Witwatersrand, with its high cost of living and dangerous working conditions, by the prospect of high wages. However, as tensions mounted between the magnates and the South African government under President Paul Kruger, the mine owners were forced to bide their time.

Cecil Rhodes and Imperial Expansion in Southern Africa

Some were more impatient—none more so than CECIL JOHN RHODES. By the 1890s, Rhodes was the wealthiest man in South Africa and served as the chairman of DeBeers, a diamond conglomerate, and the BRITISH SOUTH AFRICA COMPANY (which he had formed to spearhead expansion north of the Limpopo River). He had become prime minister of the Cape Colony in 1890 and again in 1894 with the support of the Afrikaner Bond, the most powerful political party in the colony and advocate of Afrikaner farming and commercial interests. Leading Cape Dutch-Afrikaners were not hostile to Rhodes's expansionist ideals or to the imperial connection, which brought access to metropolitan markets and credit as well as the continued deployment of British troops. While the Cape Bond retained some adherence to the notion of a unified South Africa, in general, propertied Cape Afrikaners were largely unsympathetic to pan–South African nationalist claims, fearful that they would bear the expense of any closer association. In May 1886, even a customs union with the northern republics was rejected on the grounds that it might harm local farming interests, while, in 1893, the threat of civil war between Cape and Transvaal Afrikaners loomed when President Kruger closed the crossings on the Vaal River in an attempt to block Cape produce from competing on the Transvaal market.

The alliance between Rhodes and the Bond was irretrievably ruptured on December 29, 1895, when Leander Starr Jameson, a close associate of Rhodes, invaded the South Africa Republic at the head of a column of 510 mounted police and volunteers from the Bechuanaland Protectorate. Their hopes of a simultaneous uprising by English speakers on the Rand, known as Uitlanders (foreigners), failed to materialize, and three days later their abortive coup d'état was over. The invaders were easily rounded up by South African forces and their leaders imprisoned. The raid, instigated by Rhodes, and connived by the British government, was the opening shot in the South African War.

The Origins of the South African War
All over South Africa, whites became far more starkly divided along ethnolinguistic lines. The South African Republic was far more united behind Kruger and began rearming, while, in the Orange Free State, long-standing friendships were destroyed as anti-British sentiments were roused by the jingoistic rhetoric of English speakers. A chauvinist press and political organizations promoting British supremacy attacked Kruger's refusal to enfranchise Uitlanders and the wrongs suffered by Her Majesty's COLOURED and INDIAN subjects in the Transvaal. However, these were of little concern for most Uitlanders. Few thought they would have a long-term future on the Rand, and the ferocious death toll from miners' phthisis lent a sinister reality to these expectations.

At this moment of ethnic polarization, a small group of Cape colonists came to see in the Afrikaner Bond a counterpoise imperial intervention in South Africa. They included a handful of more liberal politicians, many of whom depended on African voters for their parliamentary seats. Ironically, the divisions between whites in the Cape Colony gave rise for the first time to clearcut political parties in the 1898 election, and this lent increased political leverage to the colony's black voters as both the Progressives (as the Loyal Colonial League renamed itself for electoral purposes) and the Bond sought their support. The Rhodes-Bond alliance had been built in part on their mutual interest in subjecting Africans; when that alliance foundered, there was a brief opportunity for blacks to influence parliamentary politics, albeit modestly. This remained true until the Cape's nonracial franchise was devalued by the construction of the new white alliance that led to the formation of Union of South Africa in 1910.

With the arrival of Sir Alfred Milner in South Africa as the British high commissioner in 1897, these divisions hardened perceptibly. After Kruger's reelection as president in 1898, Milner began to push for an open confrontation with the South African Republic. A last attempt to avert war in May 1899 failed as a result of Milner's intransigence over the Uitlander franchise, an intransigence that led Kruger to remark that it was not the franchise but his state that Britain wanted. Five months later, the South African Republic issued an ultimatum to the British government: withdraw all troops or face the combined forces of the Afrikaner republics. On October 9, 1899, war broke out between Britain and the Boer republics.

The South African War, 1899–1902
Contrary to British expectations that victory would be swift, the war lasted nearly three years and had a devastating effect on the countryside for another two. After early reverses, the imperial forces were able to take the republican capitals of BLOEMFONTEIN and Pretoria. The Boers regrouped, however, and waged guerrilla war with considerable success. The British responded by destroying Boer homesteads, burning their crops, and raiding their cattle. Together with their children, the women were herded into camps in which unsanitary conditions, poor rations, and gross overcrowding led to major epidemics and frightful mortality. By the end of the war, some 28,000 out of a total of 118,000 white inmates had died of disease, the vast majority women and children—65 percent of those who died in the war were under sixteen. The horrors of this war were to

shape Afrikaner identities in complex and contradictory ways and to provide nationalists, both then and later, with a powerful metaphor for the suffering of their people.

By 1902, it was clear that the greater resources of the British army and mortality in the camps had worn the Afrikaners down, and the majority of their leaders sued for peace, realizing that they would have to sacrifice republican independence for their people's survival. Behind that recognition lay a harsher reality. Within nine months of the outbreak of war, almost 14,000 republicans surrendered to the British forces, some 40 percent of those initially mobilized and 26 percent of those liable for service; a considerable number of them joined the British army. By the end of the war, the Boer generals feared that there would soon be more Afrikaners fighting against the republican cause than for it. Even more ominously, perhaps, there were now 50 percent more armed Africans fighting with the British than there were Boers left on commando.

Equally threatening for the Afrikaner generals was their loss of control over the countryside, as Africans joined the British forces or waged their own struggles against landowners and overlords, raiding Boer farms on their own account or taking their erstwhile masters to court. As a result, in large tracts of the Transvaal, Afrikaners returned from the war to find their farms occupied by Africans, who were reasserting older rights to the land in the expectation of retaining them after British conquest. All over South Africa, master-servant relations had been subverted, leaving whites shaken and apprehensive about the impact of the conflict on Africans' mind-set. As early as January 1901, at abortive peace talks at Middleburg, Afrikaner generals stipulated that they be permitted to retain their rifles as protection against "the natives." On May 31, 1902, a treaty was signed at Vereeniging ending the war and bringing the republics—and thus all of South Africa—under imperial rule.

The Postwar Reconstruction of South Africa

The British conquest of the Afrikaner republics created the framework for the construction of the new form of state in South Africa sought by mining capital since the 1890s. Britain now held unprecedented power to intervene in South Africa and shape its future. Under the British flag, white supremacy would be assured, property rights secured, mining costs reduced, and black labor controlled.

Although British wartime propaganda claimed they were fighting for the rights of black as well as white British subjects, Africans, coloureds, and Indians, many of whom had supported the imperial army, soon found their hopes betrayed, as the British quickly restored the racial hierarchy, which had eroded during the war. Clause 8 of the Treaty of Vereeniging had already left any decision about a black franchise to self-governing white colonists. The exclusion of the black majority from South African citizenship in 1910 was the inevitable result. Africans who hoped that their lands would be restored were equally disappointed.

Even before the war was over, Milner, the British high commissioner, had appointed a closely knit circle of young men from Oxford, dubbed the "Milner Kindergarten," to join him in reconstructing the Afrikaner republics. Initially, their role was to establish an efficient bureaucracy in the new Crown Colonies, set up municipal governments, address the most obvious prewar grievances of the mining houses, and restore order in the countryside. A threatened jacquerie was quickly quelled and Africans disarmed. Pass laws, inaugurated in the 1890s at the behest of the mining industry, were more efficiently administered and taxes more systematically collected.

The appointment by Milner of the South African Native Affairs Commission in 1903 to provide a blueprint for a unified native policy that pertained to the control and management of the African population in the different British colonial states was a further indication of the centrality of native policy in the imperial reconstruction of South Africa. Rejecting overt coercion or forced labor, the commission recommended a series of policies on land and the political franchise, which were subsequently to be elaborated by the South African state under the general rubric of "segregation"—a new word that crept into official discourse at this time.

It was, however, the mining industry that was at the heart of Milner's plans for economic and political reconstruction. In 1902, a serious shortage of African mining labor had resulted from the mines' drastic reduction of black wages during the war and demands for African labor from other sectors of the economy. In response, between 1903 and 1907, some 60,000 indentured Chinese workers were imported on three-year contracts. Chinese labor had far-reaching consequences for the future of labor relations and white politics in South Africa. African bargaining power was undermined and the use of unskilled white workers to fill the labor shortage was also preempted. In response to the clamor of white workers, the "color bar," which reserved certain work for whites defined as "skilled," was greatly extended. This prevented Chinese and Africans from being recognized and paid as skilled workers and gave mine magnates a powerful incentive to employ cheap black labor rather than expensive white labor.

The importation of Chinese workers deeply divided English speakers and unified nascent Afrikaner opposition to the Milner administration in their newly formed political organization Het Volk. By closing off the possibilities for white unskilled labor, it undermined Milner's aim of ensuring British supremacy in South Africa through immigration. He may have wanted South Africa to be a white man's country but the white men had to be the right kind of Englishmen who would maintain racial purity and pose no challenge to property, stability, and order.

Milner's plans to restructure the countryside were equally contradictory. He hoped that British immigrants would stimulate capitalist agriculture among Afrikaners and gain South African support for the empire, but agricultural settlement was largely a failure. Only some 1,200 British settlers were established on the land as a result of these schemes, largely in the Orange River Colony. Most became as dependent as the Boers were on sharecropping, forced labor, and state subsidies. More generally, his plans to Anglicize Afrikaners, which began while the war was still raging, were no more successful and served to fuel demands for autonomous Christian National Schools in which Dutch would be taught and the religion of the DUTCH REFORMED CHURCH fostered.

Milner's policies and a postwar slump spurred demands from British settlers for increased political representation. When the British Liberal Party came to power at the end of 1905, it swiftly acceded to the demand for self-government, and, in 1906 and 1907 respectively, the Transvaal and Orange River Colony were granted self-governing constitutions based on white adult male suffrage. This persuaded Generals JAN SMUTS and Louis Botha, the leaders of Het Volk, of the "magnanimity" of the British government and opened the way for their collaboration with the imperial authorities.

In the elections that followed, the Afrikaner parties led by the Boer generals won handsomely, supported by their wartime followers and a literate intelligentsia, for whom language and ethnic identity were particularly important. In the decade after the war, this intelligentsia was responsible for a flurry of nationalist poetry, sermons, and historical writing, while a group of Afrikaner women began building new philanthropic institutions, designed in part to reconstitute their postwar moral order. This was all the more necessary because after the war another wave of indigent, unskilled, barely literate, mostly Afrikaner whites had flocked to the new industrial centers, where they faced competition from organized, skilled, largely English-speaking workers and from equally poor, unskilled, and illiterate black laborers who still had some access to land. Unemployed and to some extent unemployable, the poor whites constituted a major problem of social control for the government and a volatile constituency for political mobilization, whether by Afrikaner nationalists or by English-speaking socialists.

The Unification of South Africa
The electoral victories by Afrikaner parties in the Transvaal, Orange Free State, and the Cape Colony from 1907 to 1908 provided a major impetus for the unification of the self-governing South African colonies, which was already being advocated by the major interests in South Africa, if for different reasons. The British authorities,

like the mining capitalists, believed a closer union would promote economic development and a common native policy, while local settler politicians believed a more powerful nation-state would curb imperial intervention. The outbreak of a poll tax rebellion by Africans in Natal in 1906 and its brutal suppression further hastened the movement toward unification. After Milner's departure, members of the "kindergarten" began maneuvering for a closer union behind the scenes and assisted in drafting a new constitution, encouraged by his successor as high commissioner. The kindergarten saw this as the best way of retaining South Africa within the empire.

The draft constitution that emerged, with subsequent amendments recommended in the colonial parliaments, was given legal force by the British Parliament as the Act of Union in 1909. It provided for a sovereign central bicameral legislature, based on a first-past-the-post constituency model, but with considerable weighting in favor of rural areas. The legal equality of the Dutch and English languages was similarly safeguarded, both being entrenched by a clause that prevented any change without a two-thirds majority of both houses sitting together.

Natal's preference for federalism was given short shrift in favor of unification, and the Cape property-based but nonracial franchise, while also protected by a two-thirds majority, was restricted to that province. The Cape's support for the extension of its franchise was overruled, as was Natal's attempt to introduce women's suffrage. A delegation of black political leaders and the former prime minister of the Cape, the liberal W. P. Schreiner, attempted to persuade the British government to veto the color bar in the Constitution but in vain. It was to take another twenty years before white women were enfranchised and another eighty before Africans could enter the Parliament.

There were those who wished for the immediate incorporation into the union of the Basutoland, Swaziland, and Bechuanaland protectorates; that these enclaves remained under imperial control was resented by colonial nationalists. However, a combination of Africans' resistance to giving up their independence and land, British humanitarian opposition, and imperial caution prevented this. Nevertheless, a schedule to the act setting out the conditions for their ultimate transfer served over the years to ignite South Africa's demands for incorporation—and to frustrate them. Southern Rhodesia, still under chartered company rule, also had observers at the National Convention. When, in 1923, the British South Africa Company charter lapsed, Southern Rhodesians decided in a referendum to remain outside the union.

The British government, like the majority of whites in South Africa, supported the new union. Nevertheless, as an editorial in the London *Times* asserted in 1909, "A handful of leaders may fashion a state but they cannot create a nation." Reconciliation among Afrikaners, let alone between English speakers and Afrikaners, was extremely fragile. Outside the Cape, blacks were excluded from the new nation-state, and the self-governing white community underpinned by black labor envisioned by Rhodes and Milner was now a reality. Initially created by disparate social and economic interests, this political dispensation nonetheless lasted for much of the twentieth century.

—*Shula Marks*

British South Africa Company

The British South Africa Company (BSAC) was a mercantile company established by British imperialist and financier CECIL JOHN RHODES and incorporated under a royal charter in 1889. The charter was usually issued to individuals or companies to establish settlements and colonies that favored the British Empire. It was initially granted to BSAC for twenty-five years but was extended for another ten years. Modeled on the British East India Company, the BSAC sought to further British colonization and exploitation by acquiring and exercising commercial and administrative rights in southern and central Africa.

The company was empowered to trade with African rulers; to own banks; to own, manage, and distribute land; and to assemble a police force. In return, the company agreed to develop the territory under its control, obey African laws, allow free trade, and respect all religions. In reality, however, the BSAC sought to extract as much territory and mineral rights from the African population as possible, set up its own government, and establish its own laws with little regard for African laws, and was all too willing to use force to achieve its goals.

By 1900, the company had direct administrative control over both Southern Rhodesia (now ZIMBABWE) and Northern Rhodesia (now Zambia) and had acquired substantial land and mineral rights. Although the company relinquished its administrative responsibilities in the colonies in the 1920s, it still retained significant commercial interests, particularly mining rights in Northern Rhodesia. In 1964, BSAC was forced to hand over its mineral rights to the government of Zambia, and, the following year, the company merged with the Central Mining & Investment Corporation and the Consolidated Mines Selection Company to form a mining and industrial company known as the Charter Consolidated, of which slightly over one-third of the shares were owned by the British/South African mining company Anglo-American.

See also CECIL JOHN RHODES

Broederbond

An Afrikaans word meaning the "league of AFRIKANER brothers," the Broederbond was established in 1918 (first named Young South Africa) in response to the humiliating defeat of the Afrikaners at the hands of the British in the ANGLO-BOER WAR. The Broederbond operated as a secret society, composed of exclusively male, protestant Afrikaners. Its goals were to promote AFRIKANER NATIONALISM and culture, develop an Afrikaner economy, and gain control of the South African government.

While its membership was always quite small, its political and economic influence was immense. The Broederbond was largely responsible for the NATIONAL PARTY's rise to national prominence in 1948, and every prime minister and state president in South Africa from 1948 to the end of APARTHEID in 1994 was a member of the Afrikaner Broederbond. This society also formed several prominent Afrikaner businesses, including Amalgamated Banks of South Africa (ABSA), one of South Africa's largest financial institutions.

In 1993, the Afrikaner Broederbond decided to end its secrecy and open its membership to women and other races under its new name, Afrikanerbond.

See also APARTHEID; NATIONAL PARTY

Brutus, Dennis Vincent (1924–2009)

Dennis Vincent Brutus was a consistent force against racism, oppression, and imperialism. A COLOURED South African born in Rhodesia (now ZIMBABWE), Dennis Brutus was the son of two teachers. A year after his birth, the family returned to South Africa where Brutus grew up in PORT ELIZABETH. In 1946, he became a high school English teacher, as well as an advocate for equal education and sports.

Politics and poetry, teaching, and writing were all mixed together for Brutus. Increasingly confronted by APARTHEID's repression, he wrote of the ugliness of oppression and the need for people to resist. His volumes of poetry include *Sirens, Knuckles, and Boots* (1963), *Letters to Martha and Other Poems from a South African Prison* (1968), *Poems from Algiers* (1970), *Thoughts Abroad* (1975), *Strains* (1975), *China Poems* (1975), *Salutes and Censures* (1984), *Airs and Tributes* (1989), and *Still the Sirens* (1993). In the later years of apartheid, Brutus's writings were banned, and he was prohibited from teaching.

In the 1950s, Brutus led a campaign to eject South Africa from the Olympics and other international sports competitions, and, in 1958, he helped found the nonracial South African Sports Association. He also joined the Anti-Coloured Affairs Department, a nonracial, antiapartheid Trotskyist organization. In 1963, Brutus was arrested under the Suppression of Communism Act and jailed for eighteen months on ROBBEN ISLAND. Upon his release, he went into exile in the United States for the next twenty-five years and was a professor at Northwestern University in Chicago, where he helped form the African Literature Association in 1975, and later became professor emeritus at the University of Pittsburgh.

After Brutus returned to South Africa, he was based at the University of KwaZulu-Natal where he continued a life of scholarship and political activism against Third World debt, globalization, and neoliberal socioeconomic policies of the South African government. He died of prostate cancer in December 2009.

See also LITERATURE; NEW SOCIAL MOVEMENTS

Bushmen
See SAN

Buthelezi, Mangosuthu Gatsha (1928–)

A South African political leader of the INKATHA FREEDOM PARTY (IFP) and ZULU chief, Mangosuthu Gatsha Buthelezi was born August 27, 1928, in Mahlabathini, NATAL Province, to Mathole Buthelezi and Princess Magogo kaDinizulu. He inherited the chieftaincy of the large Buthelezi ethnic group in 1953. During much of the APARTHEID era, Mangosuthu Buthelezi was an important, albeit controversial antiapartheid leader, often accused of collaborating with the apartheid state.

He began his university training at the UNIVERSITY OF FORT HARE, where he joined the AFRICAN NATIONAL CONGRESS YOUTH LEAGUE and came into contact with future African leaders such as Robert Mugabe (president of ZIMBABWE) and ROBERT SOBUKWE (founder of the PAN AFRICANIST CONGRESS). Originally an activist within the AFRICAN NATIONAL CONGRESS (ANC), Buthelezi revived Inkatha (later renamed Inkatha Freedom Party), a Zulu cultural group, in 1975 as an antiapartheid political organization. In 1976, Buthelezi became chief minister of the quasi-independent KwaZulu BANTUSTAN. Although he consistently declined homeland independence or political deals until NELSON MANDELA was released from prison and the government lifted the bans on liberation organizations, he also became a prominent critic of the ANC, its support for armed struggle, and its campaign for international sanctions against apartheid. He supported an ethnic solution whereby political power would be distributed along ethnic lines rather than a democratic solution to apartheid and was often viewed as a collaborator with the state security forces, secretly supporting the buildup of paramilitary groups in KwaZulu and fomenting black-on-black violence.

After the demise of apartheid, Buthelezi initially refused to participate in the country's first democratic elections but agreed to add his name and that of the IFP to the voters' ballot at the last minute. The IFP narrowly won the provincial elections in KwaZulu-Natal, and Buthelezi was given the position of national minister of home affairs in the first government of national unity. In the 2004 elections, he lost his position as a result of corruption allegations. Buthelezi remains a member of PARLIAMENT.

See also INKATHA FREEDOM PARTY; ZULU

C

Cape Colony

The Cape Colony was a British possession in the southernmost part of Africa, beginning in 1806 until the Union of South Africa in 1910. Discovered in 1488 by a Portuguese voyager named Diaz, it was also the region settled by the Dutch in 1652. In 1795, the British briefly took over the colony for a year or so and permanently took control in 1806. Originally inhabited by indigenous groups such as the KHOIKHOI, this region later became home to Bantu-speaking African groups such as the XHOSA. When the British took control of the Cape Colony, slavery was common throughout the region. British rule of the Cape Colony brought the abolition of slavery and the institutionalization of more liberal policies and practices with regard to the native populations, a practice uncommon in other parts of southern Africa at the time. This included, for example, the granting of a limited political franchise (CAPE FRANCHISE) to certain blacks.

Cape Coloured

See COLOURED PEOPLE

Cape Dutch Architecture

Dating from the seventeenth century in the Western Cape region, Cape Dutch architecture is distinguished by H-shaped buildings, thatched roofs, curvilinear gables, and lime-washed walls. Cape Dutch architecture gets its name from the Dutch descendants who were the first settlers of the CAPE COLONY, but it draws architectural roots from medieval Holland, France, Germany, and Indonesia. The buildings were usually erected by skilled artisans imported as slaves from southeast Asia, which added to the variety of styles and decorations of the structures. Cape Dutch architecture is still common in the Western Cape's wine region in towns such as STELLENBOSCH, Paarl, and Franschoek. On suburban houses, the gables are often integrated into the front facades.

Cape Franchise

In 1853, when the CAPE COLONY was granted representative institutions by the British government, it extended the political franchise (the right to vote) on a limited basis to COLOURED men (the definition of coloured included Africans at this

Cape Dutch architecture illustrated by the KWV Vineyards in Stellenbosch.

point). Qualifications for the right to vote were either owning property worth more than £75, an earned salary of £50, or a salary of £25 if board and lodging was provided, which most coloureds could not meet. Numerous attempts by white politicians and their supporters were made to revoke this right. In 1936, African men were first removed from the Common Voters' Roll, followed in 1956 by coloureds.

Cape Malay

The Cape Malay community of the Western Cape Province are descendants of slaves brought to South Africa by the DUTCH EAST INDIA COMPANY from Indonesia, India, Sri Lanka, and Madagascar, who intermarried with Dutch settlers and the indigenous African populations, primarily the KHOIKHOI and SAN. Cape Malays are also known as the Cape Muslims because they introduced ISLAM to South Africa. The Muslim religion and culture became embedded among the slaves imported from south and southeast Asia when a prominent Muslim nobleman named Orang Cayen ("man of power and influence") and other political exiles from Asia who had opposed the Dutch colonization of their countries were exiled to the Western Cape region by the Dutch officials.

During the APARTHEID era, Cape Malays were classified as a subcategory of the COLOURED population. Linguistically, they mostly speak Afrikaans, English, or local dialects of these two languages. Currently, there are about 200,000 Cape Malays in South Africa, with most residing in the Western Cape region; 166,000 are in CAPE TOWN and another 10,000 in JOHANNESBURG. Besides religious influence, the Cape Malay culture (food and festivities) has also been incorporated into broader

South African culture. Today, the Cape Malay Quarter in Cape Town features steep cobbled streets and brightly colored buildings that were constructed in the traditional fashion.

Cape Town

Cape Town is a city of dualism and polarization. This applies to both its people and the city's topographical features. Mountains, valleys, rolling beaches, vineyards, forests, and dunes come together in breathtaking combinations to make this city one of the most beguiling places in the world, competing with iconic cities such as Rio de Janeiro and Havana. Cape Town is the capital city of the Western Cape Province and the legislative capital of the country (the national PARLIAMENT is located in Cape Town).

Uniquely in South Africa, Cape Town's three million population comprises a COLOURED majority (48.1 percent), followed by black Africans (31.7 percent), then whites (19.8 percent), and a minuscule INDIAN population (1.4 percent), according to the 2001 Census. This atypical demographic profile (coloureds comprise only 9 percent of the national population) is a direct result of the Coloured Labor Preference Policy, which was in force until 1984 and prevented African people from settling in the city without fixed employment. This heritage, one dimension of the divide-and-rule tactics of the former APARTHEID regime, has left a bitter legacy of social division and suspicion between oppressed black people (coloureds on the one hand and those historically classified as African on the other) that continues to simmer and provides the basis for racialized mobilizations. Thus, as recently as 2004, 66 percent of Cape Town's coloured community believed that the AFRICAN NATIONAL CONGRESS–led government did not care

Cape Town waterfront with Table Mountain in the background.

about them, and a staggering 35 percent of coloureds believed they would be without a job within a year due to AFFIRMATIVE ACTION policies.

From the north, the dominant impression of Table Mountain and the Waterfront development is of a stunningly located, modern, and bustling first world metropolis. However, the approach from the south takes in the vast sprawling shack settlements that make up most of the largest informal black settlements in South Africa, Khayelitsha, as well as the largest working-class area, called Mitchell's Plain, a historically coloured area. This duality goes to the heart of the city's history and its contemporary struggles to define a sense of a shared identity and future trajectory that is fundamentally different from the apartheid legacy of economic exclusion, residential segregation, and (racialized) social conflict.

Compared to any other metropolitan area in South Africa, Cape Town has the highest number of migrants, and households are growing at 3.3 percent per annum compared to a population growth rate of 2.5 percent. The majority of migrants are poor people from other regions in South Africa and other parts of Africa seeking both economic opportunities and access to essential services (which are of a better quality in the city and province compared to neighboring provinces). The faster growth rate in household formation is driven by the fact that many of the state's subsidies to the poor—in the form of free basic services or certain welfare provisions—are premised on household (as opposed to individual) need. These dynamics, in the absence of robust economic growth, produce a situation where the need for basic services by the city's poor significantly outstrips the fiscal resources available at both the municipal and provincial governments. The depth of the development challenges in the city is best illustrated by the growing housing backlog and the exclusionary dynamics of the regional economy.

Officially, the housing backlog was pegged in 2008 at 265,000 households, but even the mayor at the time intimated that this figure may have to be revised upward to 400,000. The official figure represents one-third of the total number of households of 759,765. This backlog is made up of a combination of new migrants who are settling in squatter areas, overcrowding in existing public housing (especially in coloured neighborhoods), and backyard shacks in the more established black African townships such as Langa, Nyanga, and Gugulethu. The 2006–2007 level of subsidy (R355 million, or approximately US$40 million) that the city receives from the national government enables it to build close to 9,000 units per annum, which is clearly insufficient to deal with the annual growth in the backlog, let alone reverse the apartheid legacy of destitution. These trends fuel social conflict among the poor, which can take on racial overtones, as they compete for access to new housing opportunities.

While housing needs among the poor has ballooned, the upper middle classes have been serviced by new clustered and often gated developments driven by the private sector. In fact, the sheer size of the city, in terms of land area and population, has grown by 40 percent since 1985, putting tremendous pressures on overstretched and inadequately maintained infrastructures, especially sewerage, stormwater drainage, and roads.

The housing and infrastructure challenges are exacerbated by profound economic challenges, most acutely reflected in an unemployment rate of almost 28 percent of the city's labor force. Unemployment is a systemic part of the city's economy because of the structural shift from traditional secondary sectors like manufacturing to principally tertiary sectors such as finance and business services and tourism. In 2004, the largest sectoral contributors to the city's economy were finance and business services (31.7 percent); manufacturing (17.9 percent); wholesale and retail trade, catering, and accommodation (17.2 percent); transport and communication (11.6 percent); general government services (9.4 percent); community, social, and other personal services (5 percent); and construction (a distant 3.7 percent). Due to these trends, the city's economy demands a labor force with some level of skill to ensure employment, and, moreover, a reasonably high level of skill to guarantee employment and rising incomes.

The harsh reality is that the vast majority of the city's poor are trapped in poverty due to the adverse social conditions they confront in their neighborhoods and schools, which in turn make educational attainment extremely difficult. In the Western Cape, between 48 and 55 percent of learners who enter the school system drop out before they reach grade twelve, and these learners are almost all black and poor. Furthermore, less than 10 percent of students from poor communities who complete secondary education have the right qualifications to enter the higher education system. (Dropout rates in higher education also reach 50 percent before students complete a first degree.) In this way, the poor remain structurally excluded from new employment opportunities that demand higher skill levels associated with formal education and training. In addition, extraordinarily high levels of social violence in poor households and poor neighborhoods are often the norm, in part fueled by drug-related criminal gangs that serve as important sources of alternative governance and control in these areas. In the last few years, most of the coloured townships (but not those exclusively) have been ravaged by a drug epidemic as "Tik" (crystal methamphetamine) usage has become endemic, fueling violence and further deepening the social and economic marginalization of poor youth in the city.

Despite these daunting challenges, Cape Town also displays some important comparative advantages compared to other cities in South Africa. First, the city boasts relatively high levels of access to basic services despite the massive housing shortage. In other words, even people living in informal settlements have reasonable access to water, sanitation, electricity, refuse removal, and so forth. Second, the city is supported by a significantly diversified economic base, which is admittedly vulnerable to currency fluctuations but also delinked from a mineral-driven economy, as is the case in northern South Africa. Third, Cape Town is located in the heart of the Cape Floral Kingdom (the smallest and richest of the world's six plant kingdoms), which offers tremendous opportunity in terms of tourism and fostering more sustainable patterns of growth and development. Fourth, Cape Town had an unprecedented opportunity to develop key public infrastructures such as transport, public space, public parks, mixed-income housing, and cultural industries, among others, in the buildup to the 2010 World Cup. If properly managed, these investments along with massive new investments in the renewal of the inner city and surrounding areas, will support growth in the construction and tourism sectors, both of which have less onerous entry requirements for job seekers. Last, since the Presidential Municipal Imbizo (a ZULU term for meeting) in December 2006, political agreement was reached between the provincial and the metropolitan governments to embark on a joint development planning process, which will result in a medium- to long-term agenda for coordinated public investment. The proposals contained in this program have a clear policy orientation supporting the poor, urban integration, and sustainable development. These agreements have begun to find their way into city budgets and service delivery programs, and there is a real prospect that Cape Town can overcome its deep spatial, social, and racial cleavages.

—*Edgar Pieterse*

Carnegie Commission

In 1932, the Carnegie Corporation funded and published a report entitled "The Poor White Problem in South Africa." At the time, white poverty in the United States, South Africa, and elsewhere contradicted notions of white superiority and hence became the focus of study. The Carnegie Commission report made a number of recommendations, including the establishment of "employment sanctuaries" for poor white workers and the replacement of "native" black workers in most skilled aspects of the economy with poor white workers. The authors of the report suggested that unless something was done to help poor whites, racial deterioration and miscegenation would be the outcome. It has been argued that, in many ways, the commission and its report laid the groundwork for APARTHEID.

Cetshwayo (1826–1884)

Cetshwayo was king of the ZULU nation from 1872 to 1879. The nephew of King SHAKA (son of Shaka's half-brother Mpande), Cetshwayo led the Zulu forces in the ANGLO-ZULU WAR of 1879. Like his predecessors, Cetshwayo sought to avoid conflict with the white settlers. However, an independent Zululand was clearly obstructing British imperial aims. Initially Cetshwayo was able to form an alliance with the British in NATAL so as to keep his longstanding enemies, the Transvaal BOERS, in check. In 1877, this alliance fell apart as the British annexed the Boer Transvaal Republic and supported the Boers' claims to Zulu lands.

The British regarded Zululand an imminent threat to European hegemony and soon invaded it. Cetshwayo led the Zulu to victory in the Battle of Isandlwana in 1879. Sadly this was to be the last victory of the Zulu nation. The Zulu were defeated in the crucial Battle of Ulundi that same year. Cetshwayo was subsequently exiled by the British to CAPE TOWN, bringing the demise of the Zulu Kingdom. The kingdom was divided into thirteen separate chiefdoms, irreparably fracturing the group. Cetshwayo then traveled to Britain in 1882, where he met Queen Victoria and succeeded in making his case to return to Zululand. He was reinstated as king in 1883, but never managed to bring the Zulu Kingdom back together. He died a short while later.

Champion, Allison Wessels George (A.W.G.) (1893–1975)

A trade union leader, politician, and businessman, Allison Wessels George (A.W.G.) Champion was born in Inanda, outside of DURBAN, to a Christian ZULU family. With only seven or eight years of formal schooling, Champion joined the South African police in 1913, where his most notable achievement was the formation of a policemen's union that pushed for equal treatment of black policemen. His career in the police force was short-lived as he was not comfortable spying on fellow black South Africans, a duty sometimes requested of black policemen.

In 1925, with the urging of CLEMENTS KADALIE, founding member of the INDUSTRIAL AND COMMERCIAL WORKERS UNION (ICU), Champion took the position of secretary of the ICU Transvaal branch. He was later transferred to the NATAL branch, and under his leadership this branch became the union's most powerful and energetic. Next to Kadalie, Champion became the most influential person in the ICU and later took over the position of national secretary. Like Kadalie, Champion exhibited a heavy-handed leadership style that would circumscribe the ICU's program. One of the most glaring contradictions was the leadership's inability to decide on a consistent policy for engaging with white workers and their unions. In the end, the leadership rivalry that developed between Champion and Kadalie would contribute to the union's demise.

Champion also became provincial president of the AFRICAN NATIONAL CONGRESS and later served on its executive committee. Additionally, he served on the executive committee of the ALL-AFRICAN CONVENTION in the struggle against President JAMES HERTZOG's segregation legislation. Viewed as an influential but conservative figure, Champion was a proponent of Zulu nationalism and self-government and aligned himself with the Zulu monarchy. He was also a prolific writer, publishing his own newspaper as well as numerous pamphlets and short memoirs.

See also CLEMENTS KADALIE; INDUSTRIAL AND COMMERCIAL WORKERS UNION

Chiefs and Chieftaincy
See INDIGENOUS FORMS OF GOVERNMENT

Christianity

Christianity was first introduced in the area today known as South Africa by the Dutch when they began to settle in the Cape region (contemporary CAPE TOWN) in 1652. The Dutch settlement at the Cape was initially an outpost, a stopping point for seafaring traders on their way to Asia. The first DUTCH REFORMED CHURCH minister was appointed to the Cape in 1665. Roman Catholics, French HUGUENOTS, and German Lutherans also settled in the Cape, but their religious development was largely circumscribed at the time by the

Dutch Reformed Church and the policies of the DUTCH EAST INDIA COMPANY. A Moravian mission was established in 1737, but there was almost no effort to convert Africans to Christianity before the end of the eighteenth century, as this was largely frowned upon by the Dutch Reformed Church. Beginning in the 1800s, and largely facilitated by the British takeover of the Cape, however, many missionaries began to arrive in South Africa to establish missions, with the Methodists having the largest number of African adherents. Particularly influential was the Church of Scotland mission that established LOVEDALE, an educational institution for Africans in the Eastern Cape that boasts many famous graduates, including STEVE BIKO and JOHN TENGO JABAVU. Indeed, as in many parts of Africa, the spread of Christianity was part and parcel of the project of colonization.

Christianity's relationship with South Africa's political and social history has been mixed and often contentious. With the country's independence in 1910 and the founding of the Republic of South Africa, many Christian denominations were openly opposed to some of the racist and discriminatory policies and practices that were being instituted. One exception was the Dutch Reformed Church, whose congregation was almost entirely composed of AFRIKANERS. Early on they opposed the conversion of Africans to Christianity and supported the policy of separate development that would become the cornerstone of the APARTHEID system. Indeed, it has been argued that the Dutch Reformed Church provided the theological justification for the policies of apartheid for many decades. As a result of its beliefs and teachings, the Dutch Reformed Church was removed from the South African Council of Churches and the World Council of Churches in the 1980s.

On the other hand, Christianity also played a formative role in the opposition to apartheid, primarily in the form of black liberation theology. The Anglican Church, especially under the leadership of Archbishop DESMOND TUTU, played a pivotal role in the global antiapartheid campaign. Other religious leaders and groups, including Reverends ALLAN BOESAK and Beyers Naude, were prominent leaders of the internal antiapartheid movement, particularly with the formation of the UNITED DEMOCRATIC FRONT in the early 1980s.

According to the 2001 South African Census, nearly 80 percent of South Africans are Christian. The three largest groupings within Christianity are African independent churches (31.8 percent), Protestants (25.5 percent), and Pentecostals (7.6 percent). Roman Catholics make up 7.1 percent of the population, and an additional 7.8 percent identify with various other Christian groups.

Cinema

South Africa's commercial film culture actually predates the establishment of South Africa as a country. Film production began with the ANGLO-BOER WAR (1899–1902), which brought about the production and dissemination of the first propaganda films. Prominent British cameramen and filmmakers were sent to the front lines to collect official footage that the Warwick Trading Company of London, owned by Charles Urban, gave worldwide distribution. These newsreels played a key role in making the British imperial view of history the official view of the war. For most of its history, the South African film industry was subject to British imperial domination as the British built and owned the most viable movie theaters and exercised hegemonic control over film production and distribution.

Creative artistry took a back seat to political exigency in the film industry. The first recorded act of censorship occurred in 1910, the same year as the formation of the South African Union. A documentary of the African-American boxer Joe Johnson defeating his white opponent was banned by the town clerk of JOHANNESBURG. The rationale that films had the potential to incite subversive activity among African people, and therefore should be subject to strict censorship, was repeatedly invoked. The Public Control Ordinance of 1916 prohibited films that brought any section of the public into ridicule or contempt. The Cinematograph Film Ordinance of 1917 prohibited scenes depicting antagonism between capital and labor or fights between Europeans and non-Europeans. The Entertainment Act of 1931 censored movies that depicted interracial interaction, while a 1934 amendment prevented film societies, particularly those with African members, from screening "communist propaganda." The Publications and Entertainments Act of 1963 censored locally produced films. The white South African elite strictly censored films that featured whites of low moral character, fearing that their portrayals would lower whites in the eyes of Africans and thus undermine white minority rule.

The first South African–produced drama in 1910, *The Great Kimberley Diamond Robbery*, dealt with the fundamental issue of modern South Africa: the political, social, and economic consequences of the mineral revolution of the late 1800s when diamonds were discovered around the town of KIMBERLEY and subsequently gold was discovered in the area surrounding Johannesburg. The discovery of these minerals brought thousands of prospectors from all over Europe and even farther afield. The mineral discoveries inaugurated a slew of similar films such as *A Story of the Rand* (1916), *Gloria* (1916), and *The Adventures of a Diamond* (1919). Many of these films were produced by Isadore William Schlesinger's African Film Productions, founded in 1913. Schlesinger, who was from the United States, incorporated all of the film distributors in the country and monopolized film distribution from the Cape to the Zambezi for forty-three years. Between 1916 and 1922, African Film Productions made forty-three films, and Schlesinger is considered largely responsible for the development of the South African film industry.

African Film Productions produced *De Voortrekkers/Winning a Continent* (1916), the first Afrikaans film. Directed by an American, Harold Shaw, the film was modeled on D. W. Griffith's *Birth of a Nation* and used the AFRIKANERS' GREAT TREK as the basis for constructing a narrative around the clash of civilizations between white Afrikaners and indigenous Africans as the eternal dynamic of South African history.

Because white supremacy became fused with the issue of nationhood, the New African Movement emerged a few years after the Anglo-Boer War. SOLOMON T. PLAATJE, one of its founders, articulated his worldview of South Africa as a black, African nation on the pages of the newspaper *Umteteli wa Bantu* (Mouthpiece of the Native Peoples). This newspaper also printed the first African-centered critiques of South African film culture. Plaatje and other New African Movement leaders used film as a pedagogical tool. He traveled to the major cities of South Africa showing short documentary films that detailed the achievements of black Americans or "New Negroes." In a direct affront to the racial segregationists of the time, Plaatje showed his films to mixed-race audiences.

His use of cinema for progressive racial aims brought him into direct confrontation with the American Mission Board and its leader, Pastor Ray Phillips. In the period before the introduction of APARTHEID (1920–1940), missionaries in South Africa undertook efforts to promote films for Africans with content that would model Christian values in African social life and depict traditional African culture as uncivilized and unchristian. A strong advocate of apartheid black cinema, Pastor Phillips's determination to "moralize the leisure time of the Natives" led him to inaugurate an extensive screening program aimed at all levels of African society, from the elite and literate middle classes to the poorly educated and illiterate mine workers. The Transvaal Chamber of Mines likewise used portable video systems to exhibit films in the compounds where mine workers were housed. Africans were shown films that reinforced stereotypes about white benevolence and African savagery. Many of them, such as *Allan Quatermain and the Lost City of Gold*, *King Solomon's Mines* (1918), and *Prester John* (1920) were adaptations of the fiction of empire. Documentaries of African life filmed by Europeans, such as *Africa Today* and *Witchcraft* (1927), explored the positive impact of Western civilization on Africans, which were always popular themes presented.

The first locally produced sound movie, *Sarie Marais*, was made in 1931. Soon after, a group of Afrikaner nationalists established the Reddingsdaad-Bond-Amateur-Rolprent Organisasie (Rescue Action League Amateur Film Organization), which tried to promote local film production and undermine the dominance of British and US films in South Africa. As a result, the

1940s witnessed a resurgence in the number of Afrikaans films and the rise of local stars such as Al Debbo and Frederik Burgers. In the 1950s, director Jamie Uys rose to prominence with films such as *Daar Doer in die Bosveld*. Uys would later become known for his box office hit *The Gods Must Be Crazy* (1980).

Although African actors were cast in South African feature films as early as 1916, the first full-length feature film with an all-black cast did not appear until 1949. *Jim Comes to Jo'Burg* (aka *African Jim*) adopted many of the cinematic conventions and settings of US film noirs and placed them in an African setting. The films that followed in its path, such as *Zonk* (1950), *The Magic Garden* (1951), *Cry, the Beloved Country* (1951), and *Song of Africa* (1951), likewise used night clubs, casinos, and jazz clubs as the backdrop for dramatizing the experiences of African migrants to urban areas and made clear the overwhelming influence of US music on township life.

Although apartheid and racial segregation provided the social context for these films, the devastating social and economic consequences of apartheid itself are wholly absent. Neither *African Jim* nor *Zonk* gives any sense of the socioeconomic pressures that pushed Africans from the rural areas into the cities. *Cry, the Beloved Country* reveals a fear of African political action and envisions the salvation of South Africa in religious rather than in economic or political terms.

Come Back Africa, which was clandestinely filmed in Johannesburg and SOPHIATOWN in 1958, represents a stunning departure. Cowritten by American Lionel Rogosin and *DRUM* magazine journalists Bloke Modisane and Lewis Nkosi, it critically examines the impact of apartheid on both rural migrants to the cities and on African intellectuals. A trenchant critique of the patronizing attitudes of white liberals, the film depicts the indignities of PASS LAW raids, forced removals, and township violence as well as the emergence of a politicized African consciousness.

The international release of *Come Back Africa* coincided with the SHARPEVILLE MASSACRE and renewed international outrage at the injustices in South Africa. A number of Hollywood films were made during the 1980s dramatizing the horrors of apartheid, for instance, *Cry Freedom* (1987), *A World Apart* (1988), and *Dry White Season* (1989). While these films had the admirable aim of decrying racism and promoting the ideal of interracial cooperation, they presented the white protagonists' perspectives. *Mapantsula* (1987), shot inside South Africa during the state of emergency, stands in sharp contrast in that it broke free of this stereotype. Cowritten by a white and a black South African, Oliver Schmitz and Thomas Mogotlane, this film uses the story of a gangster to protest South Africa's culture of repressive laws, chronic unemployment, and violence. The film is notable for the fact that its creators successfully deceived the censoring authorities by submitting false scripts that made it appear that the film was an apolitical gangster film—a genre that the South African government not only favored but encouraged by means of a state-financed film subsidy program.

The end of apartheid has meant that South African filmmakers are now tackling the issue of how to create a national cinema out of so many different ethnic and cultural entities. The White Paper on the Film Industry, issued by the Department of Arts, Culture, Science, and Technology in 1996, set up a statutory body, the South African Film and Video Foundation, to administer the film industry. The document outlines the postapartheid state's plan to create a film industry that is internationally competitive yet focused on promoting local talents and making films that feature local themes. Changes in the law have opened up the possibility for coproduction agreements between South African and foreign producers. The first treaty was signed with Canada in 1998.

Although the number of South African films released annually has been declining, there have been some notable successes, including *Yesterday*, a film about AIDS that was nominated for an Academy Award in 2005, and *Tsotsi,* which won an Academy Award for best foreign-language film in 2006. Charlize Theron became the first South African actor to win an Oscar for best actress in 2004. In 2009, *Invictus*, a film that chronicled how NELSON MANDELA was able to use the Springboks 1995 Rugby World Cup victory as a vehicle for nation building, garnered two Oscar nominations.

Morgan Freeman was nominated as best actor for his portrayal of Nelson Mandela, and Matt Damon was nominated as best supporting actor for his portrayal of team captain Francois Pienaar.

—Zine Magubane

Cities
See APPENDIX 4: PROVINCES AND MAJOR CITIES

Civic Associations

Civic associations began to emerge in South Africa's black communities in the late 1970s in response to APARTHEID and the specific material conditions it perpetuated. In 1979, residents of SOWETO and the black townships outside of PORT ELIZABETH formed the first civic associations (the Soweto Civic Association and the Port Elizabeth Black Civic Organization) that were specifically aimed at addressing the problems of exorbitant rents and rates for dwellings with inadequate utilities and services.

The civics, as they are called, did not emerge as antiapartheid organizations per se, although many had formed under the influence of the BLACK CONSCIOUSNESS MOVEMENT. However, they focused exclusively on local and immediate challenges of black communities and giving blacks more voice in policymaking at the local level. They sought achievable gains around bread-and-butter issues such as electricity, public transport, conditions in schools, and safety on the streets. Rent issues also became prominent after the introduction of elected black local authorities who were still controlled by the apartheid state in 1983, and the civics' preferred tactics remained petitions, marches, and engaging the services of lawyers. The tactics contributed greatly to the civics' success as local residents could be galvanized around specific and tangible causes and demands. The political structures created by the civic associations were also unique at the time as they were built on a strong ethos of participatory democracy. For example, street and block committees were established so that decisions could be made at the grassroots levels and then funneled up to the leadership.

But, as the number of civic associations began to balloon, many of the leaders recognized that the most effective way to galvanize their constituencies and effect change would be to link their local struggles to those at the national level. To this end, many civic associations joined in the formation of UNITED DEMOCRATIC FRONT, an umbrella antiapartheid organization comprising trade unions, student groups, religious leaders, women's groups, and other nongovernmental organizations, many of which were formed in the Charterist (FREEDOM CHARTER) tradition associated with the AFRICAN NATIONAL CONGRESS (ANC).

In 1992, representatives of regional civic bodies launched the South African National Civics Association (SANCO), which claimed to have approximately 2,000 affiliates. Moses Mayekiso, a leader of the Metal and Allied Workers Union (later the National Union of Metalworkers of South Africa) as well as the Alexandra Action Committee, was its first president. SANCO was created during the DEMOCRATIC TRANSITION in an effort to maintain the civics' institutional autonomy and to respond to the fear that they would be overrun by the now unbanned ANC that was reconstituting itself and securing its legitimacy within South Africa. By this time, the power and number of civics had waned. Yet, they still played an important role in the 1992–1993 DEMOCRATIC NEGOTIATIONS over local government reform. Despite some tensions between civics and the ANC, SANCO officially endorsed the ANC in the first democratic ELECTIONS in 1994 and became a fourth, informal member of the ruling tripartite alliance with the ANC, the SOUTH AFRICAN COMMUNIST PARTY, and the CONGRESS OF SOUTH AFRICAN TRADE UNIONS. Although many civic associations have since collapsed, some continue to play an active role in politics at both the local and the national levels.

See also POPULAR POLITICS; UNITED DEMOCRATIC FRONT

Civil Society

Conceptually, civil society is defined as an entity distinct from the state and from the market. Practically, civil society refers to the many nongovernmental, community-based, religious, civic, cultural, women's, and business organizations; political parties; trade unions; and even the media. In South Africa, the term became popular during the DEMOCRATIC TRANSITION in the early 1990s, in response to the increase of these types of organizations in the late 1970s and 1980s, many of which were political and opposed APARTHEID. The heightened political nature of South African civil society organizations, many of which had the explicit aim of overthrowing the apartheid state, distinguished them from theoretical understandings of civil society based on Western democratic societies. Nevertheless, commentators within and outside of South Africa saw the growth of such a vibrant civil society in the country as a prerequisite for democratic change. As a term, *civil society* was used in the context of discussions about the need for an autonomous sphere of organizations during and after the democratic transition. Furthermore, the expectation was that a vibrant civil society would continue to act as a watchdog for the new democratic government.

Although political parties, most notably the AFRICAN NATIONAL CONGRESS, have dominated South African civil society, other smaller organizations played a notable role in fomenting democracy and pushing for political change. For example, the Black Sash, founded in 1955, is a historically white, liberal, women's organization, which has been at the forefront of the struggle for women's and human rights. It entered politics by opposing the disenfranchisement of blacks in the Cape Province and the PASS LAWS of the apartheid state. The Institute for Democracy in South Africa, established in 1986 with the expressed intent of promoting democratic change, continues to act as a watchdog and collaborator with the South African government on important initiatives, including the Women's Budget and Children's Budget, and monitoring parliamentary and policy debates.

In 1995, the South African National NGO Coalition (SANGOCO) emerged to coordinate nongovernmental organization input into government policy and ensure that the rich traditions of civil society, which were forged against apartheid, continue to serve South Africans. SANGOCO has embarked on a number of campaigns to galvanize NGOs in key areas and bring national visibility to issues such as poverty, violence against women and children, and HIV/AIDS. For instance, its Speak Out on Poverty campaign, convened with the Human Rights Commission and the Commission on Gender Equality, organized a series of hearings across the country in which over 10,000 South Africans participated and presented oral testimonies or written submissions on the conditions of poverty in the country. This campaign in turn mobilized communities as well as informed and affected government policies.

The heightened political role of civil society organizations has declined since the apartheid era, however, and most civil society actors now play a more traditional role, along the lines of civil society in many established democracies.

See also NEW SOCIAL MOVEMENTS; POPULAR POLITICS

Clegg, Johnny (1953–)

Johnny Clegg is a British-born musician who was raised in southern Africa by his white Zimbabwean mother and immigrated to South Africa at the age of nine. He has a large international following and was an early exponent of world beat in his combination of European and ZULU styles (Clegg is known in French as Le Zoulou Blanc).

A former anthropology professor at the University of Witwatersrand, Clegg started two popular bands—Juluka from 1976 to 1985 (with guitarist Sipho Mchunu) and later Savuka.

See also MUSIC

CODESA
See CONVENTION FOR A DEMOCRATIC SOUTH AFRICA

Coetzee, John Maxwell (1940–)

Born on February 9, 1940, in CAPE TOWN, Nobel Prize–winning author John Maxwell Coetzee is widely regarded as one of the great contemporary writers.

Although his family is of AFRIKANER descent, Coetzee spoke English at home and at school. He studied at the University of Cape Town in the late 1950s and the early 1960s, earning degrees in English and mathematics. Wanting to be part of the wider world, Coetzee moved to England in 1962 where he worked as a computer programmer. In 1963, he married Philippa Jubber, and they had two children. Two years later, he began a PhD program in English at the University of Texas at Austin. Coetzee later taught at the State University of New York at Buffalo but was forced to leave after being denied permanent residency in the United States. He returned to South Africa where he taught literature at the University of Cape Town from 1972 until 2000.

Coetzee published his first novel, *Dusklands*, in 1974. His later works, including *Waiting for the Barbarians* (1980), *Life & Times of Michael K* (1983), and *Disgrace* (1999), garnered significant international attention. While Coetzee adamantly opposed APARTHEID, he shied away from politics and the spotlight, preferring to concentrate on his writing. He is known for his sensitivity to the human condition under colonialism and apartheid, examining the psychological and philosophical foundations of colonialism and its impact on the colonizer and the colonized. He has also written two fictionalized memoirs and numerous scholarly articles, and translated Afrikaans and Dutch literature.

In 1999, Coetzee became the first author to win the Booker Prize twice, and, in 2003, he became one of four Africans to win the Nobel Prize for Literature. In 2000, Coetzee immigrated to Australia, where he holds an honorary position at the University of Adelaide and continues to write.

See also LITERATURE

Colonialism
See BRITISH IMPERIALISM AND SETTLER COLONIALISM (1795–1870); BRITISH IMPERIALISM AND SETTLER COLONIALISM (1870–1910)

Coloured(s)
See COLOURED PEOPLE

Coloured People
Contrary to international usage, the term "coloured" in South Africa does not refer to black people in general. It instead alludes to a phenotypically varied social group of highly diverse cultural and geographic origins. The term "coloured" was previously capitalized as it was an official RACIAL CLASSIFICATION under APARTHEID, codified by the Population Registration Act of 1950 that divided the South African population into three racial groups: white, Bantu (or black, Native, or African), and coloured. (Asian was added as a fourth category in 1959. Prior to this, South Africans of Indian descent were lumped under the coloured category.) No longer an official category, more recent usage has tended toward eliminating use of the capitalized form.

Academic Kole Omotoso aptly described coloured peoples' skin color, the most important of these phenotypical features, as varying "from charcoal black to breadcrust brown, sallow yellow and finally off-white cream that wants to pass for white." Coloured people were descended largely from slaves derived from the Indian Ocean trading network, the indigenous KHOIKHOI and SAN population, and other black people who had been assimilated to Cape colonial society by the late nineteenth century. Since they are also partly descended from European settlers, coloureds are popularly regarded as being of "mixed race" and have held an intermediate status in the South African racial hierarchy, generally distinct from the historically dominant white minority by their skin color and the numerically preponderant African population by their mother tongue. (Coloureds speak Afrikaans and some English as their first language instead of the Bantu languages spoken by black Africans.) *Coloured* was used as a catch-all during the period of apartheid and institutionalized racial discrimination. However, it continues to have meaning as a social and cultural category and identity in its own right.

There are approximately four million coloured people in South Africa today. Constituting no more than 9 percent of the population throughout the twentieth century and lacking significant political or economic power, the coloureds have always formed a marginal group. There has, moreover, been a marked regional concentration of coloured people: approximately 90 percent live within the western third of the country, more than two-thirds in the Western Cape Province, and over 40 percent in the greater CAPE TOWN area. The coloured category has also generally been taken to include a number of distinct subgroups, such as Malays, GRIQUAS, Namas, and Basters.

Origins of Coloured Identity
Although coloured identity crystallized in the late nineteenth century, social amalgamation within the Cape colonial black population that gave rise to coloured group consciousness dates back to the period of Dutch rule. It was, however, only in the decades after the emancipation by the British of the Khoikhoi and San in 1828 and of slaves in 1838 that the heterogeneous black laboring class in the CAPE COLONY started integrating more rapidly and developing an incipient shared identity. This identity was based on a common socioeconomic status and a shared culture derived from their incorporation into the lower ranks of Cape colonial society.

The emergence of a full-fledged coloured identity was precipitated in the late nineteenth century by the sweeping social changes that came in the wake of the mineral revolution. The introduction of large-scale mining after the discovery of diamonds in 1867 and gold in 1886, being South Africa's equivalent of the industrial revolution, had a transformative impact on the social and economic landscape of the subcontinent. Significant numbers of Africans started going to the western Cape from the 1870s onward to find work, and assimilated colonial blacks and a wide variety of African people who had recently been incorporated into the capitalist economy were thrust together in the highly competitive environment of the newly established mining towns. These developments drove acculturated colonial blacks to assert a separate identity as coloured people in order to claim a position of relative privilege in relation to Africans on the basis of their assimilation to Western culture and being partly descended from European colonists.

Racial Discrimination Against Coloureds
Because of the marginality of the coloured people, the story of coloured political organization has largely been one of compromise, retreat, and failure under white supremacy. The most consistent feature of coloured political history until the latter phases of apartheid was the continual erosion of the civil rights first bestowed nonracially in the Cape Colony by the British administration in the mid-nineteenth century.

The attrition started with voting franchise restrictions in the late nineteenth century. A spate of racially discriminatory measures in the first decade of the twentieth century further compromised the civil rights of coloured people. The most significant were the exclusion of coloured people from the franchise in the former BOER republics after the ANGLO-BOER WAR; the promulgation of the School Board Act of 1905, which strictly segregated the Cape's education system; and the denial of the right of coloured people to be elected to Parliament with the creation of the South African state in 1910.

In the 1920s and 1930s, the economic advancement of the coloured community was undermined by Prime Minister J. B. M. HERTZOG's so-called Civilized Labor Policy as well as a number of laws designed to favor whites over blacks in the competition for employment. For example, the Apprenticeship Act of 1922 put apprenticeships beyond the reach of most coloured youths by stipulating educational entry levels that few coloured schools met but that fell within the minimum educational standard set for white schools. The 1925 Wage Act subverted the ability of coloured labor to undercut white wage demands by setting high minimum-wage levels in key industries. Furthermore, in 1930, the influence of the coloured vote was more than halved by the enfranchisement of white women only.

It was during the apartheid era, however, that coloured people suffered the most severe discrimination. Their forced classification under the Population Registration Act of 1950, which categorized all South Africans according to race, made the implementation of rigid segregation possible. The Prohibition of Mixed Marriages Act of 1949 and the Immorality Amendment Act of 1950 outlawed marriage and sex across the color line, respectively. Under the Group Areas Act of 1950, over half a million coloured people were forcibly relocated to residential areas on the periphery of cities and towns. The Group Areas Act was the most hated of the apartheid measures among coloureds because property owners were meagerly compensated, long-standing communities were broken up, and alternative accommodation was inadequate. The 1953 Separate Amenities Act, which segregated all public facilities, also created deep resentment. Moreover, in 1956, after a protracted legal and constitutional battle, the Afrikaner-led NATIONAL PARTY succeeded in removing coloured people from the common voters' roll.

Coloured Political Organization

Because their primary objective was to assimilate into the dominant society, coloured people initially avoided forming separate political organizations. By the early twentieth century, however, intensifying segregation forced them to mobilize politically in defense of their rights. Although the earliest coloured political organizations date back to the 1880s, the first substantive coloured political body, the African Political Organization (APO), was established in Cape Town in 1902. Under the leadership of the charismatic ABDULLAH ABDURAHMAN, who served as president from 1905 until his death in 1940, the APO dominated coloured protest politics for nearly four decades. It became the main vehicle for expressing this community's assimilationist aspirations, as well as its fears at the rising tide of segregationism, until its demise in the mid-1940s.

Intensifying segregation and the failure of the APO's moderate approach contributed to the emergence of a radical movement within the better-educated, urbanized sector of the coloured community during the 1930s. The National Liberation League, founded in 1935, and the NON-EUROPEAN UNITY MOVEMENT, established in 1943, were the most important of these organizations. Prone to fissure and unable to bridge the racial divisions within society, the radical movement failed in its quest to unite blacks in the struggle against segregation. Organized opposition to apartheid from within the coloured community was quelled by state repression following the SHARPEVILLE MASSACRE of March 1960, which initiated a harsh crackdown on the extraparliamentary opposition by the apartheid state. Organized coloured resistance only reemerged in the wake of the SOWETO STUDENT UPRISING OF 1976.

Recent Developments

From the latter half of the 1970s, with the popularization of BLACK CONSCIOUSNESS MOVEMENT ideology within the coloured community, the nature of coloured identity became a highly contentious issue, because growing numbers of politicized people who had been classified as coloured rejected this identity. The Soweto revolt greatly accelerated this trend because it fomented a climate of open resistance to apartheid and fostered a sense of black solidarity. Colouredness increasingly came to be viewed as an artificial categorization imposed on the society by the ruling minority as part of its divide-and-rule strategies. The burgeoning of the mass, nonracial democratic movement in the 1980s under the leadership of the UNITED DEMOCRATIC FRONT fed coloured rejectionism. Within the western Cape, an epicenter of resistance to apartheid, coloured identity became a highly charged issue, and any recognition of it was repudiated as a concession to apartheid thinking.

In spite of this, the salience of coloured identity has endured. During the four-year transition to democratic rule under President F. W. DE KLERK, political parties across the ideological spectrum made ever more strident appeals to coloured identity for support. Once again, it became politically acceptable to espouse a coloured identity. Moreover, postapartheid South Africa has witnessed a rapid retreat of coloured rejectionism and a concomitant coloured assertiveness. This was partly due to coloureds' desire to project a positive self-image in the face of the pervasive negative racial stereotyping and partly due to attempts at ethnic mobilization to take advantage of the newly democratic political environment. The resurgence of colouredism has also been motivated by a fear of African majority rule and the perception that, as in the old order, coloureds were once again being marginalized. Though far from allayed, these anxieties have been alleviated by the fading influence of black peril tactics in South African politics (tactics that whites adopted to scare coloured and white constituents into thinking blacks could not govern and that there would be tyranny under a black majority) and by all South Africans' acclimatization to the new political order.

Bibliography
Adhikari, Mohamed. *Not White Enough, Not Black Enough: Racial Identity in the South African Coloured Community.* Athens: Ohio University Press, 2005.
Erasmus, Zimitri. *Coloured by History, Shaped by Place: New Perspectives on Coloured Identities in Cape Town.* Cape Town, South Africa: Kwela Books, 2001.
February, Vernon. *Mind Your Colour: The "Coloured" Stereotype in South African Literature.* London: Kegan Paul, 1981.
Goldin, Ian. *Making Race: The Politics and Economics of Coloured Identity in South Africa.* Cape Town, South Africa: Maskew Miller Longman, 1987.
Lewis, Gavin. *Between the Wire and the Wall: A History of South African "Coloured" Politics.* Cape Town, South Africa: David Philip, 1987.
Omotoso, Kole. *Cape Times*, editorial. January 14, 2002.
Van der Ross, Richard E. *The Rise and Decline of Apartheid: A Study of Political Movements Among the Coloured People of South Africa, 1880–1985.* Cape Town, South Africa: Tafelberg Publishers, 1986.

—Mohamed Adhikari

Congress of South African Trade Unions

Formed in 1985, the Congress of South African Trade Unions (COSATU) is the largest South African trade union federation. Today, COSATU has approximately twenty-one affiliated unions, the largest being the National Union of Mineworkers, and represents over two million workers, making it one of the fastest growing trade union movements in the world. Since its formation, COSATU has been aligned with the AFRICAN NATIONAL CONGRESS (ANC) and the SOUTH AFRICAN COMMUNIST PARTY, and is currently part of the ruling tripartite alliance with them.

At its inception, COSATU brought together a number of nonracial trade unions opposed to APARTHEID, combined the aims of political democracy and workers' rights, and played a major role in the mass democratic movement in the late 1980s.

With the DEMOCRATIC TRANSITION from 1990 to 1994, some within COSATU sought to end its alliance with the ANC and forge a workers' party. This was a minority view that did not materialize. However, COSATU was instrumental in drafting the RECONSTRUCTION AND DEVELOPMENT PROGRAM (RDP), the broadly leftist manifesto upon which the ANC campaigned in the 1994 ELECTIONS. Its members also secured a number of positions on the ANC's party lists, from which members of PARLIAMENT and other government officials were selected. After 1994, COSATU lost many of its best and brightest to the new democratic government, leaving it organizationally and ideologically in flux. Historically, COSATU was at odds with the state and with the system of capital ownership but was now having to forge a new relationship with this comrade state and with capital whose role and future had been legitimized through the DEMOCRATIC NEGOTIATIONS.

Many among COSATU's leadership have taken up prominent positions in the post-1994 government. Alec Irwin was the minister of public enterprises and minister of trade and industry. CYRIL RAMAPHOSA was the ANC's key negotiator in the 1991–1993 talks with the NATIONAL PARTY to forge a new democratic dispensation. Former COSATU general secretary Jay Naidoo was the minister of the RDP during NELSON MANDELA's presidency. Mbhazima Sam Shilowa, also a former COSATU general secretary, was the premier of the Gauteng Province.

See also CYRIL RAMAPHOSA

Congress of the People

The Congress of the People (COPE) political party has its origins in the split within the

AFRICAN NATIONAL CONGRESS (ANC) between supporters of THABO MBEKI and JACOB ZUMA, both competing for the presidency of the ANC and therefore the presidency of South Africa, which openly surfaced during the fifty-second ANC national conference held at Polokwane in December 2007. This split was caused in part by the different economic and political ideologies between Mbeki and Zuma, with the former espousing neoliberal economic policies while the latter embraced a more leftist and populist ideology that aligned him more closely with the SOUTH AFRICAN COMMUNIST PARTY and the CONGRESS OF SOUTH AFRICAN TRADE UNIONS. The divide between these two figures also reveals underlying ethnic tensions between isiZULU (represented by Zuma) and isiXHOSA (represented by Mbeki) speakers. The ANC leadership, in recent decades, has been heavily stacked with isiXhosa speakers, including former president NELSON MANDELA, causing a degree of disgruntlement among the party's Zulu membership and contributing to the demise of Mbeki and several of his key allies within the party.

Thus, Mbeki's allies within the ANC, including Mosiuoa Lekota and Mbhazima Shilowa, two of COPE's deputy presidents, chose to found a new party, comprising primarily ex-ANC members and taking its name from the 1955 Congress of the People where the FREEDOM CHARTER was adopted. COPE officially came into being on December 16, 2008.

During the April 2009 elections, COPE campaigned on a platform of political reform, the promotion of a multiracial and multicultural society, and free market capitalist principles. The party won over 1.3 million votes, representing approximately 7.4 percent of the electorate, and securing thirty seats in Parliament.

Constitution

South Africa's 1996 Constitution is widely recognized as the crowning achievement of the country's dramatic transition from apartheid and racial segregation to democracy. This transition began with the lifting of the bans on the black liberation movements and the release of NELSON MANDELA from prison in February 1990. Adopted by an elected Constitutional Assembly, the Constitution was promulgated into law by President Mandela at Sharpeville on December 18, 1996, and went into effect on February 4, 1997. Not only is this democratic South Africa's founding Constitution, it also marks the shift, together with the 1993 interim Constitution, from parliamentary sovereignty to constitutional supremacy, thus fundamentally changing the role of the judiciary and the significance of constitutional law in the country's governance. Although there are significant continuities between the interim Constitution and the final Constitution, there are also important differences. These include such innovations as the idea of cooperative government, which structures the relationship between the national, provincial, and local spheres of government; the creation of specific institutions to promote democracy; and the explicit inclusion of socioeconomic rights in the BILL OF RIGHTS, all reflecting this Constitution's unique character.

History

The 1996 Constitution is South Africa's fifth constitution but only the first to be produced by a democratically elected constitution-making body. While indigenous South African communities and kingdoms as well as the British colonial governments and BOER settler republics all had their own systems of governance and even written constitutions, the country's first national constitution was negotiated at an exclusively white National Convention in the first decade of the twentieth century. Formally, the SOUTH AFRICA ACT passed by the British Parliament in 1909 brought together four settler colonies into a single Union of South Africa, but in effect, it created a fundamentally divided state. On the one hand, the Union Constitution granted the white minority representative democracy, while, on the other hand, it subjugated the majority—black South Africans—to autocratic administrative rule. Excluded from the National Convention, black leaders protested but were rebuffed as unrepresentative by colonial authorities who portrayed African society as essentially "traditional," hierarchical, and undemocratic. Thus, chiefly rule, incorporated into the colonial state as a system in which executive authorities, namely chiefs or traditional leaders, exercised unfettered power—free of even minimal judicial review—was constitutionally enshrined as the form of government for the black majority.

As this system of indirect colonial rule gave way to formal APARTHEID, international criticism of the South African government increased and the AFRIKANER-led apartheid regime broke with the British Commonwealth, adopting a Republican Constitution in 1961. Despite its break with the United Kingdom, the main feature of the 1961 Constitution was its explicit adoption of the British constitutional principle of parliamentary sovereignty. Although racial discrimination and segregation had become embedded in South African society and law from the earliest days of colonial penetration, the policy of apartheid adopted by the Afrikaner-led NATIONAL PARTY government in 1948 introduced a series of laws that together created an elaborate legislative scheme of racial oppression. When apartheid legislation eventually discriminated against black South Africans in virtually all aspects of social life, from birth to death, international political pressures led the apartheid regime to introduce a second legislative scheme of "internal decolonization." The Bantu Authorities Act of 1951 and the Promotion of Bantu Self-Government Act of 1959 introduced the policy of separate development under which the black majority was to be eventually divided into ten "ethnic" groups and granted "self-government" or "independence," on paper but not in practice, within the overall framework of apartheid. Although this process led to the creation of four new constitutions between 1976 and 1983—one for each of the ethnic BANTUSTANS, or homelands—none of these ever gained international recognition. The original plan was to establish independent homelands for the remaining six ethnic groups as well. However, this was thwarted by the failure of the policy of separate development and the unrest that gripped the country by the late 1970s.

In the face of increasing internal resistance and international isolation, the South African government moved in the late 1970s to politically incorporate the INDIAN and the COLOURED communities as a means of broadening its social base. The outcome of this shift in apartheid policy was the adoption of the 1983 Constitution, which extended the franchise to Indians and coloureds in a tricameral legislature with its jurisdiction distributed according to a vague distinction between "own" and "general" affairs. The ratio of elected representatives and a concentration of power in the hands of an executive president ensured, however, that power remained safely in the hands of the dominant white party. The exclusion of the African majority from this scheme and resistance from within the two target communities—Indian and coloured—meant that the 1983 Constitution was practically stillborn. The escalation of resistance and rebellion by African, Indian, and coloured communities, which began in late 1984 and led to the imposition of repeated states of emergency from mid-1985, sealed its fate.

Constitutional Transition
The publication of constitutional guidelines by the exiled AFRICAN NATIONAL CONGRESS (ANC) in 1988 marked the first public expression of an initiative aimed at achieving a negotiated settlement in South Africa. By publicly committing itself to the adoption of a Bill of Rights enforceable through the courts, the ANC assured South Africa and the world of its commitment to constitutional government. This led to the adoption of the Harare Declaration by the Organization of African Unity in August 1989, which outlined the minimum principles of a postapartheid constitution acceptable to the international community and was subsequently adopted by the Non-Aligned Movement and the United Nations General Assembly. The process of negotiations that followed led to the adoption of an interim Constitution in 1993, which went into force with the country's first democratic election in April 1994.

The interim Constitution provided in turn for the creation of a final Constitution within two years from the first sitting of the newly elected National Assembly. Chapter 5 of the interim Constitution required that at least two-thirds of all members of the Constitutional Assembly vote for the new Constitution. In addition, sections of a final Constitution dealing with the boundaries, powers, and functions of the provinces had to be adopted by two-thirds of all the members of the regionally constituted Senate. Once the new legislature, with both houses sitting together as a Constitutional Assembly, agreed on a draft, it would then have to be submitted to the Constitutional Court for certification. This required the Constitutional Court to certify that the provisions of the final Constitution were substantially in accordance with the constitutional principles agreed upon during the multiparty negotiations and enshrined in Schedule Four of the interim Constitution. Only then would the final Constitution be promulgated into law. In fact, the Constitutional Court at first declined to certify the text of the draft Constitution and certified it only when the Constitutional Assembly amended the draft. Although the interim Constitution had made elaborate provisions, through a series of deadlock-breaking devices, for the possibility that the Constitutional Assembly would fail to achieve sufficient consensus to reach the required two-thirds vote, the threat these provisions held, in terms of delay and an eventual reduction of the threshold from two-thirds down to 60 percent, helped ensure that a spirit of eventual compromise endured.

Structure of the 1996 Constitution

The main features of the 1996 Constitution include its founding provisions, the Bill of Rights, and the chapter on cooperative government. In addition, the Constitution, similar to other post–Cold War constitutions, includes specific chapters on public administration, the security services, and finance. More unique are the chapters on "State Institutions Supporting Constitutional Democracy" and on "Traditional Leaders." While the founding provisions define the nature of the postapartheid state—emphasizing principles of democracy, human rights, and equality—a key feature is the specific provision that this "Constitution is the Supreme Law of the Republic" and that any "law or conduct inconsistent with it is invalid." Reflecting this commitment to constitutional democracy are the provisions in the chapter on "State Institutions Supporting Constitutional Democracy," which established a series of independent constitutional bodies, including a public protector, human rights commission, auditor general, and electoral commission, as well as a commission for the promotion of the rights of cultural, religious, and linguistic communities, and a commission for gender equality. In contrast to these, the chapter on traditional leaders as well as the general provisions guaranteeing self-determination and the option of adopting additional charters of rights "in order to deepen the culture of democracy," reflect less the global constitutional paradigm of the late twentieth century and more the specific concerns flowing from South Africa's own negotiated transition.

Institutions to Promote Constitutional Democracy

Establishing institutions formally separate from and independent of the government of the day to support democracy is an innovation that originated in the negotiated transition from apartheid. Based on their concerns that the apartheid government would attempt to control the process, both the black liberation movements and the international community initially demanded the creation of an interim government to oversee the transition to democracy. Recognizing that this demand would require taking responsibility for governing with little power to make important changes while negotiations could potentially drag on for many years, the ANC embraced the idea of establishing interim mechanisms to ensure a level political playing field in the campaign and conduct of the first democratic election. The transitional mechanisms created by law included an Independent Electoral Commission to ensure free and fair elections and an Independent Broadcasting Authority to ensure fair use of public radio and television, as well as an Independent Media Commission and a Transitional Executive Council. While only the Independent Broadcasting Authority was initially designed to outlast the transitional period, the idea of independent institutions became part of democratic South Africa's political and constitutional landscape.

See also BILL OF RIGHTS; CONVENTION FOR A DEMOCRATIC SOUTH AFRICA; DEMOCRATIC TRANSI-

TION/NEGOTIATIONS, 1990–1994; GOVERNMENT STRUCTURES; TRUTH AND RECONCILIATION COMMISSION

Bibliography

Ashforth, Adam. *The Politics of Official Discourse in Twentieth-Century South Africa.* Oxford, UK: Clarendon Press, 1990.

Chanock, Martin. *The Making of South African Legal Culture 1902–1936.* Cambridge, UK: Cambridge University Press, 2001.

Ebrahim, Hassen. *The Soul of a Nation: Constitution-making in South Africa.* New York: Oxford University Press, 1998.

Klug, Heinz. *Constituting Democracy.* Cambridge, UK: Cambridge University Press, 2000.

———. *The Constitution of South Africa: A Contextual Analysis.* Oxford, UK: Hart Publishing, 2010.

—*Heinz Klug*

Convention for a Democratic South Africa

The Convention for a Democratic South Africa (CODESA) was a negotiating forum established at the end of 1991 to facilitate the creation of a new constitutional dispensation for South Africa after APARTHEID. The negotiations took place against the backdrop of increasing violence in the country, which threatened to devolve into civil war.

The NATIONAL PARTY, the ruling party of the apartheid government, the AFRICAN NATIONAL CONGRESS (ANC), and other liberation movements, excluding the PAN AFRICANIST CONGRESS and the Azanian People's Organization, participated in the CODESA talks. Like the black Africanist movements, the white right wing boycotted the talks. In theory, each party had an equal vote. However, the National Party and the ANC were clearly the two dominant parties, and the talks quickly adopted the principle of "sufficient consensus," whereby, if the National Party and the ANC agreed, the talks could proceed. These talks took place in closed-door working groups around key issues pertaining to the drafting of a new CONSTITUTION and the setting up of an interim government.

The first session of negotiations, CODESA I, was followed by a second, CODESA II, which quickly broke down in May 1992 after the parties could not agree on the majority required at the Constitutional Assembly. In reality, CODESA failed because the National Party had not yet accepted the idea of black majority rule, which was nonnegotiable for the ANC, and both parties had not yet come to terms with the extent to which they would have to compromise. Further violence erupted in the coming months with the Boipatong and the Bisho massacres, which some have described as black-on-black violence. However, the ANC argued that the National Party and the apartheid government were complicit. Whatever the cause, the violence reinforced the urgency of successful talks, and the two main parties worked to resume negotiations. Following the collapse of CODESA II, bilateral negotiations between the National Party and the ANC became the main negotiation channel, with the ANC's CYRIL RAMAPHOSA and the National Party's ROELF MEYER as the main negotiators. A multiparty negotiating forum, which included parties from both ends of the political spectrum, was convened in April 1993 and hammered out an interim Constitution, paving the way for the first democratic elections in April 1994.

See also DEMOCRATIC TRANSITION/NEGOTIATIONS, 1990–1994

COPE

See CONGRESS OF THE PEOPLE

COSATU

See CONGRESS OF SOUTH AFRICAN TRADE UNIONS

Customary Law

Customary law is made up of the written and unwritten rules that have developed from the customs and traditions of African communities. In South Africa, customary law exists alongside common or Dutch-Roman law, and a majority of the country's population falls under the jurisdiction of customary law. It is predominantly carried out by the chiefs in rural communities but can also be administered by judges or magistrates in the courts. Historically, customary law as distinct from common law reflected a dual system of justice and punishment for black versus white South Africans. Critics have accused customary law of being undemocratic and distorted by colonialism to support oppressive regimes. For example, customary law during colonialism and APARTHEID tended to privilege elder males and diminish the power and participation of women and youth. Today, customary law must conform to the principles set out in the CONSTITUTION and the BILL OF RIGHTS. Customary land tenure and customary marriage arrangements continue to be two areas of debate and contestation in trying to synchronize customary law with common law. Inheritance, for example, with the death of the husband under customary law very often goes to his family (siblings, parents, children) and does not recognize the role of the wife to inherit. This contradicts women's rights under the new Constitution, and many women who were married customarily are seeking the protection of common law.

See also LAW AND SOCIETY

D

DA
See DEMOCRATIC ALLIANCE

Dadoo, Yusuf (1909–1983)
A leading figure in the political fight against APARTHEID, Dr. Yusuf Dadoo, popularly known as "Mota" or "Doc," was born in Krugersdorp in Transvaal Province on September 5, 1909. As a schoolboy growing up in the Indian community of South Africa, Dadoo attended political meetings, was inspired by the growing nationalist movement in India, and influenced by MAHATMA GANDHI and other stalwarts in the struggle at the time. Dadoo went to London to study medicine, became involved in political campaigns there, and, at his father's urging, transferred to Edinburgh, Scotland, where he completed his medical degree. Dadoo returned to South Africa in 1936 and helped to rebuild a liberation struggle that was in some disarray at the time. In 1938, he helped found the NON-EUROPEAN UNITY MOVEMENT, which called for united mass action among blacks, INDIANS, and COLOUREDS. He also became the leader of the Transvaal Indian Congress. In 1939, Dadoo joined the Communist Party of South Africa, later renamed the SOUTH AFRICAN COMMUNIST PARTY, and was instrumental in assisting party leader Moses Kotane in building the party. Dadoo was arrested and imprisoned several times for distributing leaflets and inciting demonstrations, as well as for leading the passive resistance campaign against the apartheid regime. In 1950, Dadoo became president of the SOUTH AFRICAN INDIAN CONGRESS and was instrumental in forging a Congress Alliance with the AFRICAN NATIONAL CONGRESS (ANC, of which he was also a member), the SOUTH AFRICAN COLOURED PEOPLE'S ORGANIZATION, and the Congress of Democrats. In concert with the ANC, Dadoo helped to plan the DEFIANCE CAMPAIGNS that saw more than 8,500 South Africans defy the new unjust apartheid laws. As he grew in political prominence, he increasingly became a target of state oppression and was repeatedly arrested and banned from attending political meetings. In 1960, Dadoo went underground and fled into exile via Botswana. He traveled around much of Africa promoting the establishment of Peace Committees. In exile, he traveled and spoke often, representing the South African Communist Party as well as the ANC at many gatherings. Dadoo died

in Britain at the age of seventy-four on September 19, 1983, after twenty-three years in exile.

Defiance Campaigns

The Campaign of Defiance Against Unjust Laws was jointly launched in 1952 by the AFRICAN NATIONAL CONGRESS (ANC) and the SOUTH AFRICAN INDIAN CONGRESS (SAIC). Modeled after MAHATMA GANDHI's nonviolent, passive resistance strategy, the defiance campaign was the largest mass action against the APARTHEID regime and its repressive and racist policies to date. Over 8,500 people defied apartheid policies and courted arrest by contravening PASS LAWS and curfew regulations, as well as whites-only stipulations for public facilities. Demonstrations and protests were held throughout the country.

The significance of this campaign is that it was the first time that blacks, COLOUREDS, and INDIANS worked together to oppose apartheid and foster a new era of cooperation among antiapartheid activists. This campaign also gained international attention and spurred growing support for antiapartheid groups from abroad. The defiance campaign was also an inspiration to the burgeoning civil rights movement in the United States, as it influenced the actions and strategies of civil rights leaders, including Dr. Martin Luther King Jr. The campaign was also significant in that it raised the consciousness of many black South Africans, who began to publicly oppose apartheid. This was evident in the dramatic increase in membership of antiapartheid organizations such as the ANC and the SAIC.

In 1989, a second defiance campaign was launched, which turned out to be a watershed in South African politics. It was launched by the Mass Democratic Movement and by a conglomeration of grassroots, civic organizations, trade unions, and political groupings. The 1989 defiance campaign signaled a revival of mass-based politics after several years of state repression and crackdown. Tens of thousands of people took to the streets to call for the end to apartheid and to defy states of emergency that imposed detentions, curfews, and heavy movement restrictions on blacks. Activists took the battle to the city centers, highlighting the extent to which the people's power could overcome apartheid through their numbers.

De Klerk, F. W. (Frederik Willem) (1936–)

The last APARTHEID-era state president, F. W. (Frederik Willem) de Klerk, was awarded a Nobel Peace Prize in 1993, along with NELSON MANDELA, for negotiating the dismantling of apartheid and the transition to a nonracial democracy. De Klerk was born into a prominent political AFRIKANER family in JOHANNESBURG on March 18, 1936. He graduated with a law degree from Potchefstroom University in 1958 and practiced law in Vereeniging in the Transvaal. In 1969, he married Marike Willemse, with whom he has two sons and a daughter.

De Klerk was elected to Parliament in 1972 as a NATIONAL PARTY member and was appointed minister of posts and telecommunications and social welfare and pensions in 1978 by Prime Minister John Vorster. He later held a number of ministerial posts during P. W. Botha's administration, including posts and telecommunications and sports and recreation (1978–1979); mines, energy, and environmental planning (1979–1980); mineral and energy affairs (1980–1982); internal affairs (1982–1985); and national education and planning (1984–1989). Throughout much of his political career, de Klerk advocated for apartheid and racial segregation. As minister of national education, de Klerk was a proponent of segregated education, and, until his election as state president in September 1989, he was not known as an advocate of reforming apartheid or South Africa's political system. This leads some commentators to argue that de Klerk's subsequent actions in repealing apartheid laws and negotiating the drafting of a new CONSTITUTION were done out of necessity and with considerable pressures from international as well as domestic forces.

In his first speech as president, de Klerk lifted the bans on liberation organizations such as the AFRICAN NATIONAL CONGRESS (ANC), the PAN AFRICANIST CONGRESS, and the SOUTH AFRICAN COMMUNIST PARTY, and unconditionally released political prisoners including Mandela. With his actions, he set in motion a process of political negotiations that culminated with the country's first nonracial elections in April 1994 and an arrangement in which the victorious ANC agreed to share power with other political parties, including the Afrikaner-led National Party. After the 1994 ELECTIONS, de Klerk was one of the two deputy presidents in the new Government of National Unity (GNU). In 1996, de Klerk and other National Party leaders withdrew from the GNU in order to establish the National Party as a formal opposition party. In September 1997, he stepped down as leader of the National Party and retired from politics.

See also DEMOCRATIC TRANSITION/ NEGOTIATIONS, 1990–1994; NATIONAL PARTY

De Lille, Patricia (1951–)

Patricia de Lille has been an outspoken and influential political figure in South Africa, particularly following the APARTHEID era. She was a member of PARLIAMENT, elected first as a member of the PAN AFRICANIST CONGRESS (PAC) and later as leader of the Independent Democrats, a political party she formed in 2003 after breaking away from PAC. In 2010, de Lille's Independent Democrats signed a memorandum of understanding with the official opposition party, the DEMOCRATIC ALLIANCE (DA), setting the stage for a merger of the two parties by 2014. That same year, de Lille joined the Western Cape provincial government as the minister of social development. In 2011 she was installed as mayor of CAPE TOWN after the DA won the municipal elections.

Born on February 17, 1951, in Cape Town, de Lille has been involved in politics for more than twenty-five years. While working in Cape Town as a laboratory technician, she become involved in the Chemical Workers Union and was elected to its National Executive in 1983. In 1988, she was elected as the national vice president of the National Council of Trade Unions, the highest position held by a woman in the trade union movement at the time.

In addition to being a labor organizer, de Lille was a staunch activist against apartheid and supporter of PAC, one of the more radical liberation movements that promoted a black African agenda for change. In 1990, de Lille was elected to PAC's National Executive and led its delegation in the constitutional negotiations during South Africa's transition to a nonracial democracy. After the first democratic elections in 1994, she was appointed chairperson of the Parliamentary Committee on Transport (1994–1999) and also became PAC's chief whip. As a member of Parliament, de Lille has been a vocal and progressive, but controversial politician. She has been an outspoken opponent of some policies and actions of the ruling party, the AFRICAN NATIONAL CONGRESS (ANC), and has made use of parliamentary privilege to be a whistleblower on controversial issues such as the South African Arms Deal, which implicated high-level ANC officials in corruption and accepting bribes. De Lille has also been a vocal leader on sensitive issues such as HIV/AIDS, criticizing the government's contentious position, especially its initial lack of support for the use of antiretroviral treatment. Some of her actions have sparked criticism, particularly from other opposition parties, including her relationship with the anticrime, vigilante group People Against Gangsterism and Drugs (PAGAD) and her willingness to support squatters occupying lands illegally.

Democratic Alliance

The Democratic Alliance (DA) is South Africa's second largest political party after the AFRICAN NATIONAL CONGRESS (ANC), with 16.7 percent of the popular votes in the 2009 general election. This party was founded by TONY LEON, one of South Africa's most prominent politicians, on June 24, 2000, when it entered into a short-lived alliance with the AFRIKANER-led New National Party, the new name for the old NATIONAL PARTY that had implemented APARTHEID. The tenets of its political ideologies and platforms are federalism, free enterprise, and protection of human rights. Despite being a new political party, the Democratic Alliance has roots in previous political parties dating back to the founding of the UNION OF SOUTH AFRICA in 1910. Its ancestor parties include the South African Party, the United Party, the Progressive Party (where its member of Parliament HELEN SUZMAN was the only visible opponent to the apartheid regime in the Parliament for thirteen years), the Progressive Reform Party, the Progressive Federal Party, and the Democratic Party. The Democratic Alliance is based in CAPE TOWN, as it has the largest number of supporters there. During the 2000 elections, this party won approximately 52.3 percent of the votes in the Western Cape Province. Its current leader, Helen Zille, was elected the premier of the Western Cape Province in the 2009 elections.

With Leon's retirement in 2007, the Democratic Alliance entered into a new era. It is trying to change its image of an all-white political party by adopting the slogan "One Nation, One Future," which emphasizes a nonracial South Africa with equal opportunities for all. Additionally, it wants to present itself not only as a major political opposition but also as a viable alternative to the ANC. The Democratic Alliance has expanded its voter base by gaining political support among the COLOURED population. It signed a memorandum of understanding in 2010 with PATRICIA DE LILLE's Independent Democrats, signaling a future merger between the two parties and further expanding the DA's base, particularly in the Western Cape Province. Its other major party platform is campaigning for the extension of voting rights in both the national and the provincial elections to South African nationals abroad. The party has also recently formed a youth wing, the Democratic Alliance Youth, under Zille's leadership.

See also APPENDIX 5: POLITICAL PARTIES IN THE APRIL 2009 NATIONAL ELECTIONS

Democratic Party

See DEMOCRATIC ALLIANCE

Democratic Politics Since 1994

South Africa has moved from a racist, deeply divided, and violently unequal society to an inclusive, democratic polity, beginning with the first open ELECTION in 1994. In less than two decades, political elites and citizens are still adapting to the newly introduced democratic political institutions while responding to the legacies of racial inequalities deeply imprinted in society. The electoral dominance of the black-led AFRICAN NATIONAL CONGRESS (ANC) and weak opposition parties stand out as the distinctive feature of the post-1994 period, and in this context significant battles over transforming inherited social relations characterize the political field. Additionally, the black majority, eking out a living in townships and informal squatter camps, have had their expectations disappointed, with frustration building against the political elite. Against this backdrop of increased social mobilization of the poor, who are increasingly resorting to violent political discourse to articulate their interests, the liberal democratic political order and all that was expected of it sits uneasily.

Precursor to 1994

In 1990, the APARTHEID regime, led by F. W. DE KLERK, set the tone for a negotiated settlement by releasing NELSON MANDELA and other political prisoners, lifting the bans on antiapartheid nationalist organizations, and allowing for the return of political exiles. The onset of negotiations was itself the product of a deep crisis of social control, related to the structural failings of apartheid, splits in the ruling elite, and the development of a national protest culture together with a qualitatively sophisticated antiapartheid movement that had acquired enormous powers of mass mobilization.

This maturation of internal resistance, the key visible factor expressive of the political terrain, can be traced to the late 1960s. Beginning with the 1976 SOWETO STUDENT UPRISING, the AFRIKANER-led NATIONAL PARTY leaders grudgingly began to recognize the importance of negotiations with the black liberation movements and political reform to avert further radicalization of the struggles waged against it. The apartheid system was in crisis, as evidenced in lower productivity and profit rates, increased unemployment, growing resistance to apartheid, and a general breakdown in social order; all of which caused a distinct concern for the apartheid regime's Western allies. Following the release of Mandela, at various formal negotiating forums the National

Party and the ANC entered into a series of compromises, and after many unpredictable setbacks and uncertainties, characteristic of the negotiations between 1990 and 1994, a democratic CONSTITUTION was produced with both majoritarian and consensus features.

The Constitutional Assembly (the national PARLIAMENT constituted itself as the assembly after the first elections in 1994) had to design a Constitution compatible with thirty-four constitutional principles agreed to at the key negotiating forums. The most important were the separation of powers between different branches of government (the executive, legislative, and judicial); regular elections; recognition of population diversity; multiparty political system; three—national, provincial, and local—levels of government; provincial governments having both exclusive and concurrent powers; various independent democratic-enhancing commissions; and an electoral system following proportional representation in general. The negotiators agreed to a universal adult voter franchise in exchange for a complex system of checks and balances, the protection of private property rights, and the cultural recognition of minorities as well as promises by the ANC to form a coalition government and to preserve the white civil service for a period of five years after the first election.

Political Framework Post-1994
South Africa is best characterized as a qualified majoritarian system, having some key consensus features such as the proportional representation electoral system, weak federalism, a written Constitution, and watchdog agencies, all of which disperse the centralization of power. There is no formal separation of powers between the Parliament and the executive; the executive is dependent on its support in the legislature, which makes South Africa a parliamentary rather than a presidential system. The dominance of the ANC in Parliament makes executive power sharing (following the end of the Government of National Unity of the first election) dependent on the ANC's goodwill rather than forced coalitions, a feature occurring more frequently at local government level. The formation of coalition arrangements at the provincial level has been less common—in the KwaZulu-Natal Province between 1999 and 2004 and various combinations between the ANC, National Party, and DEMOCRATIC PARTY—with the ANC and Democratic Party entering into coalitions with the National Party but not with each other in the Western Cape.

The proportional representative electoral system has provided the basis for over thirteen parties winning seats in Parliament, but their representation is dwarfed by the ANC. In the 1994, 1999, 2004, and 2009 elections, the ANC won resounding victories, although with fewer eligible voters going to the polls each time. In 1994, it won 62.6 percent of the vote (a full 42 percent ahead of its nearest rivals). In 1999, it increased its lead to 66.5 percent, winning another 14 seats, controlling 266 seats. In 2004, it won 4 additional seats, bringing its total to 279 (after the last "floor crossings" of elected representatives between parties allowed by legislation) of the 400-seat legislature. In the 2009 election, the national seat control of the ANC in Parliament fell slightly to 264, although the party retained close to 66 percent of the vote. The proportional representation party list system leads to strong party control over parliamentary representatives; party leaders select members who will qualify for public office. Under the now-ended controversial legislation that allowed for defections in between elections, members who wanted to defect would lose their seats unless they did so during the floor-crossing window period, allowed twice in between elections and where at least 10 percent of a party's members decide to leave. These rules enhance the power of party bosses over ordinary members, which negatively affects internal party dissent. This, together with the long-held cultural practice within the ANC to value internal unity at all costs, serves to discourage internal party dissension, especially on issues considered controversial, such as, for example, President THABO MBEKI's querying of the causal links between HIV and AIDS.

Party Politics
Since the 1999 elections, the ANC and DEMOCRATIC ALLIANCE represent the two largest parliamentary political parties and occupy the center

position in the political party spectrum, indicating voter support moving away from the margins. At the same time, the opposition parties remain divided and weak. The ANC holds a clear majority with the remaining seats divided between fifteen opposition parties (with most having fewer than ten seats). The Democratic Party (which became the Democratic Alliance after it struck an alliance agreement in 1998 with the New National Party [NNP], which eventually merged into the ANC in 2004), representing the long conservative tradition of white South African liberalism (i.e., far more liberal on economic issues than on political ones), is considered the official opposition in government with some long-term viability. It fared unexpectedly badly in 1994 with only 1.75 percent of the vote (only seven seats), increasing this to 9.5 percent in 1999, and further to 11 percent in 2004 with fifty-two parliamentary seats. In 2009 the party received 17 percent of the national vote, increasing its seat share in Parliament to sixty-seven. Political parties that explicitly vie for the black vote with the ANC—the PAN AFRICANIST CONGRESS (PAC), Azanian People's Organization (AZAPO), and the Socialist Party of Azania, among others—failed to mount a significant electoral challenge to the ANC. Despite the expectations, particularly in the first election, that PAC was going to compete closely with the ANC, it and the black consciousness party AZAPO received less than 1.5 percent, and this trend has not changed in succeeding elections.

The parties on the white far right also failed to accomplish the threats to secede or destabilize the new government they claimed was against the democratic order and have steadily declined in support. The Freedom Front, representing mainly Afrikaans speakers who were once sympathetic to demands for an Afrikaner homeland, has seen its votes decline from 2.25 percent to 0.75 percent in the 1994 and 1999 elections. The parties to the extreme left and right of the ANC pose an insignificant threat to its electoral dominance.

The demise of the party of apartheid, the National Party (later the NNP), and its subsequent merger with its traditional arch-enemy the ANC, demonstrates the fluidity and unpredictability of South African politics. In a relatively short period, the NNP dramatically lost its support, with most of its white and COLOURED Afrikaans-speaking supporters joining the Democratic Alliance, which has campaigned against the ANC's AFFIRMATIVE ACTION policies, BLACK ECONOMIC EMPOWERMENT, in business; widespread corruption; ineffective implementation of policies, especially in combating crime, high unemployment, and HIV/AIDS; and conciliatory stance toward Robert Mugabe's government in ZIMBABWE. Newly formed parties under charismatic personal leaders, such as the United Democratic Movement and the African Christian Democratic Party, tended to perform well in the first elections but were unable to consolidate or increase their support in the subsequent ones. These parties, however, have contributed to the diversity of views represented in the national Parliament.

The grand coalition between the ANC, the National Party, and the INKATHA FREEDOM PARTY (IFP) at the executive level lasted between 1996 and 1999 and changed with National Party withdrawal, but the Inkatha Freedom Party remained until it also pulled out when Thabo Mbeki of the ANC and MANGOSUTHU BUTHELEZI of the IFP had a falling-out over a possible coalition government in KwaZulu-Natal, which local ANC members opposed. The ANC's internal diversity has been described as a "grand system of power sharing," and ANC dominance does not pose a threat to democratic accountability. The proportional representation (PR) election system makes single-party dominance difficult over the long term, and the written Constitution seriously undermines the ANC's centralization of power. Finally, the various democratic-enhancing Chapter Nine bodies (referring to Chapter 9 of the Constitution), such as the Human Rights Commission, Auditor General, and Public Protectors Office, serve as important watchdog agencies, although even these bodies increasingly struggle to resist being drawn into ANC factional battles.

Race and Electoral Politics
Some observers conclude that post-1994 elections have not broken the racial and ethnic divisions of the past and interpret these elections as a "racial census," with citizens voting according to their

racial identity. Although there are significant shifts in party affiliation, and racial blocs are by no means self-evident without important complex factors motivating and explaining local political behavior, there are significant overlaps between existing racial/ethnic group categories and party affiliation. It is difficult to comment with any certainty about the racial census interpretation of voting behavior because in South Africa other compelling factors, such as education, ideology, class, urban-rural, culture and tradition, and status, correlate fairly closely with past racial classification. Problematically, there is a tendency to identify race as the key explanatory factor when other factors may be more salient or, at the very least, to acknowledge that race combines with these other factors to complicate analysis of voting political behavior. According to the dominant view on voting behavior, the ANC, which receives its support primarily from the African majority, will remain in power for many decades unless black Africans divide along the lines of class, interest, ideology, and perhaps local cultures and traditions.

As a government representing the majority of citizens in a democratic South Africa after centuries of white supremacist rule, the ANC had to confront three major challenges: to keep the society together despite disgruntled supporters of the old regime and ethnic leaders demanding separate territorial jurisdictions, to address the massive legacies of race- and class-based socioeconomic inequality in virtually all aspects of social life, and, finally, to create conditions to reproduce, legitimize, and institutionalize the newly won democratic structures, practices, and values. The ANC feared that the apartheid civil service would resist the ANC's intentions to reorganize the state and civil society in the majority's interests. This fear has not been verified, and the civil service has supportively implemented the ANC government's policies. Over the years, many of the top positions (directors and deputy directors) of government departments have been gradually filled by ANC members. The old order still survives in some areas, but the slow delivery of services, initially blamed on the "conservative bureaucracy," has focused increasingly on the "lack of capacity," in terms of skills and experience of the ANC's own appointees in what is now an overwhelmingly black civil service.

The negotiations and the democratic Constitution established that national reconciliation among all South Africans was to be a priority value of the democratic order, and mechanisms to address past human rights violations had to enhance the importance of reconciliation and nation building. To this end, the TRUTH AND RECONCILIATION COMMISSION (TRC) was established to introduce a novel restorative justice model to address past atrocities. Perpetrators had to fully disclose their actions to receive amnesty, while the victims were allowed national forums to tell their stories and were promised some form of compensation. The commission aimed to ambiguously bridge the gap between the idea of the church confessional and legal court hearings, hoping to avoid the weaknesses of both. The process ran its course between 1996 and 1998, with first victim and later amnesty hearings that were extensively covered in the national media, reminding South Africans of grotesque stories of torture, assassination, abduction, maiming, and the loss of loved ones. The commission produced a five-volume report, and its Amnesty Committee granted amnesty to those security personnel who it believed confessed the truth of their deeds and were acting under the direct instructions of the leadership of a political entity or organization, such as the police, the military, a political party, or liberation movement.

Outstanding issues, however, still remain. These include the large number of people who did not participate in the TRC process (many still in the military and police establishments), making it difficult for the ANC government to criminally prosecute all of them without worrying about destabilizing the state; the large number of individuals who languish in prison convicted of criminal convictions despite the political motivation behind their acts, which fell outside the period adjudicated by the TRC; and, lastly, the widespread view that victims and their families did not receive adequate compensation for their sacrifices and loss. Unsurprisingly, all the key political parties conveyed strong reservations about the report's findings, and many victims have not received the promised reparations that were part of the initial incentive to testify. Yet, despite the weaknesses of the TRC process, few dispute that it contributed to the legitimacy and normalization of broader South African politics, at least to the degree of allowing the key political institutions to establish themselves. As for the aim of reconciliation, it became apparent that the commission was not going to realize this aim, which, in essence, involves a longer time period (perhaps generations) to overcome the deeply rooted legacies of apartheid.

The major challenge of widespread inequality between rich and poor, which strongly overlaps with race in South Africa, has continued to put pressure on the democratic institutions and culture. The country has one of the highest rates of inequality (by Gini coefficient, just behind Brazil), a situation that is glaringly visible in everyday interactions between citizens; shantytowns and grinding poverty sit side by side with immense expressions of wealth. This inequality trivializes the principles of equality enshrined in the Constitution and also seriously undermines the democratic political discourse. The ANC first embarked on the RECONSTRUCTION AND DEVELOPMENT PROGRAM (RDP) as its policy framework to tackle poverty and inequality. From 1994 to 1996, the RDP was considered the overall policy to guide all other policies of the government, which aimed to redistribute wealth by extensive state intervention through the provision of services and infrastructure. However, the ANC leadership, in rethinking its economic policies, favored more market-oriented solutions. Along with numerous problems in implementing RDP projects and funding shortages, the RDP was all but abandoned. Rather than focus on distribution in the context of stagnant growth, the government embraced what it called the GROWTH, EMPLOYMENT, AND REDISTRIBUTION STRATEGY (GEAR). GEAR amounted to a domestically designed structural adjustment program, advocating a variety of policies intended to inspire economic growth through increased foreign investment, rather than state-led distribution. The government's macroeconomic policy encouraged direct foreign investment and exports of South African goods, increased the role of the market in the allocation of goods and services, and expected these interventions would result in the creation of jobs and thus redistribution.

This policy has produced ambiguous results, leading to economic growth (but not as high as the predicted 6 percent) and stable inflation but growing unemployment. In general, South Africa has experienced what many call "jobless growth," and the insufficient state investment in social service delivery has not seriously dented the backlogs inherited from apartheid, increasing the frustrations of the poor majority. This has led to a series of civil society protests around poor service delivery, creating new tensions within the ANC and often between the ANC and its alliance partners in the ruling coalition. At the same time, the policy has been lauded by national businesses, which in turn created much stronger ties between the ruling party and the business sector under Mbeki's leadership. The adoption of the contentious GEAR policy encouraged the CONGRESS OF SOUTH AFRICAN TRADE UNIONS (COSATU) and the SOUTH AFRICAN COMMUNIST PARTY, two of the ANC's alliance partners who were not consulted over the policy, to support the overthrow of the Mbeki leadership at the ANC's Polokwane conference in 2008. However, these organizations, particularly COSATU, have not felt comfortable with the continued economic policy direction under the new administration of JACOB ZUMA.

Prospects for the Future

Less than two decades after the first democratic elections, few outside observers could have imagined the immense advances made by a society that was on the brink of collapse and social ruin by the late 1980s. The rules set out in the democratic Constitution have held, and have largely taken root in the evolving mainstream democratic political culture. These have certainly been accepted by the nationalist elite in power and of various political parties, with no significant group challenging them. Elite conflicts are managed through the electoral system, parliamentary debates, and votes, and, when unresolved at any of the political levels, are taken to the Constitutional Court. The legitimacy of the political system is not in question. The challenges facing the political system come from the slow pace in addressing the legacies of the past. The frustrations surrounding unrealized expectations that a postapartheid order promised permeate the society. The problems of poverty and unemployment directly feed into, and arguably produce, the high crime levels and other social ills. The latter are not intractable problems, although their psychological roots relate to the violence of settler colonialism in South Africa, and the long period of adapting and resisting the multiple dimensions will take creative strategies to overcome. However, few dispute that the foundational political institutions of democracy are in place. Rather, they question the direction of the policy agenda and the extent to which a pro-poor, redistributive policy will be implemented and, increasingly, point to an unresponsive political elite that seeks to buffer itself from the social and economic realities confronting most South Africans.

See also ELECTIONS; POLITICAL PARTIES

Bibliography

Faure, Murray, and Jan-Erik Lane, eds. *South Africa: Designing New Political Institutions*. London: Sage Publications, 1996.

Kadima, Denis, ed. *The Politics of Party Coalitions in Africa*. Johannesburg, South Africa: Electoral Institute of South Africa, 2006.

Koeble, Thomas. *The Global Economy and Democracy in South Africa*. New Brunswick, NJ: Rutgers University Press, 1998.

Lijphart, Arend. "South African Democracy: Majoritarian or Consociational?" *Democratization* 5, no. 4 (1998): 144–150.

Lodge, Tom. "The ANC and the Development of Party Politics in Modern South Africa." *Journal of Modern African Studies* 42, no. 2 (2004): 189–219.

Price, Robert. *The Apartheid State in Crisis*. Berkeley: University of California Press, 1990.

Reddy, Thiven. "The Congress Party Model: South Africa's African National Congress (ANC) and India's Indian National Congress (INC) as Dominant Parties." *African and Asian Studies* 4, no. 3 (2005): 270–300.

Sisk, Timothy. *Democratization in South Africa*. Princeton, NJ: Princeton University Press, 1995.

Southall, Roger. "The Centralization and Fragmentation of South Africa's Dominant Party System." *African Affairs* 97 (1998): 443–469.

—*Thiven Reddy*

Democratic Transition/ Negotiations, 1990–1994

Majority (black) rule came to South Africa in 1994 through a process of a negotiated transition between the APARTHEID regime headed by the NATIONAL PARTY but including several other smaller white-based parties and the black liberation movements headed by the AFRICAN NATIONAL CONGRESS. Public talks that culminated in universal voting franchise elections began in early 1990, shortly after a speech by President F. W. DE KLERK lifting the bans on liberation movements and promising the release of NELSON MANDELA from prison.

It took two years before a first attempt at constitutional negotiations could be made. The creation of a new democratic dispensation that included all South Africans required the drafting of a new CONSTITUTION to replace the previous one that recognized different systems of government and institutions for different racial groups. First, agreement was needed on preconditions that made negotiation possible—ending armed struggle that the liberation movements had been waging against the apartheid regime and releasing political prisoners. The African National Congress (ANC) also needed a mandate from members to negotiate with the apartheid regime, which it only received in June 1991, when it held its first national conference inside the country since the 1950s. At the meeting, Mandela was elected president and CYRIL RAMAPHOSA, later to become chief ANC negotiator, was elected secretary-general.

More important, the two main parties—which were the National Party and the ANC—were separated by a deep difference on the shape of negotiations. The ANC's goal was majority rule, while that of the AFRIKANER-led National Party—which presided over apartheid—was to prevent it. The ANC insisted, therefore, that a Constitution be framed by an assembly elected by all adults. The National Party replied that it could only be devised by a forum in which all political parties had equal say. Both believed that allowing the other's form of negotiations would decide the outcome in advance: An elected constitutional forum would adopt the ANC's vision of majority rule, while a multiparty conference would allow a veto for small parties with an interest in frustrating majority rule. To agree to the other's proposal was, seemingly, to concede the future to it before constitutional negotiations began.

Paving the Way

For a time, this gulf persisted while conflict increased Political intragroup violence was more intense in 1991 than in the mid-1980s, when the apartheid government declared a state of emergency. In May 1991, the ANC briefly withdrew from negotiations, charging government complicity in the violence. The path to negotiation, however, was opened by ANC initiatives, which made the negotiation possible while not acknowledging that the ANC had departed from its core goal. The key ANC innovation was a statement by Mandela in January 1991 calling for an "all-party congress" to negotiate the route to an elected assembly that would devise a new Constitution.

Later, the ANC argued that arranging an elected assembly could not be left to the apartheid government—all parties had to be involved. Multiparty talks were, therefore, not a substitute for a constituent assembly but the only way to achieve it. The ANC returned to talks after its May withdrawal, arguing that violence would continue as long as the apartheid government was in power, and that negotiations were needed to end the violence. Both ANC positions presented compromises as a means to majority rule. These changes, along with the National Peace Accord of September 1991, in which political parties and interest groups agreed on a joint peace effort, paved the way for constitutional negotiations.

CODESA: Getting It Wrong the First Time

The CONVENTION FOR A DEMOCRATIC SOUTH AFRICA (CODESA), the first multiparty talks, convened in December 1991. All parties except the white right and the Africanist or black consciousness parties attended, although the INKATHA FREEDOM PARTY (IFP) delegation's leader, MANGOSUTHU BUTHELEZI, stayed away in protest at the other parties' refusal to seat a delegation headed by the ZULU king. For the next five months, negotiations became ever more frustrating and incomprehensible. While they were supposedly kept out of the public eye by a decision to break into working groups behind closed doors, leaks ensured that the public knew of most developments. But progress was difficult to follow as intricate technical proposals were debated with no evidence that the parties were moving forward. In theory, every party at the talks had an equal say. In practice, they were a negotiation between the ANC and the National Party. The negotiators adopted the principle of "sufficient consensus": if the two major parties agreed—in other words the ANC and the National Party—then agreement had been reached.

In May 1992, the talks collapsed when the parties could not agree on the majority required at the Constitutional Assembly, reflecting the fact that the parties remained far apart. The National Party was still trying to prevent majority rule, and the ANC—although it had signaled its willingness to make concessions, including special majorities at the Constitutional Assembly—remained committed to it. One factor making a breakdown more likely was a March 1992 National Party victory in a white referendum on the negotiations. This prompted a wave of support from the West, which convinced the National Party that it could toughen its position and still retain Western sympathy—a priority for both sides. But, CODESA would probably not have produced an agreement even without the referendum. The parties had not yet tested each other's strength and had not therefore formed a realistic view of what they could achieve in negotiation.

For the next few months, they tested each other on the streets and in the court of world opinion. The result was an agreement between the apartheid government and the ANC in September 1992: the Record of Understanding. It made the resumption of negotiations possible but also more difficult since it alienated Buthelezi's IFP.

The record met ANC demands for the release of more political prisoners and measures to curb violence by migrant Zulu mine workers and IFP supporters who were often hostile to the ANC—and included National Party concessions on the Constitutional Assembly. However, days afterward, the ANC also signaled that it had shifted its position, namely on sharing power and protecting the jobs of white civil servants. SOUTH AFRICAN COMMUNIST PARTY leader JOE SLOVO published an article—probably on the instructions of the ANC Executive—suggesting that the ANC agree to "sunset clauses," offering the National Party guarantees of white civil servant job security for a limited period. The article tested the ANC membership's response to these concessions. Their reactions were largely positive, and this laid the ground for a compromise.

However, the record enraged the IFP, a minor national player but one with significant regional standing in the important KwaZulu region. The IFP wanted to win sufficient recognition to retain its power base in the KwaZulu ethnic territory that the apartheid regime created. Its exclusion from the record, and the fact that the hostel dwellers (mine workers) against whom action was to be taken were its members, convinced it that the ANC and the National Party had "ganged up" against it. The record made new talks possible—but also persuaded the IFP to form an alliance with other ethnic homeland leaders and the white right wing against the National Party and the ANC.

Multiparty Negotiations: Sealing the Deal

The first democratic Constitution was bargained at multiparty talks, which met at Kempton Park, located outside of JOHANNESBURG, from March to November 1993. The inclination to compromise was sharpened by the murder of Communist Party leader CHRIS HANI in April 1993. Both parties feared that the anger that his death triggered strongly threatened social peace and that a settlement was urgently needed. They reacted by committing themselves to a national election for a new government a year later. Once the election date was settled, the talks gained much greater urgency since agreement had to be reached within months if this promise to the country was to be kept. This commitment also shifted the balance of power. Until then, the National Party, which stayed in power as long as the talks lasted, had no interest in speeding negotiations and had less need to compromise. Once it was bound to wrap up talks by an agreed date, it was forced to make more significant compromises.

Despite a campaign by the IFP and its allies to derail the negotiations, and an incident in which white right wingers stormed the building that housed the negotiations, talks moved steadily toward an agreement, which was reached on November 17. Although much was made of the "chemistry" between Ramaphosa and ROELF MEYER, the National Party's chief negotiator, fear that failure would trigger unmanageable conflict was a powerful spur to agreement.

The parties agreed on an interim Constitution that would allow elections in 1994. The elected Parliament would agree on a final Constitution by a two-thirds majority. This met the ANC's demand for an elected Constitution-making body. However, the Constitution could only be negotiated within constitutional principles agreed at the talks. This met the National Party demand for checks on majority rule. To meet the ANC's insistence that the election needed to be preceded by a period of joint rule so that the National Party would not enjoy the advantage of government office to steer the election in its favor, a Transitional Executive Council was established, providing for the joint control of elections and shared decisionmaking on other matters. In practice, there was never a clear agreement on whether the council or the apartheid government was in charge until the 1994 elections. But, political realities forced the National Party government to refrain from acting unilaterally on many issues.

By far, the most important ANC victory was over the shape of government. While the ANC agreed early on to share the government with minority parties, the National Party had wanted a minority veto in the cabinet so that no decisions could be taken without its agreement. In the last hours of the negotiation, the ANC secured an agreement that cabinet decisions would be made by majority vote, establishing the principle of majority rule. This agreement was ratified by the white Parliament in December, opening the way for elections on April 27, 1994.

See also BILL OF RIGHTS; CONSTITUTION; CONVENTION FOR A DEMOCRATIC SOUTH AFRICA; F. W. DE KLERK; NELSON MANDELA; ROELF MEYER; POLITICAL PARTIES; CYRIL RAMAPHOSA

Bibliography
Adam, Heribert, and Kogila Moodley. *The Negotiated Revolution: Society and Politics in Post-Apartheid South Africa.* Johannesburg, South Africa: Jonathan Ball, 1993.
Friedman, Steven, ed. *The Long Journey: South Africa's Quest for a Negotiated Settlement.* Johannesburg, South Africa: Ravan, 1993.
Friedman, Steven, and Doreen Atkinson, eds. *The Small Miracle: South Africa's Negotiated Settlement.* Johannesburg, South Africa: Ravan, 1995.
Sparks, Allister. *Tomorrow Is Another Country: The Inside Story of South Africa's Road to Change.* Chicago: University of Chicago Press, 1996.
Van Zyl Slabbert, Frederick. *The Quest for Democracy.* Johannesburg, South Africa: Penguin, 1992.
Waldmeir, Patti. *Anatomy of a Miracle: The End of Apartheid and the Birth of the New South Africa* New York: W. W. Norton, 1997.

—Steven Friedman

Diamonds
See GOLD AND DIAMOND MINING

District Six

District Six was a residential, inner-city community of CAPE TOWN established in 1867. It was a heterogeneous community, home to freed slaves, artisans, laborers, and immigrants, and it quickly became a vibrant hub for social, cultural, and political activities. The community also has a history of forced removals beginning with its black residents being moved out of the area as early as 1901. The forced removals aimed at creating racially distinct neighborhoods by removing, for example, from white neighborhoods those who were black, COLOURED, or INDIAN. For the first half of the twentieth century, this district became a neglected area, as its more affluent residents moved to the suburbs.

In 1966, the neighborhood was declared a whites-only area under the Group Areas Act of 1950, and, by 1982, the life of the community had been extinguished. Primarily in the 1970s, 60,000 coloured people were forcibly removed from District Six to barren, far-away areas on the Cape Flats, twenty miles outside of central Cape Town. All the homes and buildings (except churches and mosques) were flattened with bulldozers to make way for white business development that was expanding from the city center. The emotional horrors of the forced removals touched both South Africans and foreigners, who put pressure on the government not to develop the area. Therefore, until the demise of APARTHEID, the area remained largely undeveloped. Since 1994, however, plans have been made to repopulate the area and begin construction once again.

D'Oliveira, Basil (1931–)

A world-class cricketer, Basil D'Oliveira's actions on the cricket field helped expose the world to APARTHEID's oppressive and discriminatory practices. Born in CAPE TOWN on October 4, 1931, D'Oliveira was classified as COLOURED and thus suffered the consequences of racial segregation and discrimination in the field of sports. Unable to join the national Springbok teams (at the time, all the national sports teams were for whites only), "Dolly," as he came to be known, developed his skills and love of the game in the South African Cricket Board of Control (SACBOC) organization that catered to players of color. After becoming a SACBOC cricket star, D'Oliveira was offered a contract with the Central Lancashire League in Middleton, England. Thanks to the financial support of a local businessman, he was able to move to England and become a professional cricketer. In June 1966, D'Oliveira qualified to play for England and proved himself to be a formidable talent despite his relatively advanced age at the time.

Dolly toured with the English team against the West Indies, Pakistan, Australia, and India. However, in a controversial move, he was kept off the English team touring South Africa in 1968–1969, despite the fact that his stellar performance against Australia should have sealed his spot on the team. This incident became known as the "D'Oliveira Affair," served to embarrass England, and brought apartheid South Africa into the international limelight. It had been revealed that England succumbed to pressures and bribes from the apartheid government to not include D'Oliveira on the team. D'Oliveira himself was offered a bribe to refuse a position on the touring team, but, following a huge outcry, was eventually put on the team. However, South African prime minister John Vorster declared D'Oliveira unwelcome and canceled the tour, placing South Africa on the path to international isolation and highlighting a watershed in the sporting boycott of apartheid South Africa, which barred South African teams from competing in international events such as the Olympics and the World Cups. In 2000, D'Oliveira won belated recognition from his home country when he was chosen as one of the nominees for the title of South Africa's Cricketer of the Century. Today, D'Oliveira resides in England.

DP

See DEMOCRATIC ALLIANCE

Drum

A unique and desperately needed outlet for black cultural expression in South Africa, *Drum* magazine, started in 1951 by Jim Bailey, became one of the most popularly read magazines in South Africa and throughout the continent. *Drum*'s heyday in the 1950s coincided with the political and cultural revival of black South Africans, witnessed by the launching of the 1952 DEFIANCE CAMPAIGNS by the AFRICAN NATIONAL CONGRESS and its allies, as well as the explosion of black urban dwellers in communities such as SOPHIATOWN, located outside of JOHANNESBURG. *Drum* captured the world of urban blacks through investigative reporting and scandalous stories of crime, alcohol, and sex. The magazine brought together a young, dynamic group of writers and journalists, including William Bloke Modisane, Can Themba, Henry (Mr. Drum) Khumalo, BESSIE HEAD, and Dolly Rathebe. After the banning of the liberation movements in 1961, the subsequent crackdown of internal dissent by the APARTHEID regime, and the destruction by apartheid forces of Sophiatown where many of the journalists, activists, and black socialites lived, however, many of its journalists went overseas or died, and the magazine slowly declined in prominence.

Dube, John Langalibalele (1871–1946)

A newspaper publisher, philosopher, writer, educationist, and political activist, John Dube was founding president of the AFRICAN NATIONAL CONGRESS (ANC). A product of US missionary education (he was schooled at Inanda in Natal, where he was born, and later at ADAMS COLLEGE), he studied at Oberlin College in Ohio (1888–1890), where he met the black educator and leader Booker T. Washington and was impressed by his educational philosophy that proper skills education was key to the advancement of black people. In 1901, he established the OHLANGE INSTITUTE, a ZULU-Christian industrial school that copied Washington's Tuskegee Institute. Dube's political activism against colonialism was moderated by his Christian beliefs.

In 1903, Dube founded the Zulu-English newspaper *Ilange Lase Natal*, the first newspaper published in Zulu. Dube publicly expressed his support for the Zulu king Dinizulu, who was implicated in the BAMBATHA REBELLION (1906) led by the head of the Zondi clan against British colonial rule, and traveled to London in 1909 as a member of a South African delegation to protest the imminent formation of the whites-only UNION OF SOUTH AFRICA. In 1912, he was elected president of the ANC (then called the South African Native National Congress) at its founding conference in BLOEMFONTEIN. He made a second trip to London as head of an ANC delegation in 1914 to protest the imposition of the NATIVES' LAND ACT that allocated over three-fourths of South Africa's arable land to whites. He lost his position as ANC president for insisting that the organization should oppose the details of the Land Act but not the principle of segregation, as he had bought into the idea of separate, and in his mind equal, development. He returned to teaching at Ohlange, earned a PhD from the University of South Africa, and, in 1937, much to the chagrin of his ANC colleagues, was elected to the first NATIVES REPRESENTATIVE COUNCIL, an advisory body to the white government. He also authored a number of books in Zulu and in English.

Durban

The English colonized NATAL in 1824 with the establishment of a trading post in Durban. Within the next three decades, Durban developed into a harbor town, which encouraged the expansion of secondary and tertiary economic activities. In 1854, Durban became a municipality with an elected town council. Initially, this city was dominated by mercantile interests. Between 1870 and 1890, Durban experienced rapid economic expansion, particularly in the shipping and allied industries. This was associated with increased production of raw materials, as well as with diamond and gold mining in the interior, which generally increased trade.

Durban's multicultural diversity was linked to the presence of people of English, ZULU, and INDIAN origins. The origin of South African Indians can be traced back to the agricultural labor requirements of colonial Natal in the mid-nineteenth century, which some have viewed as a form of slavery. The indentured laborers were followed by "passenger" Indians who were mainly traders. As Indians progressed economically, they were perceived as a threat to European interests. The perceived social menace associated with the presence of Africans and Indians in Durban compelled municipal officers to wrestle constantly with the real problems of crime, disease, and sanitation caused by overcrowding and poor urban planning. These issues influenced the development of segregation policies, which culminated in the Group Areas Act (1950). Historically, there was a great deal of conflict and contradictions among the local state, the white elite, and the working-class groups over labor, housing, and race issues in Durban. As Indians comprised a large portion of the nonwhite population in central Durban, the anti-Indian agitation of the Durban City Council and its white electorate played an important role in the development of segregation legislation, especially the Group Areas Act.

A local debate ensued about whether the African proletariat should be accommodated in compounds and barracks close to their place of employment or in locations outside the city. Employers (industrial capital and the municipality) supported the former, while the native affairs bureaucracy and the superintendent of police supported the latter. The local state was not prepared to finance African housing from the municipal budget. With the terms of the Native Beer Act of 1908, the local state developed a unique "Durban system" whereby African workers contributed to local state finances through the services they purchased and thus indirectly to their own subjugation. More specifically, the local state established its own African eating houses as well as a monopoly on the sale of beer. A separate Native Revenue Account was established, whereby profits from these enterprises were used to finance the native affairs bureaucratic administration.

By the 1970s, the socio-spatial structuring of the APARTHEID city of Durban was complete. Economic imperatives influenced the development of "grey areas" in the early 1980s, and rigid race-space divisions were blurred as blacks began to infiltrate white residential areas. Social movements with strong grassroots support demanded the transformation of the apartheid local state. The local authority was also forced to deal with land invasions and the development of informal settlements by Africans who would squat on vacant land and establish make-up homes and communities.

Political contestation between the AFRICAN NATIONAL CONGRESS (ANC) and the INKATHA FREEDOM PARTY (IFP) resulted in the Durban region being racked by endemic violence since the 1980s. Although democratic local government elections in South Africa took place on November 1, 1995, elections in KwaZulu-Natal Province, which is home to Durban, didn't take place until June 26, 1996, because of administrative problems and the high levels of political intolerance and violence. In spite of these troubles, the June 26 elections in KwaZulu-Natal were substantially free and fair. As expected, the ANC was success-

Durban beachfront.

ful in the major urban areas and the IFP in the rural areas. Against the background of political conflict, violence, and instability, the relatively peaceful local elections marked the beginning of a new era, which would focus on reconstruction, development, and planning. While there was a new democratic council, there was concern about the lack of delivery of social services and the people's great expectations.

In 1996, the population of the Durban metropolitan region, which includes central Durban and its outlying suburbs and communities, was 2,751,193 people. According to the 2001 Census, the population of Durban was 3,090,123, indicating a 12.32 percent population increase over a five-year span. The annual growth rate in Durban was about 2.3 percent. Recent surveys have suggested a decline in the rate of population growth, which was largely related to the impact of AIDS. About half of the province's population live and work in Durban's industrial and commercial sectors.

Durban's strategic planning initiative to form an alliance between the local government and the private sector to help save the region's ailing economy resulted in the International Convention Center and the Point Redevelopment Project (including the uShaka Marine Park) built in the 1990s. These projects were underpinned by a protocol to address past inequalities, with policies for AFFIRMATIVE ACTION, stable job creation, and leveling of playing fields. Similar rhetoric was used to justify the construction of the Moses Mabhida Stadium, the initial cost of which escalated from R1.83 billion to R3.84 billion (approximately US$1 billion).

However, in reality, the poor and disadvantaged did not benefit. Predictions of thousands of employment opportunities did not consider the cyclical nature and the low-paying and unstable jobs that were created by the tourism-convention–centered industry. New jobs were not created but were merely redistributed to white suburbanites and not to the low-income groups. Hence, direct benefits for the disadvantaged communities in the Durban region were limited from such projects. Instead, there was a vociferous campaign on the part of largely white businessmen and residents to push the poor out of the city, the most prominent example of which were attempts to destroy the Early Morning Market in Warwick Avenue, Durban.

High levels of crime and violence in the region had a major impact on growth and development. In the mid-1990s, the challenges to economic and social development in the Durban region included rapid population growth, a slow economic growth rate, housing backlogs, an increasing number of informal settlements, increasing poverty, high unemployment rates, an inadequate supply of basic services to the majority of the population, and land claims from the proliferation of informal settlements in Durban. These factors demanded that the pace of land reform and housing delivery processes increase significantly. There were also problems relating to illegal immigrants from other parts of Africa and xenophobia against Africans from other parts of the continent. As a result of their illegal status, migrants in Durban were subjected to high levels of exploitation, the most serious being the outbreak of xenophobic violence in May 2008.

Many of these problems still persist. The municipal government's Draft Integrated Development Review 2005/2006 identified the following key development challenges of the Thekwini Municipality:

- Low economic growth and unemployment,
- Poor access to basic household services,
- High levels of poverty,
- Low levels of literacy and skills development,
- Sick and dying population affected by HIV/AIDS,
- Exposure to unacceptably high level of crime and risk,
- Unsustainable development practices, and
- Ineffective, inefficient, and inward-looking local government.

There were also disputes and contestations over new Durban boundaries. Affluent authorities were opposed to the spatial extension of the city's boundaries because of the costs of providing services and infrastructures in the economically deprived margins. Similarly, there was concern that the incorporation of rural areas would result in increased municipal service charges being imposed on these communities. There appears to be neither the political will nor the economic capacity to upgrade these zones of marginalized urban communities. While the municipal demarcation was largely successful in eliminating the political geography of apartheid at a macro scale, the greater challenge for the Durban local authority is to reduce the socio-spatial and economic inequalities, which appear to be high and increasing.

Bibliography
Freund, Bill, and Vishnu Padayachee, eds. *(D)urban Vortex: A South African City in Transition*. Pietermaritzburg, South Africa: University of Natal Press, 2002.
Maharaj, Brij. "Apartheid, Urban Segregation and the Local State: Durban and the Group Areas Act in South Africa." *Urban Geography* 18, no. 2 (1997): 135–154.
Maharaj, Brij, and Kem Ramballi. "Local Economic Development Strategies in an Emerging Democracy: The Case of Durban in South Africa." *Urban Studies* 35, no. 1 (1998): 131–148.

—Brij Maharaj

Durban Strikes

In 1973, at least 50,000 African workers, including 16,000 municipal employees, went on a series of spontaneous and illegal strikes in DURBAN, demanding a living wage. Though the strike was over within one week, both government and business elites were shocked at the black workers' organizational abilities as well as their level of anger over wage discrimination vis-à-vis their white counterparts. Strike action by workers reverberated across the country, ushering in a new era of trade union organization that was more militant, democratic, and mass-based than was previously the case. The Durban Strikes are often cited as one of the catalysts for the highly successful grassroots mass democratic movement of the 1980s that opposed APARTHEID by taking on bread-and-butter issues such as a living wage, affordable utilities, transportation, and rents.

Dutch East India Company

Also known as the Vereenigde Oost-Indische Compagnie (VOC) in the Dutch language, the Dutch East India Company held trade monopolies and governed colonies as a proxy of the Dutch government between 1602 (when it was founded) and 1798 (when the Dutch government took over its assets) in Asia (Malaysia, Ceylon, and Indonesia), and established the first European settlement at the Cape of Good Hope (1652), under the administration of Jan Van Riebeeck, in what is now South Africa.

Dutch Reformed Church

Also known by its Afrikaans name Nederduitse Gereformeerde Kerk, the Dutch Reformed Church (DRC) served as the official state church during APARTHEID (1948–1994) by providing theological justifications for its policies of racial separation. D. F. MALAN, a DRC minister, was the first apartheid-era prime minister (1948–1954). Founded in 1652 by Dutch settlers, the DRC strictly enforced racial segregation even as it attracted some COLOURED, INDIAN, and African members. In 1881, it established the Dutch Reformed Mission Church for the coloured, the DRC Church in Africa for Africans in 1910, and later the Reformed Church for Indians. In the mid-1980s, the World Alliance of Reformed Churches stripped the DRC of its membership due to its support of apartheid. Following the 1994 election, the DRC has tried to apologize and distance itself from its apartheid past by entering into "unity talks" with other DRC denominations. However, the church's membership remains overwhelmingly white.

E

Early Colonial Period: The Dutch at the Cape

In 1652, the DUTCH EAST INDIA COMPANY (in Dutch, Vereenigde Oost-Indische Compagnie, or VOC) founded a station in Table Bay (CAPE TOWN) to provide a harbor and supplies for its ships on the route between Europe and Asia. Water and firewood were readily available, and company officials were soon able to establish a vegetable garden in the valley above what was to become the anchorage. In the course of the next few years, a small town grew up around the Castle, a defensive fort built between 1666 and 1679, and the harbor, which was to become Cape Town. It was the beginning of colonial settlement in South Africa.

In the early days, it was hoped that the further needs of the settlement and of the forty or so VOC ships (later augmented by many from other European nations), which put into Table Bay each year, could be met by trade with the KHOIKHOI who lived around the southwestern Cape. They could only supply, however, a limited amount of meat from their flocks of sheep and herds of cattle. Within half a century, the continual drain of stock—through trade, intra-Khoikhoi warfare, and attacks launched by the Dutch—led to the collapse of even the largest of Khoikhoi polities. While a number of Khoikhoi were able to remain independent, if impoverished, in the southwestern Cape, the great majority moved north to Namaqualand or east to the area populated by the XHOSA and became farm laborers under conditions that were generally little if at all better than those of the slaves among whom they worked, or they joined the indigenous SAN in what was in effect a long guerrilla war against colonial expansion.

In the first decade of colonial settlement, a few men who had been granted their release from the VOC service set up farms in the close neighborhood of Cape Town. Substantial agricultural expansion, however, only occurred after the southwest Khoikhoi polities had lost their power. From the 1680s, land grants began to be given out on the shale lands to the north of Cape Town, in what became known as the Swartland, and along the slopes of the Cape Fold Belt's first ranges around the town of STELLENBOSCH, which was founded in 1686. The former area became the CAPE COLONY's major wheat-growing area, while the latter produced wine as its major crop. In both cases, the market for the farmers' produce was

Cape Town, with the result that agricultural expansion was limited to the area west of the mountains because transport was too expensive. From around 1710, however, settlers of European descent began to establish farms on the plains of the southern coastal forelands and later to the north into the area known as the Karoo. These were primarily stock farms, because the cattle and sheep they produced could be driven to market and slaughtered in Cape Town.

The expansion of colonial settlement into the interior and the steady growth of Cape Town through the eighteenth century were made possible by the continued immigration of Europeans, mainly men who had been in the VOC service. However, they also included a sizable number of direct immigrants, among them the relatively few women who came from Europe to the Cape. The most notable group was a couple hundred HUGUENOTS who arrived via the Netherlands, after being expelled from France in 1685. Throughout the seventeenth and eighteenth centuries, however, there was a steady, if unspectacular, movement of men into the ranks of the "free burghers" (citizens). The women who married into their ranks were primarily of at least partial Asian descent.

These women, or their immediate progenitors, had arrived at the Cape as slaves and were generally manumitted at the moment of their marriage to free burghers. Over the course of the century and a half of the slave trade to the Cape, around 63,000 slaves, according to the best current estimate, were brought to the Cape. Of these, about 4,500 were imported by the VOC, mainly from Madagascar and MOZAMBIQUE, and remained working for the company. They were primarily housed in the slave lodge located at the center of Cape Town and were rarely sold. The other 58,500 slaves were brought in privately. Most of them came in small numbers as part of the cargo of the various ships that plied the waters between Asia and Europe, although in the latter years of the eighteenth century, there was a steady trade in Mozambican and Malagasy slaves from Mauritius to the Cape in exchange for provisions.

In general terms, the slaves who came to the Cape derived, in approximately equal numbers, from what are now Indonesia and the Malay world, the Indian subcontinent, Madagascar, and the East African coast. While many of the slaves remained in Cape Town—working as domestic labor (which included heavy work like fetching water and firewood); in the harbor and performing other heavy labor for the company; as artisans, fishermen, and boatmen in Table Bay; and, increasingly, as small business salesmen and women, particularly in the food sector—most ended up on the Western Cape's wine and wheat farms. Here, the groups of slaves could be substantial—between twenty-five and fifty on the larger farms, although, in 1750, a majority of slave owners had fewer than five slaves.

Colonial society, as it developed in the course of the eighteenth century, was at once tripartite and quadripartite. On the one hand, there was the geographical distinction between Cape Town and other towns of the Cape Colony. Throughout the period of Dutch rule, the colony's only substantial towns and major markets were the agricultural districts to the west of the mountain ranges and the pastoralist interior. On the other hand was the distinction between the company and its officials, the burghers and the slaves, and the Khoikhoi laborers. The company dominated society because of its economic power, even though it was not monopolistic. However, it could bend the rules to its advantage due to the wealth and prestige of its senior officials and because it controlled the state, made the laws, ran the courts, and generally administered the colony. The only church allowed in the colony until 1780, the DUTCH REFORMED CHURCH, was also directly under the company, and its ministers were VOC employees. At least in the countryside, however, the magistrate, or *landdrost*, was dependent on the local elite of rich farmers, who filled the offices of *heemraad* (town council) and *veldcornet* (local government official or military official) and so maintained control both over the slaves and the Khoisan as well as over the more unruly elements among the settlers. In general, the Cape countryside was ruled by a coherent oligarchy.

In Cape Town, however, a conflict of interests was always simmering between the company and its officials, on the one hand, and the burghers, on the other. The burghers' merchants and company officials, in their private capacity, were generally in competition for the same commercial opportunities, and the latter were generally able to make use of their position to take some degree of unfair advantage. Moreover, the VOC regulations made it impossible for the Cape merchants to expand their operations outside of the colony, for instance, by trading to the East Coast of Africa. It is thus not surprising that the first major political challenge to company rule, the Patriot Movement of the 1780s, was led by a group of wealthy Cape Town merchants, although it did acquire a degree of support throughout the colony.

Beneath the elite level was a substantial group of soldiers and sailors in the company's service. Within Cape Town's growing urban center, they formed a separate category of young, unmarried men whose lives were regulated by the honor codes of their trades. For instance, many worked as carpenters, coopers, and smiths in the company's workshops in the castle. The soldiers were in town the whole year, as was a complement of sailors who worked on the small craft that the company used to convey its goods between Cape Town and Simons Bay on the eastern side of the Cape peninsula. This vessel was used in the winter months when Table Bay was too dangerous to sail. These sailors were augmented by those who came on the ships of the VOC and other European companies and who were generally in the harbor for a few weeks during the first three months of the year, as the rhythms of the winds made this the most suitable time to reach Cape Town, both on the voyage from Europe and from India or Java.

Although the company officials and burghers may have been, to some extent, in structural opposition, they were united in their need to maintain control over the slaves. There was always the possibility of slaves running away and forming bandit groups, which at times made some of the roads into the interior unsafe. They also attacked farmhouses, including those in the suburbs of Cape Town, and even attempted, on one occasion, to burn the town to the ground. Even without this physical threat, slave runaways formed a considerable loss of capital to both the company and the burghers. Those who managed to reach the Xhosa could be assured of a good welcome, while others moved north to the Gariep borderlands or became sailors on ships that came into Table Bay. Order over the slaves, and to a lesser extent over the soldiers, sailors, and the Khoisan, was maintained through the use of judicial terror and the application of ferocious forms of corporal and capital punishment.

As colonial settlement expanded away from the Southwest Cape, confrontation with the Khoisan took on other forms. The established Khoikhoi polities of the southern plains and across the mountains to the north, notably the Hessequa and the Inqua, collapsed under the pressures of colonial raiding and trading, though in the latter case the coup de grace was given by Xhosa attacks. Invading settlers and their herds and flocks appropriated the grazing land by force and reduced the game to a fraction of its previous abundance. With their livelihoods reduced, the Khoisan either became farm laborers, often subject to exceedingly harsh discipline, or joined what the Dutch knew as Boschesmannen (BUSHMEN), who combined an autochthonous hunter-gatherer existence with violent resistance against colonial advance. Many of those who joined the Bushman bands in the Cape Mountains had previously worked on the farms, although some still spoke non-Khoikhoi languages and were presumably of Cape San descent. In both the late 1730s and in the 1770s, the latent guerrilla warfare became particularly vehement. In the former period, the warfare took place mainly in the western mountains; in the latter on the plains of the Bokkevelden, the Roggevelden, and the Ghoup, approximately from modern Calvinia through the mountains to Graaff-Reinet. During this war, large tracts were temporarily abandoned by the colonists, whose reaction was to launch a genocidal campaign in a succession of major expeditions, known as commandos. It was the Dutch colonial period's most violent episode in South Africa.

From the 1770s onward, two movements of the colonial population began to bring colonial influence into new areas. First, to the north, a variety of raids led to the Khoikhoi subgroup the Einiqua Khoi's destruction in the well-watered bush above the Aughrabies falls. These were led by individuals considered by the colony to be of burgher status, but most of those who came to the Orange River were themselves of partial Khoikhoi descent. Some remained living what was, in effect, a bandit life, both in what was to become the Northern Cape and to the north of the river in what is now NAMIBIA. Others eventually took on a more settled existence and formed the nucleus for the Bastard communities, later renamed the GRIQUAS, who were to establish communities on the southern borders of Tswanaland.

Second, to the east of the colony, colonists, mainly of burgher descent, came increasingly into contact with the most western of the Xhosa groups. In particular, competition arose for seasonal grazing in the upper reaches of the Fish River Valley. These conflicts led to a number of skirmishes, dignified in colonial historiography as wars, so that the VOC was forced to intervene and establish a magistracy at Graaff-Reinet. However, the magistrates did not have the power to impose their will on the region, and attempts to do so led to the local elite's revolt, which was in itself a signal for some of the Khoikhoi laborers to ally themselves with the Xhosa in an attempt to better their conditions, in what was known as the Servants' Revolt.

The expansion to the east and north was accompanied by a substantial increase in the prosperity of the colony as a whole, some of which percolated as far as the stock farmers of the eastern frontier. The colony's prosperity, however, was largely due to the improvement of the market in the southwest. As a result, shipping and sales of provisions to the slave colonies of the Indian Ocean both increased, especially during the 1780s. Also, wine was sold to the Batavia, particularly from the Constantia Estates on the eastern flanks of Table Mountain, and to Europe, where they were among the most sought after vintages for a time. Much of the new profits were invested in increasing the colony's slave labor force, but a considerable amount was also put into improving the rich farmers' houses, producing what is known as the CAPE DUTCH ARCHITECTURE style, with its white plastered gables. These iconic buildings were erected by anonymous slave artisans, working both in the countryside and in Cape Town itself.

The latter years of the eighteenth century also saw an increase in the colony's religious diversity. For the first time, in 1780, a church congregation other than the Dutch Reformed was allowed, as a Lutheran church was established. Around the same time, ISLAM began to be organized under the leadership of religious teachers banished to South Africa from Indonesia as a result of their anti-VOC political agitation. The first formal mosque would, however, only be established in 1798.

At this stage, VOC rule had given way to that of the British, who conquered the Cape in 1795. Certainly after 1790, as a commercial organization, VOC was on the verge of bankruptcy, and the French takeover of the Netherlands during the Revolutionary Wars made it impossible for the company to continue to function. The British, however, took the Cape for the same reason as the Dutch had founded the colony a century and a half earlier—not so much for itself as because of its position on the sea route from Europe to Asia. For a short period, between 1803 and 1806, the Cape Colony was returned to the Dutch under the rule of the Batavian Republic, but thereafter it became a part of the British Empire.

See also BRITISH IMPERIALISM AND SETTLER COLONIALISM

— Robert Ross

Economy

In 2009, South Africa's gross domestic product (GDP) came to R2.5 trillion, or around US$330 billion (at an exchange rate of R7.25 to one US dollar). Its per capita GDP was around US$6,500 per person, making it a middle-income developing country. According to the United Nations Development Program, South Africa's GDP per capita, adjusted for domestic purchasing power, ranked it with countries such as Croatia and Chile and slightly above Malaysia and Mexico.

Three factors make South Africa stand out among middle-income economies. First, it has unusually large economic inequalities and extraordinarily high unemployment levels. Second, it depends relatively heavily on mining-based exports. Finally, from the mid-1980s until recently, it suffered comparatively slow growth and low investment.

Key Economic Trends

After a period of relatively slow growth in the late 1990s, the economy grew steadily from 2000. By the end of 2007, South Africa had enjoyed the longest economic upswing in its history. Between 1994 and 2000, the economy grew at 2.8 percent a year, accelerating to 4.1 percent between 2000 and 2006. Through this period, the economy grew much faster than the estimated population growth of around 1.1 percent and more than three times as fast as between 1985 and 1994. Still, growth remained sluggish compared to many other middle-income economies.

Despite the upswing, investment remained below the level of around 25 percent of GDP, which is normally considered necessary for long-term development. Gross fixed capital formation (that is, investment in fixed assets) was under 20 percent from 1983 to 2006, with a low point of 13 percent during the transition to democracy in 1993–1994. It rose gradually from the mid-1990s, but only reached 21 percent in the third quarter of 2007.

Historically, South Africa depended heavily on international markets, but its integration into the world economy evolved after 1994. By 1990, trade had declined to under a quarter of the GDP—well below the levels of the 1970s—but after 1994, it rose to a third of GDP. Two-thirds of exports comprised mining products, but the composition shifted from gold to platinum and base metals.

Foreign investment also increased rapidly after 1994, reversing the disinvestment of the late 1980s and early 1990s. Most of it took the form of portfolio investments in the stock market, predominantly in the mining and financial companies. As a result, the net financial balance fluctuated substantially, with significant upturns in the mid-1990s and the mid-2000s, and a sharp decline in 1999. The inflow of short-run capital after 2003 was associated with a sharp currency appreciation and a growing balance of trade deficit. In 2005, the balance of trade deficit came to around 5 percent of the GDP, an extremely high level by world standards. The inflow of capital fell with the global economic downturn in 2008, but it soon resumed as a result of very low interest rates in the industrialized economies.

Unemployment and Poverty

From the APARTHEID era, South Africa inherited extraordinarily high levels of unemployment, poverty, and inequality. Shortcomings in the data make it hard to be sure about trends in the 1990s. Still, most observers agree that the trends worsened somewhat in the late 1990s and then improved modestly from the early 2000s as a result of the economic upswing and expanded welfare transfers to the poor.

Despite the upturn in economic indicators, high levels of joblessness persisted through the first decade of the new millennium. In September 2008, the unemployment rate stood at 23.1 percent, compared to an average of under 10 percent in middle-income countries as a group. From 2008, the economic downturn saw job losses of over a million, or around 6 percent of total employment, and the unemployment rate climbed back to 25.3 percent by September 2010. Youth unemployment was particularly high. In September 2010, the unemployment rate for young people under twenty-five was 50 percent, compared to 27 percent for those between twenty-five and thirty-five, and 14 percent for older people.

In addition, South Africa had an unusually high share of adults who did not have paid employment, but, because they were not actively looking for a job, did not count as unemployed in the official statistics. In the mid-2000s, just over 40 percent of adults had income-generating employment in South Africa, compared to an international average of almost 60 percent.

Unemployment was associated with deep inequalities in incomes. In the mid-2000s, South Africa ranked among the most inequitable economies in the world. Only a few countries in Latin America suffered sharper differences between rich and poor.

In the early 2000s, a substantial expansion in state support for indigent children, disabled, and elderly people—known as social grants—and higher employment led to a significant reduction in poverty and possibly a moderate improvement in income distribution. The share of households reporting that they suffered hunger at least sometimes dropped rapidly, from 24 percent in 2002 to 12 percent in March 2007.

Still, levels of poverty remained high by international standards, with close to half of all households reporting expenditures of under a dollar a day per person in the mid-2000s. These data probably exaggerate the problem to some extent, because they do not take into account either farming for household use or the provision of free government services. In 2007, the majority of poor households received some free electricity and water as well as free education and health care.

Racial Differentials

The available evidence suggests that, outside of the public sector, economic inequalities mostly continued to follow racial lines. The share of Africans, and especially African women, in private sector management, professional, and technical positions remained almost stagnant from the mid-1990s to September 2006.

The share of the black population in total income climbed from 33 percent in 1995 to 39 percent in 2004. (Black Africans constitute approximately 77 percent of the population, with whites making up approximately 12 percent, and COLOUREDS and Asians composing approximately 11 percent.) Most of the improvement went to a relatively small group of professionals, however, so that overall inequality remained virtually unchanged, while inequalities within the black population deepened.

Racial differences also emerged in the unemployment figures, in part because of the lingering influence of apartheid on EDUCATION. In September 2010, unemployment was 30 percent for Africans, 19 percent for coloureds and Asians, and 5 percent for whites. The average working-age African had nine years of education, compared to almost thirteen years for whites, and ten years for coloureds and Asians. Even if education is controlled for, however, unemployment was still the highest for Africans. The unemployment rate was around 15 percent for Africans with university degrees, or about thrice as high as for other graduates.

Gender differentials also persisted but were generally less pronounced than racial inequalities. Thus, white women typically earned more than black men, while black women were both more likely to be unemployed, and, if they had work, earn less than either black men or white women.

Structure of the Economy

To a large extent, economic developments after 1994 reflected structures established under apartheid. In particular, apartheid ensured the effective exclusion and impoverishment of the black majority, while the dominance of mining tended to slow down both growth and employment creation.

Apartheid effectively generated low-wage black labor for white-owned mines and farms. To that end, the state actively deprived Africans, the majority of the population, of the resources required for entrepreneurship: notably assets, access to markets and credit, education, and skills development. From the late 1970s until around 2000, however, rising capital intensity associated with increased domestic refining of minerals and the decline in agriculture meant that the economy absorbed lower levels of labor. In other words, the structure of the economy did not allow for job growth or upward mobility for the majority of the population who were African, hindering economic development and productivity in the long term.

Three economic trends reflected the long-term effects of apartheid on economic participation. First, even by 2005, South Africa had low levels of self-employment in new and micro enterprises, particularly compared to other middle-income countries. The informal sector accounted for only around a fifth of total employment and appeared to be growing no faster than the formal sector.

Second, a third of Africans still lived in the former BANTUSTANS, or pseudo-independent black homelands designated by the apartheid government, where economic activity remained severely depressed. These settlement patterns, created by apartheid restrictions, largely accounted for high levels of joblessness. Overall, around two-fifths of the population lived in the rural areas, but the systematic undermining of African agriculture before 1994 meant that only about a tenth were primarily employed in agriculture.

Finally, as noted, educational disparities persisted, although increasingly, they reflected class rather than race. Well-off black families sent their children to historically white or private schools, but it proved difficult for government to improve schools in poor black communities. The average South African still had more years of education than most in the developing world, and state spending on education was high by world standards. Still, employers complained that the quality of formal public education was weak by international standards. A new skills system based on a 1 percent payroll levy and sector-level skills provision failed to ensure the hoped-for upsurge in training. Meanwhile, diversification from minerals proved slow, with only the auto industry and private services—a mixed bag of high-level financial and information services, and low-level security and domestic work—showing a substantial upswing after 1994. In addition, retail and construction took off in the early twenty-first century.

Through 2010, although mining accounted for only about a tenth of the GDP and employment, it accounted for over half of all foreign sales. Furthermore, coal production fueled both electricity generation and the basic chemicals industry. The dependence on mining dated back to the end of the nineteenth century. The colonial and apartheid states had provided overwhelming support for mining combined with efforts to advance beneficiation and import-substituting manufacturing. In the 1980s and early 1990s, increased support for beneficiation and the arms industry, including strategic investments in oil-from-coal production to counter fuel sanctions imposed on the apartheid regime, contributed to a significant increase in capital intensity across the economy, slower employment creation, and more limited opportunities for smaller enterprises.

With the transition to democracy, the opening of the economy saw reduced tariffs as well as greater foreign interest in South African markets and investment opportunities. South Africa joined the General Agreement on Trade and Tariffs, the forerunner of the World Trade Organization, just before the 1994 elections, with an agreement to substantially cut tariffs on manufactures by 1997.

The democratic state also sought to reduce the size of its public sector. Starting in the 1920s, the colonial and then the apartheid state used direct investment to provide major infrastructure, with state monopolies on electricity, rail transport, and telecommunications, as well as encouraging investment in manufacturing, particularly in steel, petrochemicals, and arms. In addition, the bantustan administrations established a number of irrigation and forestry schemes.

In the 1980s, the state privatized its holdings in steel and heavy chemicals. After 1994, the new government privatized all but the five largest state enterprises: electricity, telecommunications, rail, merchant finance, and arms. It also reduced the size of the public service from around 1.2 million employees—predominantly teachers, health workers, and security workers—to under a million.

In the latter half of the 1990s, these developments were associated with relatively slow growth in the economy and employment, combined with increased foreign ownership in the country as well as growing investments by South African companies abroad. The only manufacturing industries to thrive were auto, which received billions of rand a year in tax subsidies from the state (nearly US$1 billion), as well as minerals refining and coal-based chemicals for export. In the mid-2000s, an economic upswing divided economists, who could not agree on its cause and, by extension, its potential for ensuring sustained and equitable growth. Three broad explanations emerged. One held that a consumer boom took off in the early 2000s, driven largely by lower interest rates and, in some versions, growth in the so-called black middle class—essentially black households earning over US$1,000 per month. A second was that the economy had undergone a successful shakeout after opening to world markets and pursuing privatization, placing it on the road to competitive and more diversified growth. The third held that the commodity boom that started in the early 2000s led to increased short-term investment in South African equity and bonds, pushing up the value of the rand and reducing inflation and consequently interest rates. The paradoxical result was that, since the strong rand limited returns to mining and manufacturing, the main growth occurred in services, retail, and construction.

Main Government Policies Since 1994

Government economic policies from 1994 onward can be divided into three main phases: (1) the RECONSTRUCTION AND DEVELOPMENT PROGRAM (RDP) until 1996; (2) the GROWTH, EMPLOYMENT, AND REDISTRIBUTION (GEAR) strategy from 1996 to 2000; and (3) a transition away from GEAR that culminated in Accelerated and Shared Growth Initiative for South Africa (AsgiSA) in 2005 and the New Growth Path in 2010. In all three phases, some economic thrusts—notably labor market regulation, employment equity, the broad-based BLACK ECONOMIC EMPOWERMENT (BEE), and land reform—remained in place.

The RDP arose as an election platform for the alliance of the AFRICAN NATIONAL CONGRESS (ANC), CONGRESS OF SOUTH AFRICAN TRADE UNIONS, the civic movement, and the SOUTH AFRICAN COMMUNIST PARTY before 1994. It sought to maintain the antiapartheid coalition by addressing the concerns of most participating groups, resulting in the inclusion of a host of proposals without much prioritization as well as some internal contradictions.

The RDP contained a threefold economic thrust. First, it assumed that a substantial expansion in government services in black communities would in itself both stimulate the economy and ensure greater participation by historically marginalized groups. Second, it committed to opening the economy while using industrial policy to support competitiveness, with an implicit agreement to avoid radical restructuring of ownership outside of land reform. Finally, it promised a sustainable fiscal policy, without much detail.

After 1994, the economics departments in government essentially interpreted their mandate from the RDP as focusing on support for growth, and in particular exports, combined with encouragement for smaller enterprises and black entrepreneurs. In 1996, the government adopted GEAR, which most observers considered a shift to the right for the ANC. This policy was initially designed to reassure foreign investors in order to avoid the kind of sudden capital outflow experienced in the mid-1990s by some middle-income developing countries.

GEAR reflected contradictions within the state, with significant differences between the summarized proposals and the detail in chapters and appendices, reflecting the uneasy marriage between the conservative economists who penned GEAR and the ANC politicians who adopted it but wanted to remain true to their social democratic roots and their promises of social transformation. Generally, both government departments and the public focused on its commitments to fiscal restrictions, privatization, reduced tariffs, and more flexible labor-market policies. In practice, only the fiscal restrictions were vigorously enforced. As a result, between 1996 and 1999, public expenditure dropped by around 1 percent a year. That made it virtually impossible to improve services to poor communities on the scale envisaged in the RDP. The major state-owned enterprises privatized noncore business and reduced employment, but the state relinquished its majority shareholding only in telecommunications.

Although GEAR's main direct impact was on the budget, it became a critical dividing line in the policy discourse. On the one hand, left-wing critics, notably in the labor movement, the South African Communist Party, and social movements, argued that it marked the state's surrender to business. On the other, GEAR embedded in government policy a preference for market-based solutions and macroeconomic restraint, in contrast to the ANC's historic bias toward statist approaches. In any case, the GEAR period from 1996 to 1999 was associated with relatively slow economic growth.

GEAR set objectives only through 2000. Thereafter, the government gradually began to introduce new policies associated with a more relaxed fiscal approach. From 2000 to 2006, government spending grew 9 percent per year in real terms, reversing the stagnation of the late 1990s.

The result was a significant upswing in provision of services.

At the same time, the government gradually adopted a more interventionist approach to the economy, culminating in the adoption of the AsgiSA in 2005, an industrial policy in 2007, and the New Growth Path in 2010. AsgiSA set the target of halving unemployment and poverty as well as raising growth to 6 percent per year by 2014, which certainly increased the emphasis on measures to generate employment across government. The New Growth Path maintained the core AsgiSA strategies with a strong emphasis on the need to support employment creation both by encouraging overall competitiveness and by targeting government support at industries able to generate large-scale employment. In practical terms, the more interventionist approach emerged from a major increase in public investment, particularly in rail and electricity; sector strategies targeting a rather uneven combination of exports and employment creation; skills development; an expansion in public employment programs; and greater support for small and micro enterprises.

In addition to these macroeconomic approaches, the government introduced major and heavily contested reforms through labor market policies and broad-based BEE. Through the late 1990s, the state fundamentally reformed labor market policy to ensure equal rights for workers across all races, industries, and regions; to support collective bargaining, the right to strike, and union organizing; to accelerate the schedule for dispute settlement and reduce its cost; to set minimum conditions in terms of working time and leave, as well as set rates of pay in poorly unionized industries.

Disagreements arose over the impact of these laws on employment creation. Businesses generally argued that employers were reluctant to hire new workers because of excessive regulations. Unions and social movements, in contrast, contended that the economic structure was the main cause of slow employment growth, and that the labor laws were critical to overcome the legacy of apartheid.

The state also pursued programs to enhance the participation of black people in the economy. In 2003, it introduced the concept of BEE, which aimed to accelerate the following: ownership by black people of productive assets, both as individuals and through collective mechanisms such as employee ownership schemes and community trusts, funded primarily by a combination of private and public loans to new investors; the representation of black people in managerial and skilled positions; incorporation of black enterprises, particularly small and micro producers in formal value chains; training for black workers; and corporate social investment. Companies that achieved targets in these areas gained a privileged position in tendering for government contracts and in obtaining licenses of all kinds. However, the regulations for broad-based BEE, known as the Codes, were only finalized around 2005, so the impact has not yet been seen.

See also BLACK ECONOMIC EMPOWERMENT; GOLD AND DIAMOND MINING

—*Neva Makgetla*

Education

Formal education in South Africa goes back to the opening of the first school for slaves by the DUTCH EAST INDIA COMPANY on April 17, 1658. In 1663, a second school was established for the children of colonists. The pattern of schooling that evolved over the next two centuries owed much to the nature of settler societies and the character of their relationships with indigenous people. Colonial and religious purposes meshed in the next two centuries to produce a haphazard array of informal, state-aided, and mission schooling practices for the children of the colonizers and the colonized. A combination of factors, including the impact of the discovery of DIAMONDS in KIMBERLEY in 1867 and gold in the Witwatersrand in 1886, led to social, economic, and political processes that were to place formal education on a footing that would shape its outcomes for the next century.

At the beginning of the twentieth century, compulsory education was introduced for white children and gradually extended to cover all children of school-going age. The introduction of compulsory schooling just before the UNION OF SOUTH AFRICA in 1910 laid the foundation for the rise of mass schooling among whites. The union of the four provinces under white suzerainty in 1910 provided the impetus for increased spending as enrollments climbed, teaching quality improved, and matric examination pass rates gradually rose. Curricula, pedagogy, and certification were modernized, and linguistic conflicts and differences between English- and Afrikaans-speaking whites were resolved through adopting the mother tongue and bilingual language policies, which allowed students to be taught in their mother tongue but incorporated bilingual language learning in the curriculum.

By contrast, education for children considered African, INDIAN, and COLOURED was neglected and remained primarily a missionary undertaking. After the formation of the union, each province was responsible for the financing and control of African education. However, parsimonious central government funding stultified its development. State grants to match local contributions remained the basis of financing black education well into the second half of the twentieth century, long after it had become an entirely state undertaking for whites. Although African enrollments in schools increased substantially during the 1920s and 1930s, educational expenditures lagged behind. A similar pattern of poorly funded, state-aided mission schooling characterized the education of coloured and Indian children.

In the early twentieth century, two main approaches to access and curriculum vied with one another in colonial education and in South Africa. One promoted a common, Western, and mainly academic curriculum, while the other emphasized an "adapted" education that would be relevant to the life that Africans were presumed and expected to lead in rural areas. Adapted education, however, found little support among the mission-educated African elite. In the context of general educational neglect for black people, the ideas remained largely rhetorical, with little happening in practice outside of isolated experimental situations in Kenya, Southern Rhodesia, and Nyasaland

Unequal educational provision resulted in opposition. Black political organizations undertook deputations and petitions and presented evidence of neglect before government; adult education was initiated by the South African Institute of Race Relations, the SOUTH AFRICAN COMMUNIST PARTY, and trade unions; independent schools were started by an African millenarian movement; and boycotts and riots at mission schools by students, mainly to protest against the food quality, increasingly became the order of the day.

In the 1930s, a welfarist discourse gradually displaced and sidelined the adaptationist discourse of the previous decade. During World War II, it found expression in improved funding for African schools and the extension of school meals to European and native primary school children. The period between 1935 and 1956 was the only time in South Africa's pre-1994 history when pupil-teacher ratios in African (private) mission schools came close to those of whites. Gradual and minimal as these improvements were, they were to be reversed and set back in the 1950s for the next forty years.

Apartheid Education
World War II was a watershed for education in South Africa. An AFRIKANER nationalist movement had emerged in the wake of the British defeat of the BOERS in the South African War (1899–1902). It spawned Christian National schools in the immediate aftermath of the war to prevent Anglicization, struggled for recognition of Afrikaans in the public service, and organized around unilingual Afrikaans schools and an exclusive racial identity in the 1930s. The political and educational vision of this movement was segregationist and hostile to mission education as it was determined to promote white Afrikaner interests and white supremacy.

The Afrikaner-led NATIONAL PARTY, which came to power in 1948, introduced the BANTU EDUCATION Act in 1953 as the first step in vertically segmenting education along racial lines. This act effectively forced the closure of mission schools, centralized the control of African education, and incorporated African children into underfunded state schools. New syllabi for African children, implemented in 1956, were similar to those for whites, but stressed obedience, communal loyalty, ethnic and national diversity, the acceptance of allocated social roles, piety, and identification with rural culture. Teachers' opposition was organized mainly through the Cape African Teachers' Association and the Transvaal African Teachers' Association. Parents' school boycotts on the East Rand and in the eastern Cape attempted to lead to the provision of an alternative educational experience for their children, through cultural clubs, but they had neither the resources nor the reach to survive.

This rise of mass public schooling for Africans occurred on terms very different from those established for whites in the first half of the century. Although African enrollments more than trebled over the next two decades, spending did not keep pace with growth, and small numbers survived to secondary levels. State resources were limited, and new organizational methods were introduced to raise necessary funds. These included increasing rents for teacher accommodation, ensuring that communities built and paid for classrooms needed, dispensing with cleaning staff and instead relying on the children's labor, introducing double sessions, employing poorly qualified African female teachers at lower pay while releasing expensive white teachers from their employment in African schools, diverting funds from school-feeding schemes, and introducing fees of various kinds. Mother tongue instruction was to be extended beyond the early years, curricula were adapted, teacher training requirements were reduced, and higher education was segregated.

While conditions in African schools deteriorated in the 1960s, both the coloured and Indian schools were removed from provincial control and placed under separate, centrally controlled departments for coloured and Indian education in 1963 and in 1965, respectively. Resources were constrained but not as much as in African education. In 1967, the National Education Policy and the Educational Services acts were passed to rationalize, reform, and enhance secondary education for whites. The passage of these acts meant that, by the end of the 1960s, the architecture of separate development in education, in the form of white, Indian, coloured, and Bantu (African) education, had been created. Spending followed this racial hierarchy.

This racial division was reinforced in the 1970s by the creation of ethnic departments of education linked to the ethnic client states created by the APARTHEID government—the so-called TBVC states (Transkei, Bophutatswana, Venda, and Ciskei) or BANTUSTANS. Whereas schools for Africans in white areas became divided into five regions, more or less on an ethnic basis, the schools for African children living in the bantustans were administered by eight different authorities. African education in white areas was run by whites with the assistance of Africans. In the bantustans, each department was under an African minister of education assisted by white administrators. By 1992, although over three-quarters of all African matriculation students were attending schools in the bantustans, spending, school quality, and attainments lagged significantly behind those of African schools in the urban or white areas as well as schools for children in the white, Indian, and coloured departments. Education outside the parameters of Bantu and homeland education thus became the notorious "forbidden pastures," in which Africans, as Prime Minister HENDRIK VERWOERD had proclaimed, were "not allowed to graze."

Education at the Crossroads
In 1976, South Africa was rocked by student revolts that began with the SOWETO STUDENT UPRISING, fanned out across the whole country, and continued for the next fourteen years, taking different forms over time and place. The immediate cause of the 1976 revolt was the introduction of Afrikaans as the language medium of study in African schools, but the underlying causes included the explosive rise in secondary school enrollments without comparable spending, the growing economic crisis in the early 1970s, the political context of racial inequality and control, the success of liberation movements in achieving

independence in Mozambique and Angola in 1975, and the spur to action given by the awakening trade union movement that was manifested in the DURBAN STRIKES of 1973.

The revolts provoked shifts in governing-party alignments and the appointment of a Human Sciences Research Council Commission of Inquiry under Professor J. P. de Lange. The commission produced a reform agenda based on principles that included "equal quality" and freedom of choice. The government accepted most of the recommendations but interpreted them within its own new reformist political dispensation that gave coloureds and Indians but not Africans a limited voting franchise. The National Policy for General Education Affairs Act of 1984 was subsequently introduced in accordance with the tricameral Parliament system that excluded Africans.

The education reform agenda stalled and the system crumbled in the 1980s under the weight of a structural slowdown in the economy, international economic pressure, and ongoing and broadening opposition as well as resistance to apartheid in all social spheres. In 1986, a Ten Year Plan and Funding Formula was introduced to increase total education expenditure but was abandoned on the grounds that it was unaffordable. By this stage, however, a broad-based DEFIANCE CAMPAIGN engineered by organizations affiliated with the UNITED DEMOCRATIC FRONT (UDF), rejecting any efforts to implement changes under the current government in township schools, was in motion. All symbols of authority associated with the apartheid state were ejected from schools by increasingly militant teachers' and students' organizations. "People's education for people's power" had become the rallying cry at a UDF conference held in 1986. In terms of this vision, opposition movements began to develop education policy in anticipation of the apartheid state's imminent demise. Between 1990 and 1994, both the incumbent and outgoing government and the ascendant movement for democracy prepared, contested, and negotiated policy for a democratic South Africa.

By 1992, almost half a century of apartheid had created an education system that mirrored the extremes of privilege and deprivation characteristic of South African society as a whole. Enrollment growth had been rapid in the 1970s and 1980s, and universal schooling of nine or ten years was being realized. But, the state was spending an average of R3,000 (US$1,000) per white child and R600 (US$200) per African child in a homeland area. The critical challenges were democratizing control, equalizing spending, and making qualitative improvements in African schools. On the eve of a democratic election, there was broad agreement that the main goals for a new government included a unified national department of education, improvement in the quality of basic education, broadening of the range and relevance of technical and vocational education, and improved adult and higher education.

Education in South Africa Since 1994

In its first two years in office, the new Government of National Unity led by the AFRICAN NATIONAL CONGRESS speedily integrated the numerous racially and ethnically defined departments of education into one national and nine new provincial departments; restaffed the upper echelons of the executive branch of government, PARLIAMENT, and the bureaucracy; and initiated processes to bring vision to reality through the new policies. The repeal of apartheid legislation and introduction of new legislation were prepared in the first year of government. By the end of 1996, a National Education Policy Act and a South African Schools Act had been legislated, and a new curriculum was due for implementation in 1997–1998. A review of education financing was initiated even as spending that had previously been allocated on a racial basis was now reoriented in terms of provincial housing, health, welfare, and educational needs, and aimed at equity between blacks and whites. A special fund was established (the RECONSTRUCTION AND DEVELOPMENT PROGRAM) to provide for primary school nutrition, school renovation, and the establishment of democratic governance structures in schools. Moves were afoot to redesign school curricula and bring teacher education within the ambit of higher education.

Under the new CONSTITUTION, education became a concurrent function of the national and provincial departments, except for higher education, which is the exclusive responsibility of the national sphere. The National Department of Education became responsible for formulating overall educational policy as well as setting norms and standards for all levels of educational provisioning. It is also responsible for monitoring and supporting educational provisioning whereas provinces became responsible for implementation. Schools are financed from the central government, which makes allocations to provinces on the basis of an equitable shares formula. Provinces themselves decide on what and where they will spend their resources.

The new government had inherited a near-bankrupt bureaucracy. Fiscal constraints led to severe stress on the system in the first few years after the transition to democracy. One of the most controversial issues was the imposition of school fees. In 1998, a fee exemption policy was introduced, but mounting evidence of the negative impacts of fees in poor communities and growing social pressures resulted in a Human Rights Commission public hearing in 2005. Its report maintained that the right to education was not being met in poor communities and that school fees and other costs were a major factor. As of 2007, fee-free schools were introduced. A century after compulsory education was introduced for whites, free schooling became a legal reality for many of the poorest learners in South African schools. The government has also increased financial allocations to poor schools and further exempted fees for all orphans and for children whose families or who themselves may be in receipt of a social grant intended to relieve poverty. Parents can still make voluntary contributions to schools if they wish to do so. By 2010, 60 percent of schools were fee free.

In 1995, the National Education Policy and the South African Qualifications acts grouped education in elementary, middle, and high schools under a General Education and Training (GET) and a Further Education and Training (FET) band instead of the traditional primary and secondary phases. The GET band (Grades R to 9) includes the following phases: foundation (Grades R to 3), intermediate (Grades 4 to 6), and senior (Grades 7 to 9). The FET band is for Grades 10 to 12 and learners in FET colleges. The Education White Paper No. 5 on early childhood education stipulates that, by 2010, all children entering Grade 1 must have participated in an accredited Reception Year Program (Grade R), equivalent to kindergarten, offered at primary schools or at stand-alone community-based sites.

In 1997, a new outcomes-based curriculum was implemented in schools. Three years later, in 2000, following criticisms and implementation difficulties, it was reviewed by a Ministerial Committee appointed to make recommendations on how to address emerging implementation problems. The fledgling curriculum was revised and a national curriculum, known as the National Curriculum Statement, became policy in 2002. It aimed at building a common citizenry through a curriculum whose values are based on the principles of the Constitution and was implemented in schools on a phased basis from 2004. But continuing criticism of its outcomes-based elements resulted in a new round of review of its design and implementation in 2010, with the new minister of basic education formally announcing the abandonment of outcomes-based education.

South Africa now has a national multilingual policy and follows an additive bilingual policy in schools. The aim is that all learners should learn their home language and at least one additional official language. Learners are expected to become competent in their additional language while their home language is maintained and developed. This policy provides for the home languages as well as for the first and second additional languages to be taught in all eleven official languages. School governing bodies determine the medium of instruction.

Enrollments overall have risen steadily in the last three decades, increasing from 5.4 million in 1975 to just over 14 million in 2008. Access is near universal for Grades 1–12, but there is considerable underenrollment in Grade R and high dropout rates further up the system, making for poor enrollments in high school and subsequent levels of education. The large majority of learners (84.1 percent) are in public schools, with only 2.6 percent attending independent schools, 3.0 percent in the public further education and training colleges, and 5.7 percent in higher education institutions. Relative to the appropriate school-age population, there are more female than male learners in the school system in many provinces, especially at the secondary level. About half the school-going population eligible for Grades 11 and 12 are not in the formal schooling system. The large majority of these students are in provinces (KwaZulu-Natal, Eastern Cape, Limpopo, and Mpumulanga) that have incorporated the former homelands where school quality, family poverty, unemployment, and high adult illiteracy rates are endemic.

The creation of a national, equitably funded system of education and near-universal enrollments to upper secondary level are among the success stories of the postapartheid government. Nonetheless, significant challenges remain. These relate to the unequal life circumstances into which children are born on the one hand and the continued poor quality of schooling in the majority of schools and high unemployment among school leavers on the other.

Evidence from international and national surveys consistently shows that performance in mathematics and reading is much poorer in South Africa than that for countries at a similar level of development. Results all too frequently reflect the previous patterns of advantage and disadvantage in education. Restructuring teacher and higher education institutions has absorbed a great deal of energy and negatively affected schools. Insufficient attention has been paid to improving the quality of teacher education now conducted in higher education institutions, although this has become a priority since the introduction of a new curriculum. The scourge of HIV/AIDS affects all members of the school community. A new curriculum, LANGUAGE POLICY, and textbooks have been developed to promote values consistent with those of a democratic South Africa, and many schools and teachers are actively seeking to change the lives of their students through learning. However, actual classroom practices in too many instances show not only the persistence of authoritarianism but also sexism and racism. Physical, social, and sexual abuse, particularly of girls, is strikingly high. Desegregation of formerly white, Indian, and coloured schools has proceeded unevenly, but faster in the Indian, coloured, and English-speaking white than in the Afrikaans-speaking schools.

The transformation of South African education is, in short, far from complete. As a recent volume of historical articles reflecting on the apartheid past show, there are more continuities between the past and present than first meet the eye, but there are also new voices and perspectives being brought to bear on that past.

See also ADAMS COLLEGE; BANTU EDUCATION; LOVEDALE; OHLANGE INSTITUTE

Bibliography

African National Congress. *The Reconstruction and Development Programme. A Policy Framework*. Johannesburg, South Africa: Umanyano Publications, 1994.

African National Congress, Education Department. *A Policy Framework for Education and Training*. Johannesburg, South Africa: South African Government Printer, 1994.

Brooks, A. J., and J. Brickhill. *Whirlwind Before the Storm*. London: International Defence and Aid Fund, 1980.

Cross, Michael, and Linda Chisholm. "The Roots of Segregated Schooling in Twentieth Century South Africa." In *The Pedagogy of Domination*, edited by Mokubung Nkomo. Trenton, NJ: Africa World Press, 1990.

Department of Education (South Africa). *A South African Curriculum for the Twenty First Century: Report of the Review Committee on Curriculum 2005*. Pretoria, South Africa. www.education.gov.za. Accessed January 2006.

Department of Basic Education (South Africa). *Education Statistics at a Glance in 2008*. Pretoria, South Africa: South African Government Printer, 2010.

Fedderke, Johannes W., Raphael de Kadt, and John M. Luiz. "Uneducating South Africa: The Failure to Address the 1910–1993 Legacy." *International Review of Education* 46, no. 3–4 (2000): 257–281.

Hartshorne, Ken. *The Making of Education Policy in South Africa*. Cape Town, South Africa: Oxford University Press, 1999.

Horrell, Muriel. *Bantu Education to 1968*. Johannesburg: South African Institute of Race Relations, 1968.

Hyslop, Jonathan. "Food, Authority and Politics: Student Riots in South Africa 1945–1976." *Africa Perspective* 1 (1987): 3–41.

———. "Social Conflicts over African Education in South Africa from the 1940s to 1976." PhD thesis, University of the Witwatersrand, Johannesburg, South Africa, 1990.

Jansen, Jonathan, and Pam Christie, eds. *Changing Curriculum: Studies on Outcomes-Based Education in South Africa*. Johannesburg, South Africa: Juta Academic Publishers, 1999.

Jones, Robert C. "The Education of the Bantu in South Africa." In *Education in Southern Africa*, edited by Brian Rose. London: Collier-Macmillan, 1970.

Kallaway, Peter. "Welfare and Education in British Colonial Africa and South Africa During the 1930s and 1940s." *Pedagogica Historica* 41 (2005): 337–356.

———, ed. *Apartheid and Education: The Education of Black South Africa*. Johannesburg, South Africa: Ravan Press, 1984.

Kane-Berman, John. 1978. *Soweto: Black Revolt, White Reaction*. Johannesburg, South Africa: Ravan Press.

MacMillan, R. G. "White Education in South Africa." In *Education in Southern Africa*, edited by Brian Rose. London: Collier-Macmillan, 1970.

Majeke, N. *The Role of the Missionary in Conquest*. Cape Town, South Africa: Society of Young Africa, 1952.

Malherbe, Ernst G. *Education in South Africa. Volume I: 1652–1922*. Cape Town, South Africa: Juta Academic Publishers, 1925.

———. *Education in South Africa. Volume II: 1923–1975*. Cape Town, South Africa: Juta Academic Publishers, 1977.

Molobi, Eric. "People's Education: Learning and Teaching Under a State of Emergency." Twentieth Richard Feetham Memorial Lecture, University of the Witwatersrand, Johannesburg, South Africa, 1986.

Molteno, Frank. "The Uprising of 16, June. A Review of the Literature on Events in South Africa Since 1976." *Social Dynamics* 5, no. 1 (1979): 54–76.

———. "Students Take Control: The 1980 Boycott of Coloured Education in the Cape Peninsula." *British Journal of Sociology of Education* 8, no. 1 (1987).

National Education Policy Investigation. *The Framework Report and Final Report Summaries*. National Education Coordinating Committee. Cape Town, South Africa: Oxford University Press, 1992.

Rose, Brian, and Raymond Tunmer, eds. *Documents in South African Education*. Johannesburg, South Africa: Ad Donker, 1975.

Soudien, Crain. "Constituting the Class: An Analysis of the Process of Integration of South African Schools." In *Changing Class: Education and Social Change in South Africa After Apartheid*, edited by Linda Chisholm. Cape Town, South Africa: HSRC Press; and London: Zed Press, 2004.

Tabata, Isaac Bangani. *Education for Barbarism in South Africa: Bantu (Apartheid) Education*. London: Pall Mall Press, 1960.

Troup, Freda. *Forbidden Pastures: Education Under Apartheid*. London: International Defence and Aid Fund, 1976.

Tunmer, Raymond. "The Education of Coloureds and Indians in South Africa." In *Education in Southern Africa*, edited by Brian Rose. London: Collier-MacMillan, 1970.

Wolpe, Harold. "Educational Resistance." In *South Africa in Question*, edited by John Lonsdale, 200–217. Cambridge, UK: James Currey, 1988.

—Linda Chisholm

Elections: 1994 to 2009

April 27, 1994, was a day most political analysts thought would never happen. Over the next three days, 19.5 million South Africans of all races, languages, classes, and generations patiently stood together in long snake-like queues to cast their votes in the country's first universal suffrage election. POLITICAL VIOLENCE, which had heightened over the preceding months and peaked in the days before the election, faded away.

With extremely high voter turnout, estimated at anywhere from 86 to 91 percent of the voting-age population, and a new electoral system of list proportional representation with a low threshold to win seats, seven POLITICAL PARTIES won seats in

"Vote" mural in Cape Town celebrating the 1994 elections.

the National Assembly. The black-led AFRICAN NATIONAL CONGRESS (ANC) won 63 percent of the votes cast, with the incumbent AFRIKANER-led NATIONAL PARTY winning 20 percent of the vote. Other longstanding political organizations won seats as well. The primarily ZULU-based INKATHA FREEDOM PARTY (IFP) took 11 percent of the vote; the white, liberal DEMOCRATIC PARTY, 2 percent; and the black, leftist PAN AFRICANIST CONGRESS, 1 percent. Two new parties also managed to win legislative representation: the Freedom Front (formed weeks before the election by elements of the white right wing) received 2 percent, and the African Christian Democratic Party won 0.5 percent. Yet, while the 1994 election was hailed around the world as a "miracle," it is easy to forget that the campaign and the election were marred by a wide range of flaws, ranging from poor electoral administration; to high levels of intolerance, intimidation, and violence; to strong racial cleavages in voter preferences.

South Africa's three subsequent national elections (in 1999, but especially in 2004 and 2009) were administered much more effectively. Yet, in other important areas, the country's electoral process took significant steps backward. By 2004, voter turnout, campaign participation, and general voter interest had all declined substantially. Over the same period, the ANC steadily increased its electoral majorities, confirming South Africa as a one-party dominant party system. Yet while the ANC was led by popular candidates and generated considerable public satisfaction through its delivery of infrastructure and development, little of its increased vote share resulted from attracting new voters to its cause but rather from declining voter turnout that was significantly higher among opposition supporters and independents than among ANC supporters. All these trends were reversed, if only marginally, in the election of 2009. Spurred by the defection of prominent black leaders following the removal of THABO MBEKI as president and the formation of a new opposition party (CONGRESS OF THE PEOPLE, or COPE) with significant potential for cutting into its African support base, the ANC fought a reenergized election campaign. Although the ANC ultimately lost significant ground in several provinces and saw its national vote share slide back under the two-thirds threshold required to pass legislation through PARLIAMENT, the reinvigorated political climate resulted in new increases, however small, in voter turnout and interest and campaign activity.

Electoral Administration
The 1994 election was marked by poor coordination, last-minute planning, and ad hoc decision-making by the Independent Electoral Commission responsible for overseeing the elections, mainly caused by far too little time to prepare for the elections. The April 1994 date had been set in June 1993 because the ANC and the National Party, after four years of constitutional negotiations and mounting political violence, had both become convinced that the bleeding of their respective support bases could only be staunched by announcing a firm date. Yet final agreement on the interim CONSTITUTION was reached only five months later in November 1993, and an Electoral Act passed by the white Parliament only in January 1994. This meant that the totally new Independent Electoral Commission (IEC) had just four months to organize itself, plan the elections, demarcate voting stations, and train and deploy 300,000 officials to staff 10,500 voting and 700 counting stations. Matters were made even worse by an April agreement that brought the boycotting IFP back into the election just one week before voting day, requiring the IEC to create 500 additional polling stations, train and deploy 14,000 officials in KwaZulu-Natal Province, and print and distribute millions of IFP stickers to be affixed to the already printed ballots.

One consequence of rushed planning was that many people who were actually ineligible under the election rules ultimately voted. Since possibly millions of rural voters lacked any form of official identification, negotiators decided to bypass the issue of registration and issue temporary voter cards to any citizen or permanent resident who did not have an identity document. Ultimately, 3.6 million cards were issued, a process that the IEC eventually admitted was plagued by massive abuse, with many people receiving cards without regard to age or nationality.

Rushed planning also meant that many polling stations opened late due to lack of personnel and materials or in unexpected places due to last-minute changes in plans, and many simply never opened. Combined with the lack of reliable census data, many polling stations were overwhelmed by unexpected droves of voters and had insufficient supplies of ballots or IFP stickers, problems that were multiplied exponentially in KwaZulu-Natal. Thus, at the end of the first day of official voting, President F. W. DE KLERK declared the next day a public holiday, and the IEC announced that voting would be extended to a second and even to a third day in some former homelands.

All of this led to a chaotic counting process. Basic rules and procedures were often not followed by the polling station staff, and key personnel were often missing from the central counting offices. In many centers, and especially in KwaZulu-Natal, arguments erupted about the validity of ballot boxes. Long delays in the count arose as a result of both arguments and of breakdowns in the IEC's computer system. Delays in announcing the results, along with rumors of "pirate" voting stations in KwaZulu-Natal operated by the IFP, set off rampant speculations that the election result was the product of horse trading between the IEC and the major political parties rather than an accurate reflection of the votes. This was exacerbated by subsequent challenges to the results from the major political parties. Ultimately, the European Union observer group called the election "free, but not fair," citing "inadequate logistics" and a "non-transparent process of dispute settling."

The transitional IEC quickly disintegrated following the 1994 election and faded into institutional history by the end of the year. It took until 1996 to replace it with a permanent commission that was given the tasks of maintaining a voter roll; demarcating voting districts; planning, organizing, and conducting all national, provincial, and local elections; and ensuring that electoral rules were implemented and respected. In contrast to the 1994 body, however, it was not given the task of campaign monitoring or adjudicating disputes.

Over the next two years, the new IEC prepared for the 1999 election by conducting a delimitation of 14,400 voting districts using sophisticated geographic information system technologies and developing a system by which people could register to vote in their own districts. However, while the chaos of 1994 was largely absent from the 1999 election, significant procedural problems still lingered. Registration drives in late 1998 were marred by so many problems in staffing and opening registration stations that the IEC had to add extra registration weekends in early 1999 to allow more people to register and deliver a clean and verified voter roll on time. There were also major disputes over which identity documents would be accepted for people to register. While the Department of Home Affairs doggedly maintained that virtually all South Africans who needed one possessed the modern bar-coded document required by legislation, multiple surveys conducted by the Human Science Research Council and by Opinion '99 (a consortium of the Institute for Democracy in South Africa, the Electoral Institute of Southern Africa, and the South African Broadcasting Corporation) consistently found significant numbers of voters lacked them. In a series of court cases, opposition-party challenges to these requirements were rejected, and Judge Johann Kriegler, who had publicly sided with the opposition parties' arguments, resigned under heavy criticism by both ANC party and government officials. Ultimately, the IEC was able to register and verify the names of 18.1 million voters in time for the election.

By 2004, last-minute planning and ad hoc decisions had become a thing of the past as the IEC operated under a predictable legislative and regulatory framework. With registration now possible on a continuous basis through Home Affairs offices (up to the announcement of the election date) and special registration weekends in the run-up to the election, the IEC was able to register 20.7 million voters for 2004. Voting went extremely smoothly, aided by sophisticated systems for distributing, storing, and deploying election materials to just under 17,000 polling stations and ensuring their security.

The IEC's institutional progress was matched by trends in public opinion, at least up until 2004. While 68 percent of respondents told Opinion '99 interviewers in October 1998 that they felt the 1994 election had been "conducted fairly," the 2000 independently conducted Afrobarometer survey found that 73 percent said the 2000 election had been "free and fair." In October 2004, 83 percent called the 2004 election "free and fair." Trust in the IEC increased from 49 percent in 2000 to 59 percent in 2004. Following the heightened partisanship of the 2009 campaign, however, the proportions telling the University of Cape Town National Election Study/Comparative National Election Study (UCT NES/CNEP) fieldworkers that the election was free and fair dipped back down to 72 percent, and trust in the IEC fell to 50 percent.

Intolerance and Intimidation
The 1994 election was conducted amid an atmosphere of intense intolerance, intimidation, and political violence. The violent conflicts between government security forces and the ANC and IFP militias, which had racked the country since 1990, reached their peak in the first few months of 1994. Violence monitors estimated hundreds of politically motivated deaths per month in the run-up to the election centered, not surprisingly given the IFP boycott, in KwaZulu-Natal, with 1,001 deaths between January and April.

Additionally, and not unconnected to the violence, much of the country consisted of one-party fiefdoms in which other parties were simply unable to canvass, organize, open offices, or hold rallies. The IEC documented 165 such "no-go zones," largely concentrated in white farming areas and in urban townships across the country, as well as in rural northern KwaZulu-Natal. Two-thirds of the 2,400 complaints received by the IEC Monitoring and Complaints Unit concerned obstacles to campaigning and voter education. Canvassing and voter education were virtually impossible in KwaZulu-Natal. In the Western Cape, the IEC reported some form of obstruction at 20 percent of Democratic Party events, 17 percent of ANC events, and 10 percent of National Party events. At the same time, fully 94 percent of respondents told interviewers in the September 1994 Institute for Democracy in South Africa National Post-Election Study that they had "felt free to decide on how to vote."

While acts following from attitudinal intolerance among ordinary South Africans, such as xenophobia and attacks on African foreigners, have remained at high levels, incidents stemming from behavioral electoral intolerance aimed at opposing-party supporters declined sharply in 1999 and was virtually gone by 2004. KwaZulu-Natal remained a hot spot in 1999, with eighty-two politically related deaths between January and April, but this was the same number of deaths as in the same four months of 1998, which suggested that the election had not added to the ongoing political violence in that province. At the same time, new hot spots emerged where the newly formed United Democratic Movement (UDM) appeared to mount a serious challenge to the ANC, especially in the Western Cape. All told, however, the number of formal complaints registered with the IEC dropped from 3,594 in 1994 to 1,032 in 1999.

By 2004, in contrast to the complaints that dominated in 1994 about the inability to campaign or educate voters, official-party complaints revolved around issues of poster vandalism. Perhaps the most telling indicator of the electoral institutionalization of South Africa's democracy was that international observer organizations declined to monitor the 2004 election. While twenty-seven African countries did send observer delegations, presumably, they were there to learn rather than to monitor.

Voter Participation
Beginning with the 1999 elections, South Africa's elections have been much better run, but far fewer South Africans choose to take part in the electoral process. Although the total number of people registered to vote increased from 18.1 million in 1999 to 20.7 million in 2004, the actual number of votes cast dropped from 19.5 million in 1994 to 16 million in 1999 and again to 15.6 million in 2004. Taking population growth into account, this constitutes a massive 29 percentage point decline in voter turnout, from 86 percent of voting-age

population in 1994 to 57 percent in 2004. Opinion surveys over the past decade also demonstrate a similar decline in all forms of electoral participation ranging from attending election rallies (44 to 23 percent), to contributing money to political parties (19 to 3 percent), to working for parties (11 to 5 percent), to simply taking an interest in the election campaign (64 to 48 percent). The 2009 election, however, reversed many of these trends, if only marginally. Voter turnout moved back upward to 60 percent, as did attendance at election rallies (31 percent) and general campaign interest (50 percent).

The best cross-national evidence strongly suggests that the country's levels of voter turnout are closely linked to the ANC's electoral dominance. With other things constant, voter turnout in a country with South Africa's age of democracy in 2004 and type of electoral system should have been between 69 to 70 percent, while the country's level of economic development should have produced a 64 percent turnout. However, countries where the winning party regularly receives over 60 percent of the vote in at least two consecutive elections, as in South Africa, have an average voter turnout of 56 percent, almost precisely the level to which South Africa's voter turnout fell in 2004. Unsurprisingly, once the electorate was presented with more credible alternatives in the form of COPE and a refashioned DEMOCRATIC ALLIANCE under the new leadership of Helen Zille, voter turnout increased in 2009.

Voter Choice

While there have been some significant shifts, the deep racial cleavages that largely characterized voter preferences in 1994 still remain. Although actual votes cannot be broken down by race, and survey results differ, the general trend is clear. Black voters have given and continue to give the lion's share of their votes to the ANC and COPE, and to the IFP and the UDM to a much lesser extent. Few blacks vote for any political party that has historical roots in the old white political system. Conversely, white voters have largely voted for the National Party and then, following its collapse, the Democratic Alliance; few support a political party that has its roots in the black-dominated liberation struggle. COLOURED and INDIAN voters, however, have been more likely to cross these historical dividing lines; splitting their votes, as a group, between the ANC, National Party, and the Democratic Alliance. At the same time, the specter of one-party dominance that resulted from the ANC's ability to win 63 percent of the vote in 1994 became a reality with election-day victories of 65 percent or more in 1999 (66 percent), 2004 (70 percent), and 2009 (66 percent).

What accounts for these cleavages and for the ANC's enduring dominance? Most analysts have incorrectly drawn conclusions about individual voter motivations from these aggregate trends, ranging from affective, primordial racial or ethnic solidarity; expressions of social identity; communal intimidation and pressure; to narrow clientelist competition for patronage. Increasing ANC vote margins have been largely seen as the result of former opposition supporters hopping on the bandwagon and switching their votes to the ANC.

The best social scientific, individual-level evidence, however, portrays voter motivation in quite different terms. First of all, voter surveys show that the vast majority of voters are *not pulled toward* a party because it represents their identity group (however defined) to the exclusion of others. Rather, they are attracted to parties that they perceive as inclusive of all South Africans. In fact, voters are *repelled* by parties that they see as exclusive to one group. Only once they are satisfied with a party's representational credentials will voters then consider issues of performance and policies.

Second, it is quite likely that far fewer voters ever switched their support to the ANC than its increasing vote share might have suggested. Although good panel data with which to investigate this conclusively is lacking, the available evidence strongly suggests that increasing ANC vote shares were a consequence of asymmetrical patterns of demobilization, where uncommitted voters and opposition supporters were progressively less likely to vote at each successive election than were ANC supporters. As a proportion of all eligible voters on the actual election day, ANC voters dropped by one-fourth between 1994 and 2004 (from 54 to 40 percent), but the number of opposition voters dropped by almost one-half (from 32 to 17 percent). Thus, the ANC won progressively larger proportions of shrinking pools of election-day voters.

Political Parties

Both of these conclusions demonstrate that, while South Africa's electoral machinery has been effectively institutionalized, the main electoral actors—political parties, especially the opposition parties—have not. An increasing number of political parties have arisen to take advantage of the low thresholds of South Africa's system: political parties can gain at least one seat in Parliament with as little as 0.1 percent of the national vote. The number of parties with national representation increased from seven to thirteen between 1994 and 2009; and those with seats in provincial assemblies went from eight to eleven. However, while represented parties have proliferated, only a few have developed into effective vote-getting institutions.

Opposition parties have low levels of voter trust. Although 50 percent told Afrobarometer interviewers in 2008 that they trusted the governing ANC, just 32 percent said they trusted opposition parties as a whole. Likewise, the 2009 UCT NES/CNEP survey found that no more than 23 percent of all citizens trusted any single opposition party. Crucially, opposition parties have failed to create the crucial image of inclusiveness. Over 70 percent of voters have told interviewers since 1994 that the ANC "look[s] after the interests of all in South Africa." But with one exception, no more than 39 percent have ever said the same about any opposition party (50 percent told interviewers in the 2009 UCT survey that COPE was inclusive).

Few opposition parties give evidence of a well-thought-out strategy to court voters on a continuous basis either by using their parliamentary platform or other events as opportunities to generate free media publicity between elections. Most wait and mount their campaign in the six to eight weeks leading up to the election, at which point it is far too late to shape or reshape their public image in any significant way. In the 2009 campaign, no opposition party was able to garner as much as 10 percent of the electorate (compared to 20 percent for the ANC), and no opposition party attracted more than 3 percent of voters to its rallies or meetings (compared to 25 percent for the ANC).

Much of this is a function of ill-considered strategy and lack of imagination. But, much of it is also due to a series of rules that systematically work against the interests of opposition parties. First, while television is one of the quickest ways that an opposition party, particularly a new one, can build an image in the public mind, television election advertising was for the most part banned until 2009 (outside of some short publicly funded spots). Indeed, the 2009 decision to allow television advertising helped opposition parties broaden their exposure (23 percent of voters polled said they saw a Democratic Alliance ad during the campaign), but it still fell short of the exposure garnered by the ANC (38 percent). Second, broadcast and print advertising is relatively expensive, and few opposition parties have the financial means to run sustained advertising campaigns (27 percent of voters saw an ANC print advertisement during the 2009 election compared to 16 percent for the Democratic Alliance, 13 percent for COPE, and less than 5 percent for any other party). Third, although public funding has been available to political parties since 1997, the lion's share of this money (90 percent) is allotted to parties based on their national and provincial legislative representation. Ten percent of the funds are divided among the provincial legislatures, depending on their size, and then given equally to each party represented in that assembly. All of this means that the ruling ANC receives the great proportion of these public funds.

Public funds, moreover, cover only a small share of all campaign expenses. In 1999, for example, all parties in total spent an estimated R300 million to R500 million (approximately US$35 million to 60 million) during the campaign, with only R53 million (approximately US$8 million) coming from the public purse. Political parties are not required to disclose any funds donated by private sources, but it is widely believed that the ANC (due to its control over public policy and state contracts) and the Democratic Alliance (due to its historical links with the business community) receive far more private donations than any other political party. Certainly, only the ANC and, to a lesser extent, the Democratic Alliance are able to employ professional, permanent staff for things like fundraising, market research, policy development, or publicity. In the 2004 campaign, these two parties dominated the rest across all forms of media advertising, with the ANC outpacing the Democratic Alliance in spending on paid outdoor advertising (such as billboards, murals, and ads on taxis) by R12 million (US$2.4 million) to just R200,000 (US$40,000), and in print advertising by R3.8 million (US$800,000) to R800,000 (US$160,000). Yet, the Democratic Alliance actually purchased more radio time than the ANC by R5.9 million (US$1.2 million) to R4.8 million (US$960,000). Other opposition parties were largely restricted to a heavy reliance on street posters that could contain only simple messages and captions.

South Africa now has a competent, effective, and largely autonomous electoral machinery. However, the institutionalization of South Africa's elections will remain incomplete until voters are presented with at least two or more effective party organizations that are able to provide voters with a visible and credible choice as well as a good reason to vote.

See also APPENDIX 5: POLITICAL PARTIES IN THE APRIL 2009 NATIONAL ELECTIONS

Bibliography

Ferree, Karen. *Framing the Race in South Africa: The Political Origins of Racial Census Elections.* Cambridge, UK: Cambridge University Press, 2010.

Giliomee, Hermann, and Lawrence Schlemmer, eds. *The Bold Experiment: South Africa's New Democracy.* Cape Town, South Africa: Halfway House and Southern Publishers, 1994.

Johnson, R. W., and Lawrence Schlemmer, eds. *Launching Democracy in South Africa.* New Haven, CT: Yale University Press, 1996.

Lodge, Tom. *Consolidating Democracy: South Africa's Second Popular Election.* Johannesburg, South Africa: Witwatersrand University Press, 1999.

Matlosa, Khabele, ed. *The Politics of State Resources: Party Funding in South Africa.* Konrad Adenauer Stiftung Occasional Paper (March 2004): 1–130.

Norris, Pippa. *The Democratic Phoenix: Reinventing Democratic Activism.* Cambridge, UK: Cambridge University Press, 2002.

Piombo, Jessica, and Lia Nijzink, eds. *Electoral Politics in South Africa: Assessing the First Democratic Decade.* New York: Palgrave Macmillan, 2004.

Reynolds, Andrew, ed. *Election '94 South Africa: The Campaigns, Results and Future Prospects.* Cape Town, South Africa: David Philip, 1994.

Southall, Roger, and John Daniel, eds. *Zunami! The 2009 South African Elections.* Johannesburg, South Africa: Jacana, 2009.

—*Robert Mattes*

Emigration

Often referred to as the "brain drain," emigration mainly involves skilled personnel—primarily in the medical (including nurses and dentists), engineering, banking, and accounting fields—leaving South Africa to reside in other countries. Although official statistics put the number of emigrants between 1997 and 2000 at 100,000, independent researchers triple that number, because many emigrants do not declare their status. Favored destinations of South African emigrants, most of whom are white, are Britain, the United States, Canada, Australia, and New Zealand. "Push" factors include concern about crime, personal safety, and financial stability, and widespread uncertainty over the future of South Africa after APARTHEID. "Pull" factors include aggressive recruiting by Western governments and employment agencies, and higher wages. By 2000, the South African government sponsored a program to woo skilled South Africans back home.

Eva

See KROTOA

F

Fanagalo

Fanagalo is a LANGUAGE of instruction first developed in the nineteenth century in NATAL Province by English colonists to communicate with their black servants. It later became widely used by white managers on gold and diamond mines in Transvaal Province to communicate with a multinational work force. The bulk of the terms and phrases relate to commands. It was also later used on work sites in ZIMBABWE, NAMIBIA, and Malawi, and mines in Zambia. Originally called "Kitchen Kaffir," it is largely derived from the South African languages ZULU and XHOSA mixed with some English and Portuguese terms and phrases.

Fassie, Brenda (1964–2004)

Known as the "Queen of African Pop," or "Ma Brr," by her fans and named as the "Madonna of the Townships" by *Time* magazine in 2001, Brenda Fassie was one of South Africa's most popular vocalists. Her MUSIC was deeply intertwined with the South African society and played a prominent role in the country's political scene. Fassie's most renowned songs, such as "Weekend Special" and "Too Late for Mama," reflected life in the black townships. She was politically outspoken and often visited JOHANNESBURG's poor townships.

Fassie was born on November 3, 1964, in Langa, a black township located in CAPE TOWN. Her mother was an amateur pianist, and because of this background, Fassie started singing at an early age and gave her first musical performance at the young age of four. Her innate musical talent attracted the attention of music talent scouts from Johannesburg. In 1980, at the age of sixteen, Fassie was recruited by Koloi Lebona, one of South Africa's top music producers at the time, who brought her onto South Africa's music scene.

After singing background vocals for other musicians, Fassie formed a music group with the Big Dudes and recorded her first and biggest album, *Weekend Special*, with them in 1986, which became an international success. As a result, Fassie was invited on international concert tours in the United States, Europe, Brazil, and Australia. She went on to a solo career and worked with the music producer Sello "Chicco" Twala. Until the end of the 1980s, she enjoyed continuous success with hit songs such as "Too Late for Mama" and "Black President," which was banned during the APARTHEID era. In spite of her career success, Fassie's personal life was troubled by scandals and battles with drug addiction. She was in and out of drug rehabilitation numerous times and became notorious for missing concerts.

In 1998, Fassie released one of her best-selling albums, *Memeza* ("Shout"), which consolidated her position as the leading Afro-pop star. For four consecutive years, Fassie won the South African Music Awards' prize for the best-selling album of the year. Tragically, Brenda Fassie died of a drug overdose on May 9, 2004, in Johannesburg. Despite her death at the young age of forty, her legacy lives on: in the Top One Hundred Great South Africans, she was voted seventeenth.

First, Heloise Ruth (1925–1982)

Journalist, academic, Communist, and activist against APARTHEID, Heloise Ruth First was born in 1925 to Jewish immigrants who were founding members of the Communist Party of South Africa (CPSA). While obtaining a BA in social studies from the University of Witwatersrand (1942–1946), First helped to found the Federation of Progressive Students, served as secretary to the Young Communist League, and then served on the JOHANNESBURG branch of the CPSA. After a short stint at the Johannesburg City Council, she became a journalist and an editor for the left-wing Johannesburg-based newspaper, *The Guardian*, where she covered bus boycotts, exploitative conditions of peasants in rural areas, the women's campaign against PASS LAWS, MIGRANT LABOR, and slum conditions. She did supporting work for the 1946 mine workers' strike, the Indian Passive Resistance campaign, and protests surrounding the suppression of communism in the 1950s.

In 1949, First married JOE SLOVO, a lawyer, labor organizer, and fellow Communist, who would later play a leading role in the development of Umkhonto we Sizwe, the military wing of the AFRICAN NATIONAL CONGRESS (ANC). They had three daughters together: Robyn, Gillian (who based her novel, *Ties of Blood,* on her family), and Shawn (who wrote the film *A World Apart* based on her mother).

Throughout the 1950s, First continued to serve as an editor for various left-wing newspapers. In addition, she helped found the Congress of Democrats, resurrected the SOUTH AFRICAN COMMUNIST PARTY (SACP), and served on the drafting committee of the FREEDOM CHARTER. Furthermore, she and her husband were defendants in the TREASON TRIAL (1956) along with NELSON MANDELA and other prominent antiapartheid leaders in which they were accused of plotting to overthrow the apartheid regime. In 1963, First was again arrested because the police believed she could provide information about the ANC's High Command and her husband's role in it. The police could then use this information to crush the ANC or at least undermine its anti-apartheid activities. She was kept in solitary confinement under the notorious 90-day clause that allowed the police to arrest individuals without cause and hold them for 90 days. She was released, only to be arrested again when she stepped outside the Marshall Square Station. Due to mounting fear about her ability to withstand interrogation, First attempted suicide but was thwarted by the authorities. The 117 days that she was held and interrogated later became the basis for her book *117 Days* (which became a BBC film in 1966, *90 Days*, in which she played herself). Upon her release from prison, First fled the country with her children and joined her husband in London. She would never set foot in South Africa again.

First helped to edit and publish the works of Nelson Mandela (*No Easy Walk to Freedom,* 1965/1989), Govan Mbeki (*South Africa: The Peasant's Revolt,* 1964/1984), and Oginga Odinga (*Not Yet Uhuru,* 1967), which led to her deportation from Kenya. The effort to research, write, and publish anything about the conditions in apartheid South Africa was itself considered treasonous, which made her political writing (and her efforts to publish the works of other political leaders) all the more dangerous and important.

First also authored and coauthored many books about conditions throughout Africa: *Power *in Africa* (1970, originally entitled *The Barrel of a Gun: The Politics of Coups d'Etat in Africa*); *The South African Connection: Western Investment in Apartheid* (1973, with Jonathan Steele and Christabel Gurney); *Libya: The Elusive Revolution* (1974); a biography of author and political activist Olive Shreiner, coauthored with Ann Scott (1980); and the posthumous and collectively authored *Black Gold: The Mozambican Miner, Proletarian, and Peasant* (1983).

On August 17, 1982, First was assassinated by a parcel bomb sent to her in Maputo, Mozambique, where she was working as a researcher at the Center for African Studies at the Eduardo Mondlane University.

See also JOE SLOVO; SOUTH AFRICAN COMMUNIST PARTY

Fischer, Abraham Louis "Bram" (1908–1975)

A prominent antiapartheid lawyer and Communist who served as NELSON MANDELA's lawyer during the 1964 RIVONIA TRIAL, Abraham Louis "Bram" Fischer came from a prominent AFRIKANER family. His grandfather was president of the Orange Free State Republic and later served in the UNION OF SOUTH AFRICA cabinet, while his uncle was a High Court judge; Fischer later married the niece of Prime Minister JAN SMUTS.

Born on April 23, 1908, in the former Afrikaner republic of the Orange Free State, he studied at Oxford University as a Rhodes Scholar and, in 1932, visited the Soviet Union. He defended the 156 antiapartheid activists in the 1956 TREASON TRIAL (including Mandela, WALTER SISULU, and HELOISE RUTH FIRST, among others) when all the accused were acquitted. At the end of the Rivonia Trial, he went underground to help regroup the banned SOUTH AFRICAN COMMUNIST PARTY. He was arrested in 1965 and sentenced to life imprisonment. In prison, he was diagnosed with cancer. After international and domestic petitions to the APARTHEID government, Fischer was released from prison a few weeks before his death and taken to his brother's home where he died in 1975.

See also RIVONIA TRIAL; SOUTH AFRICAN COMMUNIST PARTY; TREASON TRIAL

Freedom Charter

The Freedom Charter was adopted on June 26, 1955, at the Congress of the People in Kliptown, South Africa. This charter was a policy document as well as a declaration on the part of the AFRICAN NATIONAL CONGRESS (ANC) and its allies of their vision for South Africa after APARTHEID. The grassroots document reflected the will and demands of many South Africans and later became part of the basis of the new South African CONSTITUTION for the postapartheid era.

In 1955, the ANC sent 50,000 volunteers into the townships and the countryside to collect "freedom demands" from the South African people in order to design a democratic system that would give all South Africans equal rights. Ordinary people's demands—such as land for all landless people, living wages and shorter working hours, and free and compulsory education, regardless of color, race, or nationality—were incorporated into the final document. The Congress of the People brought together 2,844 delegates from all over the country and from all racial groupings, which was an important event in establishing a new system based on the people's will.

The charter's key provisions include: "The People Shall Govern," "All National Groups Shall Have Equal Rights," "All People Shall Share in the Country's Wealth," "The Land Shall Be Shared by All Those Who Work it," "All Shall Enjoy Equal Human Rights," "There Shall Be Work and Security," and "The Doors of Learning and Culture Shall Be Open."

The Congress of the People consisted of the black-led ANC, the SOUTH AFRICAN INDIAN CONGRESS, the white-led Congress of Democrats, and the South African Coloured People's Congress. In the 1956 TREASON TRIAL, the government tried 156 activists for their close association with the charter, charging them with attempting to overthrow the government. In the 1980s, the charter was revived as the central document of the UNITED DEMOCRATIC FRONT, an umbrella body composed of hundreds of antiapartheid social and political groupings, including civic associations, sports clubs, workers organizations, and student groups. The charter's tenets, for example, "The People Shall Govern," became rallying cries for the antiapartheid struggle.

Frontier Wars

Over a one-hundred-year stretch between 1779 and 1879, a total of nine wars were waged between the colonists (first the Dutch and, after 1814, the British) and the indigenous XHOSA in what is now the Eastern Cape. The result of the Frontier Wars, also known as the Cape Frontier Wars, was defeat for the Xhosa and the eventual annexation of their lands into the CAPE COLONY.

See also BRITISH IMPERIALISM AND SETTLER COLONIALISM

Frontline States

Because of their close proximity, the independent nations of southern Africa were in the "front line" of the struggle against the APARTHEID regime in South Africa. The Frontline States included MOZAMBIQUE, Tanzania, Zambia, Botswana, and ZIMBABWE. These countries often supported black, nationalist liberation movements such as the AFRICAN NATIONAL CONGRESS and the PAN AFRICANIST CONGRESS by providing bases of operation as well as financial and military support. They often paid a heavy price for this support, as the apartheid regime used its military and economic power to foment dissent and civil war in South Africa's neighboring countries, as well as economically sabotaged many of the landlocked neighbors who relied on South African ports to transport their imports and exports.

Fugard, Athol (1932–)

A pioneer in breaking racial barriers in South African theater, Athol Fugard used theater to build bridges between blacks and whites from the 1950s to the present. Many of his plays are set in PORT ELIZABETH in the Eastern Cape Province where he was raised by an English father and an AFRIKANER mother. Instead of completing his studies at the University of Cape Town, Fugard hitchhiked throughout the African continent. Two years after returning home to South Africa, in 1956, Fugard married Sheila Meiring.

The pair relocated to JOHANNESBURG in 1958 to work in theater. Fugard took a day job in the court system where he learned of the injustices of the PASS LAW system. In his spare time, he established close ties with the black artists of SOPHIATOWN, who worked with him on his first production, *No Good Friday*, in 1958, followed by *Nongogo* in 1959. Both plays featured black casts that depicted life in the townships. The many plays that followed addressed race relations in South Africa, including *The Blood Knot* (1961) and *Boesman & Lena* (1969).

In 1963, Fugard collaborated with a black performing arts group in Port Elizabeth called the Serpant Players. Fugard and two key members of this group, John Kani and Winston Ntshona, teamed up to write *Sizwe Bansi Is Dead* (1972) and *The Island* (1973). *Bansi* portrayed the hardships of South African migrant laborers, while *The Island* explored the lives of two inmates on ROBBEN ISLAND. From 1958 to 2008, Fugard wrote numerous plays, a novel, and two memoirs. Although not all of his plays discuss race and politics, his drama is known for creating interracial dialogue between groups. The 2005 adaptation of his novel *Tsotsi* was the first South African film to win an Academy Award for best foreign film.

G

Gandhi, Mohandas (Mahatma) (1869–1948)

Mohandas, also known as Mahatma, Gandhi was an internationally renowned INDIAN peace activist and civil rights leader who played an important role in leading the movement for Indian self-rule. In particular, his experience in South Africa played a pertinent role in his leadership of the Indian independence movement and struggles against British colonial rule. He was born on October 2, 1869, to a wealthy family of a high social caste in Porbandar, India. In September 1888, Gandhi left for the United Kingdom to study law at London's University College and was admitted to the British bar in 1891. After his bar admission, he returned to India and tried to establish a law practice in Mumbai but had little success. In 1893, an Indian business firm with interests in South Africa recruited him as a legal adviser for its branch office in DURBAN.

Although he had originally planned to stay in South Africa for only a year, Gandhi ended up staying for over twenty years, from 1893 to 1915, as he became involved in the country's Indian civil rights struggle. He launched campaigns to improve the legal status of Indians in South Africa and consolidated the Indian community into a homogeneous political force by forming the Natal Indian Congress. Gandhi also urged South African Indians to defy a law that required their registration and fingerprinting in 1907. As a result, he was sentenced to two months in prison by South African authorities and was released only when he agreed to voluntary registration.

It was in South Africa that Gandhi began preaching and putting into practice his philosophy of passive resistance and noncooperation; it was also where he first defined the term *satyagraha* to represent his theory and practice of nonviolent resistance. A number of Gandhi's writings detail his experiences with racism, prejudice, and injustice in South Africa, which served as a precursor to his work in India.

Garveyism

In 1914, Marcus Garvey, a West Indian immigrant to the United States, founded the Universal Negro Improvement Association and preached black unity, military-style discipline, self-help, and the

Protest march organized by Gandhi in 1913.

repatriation of US blacks to the African continent as a response to white supremacy. Garvey's message caught on among members of the AFRICAN NATIONAL CONGRESS (ANC) and the INDUSTRIAL AND COMMERCIAL WORKERS UNION in the Transkei, in what is now the Eastern Cape Province. Garveyites were behind a number of boycotts of schools and taxes, reforms in local government, and land reforms during the 1920s. Figures associated with Garveyism, such as Wellington Butelezi, told their followers that US blacks would arrive in airplanes from which they would bomb all white and African nonbelievers of Garveyism with burning lumps of charcoal. This led to clashes with the national ANC, many of whom were not followers of Garvey. By the mid-1930s, this movement had significantly declined.

GEAR

See GROWTH, EMPLOYMENT, AND REDISTRIBUTION STRATEGY

Ginwala, Frene Noshir (1931–)

Frene Noshir Ginwala is a renowned South African politician. She was born in JOHANNESBURG on April 25, 1931, to an INDIAN family with origins in the Parsi-Zoroastrian community in western India. Throughout much of her life, Ginwala has been active both against APARTHEID and for women's rights. As a student, she was exiled from South Africa when she helped arrange prominent antiapartheid activist and leading figure in the African National Congress OLIVER TAMBO's escape from the country in 1960. While in exile, Ginwala completed her university and graduate studies, earning a bachelor's degree in law from the University of London and a doctorate from Oxford University. Before and during her exile, she also worked in Tanzania, Zambia, and Mozambique, and in the United Kingdom as an AFRICAN NATIONAL CONGRESS (ANC) official, journalist, and broadcaster.

Additionally, Ginwala has written and published extensively on women's issues and on liberation struggles. She has produced authoritative reports published by the United Nations as well as edited books and monographs on these subjects. Some of her well-known publications include: "Indian South Africans," "Press in South Africa," "Workers Under Apartheid," "Sanctions in South Africa in Question," and "Gender and Economic Policy in a Democratic South Africa." Upon her return to South Africa in 1991, Ginwala was instrumental in establishing the ANC WOMEN'S LEAGUE as well as the Women's National Coalition, which comprised organizations from across the political spectrum tasked with the goal of drafting the women's charter, a document that aimed to provide a blueprint for achieving gender equity in South Africa.

Ginwala was elected as the speaker of South Africa's National Assembly during the country's first democratically elected PARLIAMENT in 1994, which she served for ten years until 2004. As speaker, she played an important role in implementing many changes in the South African Parliament. Ginwala is also the president of South Africa's Speakers' Forum, the chairperson of the Commonwealth Parliamentary Association African Region, the cochairperson of the Commonwealth Parliamentary Association and the International Parliamentary Union. In April 2005, she was appointed as KwaZulu-Natal University's first female chancellor and served a four-year term; at the time she was one of only four female university chancellors in the country.

Ginwala has also won numerous awards including: Women of the Year Award in 2000, Presidential Award from the Black Management Forum in 2000, the Global Award for Outstanding Contribution for Promotion of Human Rights and Democracy in 2000 from the Priyadarshni Academy in India, and the Grand Officer de l'Ordre National in Ivory Coast in 1998.

Global Antiapartheid Movement

The global antiapartheid movement (AAM) made a major contribution to ending APARTHEID. Composed of a diverse, complex mosaic of local, national, and international organizations, the AAM united in opposition to apartheid and in support of black-led liberation movements. This solidarity tended to overflow the narrow bounds of single nations. The AAM is characterized as a transnational social movement with national components but linked internationally by media, global movements of people, and global institutions such as the United Nations, developing at a time of emergent globalization.

History and Structure

Although apartheid was not introduced until after 1948, there had been earlier protests around the world against South African racism: in the United States by Paul Robeson and the Council on African Affairs, by New Zealand Maori against racially selected SPORTS tours, by global labor movements in support of black South African unionists, and by Indian leaders MAHATMA GANDHI and Jawaharlal Nehru. From 1946, India embargoed trade with South Africa and made South Africa's treatment of its INDIAN minority a regular issue in the United Nations. Drawing on common bonds of anticolonial resistance, India remained a major bulwark of the international AAM.

In the 1950s and early 1960s, a more coordinated antiapartheid movement developed, chiefly in response to large-scale DEFIANCE CAMPAIGNS led by the AFRICAN NATIONAL CONGRESS (ANC) and, after 1960 when the ANC was banned, by exiles. The UK AAM emerged in 1960 and grew into a centralized, highly effective organization. In the next two decades, the AAM's growth was to some extent linked to decolonization, to other social movements such as anti–Vietnam War protests, and to broader social change. By the 1970s, the AAM was truly global, with movements from Jamaica to Japan.

The AAM had three components: nation-based antiapartheid organizations, supportive international bodies, and sympathetic groups, including labor unions, churches, and student and women's associations. International labor federations were strongly supportive. As early as 1959, maritime unions imposed bans on South African shipping after ANC president ALBERT LUTHULI called for sanctions. In the mid-1980s, unions coordinated global "weeks of protest." Churches also were consistent supporters of the AAM. Some political parties played a significant role, notably nationalist parties across Africa and in India, and center and left parties across the globe.

Governments in India, Scandinavia, and Eastern Europe provided substantial material or diplomatic aid to the liberation movements. Nordic AAMs were successful in persuading their governments to give support: Danish policy focused on sanctions after 1978, and, in Sweden, extensive aid was given to victims of apartheid. Such state solidarity was in stark contrast to the United Kingdom and United States, where governments that profited from trade with the apartheid regime refused to recognize or support the movements. Britain, in particular, maintained large investments in South Africa.

The political configuration of each country influenced the form of the AAM. In the UK AAM's hierarchical model, eminent persons were at the top and local activists at the base, but in the wider spaces of North America and Australasia the pattern was more diffuse, with looser coalitions. Even in Britain there were prominent antiapartheid organizations that were driven more by local activists than well-known or influential figures, notably the International Defence and Aid Fund (IDAF). In the United States, the American Committee on Africa (networking divestment), Africa Fund (education and aid), Congressional Black Caucus, TransAfrica, and Free South African Movement, plus numerous local groups, built wide community opposition to apartheid, particularly among African Americans, churches, and labor. US divestment campaigns targeted governments and colleges, and illustrated "local activism in global politics" (see Love 1985).

Antiapartheid Campaigns and Issues

International campaigns were a major weapon of the AAM; arms, oil, sports, and investment sanctions all had success. Sanctions put economic constraints on the apartheid regime, but more importantly they weakened the morale of apartheid's followers and emboldened the black opposition. UN and (British) Commonwealth resolutions opposing apartheid and calling for a boycott of economic and political interactions with the apartheid regime were broadly implemented, yet it took decades to convince Western powers and their transnational corporations to effectively boycott South Africa. Transnational corporations used many loopholes to continue with the purchase of uranium and gold from South Africa, the sale of arms and oil to South Africa, and the participation of South African mercenary sports teams in international competitions. With Western governments slow to act, the AAM adopted people's sanctions, asking individuals and organizations to boycott companies that continued to do business with South Africa and to not buy South African products such as wine, fish, and gold kruggerands.

The AAM targeted Shell oil company in particular, which continued to profit from the sale of oil to the apartheid regime into the late 1980s, despite numerous global agreements at this time to isolate the apartheid regime and discontinue business with it. The AAM launched a global campaign against Shell that coordinated "weeks of action" in several countries in 1987 and 1988. Pressure against the apartheid regime was maintained in other areas. Codes of conduct for foreign companies still doing business in South Africa, such as the Sullivan Principles, were intended to improve economic conditions for black South Africans by prescribing fair wages and labor practices, providing training and skills transfer for black workers so they could move into management positions, and requiring foreign companies to give back to the black communities of South Africa through social responsibility programs. The codes of conduct had limited effect globally, but encouraged some companies to divest. Financial and sports sanctions, notably South Africa's expulsion from the Olympic games beginning in 1964, had a deep impact and helped modify the views of white South Africans. White South Africans as a whole were shunned from the global community, taking a heavy toll on their psyche and their desire to be part of the global community. Financial sanctions made it difficult for white South Africans to travel abroad, and sports sanctions saw their beloved sports teams shunned from international competitions. In particular, the US Comprehensive Anti-Apartheid Act of 1986, which saw President Ronald Reagan's support for

Pretoria overridden by the US Congress and the refusal of banks to roll over South African loans, was a major force dragging Pretoria to negotiations. Sanctions were used in conjunction with diplomatic pressure. In October 1985, the Commonwealth set up the Eminent Persons Group led by former prime ministers Malcolm Fraser of Australia and Olusegun Obasanjo of Nigeria, but they concluded Pretoria had no intention of negotiating in good faith. Reagan and British prime minister Margaret Thatcher continued to refuse to accept action to end apartheid, but the independence of NAMIBIA in 1990 and the end of the Cold War removed many obstacles to negotiations between the apartheid state and the black-led liberation movements.

In countries with cultural ties to South Africa, such as Britain, Australia, and New Zealand, the AAM focused on sports sanctions, which served to isolate AFRIKANERS, who dominated South Africa's whites-only national rugby team in particular and comprised many of the country's star athletes. There were major protests in 1970–1971 and 1981 against tours by South African teams selected on race. In 1981 in New Zealand, HART (Halt All Racist Tours) achieved great success in mobilizing mass protests that, per capita, were perhaps the largest in the world and which ended major apartheid sports tours. Historic ties between South Africa and Holland lent a special character to the Dutch AAM, which included hundreds of local groups and bodies such as Anti-Apartheidsbeweging Nederland and Komitee Zuidelijk Afrika. This diversity saw some duplication of effort but united people from a wide spectrum of views in campaigns such as those against Shell.

Another form of solidarity was material aid, in which IDAF played a major role, stealthily forwarding aid to political prisoners in South Africa, while the AAM sent goods to refugees in southern Africa. Eastern European and African states gave military support to the liberation movements. Military bases of the liberation movements in the FRONTLINE STATES, notably Tanzania, Zambia, and MOZAMBIQUE, relied on antiapartheid solidarity of African governments and peoples for financial support and protection. The AAM also drew great strength from the work of exiles. The ANC's OLIVER TAMBO had a global impact, charming East and West alike to support the ANC's cause. All this work was not without danger: South African embassies engaged in dirty tricks that included misinformation, destabilization, and even assassinations.

Internally, the AAM had to deal with contradictions and divisive issues: proapartheid governments such as the United States and the United Kingdom, ANC vs. PAN AFRICANIST CONGRESS tussles, different opinions about the merits of armed struggle as a key strategy, the effectiveness of sanctions as a strategy, and how to relate to racism in their countries' own societies. The Western public was more comfortable with civil rights than a liberation war, and the AAM countered by explaining the historical necessity for armed struggle. Globally, a greater problem was the unwillingness of main investors in apartheid South Africa—the United Kingdom and United States—to support sanctions or the liberation movement. Although global mobilization against apartheid was therefore a difficult task, bodies such as the UN, IDAF, and international labor and church bodies successfully coordinated regional actions against apartheid.

People, Culture, and Media
The global AAM included many remarkable people: DENNIS BRUTUS (author and activist), Prexy Nesbitt (activist), Arthur Ashe (tennis star), and Trevor Huddleston (Anglican priest), to name just a few. Leaders were backed by thousands of activists and millions of supporters worldwide, and when the AAM was able to mobilize this wider constituency in the 1980s it was most effective. Staffed by inventive, hard-working people, the AAM developed effective techniques to expose apartheid; built its own MEDIA with newsletters, cartoons, films, and posters; and adopted diverse tactics: pickets, lobbying, sports disruption, mass rallies, concerts, consumer boycotts, strikes, film festivals, and demonstrations at Shell pumps. Writers, artists, cartoonists, and musicians from Bob Marley to Stevie Wonder inspired the AAM, which used star performers, massive rock concerts, and public debate to sway the media, and nightly TV pictures of police dogs and *sjambok* whips

tearing into defenseless protesters swept around the world, destroying the credibility of pro-apartheid supporters like Thatcher and Reagan. The AAM was able to exploit an initially skeptical media because it was broad-based and united in a single aim: to destroy apartheid.

Success and Lessons

The early 1990s was a challenging if fulfilling time for the AAM. After NELSON MANDELA was released from prison, he toured widely, thanking countries for their support. The South African political situation remained volatile, and the AAM continued to monitor compliance with sanctions, but the ANC, eager to open space for negotiations with the apartheid regime, moved to support selective lifting of financial and economic bans in 1991; some argued they must remain until apartheid was gone, but the pace of change for a new political dispensation in South Africa was fast and the new course set. Most AAMs chose to maintain solidarity until the 1994 elections that brought democracy, after which, with the death of apartheid, they folded.

The AAM did not by itself bring down apartheid but rather, in conjunction with wider political forces and economic trends, helped produce an irresistible movement for change. Its individual components were part of a wider global team, and the AAM was able to turn apartheid into an international issue. It helped defeat apartheid and strengthened antiracism forces in many countries, achieving these goals through hard educational work, a close relationship with liberation movements, and by putting down deep roots. It was able to work with some governments, change others' policies, and campaign against still others. The AAM's broad lessons are that solidarity needs to be global and united, and that social without political movements are inadequate. It is no coincidence that some AAM veterans are still active today in antiglobalization protests; the AAM, which provides a model of a focused global campaign, was an early manifestation of a new kind of globalizing process.

See also AFRICAN NATIONAL CONGRESS; ARMED STRUGGLE; NELSON MANDELA; OLIVER TAMBO

Bibliography

Culverson, Donald R. *Contesting Apartheid: US Activism, 1960–87.* Boulder, CO: Westview, 1999.

Fieldhouse, Roger. *Anti-Apartheid: A History of the Movement in Britain: A Study in Pressure Group Politics.* London: Merlin, 2005.

Gurney, Christobel. "'A Great Cause': The Origins of the AAM, June 1959–March 1960." *Journal of Southern African Studies* 26 (2000): 123–144.

Herbstein, Denis. *White Lies: Canon Collins and the Secret War Against Apartheid.* Cape Town, South Africa: HSRC Press; and Oxford, UK: James Currey, 2004.

Hostetter, David L. *Movement Matters: American Antiapartheid Activism and the Rise of Multicultural Politics.* New York: Routledge, 2006.

Klotz, Audie. *Norms in International Relations: The Struggle Against Apartheid.* Ithaca, NY: Cornell University Press, 1995.

Love, Janice. *The U.S. Anti-apartheid Movement: Local Activism in Global Politics.* New York: Praeger, 1985.

Minter, William, Gail Hovey, and Charles Cobb. *No Easy Victories: African Liberation and American Activists over a Half Century, 1950–2000.* Trenton, NJ: Africa World Press, 2008.

Nesbitt, Francis Njubi. *Race for Sanctions: African Americans Against Apartheid, 1946–94.* Bloomington: Indiana University Press, 2004.

O'Donnell, Penny, and Lynette Simons, eds. *Australians Against Racism: Testimonies from the Anti-Apartheid Movement in Australia.* Sydney, Australia: Pluto Press, 1995.

Richards, Trevor. *Dancing on Our Bones: New Zealand, South Africa, Rugby and Racism.* Wellington, New Zealand: Bridget Williams, 1999.

Sellström, Tor. *Sweden and National Liberation in Southern Africa.* Uppsala, Sweden: Nordic Institute, 1999.

Shubin, Vladimir. *ANC: A View from Moscow*, 2nd ed. Johannesburg, South Africa: Jacana, 2008.

South Africa Democracy Education Trust. *The Road to Democracy in South Africa.* Vol. 3, *International Solidarity.* Pretoria, South Africa: Unisa Press, 2008.

Thörn, Håkan. *Anti-Apartheid and the Emergence of a Global Civil Society.* New York: Palgrave, 2006.

United Nations. *The United Nations and Apartheid, 1948–1994.* New York: UN, 1994.

—*Peter Limb*

Gold and Diamond Mining

Contemporary South Africa's social, political, and economic landscape has been fundamentally shaped by the discovery of diamonds in 1867 and subsequently of gold in 1887. The mining of these two minerals has been the cornerstone of the South African economy for over a century and provided a crucial impetus for the highly discriminatory and racialized labor and social policies that culminated in the APARTHEID policies implemented by the AFRIKANER-led NATIONAL PARTY in 1948. Given the labor-intensive nature of mineral extraction and the relatively rigid equipment and manufacturing costs of gold and diamonds, the need of mine owners to secure a cheap, steady pool of relatively unskilled black labor was critical to this economic endeavor. By the mid-twentieth century, South Africa was the world's largest or second largest producer of gold, diamonds, platinum, chromium, manganese, and vanadium; and it ranked high among producers of coal, iron ore, uranium, copper, silver, fluorspar, asbestos, and limestone. Once the keystone of the South African economy and accounting for, on average, over 15 percent of all economic activity in the 1970s and 1980s, the mining sector has diminished in importance since the mid-1990s as the economy has become more diversified, and as the government has sought to promote job creation in other sectors. Still quite crucial to South Africa, the mining industry still accounts for approximately 21 percent of all export earnings and remains the biggest employer in South Africa, with around 460,000 employees and another 400,000 employed by suppliers of goods and services to the industry.

Diamond Mining

Diamonds were first discovered along the Orange River in 1867, and their source was quickly traced back to an area near the then small town of KIMBERLEY in what is now the Northern Cape Province. By the early 1870s, a full-scale diamond rush had begun, adding to the four open quarries in Kimberley worked by 2,500 miners and 10,000 hired laborers who had migrated to the area from other parts of South Africa and Africa. The discovery of diamonds brought new investments and prospectors, notably CECIL RHODES, the Rothschild family of London, and other partners who in 1888 formed the DeBeers mining company. It wasn't long before DeBeers Consolidated Mines had a monopoly on the diamond industry, having quickly bought up the other major mines. Its monopoly quickly spread, and by 1939, 97 percent of all diamonds globally passed through the company. By this time, another South African entrepreneur and business mogul, Ernest Oppenheimer, had entered the picture. Chairman of the Anglo American Corporation, which already owned many of South Africa's gold mines, Oppenheimer bought shares in DeBeers, giving him a majority ownership in the company. DeBeers remains the world's largest diamond mining company, and still produces approximately 40 percent of the world's rough diamonds from its South African mines, and in partnership with the governments of Botswana, NAMIBIA, and Tanzania.

Gold Mining

First mined by Europeans in 1886 near JOHANNESBURG, gold soon became the most important sector in the mining industry. South Africa has almost one-half of the world's known gold reserves, located primarily in the Witwatersrand (Rand) region of what is today Gauteng Province in what was once a prehistoric lake. At its peak around 1970, the country's fifty-seven operating gold mines produced over 1,000 tons of gold per year, representing almost 30 percent of the world production. In 1994 and 1995, however, gold production fell below 600 tons for the first time since the 1960s. In 2008 and 2009, gold production fell an additional 13.6 percent to below 230 tons, production levels last seen in the 1920s, representing just over 8 percent of world production in 2008. The sharp decline in gold production since 1994 has a lot to do with the fact that South Africa's gold mines are aging and the ore being produced is of lower and lower grades.

Traditionally, the gold mining companies were able to earn high profits, despite the costly and labor-intensive process of extracting gold, by paying low wages to black laborers. Gold mines became known for their often exploitative labor policies, including the use of migrant workers on limited contracts, strict control over workers' social activities in company compounds that housed the workers, and difficult and dangerous working conditions. Migrant laborers came from all over southern Africa. Migrant labor still plays an integral role in the South African mining industry, now sourced from LESOTHO, MOZAMBIQUE, Botswana, and ZIMBABWE.

Transforming the Mining Industry

Transformation is a key issue facing South Africa's mining sector—the sense of needing to transform its ownership and management structure to include blacks, as well as needing to transform its economic business model to continue to be a profitable and growing industry. Equitable access to mineral resources and opportunities has been legislated, with meaningful participation of historically disadvantaged individuals the subject of the industry's BLACK ECONOMIC EMPOWERMENT (BEE) charter. Since the early 1990s, the mining industry in South Africa has seen significant restructuring and changes, with the traditional "big six" mining houses—Anglo American/DeBeers, Gencor/Billiton, Goldfields, JCI, Anglovaal, and Rand Mines—being restructured and extending their global presence. These companies traditionally controlled gold, platinum, chrome, coal, and base metal production in South Africa. The advent of South Africa's new democratic CONSTITUTION and rising costs from gold mining activities resulted in several changes in the industry.

More than 70 percent of the mining industry's labor force is black, but, up through the 1990s, less than 5 percent of managerial positions were held by black people. Targets have been set by the government and, by 2009, all mining companies were expected to have 40 percent of managerial positions held by previously disadvantaged South Africans. Other targets over the next ten years include transferring 26 percent of mining assets to black-owned companies and ensuring that 51 percent of future mining projects are controlled by black-owned firms.

Goniwe, Matthew (1947–1985)

Matthew Goniwe was part of a vibrant, new leadership fighting APARTHEID in the 1980s whose message appealed to a broad spectrum of South African society. He was born in Cradock in the Eastern Cape in 1947. After earning a teacher's diploma from the UNIVERSITY OF FORT HARE, he returned to his secondary school, Sam Xhallie, in Cradock to teach mathematics and science. In 1974, Goniwe left Sam Xhallie for a teaching post in Transkei in the Eastern Cape Province and married a social worker named Nyameka. His political involvement in the antiapartheid struggle led to his arrest in 1977, where he was convicted under the Suppression of Communism Act and was sentenced to four years in the Umtata Prison. Upon his release, Goniwe returned to teaching in Graaff-Reinet in the Eastern Cape and completed his bachelor's degree through the University of South Africa. In 1983, he led protests against high rents in Cradock, and, because of this activity, the Department of Education and Training attempted to transfer Goniwe back to Graaff-Reinet under political pressure from the apartheid government. However, its attempt led to a fifteen-month boycott by students and teachers from Cradock's seven schools, which was the longest school boycott in South African history. Goniwe helped to organize communities in the Eastern Cape under the banner of the UNITED DEMOCRATIC FRONT, a broad-based, popular democratic movement that was instrumental in bringing the demise of apartheid. Needless to say, this made him even more of a threat to the apartheid regime. On June 27, 1985, Goniwe and three other antiapartheid activists—Fort Calata, Sparrow Mkonto, and Sicelo Mhlauli—were murdered and their bodies mutilated by members of the apartheid security forces. In 2003, the South African government posthumously awarded Goniwe the Order of Luthuli in Silver Award for his contributions and dedication to the struggle for a free, just, and democratic South Africa.

Gordimer, Nadine (1923–)

An internationally renowned author, Nadine Gordimer was born on November 20, 1923, to Jewish immigrants in Springs, a mining town in the Transvaal. Her writing career spans the rise and fall of APARTHEID in South Africa, and her work explores the psychological impact of living in a racially divided society.

Gordimer's professional writing career began at the age of fifteen, and, by 1949, she had published a compilation of short stories entitled *Face to Face*. In 1951, her work appeared in the *New Yorker*, and, in 1953, she published her first novel *The Lying Days*. Gordimer describes herself as a "natural writer" and claims it is the writer's responsibility to act as society's conscience. Her work attracted an international audience seeking to understand South Africa. Common themes include the violence of apartheid, sexual politics, white privilege, and the relationship between the political and the personal. Gordimer has published fourteen novels, over 200 short stories, dozens of scholarly articles, and several screenplays, including *The Conservationist* (1974), *Burger's Daughter* (1979), and *A Sport of Nature* (1987).

Although apartheid was an experience that fundamentally shaped her life, she was not affiliated with a political party. Gordimer preferred to maintain her commitment to truth in her writing, saying, "If you write honestly about life in South Africa, the apartheid damns itself." Seeing black writers driven into exile and having three of her own novels banned because of her candid and negative accounts of apartheid, Gordimer campaigned against censorship.

In addition to winning the James Tait Black Memorial Prize and the Booker Prize, in 1991 Gordimer became the third of four Africans to win the Nobel Prize for Literature. She continues to live and write in JOHANNESBURG, taking up themes related to contemporary South Africa in her recent novels *The Pick Up* (2001) and *Get a Life* (2005).

See also LITERATURE

Government Structures

See APPENDIX 3: GOVERNMENT STRUCTURES

Great Trek

The Great Trek began in 1836 and lasted into the 1840s, as increasing numbers of BOER farmers became disgruntled with British rule in the CAPE COLONY and feared that their culture and identity were being threatened. Another major impetus for the Great Trek was the fact that Boers in the Eastern Cape were running out of land for pasture since there was little additional land to conquer. Therefore, they packed up their belongings and their servants and began the journey into the interior of South Africa, settling in areas later known as the Orange Free State and the Transvaal. In total, over 10,000 people migrated, primarily from the Eastern Cape region to the north. These Voortrekkers, as they came to be known, often came into conflict with local African ethnic groups and had to wage bloody battles for their survival, in particular with the ZULU and the NDEBELE groups.

Griqua

The Griqua people are descendants of the first African inhabitants and the first Dutch settlers of South Africa's Cape region that today encompasses the Western Cape, Eastern Cape, and Northern Cape provinces. Their origins date back to the interracial marriages and the exploitative sexual relationships between the Dutch colonists in the CAPE COLONY and the KHOIKHOI ethnic group during the seventeenth and eighteenth centuries. The Griqua were originally called Bastaards in Afrikaans, but the British in South Africa found this term offensive, and in 1813 the London Missionary Society changed their name to Griqua because they had a common ancestor named Griqua and a common ethnic heritage of Chariguriqua.

By 1730, the Griquas were already residing in the northeastern section of the Cape Colony. Under the leadership of their first leader, Adam Kok I, they migrated from the Cape Colony and settled near the Orange River, located west of the Orange Free State. Before their migration, the Griquas adopted the Afrikaans language. The second Griqua leader, Andries Waterboer, founded

Griqualand West, near KIMBERLEY in what is now the Northern Cape Province, and controlled it until the discovery of diamonds on their territory, which attracted a large influx of white settlers. Around 1843, the Griquas moved once again because of the intense competition among the British-controlled Cape Colony and the two AFRIKANER republics of the Orange Free State and Transvaal. Griqualand East was established, in what would be present-day Eastern Cape Province, under the leadership of Adam Kok III.

Both of these territories were eventually integrated into the European colonies, and the Griquas became part of the COLOURED ethnic group. Even though their mixed heritage was looked down upon during the APARTHEID era, they have maintained their identities through the Griqua Protestant Church. Their exact numbers are unknown, because they took the identity of the coloured racial category during the apartheid era due to fears of being relegated to the same status as the black South Africans. Currently, the Griqua population, which lives in both NAMIBIA and South Africa, is estimated at between 100,000 to 300,000. The South African Griquas mostly reside in the Northern and in the Western Cape, near the cities of Kranshoek and Plettenberg Bay.

Growth, Employment, and Redistribution Strategy

The Growth, Employment, and Redistribution Strategy (GEAR) is a macroeconomic strategy announced by the AFRICAN NATIONAL CONGRESS (ANC) government in 1996. It effectively replaced the RECONSTRUCTION AND DEVELOPMENT PROGRAM (RDP) as the central socioeconomic policy framework for the government and ushered in a new approach to policymaking and economic development.

Penned by a group of economists who opted for liberal orthodox policies, with no societal input but extensive consultation with the World Bank and the International Monetary Fund, GEAR was designed to find a balance between meeting the population's basic needs and finding the resources to finance those needs by spurring foreign investment and stimulating economic growth. It includes tax cuts, government fiscal and monetary discipline, financial liberalization, and privatization of publicly owned companies.

Reducing unemployment is the strategy's linchpin, and making significant progress on this issue looms as one of the government's biggest political, economic, and social challenges. In 1994, unemployment was estimated by the Central Statistical Service to be around 32.6 percent. The government calculated that in order to address this serious challenge, the country's economy would need to grow at a minimum rate of 6 percent per annum. Whereas the ANC had previously held that rapid increases in government spending would provide both the stimulus for economic growth and means to reduce inequities, its new strategy is strikingly similar to those widely prescribed by the World Bank for other countries in transition from authoritarianism, central planning, and underdevelopment. South Africa's comprehensive plan to transform the economy includes

- A competitive platform for exports,
- A stable environment for a surge in private investment,
- Restructured public services and government capital expenditure,
- New emphases in industrial and infrastructural development,
- Greater labor market flexibility, and
- Enhanced development of human resources.

Thus, economically, this program's success hinges on greater engagement with the global economy.

To date, this strategy has received mixed reviews. Praised by international donors and financial institutions, under GEAR, South Africa has achieved sustained levels of economic growth even though foreign investment has not been as forthcoming as anticipated. In contrast, critics of GEAR point to the growing levels of inequality in South Africa, especially income, as a consequence of this particular growth strategy.

Hani, Martin Thembisile (Chris) (1942–1993)

An extremely popular and influential figure in the fight against APARTHEID, Martin Thembisile (Chris) Hani was the leader of the SOUTH AFRICAN COMMUNIST PARTY (SACP) and the chief of staff of Umkhonto we Sizwe, the armed wing of the AFRICAN NATIONAL CONGRESS (ANC). He was born on June 28, 1942, to a family of six children in the small town of Cofimvaba, which is located in a rural village of KuSabalele in Transkei. Hani was the penultimate child of a migrant worker. He attended the LOVEDALE school and joined the ANC YOUTH LEAGUE at age fifteen. Hani studied modern and classical literature at the UNIVERSITY OF FORT HARE, where he earned his bachelor's degrees in English and Latin. While at Fort Hare, he was exposed to Marxist philosophy and was active in protests against the BANTU EDUCATION Act. After earning his bachelor's degree, Hani joined the SACP in 1961 and, a year later, became a member of the ANC's militant wing, Umkhonto we Sizwe (MK). Hani was active in the ANC's Eastern and Western Cape branches.

In 1963, Hani went into exile in LESOTHO following his arrest under the Suppression of Communism Act. While in exile, Hani received military training in the Soviet Union and served in the military campaigns against Rhodesia's Bush Wars in ZIMBABWE. As a result of his militant campaigns against the apartheid government, he became a target of several assassination attempts, which led him to move MK's headquarters from Botswana to Lusaka, Zambia, in 1982. In 1987, Hani became the commissar and the deputy commander of Umkhonto we Sizwe. As the head of this organization, he was also responsible for the suppression of a mutiny by dissident ANC members who were accused of being undercover agents of the apartheid regime and held in the ANC detention camps. Nevertheless, Hani denied any responsibilities for human rights abuses (purportedly including torture and murder) that were alleged by some former ANC members in the late 1980s and that surfaced again during the TRUTH AND RECONCILIATION COMMISSION hearings in the mid-1990s. In 1990, he returned to South Africa after both the ANC and the SACP had been recognized as legitimate political parties. By this time, not only had Hani become a charismatic and popular speaker in the black townships, he had also become a close associate to SACP general-secretary JOE SLOVO.

When Slovo announced that he had cancer, Hani took over as the SACP's general-secretary in 1991. During this time, he supported ending the ANC's armed struggle in favor of negotiations with the apartheid government to pave the way for the transition to black majority rule by 1994. His support for the negotiation process was crucial in pacifying many ANC militants. In 1992, Hani resigned as Umkhonto we Sizwe's chief of staff in order to dedicate more time to the SACP. He actively campaigned for this party in the townships throughout the country as a way to redefine SACP as a national political party that could rival the ANC. In some ways, the SACP was more popular than the ANC, especially among the black youths who did not live through the preapartheid era and had no commitment to NELSON MANDELA's democratic ideals. Furthermore, Hani was the only political leader who could exert influence over the radical township self-defense groups that broke away from the ANC.

Chris Hani was assassinated on April 10, 1993, in a racially mixed suburb of Dawn Park in JOHANNESBURG by Januzs Walus, an anti-Communist Polish refugee who had close ties to the AFRIKANER WEERSTANDSBEWEGING (Afrikaner Resistance Movement). Also implicated in the killing was Clive Derby-Lewis, a Conservative Party member of Parliament.

Head, Bessie (1937–1986)

Author Bessie Head was born Bessie Amelia Emery on July 6, 1937, in Pietermaritzburg, KwaZulu-Natal Province, as a result of an illicit interracial affair. While pregnant, her mother was placed in an insane asylum and committed suicide six years later. Head was adopted by a COLOURED family with whom she resided until she was sent to boarding school at the age of twelve.

Head rejected the APARTHEID state's obsession with racial categorization, claiming she felt like an outsider within her own country. After a brief stint in teaching, she moved to CAPE TOWN in 1958 to write for the *Golden City Post*. Head joined the PAN AFRICANIST CONGRESS and was arrested following the SHARPEVILLE MASSACRE. While detained, she provided the police with evidence implicating a friend in antiapartheid activity. Soon after this incident, Head was sexually assaulted. These events led to a suicide attempt. In 1961, she married political activist Harold Head, and they had a son together, but the marriage ended by 1964.

Hoping to escape what she has referred to as the "racial sickness of South Africa," Head moved to Botswana in 1964. Her short story, "The Woman from America," caught the attention of publisher Simon and Schuster, and she was offered a publishing deal in 1966. Head wrote three critically acclaimed novels: *When Rain Clouds Gather* (1969), *Maru* (1971), and *A Question of Power* (1973). All three works were set in Botswana and influenced by her personal experiences with racism, social alienation, patriarchy, and psychosis. Despite her success as a writer, she suffered an ongoing battle with depression and hallucinations and was institutionalized on several occasions. Nevertheless, Head continued to produce short stories, as well as autobiographical and historical writings. At the time of her death in 1986, she was considered a significant figure in African literature, and a number of her writings have been published posthumously.

See also LITERATURE

Health

As a developing country, South Africa is grappling with both a high level of poverty-related communicable diseases and chronic diseases associated with Western lifestyles. Approximately 19 percent of the adult population is living with HIV, and the number of tuberculosis cases almost doubled between 1996 and 2002, largely as a result of HIV/AIDS. At the same time, hypertension, diabetes, and heart disease are growing as a result of rapid urbanization, a change in diet to food with high fat and sugar content, and a more sedentary lifestyle.

Racial inequality and inequity between better-resourced urban areas and relatively poorer rural areas are still taking their toll on health. While high numbers of African and COLOURED youth are physically stunted, obesity is rising among INDIAN and white children. In addition, the province with the lowest level of sanitation and piped water, the Eastern Cape, has a high incidence of diarrhea. Although tuberculosis is an infectious disease that can be cured after six months of treatment, the country's overall cure rate by 2010 was 65 percent, a clear indication of weaknesses in the health system.

In 1994, the new democratic government inherited a highly fragmented, inequitable health system with health departments for four different racial groups as well as for each of the ten BANTUSTANS (so-called independent black homelands). Health resources were heavily skewed toward whites, a mere 12–15 percent of the total population. The transformation of the country's health-care system into one that meets the needs of all citizens is a massive and slow task. Some 84 percent of the population is entirely dependent on the public health system for medical treatment.

Thus, a huge burden of responsibility for health care falls on the government. By 2010, only 16 percent of South Africans had health insurance and could access private health care. However, from 2009 to 2010 more money was spent on health care in the private sector (R122 billion, US$13.6 billion) than in the public sector (R102 billion, US$11.3 billion). The government has intervened in private health care, in an attempt to get the private sector to take responsibility for more citizens. In 1999, it became illegal for medical or health insurance plans to reject any paying customer or dependent. In 2004, medical (health insurance) schemes were compelled to cover a range of chronic care as part of their basic packages. However, the membership of private schemes has remained stagnant, largely as a result of above-inflation increases in premium contributions. As a result, the government has announced that it will phase in a compulsory national health insurance scheme for all citizens over fourteen years old, starting in 2011. This is aimed at bringing the private sector into a common health funding framework, according to health minister Aaron Motsoaledi.

On assuming office in 1994, the democratically elected government immediately offered free health care to pregnant women and children under the age of six. In 1996, free primary care was extended to all those who needed it. In 2003, free specialized services were offered to the disabled. Few people who attend government hospitals can afford to pay for their services and usually pay only a small admission fee. Reforms also have been made in reproductive health, and, since 1996, women have had the right to abortion services before their twelfth week of pregnancy. Additionally, the incidence of malaria has been reduced dramatically by spraying households in areas vulnerable to malaria with the controversial pesticide DDT.

According to the BILL OF RIGHTS, every South African has "the right to have access to healthcare services and sufficient food and water," and the state is compelled to "take reasonable measures within its available resources to achieve the progressive realization of these rights."

Other explicitly health-related rights in the Bill of Rights:

- No one may be refused emergency medical treatment.
- Everyone has the right to "bodily and psychological integrity," including the right to make decisions about reproduction.
- Everyone has the right to "security in and control over their body" and "not to be subjected to medical or scientific experiments without their informed consent."

In order to progressively realize the right of citizens to access health care, the AFRICAN NATIONAL CONGRESS–led government has tried to transform the health-care system from a doctor-dependent, hospital-based medical service focused on curing existing diseases to a primary health-care (PHC) system based on clinics and nurses spread throughout the country, and a philosophy of disease prevention through education and the provision of services such as clean water and sanitation. Under the PHC system, local clinics are the first option for citizens who use government health services. If the health problem cannot be handled by the clinic, the patient is referred up the system to district, regional, and then tertiary hospitals for more specialized treatment. Since 1994, more than 700 clinics have been built or upgraded. A package of PHC services has been developed to standardize care across the country. As a result of better access to primary health services, the immunization of children has improved. Tetanus in babies has been eliminated, and the last polio case was recorded in 1989.

However, the system is far from perfect and—with overcrowded hospitals and a shortage of health staff—many people get stuck in the system and fail to get the specialized care they need. In addition, the shift to PHC has not eased the burden on hospitals. Instead, admissions have increased by about 100,000 a year since 1994—primarily due to the AIDS epidemic. By 2000, AIDS was the leading cause of death in the country, responsible for an estimated 43 percent of deaths. AIDS patients require a higher level of care and longer hospital stays than non-AIDS patients, and they are crowding out other patients—particularly the elderly with chronic conditions. There is some evidence that the AIDS epidemic is slowing. Between 2006 and 2009, there was virtually no increase in HIV among pregnant women attending government health facilities, and the infection rate appears to have stabilized at 29.4 percent. Women between ages thirty and thirty-four are most affected by HIV, with over four in ten (41.5 percent) pregnant women in this age group living with the virus.

The country's high levels of homicide and vehicle accidents also put strains on hospital services, with homicide and violence being the second highest cause of death in 2000. In addition, poor management at many clinics leading to long wait times and insufficient treatment has resulted in many people choosing to go to the hospitals' outpatient departments for treatment rather than to their local clinics.

At the same time, since 1994, there has been a serious "brain drain" of South African healthcare workers to developed countries where they are offered significantly better salaries and working conditions. By March 2010, 42.5 percent of all health posts in the country were vacant. Staff shortages are particularly bad in rural areas. Rapid urbanization over the past decade has also put a strain on health services in urban townships, with those living in informal settlements particularly susceptible to diseases.

The shortage of professional nurses, doctors, and specialists is particularly acute. In 2002, there were 4 percent fewer professional nurses in the public service than in 2000. Ironically, it is easy for overseas countries to poach South African doctors and nurses, but red tape makes it difficult for foreign health professionals to work in South Africa.

In a bid to address the crisis, the government has introduced compulsory community service for a range of health professionals such as doctors, dentists, pharmacists, and psychologists. This has served to alleviate the skills shortage, but these community service health workers are inexperienced and cannot replace those with years of experience who have left the country. The government also introduced special "scarce skill" and rural allowances ranging from 10 to 37 percent of annual salaries in 2004 to increase the salaries of health-care categories that are in particular short supply. In an effort to improve hospital efficiency, the government has also committed itself to the decentralization of hospital management, with hospital managers getting more decisionmaking powers and with service delivery becoming their responsibility rather than that of the government.

Constitutionally, health is a concurrent function of both national and provincial governments, with the national sector largely responsible for setting policies and the provinces largely responsible for implementing them. In 2010, the national minister of health signed performance agreements with all provincial heads of health that committed them to a program aimed at improving health outcomes by increasing life expectancy, reducing maternal and child mortality, increasing the tuberculosis cure rate to 80 percent, halving the rate of new HIV infections and reaching 80 percent of those who need antiretroviral treatment.

Ensuring that health services are equitable, both between and within provinces—particularly across rural and urban areas—is complicated by fiscal federalism. There is a tendency, especially in weaker provinces, for funds to be diverted from social service delivery to salaries. In the 2003 Health Act, the government committed itself to the gradual devolution of more health responsibilities to the local governments, starting with environmental health services in July 2004.

Another major policy challenge is the regulation of traditional healers. More South Africans are believed to consult traditional healers than doctors, yet the sector is unregulated, and there have been many reports of patients being exploited by unscrupulous healers. As a first step to regulation, the government is compiling a register of traditional healers.

See also AIDS

Bibliography

Department of Health. *National Antenatal Sentinel HIV and Syphilis Prevalence Survey in South Africa 2009*. Pretoria, South Africa: Department of Health, 2010.

———. "Strategic Plan 2010–2013." Pretoria, South Africa: Department of Health, 2010.

Department of National Treasury. *Provincial Budgets and Expenditure Review 2005/6–2011/12*. http://www.treasury.gov.za.

—*Kerry Cullinan*

Hertzog, James Barry Munnik (1866–1942)

James Barry Munnik Hertzog was South Africa's prime minister from 1924 to 1939. Throughout his life and especially during his political career, Hertzog encouraged the development of AFRIKANER culture and was determined to protect the Afrikaner population from colonial British influence. He was born on April 3, 1866, in Wellington in the CAPE COLONY to parents of German ancestry. Hertzog received his bachelor's degree in law at Victoria College in STELLENBOSCH, the Cape Colony, in 1889, and pursued doctoral studies in law at the University of Amsterdam in the Netherlands, receiving his PhD in law in 1892. After his return to South Africa, Hertzog had his own law practice in Pretoria from 1892 to 1895 and was appointed to the Orange Free State High Court in 1895 to serve as a judge, a position he renounced in 1899 to participate as a soldier in the ANGLO-BOER WAR. During the war, he rose to the rank of a general and became the assistant chief commander of the Orange Free State military forces.

After the end of the war, he served as the chief organizer of the Orangia Unie Party, and when the Orange Free State formed its own government in 1907, Hertzog joined the governmental cabinet as an attorney general and was eventually promoted to the post of state's minister of education. During his term as education minister, he proposed a bilingual policy that advocated equal status for both English and Afrikaans, but it was fiercely opposed by nonbilingual school teachers. When the UNION OF SOUTH AFRICA was formed, Hertzog next became the justice minister for two years, from 1910 to 1912. During this time, Prime Minister Louis Botha invited Hertzog to join his cabinet. However, in 1913, Hertzog led a secession of the old Afrikaner and anti-imperialist sections from the South African Party against Botha. In 1914, the NATIONAL PARTY came into being and formed an alliance with the predominantly English-speaking Labor Party after the RAND REVOLT in Witwatersrand in 1922. This rebellion brought both Hertzog and F. H. P. Creswell, the leader of the South African Labor Party, together as they both supported strikers against General JAN SMUTS. The alliance between the National and the Labor parties emerged victorious in the 1924 general elections and allowed Hertzog to become the country's prime minister. During his term, his government introduced measures to isolate and silence political dissent, passed legislation to uphold the industrial color bar that reserved management and skilled jobs for whites and confined black workers to low-wage jobs, isolated the black population from participation in the political process by removing them from the voters' list in the Cape Province, and established the groundwork for the APARTHEID system by allowing the white minority to economically, politically, and socially oppress the black majority.

In 1934, the South African Party merged with the National Party to form the United Party, with Hertzog the head of the new party. However, on September 4, 1939, the United Party caucus refused to accept Hertzog's neutral position in

World War II and removed him in favor of Jan Smuts as South Africa's prime minister. Three years later, he died in Pretoria on November 21, 1942. In 2007, a building named after him was built in Paarl in the Western Cape to honor his legacy.

Holomisa, Bantubonke Harrington (Bantu) (1955–)

Bantubonke Harrington (Bantu) Holomisa is currently a member of the South African PARLIAMENT as well as the president of the United Democratic Movement (UDM), the country's first multiracial political party established following APARTHEID. A former member of the AFRICAN NATIONAL CONGRESS (ANC), Holomisa cofounded the UDM in 1997 with ROELF MEYER, a former NATIONAL PARTY cabinet minister. In 1999, Holomisa and thirteen other UDM members were elected to the Parliament.

Holomisa was born on July 25, 1955, in the town of Mqanduli in the Eastern Cape. In 1976, he joined the Transkei Defense Force and became its commander in 1985. Holomisa was also one of the first two black persons accepted into the South African Army College for a one-year senior staff course for officers in 1984. After ousting Transkei prime minister Kaizer Mantanzima in 1987, on the basis of corruption, he became the head of Transkei, currently part of the Eastern Cape Province, but which was a so-called independent homeland for blacks under the apartheid regime. Serving from 1987 to 1994, Holomisa unbanned between 1988 and 1989 around thirty-nine political organizations that were prohibited by the previous government leaders, as well as worked closely with the antiapartheid movement. He also led the Transkei delegation to the CONVENTION FOR A DEMOCRATIC SOUTH AFRICA, which helped smooth Transkei's integration into the post-apartheid South African state before the 1994 general elections.

In 1994, Holomisa was elected to the ANC National Executive Committee and was chosen by its Election Committee to campaign nationwide alongside leading ANC leaders such as NELSON MANDELA and THABO MBEKI. However, in 1996, he was expelled from the ANC after testifying to the TRUTH AND RECONCILIATION COMMISSION about his activities as the head of the Transkei government and publicly accusing his ANC colleague, Stella Sigcau, of corruption when she was a minister in Kaizer Mantanzima's cabinet. Besides founding the UDM and serving as its president after his expulsion from the ANC, he has been an active participant in many global forums since 1989, including the United Nations Security Council, the World Tourism Association, the Convention on Biodiversity, and the Confederation of British Industry. In 2007, the Independent Electoral Commission invited him to act as an electoral monitor in East Timor's June elections.

Homeland
See BANTUSTAN

Hottentot Venus
See SARA BAARTMAN

Huguenots

The Huguenots were French Protestants who suffered persecution by the Roman Catholic Church in France during the sixteenth century for their religious beliefs. As a result, they immigrated to neighboring countries, to South Africa, and to North America. The Huguenots first came to South Africa after the Edict of Nantes was revoked in 1685, taking away their political rights and religious freedoms. Between 1688 and 1689, under the auspices of the Dutch government, Huguenots migrated to the Cape of Good Hope. The DUTCH EAST INDIA COMPANY had encouraged the migration of Huguenots to South Africa because they shared the company's religious beliefs and also because most of them were highly skilled craftsmen and experienced farmers who specialized in wine production, economic activities the company could benefit from. The Hugenots contributed greatly to South Africa's wine industry, and many wineries in the country still have French names.

Today, a large number of white South Africans are Huguenot descendants. Although many originally settled in the CAPE COLONY, they were quickly assimilated into the AFRIKANER population. The Huguenots gradually lost their French language as well as their distinct religious identity after the Dutch East India Company mandated in 1701 the exclusive use of Dutch in the schools. In addition to agriculture and the wine industry, the Huguenots also made significant contributions in all fields—from science to politics to sports.

On April 17, 1948, a large monument commemorating the arrival and presence of Huguenots in South Africa was erected at Franschhoek, also known as the French corner, which is a small town in the winelands region of the Western Cape Province. Famous South Africans of Huguenot descent include F. W. DE KLERK, DANIEL FRANCOIS MALAN, Pieter de Villiers (rugby coach), and Charlize Theron (film actress).

I

Ibrahim, Abdullah (1934–)

An acclaimed jazz pianist and composer, Abdullah Ibrahim was born Adolph Johannes Brand on October 9, 1934, in CAPE TOWN. He began playing piano at age seven and was heavily influenced by the Western Cape's multicultural landscape—from traditional African songs, to gospels of the African Methodist Episcopal church, to ragas and more Western-influenced MUSIC. Under the name Dollar Brand, Ibrahim played with a swing band, with his own trio as well as with several other bands, and then, in the mid-1950s, joined the Jazz Epistles with HUGH MASEKELA, KIPPIE MOEKETSI, and Jonas Gwangwa.

After the SHARPEVILLE MASSACRE in 1960 and the subsequent crackdown by the APARTHEID state on all antiapartheid activity, Ibrahim moved to Switzerland, played in a trio, and accompanied the singer Sathima Bea Benjamin, whom he later married. He recorded the album *One Morning in Paris* with Duke Ellington, which launched a successful touring career. In the late 1960s, he spent time in South Africa, Europe, and the United States. It was also during this time that he converted to ISLAM and changed his name to Ibrahim. In the early 1970s, he played and recorded with several well-known Cape Town musicians, including Basil Coetzee, with whom he wrote and recorded the song "Manenberg," a popular song at the time that has become a South African jazz classic. In 1976, he joined the AFRICAN NATIONAL CONGRESS and publicly expressed his antiapartheid politics, which caused him to go into exile in the United States. Based in New York, Ibrahim played with many jazz luminaries, including Max Roach and Duke Ellington.

With the transition to democracy, Ibrahim returned to South Africa. In 1994, he performed at NELSON MANDELA's inauguration as South Africa's first democratically elected president. Ibrahim now resides in Cape Town and continues to compose and play music.

See also MUSIC

IFP

See INKATHA FREEDOM PART

Immigration

At the formation of the UNION OF SOUTH AFRICA in 1910, the country's immigrant population, defined as permanent residents born outside of the country, comprised 200,000 whites from Europe, 200,000 blacks from neighboring countries, and 150,000 migrants from India. All of the 1.2 million white residents in the country around 1910 were either immigrants or descendants of immigrants who had come to South Africa from Europe in various settlement waves since the mid-seventeenth century. Twentieth-century racism, however, dictated a different approach toward continued immigration by these three foundational immigrant groups. In 1913, the new state passed its first racist immigration legislation, the Immigrants Regulation Act, which laid the foundation for all subsequent legislation concerning immigrants up to the Immigration Act of 2002.

The 1913 act established "whiteness" as the basic criterion for immigration. From then until 1991, all immigrants had to be "assimilable" by the white population, which effectively denied all foreign blacks the legal right to immigrate to South Africa. Mechanisms, such as bilateral agreements with neighboring British and Portuguese colonies, were put in place to facilitate the temporary importation of black Africans to work on South Africa's mines and farms. Their numbers were augmented by clandestine migrants, including many women from countries such as LESOTHO and Botswana. The black foreign-born population of South Africa peaked at around 600,000 in 1948 but declined under APARTHEID to less than 320,000 by 1985.

Between 1860 and 1911, 152,000 INDIANS landed in South Africa, some as INDENTURED LABORERS while others came with money and started businesses, adding to the Indian immigrant population. By 1911, an additional 30,000 Indian immigrants contributed to a total of 200,000 Indians in all of South Africa. The 1913 act was designed to also prevent any further immigration to South Africa from the Indian subcontinent. Although it prompted a passive resistance campaign from Indians in 1913, this act had its desired effect and effectively stopped further immigration by Indians. In contrast, the white immigrant population of South Africa continued to increase throughout the twentieth century as the state aggressively pursued recruitment strategies to boost the number of whites coming mainly from Europe, Australia, and New Zealand. The increase was neither consistent nor regular. Immigration tended to drop during periods of political unrest and uncertainty in South Africa (such as the early 1960s, the mid-1970s, and the 1980s) and increase during periods of internal political suppression (such as the late 1960s and the late 1970s).

Definitions of immigrant desirability shifted during the twentieth century. Having successfully curbed Indian immigration in the decade after 1910, the state introduced measures to restrict the volume of Jewish immigration from Europe in the 1920s and the 1930s. These included the Immigration Quota Act in 1930 and the Aliens Act in 1937. The Jewish population of South Africa, which had reached 50,000 by 1911, hardly increased thereafter as restrictive measures took hold. Ironically, many descendants of Jewish immigrants later emerged as leaders in the nonracial struggle against apartheid. Anxieties about Jewish immigration lessened after World War II. Until 1948, the most desirable immigrants, targeted in state-sponsored recruitment drives, were British. The AFRIKANER-led NATIONAL PARTY government shifted its emphasis after 1948 toward the Netherlands and Germany as sources of immigrants. In 1948, 70 percent of immigrants came from Britain and 8 percent from the Netherlands, but, in 1953, 33 percent were from Britain, 21 percent from the Netherlands, and 17 percent from Germany. In the 1950s and the 1960s, the apartheid government included Catholicism as a measure of undesirability and dissuaded immigrants from Mediterranean Europe. After 1960, white immigration from independent Africa to South Africa gathered momentum, as white settlers in former African colonies feared the prospects of black rule at independence.

In 1991, the apartheid state passed its final piece of immigration legislation, the Aliens Control Act, designed to give the state sweeping powers to rid the country of black migrants. It also reaffirmed the state's commitment to continued immigration even though the explicit racial criteria of "assimilability" was dropped. Because white immigration had fallen dramatically during the late 1980s, the Aliens Control Act was a last-ditch effort to keep South Africa's doors open to white immigrants. After 1994, with a new black-led government, the whole issue of immigration became highly politicized. Even though the Aliens Control Act remained in force until 2002, the number of immigrants coming to South Africa declined dramatically after 1991. South Africa was no longer viewed as a destination of choice for prospective European immigrants. The new government also took active measures to restrict all forms of immigration, including from the rest of Africa, in part because immigration was tainted by its racist past. More importantly, immigration was perceived as a threat to the interests of newly enfranchised citizens. Immigrants were viewed as takers of jobs and consumers of resources and became the target of xenophobic media reporting as well as verbal and physical abuse.

Between 1994 and 2002, a long and protracted process of developing a new South African immigration policy took place. By the late 1990s, it had become apparent that the country was experiencing a significant outflow of skills, which was seriously compromising public service delivery and economic growth. As a result, attitudes toward immigration began to change. The 2002 Immigration Act established a new set of procedures designed to make South Africa more accessible to prospective immigrants, including new forms of permits and quotas for desirable skills. However, the act proved cumbersome and difficult to implement and was amended in 2004. Since then, immigration has been seen as an integral part of the government's Joint Initiative on Priority Skills Acquisition. Immigration is likely to increase considerably again in the next decade, especially by Africans from the rest of the continent and others attracted by the economic opportunities and state services offered in South Africa. The implications of recruiting immigrants from African countries that cannot afford to lose their skills have not been fully debated.

Most of South Africa's post-1994 immigrants do not view the country in a particularly positive light. On almost every measure, with the exception of economic opportunity, they prefer their home countries. African immigrants find South Africans extremely intolerant and even xenophobic in their attitudes. After 1994, xenophobia intensified markedly, culminating in widespread violence against foreigners across the country in May 2008. Most citizens remain highly skeptical about South Africa's new focus on immigration. The government will need to do a lot more public education and highly visible policing in order to put an end to the xenophobic rhetoric and attacks on foreigners.

Bibliography

Crush, J., and D. Tevera, eds. *Zimbabwe's Exodus: Crisis, Migration, Survival*. Cape Town, South Africa, and Ottawa, Canada: SAMP and IDRC, 2010.

McDonald, David, ed. *On Borders: Perspectives on International Migration in Southern Africa*. Cape Town, South Africa, and New York: SAMP and St. Martin's Press, 2000.

Peberdy, Sally. *Selecting Immigrants. National Identity and South Africa's Immigration Policies, 1910–2008*. Johannesburg, South Africa: Wits University Press, 2009.

—*Jonathan Crush*

Indentured Labor(ers)

A form of cheap, contract labor, indentured labor was common in the British Empire, particularly in the Caribbean and in Africa during the nineteenth century. At the end of their service term, workers were required to return to their countries of origin, although many of them stayed in their new homes. In 1860, thousands of INDIAN migrants were shipped to South Africa's northeast coast where they worked on the sugar cane farms in NATAL. Some estimates put the total number of indentured laborers who arrived over a fifty-year period at over 150,000 people. Brought in after Africans refused to work for the low wages offered, these new laborers were poorly housed and malnourished and worked long hours. The bulk of the large Indian population in South Africa traces its origins to these migrants.

Indian(s)

See INDIAN SOUTH AFRICANS

Indian South Africans

Numbering about 1.5 million and composing about 2.5 percent of South Africa's population, South Africans of Indian ancestry constitute one of the largest diasporan Indian communities in the world. Some researchers suggest that Indians may have arrived as slaves in South Africa as early as the seventeenth century, brought to South Africa by Dutch settlers and traders when they began to colonize the Cape region in 1652. However, the Indian arrival in South Africa is more often traced to the needs of agricultural capital in the mid-1800s. As SLAVERY was being abolished throughout the British Empire, colonies producing agricultural commodities, such as sugar, needed labor. To meet this need, Indian indentured servitude, often likened to slavery, was introduced. After its institutionalization in Mauritius and the Caribbean in the 1830s, South Africa adopted the system in 1860. A second wave of Indian migrants, known as "passenger" Indians (because they were mainly traders and merchants who paid for their own passage), arrived in the late 1870s and constituted about 10 percent of the original Indian migrants to South Africa.

Upon arriving in South Africa, Indian INDENTURED LABORERS were subjected to extremely harsh working conditions. In 1881, the first group of repatriated laborers informed the Indian colonial government of exploitation and abuses such as flogging, inadequate medical treatment, and excessive fines for minor offenses. In addition to degrading work conditions, these Indians found themselves increasingly entangled in the emerging racial hierarchy of South African society. Consequently, they had to devise various political strategies to survive and preserve their identities, as neither black nor white but nevertheless South African.

White attitudes, AFRIKANER and English, toward Indians were reflected in the Afrikaner-led NATIONAL PARTY's election slogan "Die Kaffer op sy plek en die Koelie uit die land" (Afrikaans for "The kaffir [African] in his place and the coolie [Indian] out of the country"), which propelled the National Party to victory in the 1948 election. Repatriation, pursued briefly, proved to be an unrealistic option for Indians because most were already deeply rooted in South Africa by the mid-1940s. In fact, most Indians who came to South Africa as indentured laborers had made the journey to escape caste and class oppression in India in the first place. On the other hand, many Africans viewed Indians as interlopers. Black Africans' attitudes varied depending on the nature of political leadership, which led to hostility and violence at times but also cooperation and solidarity at other times in the struggle against APARTHEID. Thus, the place of Indians in South African society has always been, and continues to be, contested.

With neither the numerical superiority of the African population nor the political and economic might of the whites, Indians have had to carve out a political and cultural space in South Africa under extremely hostile conditions. As white power became entrenched in the nineteenth century, communities of color found themselves increasingly marginalized politically, economically exploited, territorially displaced, and culturally maligned. Apartheid, the emergent racial hierarchy of South African society, led Indians to see themselves increasingly as "Indians," aggregated and collectively creolized, rather than in terms of the religious, caste, ethnic, or linguistic identities with which they left India. The political history of South African Indians is characterized by the constant tension between four tendencies: individualism, legalism, accommodationism, and militancy.

Indian Militancy

MAHATMA GANDHI played a major role in Indian activism and resistance to racism in the late 1800s and early 1900s. In 1894, one year after his arrival in South Africa, Gandhi was instrumental in forming the Natal Indian Congress (NIC), a political organization, to fight a bill threatening Indian disenfranchisement. Gandhi tested his strategy of *satyagraha*, or nonviolent noncooperation, in South Africa before deploying it in the independence struggle in India. As racial segregation intensified in the 1930s in South Africa and apartheid policy eventually was formalized by the 1950s, Indians continued to be subjected to a number of racist laws, including the Group Areas

Act, which forcibly moved and segregated Indians into racial enclaves. (Indeed, a forerunner to the Group Areas Act was the Pegging Act in NATAL in the 1940s, which was aimed at getting rid of Indian businesses in the downtown business district.) During this period, a new generation of Indian activists vied for leadership positions within the NIC, giving rise to a more militant politics in the post–World War II period. Their increasing realization that Indians needed to form partnerships with Africans in order to oppose apartheid led to the 1947 pact between the SOUTH AFRICAN INDIAN CONGRESS, the NIC, and the AFRICAN NATIONAL CONGRESS (ANC) to form a united front against segregation and oppression. The pact was an important symbol of unity between Indians and Africans. The Indian activists and political leaders of the 1950s emphasized that the problems faced by the Indian community could only be solved as part of the wider solution to racism and apartheid in South Africa.

Unified opposition to apartheid by Indians and Africans resulted in substantial gains despite the white government's attempts to divide the various communities along ethnic lines. As early as 1946, the Indians rejected the state's offer of communal representation in the government of South Africa. They saw it as a cooptation strategy, especially because it did not include the African majority. Africans and Indians worked together in the DEFIANCE CAMPAIGNS of the 1950s against apartheid laws. Indians were instrumental in formulating and incorporating the concerns of all three "black" groups (COLOURED, African, and Indian) into the FREEDOM CHARTER, a policy document that envisioned a multiracial, democratic, postapartheid South Africa. When the military wing of the ANC, Umkhonto we Sizwe, was formed in the early 1960s to challenge the white regime, many Indians were reluctant to support armed struggle in light of their Gandhian philosophy of nonviolence. However, Ahmed Kathrada, one of the founding members of Umkhonto we Sizwe, and a number of other Indians in the ANC who either served life sentences with NELSON MANDELA or dedicated their lives to ending apartheid, thought otherwise. The 1973 labor strikes, which are often described as African strikes, included numerous Indian participants. The solidarity of Indian students at the University of Durban–Westville (the university for the Indian population, which was not permitted to attend white universities under apartheid) with the African struggle and the joint actions by both the Indian and African communities in boycotting rent increases in DURBAN are examples of successful joint mobilizations of politically and economically marginalized communities in South Africa.

One of the most successful instances of Indian-African coalition was in 1984, when Indians overwhelmingly rejected attempts by the ruling National Party to incorporate them into the apartheid government. In the early 1980s, the government proposed a tricameral system, which allowed whites, Indians, and coloureds (people of mixed race ancestry) to become part of the national legislative structure, albeit in racially separate chambers of PARLIAMENT. Whites had the automatic majority in this structure, while Africans were excluded. Most Indians rejected the offer, arguing that it was a mechanism to make them junior shareholders in apartheid, with no real power to change the system from within. A revived and rejuvenated NIC spearheaded a national campaign to boycott the election of delegates to the tricameral Parliament. In its aftermath, the NIC and its affiliate, the Transvaal Indian Congress, were crucial in the establishment of the UNITED DEMOCRATIC FRONT, a national alliance of civic associations, trade unions, and women's, students', religious, and other democratic organizations against apartheid.

Indian and African Relations

Despite their shared histories of economic exploitation, political marginalization, and resistance, Indians evoke African resentment because of their seemingly privileged position in the South African pecking order. Sandwiched between the powerful, affluent white minority and the disadvantaged, poor African majority, Indians are perceived by the Africans as "middle man" beneficiaries of the hierarchy. These emotive accusations have often served as rallying points for Africans. In January 1949, riots broke out between the

African and Indian communities around Durban, killing 50 Indians and 87 Africans, and injuring 503 Indians and 541 Africans. Thousands of Indian stores and dwellings were destroyed or damaged. Memory of the 1949 riots created a climate of fear and apprehension among some Indians over the viability of cooperating with Africans in the political struggle.

There was violence once again in 1985 in Inanda, KwaZulu-Natal Province, near the historic Gandhi settlement, which was all but destroyed during the rioting. The violence and looting had clear racial overtones; looting African mobs faced Indian vigilantes over screams of "Kill the kaffirs" or "Kill the coolies." The circumstances and causes of the 1985 riots, in which 70 people died, were similar to those of the 1949 riots. The riots partially confirm the success of the state in alienating the different communities from each other through separate institutions and differential incorporation into the apartheid system. Given the divide-and-rule strategy deployed against them by the white government, the question that arises is not why the riots occurred but why there was not more serious conflict during the apartheid years between Indians and Africans. The absence of continued racial violence between Indians and Africans attests to the success of political movements in building interethnic coalitions.

When South Africa's first democratic elections were held in 1994, it was expected that Indians would overwhelmingly support the ANC, given their disenfranchisement under white rule and their history of antiapartheid activism. However, in contrast to this expectation, many Indians voted for the National Party of F. W. DE KLERK, not to support the apartheid order but to defend their group interest and identity, which they felt were being dissolved in African-led agendas such as nonracialism, black consciousness, and Africanism. Opinion polls showed that, despite their support of universal voting franchise, both the Indian and coloured communities wanted some form of guaranteed representation for minorities in Parliament for fear of exclusion as well as dispossession. In light of these anxieties, white parties attempted to manipulate the fears of the Indian and coloured minorities, with the National Party successfully garnering a significant number of their votes.

The neoliberal policies pursued by the ANC government since that first electoral victory have disproportionately benefited the upper classes of all races. Thus, the ambivalence of working-class Indians toward the ANC stems from their class vulnerability in the South African economic order. Although they recognize that AFFIRMATIVE ACTION is an important and necessary mechanism for addressing past inequities, they feel particularly disadvantaged as a minority because it pits low-income Africans and Indians against one another in competition for jobs and government services. The fact that affirmative action is being implemented simultaneously with neoliberal economic policies in an era of corporate downsizing, outsourcing, restructuring, and eradication of welfare support mechanisms across the board means that just outcomes of affirmative-action policy remain to be seen.

The 2004 and 2009 national ELECTIONS, however, defied the trend established by previous elections, as the ANC received significant support from the same segments of the Indian community that had shied away previously. These electoral outcomes were regarded by the press as a sign of Indian identification with the African majority. However, such optimism for overcoming the racial divide between Africans and Indians has been dampened by a series of xenophobic statements made by certain prominent Africans in the media. Their calls for Ugandan-style expulsion of Indians, dispossession, and violence contrast with the inclusive rhetoric of "the Rainbow Nation" promoted by Archbishop DESMOND TUTU, Mandela, and other visionaries. It remains to be seen how South Africa will deal with its specter of anti-Indianism, as well as the alienation and anxiety it causes among Indians. One possibility is to draw upon the political bond between Indians and Africans, which was founded on shared political grievances. Thus, the challenge for contemporary South Africa lies in translating the shared memory of joint political struggles into greater sociocultural understanding and cooperation while respecting cultural identity and diversity in government and society.

Bibliography

Bhana, Surendra, and Goolam Vahed. *The Making of a Political Reformer: Gandhi in South Africa, 1893–1914*. New Delhi, India: Manohar Publishers, 2005.

Dhupelia-Mesthrie, Uma. *From Cane Fields to Freedom: A Chronicle of Indian South African Life*. Cape Town, South Africa: Kwela Books, 2000.

Govinden, Devarakshanam. *Sister Outsiders: The Representation of Identity and Difference in Selected Writings by South African Indian Women*. Leiden, Netherlands: Brill Academic Publishers, 2008.

Ramsamy, Edward. "Post Settlement South Africa and the National Question: The Case of the Indian Minority." *Critical Sociology* 22, no. 3 (1996): 57–78.

Vahed, Goolam, and Aswin Desai. *Inside Indenture: A South African Story, 1860–1914*. Durban, South Africa: Madiba Publishers, 2007.

—Edward Ramsamy

Indigenous Forms of Government

Chieftancy is a political institution that dates back to the precolonial era and is widespread throughout South Africa and across all indigenous groups. However, modern chieftancy can more accurately be seen as a creation of the colonial, postcolonial, and APARTHEID state. An indigenous form of government, chieftaincy, took different forms under various historical contexts, spurred by political motif. A constant feature, however, has been that succession is determined by genealogy and patrimony, with the exception of the Lobedu people in the northern part of South Africa, who are matrilineal. In a patrilineal chieftaincy, the heir must be a first-born male to the royal wife.

Fear of a power struggle tended to influence chiefs to postpone taking a royal wife, a woman from a royal family herself, until their senior years. This meant fathering an heir in old age, thereby assuring that the father reigns until death. When an heir came of age while his father was still sitting, he tended to be impatient for his father to die so he could assume the title. Oftentimes, this impatience translated into political instability in the form of a breakaway to form an independent and a rival chieftaincy, with the extreme case being the assassination of the father. In the case of the reigning chief dying while the heir was still too young to inherit the title, a regent would be inaugurated instead. Uncles tended to fill this role, with the understanding that they would abdicate once the heir came of age. But it did not always happen that way. Oftentimes, a regent would refuse, forcing the heir to compel him out of power. Now, the trend is to put the heir's mother as a regent, since she is likely to step down in favor of her own son.

Sources of Legitimacy

Precolonial chieftaincy derived legitimacy from three sources: wealth, military, and spiritual powers. Chiefs were believed to have rare spiritual powers, which enabled them to communicate with ancestral spirits or break a spell of drought. Such powers were sustained by the periodic doctoring of a *sangoma*, a medicine man. The more respected the *sangoma*, the greater the chief's powers were believed to be.

Wealth complemented religion. Patronage played a key role in chief-subject relations. Chiefs catered to the material needs of their subjects. Where a chief failed, subjects left for one who could. So politics and economics coincided. Those who controlled cattle, a primary form of wealth during the precolonial era, also controlled men.

Military strength provided security and secured resources. War was a common method of acquiring more land and cattle that could be dispensed to subjects, assuring their loyalty and reducing the chances subjects would desert the chief for another more powerful chief. A large population also meant more revenue for the chief.

Thus, a chief occupied an omnipotent position, which opened the possibilities for abuse of power. However, this was checked through a myriad of mechanisms. A chief ruled in consultation with councilors, whose advice he had to take. Councilors, in turn, were obliged to exercise positive influence on the chief, for whatever decision he made reflected on them. An unpopular decision could easily bring punishment from the people onto the councilors. The councilors did enjoy leverage over their chief, because, as hereditary heads of commoner clans, the councilors recruited military men and a chief relied on them for that. Therefore, a chief had to be on good terms with his councilors lest they desert him during wartime.

Subjects too exercised some measure of restraint on chiefly power. They could openly criticize their chief at public gatherings, during which a chief would recuse himself and only return to pronounce a decision made by consensus. That said, fear of appearing disloyal could restrain others from criticizing the chief. Also, not everyone's views held sway in a public gathering. Age and wealth, which were associated with wisdom and patronage, respectively, determined one's influence. Hence, chiefs tended to consider wealthy men rivals, whose wealth they kept in check. Oftentimes, wealthy men had to give livestock to the chief as penalty arising from an unproven conviction that they practiced witchcraft, which was only to be practiced by the chief and his *sangoma*.

Chieftaincy Under Colonialism: Tool for Control

COLONIALISM dramatically changed chieftaincy beginning in the 1800s. For starters, it ceased being independent and was subject to colonial authority to advance imperial objectives, to the detriment of the chiefs' own subjects at times. However, the colonial impact was not uniform. None illustrated this diversity better than the CAPE COLONY and NATAL.

Colonial authority in the Cape sought to transform chieftaincy into a more decentralized form of government. Chiefly powers and scope of responsibilities dwindled in favor of elected headmen and location boards, operating at the village level. Village administration fell to the headman and the board. Ownership of property was a prerequisite for voting franchise and for candidature for either position. Headmen served a mediatory role between the board and the populace. Hence, in addition to ownership of property, they had to be literate since they interpreted and enforced colonial policies. Headmen also acted as interpreters at the colonial magistrates' court.

Chiefs retained a role only in legal administration. They arbitrated over civil cases, while criminal cases were the magistrate's preserve. Even over civil matters, chiefs competed with the headman's court. Complainants could choose either the chief or the headman's court to lay their charges and, if they wished, appeal to the magistrate against a verdict passed by a chief. CUSTOMARY LAW, based on unwritten, indigenous cultural norms and practices, remained the only area where chiefs exercised sole authority. That authority, however, was conditional. The chiefs applied customary law only to the extent that it did not conflict with common law or civilized standards.

Thus, the colonial administration sought to modernize the administration and the legal system among the indigenous population in the Cape. This stemmed from the liberal ideology of the ruling elite, most of whom tended to be career bureaucrats and scholars influenced by Victorian ideas of civilization. They felt a sense of mission to lead their conquered subjects into civilization.

If the Cape administration weakened chieftaincy, Natal's British colonial authority strengthened it to shore up colonial control over the conquered population. Chiefs remained the sole administrators and legal enforcers in villages. Although they administered customary law, without any limitations or conditions, that law was of a colonial nature. The 1878 Code of Native Natal, which evolved to the Natal Code of Native Law in 1891, made the Natal governor general supreme chief, empowering him to appoint and dismiss chiefs, and break and remake tribes. Chiefs were no longer subject to the checks and balances that historically existed within the system of chieftaincy but became accountable to the colonial administration and despotic toward their subjects. The long-held customary practices of consultation and consensual decisionmaking no longer applied.

By the 1890s in the Cape, the civilizing zeal stalled in the face of African colonial resistance. Customary law regained full status and could be applied without restrictions. Here, the Cape government was following the Natal administration's advice: to use customary law as a form of native control. Natal reckoned that common law offered natives too many rights (and recourse), including voting franchise, even though it was highly restricted in order to reduce the number of African voters to a minuscule amount. Customary law divested the colonial authority of the responsibility to grant Africans civil rights, since they were essentially defined as subjects with rights vested within the domain of customary law. Natalian influence came full circle in 1927, after formation of the UNION OF SOUTH AFRICA, in the form of the Native Administration Act, an offshoot of the 1878 Code of Native Natal. It decreed that, henceforth, all Africans were tribespeople, whose natural habitat was a village under a chief's rule. If a person did not have a tribe, then the native commissioner would assign him or her to one. The commissioner could even constitute or disband a tribe as well as inaugurate or dethrone a chief.

Despite rejuvenating customary law, officialdom still confined its custodians—that is, the chiefs—on the margins of village government. Headmen and location boards remained in charge, but this changed after 1948 following the electoral victory of the NATIONAL PARTY—the architect of apartheid. The Bantu Authorities Act of 1951 put chieftaincy at the center of village administration. This was a manifestation of the apartheid rationale that each ethnic group must be granted its own state within which to practice its culture. In that regard, the apartheid government sought to grant full expression to chieftaincy, albeit in a perverted form. Now, the chiefs could appoint their own headmen. Although this position had ceased being elective back in the early nineteenth century, the old proviso still applied. As the ultimate authority rested with the native commissioner, he could appoint or dismiss chiefs and instruct them to implement government polices, however unpopular they might be among their subjects.

Postapartheid Chieftaincy
Post-1994, the chieftaincy became largely a symbolic institution with a limited institutional role. The South African CONSTITUTION recognizes it as a cultural institution and not as a political one. The chief's institutional role is both advisory and subject to elected representatives. This means making inputs on any legislation related to rural communities through the House of Traditional Leaders, which are established both at the provincial and at the national levels. But, legislators are not obliged to heed or incorporate that advice into legislation.

Governance at the village level rests entirely with elected councilors and municipalities. The dichotomy of a (urban) citizen with rights to elect his or her own local representative, on the one hand, and a (rural) subject under (unelected) tribal authority on the other, no longer applies, at least on paper. Chiefs only have symbolic representation within district councils, the most decentralized form of local government in South Africa, where they assume 20 percent of the seats but without voting powers.

That said, chiefs still retain a limited role in the administration of communal land. Formerly, they had undue authority to decide who received land plots, but the Communal Land Rights Act of 2004 limited their role while expanding community and official participation in land matters. Administration of land has been divested from tribal authorities (chiefs) and reassigned to the Land Rights Boards. The boards' composition is skewed in favor of community representation—five elected residents, one government official, and two chiefly representatives. A greater community representation is thus intended to ensure public accountability and ownership of the land allocation process.

The postapartheid state has also taken to scrutinizing the credibility of certain traditional leaders and tribal authorities. Hardly two years in office, in 2010 President JACOB ZUMA stripped six traditional communities of their kingship on the basis that their titles were a colonial fabrication, and thus not customarily legitimate. The decision was based on the findings of the Nhlapho Commission, which had been set up in 2004 to establish the legitimacy of South Africa's kings. Amongst those stripped of the title were the Matanzima and the Sigcawu families, which had dominated BANTUSTAN politics in the former Transkei homeland. Audits are still ongoing to establish the legitimacy of other traditional leaders below the level of king. This suggests that the postapartheid state is determined to weed out traditional leaders that were imposed by the pre-1994 government, many of whom collaborated with the oppressive, apartheid state.

See also CUSTOMARY LAW

Bibliography

Hailey, Lord. *African Survey*. London: Oxford University Press, 1958.
Hammond-Tooke, D. *Command and Consensus*. Cape Town, South Africa: David Phillip, 1975.
Mamdani, Mahmood. *Citizen and Subject*. Cape Town, South Africa: David Phillip, 1996.
Ntsebeza, Lungisile. *Democracy Compromised*. Leiden, Netherlands: Brill Academic Press, 2005.
Peires, Jeffrey. *The House of Phalo*. Johannesburg, South Africa: Ravan Press, 1981.
Rogers, Howard. *Native Administration in the Union of South Africa*. Johannesburg, South Africa: University of the Witwatersrand Press, 1936.
Schapera, Isaac. *Government and Politics in Tribal Society*. New York: Schocken Books, 1967.
Soga, J. H. *Xhosa Life and Custom*. Alice, South Africa: Lovedale Press, 1939.

—Mcebisi Mdletyana

Industrial and Commercial Workers Union

Founded in 1919 in CAPE TOWN with twenty-four members, mainly dockworkers, the Industrial and Commercial Workers Union (ICU) grew into South Africa's first mass-based majority black trade union. From its inception, the ICU organized a number of successful wage- and work-related strikes. By 1927, it had an estimated 100,000 members countrywide, and its popularity eclipsed the AFRICAN NATIONAL CONGRESS. The majority of its members were black, but there were a few thousand COLOURED members and some white members as well. Sensing its growing impact, the South African government harassed and imprisoned ICU leaders and supporters. Its main leaders included founder CLEMENTS KADALIE, as well as A.W.G. CHAMPION, James La Guma, and Selby Msimang. In 1929, Kadalie broke away to form a smaller rival union, and the ICU declined soon after. Other factors accounting for its decline were internal (regional) rivalries, corruption, and union money diverted to take on farmworkers' legal cases. The ICU is remembered for raising blacks' awareness of their exploitation and for being one of the first organizations to mobilize South Africans as workers across racial lines.

Inkatha Freedom Party

Founded in 1975 by MANGOSUTHU BUTHELEZI, then chief minister of the KwaZulu self-governing territory, the Inkatha Freedom Party was originally known as the Inkatha National Cultural Liberation Movement and focused on the ZULU culture. It was also initially limited to NATAL Province and among Zulu migrants to the then Transvaal Province. Buthelezi wanted to mimic an organization by the same name founded in the 1920s by Zulu king Solomon Dinuzulu. By the late 1970s, Inkatha, despite its ostensibly cultural focus and Buthelezi's position in black homeland politics, had developed close relations with the AFRICAN NATIONAL CONGRESS (ANC) (Buthelezi had met with the ANC leader-in-exile OLIVER TAMBO). However, in the early 1980s, it broke away from the ANC because of Inkatha's antisanctions stance and the ANC's use of armed struggle against APARTHEID, which Inkatha opposed. When the UNITED DEMOCRATIC FRONT (UDF), which had close ties with the ANC, was formed in 1983, it soon clashed with Inkatha, especially in the black townships and in the rural areas of Natal Province (later KwaZulu-Natal) and around JOHANNESBURG. Thousands of people were murdered and tens of thousands left as refugees due to the violence, which continued well into the early 1990s. During the TRUTH AND RECONCILIATION COMMISSION hearings (1996–1998), it emerged that the apartheid South African government armed Inkatha in its conflict with the UDF. In 1990, Inkatha changed its name to the Inkatha Freedom Party (IFP). On the eve of the April 1994 ELECTIONS, Inkatha, along with two other homeland governments and a smattering of white right-wing groups, threatened to boycott the democratic elections but relented at the last minute. Although it won a heavily disputed provincial election in KwaZulu-Natal, the IFP fared less well nationally.

Buthelezi and a number of IFP leaders were invited to serve in NELSON MANDELA's cabinet. Following the 1999 election, the new president, THABO MBEKI, did not retain the IFP cabinet ministers, and Inkatha has suffered an electoral decline since then.

Isicathamiya

Isicathamiya is a form of male choral MUSIC developed among ZULU-speaking migrant mine workers from South Africa's KwaZulu-Natal Province. The music has its roots in Zulu music and in US minstrel shows. Isicathamiya competitions among mine workers who live in hostels near the mines in Gauteng Province are common. The singers are called "tip-toe guys," as their choreography demands that they often stand on their toes or do high kicks. Usually associated with LADYSMITH BLACK MAMBAZO, the music became well known in the West with its inclusion on singer/songwriter Paul Simon's *Graceland* album.

See also LADYSMITH BLACK MAMBAZO; MUSIC

Islam

In April 1994, South Africa held its first democratic ELECTION and also marked the three hundred years of Islamic presence in the country. From the CAPE COLONY's inception in the mid-seventeenth century, Dutch colonists brought Muslim slaves from territories around the Indian Ocean. In 1994, President NELSON MANDELA's presence at the 300th anniversary celebrations showed that Islam formed part of the new nation's vision of itself as diverse and inclusive. This vision has been sustained despite crises around Islam and the global impact of the September 11, 2001, World Trade Center attacks in New York.

Islam and SLAVERY are central to understanding South Africa's history. The DUTCH EAST INDIA COMPANY founded the Cape Colony in 1652 to provision ships on the spice trade from the East. Prohibited from enslaving the indigenous KHOIKHOI and SAN, the Dutch brought Muslim slaves to the colony from India, East Africa, and Southeast Asia; eventually, slaves (known as "Malays") outnumbered the colonists. Colonial writers portrayed Malays as submissive, obedient, and exotic in contrast to the indigenous Khoikhoi and San people, whom they characterized as lazy and unreliable. In addition, a small number of resistance leaders from Southeast Asia were sent into exile at the Cape Colony. Among them was Sheikh Yusuf, whose arrival in 1694 was chosen as the starting point to mark the 300th anniversary of Islam in South Africa in 1994. From 1860, the second wave of Muslim migration began when the British brought INDENTURED LABORERS and traders from India to NATAL on the east coast of South Africa.

Because of slavery, Islam is crucial to understanding notions of race and sexuality in South Africa. Due to the small proportion of European women at the Cape, white male colonists and sailors were given sexual access to female slaves. This generated an extraordinary racial heterogeneity in the colony and discourses about sexuality and race that have profoundly shaped contemporary notions. The racial diversity of the Cape led in the nineteenth century to laws regulating the meanings of skin color. Due to the history of enforced prostitution, the memory of slavery is associated with intense shame for its descendants, and only recently has slavery gained broader cultural visibility. Indenture has been similarly neglected, but recent scholarship has addressed the role of Indian Ocean migration in the formation of South African Islam.

The creole language, Afrikaans, emerged from the "kitchen" language used by slaves, who spoke Behasa Melayu, the lingua franca of the Indian Ocean region, combined with Dutch, French, English, Portuguese, Arabic, and indigenous African languages. The first book published in Afrikaans was written using ajami, or Arabic script, similar to written Hausa. Friday sermons have been delivered in Afrikaans for decades, and the Quran has been translated into Afrikaans.

Under Dutch rule, the public practice of Islam at the Cape was punishable by death. In 1795, when Napoleon invaded the Netherlands, the Dutch passed control of the Cape to the British, who were more accommodating of Muslims. The Awwal mosque, the first in South

Africa, was founded in 1798 by Imam Abdulllah Kadi Abdus Salaam, known as Tuan Guru, and was built on ground donated by Saartjie van de Kaap, a freed slavewoman. In 1887, the first mosque in the Transvaal was built by Indian traders, who established further religious institutions in the province despite opposition from the AFRIKANER and British authorities.

Muslims constitute only 1.5 percent of South Africa's population and are diverse in race, class, language, and ethnicity. Most Muslims live in the country's urban centers and maintain strong regional identities. Both CAPE TOWN and DURBAN have the largest Muslim populations, with smaller communities in JOHANNESBURG and in PORT ELIZABETH. South Africa's terminology for Muslims manifests the country's colonial legacy. The term CAPE MALAY, used for about 80 percent of Muslims in South Africa today, is a portmanteau phrase first used during the colonial period to mean both "slave" and "Muslim." While some of the Malays came from Southeast Asia, the term also included people from India, Mozambique, Malagasy, Tanzania, and Zanzibar. After the abolition of slavery, Malay came to mean Muslim and was used even for indigenous Khoikhoi who converted to Islam.

The second largest group of Muslims, around 20 percent, are called "Indian Muslims" and are descendants of indentured laborers and merchants who arrived in South Africa from 1860. The number of African converts is very small but growing, and immigrants and refugees from other parts of the continent make up the rest of the Muslim population, bringing distinctive Islamic practices with them. Debates about Islam—for instance, Sufism and Sharia—have been enriched and made more complex by the presence of an increasingly diverse range of Muslims from other parts of the world. African immigrants include Malawians, who have worked for decades as migrant laborers in South Africa; the Senegalese Mourides and Ethiopians; Somalis; and Hausa Muslims from northern Nigeria. Of concern is that Muslim Africans and Asians who recently immigrated to South Africa have been subjected to xenophobia from South Africans.

Cape Malay and Indian Muslims are integrated into South Africa's political and cultural identity, serving in the government at senior levels, operating vocal media outlets, and engaging with the state on matters of law and culture. Internationally, South African Muslims have contributed to progressive debates in Islam regarding gender equality, antiracism, and the Israeli-Palestinian conflict, though conservative figures such as Ahmed Deedat, who is well known in the Muslim world for his debates with US televangelist Jimmy Swaggart and who died in 2005, also form part of the panoply of South African Muslim voices.

Most South African Muslims are Sunnis who follow the Shafii and Hanafi schools of Islamic law dominant in South and Southeast Asia; Shiites form a small proportion of the population, and many identified with Iran after the Islamic Revolution. Because of South Africa's distance from the centers of the Muslim world as well as the presence of revered local teachers, religious authority shifts between the local and the global. During the colonial period, Islam was propagated through the faithful memorizing of the Quran and communal prayers and rituals hidden from Dutch authorities. Islamic schools, or madrassas, were among the earliest schools for blacks in South Africa. The Sufist Islam, brought to the Cape by its earliest adherents, is still reflected in the observation of *Mawlid* (the birthday of the Prophet) and *thikr* prayer gatherings.

Scholars of South African Islam have noted the structural tendency within local Muslim communities toward schism. Control over mosque committees and the administration of the pilgrimage to Mecca cause perennial controversy. A strong imam-centered discourse operates in South Africa, and the ulema (religious leaders) hold a significant degree of power in Muslim communities through bodies such as the Muslim Judicial Council.

Since 1996, the rise of Muslim community radio stations such as Radio Islam, the Voice of the Cape, and Radio 786 has generated new forms of visibility and social cohesion among Muslims. This new Muslim public sphere is also marked by consumerism and political partisanship. In the cultural realm, the Creole cuisines known as South African Indian cooking and Cape Malay food are widely admired.

In the mid-twentieth century, the Afrikaner folklorist I. D. du Plessis promoted an Orientalist vision of the Malay as a separate race. Under APARTHEID, Muslims were categorized under the Population Registration Act as subgroups of the COLOURED and native groups. The major apartheid acts—the Group Areas Act, the Mixed Marriages Act, and the Immorality Act—devastated the mixed neighborhoods in which many Muslims lived. In the postapartheid period, Muslims remain divided by race, ethnicity, class, language, and region.

Muslim political engagement has swung between a focus on the right to worship and active resistance to prevailing political conditions. Many Muslims resisted apartheid and rejected its divisive racial labels and instead adopted a black identity. The revered Imam Abdullah Haron staunchly resisted apartheid's racial divisions and preached in black townships. He was arrested and murdered in prison in 1969, leaving an antiracist legacy within the Muslim community. In the 1980s, the Call of Islam, a progressive Muslim organization allied with the UNITED DEMOCRATIC FRONT, challenged quietist responses among some Muslims. Through the antiapartheid struggle, South African Muslim activists embedded religion in broader historical and social issues.

Two years after the transition to democracy, the controversial anticrime group People Against Gangsterism and Drugs (PAGAD) generated an unprecedented level of anxiety about Islam in South Africa. This group came to prominence after the public murder on August 4, 1996, of Rashaad Staggie, an alleged gang leader in Cape Town who was brutally murdered by PAGAD members. PAGAD drew on a bricolage of Islamic rhetoric for its anticrime stance, and media reports of its activities—accompanied by images of masked men, violence, and militancy—decisively disrupted the picturesque portrayal of Islam. Public anxiety about crime, VIGILANTISM, and militant Islam coalesced around PAGAD. The South African state initially struggled to deal with this group's populist appeal, especially given an overburdened judicial system. However, the strategy of prosecuting perpetrators of violence rather than casting them as ideological enemies meant that the state was able to contain the nascent combination of vigilantism, rhetoric associated with Islam, and antistate tendencies. Despite its deft response to the rhetoric of Islamic militancy, the South African government also expanded its antiterrorism legislation in ways that disturbed internal critics, and it was accused of complicity with the US policy of extraordinary rendition, a covert US Central Intelligence Agency program established during the early years of the War on Terror that sent foreign nationals to detention and interrogation camps outside the United States and whose activities did not fall under the jurisdiction of US laws of due process and right to counsel, for example. Nonetheless, the debates about PAGAD led to a more reflective view of Islam in South Africa.

In the twenty-first century, theological debates in South Africa have gained increasing international weight. Islamic activists and scholars such as Farid Esack, Rashid Omar, Abdulkader Tayob, Ebrahim Moosa, and Sa'diyya Shaikh have not only confronted racial discrimination in South Africa but also grappled with issues such as social justice, poverty alleviation, advocacy about HIV/AIDS, and progressive perspectives on gender. Muslims in South Africa are also increasingly nurturing their identity as Africans, engaging with intra-Muslim conflicts in other parts of the continent, and contributing to the preservation of Islamic manuscripts at Timbuktu.

Important Muslim public figures include several ministers in the governments of Nelson Mandela, THABO MBEKI, and KGALEMA MOTLANTHE. Leaders such as Ebrahim Rassool, who is the former premier of the Western Cape and since 2010 is South African ambassador to the United States, participated in interfaith efforts during periods of crisis following the September 11, 2001, attacks. In the arts, the late Tatamkhulu Afrika combined religion, empathy, and activism in his poetry and novels; Nadia Davids wrote groundbreaking plays about Muslim women in South Africa, such as *At Her Feet* and *Cissie*; Shamiema Shaikh and

Na'eem Jeenah articulated a progressive Islamic feminism; and Farid Esack established the advocacy group Positive Muslims to deal with the HIV/AIDS pandemic.

To face Mecca from South Africa, one must turn "north-north-east," and "bluegum trees [are] our substitute for olive," writes the poet Rustum Kozain in his epic poem "Brother, Who Will Bury Me?" (2005). He and his fellow poets Malika Ndlovu, Mphutlane wa Bofelo, and Shabbir Banoobhai portray a complex and compelling view of Islam in South Africa.

Bibliography

Bradlow, Frank Rosslyn, and Margaret Cairns. *The Early Cape Muslims: A Study of Their Mosques, Genealogy, and Origins.* Cape Town, South Africa: A. A. Balkema, 1978.

Da Costa, Yusuf, and Achmat Davids. *Pages from Cape Muslim History.* Pietermaritzburg, South Africa: Shuter and Shooter, 1994.

Davids, Nadia. *At Her Feet: A Play in One Act.* Cape Town, South Africa: Oshun, 2006.

Desai, Ashwin, and Goolam Vahed. *Inside Indenture: A South African Story, 1860–1914.* Durban, South Africa: Mabiba Publishers, 2007.

Du Plessis, Izak David. *The Cape Malays: History, Religion, Traditions, Folk Tales of the Malay Quarter.* Cape Town, South Africa: A. A. Balkema, 1972.

Galant, Raashied, and Fahmi Gamieldien, eds. *Drugs, Gangs, People's Power: Exploring the Pagad Phenomenon.* Claremont, South Africa: Claremont Main Road Masjid, 1996.

Gqola, Pumla Dineo. "Shackled Memories and Elusive Discourses? Slave Pasts and the Contemporary Cultural and Artistic Imagination in South Africa." Diss., University of Munich, Germany, 2004.

Jeppie, Shamil. "Reclassifications: Coloured, Malay, Muslim." In *Coloured by History, Shaped by Place: New Perspectives on Coloured Identities in Cape Town.* Edited by Zimitri Erasmus. Cape Town, South Africa: Kwela, 2001.

Kozain, Rustum. *This Carting Life.* Cape Town, South Africa: Kwela, 2005.

Tayob, Abdulkader. *Islam in South Africa: Mosques, Imams, and Sermons.* Gainesville: University of Florida Press, 1999.

Worden, Nigel. *Slavery in Dutch South Africa.* London: Cambridge University Press, 1985.

—Gabeba Baderoon

Jabavu, Davidson Don Tengo (1885–1959)

Davidson Don Tengo Jabavu was born in the CAPE COLONY in 1885, and was the eldest son of JOHN TENGO JABAVU, a famous black South African journalist who was one of the founding members of the South African Native College, which later became the UNIVERSITY OF FORT HARE. Davidson Jabavu's life encompassed several distinct careers. He was an educator, social activist, and politician as well as a writer and Methodist lay preacher. Jabavu pursued his university studies in the United Kingdom where he received his bachelor's degree from London University and a teaching certificate from Birmingham University. In 1920, he earned an honorary doctorate from Rhodes University. After completing his university studies, he returned to South Africa and took up a teaching position in languages. Jabavu became the first black professor at the University of Fort Hare, where he taught for more than thirty years and eventually founded a black teachers' association, which advocated better farming methods, stressed the value of manual work, and pleaded for racial cooperation. Jabavu transformed the university from its reputation of being little more than a glorified high school into a famous educational institution for higher learning for black South Africans.

Additionally, Jabavu cofounded the ALL-AFRICAN CONVENTION (AAC), an umbrella organization that consisted of several groups opposing the JAMES HERTZOG government's racial segregation legislation passed in 1936. He also served as the AAC's president until 1948. In 1943, Jabavu helped to establish as well as lead the NON-EUROPEAN UNITY MOVEMENT (NEUM), aimed at fighting racial discrimination against blacks. In spite of his repeated efforts, he could not unite both the AAC and the NEUM with the AFRICAN NATIONAL CONGRESS into a broad alliance against APARTHEID.

The defining characteristic of Jabavu's political philosophy was his lifelong commitment to the Cape liberal tradition, as he believed that equal rights should be extended to all civilized men regardless of their race. He continued to uphold this ideal in the midst of sociopolitical developments that gradually took away all the basic civil and political rights from black South Africans. Jabavu retired from active political life in 1949 after realizing that his moderate approach to political protest conflicted with the more radical and assertive strategies espoused by the younger generation of black political activists. Furthermore, like many elite, mission-educated black South Africans of his generation, Jabavu was unable to discard his liberal ideological commitment in favor of grassroots radicalism. Despite pressures from younger political leaders who entered the ranks of AAC and other black opposition movements during the 1940s, Jabavu resisted attempts to make AAC more responsive to a mass membership because he believed that he and other elite Africans were uniquely qualified to lead their black constituencies. His remaining years were spent in isolation as he devoted himself to writing and making public appearances only on an occasional basis. His literary publications include *The Black Problem* (1920) and *The Segregation Fallacy and Other Papers* (1928).

Jabavu, John Tengo (1859–1921)

John Tengo Jabavu was born on January 11, 1859, in Healdtown in the Eastern CAPE COLONY. He played multiple roles as an educator, journalist, and founder of the first Bantu-language newspaper in South Africa. In 1881, Jabavu was invited by Reverend James Stewart of the LOVEDALE Institution to become the editor of *The Xhosa Messenger*, also known as *Isigidimi Sama Xhosa*, due to Jabavu's commitment to the black community's development. One of his sociopolitical campaigns was to alert his fellow black South Africans to the new political reality of that era, in which the British colonial government was instituting more concerted efforts to discriminate against and control blacks, further driven by the discovery of gold and diamonds in the 1860s. He viewed an enlightened mind and political awareness as an important vehicle for the black people's liberation and socioeconomic development, and did his best to ensure that black South Africans were exposed to propitious conditions favoring their intellectual and political development by facilitating media outlets targeted toward black South Africans.

In 1884, at the age of twenty-five, Jabavu established his own newspaper called *Black Opinion*, or *Imvo Zabantsundu*, in XHOSA, the local language. The principles of this newspaper were love, peace, and Christian justice with the objective of serving as a voice for voiceless black South Africans. He also turned the *Black Opinion* into a forum of ideas for both the Native Educational Association and the Lovedale Literary Society intellectuals. At the same time, the *Black Opinion* also drew negative attention from the Cape Parliament, because it served as a tool against white domination by helping to foment the black community's sociopolitical consciousness. Additionally, Jabavu played a crucial role in the formation of the South African Native College, which later became the UNIVERSITY OF FORT HARE. At the same time, he was also an advocate of women's access to higher education.

In 1909, he was part of a delegation that traveled to London to protest against the draft constitution that led to the formation of the UNION OF SOUTH AFRICA, because it did not safeguard the black people's franchise and rights. In 1911, Jabavu was elected to attend the Universal Races Congress. Overall, he was highly respected by both white and black South Africans, as he promoted racial unity by persuading black voters at the Cape Province to support white liberals. However, his influence in the black community began to decline as he opposed the formation of the South African National Native Congress, which later became the AFRICAN NATIONAL CONGRESS, and he was eventually viewed by many blacks as favoring the white establishment too much. Similarly Jabavu's action in contesting the Tembuland Cape Provincial Council seat against W. B. Rubusana, which led to the defeat of the latter by a white candidate, caused Jabavu to lose the approval of many blacks. He also showed open COLOURED support for the Afrikaner BROEDERBOND, an exclusive club for AFRIKANER elite aimed at promoting Afrikaner interests, as well as the 1913 NATIVES' LAND ACT that divided land in South Africa along racial lines, designating the overwhelming majority of arable land for whites only.

Johannesburg

Johannesburg is the largest city in South Africa. It is also the provincial capital of Gauteng Province, the wealthiest province and the economic hub of the country. Settled in 1886, Johannesburg has its roots in the discovery of gold on the Witwatersrand, the area surrounding Johannesburg. This city takes its name from the two commissioners, Johannes Rissick and Christian Johannes Joubert, who confirmed the discovery of gold in the area. Johannesburg quickly attracted prospectors from near and far, and the town's population quickly grew with large influxes of AFRIKANER settlers as well as black migrant laborers working on the mines. Today, this metropolis, fondly referred to as Jo'burg or Egoli (city of gold), is one of the largest and most vibrant cities in the world.

The area where Johannesburg is located was first settled by the SAN as well as by other indigenous groups whose numbers reached as high as 150,000 by the early 1800s. However, by the 1860s, the displacements caused by the MFECANE political turmoil and the influx of BOER farmers from the GREAT TREK had pushed most Africans out of this area. Attracted by the prospects of work and higher wages, Africans returned to the area beginning in the 1880s, contributing to the enormous growth of Johannesburg and creating a large labor pool of unskilled, predominantly male workers, who found work as domestic servants and in the mines.

The geography of Johannesburg reflects nearly a century of racially driven social engineering that reached a climax under APARTHEID. The result is a city of extraordinary contrasts: of glass and steel skyscrapers and squalid shantytowns, of internationally recognized universities and widespread illiteracy, and of glittering abundance and desperate poverty. With an official population of nearly four million (2007 estimates), Johannesburg is surrounded by sprawling black townships (including the most well known, SOWETO), which are home to another several million people, raising the population of the Greater Johannesburg Metropolitan Area to over seven million.

During the early 1990s, the city was once again transformed—by urban blight and suburbanization. With the transition to democracy, poor blacks who historically were not allowed to live in the city flocked into the urban center looking for work and convenient accommodation. Neighborhoods such as Hillbrow, once known for its socioeconomically and racially diverse population, became overrun by criminal elements. The poor remained, but those who had the means flocked to comfortable suburbs such as Sandton, along with most businesses. The downtown city center became somewhat of a wasteland, as all of the economic activity, including the stock exchange and economic resources, moved to the suburbs. Currently, there is a plan to revitalize downtown Johannesburg, and significant strides have been made in reducing inner-city crime.

Joseph, Helen (1905–1992)

A leading female activist against APARTHEID, Helen Joseph was born Helen Beatrice May Fennell in Sussex, England, in 1905. She graduated from King's College in 1927 and traveled to India, where she taught English for three years. In 1931, she moved to DURBAN and married a dentist, Billie Joseph. In 1948, Joseph divorced and moved to JOHANNESBURG. In 1951, she began working as the secretary of the Medical Aid Society, which served the garment workers. Through her association with the Garment Workers' Union, she met Solly Sachs and LILLIAN NGOYI, both of whom influenced Joseph's political ideology and activism.

A founding member of the Congress of Democrats and the Federation of South African Women, she also served as the representative for the Congress of Democrats on the Congress Alliance's national consultative committee. In 1955, she was the only woman selected to take part in the reading of the FREEDOM CHARTER at the Congress of the People in Kliptown in Gauteng Province. Alongside Ngoyi and others, Joseph led the demonstration against PASS LAWS, which brought 20,000 women to the Union Buildings in Pretoria on August 9, 1956, an event that subsequently has been commemorated as Women's Day. Later that year, Joseph was arrested and imprisoned, alongside NELSON MANDELA, WALTER SISULU, and others in the TREASON TRIAL (1956–1961) and charged with plotting to overthrow the apartheid government.

Banned from public gatherings and public buildings in 1957, Joseph was the first antiapartheid activist to be placed under house arrest. Throughout the next thirty years, she lived through various imprisonments, banning orders, house arrests, and an attempt on her life. Throughout her life, Joseph was keenly aware of the privilege her white skin gave her. As a leader in the liberation struggle, her race was both a source of shame and inspiration. Joseph wrote three books: *If This Be Treason* (1963), *Tomorrow's Sun* (1966), and *Side by Side* (1986). She received the AFRICAN NATIONAL CONGRESS's highest award, the Isitwalandwe/Seaparankoe Medal, commemorating her sacrifice and commitment to the liberation struggle. At the age of 87, she suffered from a stroke and died on December 26, 1992.

See also WOMEN AND POLITICS

Judaism

Judaism in South Africa has been shaped by several countervailing impulses: maintaining an idealized religious sensibility developed in the yeshivot (houses of learning) of Tsarist Lithuania while aspiring toward social acceptance in the broader white community; investing in communal institutions to limit assimilation while claiming a national identity to offset the anxiety of a small, vulnerable community; and balancing a deep ambivalence about the social injustice of APARTHEID with the fear that vociferous protest would provoke the AFRIKANER-led NATIONAL PARTY government. Postapartheid Jews struggle with identifying themselves as citizens of a democratic South Africa while maintaining a strong affiliation to the State of Israel, and with increasing religious observance, particularly as the rate of emigration has stabilized.

Although this community's origins lie with the arrival from the 1820s onward of Jews from Great Britain and Germany who formed part of the CAPE COLONY's social and economic elite, it was the Yiddish-speaking Jews from Tsarist Lithuania, arriving from the 1880s to the 1920s in the thousands, who would define the community's character. While religious observance and participation (along with a strong Zionist orientation) have developed as the defining communal characteristics, many of the Jews who arrived in South Africa, particularly in the later waves of immigration, were members of the Bund—the Socialist General Jewish Workers Union—that was founded in Wilno, Lithuania, in 1897. Lithuanian Jews were prominent in the establishment of the SOUTH AFRICAN COMMUNIST PARTY (and, indeed, also active participants in later years, as JOE SLOVO, Ronnie Kasrils, and RUTH FIRST exemplify), as well as many of South Africa's first trade unions (for example, Ray Alexander [originally Alexandrowich] and Solly Sachs among textile workers).

The socialist ideal, what many felt to be Judaism's guiding principle of social justice and a history of oppression, resulted in the disproportionate representation of Jews, relative to the overall white population, in the antiapartheid struggle. However, the religious and the communal expressions of Jewish identity ultimately prevailed, with political activism taking place on an individual, secular basis.

Statistics and Origins

Jews account for roughly 0.2 percent of the South African population. According to the 2001 Census data, 75,745 South Africans identified themselves as Jews. The largest concentration is in JOHANNESBURG, with a population of 36,000, followed by CAPE TOWN with 15,628. Economic growth and opportunities have led to a stabilization of the overall population. However, the numbers are gradually decreasing as emigration has declined and the overall population has aged.

The first organized community (Tikve Israel, or "Hope of Israel") was established in 1841 in Cape Town by the culturally assimilated, English-speaking Jews from Great Britain and Germany, followed by the construction of a synagogue in 1849 in the Botanical Gardens District. The Great Synagogue, which was the seat of the South African chief rabbi, was constructed in Johannesburg in 1914.

South Africa's founding Jewish community was subsumed by the successive waves of Lithuanian immigrants from the 1880s onward. They were mostly Yiddish-speaking, impoverished, working class, and entirely unfamiliar with the Anglo-Saxon culture. However, they placed a strong emphasis on *landmannschaft* (hometown society immigrants from the same town or region) as a means of overcoming the challenges of immigration.

The majority of Jewish South Africans follow the Ashkenazi practice, custom, and liturgy derived from pre-Holocaust Eastern Europe. Approximately 80 percent of the community identifies themselves as Orthodox, although the definition is by and large restricted to synagogue rites as opposed to the level of observance, as the term may be understood elsewhere. However, surveys conducted since 2000 suggest an increase in levels of observance, with as much as 60 percent of households maintaining homes that conform to the stipulations of dietary laws (*kashrut*) and at least some regular observance of the ritual marking the Jewish Sabbath (Shabbat).

A small number of Reform synagogues exist, as do visible communities of Sephardim (Jews who trace their ancestry to Spain prior to the 1492 expulsion) in both Johannesburg and Cape Town. The black VENDA-speaking BaLemba, who claim Jewish ancestry, have also grown increasingly more visible.

While the community has supported primary and secondary Jewish day schools since the 1950s, its tertiary educational institutions have historically focused on the ordination of religious leaders or continued adult learning. Only since 1994 have institutions been founded to focus exclusively on the study of religious texts to produce scholars trained in the Lithuanian intellectual tradition. The renewal in religious study is likely in response to the growth of Habad or the Lubavitcher branch of Hasidism, which has attracted many Jews who are not from traditionally observant households, by means of active outreach activities. In the late eighteenth century, the Lithuanian communities opposed the growth of Hasidism on the basis of its rejection of scholarship.

Although not universally affluent, this community is prosperous, with status attached to membership in professional and entrepreneurial groups. Economically, the community could be categorized as middle to upper-middle class, but it has encountered mild anti-Semitism from the generally English-speaking, Protestant upper-middle class at times.

Even though for many decades the chief rabbi of southern Africa (including ZIMBABWE, Zambia, NAMIBIA, and Botswana) was nominally held to the rulings of the chief rabbi of the Commonwealth resident in the United Kingdom, South African Jews have by and large tended to follow local rulings on matters of Jewish law (*halachah*).

The communal lay governing body is known as the South African Board of Jewish Deputies. Since the 1970s, the board has debated taking a principled stance against apartheid. Board members sought to balance an antiapartheid position, based on Jewish teachings that emphasized the dignity of the individual and opposition to unfair discrimination as well as the historical legacy of oppression, with the pragmatic concern that raising a voice of opposition would intensify anti-Semitism and endanger the Jewish community stance vis-à-vis the apartheid government and the wider white public opinion. It was not until the mid-1980s that the Board of Deputies issued a statement that made a negative moral judgment on apartheid, with the chief rabbinate following shortly thereafter. However, the statement was seen as a compromise by antiapartheid political activists.

Slippages Between Religious, Cultural, and Political Identities

An unresolved debate within the community revolves around self-identification: Should the term be *Jewish South African* or *South African Jew?* The preferred term is *South African Jew*, reflecting a primary affiliation with the religious and cultural identities as opposed to the national identity. This has, in turn, intensified the notion of an idealized "Litvak" (Lithuanian Jewish) identity. However, at the turn of the twentieth century, many Jews identified with Afrikaners, on the basis of a strong integration of religion into daily life, by participating in BOER commandos and by providing military intelligence during the conflict with the British Empire. In fact, in the 1950s, the *siddur* (prayer book) was printed in Afrikaans for Jews living in rural communities. The National Party's anti-Semitic platform undermined the mutual affinity but was not replaced by identification with the African majority.

The South African Jews' strong affiliation with Israel and their association of Judaism with Zionism has proven to be a source of friction with Muslims and with the left wing of the AFRICAN NATIONAL CONGRESS (ANC), which identifies with the Palestinian cause. Historically, Jews experienced either social exclusion by English-speaking South Africans or Afrikaner anti-Semitism on an economic, political, or religious basis. The new strain of anti-Zionism is qualitatively different because it plays across racial boundaries. While former president THABO MBEKI was perceived as being sensitive to Jewish concerns, the ANC's longstanding sympathies for the Palestinian quest for self-determination and its seeming inactivity in reining in Islamic fundamentalism, mixed with general discontent with the ANC government's treatment of crime, has contributed to a deteriorating relationship between the state and the Jewish communal institutions.

Although the Jewish population appears to be stabilizing at around 200,000 after decades of emigration, the question remains on how to engage with the broader society and retain a specific religious sensibility at the same time. The anxiety of anti-Semitism fueled by opposition to Israel's policies and the growing visibility of Islamic fundamentalism suggest that the response will be tilted toward continued emphasis on internal interests, particularly as social injustice has assumed more diffuse manifestations.

Bibliography

Adler, Franklin Hugh. "South African Jews and Apartheid." *Patterns of Prejudice* 34, no. 4 (2000): 23–36.

Gilman, Sander, and Milton Shain, eds. *Jewries at the Frontier: Accommodation, Identity, and Conflict*. Chicago: University of Illinois Press, 1999.

Mantzaris, Evangelos. *Labor Struggles in South Africa: The Forgotten Pages, 1903–1921*. Windhoek, Namibia: Collective Resources Publication, 1995.

Mendelsohn, Richard, and Milton Shain, eds. *Memories, Realities, and Dreams: Aspects of the South African Jewish Experience*. Johannesburg, South Africa: Jonathan Ball, 2002.

Shimoni, Gideon. *Community and Conscience: The Jews in Apartheid South Africa*. Cape Town, South Africa: David Philip, 2003.

Stier, Oren Baruch. "South Africa's Jewish Complex." *Jewish Social Studies* 10, no. 3 (2004): 123–142.

Tatz, Colin, Peter Arnold, and Gillian Heller. *Worlds Apart: The Re-Migration of South African Jews*. Dural, Australia: Rosenberg, 2007.

—*Steve Coplan*

K

Kadalie, Clements (1896–1951)

Clements Kadalie was one of South Africa's first black national trade union leaders. He was born in April 1896 in Nyasaland, located in present-day Malawi, north of South Africa. The grandson of Chiweyu, a paramount Nyasaland chief, he attended a mission school and was educated by the Church of Scotland missionaries. After teaching elementary school for a short time, in 1915 he found work in MOZAMBIQUE and Rhodesia (currently ZIMBABWE). In 1918, he settled in CAPE TOWN, where he met and befriended Arthur Batty, an emerging white political activist and trade unionist. With Batty's advice, Kadalie founded the INDUSTRIAL AND COMMERCIAL WORKERS UNION (ICU) in January 1919 during black dockworkers' meetings in Cape Town. Under his leadership, the ICU expanded and attracted a large membership. In 1924, it became a focal point for national politics when Kadalie urged black voters to vote for General JAMES HERTZOG of the AFRIKANER-led NATIONAL PARTY. However, both Kadalie and the ICU felt betrayed when the successful Nationalist-Labor coalition government made "civilized labor" its policy, privileging white workers over black workers. Through the mid-1920s, the ICU spread rapidly throughout South Africa. By 1927, this organization had around 100,000 members, making it the largest trade union on the African continent, with more members than the well-established white trade unions. Its rapid growth and large membership also caused backlashes among white farmers and politicians, who called for government action against the ICU. However, the ICU was able to attract support from the government's opponents and white liberals, which allowed Kadalie to travel to Geneva in May 1927 to represent South African black workers at the International Labor Conference. Even though the International Labor Organization had denied the ICU official recognition, Kadalie was warmly received by the European social democrats and trade unionists. From extensive discussions with key members of the British labor movement, he obtained a British labor union adviser's promise to assist the ICU to efficiently establish itself based on a European trade union's model.

However, in 1928, Kadalie was fired from the ICU as a result of internal fighting and formed an independent Industrial and Commercial Union in East London in the Eastern Cape Province. In

1930, he organized a local general strike, which landed him in jail for two months. Throughout the 1930s and the 1940s, Kadalie sought to reassert himself nationally, but without success because during this time period, no national black trade union organization had been consolidated to serve as a legacy for the future generation of trade unionists. Nonetheless, Kadalie united South Africa's new black proletariat and wage earners for a brief period into a formidable large-scale movement, which posed significant challenges to the country's white economic and political domination. He remained a respected community leader in East London and also served as the provincial organizer for the AFRICAN NATIONAL CONGRESS.

Khoi/Khoe
See KHOIKHOI

Khoikhoi
The Khoikhoi are believed to be the original inhabitants of the southernmost parts of South Africa and NAMIBIA. Their archaeological history can be traced back to 25,000 years B.C. They were referred to as Hottentots by the white settlers who came in contact with them shortly after their arrival in 1652. Today, approximately 55,000 Khoikhoi people live in parts of South Africa and Namibia.

In language and in physical type, the Khoikhoi appeared to be related to the SAN, who were also derogatorily referred to as Bushmen by the white settlers. Both indigenous groups speak variations of Khoisan, an African language known for its many clicks. They are also known for their rock paintings that have endured for thousands of years and have given scientists many clues as to the plants and animals that existed in southern Africa centuries ago. The Khoikhoi are a pastoral people and inhabited much of the southwestern coastal areas when the Dutch settlers first arrived. Historically, the Khoikhoi were herders who took up cattle rearing but also acquired food through hunting and gathering; the San were primarily nomadic hunters. Khoikhoi villages could be relatively large with well over a hundred villagers led by a headman. Each village consisted of members of the same patrilineal clan. The whites, however, quickly dispossessed the Khoikhoi of much of their land and pushed them farther into the interior of South Africa and up into Namibia.

Kimberley
The capital of the Northern Cape Province, Kimberley is located near the intersection of the Vaal and Orange rivers. Historically significant as one of South Africa's major mining towns, the city is known for its diamond mines that were first discovered in 1867. After the discovery of diamonds, the area was quickly annexed into a British colony named Griqualand West. Under the leadership of CECIL RHODES, the DeBeers Consolidated Mines was founded in 1888. Kimberley quickly grew into the largest city in the area, attracting many African workers needed as cheap labor for the mines. In total, five mine holes were dug in the area. The "big hole," closed in 1915, is still the largest tourist attraction in Kimberley. During its forty-four years of active life, it yielded fifteen million carats of diamonds. Overall, diamond mining has declined in Kimberley, but the discovery of other minerals, including limestone, asbestos, and manganese, has ensured that mineral mining continues. Kimberley's population has remained rather steady in recent years, with 2004 estimates putting the total at approximately 170,000.

Kimberley also featured prominently in the ANGLO-BOER WAR, when the BOERS besieged the city from 1899 to 1900.

Krotoa (1643–1674)
Known as Eva by Dutch colonists, Krotoa was a KHOIKHOI slave (related to Autshumato, the Khoikhoi chief) who first worked as a domestic (from the age of ten) for JAN VAN RIEBEECK, the first governor of the Cape region where the Dutch originally landed in 1652, and later as an interpreter (she spoke Portuguese and Dutch fluently). Following her baptism in the DUTCH REFORMED CHURCH, she married Pieter van Meerhoff, a Dutch surgeon, who became the superintendent of

ROBBEN ISLAND prison. When he died, she returned to the mainland with their children but was arrested for being an alcoholic and subsequently imprisoned at the Castel (the colonial headquarters). She was later banished to Robben Island where she died. Upon her death, the Dutch colonists described her as "this brutal aboriginal, [who] was always still hovering between" Dutch and Khoikhoi cultures. Krotoa is believed to be the first Khoikhoi woman to live among the Dutch settlers and is seen as the first in a long line of black leaders who sought a multiracial union in South Africa.

Kruger, Stephanus Johannes Paul (1825–1904)

President of the Republic of South Africa from 1880 through the ANGLO-BOER WAR, Stephanus Johannes Paul Kruger was born near Cradock in the Eastern Cape, but his family later became part of the Afrikaners' GREAT TREK north into the country's interior. He became involved in politics at an early age, first as a commandant of Rustenburg in 1854 and subsequently as a commandant-general of the AFRIKANER Republic of the Transvaal army. After leading the Transvaal's fight for independence from Britain, he was named the state president of the Republic of South Africa in 1883. The discovery of gold in the Transvaal again put the Afrikaners and Kruger's administration in conflict with the British. In the Anglo-Boer War, he led BOER forces against the British and became a battle hero. However, as the British advanced on the capital, Pretoria, Kruger fled overseas. He never returned to South Africa but died in Switzerland in 1904.

Kuruman

Kuruman, located in South Africa's Northern Cape Province, was founded in 1821 by Robert Moffat of the London Missionary Society, although the town's name came from a chief called Kudumane. In 1824, the Missionary Society built a new mission station for the local community, which became a well-known frontier post as well as the foundation of CHRISTIANITY on the African continent. In 1841, a famous British explorer named David Livingstone came to Kuruman to serve his first missionary post.

Today, this town is an important agriculture and mining district, and the original churches, mission posts, and historical sites are well preserved. In terms of demographics, Kuruman has a mixture of blacks, COLOURED, and AFRIKANERS and is the home of Credo Mutwa, a well-known author and traditional ZULU healer. The local languages are TSWANA and Afrikaans.

Compared to other Northern Cape towns, Kuruman's weather patterns are relatively mild, and the town is surrounded by lush vegetation. One of South Africa's tourist destinations, it is famous for its scenic beauty and a renowned geyser, also known as the "eye" or "oog." This geyser is the Kuruman River's source as it brings underground water to the surface in the Kalahari Desert and serves as a water source for Kuruman as it gushes about twenty million liters of water daily.

Kwaito

Kwaito is South Africa's equivalent of hip-hop or rap and plays a prominent role in South African youth culture. It emerged in JOHANNESBURG's black townships during the early 1990s. The origins of its name came from Amakwaito, the name of a group of gangsters located in a Johannesburg township named SOPHIATOWN during the1950s. Amakwaito derived its name from *kwaai*, an Afrikaans word for angry or vicious, and, because of its origins, kwaito is also referred to as gangster music or the "sound of the ghettos." This MUSIC is a distinctly homegrown style of popular dance music that is rooted in Johannesburg's urban culture. Its lyrics are usually sung in English or in South Africa's indigenous languages, featuring rhythmically recited vocals over an instrumental backing with strong bass lines. Kwaito is not performed using live instruments but is first composed in a music studio and then played as a backup on stage or in clubs for the musical artists to sing it live.

Kwaito's origins are inseparable from South African politics, as its inception took place around the time that NELSON MANDELA became the country's president. The themes of this music are the townships' angry voices and key social issues that black township youths face on a daily basis. Its lyrics reflect ghetto life by asking questions such as "why is the divorce rate so high?" and by talking about single mothers struggling to raise their children. Besides serving as a voice for black urban youths, the development of kwaito has also created business opportunities for black musicians in South Africa's mainstream music industry. This music dominates South Africa's airwaves and can be heard everywhere—from minibuses to radios, clubs, and parties. Kwaito has become popular outside of South Africa, with some artists selling records in the United States, Australia, and Europe, and eventually in China and Japan as well. Kwaito is not just music but is both an expression and validation of South Africa's lifestyle, reflecting the ways people dress, talk, and dance.

Kwela

Kwela is a South African form of MUSIC originating in 1950s JOHANNESBURG. The primary instrument is the pennywhistle, a simple, cheap instrument that is ubiquitous among street performers in South Africa's black townships and city centers. The word *kwela* derives from *ikhwelo*, a XHOSA word translated in English as "shrill whistle." It also refers to a term used to encourage musicians to join in a performance. The most recognized exponents of pennywhistle kwela, which has a swing jazz feel, are Spokes Mashiyane (in the 1950s), "Big Voice" Jack Lehore (who had a late 1950s international hit, "Tom Hark," as Elias and his Zig Zag Jive Flutes), and Robert Gumede (in the 1970s and 1980s). Some internationally recognized musicians such as HUGH MASEKELA incorporate kwela elements into their music, as do younger performers in genres like KWAITO, such as Mafikizolo.

See also MUSIC

L

Ladysmith Black Mambazo

Ladysmith Black Mambazo is a Grammy-winning, a cappella singing group that has served as an emissary for South African MUSIC at home and abroad. The traditional ZULU music sung by the group is called ISICATHAMIYA, which originated from the mine workers who spent many months away from their families working in poor conditions.

Formed by Joseph Shabalala in 1960, the group began to make recordings for Radio Zulu in 1967. Ladysmith's first album, titled *Amabutho*, was released in 1968 and quickly reached gold status. Since landing their first record contract in 1970, they have recorded over forty albums and sold more than six million records, both inside and outside of South Africa, making them the number one record-selling group from the African continent.

They rose to international prominence by the mid-1980s, working with singer/songwriter Paul Simon on his album *Graceland*. Ladysmith Black Mambazo has also won numerous nominations and awards from major arts groups, such as the Grammys and the Academy Awards. They received their first Grammy Award in 1988 for the album *Shaka Zulu*, which was their first release recorded for the US market. In 2005, they won another for *Raise Your Spirit Higher*. In total, the group has received twelve Grammy nominations.

In 1993, they accompanied NELSON MANDELA to the Nobel Peace Prize ceremony in Oslo, Norway, and performed at his presidential inauguration in 1994. Additionally, they have performed at numerous prestigious events such as South Africa's presidential inaugurations, the 1996 Summer Olympics, and functions hosted by Britain's royal family. Its current choir members are Joseph Shabalala; his sons Thamsanqa, Msizi, Thulani, and Sibongiseni; his cousins Albert and Abednego Mazibuko; and his close friends Russel Mthembu and Mfanafuthi Dlamini. In January 1999, Joseph Shabalala founded the Ladysmith Black Mambazo Foundation to teach young Zulu children about their traditional culture and music. The Mambazo Academy is being built with an anticipated completion date in 2011. The academy will house a rehearsal hall, teaching areas, and a professional recording studio.

La Guma, Alex (1925–1985)

Alex La Guma was a renowned South African writer and political activist. He was born in CAPE

Town on February 20, 1925, to a COLOURED family. His political activism and literary career were heavily influenced by his parents, who were active in left-wing politics and in the labor movement. La Guma was a leader of the SOUTH AFRICAN COLOURED PEOPLE'S ORGANIZATION as well as one of the defendants in the TREASON TRIAL (1956–1961) of APARTHEID opponents. After he turned thirty, he became a writer and published his first short story, "Noctum," in 1957 and his first novel, *A Walk in the Night,* in 1962. He wrote both fiction and nonfiction works focusing on racial conflicts and dealing with issues of apartheid. Throughout his work, La Guma stressed the importance of collective action and the need to care for others.

As his writings criticized the apartheid government, like many political activists, La Guma was constantly harassed by the police, which prompted him to emigrate to the United Kingdom in 1966 at the age of forty-one. Even though La Guma never returned to South Africa, he continued writing about his native country and was awarded the Lotus Prize for Literature in 1969. His three most famous novels are *A Walk in the Night* (1962), *And a Threefold Cord* (1964), and *In the Fog of the Season's End* (1972). Not only did La Guma's literary publications characterize the sociopolitical movements against the apartheid government, his vivid style and distinctive dialogue, along with his realistic and sympathetic portrayal of oppressed groups, have made him one of the most notable South African writers of the twentieth century. La Guma died on October 11, 1985.

Land Tenure and Dispossession

"Awaking on Friday morning, June 20, 1913, the South African native found himself, not actually a slave, but a pariah in the land of his birth." In many ways, the memorable words by SOL PLAATJE, referring to the NATIVES' LAND ACT, sums up the effects of colonialism and land dispossession on the indigenous people of South Africa. Promulgated on June 20, 1913, the Natives' Land Act was the finalization in legislative terms of a process that began during the seventeenth century, with the first white settlers' arrival in the Cape region surrounding CAPE TOWN. In this region, the indigenous people were robbed of their land as early as the end of the seventeenth century. For black Africans in the rest of South Africa, land was systematically and often violently taken away from them, culminating with the 1913 Land Act. More than 90 percent of the land surface in South Africa was appropriated from the indigenous people, whose rights to land were restricted to the remainder of the country, dubbed "reserves," which accounted for about 7 percent of the landscape. Compared to other countries on the African continent, the extent of land dispossession in South Africa has little parallel.

Prior to COLONIALISM, the indigenous people made a living from their land. With the advent of colonial conquest, colonialists in the CAPE COLONY, in particular, introduced commodity farming, which challenged indigenous agricultural systems that were not geared for the market. Scholars such as Archie Mafeje and Colin Bundy have argued that Africans adapted quite remarkably to commodity farming and were the most dynamic agricultural producers in South Africa. In what is now referred to as the Eastern Cape, the colonial government and missionaries went further and attempted to establish a class of African farmers in the reserves.

However, this colonial strategy changed with the discovery of minerals, particularly gold in the 1880s. GOLD AND DIAMOND MINING required cheap labor, something that changed how colonialists viewed their relationship with black Africans. Because the colonists forced black Africans to pay arbitrary "head" and "hut" taxes imposed by the colonial authorities, black Africans had to become wage laborers. The reserves were destined to play an important role in supplying this labor. On the reserves, black Africans were restricted to one plot per household with severe limits on the size of the plot. These measures were first promulgated in the notorious Glen Grey Act of 1894, which applied to the British-controlled Cape Colony, but when the four provinces—NATAL, Transvaal, Orange Free State, as well as the Cape—came together under the independent UNION OF SOUTH AFRICA in 1910, the major provisions of the Glen Grey Act were incorporated in the Natives' Land Act of 1913.

Apart from confining black Africans to the reserves, the 1913 Land Act also abolished the sharecropping system and labor tenancies that were blacks' alternative strategies to access and use land outside the reserves (see van Onselen on sharecropping). These developments, according to Bundy and other scholars, by and large accounted for the fall of the peasantry in South Africa. Over time, a significant number of rural people became fully proletarianized, but others remained in the rural areas of the reserves and became migrant workers with a tenuous link to land.

Outside the rural areas of the reserves, colonialists established commercial farms, which were owned by whites on a freehold title basis. As of 1994, the end of white minority rule in South Africa, there were about 55,000 almost exclusively white commercial farmers with varying degrees of land concentration. The success of white commercial farming was largely due to massive and substantial state subsidies as well as the availability of cheap black labor in particular. After the discovery of minerals, farming in the reserves never took root but crumbled, mainly due to overcrowding and the fact that men were forced to become migrant workers. Overcrowding in the reserves never improved despite the adoption in 1936 of the Native Trust and Land Act, which sought to increase the landholding of black Africans to about 13 percent of the landscape, still far too little to adequately accommodate the housing and nutrition needs of the African population. At the dawn of democracy in South Africa in 1994, state social grants were the dominant source of rural existence.

Up until 1994, there were two common features in South Africa's countryside. First, farmworkers and dwellers on commercial farms and residents in the rural areas of the former reserves (the term used to designate land set aside for black occupancy prior to 1948) did not have security of tenure. Farm dwellers and workers stayed on land that was legally owned by commercial farmers, while land in the rural areas of the former reserves was legally owned by the state, and residents did not enjoy land rights comparable to freehold title. Second, the families of the immense majority of farm workers and residents in the former BANTUSTANS (so-called independent homelands for each of the African ethnic groups that were established post-1948) occupied land on which they and their ancestors resided for decades and even centuries.

Land Reform in South Africa

Following its victory in the first democratic ELECTIONS in 1994, the AFRICAN NATIONAL CONGRESS (ANC), the dominant party in the Government of National Unity, committed itself to a land reform program. The program revolved around three components: land restitution, land redistribution, and land tenure reform. These legs were based on Section 25 (5), (6), and (7) of the South African CONSTITUTION of 1996. Land reform in South Africa not only committed the government to a market-led program, but the land reform policy was based on a willing-seller–willing-buyer condition. However, this principle had, by the mid-1990s, proved to be a failure in neighboring ZIMBABWE, for example. In the first fifteen years of democratic, black majority rule, the ANC government had managed to redistribute only a tiny fraction of South Africa's land to black farmers. Likewise, its land restitution program had failed to adequately compensate those who were dispossessed of their land.

To understand why market-led land reforms are likely to be unsuccessful, the broader context within which democracy was attained in South Africa needs to be understood. The transition to democracy in the early 1990s and the subsequent launch of the land reform program took place after the fall of Soviet communism and at a time when the global order was dominated by neoliberal capitalism. This put the ANC, which received a great deal of support from the Soviet Union and its satellites, in a dilemma. Up to the beginning of the political negotiation process in the early 1990s, the FREEDOM CHARTER, which was adopted in 1955, was the ANC's leading manifesto and incorporated radical clauses such as the nationalization of big industries and the redistribution of land.

But the rhetoric of the Freedom Charter increasingly became difficult to sustain as the

APARTHEID regime and the liberation movements negotiated a new democratic dispensation. The conflict in which the ANC found itself was reflected in its 1994 election manifesto, the RECONSTRUCTION AND DEVELOPMENT PROGRAM (RDP), which fundamentally reversed the Freedom Charter's call for the nationalization of land. Although the RDP had redistributive elements, the document equally committed the ANC, albeit cautiously, to a market-led land reform program. Two years later, in 1996, an ANC-led government formally embraced the conservative neoliberal economic policies in the form of GEAR (GROWTH, EMPLOYMENT, AND REDISTRIBUTION STRATEGY). In the same year, the Property Clause, which protected property rights originally acquired through colonialism and land dispossession, was entrenched in the final Constitution.

South Africa's market-led approach to land reform is, however, nuanced. First, it could be said that the state, in terms of the South African Constitution, is expected to take steps to ensure that citizens in need of land should gain access to it. This means that the state should not be passive in the process of redistributing land. Second, the protection of private property and the entrenchment of the willing-seller–willing-buyer condition in policy must be balanced with the constitutional provision that gives the state the power to expropriate land with compensation.

In keeping with the Constitution's spirit, legislation was promulgated to address tenure problems affecting farmworkers and dwellers on commercial farms, on the one hand, and residents in the rural areas of the former bantustans on the other. With regard to farmworkers and dwellers, the critical pieces of legislation are the Extension of Security of Tenure Act (1997) and the Labor Tenants Act (1996). For communal areas (the rural areas of the former reserves), the crucial laws are the Traditional Leadership and Governance Framework Act (2003) and the Communal Land Rights Act (2004).

Despite the laws that were supposed to provide farmworkers and dwellers with secure tenure rights, the workers' position has not improved. If anything, conditions have become worse for a significant portion of farmworkers. For example, farm owners evict workers even in situations where the latter are not offered alternative lands, contrary to what the law stipulates.

It is too early to say how the recent legislation is going to affect people living in the rural areas of the former reserves. However, the laws effectively give unprecedented powers to the apartheid-created Tribal Authorities, now referred to as Traditional Councils, which are dominated by chiefs and their appointees. Under these laws, the Traditional Councils are given administration powers over land and even acquired land ownership. At the same time, the pace of land redistribution has turned out to be exceedingly slow. Only about 4 percent of the land has been transferred to black farmers in the years since the fall of apartheid.

Contemporary Debates Around the Land Question

A number of issues arising out of the land reform program are currently being debated. One dominant debate, about the reasons for the slow pace of land reform, has two main arguments. There are those who cite two key problems: poor implementation of government policies coupled with the lack of political will on the government's part. Others, while not disagreeing with that argument, emphasize the entrenchment of the Property Clause in the Constitution as the main reason for the failure of land reform in South Africa. The Property Clause, it is argued, protects existing property rights acquired through violent processes, thus creating problems for sustaining the Freedom Charter's rhetoric, notably the redistribution of land. Although expropriation of land is a possibility entrenched in the Constitution, those opposed to the inclusion of the Property Clause argue that the formula to compensate white farmers, which is based on market prices, makes it difficult for the state to budget for land purchases, given the unpredictability of market prices.

The other debate revolves around the beneficiaries of land reform. In the first five years of South Africa's democracy, poorer communities were targeted. However, since 1999, land reform has encouraged the promotion of a class of black commercial farmers, using the existing large-scale farming approach and producing for the market as key criteria for qualification. In short, the new approach to land reform aims at deracializing the existing agricultural model.

Land reform in South Africa has also been criticized for not giving adequate support after the transfer of land—in the form of training and resources to beneficiaries. This, in many ways, makes it extremely difficult for new black farmers to make productive use of the land, subjecting them to criticisms about their farming skills.

Last, but perhaps the most important, is the tendency to relate land reform to agriculture and to make it a rural issue. This leaves out many needy people in South Africa, especially in the urban areas where, given how the country's political economy has evolved, an urban-based proletariat has been created that needs land for various reasons other than agriculture—for example, to be able to have a homestead to retire to and to pass on to one's children.

Bibliography
Bundy, Colin. *The Rise and Fall of the South African Peasantry.* Cape Town: David Philip, 1988.
Mafeje, Archie. "The Agrarian Question and Food Production in Southern Africa." In *Food Security Issues in Southern Africa: Selected Proceedings of the Conference on Food Security Issues in Southern Africa.* Maseru, January 12–14, 1987. Edited by Kwesi K. Prah. Southern Africa Studies Series no. 4. Lesotho: Institute of Southern African Studies, National University of Lesotho, 1988.
Van Onselen, Charles. *The Seed Is Mine: The Life of Kas Maine, a South African Sharecropper, 1894–1985.* Oxford: James Currey, 1988.

—Lungisile Ntsebeza

Language/Language Policy

South Africa's sociolinguistic landscape, as we know it today, is the result of different groups of people speaking different languages at different stages, propelled by sociohistorical forces that, to a large extent, determined the ways in which those who came later related to those who had arrived earlier. Before colonial conquest, the different people who at different times inhabited the present territory of the Republic of South Africa interacted with one another in both cooperative and conflictual ways. Their languages influenced one another, as is most evident in the clicks that characterize both the indigenous Khoisan and Nguni languages.

The Bantu languages, the broader category for most southern African languages according to Greenberg's classification of Africa's languages, derive from the Niger-Kordofanian language family, which encompasses most of the languages spoken in Africa south of the Sahara. They have been spoken in the southern African region since the dawn of the modern era. With episodic exceptions, the languages of the KHOIKHOI and the SAN are no longer spoken in South Africa, although highly endangered varieties of these are still extant in NAMIBIA, Angola, and Botswana. The dispossession, bondage, or extermination of the speakers of these languages inexorably led to many of the survivors being integrated into the evolving colony and, incidentally, becoming integral to the evolution of the Afrikaans language, or being forced into the arid northern parts of what eventually became South Africa.

The two Germanic languages, Afrikaans and (South African) English, are directly traceable to the country's colonial conquest and occupation during the seventeenth and nineteenth centuries, respectively. Afrikaans, despite the often passionate debates about its real—that is, European or non-European—origins, is essentially a Dutch-based creole. Other languages spoken in South Africa are vestiges of the mother tongues of earlier (Asian and European) or recent (mostly African) immigrant groups, many of whom arrived in South Africa in search of work or of a better life. Most, however, were the result of forced migrations emanating from economic or political pressures in their homelands. Of these, the most prominent are the INDENTURED LABORERS who were transported to NATAL from India between 1860 and 1913. As with the people of Indonesian, Malaysian, INDIAN, and East African origin, who constituted the bulk of the slaves that were brought to the CAPE COLONY by the DUTCH

EAST INDIA COMPANY in the seventeenth and eighteenth centuries, the linguistic result was that the progeny of the slaves adopted a variety of their masters' language: Dutch (Afrikaans) at the Cape and English in Natal. Three-hundred-and-fifty years after the colonization of South Africa by Holland and Britain, the sociolinguistic map of the country has become relatively stable.

Language Policy Before 1910

Colonial language policy under both Dutch and British overlords was based on the imperial principle: "The natives should learn our language rather than we (learn) theirs." The Dutch East India Company more or less ignored the indigenous peoples' languages. Under British rule, however, especially beginning with Lord Charles Somerset's governorship, a century of Anglicization ensued, which was specifically aimed at the Dutch/Afrikaans-speaking population. In spite of sporadic, but increasingly violent, resistance on the latter's part to the English-only policy, it was extremely successful.

For the one-and-a-half centuries between the British occupation of the Cape in 1806 and the AFRIKANER-led NATIONAL PARTY's victory at the (white South African) polls in 1948, which inaugurated the APARTHEID era, the development and use of the indigenous peoples' languages in those domains that were relevant to the colonial system—especially education and religion—were viewed as the responsibility of the Christian missionaries. Until 1910, the colonial state at the Cape and in Natal, insofar as it concerned itself directly with language matters, was intent on ensuring that English was the language of power and high status in all the key social domains. Resistance to British imperialist strategy in southern Africa was initiated from the independent BOER REPUBLICS of the Transvaal and the Orange Free State as the direct result of the discovery of diamonds and gold in the territories of those republics. Britain's policy of annexing the republics in order to gain control of the region's mineral wealth engendered antagonistic contradictions that resulted in the ANGLO-BOER WAR (1899–1902). From the point of view of language policy, the significance of this struggle (against Lord Alfred Milner's policy of forced Anglicization) is that it firmly entrenched the notions of mother tongue education among Afrikaans-speaking white South Africans. This fixation was to have a decisive influence on language policy and practice in the twentieth century.

The missionaries, just as they did elsewhere on the African continent, reduced the indigenous languages to writing in the course of translating the Bible and the Christian hymnal, among other proselytizing texts. Not only did their literacy activities open the possibilities of these languages becoming the languages of teaching and learning in modern educational institutions such as the school and the church, they also constituted an important part of the political platform on which the subsequent African groupings, and thus some of the most taken-for-granted ethnic entities of modern times, were based. Besides church and school-related texts in the African languages, the first creative works appeared in languages such as isiZULU, isiXHOSA, seSOTHO, and seTSWANA from about the middle of the nineteenth century.

Union of South Africa: 1910–1948

After the Treaty of Vereeniging in 1902, which marked the British military victory of the Anglo-Boer War, all social policy in the British colonies, which now included the Cape Colony, Natal, and the two former Afrikaner republics of the Orange Free State and Transvaal, was geared toward the reconciliation of both the BOERS and the British. In the domain of language policy, therefore, in spite of the immediately preceding hated policy of Lord Milner, the British high commissioner in the period from 1901 to 1905, both Dutch and English were elevated to the position of the UNION OF SOUTH AFRICA's official languages. In 1925, under General JAMES HERTZOG's administration, Afrikaans became a third official language by means of an expanded definition of Dutch and gradually displaced Dutch altogether as the second official language.

This period of segregation, roughly between 1910 and 1945, saw the rapid advancement of Afrikaans as a public language, fueled by a combination of government and civil society initiatives as well as the flowering of an ethnic white

Afrikaner literature. In the public service, although Afrikaans gradually became more pervasive, most transactions and communication continued to be conducted in English. In the private sector, with the exception of the militant Afrikaner-empowerment enclaves, all activities were conducted and documented in English. The indigenous African languages were mostly ignored or, at best, neglected, even though liberal and philanthropic groups, especially those motivated by their religious or educational missions, assisted individual efforts at publishing sporadic works. Virtually all non-textbook works in local African languages saw the light of day through the financial and editorial mediation of a mission-related enterprise. One of the most prolific and enduring of these publishers was the LOVEDALE Press.

These publications and related developments were important for the future of the African languages, but the "mission elite," including many of the founding members of the AFRICAN NATIONAL CONGRESS (ANC), as well as other formally educated black South Africans became almost completely oriented toward English as the language of aspiration. It came to be viewed as the language of political unity and later of liberation.

The Apartheid Era

In the domain of language policy, as in most other domains, apartheid amounted to the formal legal institutionalization of the racial order and the intensification of the social practices of the segregation era. This had the paradoxical consequence that much more attention was given to African languages given apartheid's emphasis on defining South Africa's population along racial and ethnic lines. At the same time, Africans were deprived of the necessary material and skilled human resources, through inferior black education and the relegation of Africans to low-paying, unskilled work and professions, that would have made it possible for at least some of them to emulate "the miracle of Afrikaans" that was transformed into a dominant language by virtue of the prevalence of wealthy, educated Afrikaners in top business and government positions. In language terms, the National Party's victory in the elections of 1948 marked the final acknowledgment of Afrikaans as a public language of high status. This party's entire history up to 1990 can be read in terms of a strategy to Afrikanerize South African society by, among other things, making Afrikaans equal to English as the preferred official language in the public sector. By the mid-1960s, there were five fully fledged Afrikaans-medium universities. There were also vibrant, if mostly racist and reactionary, radio and print media along with many giant private and parastatal corporations with a decidedly Afrikaans orientation.

With regard to the African languages, the situation was very different and much more complex. They were deliberately developed as Ausbau languages—that is, even where it was possible in either linguistic or political terms to allow the varieties of a particular language cluster or subgroup, such as the Nguni group, to converge into a more embracing standard written form, these languages were systematically kept separate through lexical and other corpus-planning maneuvers. This was an integral aspect of the more general policy of using linguistic diversity to divide and rule people who were being driven into unity by the apartheid state's oppressive racist policies. For the same reason, the universally valid and generally applied pedagogical principle of mother tongue education was not only abused in this way but came to be associated in the minds of native speakers of the indigenous languages with the inculcation of an inferior, racist, and divisive curriculum. BANTU EDUCATION was the most devastating blight to affect South African life in the second half of the twentieth century. The African languages were deliberately starved of essential material and human resources so that they could not in any sense become languages of real power. There were very few teachers of African languages and very few texts translated into African languages. Social and political policies ensured that they remained languages of low status throughout the era of high apartheid.

Widespread and continuous resistance to Bantu education by all the forces active in the national liberation struggle culminated in the SOWETO STUDENT UPRISING OF 1976, which was triggered by the National Party's policy of insisting that both

English and Afrikaans not only had to be learned as subjects by African language–speaking pupils but also had to be used as languages of teaching (media of instruction) in the higher primary and junior secondary schools. The waves of revolutionary, antiapartheid mobilization that followed the uprising heralded the end of the policy of Afrikaans and English as the media of instruction and, in the early 1980s, gave rise to grassroots educational movements that were inspired and mostly organized by BLACK CONSCIOUSNESS MOVEMENT activists. One manifestation of this movement was a strategic move in 1983 to systematically address the language question in South Africa. The ephemeral Education Coordinating Council of South Africa was created, and one of its initiatives, the National Language Project, came to play a significant catalytic role in language policy debates and democratic language policy formulation in the years leading up to and immediately after the negotiations that gave birth to the new South Africa in 1994.

By the time the negotiations between the African National Congress and the Afrikaner nationalists began, waiting in the wings were two sets of language policy and planning specialists. On the Afrikaner side were men and women who in practice and in some cases with deep theoretical understandings had been planning language and formulating policy in the apartheid regime's interest. On the side of the liberation movement were those who, because of the consequences of Bantu education, had to learn about language planning as an instrument of liberation.

Without Afrikaner insistence on the maintenance of equality between English and Afrikaans, it is unlikely that postapartheid South Africa would have ended up with the democratic language provisions that adorn its CONSTITUTION. These are reflected in legislation such as the Pan South African Language Board Act of 1995 (amended in 1999), the Language in Education Policy of the National Education Policy Act (1996), and the National Language Policy Framework (2002). Like most other postcolonial African elites, the representatives of the African majority at the negotiations, with some exceptions but including the ANC, would probably have chosen the path of one official language, that is, English, rather than the apparently impracticable final decision to have eleven official languages.

Language Policy in Postapartheid South Africa

As the result of Afrikaner intransigence on the language question, the new South Africa not only has eleven official languages but one of the most progressive sets of constitutional provisions on language. In terms of Section 6 of the Constitution (Act 108 of 1996), the official languages are: Afrikaans, English, isiNdebele, isiXhosa, isiZulu, sePedi, seSotho, seTswana, siSwati, tshiVENDA, and xiTSONGA. (For a demographic breakdown, see chart on "Eleven Official Languages of South Africa.") Other significant sections of the Constitution protect and promote the right of the individual or the relevant "linguistic community" to use their mother tongue or another official language of their choice in all interactions among themselves as well as between themselves and the state.

Because of the hegemonic pro-English attitudes that prevail among most of the middle-class elites and other formally educated South Africans, with the significant exception of a majority of Afrikaans-speaking citizens in these categories, the translation of these provisions into daily practice has been beset with serious problems. The shaping of a genuinely democratic multilingual language policy and practice reflecting the values

Home Language Distribution of the Eleven Official Languages of South Africa (in percentage)

isiZulu	23.8
isiXhosa	17.6
Afrikaans	13.3
sePedi	9.4
English	8.2
seTswana	8.2
seSotho	7.9
xiTsonga	4.4
siSwati	2.7
tshiVenda	2.3
isiNdebele	1.6

Source: 2001 Census, Statistics South Africa, www.statssa.gov.za.

and the aspirations of the Constitution will require decades, perhaps even generations, of see-saw progress.

Since democratization, the beginnings of the requisite language infrastructure have been put in place:

- The Pan South African Language Board (PANSALB), representative of all the official languages as well as the South African sign language, responsible for advising government on language policy;
- Nine Provincial Language Committees, whose main task is to represent PANSALB and to oversee the implementation of official language policy at the provincial level;
- Thirteen National Language Bodies, whose main task is to promote the corpus development of their respective languages; and
- Eleven Lexicographic Units, each of which ultimately creates and maintains a comprehensive monolingual explanatory dictionary for the respective language.

Two important language policy initiatives include the National Language Policy Framework, approved by the cabinet in 2002, and the South African Languages Bill, similarly approved by the cabinet but not yet placed before the National Assembly. Given the long delay in passing the bill, in March 2010 a court ruled that the government must pass a language act by 2012.

Except for the South African Broadcasting Corporation, which has an improving record as far as the use of indigenous languages, most media, the public service, and the vital tertiary education sector have tended to join the slide toward a unilingual public policy delivery, in spite of the fact that this disposition favors the English-speaking elite and thus deepens the asymmetry of power relations in South Africa. Because each province has its own official language, the Provincial Language Committees play a potentially decisive role with respect to developments on the ground. In practice, however, few of them have the necessary skills and resources at present, and the de facto language policy in most provinces is a laissez-faire English-mainly policy.

The key challenges that have to be addressed at the beginning of the twenty-first century are the increasing hegemony of English; the need to raise literacy levels by means of, among other things, the successful implementation of appropriate language-medium policies in both the schools and the universities; and the need to demonstrate the positive relationship between functional multilingualism and economic efficiency and productivity. The inculcation and nurturing of a culture of reading in African languages is the key to all of these issues.

Bibliography

Alexander, Neville, and Kathleen Heugh. "Language Policy in the New South Africa." In *Cultural Change and Development in South Africa. Culturelink Special Issue, 1998–1999*. Edited by Abebe Zegeye and Robert Kriger. Zagreb, Croatia: Institute for International Relations, 1999.

Cooper, Robert. *Language Planning and Social Change*. Cambridge, UK: Cambridge University Press, 1989.

Davenport, Rodney, and Christopher Saunders. *South Africa: A Modern History*. London: Macmillan Press, 2002.

Giliomee, Hermann. *The Afrikaners: Biography of a People*. Charlottesville: University of Virginia Press, 2003.

Greenberg, Joseph H. 1963. *The Languages of Africa*. Bloomington: Indiana University Center in Anthropology, Folklore, and Linguistics; The Hague, Netherlands: Mouton.

Mesthrie, Rajend, ed. *Language in South Africa*. Cambridge, UK: Cambridge University Press, 2002.

Vail, Leroy. *The Creation of Tribalism in Southern Africa*. Berkeley: University of California Press, 1989.

Wilson, Monica, and Leonard Thompson, eds. *The Oxford History of South Africa,* Vol. 1. Oxford, UK: Oxford University Press, 1969.

—*Neville Alexander*

Law and Society

The relationship between law and systems of social domination in modern South Africa can be closely tracked. The legal system was intimately integrated into COLONIALISM and the system of racial exploitation known as APARTHEID, which emerged after World War II. While the law and the legal system have been considerably reformed since the advent of democracy in 1994 and have created opportunities of redress for previously exploited individuals and communities, the system faces new challenges.

Law and Apartheid

The system of apartheid, underpinned by a racial ideology of white supremacy and implemented by a minority white government in South Africa in 1948, increasingly became one of the most reviled legal system of the twentieth century. Apartheid was implemented at the same time that the United Nations Charter was adopted by the international community of states and negotiations were under way for the drafting of the Universal Declaration of Human Rights. Subsequently, apartheid evolved as a contrast to the principles underlying the human rights declaration and was deemed as a crime against humanity by the United Nations in 1973.

The apartheid system violated the most basic tenets of international human rights law and policy, embodying a harsh combination of state-sponsored authoritarianism, militarism, race and gender discrimination, and economic exploitation. Therefore, the South African legal system was always of great concern to the international community, with some international legal scholars arguing that apartheid was a key factor in the development of international law as it relates to the principle of nondiscrimination and state sovereignty.

The processes of law underpinned the apartheid political project and largely kept the project intact throughout its duration. The law regulated every aspect of people's lives—for example, where they lived, where they went to school, whom they married, the association(s) they belonged to, and what they read. The legal system existed to bolster white rights and white privileges and, despite its formal edifice, was entirely stacked against the black majority population. The trappings of law and legality performed an important symbolic role for the white minority government, allowing it to believe that it belonged to the Western democratic world. It also allowed white South Africans the psychological reassurance of living in a "civilized" state regulated by law.

Of particular relevance were the ubiquitous pass courts, which rendered life enormously insecure for millions of Africans over the entire period of apartheid. Part of the legal system, the pass courts enforced the PASS LAWS and the system of influx control, which regulated the movement of Africans from the so-called homelands to the white urban centers. Africans were only allowed in South Africa's cities to provide labor, and permission was only granted under the most stringent and often arbitrary conditions. Some historians have argued that the pass system was the most hated aspect of the apartheid legal system, rendering the majority of black South Africans aliens in their own country. It also caused Africans to be labeled criminals for merely pursuing activities, such as traveling to seek work or to live with a spouse, regarded as legal in any democratic society.

Transition to Constitutional Democracy

The end of apartheid in South Africa came with the establishment of a constitutional democracy in 1994. In its founding provisions, the new CONSTITUTION outlines the human rights principles on which the new democratic state is premised, including nonracialism, nonsexism, and human dignity. The South African Constitution reflects the influence of the global human rights framework and is a byproduct of that framework. For example, the Constitution embraces international law in several ways, and the Constitution's comprehensive BILL OF RIGHTS is drawn entirely from several human rights instruments, including the Universal Declaration of Human Rights, the International Covenant on Civil and Political Rights, and the International Covenant on Economic, Social, and Cultural Rights. The Bill of Rights is expansive, incorporating a wide range of civil and political rights, as well as economic, social, and cultural rights.

The second way that the Constitution incorporates international law is that it specifically directs the South African courts to consider international law in their deliberations. In addition, it provides for the direct incorporation of international law into the South African legal system. South Africa is party to several international human rights instruments that include the elimination of racial discrimination, SLAVERY, and genocide; the suppression of human trafficking; and the rights of women, children, and refugees.

The Constitution, and particularly its Bill of Rights, has been universally heralded for the range of protections it affords and the purposive manner in which it affords such protections. In addition, it also incorporates the right of access to information, to due process, to a fair trial, and access to the courts.

Under South African law, in addition to the Constitutional Court and other courts, several bodies are mandated to pursue the human rights embodied in the Constitution. These include the Public Protector, the Human Rights Commission, the Commission for Gender Equality, the Electoral Commission, and the Commission for the Promotion and Protection of the Rights of Cultural, Religious, and Linguistic Communities.

South Africa's System of Courts

The transition from the colonial and apartheid systems of parliamentary supremacy to a constitutional democracy in 1994 placed the Constitution as the supreme legal authority in the country and provided for a system of separation of powers. The Constitution binds all state organs, including both the executive and the legislature, which is a significant shift from the days of executive prerogative that typified apartheid. Specifically, it provides for independent courts, "subject only to the Constitution and the law." The system of courts outlined in the Constitution encompasses the Constitutional Court (the highest court in the country), the Supreme Court of Appeals (the highest appeals court except in constitutional matters), the High Courts (provincial supreme courts), and the Magistrates' Courts (lower courts).

Several other specialized courts are in operation as well, including the Labor and the Labor Appeal Courts, Land Claim Courts, Small Claims Courts, Special Income Tax Courts, Divorce Courts, Sexual Offenses Courts, Community Courts, the Water Tribunal, and the Chiefs' Courts.

The Constitution creates a Constitutional Court that sits at the apex of the court structure, and which is the final court of appeal on all matters constitutional. It authorizes a restructuring of the entire legal system to render the system representative, accountable, and accessible, and one that will provide justice to all South Africans irrespective of race, gender, and ethnicity. These values impact all aspects of the legal system but especially the structure and operation of the courts as well as the appointment of judges.

The Constitution provides that "any appropriately qualified woman or man who is a fit and proper person" is eligible for appointment as a judge, and that the racial and gender composition of judges should broadly reflect South Africa's racial and gender composition. The consideration of racial and gender diversity (and, to a lesser extent, disability and sexual orientation diversity) has propelled this country's judicial transformation as it rejects the apartheid legal order that appointed only white, and overwhelmingly male, judges.

Under the apartheid system, which lacked transparency and required no public input, the process of appointing judges was at the president's discretion based on the minister of justice's recommendation. The Constitution makes provision for the establishment of a Judicial Services Commission made up of the chief justice, one judge president, the minister of justice, members of the legal profession and the legal academy, politicians, and lay persons. The commission's process of appointing judges is required to be transparent and open to public scrutiny.

Constitution and Indigenous Law

With the advent of democracy in South Africa, a challenge was to incorporate the remnants of indigenous laws, institutions, and policies within the new legal framework. During several centuries of colonialism and four decades of apartheid, indigenous law was marginalized, trivialized, denigrated, and increasingly existed to bolster both colonial and apartheid rule. Indeed, African laws and customs, when accorded authority through the BANTUSTAN political structure and surrogate administrators such as traditional chiefs, actually served a useful purpose in administering apartheid. This was so despite a significant proportion of the African population having certain aspects of their lives, particularly their private lives, still governed by indigenous law. Interaction and engagement between South African law, on the one hand, and indigenous law, on the other, were almost nonexistent.

The Constitution provides for the recognition of the traditional leaders' roles and mandates the courts to apply customary law when applicable. It also provides that "everyone has the right to use the language and to participate in the cultural life of their choice, but no one exercising these rights may do so in a manner inconsistent with any provision of the Bill of Rights." Similarly, the Bill of Rights makes provision for legislation that recognizes marriages concluded under indigenous law, provided that such marriages do not contradict the principle of equality.

Constitutional Jurisprudence

The legacy of apartheid has meant that the Constitutional Court has, since its inception in 1995, almost overwhelmingly adjudicated human rights issues. By incorporating international human rights law in its interpretation of the Bill of Rights, as mandated by the Constitution, the court has spawned an international human rights jurisprudence that continues to be cited in many jurisdictions.

The use of the death penalty, particularly against political opponents of apartheid and disproportionately against black males, was one of the first legacies of apartheid to be confronted by the court. Invoking the right to life and the right to dignity found in the Bill of Rights and international human rights law, the court struck down the death penalty as unconstitutional.

The Constitutional Court has also examined in some detail the issue of equality—the paramount principle in the Bill of Rights. The court has formulated a substantive vision of equality by exploring a range of factual situations, including those involving the rights of HIV-positive persons not to be discriminated against in their employment; the right of prisoners to vote; the rights of unmarried fathers in relation to adoption of their children; the rights of permanent residents not to be treated unfairly in the workplace compared to citizens; the rights of homosexuals to engage in consensual sexual conduct; and the rights of African girls and women not to be discriminated against under indigenous customary law.

Addressing the issue of violence, the court held the state accountable for failure to protect citizens. Regarding violence against women in both the public and the private spheres, the court has rendered judgments that reflect its constitutional commitment to eradicating violence against women.

Between the competing rights of privacy and state regulation, the South African Constitutional Court has struck a balance and has also deliberated on the sometimes competing claims of religious rights and equality. It has attempted to balance the rights of criminals in a violent society such as South Africa and the rights of individuals to personal security.

Of significance has been the court's incremental adoption of a socioeconomic rights jurisprudence that strives to grapple with the dire economic conditions in which a large number of South Africans still find themselves. Mindful of the doctrine of separation of powers and reticent to usurp the PARLIAMENT's prerogative, in addition to its concerns about institutional capacity, the court has nonetheless attempted to ensure that the government pays attention to the needs of the poor. For example, in a landmark judgment in 2000, the court outlined in great detail the government's obligations to provide housing for those most in need of shelter. It has also mandated that the government, in compliance with the right to health as delineated in the Bill of Rights, provide antiretroviral drugs to HIV-positive pregnant women at public hospitals throughout South Africa.

The effectiveness of the court in this human rights venture has been somewhat compromised by some of the lower courts' inabilities to fully effectuate the constitutional rights. Many of the lower courts, particularly those in the rural areas, are underresourced and lack properly trained and experienced personnel. In addition, the Constitutional Court is dependent upon the willingness of government officials and members of civil society to catalyze and enforce its judgments.

For the most part, the court's judgments have been respected by both the government and society at large, although many South African citizens are still skeptical of the new rights environment, particularly as it pertains to criminals. The government has sometimes been lacking in acting on or implementing the court's socioeconomic judgments. Such omissions are often a result of incompetence, hostility, or indifference. The success of the human rights legal enterprise in South Africa is dependent upon a productive collaboration between the legislature, bureaucracy, and the courts, especially the Constitutional Court. This is especially crucial in the area of socioeconomic rights, where failure to act on or implement courts' judgments may discredit the entire constitutional endeavor.

See also BILL OF RIGHTS; CONSTITUTION; CUSTOMARY LAW

Bibliography

Chanock, Martin. *The Making of South African Legal Culture, 1902–1936: Fear, Favour, and Prejudice*. Cambridge, UK: Cambridge University Press, 2001.

Dugard, John. *Human Rights and the South African Legal Order*. Princeton, NJ: Princeton University Press, 1978.

Klug, Heinz. *Constituting Democracy: Law, Globalism and South Africa's Political Reconstruction*. Cambridge, UK: Cambridge University Press, 2000.

Matua, Makau W. *Human Rights: A Political and Cultural Critique*. Philadelphia: University of Pennsylvania Press, 2002.

Worden, Nigel. *The Making of Modern South Africa: Conquest, Apartheid, and Democracy*. Malden, MA: Blackwell Publishing, 2007.

Zimmerman, Reinhard, and Daniel Visser. *Southern Cross, Civil and Common Law in South Africa*. Oxford, UK: Oxford University Press, 1996.

—Penelope Andrews

Lembede, Anton Muziwakhe (1914–1947)

Founding president of the AFRICAN NATIONAL CONGRESS YOUTH LEAGUE in 1944, as well as teacher, lawyer, intellectual, political philosopher, and strategist, Anton Muziwakhe Lembede played a crucial role in defining and articulating the philosophy of the Black Nationalist Movement during the 1940s. He was born in 1914 into a ZULU peasant family in the rural district of Georgedale in NATAL. Lembede's father was a farmworker, and his mother taught him at home. From the age of thirteen, he attended school and excelled, securing a bursary to study at ADAMS COLLEGE under ALBERT LUTHULI and others.

After matriculating in 1937 with a distinction in Latin, Lembede taught in Natal and the Orange Free State. During this period, he was exposed to AFRIKANER nationalism, learned seSOTHO and Afrikaans, and studied both philosophy and law through University of South Africa correspondence courses. He received bachelor of arts and bachelor of law degrees and clerked for Dr. Pixley ka Isaka Seme, a founder and member of the AFRICAN NATIONAL CONGRESS (ANC), in JOHANNESBURG before becoming a legal partner. It was there that friends Jordan Ngubane and A. P. Mda introduced him to the ANC; the three would play an integral role in reshaping the ANC's direction.

In 1944, Lembede helped found the ANC Youth League and helped pen its manifesto, reflecting a younger, more radical emerging leadership. As president, he urged Africans to unite and fight against their oppression by asserting their right to self-determination. With WALTER SISULU and OLIVER TAMBO, he advocated the expulsion of Communists from the Transvaal Congress in 1945. Rejecting "foreign ideologies," Lembede believed that a greater militancy was needed among Africans, "the only legitimate owners" of the land. He climbed the ranks of the ANC and in 1946 served on the ANC National Executive Committee and its National Working Committee under the leadership of Dr. Alfred Bitini Xuma. He was regarded as the primary architect of the ANC Youth League's 1949 Program of Action and was reportedly proficient in seven or more languages.

In July 1947, after only four years of political activism, Lembede died suddenly at the age of thirty-three. On October 27, 2002, Lembede's remains were removed from Johannesburg and reburied in his hometown of Mbumbulu.

See also AFRICAN NATIONAL CONGRESS; AFRICAN NATIONAL CONGRESS YOUTH LEAGUE

Leon, Anthony James (Tony) (1956–)

Anthony James (Tony) Leon was the longest-serving leader of the opposition in PARLIAMENT, leading the DEMOCRATIC ALLIANCE and its predecessor for thirteen years. Although no longer head of his party, Leon remains active in politics and in 2009 was appointed South Africa's Ambassador to Argentina by President JACOB ZUMA.

Leon was born in 1956 in NATAL Province to middle-class Jewish parents. When he was only twelve years old, he became obsessed with politics and started campaigning for the liberal, English-speaking, white opposition to the APARTHEID regime. At the age of eighteen, in 1974, Leon became an organizer for the Progressive Party, one of the two opposition parties represented in the Parliament at that time. He studied at the University of Witwatersrand in JOHANNESBURG, where he earned a bachelor of law degree. Before being elected to Parliament in 1989, Leon's first official political post was on the Johannesburg City Council. Since his election to Parliament, he has led both the Democratic Alliance and the former DEMOCRATIC PARTY (now part of the Democratic Alliance) (1994–2007). Leon was also the leader of the official opposition in the South African Parliament for seven years (1999–2007).

From 1990 to 1994, he chaired the Democratic Party's BILL OF RIGHTS Commission and served as adviser to the CONVENTION FOR A DEMOCRATIC SOUTH AFRICA as well as a delegate to the multiparty negotiations that led to the end of apartheid and the establishment of a multiparty democracy in 1994. After being reelected to Parliament during the 1994 general elections, Leon became both the leader of the opposition Democratic Party and the chairman of the Theme Committee on Human Rights in the Parliament's Constitutional Assembly. Under Leon's leadership, political support for the Democratic Party grew from 1.7 percent to 12.7 percent, making it the second largest opposition party to the ruling AFRICAN NATIONAL CONGRESS (ANC). On May 5, 2007, he retired as the leader of the Democratic Alliance and is in his last term as a member of Parliament. As an opposition leader, Leon has built a high media profile through his vocal criticisms of the ANC government for failing to address the problems of poverty, unemployment, and AIDS. He strongly believes that South Africa needs a robust opposition to the ANC in order to deepen the country's democracy.

Leon has also published two autobiographies: *Hope and Fear: Reflections of a Democrat* (1998) and *On the Contrary: Leading the Opposition in a Democratic South Africa* (2008).

Lesotho

Officially named the Kingdom of Lesotho, this tiny, landlocked country is entirely surrounded by South Africa. Lesotho was a former British colony known as Basutoland and gained its independence in 1966. However, since 1822, the area now known as Lesotho has been a unified polity, formed under the leadership of King MOSHOESHOE. Today a constitutional or parliamentary monarchy, the government is headed by Prime Minister Pakalitha Mosisili, while King Letsie III plays more of a ceremonial role.

Lesotho has strong historical, cultural, political, and economic ties to South Africa. The indigenous Basotho remain a significant minority group in South Africa, and seSOTHO, the language of the Basotho, is one of the eleven official languages of South Africa. Historically, migrant workers from Lesotho were used on the mines and farms in South Africa. Many Basotho who reside in Lesotho continue to travel to South Africa for work. Lesotho, however, is rich in diamonds and water, and it services the Free State Province (formerly the Orange Free State Province) and the greater JOHANNESBURG area through its Lesotho Highlands Water Project.

Because of their geography, Lesotho and South Africa are inevitably drawn into each other's political developments. During APARTHEID, Lesotho was a strong public supporter of the liberation movements and provided refuge to many antiapartheid activists. More recently, South Africa was drawn into the political turmoil that followed the 1998 elections in Lesotho. Socially, the two countries also share a ravaging AIDS epidemic.

See also FRONTLINE STATES

Literature

Historically, South Africa's literary landscape has been as diverse and multicultural as its people. Changes within the political and social order have continually affected South African literature and the arts. The linguistic recording of the African oral tradition, the emergence of Afrikaans as a new world language, and the international influence of the APARTHEID novel are all examples of how changing social relations have influenced South African literary traditions.

Indigenous Tradition

European COLONIALSIM profoundly affected precolonial, indigenous oral literature, which was expressed in varying genres, including proverbs, mythic tales, prayers, and songs. In the nineteenth century, European settlers engaged in the transcription and translation of African oral stories. Their interest in collecting information on African languages was linguistic, evangelical, and administrative, and the linguistic data led to the organization of written grammars, vocabularies, and dictionaries. Beginning in the 1850s, German linguist Dr. W. H. I. Bleek and Lucy Lloyd began an oral study of the SAN and the KHOIKHOI people, and their collection was published in 1956 as *The Bushman Dictionary*. The Reverend Henry Callway collected information from the ZULUS in the 1860s, which became *Zulu Narratives of Nursery Tales, Traditions, and Histories of the Zulus* in 1868. Callway's linguistic collection of the Zulu language recorded varying accounts of the activities and the course of the great King SHAKA Zulu.

Each genre of the indigenous African oral tradition has a specific form and function in society. Proverbs are short, witty expressions used to impart knowledge in the community. Myths are much longer, historical narratives used to relate creation stories. Like proverbs, folktales impart knowledge through a story. While prayers are lamentations to the ancestors, praise poems are used to honor great leaders in society. As part of ceremonies, songs are normally used. Stories normally feature animals with human characteristics. The XHOSA folktale style known as *iintsomi* is presented not only as a repetition of a story, but also every teller of the story may add his or her own embellishments to each rendition. This performance method encourages audience participation and discussion about the story.

Although the oral tradition in South Africa is used less today, it still influences contemporary literary art forms. For example, the praise poems performed to honor Shaka Zulu and the earlier heroes of society were also used during later social movements for change. For example, in the 1970s, scholar Elizabeth Gunner recorded praise poems of Zulu women who were addressing issues of identity and marginality in the home. The praise poem structure allowed women to have a socially acceptable means of voicing concerns, as the format was a public form of discourse. Praise poems and other elements of the oral tradition were also used in society during trade union movements. Singing protest songs against apartheid and spirituals in African churches provided outlets for storytelling and for building strength within the community up through the 1980s. This is a tradition that continues today.

Afrikaner and British Literature

In AFRIKANER society, the written tradition of literature provided a means to define Afrikaner identity through the creation and codification of a new Afro-European language. The origins of Afrikaans have been traced to the settlement activities of the DUTCH EAST INDIA COMPANY of Holland in 1652. The merger of Dutch and the language of the servant classes of the Khoikhoi and the CAPE MALAY ethnic groups created the Afrikaans language. Although Afrikaans became the spoken language of the Dutch settlement, the literary and the official languages remained authentic Dutch throughout the turn of the century to the 1800s. The ruling authority of the British in 1806 complicated the linguistic structure of the

Dutch settlement, as the British imposed English as the society's official language. In part an attempt to protect the Afrikaans language and culture, but also to escape the imposition of British laws and taxes and in search for more land, in 1835 many Dutch descendants, or BOERS, migrated in the GREAT TREK northward to establish the republics of the Orange Free State and the Transvaal in order to escape Anglicization.

The strengthening of the Afrikaner identity and language during this time period resulted in the First Afrikaans Language Movement from 1875 to 1898. There is evidence to suggest that writing in Afrikaans emerged first among Cape Muslims. One of the earliest Afrikaans texts was *Bayaan-ud-djyn*, an Islamic tract written in Arabic script by Abu Bakr Effendi in 1871. However, among Afrikaners, beginning in 1874, Reverend S. J. du Toit called for the use of Afrikaans as a written language and founded a group called Die Genootskap van Regte Afrikaners (The Society of True Afrikaners) in order to preserve the Afrikaans language in a written form. The society published a written newspaper called *Afrikaanse Patriot*, and, by 1933, also a dictionary, grammar school book, and translation of the Bible. The Second Language Movement, from 1903 to 1919, was a literary assertion of Afrikanerdom over British imperialism. The height of the culture clash between the Afrikaners and the British, in the form of the ANGLO-BOER WAR (1899–1902), was followed by the victorious British unification of the country into the UNION OF SOUTH AFRICA in 1910. However, Afrikaners maintained their ethnic identity through the continued use and the encouragement of the Afrikaans language, literature, and culture. One of the most popular Afrikaner writers during the Second Language Movement was C. J. Langenhoven, who wrote poetry, prose images, and sentimental ideals related to the Great Trek.

During this time period, South Africans of British origin also established a literary tradition based on stories of migration and their new frontier. The South African colonial novel defined a landscape of white South Africans from Britain arriving in a new land and establishing an identity of their own. OLIVE SCHREINER's debut novel, *The Story of an African Farm* (1883), was one of the first narratives to define issues of self and identity in a new place. Sir Henry Rider Haggard's *King Solomon's Mines* (1885) described a land of adventure laden with the promises of gold and riches. Sarah Gertrude Millin's *God's Stepchildren* (1924) grappled with race issues in regard to white South African identity and miscegenation.

The British colonial novel of the frontier normally represented blacks as savages and whites as imperialists destined for leadership in a land of plenty. To counter these images, mission-educated black writers such as S. E. K. Mqhayi and SOL T. PLAATJE wrote from a black point of view, which highlighted the humanity of the black experience. Mqhayi is credited as being the father of modern Xhosa literature, and his novel *Ityala Lamawela* (The Lawsuit of the Twins, 1914), among his biographies, allegories, poetry, and essays, helped to chronicle Xhosa history. Plaatje's first novel, *Mhudi*, written in 1920 and later published in 1930, also chronicled early South African life from the perspective of the black experience. H. I. E. Dhlomo's play *The Girl Who Killed to Save: Nonquase the Liberator* (1936) was a native's account of the controversial history of the Xhosa cattle killing. The early works of Dhlomo, poet B. W. Vilakazi, and novelist A. C. Jordan combined the creative expression of writing with political activism. This literary tradition of political activism continued throughout the 1940s and after the implementation of apartheid rule in 1948.

Apartheid-Era Novels
Early apartheid-era novels included Peter Abraham's *Mine Boy*, published in Britain in 1946, and Alan Paton's *Cry, the Beloved Country*, published in the United States in 1948. The apartheid novel was a device used to inform the international community about the injustices inherent in the apartheid system. In the 1950s, NADINE GORDIMER began writing novels that discussed apartheid from the point of view of white liberal consciousness, beginning with the novel *The Lying Days* (1953). Gordimer continued writing novels against apartheid throughout the 1990s. Along

with the novel, the South African theater also provided a voice against apartheid, projecting issues of injustice to international audiences. The plays of ATHOL FUGARD garnered international attention beginning in the 1950s. His methods of racially integrated theater, as seen in *The Blood Knot* (1961) and *Master Harold and the Boys* (1982), spoke out against apartheid while defying the segregationist laws at the same time.

The 1960s rise of the BLACK CONSCIOUSNESS MOVEMENT also engendered a black "theater of resistance," as well as an oral tradition of communicating black identity through poetry. The South African Student Organization was instrumental in providing venues showcasing black arts as a tool for strengthening black identity. The plays of ZAKES MDA, Lewis Nkosi, and Matsemela Manaka highlighted issues relevant to asserting resistance against apartheid and oppression. The poetry of Oswald Mtshali and Es'kia Mphahlele as well as Mphahlele's autobiography *Down Second Avenue* served as catalysts for strengthening black solidarity in the 1970s.

In addition to black theater and poetry movements in the 1960s and 1970s, white poets such as BREYTEN BREYTENBACH wrote poetry dedicated to questioning oppression. Due to government restrictions on speech and communication through the arts, many writers like Mda, Nkosi, and Breytenbach wrote in exile. In addition to writing about the social injustice of apartheid, women writers expressed issues related to domestic injustice and the roles of women in society. Lauretta Ngcobo's *And They Didn't Die* (1990) specifically discussed the hardships faced by black women during apartheid from the 1950s to the 1980s. While Ngcobo's work depicts issues in rural South Africa, Miriam Tlali's earlier work *Muriel at Metropolitan* (1975) gives an urban account of social injustices.

The period of the transition to democracy, from 1989 to 1994, provided an opportunity for artists and writers to begin the process of telling new stories within a new South Africa. Njabulo Ndebele called on writers to rediscover the ordinary within the South African context. During this period, truth and reconciliation became a dominant theme in many writers' works. Writer Antjie Krog wrote a comprehensive, nonfictional account of the TRUTH AND RECONCILIATION COMMISSION called *Country of My Skull* (1999). Writers such as Mda and J. M. COETZEE explored topics pertinent to South African society during the postapartheid age, including issues related to crime and economic development. Phaswane Mpe's *Welcome to Our Hillbrow* (2001) explored the taboo subject of the impact of AIDS on society. South Africa's continually changing literary traditions continue to be a vehicle for outreach and creativity, as well as communicating social and personal issues in society.

Bibliography
Attridge, Derek, and Rosemary Jolly, eds. *Writing South Africa: Literature, Apartheid, and Democracy, 1970–1995*. Cambridge, UK: Cambridge University Press, 1998.
Chapman, Michael, ed. *Southern African Literatures*. Durban, South Africa: University of Natal Press, 2003.
Kruger, Loren. *The Drama of South Africa: Plays, Pageants, and Publics Since 1910*. New York: Routledge, 1999.
Owomoyela, Oyekan. *African Literatures: An Introduction*. Waltham, MA: Crossroads Press, 1979.

—Kari Miller

Lovedale

The Lovedale Institution, located in the Eastern Cape, was established by Church of Scotland missionaries in 1841 as a small secondary school for black South Africans and their own children, one of a very few at the time. Since its inception, this institution has educated well-known black political and social activists such as STEVE BIKO and JOHN TENGO JABAVU, former president THABO MBEKI, and writer SOLOMON PLAATJE—and some whites in the early twentieth century including William Solomon, chief justice of South Africa, 1927–1930; his brother Richard, first South African high commissioner to London, 1910–1913; and the eminent anthropologist, Monica Hunter Wilson.

Luthuli, Albert (1898–1967)

Leading APARTHEID opposition leader and Nobel Peace Prize recipient Albert Luthuli, also known as Mvumbi in ZULU, was born in 1898 at a Seventh Day Adventist Missionary near Bulawayo, located in current-day ZIMBABWE. He returned to his ancestral home of Groutville, located in what is now the KwaZulu-Natal Province, in 1908 to attend mission school. After completing a teaching course at Edendale, Luthuli ran a small primary school in the NATAL Uplands. At the same time, he also became a lay preacher at a Methodist church. After pursuing further studies in 1920, he took a teaching post at ADAMS COLLEGE. In 1928, he became the secretary of the African Teachers' Association and then its president in 1933.

His entry into South African politics and the antiapartheid struggle began in 1935 when he accepted the chieftaincy of the Groutville Reserve, where he was exposed to the realities and injustices of the apartheid system. Luthuli joined the AFRICAN NATIONAL CONGRESS (ANC) in 1945 and was elected as its Natal provincial president in 1951, the same year he also joined the NATIVES REPRESENTATIVE COUNCIL. In 1952, Luthuli led the DEFIANCE CAMPAIGNS to protest the PASS LAWS. As a result, the apartheid government removed his Groutville chieftaincy because he refused to resign from the ANC. In the same year, he was elected as the ANC's president-general. Six days after the SHARPEVILLE MASSACRE, in which South African police killed sixty-nine black protesters, Luthuli mobilized black South Africans to resist the apartheid government by publicly burning his pass in PRETORIA and calling for a national day of mourning. Subsequently, on March 30, 1960, he was detained and held until August of the same year when he was tried and given a six-month suspended sentence.

In 1961, Luthuli was awarded the 1960 Nobel Peace Prize for his role in leading the nonviolent antiapartheid struggle. In 1962, he was elected by the students of Glasgow University in Scotland as the university's rector. Since Luthuli was banned by the apartheid government from traveling abroad, the Glasgow Student Council established a scholarship fund in his name to allow black South African students to study at the university. In 1963, he published an autobiography entitled *Let My People Go*.

In 1966, a year before his death, Luthuli met with US senator Robert Kennedy during his visit to South Africa to discuss the ANC's vision of a united South Africa. Kennedy's visit to the country and his meeting with Luthuli increased international awareness of black South Africans' struggles.

In 1967, Luthuli was struck and killed by an oncoming train near his home in Natal. In August 2004, his home, which used to be a meeting place for antiapartheid activists, was converted into a museum.

Makeba, Miriam Zenzi (1932–2008)

Born in JOHANNESBURG on March 4, 1932, Miriam Zenzi Makeba is a Grammy Award–winning singer whose long and successful career has earned her the title of "Mama Afrika."

Her professional career began in the 1950s when she performed with the Manhattan Brothers, after which she formed her own group, the Skylarks. In 1959, they performed in the hit musical *King Kong*, alongside HUGH MASEKELA (to whom she was married from 1964 to 1966), ABDULLAH IBRAHIM, and KIPPIE MOEKETSI, which toured throughout Europe. That same year, she starred in the documentary *Come Back Africa*, a film exposing APARTHEID, which also took her to Europe for the opening premiere. She decided not to return to South Africa and eventually, with the assistance of singer Harry Belafonte, gained entry into the United States, where she would record many of her most famous songs, including "Pata Pata" and "Malaika."

For Makeba, as for many other black South African musicians, politics and MUSIC were often intertwined. In 1963, she gave an impassioned speech before the United Nations Special Committee Against Apartheid, which led to the banning of all of her songs in South Africa and the revocation of her citizenship and right of return. She later received a Grammy Award with Belafonte for best folk recording for *An Evening with Belafonte/Makeba*, an album that dealt with the plight of black South Africans under apartheid.

In 1968, Makeba married the Black Panther activist Stokely Carmichael, which caused considerable controversy in the United States given Carmichael's reputation within mainstream and government circles as a radical revolutionary intent on fomenting violence, and cost her several recording deals and performance dates. After she and Carmichael became persona non grata in the United States, the couple moved to Guinea. Even after the couple separated in 1973, Makeba primarily remained in Africa and became one of the most influential female African vocalists. In the 1980s, she again rose to prominence on Western stages after guest singing on singer/songwriter Paul Simon's *Graceland* tour. In 1990, after apartheid's demise, Makeba returned to her native country. In 1992, she starred in the hit musical *Sarafina*, commemorating the 1976 SOWETO STUDENT UPRISING. Makeba completed her international farewell tour in 2007, a year before she died.

See also MUSIC

Malan, Daniel Francois (D. F.) (1874–1959)

Daniel Francois (D. F.) Malan was the first prime minister of the APARTHEID era and a renowned AFRIKANER nationalist. He was born on May 22, 1874, in the town of Riebeek-Wes, located in the Cape Province. Malan attended Victoria College in STELLENBOSCH, where he earned a bachelor's degree in science and mathematics and then a master's degree in philosophy while training to become a minister for the DUTCH REFORMED CHURCH. In 1900, Malan left for the Netherlands to pursue a doctorate degree in divinity at the University of Utrecht. After earning his PhD in 1905, he returned to South Africa and became ordained as a minister of the Dutch Reformed Church.

In 1915, Malan left his position as a minister to become the editor of *Die Burger*, the NATIONAL PARTY's newspaper. That position led to his involvement in the political arena as he became the provincial leader of the National Party's Cape branch in 1915 and then a member of Parliament in 1918. After the National Party came to power in 1924, Malan became the minister of the interior, education, and public health, a post he held until 1933. In 1925, Malan was at the forefront of a campaign to replace Dutch with Afrikaans in the Constitution and instituted bilingualism (English and Afrikaans) throughout the country's civil service, which greatly expanded career opportunities for the Afrikaans-speakers. This measure was instrumental to the future political developments of AFRIKANER NATIONALISM.

When both JAMES HERTZOG's National Party and JAN SMUTS's South African Party formed the United Party in 1934, Malan strongly opposed the merger and established a new National Party along with nineteen other members of Parliament. The new National Party became the country's strongest opposition under his leadership. Meanwhile, he also opposed South Africa's participation in World War II, which was unpopular among the country's Afrikaner population. His opposition to the war increased his political popularity and allowed him to become South Africa's prime minister in 1948 after he successfully defeated Smuts and the United Party. During his term as prime minister, Malan's government laid a firm foundation for the apartheid system as the National Party implemented comprehensive measures of racial segregation. He retired from politics in 1954 at the age of eighty. Malan died at his home in Stellenbosch in 1959, the same year his book *Afrikaner Nationalism and My Experiences on the Road to It* was published.

Mandela, Nelson Rolihlahla (1918–)

Nelson Rolihlahla Mandela was the leader of the prolonged African struggle against APARTHEID before becoming South Africa's first democratically elected president in 1994. Beyond this, he was one of the most prominent and widely respected persons in the world by the century's end and won the 1993 Nobel Peace Prize.

The Early Years

Mandela was born on July 18, 1918, in the village of Mvezo in Transkei, which is located in the Eastern Cape Province, to Henry Gadla Mphakanyiswa Mandela and Nonqaphi Fanny Mandela. Named Rolihlahla (figuratively "troublemaker") at birth, he received the English name Nelson when he began attending school in 1926. His father belonged to the Madiba clan of the Thembu; hence, Mandela's friends and associates have long called him Madiba, as do many South Africans.

Mandela was born into a conquered and subjugated community in which even the most promising individuals had limited prospects. Fortunately for Mandela, his father had close ties to the Thembu regent, Jongintaba Dalindyebo. Shortly before his death, Mandela's father placed him with the regent as his ward and a companion for his son Justice. Even with such an advantage, the best that a young man could aspire to in the rural Transkei of the 1920s and 1930s was a position of moderate wealth and social standing among his own people.

Jongintaba saw to it that his ward received the best education available at the time, sending

Former president Nelson Mandela in 2008.

him first to the Methodist boarding school, Clarkebury, and then, in 1937, to another Methodist school, Healdtown. Two years later, Mandela enrolled at the UNIVERSITY OF FORT HARE, the country's sole institution of higher education for Africans. He had his heart set on being an interpreter or a clerk in the Native Affairs Department, for a career as a civil servant was a glittering prize for an African. Expelled for involvement in a student protest, he ultimately graduated in 1942.

Perhaps Mandela would most likely have ended up as a civil servant in the Transkei and eventually have held a senior position in the ersatz, independent Transkei headed by his close kinsman Kaiser Matanzima. However, under the circumstances of impending marriages that Jongintaba had arranged for Mandela and Justice without consulting them, Mandela and Justice decamped to JOHANNESBURG and abandoned their rural existence. His formal and informal education had well prepared him to adjust to the fast-paced life of South Africa's principal city. Mandela also carried with him an understanding of the Thembu leadership's consensus-building process as well as the British cultural and intellectual values that permeated his education. Both of these traditions became key components of his eventual leadership style.

Soon after arriving in Johannesburg, Mandela had the good fortune of meeting WALTER SISULU. It was the beginning of his most enduring friendship, as well as a life-long political partnership. As a real estate agent, Sisulu had excellent contacts not only within the African community but with whites as well and was able to facilitate Mandela's placement as a clerk with the law firm Witken, Sidelsky, and Eidelman, a step that was crucial to Mandela becoming a lawyer a decade later. Among others whom Sisulu aided was OLIVER TAMBO, Mandela's eventual law partner and later president of the AFRICAN NATIONAL CONGRESS (ANC). Mandela soon began studying law part-time at the University of the Witwatersrand and, in 1947, became a full-time law student. His increasing political activism, however, interfered with his studies to the extent that, in 1948, he failed his law degree exam, but by taking a qualifying exam he was able to become a practicing attorney.

Sisulu and his wife, Albertina, befriended Mandela in numerous ways, including introducing him to Sisulu's first cousin, Evelyn Ntoko, who was training as a nurse. Nelson and Evelyn married in 1944. Within a year, they had a son named Thembekile (Thembi) Madiba, who died in an auto accident in 1969 while Mandela was in prison. Their daughter Makaziwe died in infancy. A second son, Makgatho Lewanika, arrived in 1950 (he died in 2005), followed by a second daughter, Pumla Makaziwe (Maki) who bore her departed sister's name. Though family finances were often precarious, Mandela enjoyed the early years of family life. However, his professional commitments and, even more so, his political involvement led to the dissolution of their marriage in 1957. "A man involved in the struggle was a man without a home life," he later wrote. The next year, he married WINIFRED NOMZAMO MADIKIZELA (MANDELA), thus initiating a prominent and yet ultimately ill-fated union. Winnie, as she was known, bore two daughters: Zenani (Zeni) in 1958 and Zindziswa (Zindzi) in 1960.

By the mid-1950s, Mandela had become a major political leader and gained considerable social prominence. His work as a lawyer in partnership with Tambo from 1952 to 1961 would alone have provided him with high visibility and great social prestige, placing him at the pinnacle of Johannesburg's African society. There were few lawyers to whom Africans could turn for legal representation when ensnared in the increasingly complex legal apparatus of apartheid or even regarding the more prosaic aspects of civil law. Mandela held the law and its institutions in high regard. Even, in 1962, when he was arrested for leaving South Africa illegally and argued, "I will not be given a fair and proper trial" because it was a political trial, he sought to make clear that he was not challenging the integrity of the court itself.

Mandela's legal practice no doubt heightened his awareness of the injustices and the suffering Africans had endured under apartheid. The roots for his political involvement, however, lay primarily within the social network of younger well-educated Africans who became increasingly dismayed with the ineffectiveness of the older generation of African leaders in challenging the white political order. In 1944, they formed the AFRICAN NATIONAL CONGRESS YOUTH LEAGUE and began to press for more direct action. Mandela, Tambo, and Sisulu were among the original members, along with ANTON MUZIWAKHE LEMBEDE, the later PAN AFRICANIST CONGRESS (PAC) president ROBERT SOBUKWE, journalist Jordan K. Ngubane, and the Black People's Convention's founder William Nkomo. The ANC Youth League believed that Africans suffered from national oppression, were responsible for achieving their own liberation through direct action, and should engage in struggle to create a truly democratic society. These themes subsequently resonated in Mandela's political thought, but he discarded his initial Africanist position of racial exclusiveness. Indeed, Sobukwe and others broke with Mandela, Sisulu, and Tambo in 1959 over this issue and founded PAC to oppose the more multiracially inclined ANC. The ensuing rivalry spurred PAC into the precipitous demonstration against the PASS LAWS that led to the SHARPEVILLE MASSACRE on March 21, 1960, in which South African police killed sixty-nine black protesters and which became a crucial turning point in South African political history.

Mandela grew steadily in political prominence. He was a member of the ANC Youth League executive committee that drafted the Program of Action, which the ANC adopted in 1949, and he then joined the ANC National Executive Committee. In 1950, he became president of the ANC Youth League, which placed him at the center of the decision to launch the 1952 DEFIANCE CAMPAIGNS against apartheid laws. In the same year, he was elected as president of the ANC's Transvaal branch. However, he was also charged and convicted under the provisions of the Suppression of Communism Act, for which he received a suspended sentence and an order confining him to Johannesburg. These events led to the pattern of arrests and trials that included his arrest in 1956 along with 155 other ANC leaders on the charge of treason, and the subsequent TREASON TRIAL that ended only in 1961 with the acquittal of all of the defendants. Mandela was arrested again in 1962 and was convicted for leaving South Africa illegally (he had spent six months traveling around Africa and to London). He received a three-year sentence and was sent to ROBBEN ISLAND prison, for the first time, in May 1963. Since he was banned, Mandela did not attend the 1955 Congress of the People, in which the hallmark FREEDOM CHARTER was produced, but, as an ANC National Executive Committee member, he had read and approved the document's draft. In the aftermath of the government's post-Sharpeville crackdown and its banning of both the ANC and the PAC in 1961, Mandela helped organize the All-in-Africa Conference, which called for a national constitutional convention and a three-day stay-at-home national strike to coincide with the country's declaration of becoming a republic. This represented one last effort at peaceful protest designed to dissuade the government from its apartheid strategy.

The government's perseverance in its policy and the use of violence against its opponents led African political organizations to pursue a counter-policy of armed struggle. Mandela, who was by now in hiding from the apartheid authorities, became a key advocate of adopting violence as a strategy and of creating a military arm for the ANC known as Umkhonto we Sizwe (Spear of the Nation). In late 1961, Umkhonto launched a sabotage campaign in which it would militarily attack key pillars of apartheid such as police stations and oil refineries, though for the most part it proved to be ineffective except for its initial psychological impact on whites. In 1962, Mandela had toured independent African countries to promote the ANC over the rival PAC and to garner financial and diplomatic support as well as access to military training for the struggle for freedom and democracy.

In mid-1963, he was again brought to trial when the arrest of Umkhonto leaders at Rivonia farm, an ANC hideout outside of Johannesburg, produced evidence that Mandela was a key member of that organization's leadership. At the RIVONIA TRIAL, he delivered an articulate, lengthy, and widely publicized statement explaining the reasoning behind the creation of Umkhonto and its ultimate objective of creating "a democratic and free society." "It is an ideal which I hope to live for and to achieve," he concluded. "But if needs be, it is an ideal for which I am prepared to die." The court found the Rivonia defendants guilty of preparing for guerrilla warfare and acts of sabotage against the government, and furthering the aims of communism but imposed a life sentence instead of the death penalty.

A sentence of life imprisonment on ROBBEN ISLAND brought dramatic changes. It not only entailed the loss of personal freedom but also cost Mandela his family life and ultimately his marriage. Especially in the early years, political prisoners were subjected to an arbitrary, harsh, and, on occasion, quite brutal prison regime. Paradoxically, however, Robben Island proved to be an environment conducive to the further development of Mandela's inner personal strength and outward leadership qualities. It took great physical and moral courage, stamina, and fortitude to survive those first years, a period Mandela terms "the dark years" in his autobiography. The prisoners also learned the value of relying on and trusting each other. Not doing so could mean withering away in isolation. Through winning a host of small battles that added up to a change in the atmosphere of the island, gradually the inmates, rather than the authorities, seemed to be running the prison. Mandela became their leader, recognized by both the prisoners and the prison authorities alike. His leadership was not that of a single individual but rather more of the first among equals who made up the High Organ that the prisoners created to run their internal affairs. It also served as the contact point for the prisoners' intermittent communications with the resistance movement within South Africa and abroad. Although there were some significant personal and political differences and disputes, as in the case of the tension between Mandela and GOVAN MBEKI, the internal governance structure managed to contain them.

On March 31, 1982, prison officials transferred Mandela, Sisulu, and two other Rivonia defendants, Raymond Mhlaba and Alfred Mlangeni, to Pollsmoor Prison. This enabled the government, which needed to defuse the escalating African challenge to its authority, to interact with Mandela more directly. In early 1985, President P. W. Botha offered Mandela conditional release from prison, which he promptly rejected. "I [am not] prepared to sell the birthright of the people to be free" was his public response. Next came an informal meeting with Minister of Justice Kobie Coetsee, who visited Mandela later that year when he was hospitalized. Officials allowed Mandela to communicate with Tambo, then ANC president in exile in London, about Mandela's plans to directly meet with government representatives. In 1986, he and Coetsee met with the Commonwealth's Eminent Persons Group, a group of distinguished former politicians brought together to try to initiate dialogue between the apartheid regime and the liberation movements. Additional interaction with Coetsee followed over the course of 1987, and, in 1988, Mandela met with a special committee comprising government officials and leading Afrikaner businessmen and community leaders that Coetsee had assembled forty-seven times. Increasingly, it would seem, the government came to regard Mandela as indispensable to achieving some sort of viable internal settlement. This underlay the government's transfer of Mandela to Victor Vorster Prison and putting him in a house, with a warden as a personal aide, following his hospitalization in 1988 for tuberculosis. The culmination of these discussions came on July 5, 1989, when Mandela, elegant in a new suit, had tea and posed for photographs (which were not published until well after his release from prison) with Botha at his presidential office. This promising start at personal negotiations ended with Botha's resignation in August and F. W. DE KLERK becoming president.

De Klerk realized that continued efforts at suppression and repression were doomed to failure and thus embarked on a new direction. The international environment also became increasingly intolerant of authoritarian regimes following the fall of the Berlin Wall in 1989. Thus, in February 1990, de Klerk surprised Parliament and the world by releasing Mandela and by unbanning the ANC and the other proscribed organizations. Already an international public figure, Mandela strode fully onto the international stage on February 11, 1990, with the global telecast of his release from prison and his subsequent public address in CAPE TOWN. Except for a single photograph taken in 1965, it was the first time the public had seen or heard him since the 1964 Rivonia Trial His international stature provided the ANC with a distinct edge in its subsequent negotiations with the government. While he shared the 1993 Nobel Peace Prize with de Klerk, he received greater attention, both internationally and domestically. Indeed, his international standing was somewhat of a stumbling block in his working relationship with de Klerk, which perhaps served to prolong the process in achieving a negotiated settlement for a new democratic dispensation.

Initial formal talks began in May 1990, and in December 1991 the CONVENTION FOR A DEMOCRATIC SOUTH AFRICA got under way. The talks collapsed over the ANC's distrust of the government's involvement in fomenting intra-African discord and violence but resumed after a lapse of several months. Ultimately, a new format, the Multi-Party Negotiation Process, brought an agreement on a transitional CONSTITUTION and democratic ELECTIONS. As the ANC president (elected in 1991), Mandela played a guiding role in this long process. However, he usually was not involved in direct negotiations. His more important contribution was his general guiding role in the overall political process, including appealing for public calm after the assassination of CHRIS HANI, a highly popular and influential anti-apartheid figure.

The ANC's overwhelming electoral victory in April 1994, with 62.6 percent of the vote, and Mandela's election to a five-year term as the country's first black president set South Africa on a new course. Initially, there was great uncertainty, for the tensions and inequities of the apartheid era persisted. Mandela's biggest challenge as president was to steer the country away from its violent past and point it in a new direction. His inaugural address set the tone: "We enter into a covenant that we shall build a society in which all South Africans, both black and white, will be able to walk tall, without any fear in their hearts, assured of their inalienable right to human dignity—a rainbow nation at peace with itself and the world." His 1994 autobiography, *Long Walk to Freedom*, while depicting the harsh nature of African life under apartheid and the prolonged struggle to end it, also delivered a message of reconciliation. "When I walked out of prison, that was my mission, to liberate both the oppressed and the oppressor." His approach worked. South Africa successfully made the transition from apartheid to democracy and achieved considerable national reconciliation. Mandela also rehabilitated South Africa's international image and was active in its foreign affairs, while much of the conduct of the government's day-to-day affairs and areas such as its economic policy rested with his deputy president and successor THABO MBEKI.

Mandela thought that one term as president fulfilled his responsibilities to his people and his country and thus willingly relinquished office. After leaving the presidency, he continued his international involvement, as exemplified by his facilitation of the Burundi peace process.

Although his wife, Winnie, had played a crucial role in keeping her husband's name in the public arena during his long imprisonment, the enforced separation and isolation proved too much to overcome. They separated two years after Mandela's release from prison in 1990 and finally divorced in 1996. In 1998, he remarried, to Graca Simbine Machel, widow of the late Mozambican president Samora Machel, and a major public figure in her own right. At last, he could enjoy a domestic life.

Since leaving office, much of his public life has been under the auspices of the Nelson Mandela Foundation. Established in 1999, it has provided him with a logistical and administrative base that has allowed him to continue to put into practice his ideals and values not only for the benefit of South Africa, but for the world. In the face of the government's neglect of the HIV/AIDS crisis that has beset South Africa both during and after his presidency, the foundation has made this issue a priority. In 2003, for example, it launched the 46664 [his prison number] Campaign and enlisted high-profile musicians to heighten AIDS awareness globally. The death of his surviving son, Makgatho, from AIDS in 2005 injected a highly personal dimension onto this effort. The foundation's other principal focuses are education and rural development.

Now in his early nineties, Nelson Mandela is less active in the public sphere. Yet he remains South Africa's most prominent citizen and among the most widely respected and revered figures in the world. His stature is surely due to his own impressive personal qualities. At the same time, it also reflects the tremendous changes that have taken place not only in South Africa but around the world as a whole over the course of his lifetime. The enthusiastic reception he received at the July 2010 World Cup final match in Johannesburg testified to his national and international standing.

See also AFRICAN NATIONAL CONGRESS; RIVONIA TRIAL; ROBBEN ISLAND; TREASON TRIAL

Bibliography
Beinart, William. *Twentieth Century South Africa*. Oxford, UK: Oxford University Press, 2001.
Lodge, Tom. *Mandela: A Critical Life*. New York: Oxford University Press, 2006.
Mandela, Nelson. *Long Walk to Freedom: The Autobiography*. Boston, MA: Little, Brown, 1994.

———. *Conversations with Myself*. New York: Farrar, Straus and Giroux, 2010.

Meredith, Martin. *Nelson Mandela: A Biography*, 2nd ed. New York: Public Affairs, 2010.

Sampson, Anthony. *Mandela: The Authorized Biography*. London: HarperCollins, 1999.

Smith, David James. *Young Mandela: The Revolutionary Years*. Boston, MA: Little, Brown, 2010.

—*R. Hunt Davis Jr.*

Mandela, Winifred Nomzamo (Winnie) Madikizela (1934–)

Winifred Nomzamo (Winnie) Madikizela was born on September 26, 1934, at Bizana in Pondoland, Transkei, a native reserve. In 1952, she matriculated and attended the Jan Hofmeyr School in JOHANNESBURG. She then took a position as a social worker at the Baragwanath Hospital. Several years later, she earned a bachelor's degree in international relations from the University of Witwatersrand. She met NELSON MANDELA in 1957, and they were married a year later. Their first daughter, Zenani (Zeni) was born in 1958, and their second daughter, Zindziswa (Zindzi), was born in 1960.

When they married, Winnie was only twenty-three and new to the liberation struggle, whereas Nelson Mandela, sixteen years her senior, was already a successful lawyer and a prominent leader of the AFRICAN NATIONAL CONGRESS (ANC). Through her marriage, Winnie was immediately propelled into a life of full-time revolutionary activism. She was arrested during her first political protest, a demonstration against the PASS LAWS organized by the AFRICAN NATIONAL CONGRESS WOMEN'S LEAGUE in 1958.

In the 1964 RIVONIA TRIAL, Nelson Mandela was sentenced to life imprisonment on ROBBEN ISLAND. During the twenty-seven years that Mandela was in jail, Winnie endured the isolation of house arrests and banishment, as well as constant repression from state authorities. In 1969, she was arrested under the Terrorism Act for engaging in politics against APARTHEID and placed in solitary confinement for seventeen months. In 1970, she was put under house arrest. During the 1976 SOWETO STUDENT UPRISING, she established the Black Women's Federation and the Black Parents' Association. In 1977, she was detained under the Internal Security Act again for fomenting antiapartheid activities and then banished to Brandfort in the Orange Free State. While there, she helped to set up a preschool and clinic. In 1986, she returned to Orlando Township, located outside of Johannesburg, and resumed her ANC activities. In 1991, she was elected to the ANC's National Executive Committee and subsequently served as president of the ANC Women's League from 1993 to 2003. During Nelson Mandela's imprisonment, Winnie was considered his political heir, and the ANC promoted her as a symbol of the struggle against apartheid, earning her the title "Mother of the Nation." But her politics were often considered more militant and extreme than those of the ANC.

Since the early 1990s, Winnie's life has been steeped in controversy, and she has become one of the most contentious figures in postapartheid South Africa. She was accused of ordering the kidnapping and brutal assault of four youths, who were suspected of collaborating with the apartheid regime, which led to the death of fourteen-year-old "Stompie" Moeketsi Seipei in 1989. She and one of her bodyguards stood trial in 1991 for murder. She denied the allegations but was found guilty of kidnapping and sentenced to six years' imprisonment, later reduced to a fine by an appeals court.

She and Nelson Mandela separated in 1992, just two years after his release from prison, and they divorced in 1996. After the 1994 ELECTIONS, Winnie was appointed as the deputy minister of arts, culture, science, and technology, but, following allegations of financial mismanagement, was dismissed by her former husband. Despite these controversies, Winnie Mandela has consistently retained tremendous grassroots support. In the 2007 ANC elections, she won first place in the election of the ANC National Executive Committee with 2,845 votes.

See also AFRICAN NATIONAL CONGRESS; WOMEN AND POLITICS

Mapungubwe

Mapungubwe was the center of southern Africa's largest kingdom from 1050 to 1270 A.D. and the progenitor of the Zimbabwean civilization. Located in the northern part of South Africa, bordering Botswana and ZIMBABWE, it had a prosperous agricultural industry, and life was centered on family and farming. Mapungubwe also functioned as a major sophisticated trading center where luxurious commodities such as gold and ivory were traded with Egypt, China, and India from 1220 to 1300. This city was home to the ancestors of the Shona people in present-day Zimbabwe. At its height, Mapungubwe had a population of up to 5,000 inhabitants. Additionally, the kingdom had one of southern Africa's most complex societies with a social structure that separated the elites from the masses and sites designated for special ceremonies and occasions. However, the kingdom only lasted a short time, as its population gradually declined after the 1300s due to drastic climate changes, which made the area colder and drier. Over the years, Mapungubwe was forgotten until its rediscovery by a local farmer named E. S. J. Van Graan and his son on New Year's Eve of 1932.

Van Graan and his son found a plethora of artifacts including pottery, glass trade beads, gold ornaments, ceramic figures, iron, and other organic remains on a hilltop. They reported their findings to a University of Pretoria professor named Leo Fouché, which led to a series of archaeological excavations that continue today. However, the archaeological findings of Mapungubwe were kept quiet during the APARTHEID era as they contradicted the NATIONAL PARTY government's racist ideology of black inferiority.

Mapungubwe's archaeological site is an area of open savannah located at the confluence of the Limpopo and the Shashe rivers. It is a testament to the existence of a flourishing African civilization before European colonization, as it represents the most sophisticated southern African society of its time and the origins of Zimbabwean culture.

In 2001, the South African Heritage Resources Agency declared Mapungubwe one of the country's national heritage sites. Additionally, on July 3, 2003, the United Nations Educational, Scientific, and Cultural Organization declared it as a world heritage site. Currently, Mapungubwe is one of South Africa's most renowned national parks, which opened to the public in September 2004, where visitors can see a diverse cultural and animal life as well as a significant view of South Africa's landscapes.

Masekela, Hugh (1939–)

Trumpeter, singer, and composer, Hugh Masekela was born on April 4, 1939, in Witbank, located outside of JOHANNESBURG. An internationally recognized musician, Masekela has performed all over the world, and his MUSIC has won acclaim from a global audience.

He developed a love for music at an early age and, at fourteen, started playing the trumpet after being introduced to this instrument by an activist fighting APARTHEID named Archbishop Trevor Huddleston. Early on, Masekela played with other up-and-coming musicians, including ABDULLAH IBRAHIM (then known as Dollar Brand), KIPPIE MOEKETSI, and Jonas Gwangwa. His unique musical style was influenced by the rhythms and activities of township life, including church, protest, and workers' songs, as well as great African-American jazz musicians such as Louis Armstrong, Ella Fitzgerald, Dizzy Gillespie, and Duke Ellington.

The antiapartheid movement became an important influence in Masekela's life. After the 1960 SHARPEVILLE MASSACRE, in which South African police killed sixty-nine black protesters, and the banning of the AFRICAN NATIONAL CONGRESS and other liberation movements, along with tightening state repression, Masekela left South Africa to study music in London. He then moved to the United States with the help of fellow South African musician MIRIAM MAKEBA (to whom he was married from 1964 to 1966) and Louis Armstrong. His career began to take off quickly, particularly with his 1968 hit "Grazing in the Grass" (which rose to number one on the Billboard chart). In the 1970s, his African roots called him back home, and he subsequently lived in Guinea,

Hugh Masekela in 2007.

Liberia, and then Ghana. In the 1980s, he helped to conceive the Broadway hit musical *Sarafina* and in 1986 recorded the hit song "Bring Back Nelson Mandela, Bring Him Back Home to Soweto," which became a staple at antiapartheid gatherings. In 1991, Masekela returned to South Africa, where he continues to compose and perform.

See also MUSIC

Matthews, Zachariah Keodirelang (Z. K.) (1901–1968)

Zachariah Keodirelang, also known as Z. K. Matthews, was one of the AFRICAN NATIONAL CONGRESS's (ANC's) most influential members. He was born in Winter's Rush, a town near KIMBERLEY in the Northern Cape. Besides being an avid political activist, Matthews was a prominent academic. He was the first black South African to earn both a bachelor of arts and a bachelor of law in South Africa during the British colonial era. He also earned a master's degree at Yale University in the United States and studied anthropology for a year at the London School of Economics. After pursuing graduate studies abroad, Matthews returned to South Africa in 1935 and taught both law and social anthropology at the UNIVERSITY OF FORT HARE for over two decades.

In 1940, Matthews joined the ANC and eventually became the president of the ANC's Cape Chapter and was elected to its National Executive Committee in 1943. His most significant contribution to the struggle against APARTHEID was organizing the Congress of the People in August 1953, which led to the drafting of the FREEDOM CHARTER in 1955. The charter outlined the ideologies and principles for the postapartheid government, as it declared that South Africa belongs to all South Africans, regardless of race, and brought together all the progressive forces in the country to struggle for racial equality.

Matthews and several other political activists were subsequently arrested and indicted for treason, along with many of the organizers of the Congress of the People. After he was released in 1958, Matthews returned to his original teaching post at Fort Hare but later resigned to protest against the apartheid government, turning Fort Hare into an ethnic university for the XHOSA community. In 1961, Matthews left South Africa and took the secretarial post at the African division of the World Council of Churches located in Geneva, Switzerland. In 1966, he served as the Botswanan ambassador to the United States, where he died in Washington, DC, in 1968.

Mbaqanga

Mbaqanga is a popular 1960s-style South African MUSIC drawing on a number of earlier urban music styles—KWELA (swing jazz), township jive (saxophone driven), ISICATHAMIYA, and marabi, the latter akin to American ragtime music. Mbaqanga spawned a number of later styles including 1980s "bubblegum" pop music and the hip-hop– and dance music–oriented KWAITO. The most internationally recognized exponents of mbaqanga are Mahlatini and the Mahotella Queens.

See also MUSIC

Mbeki, Govan Archibald Mvuyelwa (1910–2001)

Prominent activist in the fight against APARTHEID and leader within the AFRICAN NATIONAL CONGRESS (ANC), Govan Archibald Mvuyelwa Mbeki was born on July 9, 1910, in Transkei, located in the country's Eastern Cape Province. He attended UNIVERSITY OF FORT HARE and received his bachelor's degree in politics and psychology as well as earning a teaching diploma. It was also where he met other antiapartheid activists such as ZACHARIAH KEODIRELANG (Z. K.) MATTHEWS, as Fort Hare was known as the intellectual bastion of South Africa's antiapartheid movement. He joined the ANC in 1935, becoming its national chairman in 1956, and joined the SOUTH AFRICAN COMMUNIST PARTY (SACP) in 1961. Besides being politically active in the ANC and in the SACP, Mbeki was also active in local politics and in grassroots movements. In 1938, he moved back to Transkei to become involved in local politics and writing. He helped the black farmers to organize agricultural cooperatives in rural areas and wrote a pamphlet explaining how to continue his grassroots work. In 1943, Mbeki assisted in the drafting of a document called "Africa Claims" that later formed the basis of the FREEDOM CHARTER in 1955, which outlined the principles for a postapartheid government. Additionally, he wrote a book called *South Africa: The Peasants' Revolt*, which documented the uprising of peasants against the APARTHEID government between 1956 and 1960.

In 1954, he joined the editorial board of *The New Age* newspaper and wrote about the conditions, demands, and aspirations of the country's black population. In November 1962, Justice Minister John Vorster banned the newspaper's publication. When *New Age*'s editors and writers formed a new paper called *Spark*, Vorster banned both the newspaper and its staff from engaging in journalism. In 1963, Mbeki along with nine other defendants—including Denis Goldberg, Ahmed Kathrada, NELSON MANDELA, Raymond Mhlaba, Andrew Mhlangeni, Elias Motsoaledi, and WALTER SISULU—were arrested in what came to be known as the RIVONIA TRIAL, named after the ANC hide-out in Rivonia, near JOHANNESBURG, where most of the activists were arrested. They were indicted and incarcerated for life on ROBBEN ISLAND on charges of preparing for guerrilla warfare and furthering the aims of communism.

After spending twenty-three years in jail, Mbeki was released in 1987 and continued his antiapartheid activism. In the 1994 elections, he won a parliamentary seat and then became the Senate's deputy president. In 1999, Mbeki retired from South African politics and lived to see his son, THABO MBEKI, become president on June 14,

1999, before his death on August 30, 2001, in PORT ELIZABETH at the age of 91.

Mbeki, Thabo Mvuyelwa (1942–)

A key player in the struggle against APARTHEID and postapartheid political leader, Thabo Mvuyelwa Mbeki was South African president from 1999 until 2008 when he was forced to resign before the end of his second term in office.

He was born in Idutya in the Transkei, a native reserve, on June 18, 1942. From birth, Mbeki has been closely linked to the AFRICAN NATIONAL CONGRESS (ANC). He is the son (one of four children) of the leading ANC and SOUTH AFRICAN COMMUNIST PARTY activist GOVAN MBEKI (1910–2001) and Epianette Mbeki (1916–). At the age of fourteen, Mbeki joined the AFRICAN NATIONAL CONGRESS YOUTH LEAGUE. Following a strike at his school, LOVEDALE, he completed his high school by correspondence and began a degree in economics (also by correspondence) with the University of London.

In 1962, as state repression against opponents of apartheid and blacks in general intensified, Mbeki left the country under the ANC's orders. In 1964, Govan Mbeki was convicted of treason, along with NELSON MANDELA and six other political activists, and sentenced to life imprisonment in the 1964 RIVONIA TRIAL. In Britain, Thabo Mbeki continued his studies at Sussex University and graduated with a master's degree in economics in 1966.

In 1970, Mbeki underwent military training in the Soviet Union—not unusual for young ANC leadership material at the time, given that the West remained cold to the struggles of South Africa's majority—but did not serve in the ANC guerrilla army. Instead, in the early 1970s, Mbeki began a career as an ANC administrator and public official. During the 1970s, he was based in Zambia, Botswana, SWAZILAND, and Nigeria, among other countries. In 1974, Mbeki married Zanele Dlamini.

In 1978, he was appointed as political secretary to OLIVER TAMBO and as the ANC's director of information. In the latter capacity, he was credited for turning around the organization's image in Western capitals and oversaw the establishment of an ANC office in Washington, DC, in 1989.

In the mid-1980s, Mbeki emerged as central to secret negotiations with emissaries of the apartheid government in various European, North American, and African capitals as well as with delegations of white South Africans visiting the exiled ANC's headquarters in Lusaka, Zambia.

In 1989, he was appointed head of the ANC's department of international affairs. However, Mbeki was soon eclipsed by former trade unionist CYRIL RAMAPHOSA as the ANC's chief negotiator in formal talks with the apartheid government in the early 1990s. He also faced political competition from CHRIS HANI, head of the ANC's armed wing, in the race to succeed Tambo and Mandela. However, Mbeki quickly rebounded by edging out Hani in an ANC party election in 1991. Even though Ramaphosa was purportedly favored by Mandela to succeed him, Mbeki was elected as Mandela's deputy president after the 1994 ELECTIONS. (Hani was murdered by white extremists and Ramaphosa soon left politics for business.)

Between 1994 and 1999, as Mandela took a hands-off approach to his presidency—playing more the role as "father of the nation" and softening up the country's whites, Mbeki presided over the more fundamental transformations of South Africa's political and economic life. These included defining the government's economic approach; turning the ANC into a modernized, conventional political party; and ensuring a greater role for South Africa on the continent.

In mid-1996, the ANC government, largely under the stewardship of Mbeki and encouraged by business advisers and the World Bank, abandoned its existing economic policy framework, the RECONSTRUCTION AND DEVELOPMENT PROGRAM, for the GROWTH, EMPLOYMENT, AND REDISTRIBUTION STRATEGY (GEAR). The latter tied economic growth to foreign investment and promoted cuts in social spending. Accompanying this policy was BLACK ECONOMIC EMPOWERMENT (BEE), a deliberate attempt to tackle South Africa's racially exclusive economic ownership patterns by creating a black middle class. Mbeki became synonymous with these two policies.

Between 1996 and 2004, GEAR resulted in modest growth but was accompanied by growing poverty, unemployment, and underemployment.

BEE failed to address skewed racial ownership of the economy but instead exacerbated income inequalities among blacks in the process. This policy also brought allegations of corruption and, according to its critics, served to mask continued white ownership and control of the mainstream economy.

In transforming the ANC from a mass movement to a professional political party in the vein of the average Western European social democratic party, Mbeki was accused of moving the party toward the right on the political spectrum and imposing a top-down leadership style. At the same time, he has been credited for actively opposing populism and corruption within the ANC. On the continent and internationally, Mbeki has emerged as the face of African resurgence—with the reenergized AFRICAN UNION and a continental growth plan, New Partnership for Africa's Development (NEPAD), being his most important achievements. He also served as the head of the Non-Aligned Movement and has been one of the most prominent leaders from the South to engage in global debates on democratic reforms of global governance structures such as the United Nations and the World Trade Organization.

According to many, Mbeki's most serious domestic failing has been his recalcitrance in providing the necessary leadership in the face of the AIDS pandemic. Mbeki was heavily criticized both domestically and internationally for engaging in scientific debates on HIV and AIDS, and questioning the causal link between the two. He is also perceived to be directly responsible for stalling the implementation of a viable treatment program in the public sector, which was finally introduced in 2003. His policies of "quiet diplomacy" in dealing with the political violence and repression since 2000 of ZIMBABWE's President Robert Mugabe and his ruling party, the Zimbabwe African National Union–Patriotic Front, also dented his long-term reputation.

In 2005, Mbeki fired his deputy JACOB ZUMA over allegations that Zuma was implicated in corruption, although Zuma's supporters within the ANC claimed the charges were politically motivated. At the ANC's 2007 national conference, Zuma defeated Mbeki by a clear majority to become the new ANC president. In early 2008, party officials demanded Mbeki step down as South African president. ANC secretary-general KGALEMA MOTLANTHE was appointed interim president until the next general elections in April 2009. When the ANC won the elections, Zuma was installed as president and quickly set about dismantling some aspects of Mbeki's legacy by, among others, declaring a change in AIDS policy, appearing more evenhanded in his dealings with Mugabe and the Zimbabwean political opposition, and setting out to make the presidency more accessible. Mbeki moved on to work on the Sudan peace process and develop an academic center at a local university.

See also AFRICAN NATIONAL CONGRESS; GOVERNMENT STRUCTURES

Bibliography
Gevisser, Mark. *Thabo Mbeki: A Dream Deferred.* Johannesburg, South Africa: Jonathan Ball and HarperCollins, 2007.
Gumede, William. *Thabo Mbeki and the Battle for the Soul of the ANC*. Pretoria, South Africa: Zebra Press, 2005.
Jacobs, Sean, and Richard Calland. *Thabo Mbeki's World: The Politics and Ideology of the South African President.* New York: Zed Books, 2003.

Mda, Zakes (1948–)

Novelist, playwright, and scholar, Zakes Mda is a leading voice for the arts as an agent of social change in Africa. His dedication to the arts as a vehicle for development and resistance to oppression has spanned nearly forty years. Zanemvula Kizito Gatyeni Mda was born in 1948 in the Herschel District of the eastern Cape Province. His father, A. P. Mda, was involved in the AFRICAN NATIONAL CONGRESS YOUTH LEAGUE and later helped to develop the PAN AFRICANIST CONGRESS. In 1963, the family went into exile in the British Basotholand Protectorate, which became the newly independent LESOTHO in 1966.

While living in Lesotho, Mda was heavily influenced by musical theater. However, instead of musical theater, he wanted to write plays with political messages. He wrote a series of plays that dealt with racism, including *The Road* (1982) and *The Hill* (1980). Other plays, such as *We Shall Sing for the Fatherland* (1978) and *And the Girls and Their Sunday Dresses* (1988), focused on issues of inefficiency and corruption in postindependent Africa. The multifaceted Mda published not only plays but also a wide range of poems, short stories, and film scripts.

In 1991, Mda turned his attention to novels with themes relevant to South Africa after APARTHEID. His first novel, *Ways of Dying*, focused on crime and poverty in the inner cities. In addition to writing novels, he is involved in community development initiatives, including a honey and a beekeeping cooperative, which he developed in 2001 with women in the rural Eastern Cape village of Lower Telle. He also works with the Market Theater in JOHANNESBURG on the traveling play, *Broken Dreams*, which was produced for black township youths. Mda returned to his alma mater, Ohio University, in the mid-2000s to teach creative writing and has been dividing his time between South Africa and the United States.

Media

The history of media in South Africa has been one of contestation from the beginning. From their inception, the different forms of South African media have reflected broad political, cultural, and social power relationships and continue to do so.

As in many other African countries, the first newspapers were aimed at colonial/postcolonial elites. The first newspaper in the country, the bilingual *The Cape Town Gazette and African Advertiser/Kaapsche Stads Courant en Afrikaansche Berigter*, was published on August 16, 1800, serving the white settler communities in the CAPE COLONY. Later renamed the *Kaapsche Courant* and subsequently *The Cape of Good Hope Government Gazette*, it remained the only newspaper in the Cape until the founding of the *South African Commercial Advertiser* in 1824. The latter, South Africa's first privately owned and independent weekly paper, was edited by Thomas Pringle and John Fairbairn. After publishing stories with political implications, they clashed with the British colonial governor of the Cape, Lord Charles Somerset, who ordered the publication to cease.

This was the start of a prolonged struggle with the authorities, which was eventually won by the press when the "Magna Carta" of freedom of the press in South Africa, Ordinance No. 60 of May 8, 1829, was decreed and allowed it to publish freely, albeit under certain conditions. The arrival of large numbers of British settlers (and their printing presses) in 1820 provided impetus to the news industry with papers such as the influential *Graham's Town Journal* in the eastern Cape Colony.

Black Media

The Christian missions established by the British provided a crucial impetus for the development of a black press. The first newspaper aimed at a black audience was *Umshumayeli Wendaba* (Publisher of the News) in the eastern Cape Colony in 1837. Several other missionary newspapers followed, with *Isigidimi Sama Xosa* credited as the first to be edited by blacks. Although some muted political resistance in these papers was evident, the mission press also contributed to a widening gap between a minority, mission-educated black elite and the rural-based majority.

In 1884, the black press moved into a new independent phase with the publication of *Imvo Zabantsundu*, founded by JOHN TENGU JABAVU. This was the first paper that was not only written by blacks and aimed at a black readership but also owned by blacks. Additionally, it clearly expressed political points of view. Stronger, if still cautious, political positions were taken up by subsequent papers such as *Izwi la Bantu* and *Ilanga lase Natal*. Soon after its founding in 1912, the AFRICAN NATIONAL CONGRESS (ANC) established *Abantu-Batho* as a mouthpiece, but the stirrings of political sentiments in the independent black press were later subsumed by the major interventions of white capital into the black newspaper market. The establishment of *Bantu World* in 1932 redefined the mass black press in terms of the profit motive recognized by white owners of capital and was based on the Western tabloid format.

The iconic *DRUM* magazine also appealed to popular sentiments in the 1950s. Owned by the white British journalist Jim Bailey, it showcased some of the best writers of the era (for example, Can Themba, Casey Motsisi, ALEX LA GUMA, Henry Nxumalo, Nat Nakasa, and Todd Matshikiza). Its critics point out that it glamorized life in the black townships rather than provide political resistance, although some investigative reporting did highlight the plight of blacks. The media company Naspers, built on AFRIKANER capital, bought *Drum*, along with other black titles like *City Press* and *True Love* in 1984.

An alternative black press aimed at political resistance rather than profit emerged in the same era as the white-owned black press, reaching its zenith in the 1980s when APARTHEID was at its fiercest. The first Africanist (*The Africanist*) and Marxist (*Inkululeko*, later renamed *Umsebenzi*) publications were established in the 1930s, but these dwindled by the 1960s as state repression increased. In the 1960s, the BLACK CONSCIOUSNESS MOVEMENT led to the reemergence of alternative publications and laid the foundations for the development of an active resistance press in the 1980s. *Grassroots, New Nation,* and the *Weekly Mail* were well-known examples of, respectively, a left-wing community press, a left-commercial press, and an independent social-democratic press.

White Media

Under apartheid, the mainstream white press was divided across political allegiances that correlated with English or Afrikaans, with limited attempts to cater to black or COLOURED audiences (for example, in separate, "extra" editions). While English-language newspapers linked to mining capital provided a limited, procapitalist critique of apartheid, Afrikaans-language newspapers (most of them owned by Nasionale Pers, or Naspers as it is known today) supported AFRIKANER NATIONALISM and the apartheid state, albeit later in a reformist mode. A limited number of smaller Afrikaans newspapers and magazines (for example, *Saamstaan* and *Vrye Weekblad*) counted among the alternative press. Alternative or resistance publications (mainly in English, but also in ZULU and in Afrikaans) were constantly harassed, and, under the states of emergency in the late 1980s, journalists were often arrested and publications banned.

Under apartheid, the broadcasting sector reflected the state's racial policies in structure and content. The white language groups used the medium to maintain their cultural and linguistic identities while imposing the ideology of distinct ethnicities. The South African Broadcasting Corporation (SABC) was dominated by white interests but catered to the nonwhite ethnic groups through a network of stations and channels that followed the apartheid logic of "separate development." Television was kept out of the country until 1976, because of the perceived threat to Afrikaans culture and fears of exposing black audiences to international democratic discourses that could incite further political resistance. SABC television supported state policies through self-censorship, often succumbing to direct government intervention in content.

The Media After 1994

The country's democratization and end of apartheid brought some significant shifts in the media landscape. Freedom of expression was guaranteed in the new CONSTITUTION, adopted in 1996, which created an open society where the media enjoyed unprecedented liberties. Ethical codes for the media were drawn up as part of a system of self-regulation, through complaints bodies such as the Press Ombudsman and the Broadcasting Complaints Commission of South Africa. Despite these constitutional guarantees and self-regulatory landscapes, tensions between media and government continue and from time to time boil over in conflicts. The ANC government has often been accused by members of the media industry of not taking press freedom seriously enough.

Formal regulation of the broadcast industry now takes place through the Independent Communications Authority of South Africa on three levels: public, private, and community. Since the early 1990s, the SABC went through a complicated transformation in an attempt to reposition itself as a public broadcaster, while having to stay afloat financially with minimal government subsidy. Increased global competition, facilitated through the free-to-air entertainment channel e.tv, global commercial content carried on pay-television channel M-Net, and the satellite service DSTV, increased this pressure. Although now governed by a board answering to PARLIAMENT, the SABC remains under constant attack from critics pointing to perceived bias toward the ANC and political interference in editorial content.

Additionally, the industry saw some major shifts in ownership and, in some cases, shareholding passed onto black owners through a series of BLACK ECONOMIC EMPOWERMENT deals. Editorial staffs also became more representative of the country's demography, with black editors taking charge of most of the major print titles in the country. A professional body of journalists, the South African National Editors' Forum (SANEF), was formed in 1996 out of the White Conference of Editors and the Black Editors' Forum. This body actively engages the government on issues pertaining to press freedom and sets standards for journalistic professionalism. On occasion, the boundaries of what constitutes journalistic professionalism in a nascent democracy have been tested. One example includes a range of new tabloid newspapers, which emerged from 2001 onward, that were aimed at the poor black majority and enjoyed phenomenal commercial success. Their popularity suggests that, for the first time since democratization, the majority of the South African population found a space in the print media where their interests and lived experiences were articulated. The tabloids, however, are reviled for their sensationalist approach, which brought them into conflict with SANEF, which demanded that they comply with the mainstream ethical guidelines.

After the demise of apartheid, the alternative media sector dwindled, leaving the public sphere dominated by commercial mainstream media. Attempts have been made with varying degrees of success to broaden the media sphere to include previously marginalized voices through the licensing of community radio stations and the establishment of the Media Diversity and Development Agency, which can provide startup funding for grassroots publications.

South Africa also leads the continent in the adoption of new media technologies, with increasing convergence between media platforms. Access to these new formats, however, remains highly unequal across racial and class groups. As in other parts of the continent, mobile telephony has enjoyed a high penetration rate and is becoming a significant vehicle for Internet access.

Although the media industry in postapartheid South Africa continues to grow, with new outlets continually added to the already pluralist offering, critics have pointed out that this diversity does not always imply a wide enough range of viewpoints. Participation in the mediated public sphere remains dominated by elite interests, and attempts to bring about structural change have proved limited.

More than a decade after democracy, the South African media continue to be the continent's powerhouse. Aided by sophisticated technologies and big capital investment, the South African media continue to broaden their sphere of influence by penetrating other African countries and even spreading globally. Using their advanced technological sophistication and organizational infrastructure to further broaden the public sphere at home remains a challenge for the South African media.

See also DRUM

Bibliography

Claassen, George. "Breaking the Mold of Political Subservience: Vrye Weekblad and the Afrikaans Alternative Press." In *South Africa's Resistance Press: Alternative Voices in the Last Generation Under Apartheid.* Edited by Les Switzer and Mohamed Adhikari. Athens: Ohio University Press, 2000, 404–457.

De Beer, Arrie S., ed. *Mass Media for the Nineties.* Pretoria, South Africa: Van Schaik, 1993.

Horwitz, Robert Britt. *Communication and Democratic Reform in South Africa.* Cambridge, UK: University of Cambridge Press, 2001.

Switzer, Les, ed. *South Africa's Alternative Press: Voices of Protest and Resistance, 1880–1960.* Cambridge: Cambridge University Press, 1997.

Switzer, Les, and Mohamed Adhikari, eds. *South Africa's Resistance Press: Alternative Voices in the Last Generation Under Apartheid.* Athens: Ohio University Press, 2000.

Tomaselli, Keyan, and Hopeton Dunn, eds. *Media, Democracy, and Renewal in Southern Africa.* Colorado Springs, CO: International Academic Publishers, 2001.

Tomaselli, Keyan, and P. Eric Louw. *The Alternative Press in South Africa.* Bellville, South Africa: Anthropos, 1991.

Wasserman, Herman. *Tabloid Journalism in South Africa: True Story!* Bloomington: Indiana University Press, 2010.

—Herman Wasserman

Meyer, Roelof (Roelf) Petrus (1947–)

Roelof (Roelf) Petrus Meyer is a South African businessman and former politician who played an important role in negotiating his country's transition from a NATIONAL PARTY–dominated APARTHEID government to the 1994 democratic ELECTIONS, which paved the way for the victory by the AFRICAN NATIONAL CONGRESS (ANC). Meyer was born in PORT ELIZABETH in the eastern Cape Province on July 16, 1947. He attended the University of the Free State, where he earned bachelor degrees in commerce in 1968 and in law in 1971. Upon receiving his university degrees, he worked as an attorney in PRETORIA and in JOHANNESBURG until 1980. Meyer entered the political scene in 1979 when he became a member of Parliament for the ruling National Party. He later served as the deputy of law and order in 1986 and then as the deputy minister of constitutional development until 1991. Meyer also served as the minister of defense for a year, from 1991 to 1992, under President F. W. DE KLERK's government. After resigning from his post as the defense minister in May 1992, he became the minister of constitutional affairs and also the minister of communication, which brought him into the negotiation process with the ANC to prepare for the country's transition into the postapartheid era.

Meyer became well known when he served as the National Party's chief negotiator in the Multiparty Negotiating Forum in 1993. As the party's chief negotiator, he was able to establish an effective and amicable relationship with the ANC's chief negotiator, CYRIL RAMAPHOSA. After the end of the political negotiations between the two parties in 1993, Meyer became the National Party government's key representative in the Transitional Executive Council. After the 1994 elections, he became the minister of constitutional development and provincial affairs in President NELSON MANDELA's administration. In 1996, Meyer became the secretary-general of the National Party when it withdrew from Mandela's government after the new CONSTITUTION was ratified in the same year. However, a year later he resigned as the party's secretary-general and withdrew his membership in 1997 because strong resistance from its conservative faction thwarted the party's adaptation to South Africa's new political environment.

After leaving the National Party, Meyer cofounded the UNITED DEMOCRATIC MOVEMENT (UDM) with BANTU HOLOMISA, a former Transkeian leader. In the 1999 elections, the UDM won fourteen seats in the South African PARLIAMENT and became one of the country's main opposition parties. In 2000, Meyer retired from the political arena and became active in the business world, serving as the director and later as the deputy executive chairman of the TILCA Infrastructure Corporation. He became a member of Armscor's board of directors. Meyer also serves as a consultant on peace processes around the globe: in Northern Ireland, Sri Lanka, Rwanda, Burundi, Kosovo, Bolivia, Spain's Basque Region, and the Middle East. Additionally, he has held and holds a number of international positions, which include the Tip O'Neill Chair in Peace Studies at the University of Ulster in Northern Ireland in 2001 and membership in the Strategy Committee of the Project on Justice in Times of Transition at Harvard University as well as chairman of South Africa's Civil Society Initiative.

Mfecane

Mfecane refers to a period of political turmoil, social upheaval, and migration in southern Africa from 1815 to 1840, which is often ascribed to the emergence of a centralized and militarized ZULU state under the leadership of King SHAKA. *Mfecane,* or *Difiqane,* are two words of uncertain origin that are most commonly translated into English as "the crushing" or "the scattering." The creation and consolidation of other indigenous groups, including the NDEBELE, the MFENGU, and the Makololo, as well as the creation of the LESOTHO state, have also been attributed to the Mfecane.

The meaning, causes, and reading of the Mfecane remain an issue for considerable debate. Some have attributed the political turmoil to the growing population in Zululand and the introduction of maize (corn) by Portuguese settlers, which augmented the food supply and contributed to the increased population. However, by the 1800s, declining rainfall and a multiyear drought made arable land and food again a prized commodity, as well as the source of great competition. By 1830, population pressures also came from an encroaching white settler population as they were increasingly moving into the area.

Another contributing factor cited for the Mfecane was the change in Zulu military tactics and strategies. It was during this time that Shaka was able to amass a standing army and introduced a process of conscription for all adult males. In addition, the Zulu began using shorter stabbing spears instead of longer throwing spears, which made them more effective in close combat. Shaka defeated many other Nguni groups in the area, incorporated some of the women and children into the Zulu nation, and forced the men to flee.

Some within the Zulu nation, most notably MZILIKAZI's Ndebele, became increasingly disgruntled with Shaka's stern rule. The Ndebele migrated northwestward, taking with them many of the Zulu's devastating military tactics. Under Mzilikazi's leadership, the Ndebele battled many African groups and white settler groups on their migration north and finally settled in Matabeleland, located in the southern part of present-day ZIMBABWE. The flight of other groups from Zululand, such as the Hlubi and the Ngwane, also left a path of destruction in its wake. In fact, the mass migrations out of Zululand were a major source of chaos and destruction at the time, with some groups being scattered in the process while others were able to consolidate into new kingdoms, most notably the kingdoms of SWAZILAND and Gaza in present-day MOZAMBIQUE under the leadership of Soshangane, a former general in Shaka's army.

See also BRITISH IMPERIALISM AND SETTLER COLONIALISM (1795–1870); SHAKA; ZULU

Mfengu

The Mfengu were refugees of the MFECANE who traveled from the interior of southern Africa to the eastern frontier of the CAPE COLONY and settled there around 1823. The Mfengu ethnic group comprised members from the Bhaca, Bhele, Zizi, and Hlubi chiefdoms. For the British, the Mfengu played an important role in serving as a buffer between the indigenous XHOSA and the BOER settlers. They assisted Governor Benjamin D'Urban in his campaigns against the Xhosa chief. When the war with the Xhosa was over, D'Urban's army escorted the Mfengu and helped them settle on former Xhosa lands in the Ciskei in present-day Eastern Cape Province. Besides providing both labor and military assistance for the British, this group also established a flourishing trade business by selling grain, tobacco, cattle, milk, and firewood. Additionally, they adopted farming techniques from white farmers, which allowed them to become better integrated with the colonial mercantile economy. The Mfengu militia partook in Britain's three frontier wars of territorial expansion and were rewarded with large parcels of land taken from the Xhosa by the British colonial forces in return for their loyalty.

See also MFECANE

Migrant Labor

In the history of South Africa's capitalism, white minority rule, and racial discrimination, the expression "migrant labor" has a highly specific meaning, which is not limited to the economic and labor market dynamics of migration. Opponents of segregation and APARTHEID have usually and significantly employed the expression "migrant labor system" to define the interactions between the socioeconomic dynamics of migration, the institutional processes, and the juridical constructs that reproduced a migrant black (predominantly African) working class as a low-wage, vulnerable, and exploitable workforce.

Labor migrations are a long-standing feature of South African history. As such, they precede the establishment of racial segregation by European settlers. Unfree employment has, however, shaped black labor's mobility since the beginning of European colonization: Asian and African slaves were employed by the DUTCH EAST INDIA COMPANY in the CAPE COLONY, while British sugar plantations in nineteenth-century NATAL used migrants from MOZAMBIQUE and INDENTURED LABORERS from India in a racially segregated labor process.

It was only after the mineral discoveries during the second half of the nineteenth century, particularly with the beginning of gold mining in the Witwatersrand in 1886, that the migrant labor system acquired its modern characteristics and its linkages with fully fledged institutions of racial segregation. Challenging conventional views that saw migration as primarily determined by economic necessity and individual worker choices, scholars such as Norman Levy, Marian Lacey, and RUTH FIRST emphasized that the profitable exploitation of South Africa's mineral reserves required regular flows of a migrant labor force with remunerations kept artificially low. Labor migration and racial segregation provided the means through which African populations, impoverished by the colonial destruction of local peasant economies, could be turned into cheap wage laborers in conditions of permanent vulnerability. In this way, the mining industry could expand its profit margins eroded by high capital costs and the predominance of highly paid European migrants in artisan and supervisory positions.

By the 1880s, wars, taxation, and white settler occupations had decisively undermined the African people's political independence and economic prosperity. Under rural conditions that continued to worsen, work in the mines came to represent for many Africans the sole available income to cope with a monetary capitalist economy. The control of African miners in the workplace was initially guaranteed by measures modeled after the Masters and Servants Acts adopted in the Cape Colony since 1856, which made workers' defections and associations criminal offenses. The fixed duration of the miners' contracts (gradually moved to ten or twelve months) also made their continuous employment discretionary upon the mining companies' demands. Recruitment was initially performed by independent agents, or "touts," scouting in the rural areas. The system proved, however, to be inefficient in reducing wage costs, and mining companies devised methods to coordinate African recruitment and wage fixing. The highly centralized, monopolistic nature of the industry facilitated such efforts, particularly after the establishment of the Chamber of Mines in 1889. The chamber's agreements centralized determinations of African miners' wages, undercutting competition among the mines. Government policies confined Africans to low-skill and low-wage jobs, starting with the 1911 Mines and Works Act.

The Chamber of Mines established two organizations that centralized the recruitment of migrant workers on a continental scale. The Witwatersrand Native Labor Association, founded in 1901, recruited workers in neighboring countries and across the region. By the 1930s, the northern limit of its operations was near the equator. The Native Recruitment Corporation, founded in 1912, hired migrants inside South Africa and the protectorates of Bechuanaland (Botswana), Basutoland (LESOTHO), and SWAZILAND. The internationalization of South Africa's migrant labor system required the participation of various colonial states and local administrations. Taxation on migrants' remittances and the practice by South African mines to "defer" to countries of origins a share of workers' wages, in the form of lump sums to be cashed at retirement, rewarded European COLONIALISM's collaboration with South African mining capital.

Mining companies and colonial states, however, were not the only ones benefiting from African labor migration. Despite reinforcing their subordinate position within South Africa's nascent capitalist economy, migration also carried gains for African societies. Local chiefs were rewarded for their collaboration in recruiting migrants. For many workers, migration was a way out of rural poverty, as remittances counterbalanced the decline of peasant economies to some extent. African migrants, therefore, tried to use migration and mobility as ways to cope with the impact of proletarianization.

Migrant labor led to the emergence of distinctive workers' cultural expressions. New musical and dancing styles—as analyzed, for example, by Deborah James's study of *kiba* performances among northern SOTHO-speaking migrants—showed innovative aesthetic patterns where tradition and modernity coexisted. Workers' nostalgia for home tended to be structured in diasporic ethnic identities, which transcended regional differences. At the same time, life in urban townships and mining areas was increasingly seen as a formative experience and as a testing ground for individual prowess and morality. Therefore, rural identities were translated into migrant workers' urban strategies, which, while condemning the alienation and corruption of urban society, maintained waged work as a vehicle to improve rural living conditions.

Migrant Labor, Racial Segregation, and Apartheid

African labor migration has been linked to racial segregation since the early stages of South Africa's capitalist agriculture. Only after the 1880s minerals revolution, however, did systematic segregation become functional to the control of nationwide flows of migrant workers. The institution that symbolizes this development is the African single-sex compound, a form of accommodation enabling the centralized surveillance of a labor force ethnically segregated and bound to the workplace. The compounds, which could house more than twenty workers per room, did not usually provide family accommodations. Women were in fact expected to remain in the rural areas to ensure a local economic base, which could absorb part of the labor force's reproduction. Therefore, the compound both served to compress African miners' wages and to enforce short-term migrant labor contracts.

The diversification and industrialization of South Africa's economy in the first three decades of the twentieth century saw the extension of segregated migrant labor from mining to other sectors. Mining provided the model with which migratory flows were channeled to different industries. Already before the SOUTH AFRICAN WAR (1899–1902), tensions had emerged between British capitalists and AFRIKANER farmers, who were afraid to lose their African workers to mining migration. The newly established UNION OF SOUTH AFRICA (1910) made the development of national regulation of African labor migration a policy priority. The Native Affairs Department was established in 1927 to administer the so-called native reserves and to balance rural subsistence economies with the capitalist sector's migrant labor requirements. With urbanization it also became imperative for mining capital to prevent African miners' defection to the cities. The early provision of municipal services was also premised on the recruitment of African migrants for low-wage menial occupations, as in the case of JOHANNESBURG's "bucket boys": sanitation workers recruited among the amaBhaca of the Transkei. Additionally, more migrants were needed in agriculture, which knew a period of intense, state-subsidized growth in the 1910s and the 1920s.

From the early 1920s, the PASS LAWS, which restricted and carefully monitored the movement of Africans in the urban areas, were being slowly systematized on a national scale and played a decisive role in channeling migrant workers to different economic sectors. Even if the passes proved largely ineffective in limiting African urbanization, they contributed to the supply of an abundant labor force to the mines. At the same time, demands for stricter racial segregation were now coming from a poor white population that was also migrating to the mines and to the cities. Particularly after the 1922 RAND REVOLT, in which white mine workers staged an armed insurrection demanding better wages and better treatment than their black counterparts, the African migrant workers' continuous vulnerability helped to strengthen the collaboration between the white workers' demands and the segregationist state. The Stallard Commission's 1923 report defined Africans in "white" South Africa essentially as temporary visitors, whose residential status was determined by their employment contract. The

1932 Holloway Commission and the ensuing land legislation reinforced the principle that reserves were the natural residences of African migrants, as urban segregation became more ruthless and systematic, aided by local policies of slum clearance.

During the 1940s, migrant labor was at the center of political divisions within the white establishment. In a context of growing industrial production and rising African wages, the government of JAN SMUTS was favorable to the introduction of a limited layer of semiskilled urban African residents to meet the requirements of manufacturing. However, Afrikaner nationalists and mining and agricultural capitalists maintained a rigid, "Stallardist" view of segregation, which propelled the NATIONAL PARTY's program of apartheid to electoral success in 1948. The National Party government continued, nonetheless, to debate ways to accommodate its segregationist ideology with the often divergent requirements of different capitalist sectors and with a social reality of rapid African urbanization.

The apartheid policy of "influx control" tried to further constrain the possibilities for Africans to gain urban residential rights while creating incentives to locate manufacturing sites on the borders of the BANTUSTANS (later "homelands") that replaced the old native reserves. At the same time, African migrants' employment in the mines soared from 200,000 in 1920 to 427,000 in 1961 and up to 500,000 in the 1970s, with the majority coming from neighboring countries ruled by apartheid-friendly colonial regimes. Before 1975, Mozambicans provided 60 percent of the total labor force in the sector. In agriculture, forced removals and rural deportations eliminated the last vestiges of African peasantry ("black spots") outside the legislatively demarcated bantustans during the 1960s and the 1970s, which satisfied the white landholders' requirements. The government became increasingly interdependent with the mining and agricultural capital. Industrialists, however, started to complain that short-term migration inhibited the productivity and skills of needed African factory workers. The homelands, moreover, suffered a constant economic decline as poverty and overcrowding eroded their agricultural base. In this context, as Doug Hindson explained, influx control had more to do with segmenting the labor market by insulating an African minority with urban residential rights, rather than with shifting the costs of reproduction to the rural homelands. Others have suggested that, by keeping mining and agricultural migrants in a permanently inferior juridical and economic status, the late apartheid migrant labor policies placed an additional downward pressure on African urban wages.

Labor Migrations Between Crisis and Transformation
In the 1970s, resurgent African working-class militancy was deeply influenced by the deteriorating living conditions of African migrants in industry and mining, which reflected the economic collapse of the homelands. Migrant workers played a decisive role in the revitalization of independent labor organizations following the 1973 DURBAN STRIKES by African workers. The migrants' compounds and hostels became crucial sites for the recruitment and mobilization by trade unions. Urbanization and unionization profoundly affected the migrant workers' cultural formations. During the 1970s and the early 1980s, trade unions successfully challenged ethnic loyalties and hierarchies in migrants' hostels and compounds. As a result, the migrants' opposition to workplace discipline and capitalist alienation combined rural identities and morality with proletarian consciousness and radicalism. Conversely, the weakening of union organizations in the compounds during the late 1980s facilitated a resurgence of ethnic sentiments and animosities, which escalated into widespread violence in places like Witwatersrand and NATAL.

The labor reforms prefigured in 1979 by the Wiehahn and Riekert Commissions Reports in response to the black workers' mobilization resurrected an agenda of urban stabilization and trade union rights for Africans with permanent employment. However, the abolition of influx control in the mid-1980s did not earn the collaboration of African urban dwellers for the apartheid regime. Moreover, new waves of migrants from within South Africa and without residential rights moved to the outskirts of urban areas, which saw the proliferation of informal squatter settlements. To deepen the crisis of the migrant labor system, the migrant workers' unionization led to substantial wage increases, which in part were also caused by labor shortages resulting from the apartheid regime's growing international isolation. As a result, migrant labor was no longer necessarily synonymous with cheap labor.

Higher wages, rising unemployment, and the abolition of influx control led black migrant workers, particularly in the mines, to spend longer periods of time near their places of employment. They started to regard their job as a career rather than as a circular, short-term movement. Moreover, the government and employers reacted to the loss of foreign migrants by further decentralizing production closer to the homelands and by building more family accommodations on work premises. As a result, much migrant work took the form of weekly or monthly commuting from rural residences to urban workplaces. Permanent residence near the workplace remained, however, an option reserved for highly skilled sectors of the black working class. On the other hand, low-skilled migrants had to adapt to precarious employment and the requirements of flexible labor markets.

Apartheid's final years and the onset of the DEMOCRATIC TRANSITION witnessed a profound redefinition in the meanings of migrant labor. No longer subject to the institutional constraints of influx control and the pass system, labor migration became increasingly dependent on market dynamics of employment stratification that accompanied the emergence of new class divides. Long-distance mining migration declined during the 1990s and the early 2000s. However, persistent poverty and high unemployment continue to make remittances from short-term circular migration between the rural and urban areas an important source of income for rural households. During the 1990s, the number of families with migrant members actually increased, reaching up to one-third of rural African households. The migrant labor's composition has become, at the same time, more female and directed at the informal sectors of the urban economy. The end of apartheid has also meant a resumption of foreign migrant flows from both the region and from more distant areas such as West Africa.

Cross-border migration has revealed new features as well. Movements from neighboring countries are driven by international economic inequalities and show a wide variety of employment forms. Agriculture still employs many cross-border migrants for its low-wage and more exploitative occupations, while a growing migrant entrepreneurship is linked to trade and to small, often informal, productions conducted by foreign citizens who are not aiming to settle in South Africa. Despite not being easily quantifiable, the undocumented nature of many of these movements recursively raises media hysteria about the "invasion" of "illegal" immigrants. In a context of high unemployment, anti-immigration rhetoric has often fueled episodes of xenophobia, which remains an urgent problem today.

See also ECONOMY; GOLD AND DIAMOND MINING

Bibliography

Crush, Jonathan, Alan Jeeves, and David Yudelman. *South Africa's Labor Empire: A History of Black Migrancy to the Gold Mines*. Boulder, CO: Westview Press, 1991.

First, Ruth. *Black Gold: The Mozambican Miner, Proletarian, and Peasant*. Brighton, UK: Harvester Press, 1982.

Hindson, Doug. *Pass Controls and the Urban African Proletariat in South Africa*. Johannesburg, South Africa: Ravan Press, 1987.

James, Deborah. *Songs of the Women Migrants: Performance and Identity in South Africa*. Edinburgh, UK: Edinburgh University Press, 1999.

Lacey, Marian. *Working for Boroko: The Origins of a Coercive Labor System in South Africa*. Johannesburg, South Africa: Ravan Press, 1982.

Levy, Norman. *The Foundations of the South African Cheap Labor System*. London: Routledge and Kegan Paul, 1982.

McDonald, David. *On Borders: Perspectives on Migration in Southern Africa*. New York: St. Martin's Press, 2000.

Moodie, T. Dunbar. *Going for Gold: Men, Mines, and Migration*. Berkeley: University of California Press, 1994.

—*Franco Barchiesi*

Moeketsi, Kippie Morolong (1925–1983)

Legendary saxophonist and jazz musician Kippie Morolong Moeketsi was arguably the defining voice and symbolic representation of South African jazz during the period of the SOPHIATOWN renaissance in the 1950s. Born on July 27, 1925, into a musical family, his first instrument was the clarinet. In his youth, he was greatly influenced by his older brothers, especially pianist Jacob Moeketsi.

The roots of Moeketsi's musical style were diverse. He admired classical MUSIC and African tradition as well as jazz. After discovering bebop and the work of Charlie "Bird" Parker, he pioneered modern jazz in South Africa. His musical career began in the shebeens (beer halls) and later as a session recording artist. He joined ABDULLAH IBRAHIM, HUGH MASEKELA, and Jonas Gwangwa to form the Jazz Epistles, who made South Africa's first modern jazz LP. Often introduced as Bra Joe from Kilimanjaro, Moeketsi, along with Masekela and Gwangwa, joined the cast of *King Kong* (1956), a jazz-inspired musical that took them to London. Back home, he continued to play and compose prolifically, working with musicians such as pianist Chris McGregor.

A passionate nationalist, Moeketsi rejected the exile option. He worked in South Africa and toured the region. After one tour in the 1970s, his saxophone was confiscated by the border authorities, which prevented him from performing for four years. However, shortly before his death, he returned to the stage with the African Jazz Pioneers. After his health was destroyed by poverty and by alcohol abuse, Moeketsi died bitter and penniless in 1983, but his compositions still remain in the South African jazz canon, and a popular JOHANNESBURG jazz club, Kippies, was named in his honor.

See also MUSIC

Moshoeshoe (1786–1870)

Moshoeshoe I was the founder and king of Basutoland, which is modern-day LESOTHO. He received the name Moshoeshoe, which means shaver, after he shaved off the beard of a cattle thief. From the 1820s to the 1830s, Moshoeshoe formed the Basuto nation by unifying a number of smaller SOTHO clans. Besides being the founder, he also played important roles both as a diplomat and as a military strategist. He resorted to diplomacy to diffuse the ZULU threat and sought British protection against the BOER settlers' advances. Moshoeshoe instilled a sense of identity and unity among the Basuto people and motivated them to defend their kingdom against external threats to their independence. He also invited Christian missionaries to Basutoland to promote literacy and knowledge about the outside world. Moshoeshoe displayed acts of friendship toward his defeated enemies and incorporated them into the Basuto Kingdom by providing them with land and protection as a way to expand Basutoland's frontiers. Around the 1830s, the Boer trekkers from the CAPE COLONY came to Basutoland's western borders and claimed land rights to this area, which in turn led to territorial conflicts for the next thirty years, from the 1830s to the 1860s.

In 1858, Moshoeshoe I defeated the Boers in the Free State–Basotho War. However, after another war in 1865, he lost a sizable portion of the western lowlands to the Boers. Meanwhile, Moshoeshoe signed a treaty with the British and then attacked the Boers. However, he did not realize that the Boers had also signed a peace treaty with the British. Therefore, his action prompted the British to attack Basutoland, but he was able to fend off the British aggression. By 1868, realizing that continued pressure from the Boers would eventually lead to the disintegration of his kingdom, Moshoeshoe placed Basutoland under British protection. In 1869, the British signed a boundary treaty with the Boers, which in turn forced Moshoeshoe to relinquish more of his territories. The reduction of Basutoland to half of its original size also marked the Lesotho state's current national boundaries, which became independent from Britain in 1966. Currently, Moshoeshoe Day is a national holiday in Lesotho, celebrated annually on March 11, to commemorate Moshoeshoe's death. The country's international airport, Moshoeshoe I International Airport, is named in his honor.

Motlanthe, Kgalema Petrus (1949–)

Kgalema Petrus Motlanthe was South Africa's interim president from September 2008 until the April 2009 general elections. On September 25, 2008, he became the country's third president following the end of APARTHEID after NELSON MANDELA and THABO MBEKI. The AFRICAN NATIONAL CONGRESS (ANC) nominated Motlanthe to serve as the interim president after Thabo Mbeki resigned his presidential post after being found guilty for political interference in the corruption trial against JACOB ZUMA. Motlanthe is South Africa's first TSWANA-speaking president and is also the country's current deputy president.

Motlanthe was born in the township of Alexandra in JOHANNESBURG on July 19, 1949. His father was a mine worker, and his mother was a garment worker. In 1959, his family was forcibly relocated to SOWETO by the apartheid government. For many years, Motlanthe served as an altar boy at the Anglican Church and thought about becoming a priest, as the church had a profound impact on the early years of his life.

While working for the Johannesburg City Council during the 1970s, Motlanthe was recruited into Umkhonto we Sizwe. After joining the ANC's militant wing, he formed a unit responsible for recruiting additional participants for military training. As a result of his participation in Umkhonto we Sizwe, Motlanthe was arrested on April 14, 1976, and was subsequently detained for eleven months. In 1977, he was found guilty of three charges under the Terrorism Act and was sentenced to ten years on ROBBEN ISLAND prison. Despite the hardships of serving a decade-long sentence, Motlanthe recalled that the prison years were one of the most memorable times of his life, as he had opportunities to interact with people from all walks of life, ranging from the illiterate to the highly educated, and they all shared the same goals of the antiapartheid struggle.

After his release in 1987, Motlanthe became active in trade union activities and was responsible for education and worker training for the National Union of Mineworkers (NUM). In 1992 he was elected secretary-general of NUM. Five years later, in 1997, he became the ANC's secretary-general and was elected as its deputy president in 2007.

Motlanthe is regarded by many as a moderating influence on the ANC leadership under Jacob Zuma. While he had defended and implemented Thabo Mbeki's ANC agendas and had denounced Archbishop DESMOND TUTU's criticisms of Mbeki's authoritarian leadership style, Motlanthe also vociferously spoke out against corruptions within the ANC party and the national government.

Mozambique

Bordering South Africa to the northwest, Mozambique was formerly a colony of the Portuguese, who maintained close relations with colonial and then local white rulers in South Africa. Following a guerrilla war, Mozambique became independent in 1975.

Beginning with Portuguese colonialism, South Africa relied on cheap, black Mozambican labor for its GOLD AND DIAMOND MINING around JOHANNESBURG (since the 1860s) and sugar cane plantations in what is now KwaZulu-Natal Province. The Portuguese colony's capital Lourenço Marques (renamed Maputo at independence), as well as its pristine beaches, was a favorite, cheap holiday destination for white South Africans. At independence, many white Portuguese settlers fled to South Africa. In the 1970s and 1980s, the foreign policy of Mozambique was intertwined with the struggle for black majority rule in South Africa and Rhodesia. Mozambique's ruling Frelimo Party maintained official links to the South African resistance movement, the AFRICAN NATIONAL CONGRESS (ANC). The South African APARTHEID government attempted to destabilize Mozambique by providing arms and financial assistance to the Resistência Nacional Moçambicana (Mozambique Resistance Movement, or Renamo), a conservative, anti-Marxist organization also supported by the US Central Intelligence Agency, which began a bloody and protracted civil war with Frelimo soon after independence.

A 1984 accord between the two governments failed to curb South African support for Renamo (and Mozambican support for the ANC). In 1986,

Mozambique president Samora Machel was killed in a plane crash near the South African border. Since then, there has been widespread speculation—never proven—of foul play in Machel's death on the part of the South African government. At least one million people were killed and five million left homeless by this destabilizing civil war that lasted until 1992.

Only after political reforms were initiated in South Africa did relations between the two countries improve, with full diplomatic relations established in 1993. Since the end of apartheid, Mozambique's economy has been dominated by South African capital, including retail, construction, finance, and telecommunications. Mozambican economic migrants and traders, however, have faced a hostile reception in South Africa. A mass outbreak of xenophobic violence in South Africa's black townships in May 2008 mostly targeted Mozambicans (and Zimbabweans).

See also FRONTLINE STATES

Music

While the development of modern urban music in South Africa is usually dated from the 1920s, a rich foundation of traditional styles, performances, ceremonies, and instruments predated the arrival of the first colonizing explorer, Vasco da Gama, in 1497 and still survives in modified forms in the rural areas at the start of the twenty-first century.

European musical traditions have existed in parallel to African ones for many centuries. The folk music of the AFRIKANERS, for example, originated with the Dutch settlers in the CAPE COLONY in the 1700s, and also has roots in the Indonesian archipelago, from where slaves were imported. During the Afrikaner nationalist era, the first half of the twentieth century, much music was "borrowed" from Europe, especially Germany. Also heavily influenced by their Christian faith, the Afrikaner community today continues with a rich and distinctive musical tradition.

African Musical Traditions

Early indigenous music included elaborate court ritual music (in the VENDA tradition, for example), the complex rhythmic and harmonic structures of Nguni bow music and overtone singing, the social and work-related songs, and the simple pipe tunes of farming communities and herdsmen. Over the centuries, these received infusions of new ideas and instruments through the travels and sharing of ideas (and cash-economy purchases) facilitated by the MIGRANT LABOR system, especially with the arrival of the guitar and later the wind-up gramophone. One example is the development of the ISICATHAMIYA style of ZULU, choreographed close harmony singing, developed in the mine hostels during the twentieth century as a blend of hymns, vaudeville music, and village song. Later, isicathamiya further modernized into an extremely successful world music by the group LADYSMITH BLACK MAMBAZO.

There were significant elements of Indonesian music ("Malay" choirs) in the Cape Colony that came from South Asian slaves and from political prisoners held by the DUTCH EAST INDIA COMPANY. In the Eastern Cape region, a strong choral tradition grew up in areas where mission stations had been established (one of the most significant was LOVEDALE) as early African converts trained in Scotland brought the pentatonic hymn with them from back home. South Africa's national anthem, "Nkosi Sikelel' iAfrika," which was a hymn composed by Enoch Sontonga, is an example of this type of influence.

In the early 1820s, COLOURED bands of musicians began parading through the streets of CAPE TOWN, in a style similar to that of British marching military bands. This tradition was given added impetus by the traveling minstrel shows of the 1880s and has continued to the present day with the great carnival held in Cape Town every New Year. Also around this time, African Christian trainees who studied in the United States were impressed and influenced by African-American spirituals.

In the nineteenth century, a nascent black middle class—successful farmers in the countryside and clerks, teachers, and other freeholders in the early towns—was devoting its social hours to composition, musical evenings, and choral activities encompassing both modern arrangements of traditional music and original compositions inspired by growing nationalism and works by European composers.

By the start of the twentieth century, performance and music education spaces such as JOHANNESBURG's Bantu Men's Social Center (founded in 1924) were developing. Vaudeville and dance bands, influenced by the African-American minstrel tours to some extent, found a ready audience; the earliest was the Japanese Express, founded in 1929.

In the 1930s, music called marabi was being developed in crowded, informal urban settlements. It employed a keyboard or an accordion plus homemade percussion and a three-chord structure (I: IV: V), and took its melodic inspiration from all ethnic groups and from contemporary imported popular music. Marabi added value to shebeens (illegal neighborhood drinking places) and to working-class social life but also developed a syncretic style that gradually became increasingly modernized, especially after the demolition of many informal settlements at the end of the decade.

Thereafter, in the cities, came a relatively rapid transition from folk-based forms to an urban, swing-based dance band sound using jazz band instrumentation and employing female vocalists who attracted huge fan bases. The form was initially still called marabi, but later tsaba-tsaba, "concert and dance," was the dominant performance form: a vaudeville-type act before midnight and a jazzier dance session after midnight. Different types of bands—some more musically literate and refined, others wilder and more modernist—reflected different social strands within black urban society. Different areas had different styles, too: in DURBAN, for example, the concert segment featured string bands.

At the same time, US movies and the music they featured became influential. The 1936 British Empire Exhibition brought South African black music to world attention as a stimulus to both performance and the recording industry, although no recordings were made in South Africa until the end of the decade. In 1939, "Imbube" (a Zulu traditional song) was recorded by Solomon Linda and his Original Evening Songbirds, and The Jazz Maniacs led by "Zuluboy" Cele recorded *Tsaba/Izikhalo Zika Zuluboy*, identified as the country's first "jazz" recording.

In 1948, the newly elected, Afrikaner-dominated NATIONAL PARTY government codified and extended the various forms of racially based segregation, black disenfranchisement, and dispossession known as APARTHEID. At the same time, marabi and tsaba-tsaba were being reshaped into a more modernist, improvised form known first as majuba and later as KWELA or (in a titling that reflected a growing nationalist consciousness) African jazz. The forms were sometimes very different: kwela was a street pennywhistle music while African jazz was a music of high-level improvisation in performance settings. But they intertwined and fed off one another so that the terms were often used interchangeably.

Areas that were historically home to a mixture of racial groups such as DISTRICT SIX in Cape Town and SOPHIATOWN in Johannesburg survived for a while, but Sophiatown was finally cleared in line with residential segregation laws in 1955. They provided a setting for performance and musical education and growth, while magazines such as *DRUM* and *Zonk* documented and spread news of the music to raise "African awareness." The state broadcaster, the SABC, gave one hour a week to jazz. By the middle of the decade, some of the stars now identified with South African jazz had begun their careers. MIRIAM MAKEBA was singing, and a schoolboy named HUGH MASEKELA was playing in the Huddleston Jazz Band in Sophiatown. At the same time, other music heroes were admired, including a risk-taking saxophonist called KIPPIE MOEKETSI, now considered the father of South Africa's modern jazz.

In 1958, the pioneering black musical *King Kong* premiered, starring Makeba and Masekela, among others, and composed by *Drum* journalist and jazz pianist Todd Matshikiza, who used both jazz and choral idioms. However, lesser-known artists often sold complete rights to their compositions for a small flat fee or for gifts, radio recordings were unpaid, and royalties for black artists were unknown. Also, as segregation tightened, such creative opportunities for mixed production companies and for mixed audiences shrank.

However, black music theater continued to flourish into the 1960s and the 1970s. Male vocalists ousted female big-band singers as the stars. Kwela and African jazz sounds were gradually squeezed by both overseas-influenced soul and pop music and by neotraditional sounds encouraged by the apartheid regime as part of its project of retribalization. As part of the disenfranchisement of the black majority population, cultural ideologues within the regime aimed to erase nontribal urban identity. Labor policies treated South Africans of color as temporary urban residents whose real home was under a rural tribal leader, and cultural policies reinforced this as well. Modern popular music and especially jazz seemed to typify sophisticated, urban black life and was associated with community protest and political awareness. The shebeens where the music played represented gestures of defiance, for prohibition was in force for black South Africans.

In 1960, the SABC created "Radio Bantu"—seven, full-time ethnic services focused on traditional, neotraditional, and religious music—and discouraged black musicians from playing hybrid music (like jazz) that did not fit into an apartheid-defined tribal authenticity. Record companies colluded by churning out apolitical pop tunes in neotraditional styles.

In a last breath of innovation, the most daring modern jazz experiments took place: ABDULLAH IBRAHIM, Masekela, and Moeketsi combined bebop-style improvisation with African melodic and harmonic ideas as well as challenging titles (for example, "Scullery Department") in the Jazz Epistles recording. In other cities, other small groups and musicians, such as Winston Mankunku Ngozi in Cape Town, were doing similar work. In 1965, Winston Mankunku recorded *Yahkal'Inkhomo* ("The Bellowing Bull" for, he said, the "black man's pain"), the top-selling jazz record of that and subsequent years.

Black musicians began a major move into exile. The first jumped ship when the *King Kong* musical toured overseas in the early 1960s. Others left independently as soon as they could secure travel permits. Some, such as Miriam Makeba and Dorothy Masuka, were banned from returning while touring because the authorities disliked songs they had composed or statements they had made against apartheid.

In the shrinking music scene, the white musicians' unions sought to exclude their black counterparts from work opportunities. This, plus apartheid segregation, led to absurd situations where black artists performing with white bands played behind a screen while white players mimed. For instance, the black Winston Mankunku at the upscale Cape Town City Hall became, for white audiences, Winston Mann.

Eventually, the government legalized "white" liquor for black drinkers as it recognized the inevitable, sought wider revenue profits, and hoped to anesthetize dissent. To stimulate sales and win customer loyalty, liquor companies sponsored jazz festivals, at which the new music received what was often its first—and sometimes its last—performances. Artists at liquor company–sponsored events were often paid with a case of the product instead of cash, which entrenched alcoholism in the sector. At the Cold Castle Festival in 1964, Eric Nomvete played "Pondo Blues," an assertively African modern jazz tune, to rapturous applause. But as the festivals (accidentally) showcased musical nationalism, the authorities' attitudes hardened. This creative mood emerging from the festivals did not survive the decade, and the later festivals were more tightly controlled and became more musically conservative.

Overseas, the South African music and struggle were receiving ever-wider recognition and support. Makeba addressed the United Nations and was nominated for a Grammy for her recording with Harry Belafonte. Abdullah Ibrahim played at the Newport Jazz Festival and recorded with Duke Ellington.

At the end of the 1960s, the SOWETO soul style was born, influenced by both African-American musical trends and by a growing cultural and political awareness of the African continent. One famous South African soul group called itself Harari, and its music took ideas from both Motown and Osibisa, a British Afro-Pop band. Eventually, the sound slid into formula, while broadcasting authorities still favored harmless pop forms such as the "sax jive."

However, by the 1970s, new forms of modern jazz emerged and explored the same territories as overseas fusion groups such as Earth, Wind, and Fire. These included Sean Bergin's Abstract Truth in Natal, Pacific Express with Robbie Jansen in Cape Town, Spirits Rejoice, and others. However, censorship and control of radio airplay tightened, and "pure" tribal music forms were more consciously fostered. Modern jazz groups and composers continued to work, but, especially after the tightening of public order regulations following the 1976 Soweto Student Uprising, they found increasingly fewer performance venues and received no airplay. Therefore, musical developments were often undocumented. It has been said that South African jazz died in the 1970s; it certainly lost much of its public arena. The Pelican in Orlando (opened in 1972) was one of the few jazz clubs in the whole country. Mixed clubs were regularly raided and closed under the licensing and the so-called immorality (race mixing) laws.

With the growth of independence in the rest of Africa and the Black Consciousness Movement led by Steve Biko at home, there was more seeking after South African and pan-African musical roots. This was seen in groups such as Philip Tabane's Malombo and Bruce Sosibo and Pat Sefolosha's Malopoets.

Meanwhile, South African jazz flourished in exile: with Masekela in the United States; Makeba in Guinea; Chris McGregor, Dudu Pukwana, Lucky Ranku, and many others in the United Kingdom and northern Europe; and Jonas Gwangwa creating the African National Congress's touring Amandla Cultural Ensemble. The notion of music as a weapon of struggle was growing and became a major feature in the following decade.

Formulaic neotraditional pop styles (Mbaqanga, smanje-manje) still dominated the airwaves, but they had become so insubstantial that, by the 1980s, the term for them was "bubblegum." However, independent labels such as Shifty, Mountain, The Sun, and others recorded everything from jazz and poetry to the political jazz of Basil Coetzee's Sabenza and diverse, avant-garde bands like Abstractions. Many progressive, young, white musicians rejected segregation in music; one was the sociology student Johnny Clegg, who developed a lively, questioning form of pop music based on Zulu tradition with guitarist Sipho Mnchunu in the group Juluka.

At the same time, choral music, which still flourished in black communities, took a new twist with the emergence of "worker choirs," which were often attached to trade union branches. These used the time-honored choral forms to call for solidarity, praise strikers and martyrs, or denounce informers.

Festivals and coaching schools in places such as Swaziland and Botswana—for example, the 1982 Culture and Resistance Festival in Gaborone—were accessible to South African musicians, who could share ideas with overseas counterparts. However, repressive censorship also intensified. In one case, a man was jailed for eight years for owning an Amandla music cassette.

As the regime fought an increasingly rearguard action against political change, "Third Force" violence (sponsored but not openly acknowledged by the state) more or less killed nightlife in the townships, robbing aspiring jazz players of a local scene where they could hone their skills before aiming for the big time. But, as both censorship and labor and residential zoning restrictions weakened under commercial pressures (enforcing apartheid racial policies became increasingly unprofitable), new venues opened, even if they were short-lived. New styles looked at both traditional roots (Sakhile, Bayete, The Genuines, Amampondo) and older jazz styles (the African Jazz Pioneers was formed in 1981). Although the UN cultural boycott distanced South African musicians from much that was happening in the United States and Europe, it also fostered self-reliance as well as the mining of indigenous identity and character. This was seen across the musical spectrum, from the proudly nationalist classical compositions of Professor Mzilikazi Khumalo to the sassy, assertively African pop style of a young singer named Brenda Fassie, who would go on to become the biggest pop star the country had ever seen. In 1986, singer/songwriter Paul Simon collaborated with South African musicians on the *Graceland* project, which reopened some of those doors (though not without controversy, for the cultural boycott was not yet over and political change had not arrived).

When the negotiated settlement ending apartheid did arrive in the early 1990s, it saw the end of censorship and isolation but also of protected local markets for music. Exiled musicians returned and new young voices emerged, as well as new African styles. Though distinctively South African, these styles were influenced by immigrants from the rest of the continent. A number of independent record companies seized the gap left by the conservative record industry majors, and one of these, Sheer Sound, produced the first major crossover hit from the black to the white music markets in 1997: the jazz album *Trains to Taung* by pianist Paul Hanmer.

Today, South Africa's music scene has vastly diversified. Classical music is no longer the exclusive domain of the white elite and has attracted increasing numbers of black musicians and audiences. The Soweto String Quartet, for example, was formed in 1989 by the three Khamese brothers, violinists Sandile and Thami and cellist Reuben, as well as Makhosini Mnguni on viola—four classical musicians from Soweto township. Originally criticized for their adherence to traditional European instruments, the Soweto String Quartet imbues their music with native African rhythms and intonations. Their talents went unrecognized until the demise of apartheid. However, the foursome have now taken South Africa, and the international stage, by storm.

Top-selling jazz sounds stretch from the fusion-influenced, dance-oriented guitar sounds of Jimmy Dludlu to the committed improvised music of saxophonist Zim Ngqawana. Popular music includes groups that clone international sounds as well as indigenous inventions such as KWAITO ("township house") with its chanted lyrics and heavy bass beats. The kwaito boom peaked in South Africa in the mid-1990s, but reached international markets in the early 2000s through a successful kwaito soundtrack to the Oscar-winning film *TSOTSI*. At home, the South African equivalents of nu-soul and hip-hop (with sharply observant African-language lyrics) and new genres such as motswako (mixup) dominate. Demonstrating how South African traditions adapt but do not easily die, the top-selling recorded genre in the country remains gospel music: the modernized godchild of the historic choral tradition. Sales of indigenous music by 2010 exceeded in units (though not currency value) those of imported sounds.

See also BRENDA FASSIE; ABDULLAH IBRAHIM; LADYSMITH BLACK MAMBAZO; MIRIAM MAKEBA; HUGH MASEKELA; KIPPIE MOEKETSI

Bibliography
Ansell, Gwen. *Soweto Blues: Jazz, Popular Music and Politics in South Africa*. New York: Continuum Books, 2004.
Lucia, Christine, ed. *The World of South African Music: A Reader*. Newcastle, UK: Cambridge Scholars' Press, 2005.
Meintjies, Louise. *Sound of Africa! Making Music Zulu in a South African Studio*. Durham, NC: Duke University Press, 2003.
Titlestad, Michael. *Writing the Changes: Jazz in South African Literature and Reportage*. Pretoria, South Africa: University of South Africa Press, 2004.

—Gwen Ansell

Mzilikazi (1790–1868)

Mzilikazi was a southern African king whose name means "The Great Road." He was also called Mosilikatze at times and was the founder of the NDEBELE, or, as it is sometimes called, the Matabele kingdom, located in current-day ZIMBABWE. Mzilikazi was considered by many southern African historians to be the greatest southern African military leader after the ZULU king SHAKA, because he united his own people and many ethnic groups that he had conquered into a diverse but centralized kingdom. However, he also had a reputation of being ruthless toward his opponents.

Mzilikazi was born around 1790 in Mkuze, Zululand. He was originally King Shaka's lieutenant and had sworn allegiance to him. But Mzilikazi later had a falling out with Shaka, because he had ambitions of his own and felt dissatisfied with his subservient position. To avoid execution, he escaped toward the north with his ethnic group.

Mzilikazi first established his kingdom, Mhlahlandela, located outside present-day Pretoria, in the 1820s. After facing a series of attacks, he then moved his kingdom northward to current-day MOZAMBIQUE in 1826 and later moved again to AFRIKANER Republic of Transvaal, around present-day JOHANNESBURG, as attacks on his kingdom continued.

Gradually, Mzilikazi conquered and dominated Transvaal and absorbed other ethnic groups in the process. While conquering Transvaal, he also massacred and systematically eliminated his enemies, which in turn depleted this region's population and facilitated the BOER trekkers' occupation of Transvaal's best lands around the 1830s. In 1836, large numbers of Boers began arriving in Transvaal and became engaged in conflicts for the next two years with Mzilikazi over land. By early 1838, Mzilikazi and his forces had to leave Transvaal as they suffered heavy losses in their clashes with the Boer settlers. After unsuccessful attempts to settle in Botswana and in Zambia, Mzilikazi then traveled southeast to present-day Zimbabwe and established the Ndebele kingdom there in 1840. Once the kingdom came into being, he organized his followers into a strong military system to fight off the Boer incursions from 1847 to 1851 and was able to persuade the government of the South Africa Republic to sign a peace treaty with him in 1852.

As the Ndebele kingdom grew and became militarily strong, Mzilikazi carried out raids to remove potential enemies as well as to expand his kingdom's military power and human resources by capturing women and children. At the same time, he also established social structures to make his captives assimilate and conform to the Matabele culture.

Mzilikazi died on September 9, 1868, at Ingama, near present-day Bulawayo in Zimbabwe. Although he had a successor, Lobengula, in 1870, conflicts between contesting ethnic groups along with the British territorial expansion led to the collapse of the Ndebele kingdom. Despite the fall of the kingdom, both the Ndebele language and culture have survived.

Namibia

Namibia is a country in southern Africa, bordering the South Atlantic Ocean to the west, Angola to the north, South Africa to the south, and Botswana to the east. Under German COLONIALISM and later South African occupation, the territory was known as South West Africa (SWA). Since the 1960s, African nationalists, the United Nations, and others have used the name Namibia to refer to the region, although the Republic of Namibia was only established in 1990.

The early inhabitants of Namibia included ancestors of the SAN and the Damara, who developed hunting and gathering economies adapted to the region's arid environment. More concentrated settlement can be linked to two migrations. In the early first millennium A.D., pastoral migrants entered Namibia by traveling west along the Orange River. Collectively, descendants of these people are known as the KHOIKHOI, and those who remained in southern Namibia, as the Nama. Toward the end of the first millennium, agropastoralists of Bantu origin entered the area between the Kunene and Okavango rivers. Those who traveled farther south developed an exclusively pastoral economy adapted to dry conditions in central Namibia and are ancestors of the Herero. Others who remained in northern Namibia's more fertile Kunene-Okavango floodplain along the contemporary Namibian-Angolan border are ancestors of the Ovambo, Namibia's largest ethnic group.

Compared to South Africa, Namibia remained relatively isolated from European expansion for many years. Although Portuguese ships landed on the Namibian coast as early as 1486, Namibia was largely shielded from European trade until the nineteenth century. The immediate catalyst for change was the Oorlam, people of mixed Khoikhoi and European descent, who migrated north of the Orange River into Namibia during the early 1800s. Through their connections with the CAPE COLONY, the Oorlam amassed firearms, ammunition, and horses; developed a society that centered on military oligarchies; and lived off spoils from hunting, trading, and raiding. The Oorlam migration pushed southern and central Namibia's inhabitants to develop similar forms of social organization and made them increasingly reliant on traders and missionaries entering the region. By the 1840s, Jonker Afrikaner, an Oorlam leader, asserted his authority over much of southern and central Namibia, controlling trade along the roads leading from both the Cape and the Namibian harbor at Walvis Bay to his settlement in Windhoek. In the 1850s, traders and missionaries first entered the Kunene-Okavango floodplain, gradually integrating the Ovambo and others in northern Namibia into southern Africa's mercantile capitalist system.

In 1884, SWA was declared a German colony at the Conference of Berlin. The colony consisted of current-day Namibia with the exception of the coastal enclave Walvis Bay, which Britain had previously annexed in 1878. (Walvis Bay was integrated after separate negotiations between the South African and the Namibian governments on April 1, 1994.) Few Germans resided in the colony at the time of its colonization outside the Rhenish Mission Society, which had established itself as the dominant missionary presence in southern and central Namibia since mid-century. Gradually, German traders and colonial officials forced treaties with local leaders, allocating areas for German settlement in return for protection from African rivals. By the end of the nineteenth century, Germans had established Windhoek as the colony's administrative capital and inhabited large swaths of southern and central Namibia, which became known as the SWA Police Zone. By contrast, the Germans never controlled the northern part of Namibia and white settlers did not inhabit the region throughout the colonial period.

African resistance to German rule commenced in the 1890s, and between 1903 and 1907, Africans in the Police Zone initiated a series of large rebellions against the German government. In October 1903, the Bondelswart Nama led an armed revolt, and in January 1904, fighting broke out between Germans and Herero under the Paramount Chief Samuel Maherero. With security concerns rising among settlers, German kaiser Wilhelm II replaced Theodor Leutwein with Lothar von Trotha as the colony's military commander. Whereas Leutwein had exercised divide-and-rule tactics, his successor pursued a military confrontation and eventually ordered the extermination of the Herero people. On August 11, 1904, the German army encircled and attacked the Herero at the Waterberg Plateau. Many Hereros evaded the attack and fled through the Kalahari Desert into Bechuanaland, but due to the German pursuit and the occupation of waterholes, tens of thousands died in a mass genocide.

In October 1904, Nama communities under Hendrik Witbooi led a guerrilla war against the Germans, and following Witbooi's death in October 1905, some continued to fight under Jacob Marengo and other local leaders. Following the wars, thousands of Herero and Nama were interred in concentration camps where many perished. Those Africans in the Police Zone who survived the wars were expropriated from most of their land and livestock. They were forced to live in defined native reserves and had to work on settler farms to earn a living. Ovambo migrant laborers also became increasingly important to the colonial economy, particularly to diamond mining, which developed along Namibia's southern coast from 1908.

Germany's rule over SWA ended with World War I. In 1915, the South African forces defeated German troops defending the colony, and in 1919, the region was transferred to South Africa as a League of Nations mandate. South Africa's interwar policy toward SWA focused largely on ensuring a cheap and steady supply of African labor. The regime set aside more native reserves for Africans who had been displaced in the previous wars, enabling some resurgence in African pastoral economies but providing insufficient territories to support them. Both South African officials in the Police Zone and the Ovambo headmen propped up by the South African regime administered taxes, effectively coercing Africans to join the colonial workforce. Only white settlers, including German and new AFRIKANER migrants to SWA, were represented in the South African Parliament.

Following World War II, South Africa's rule in SWA became a matter of international controversy. In 1945, the newly formed United Nations established a trusteeship system to administer those territories that had been mandated under the League of Nations. South African officials refused to hand over SWA to the United Nations, arguing that the mandate had expired following the league's dissolution and that South Africa should annex SWA as the country's fifth province. In response, Herero chief Hosea Kutako, Nama chief Samuel Witbooi, and Anglican reverend Michael Scott initiated a petition campaign at the United Nations to contest the annexation. Although the United Nations turned down South Africa's proposal, it was unable to force South Africa to place SWA under the new trusteeship system. South Africa's policy toward SWA became increasingly controversial in conjunction with African decolonization, the adoption of APARTHEID policies in South Africa (1948) and in SWA (1964), and South Africa's increasingly violent forms of governance.

It is in this context that Namibia's national liberation movements formed during the late 1950s and early 1960s. Of Namibia's two primary movements, the South West African National Union and the South West Africa People's Organization (SWAPO), SWAPO emerged as the most powerful, drawing from a popular support base among Ovambo contract laborers and diplomatic victories achieved by the organization's exiled leadership under Sam Nujoma. On August 26, 1966, SWAPO commenced a guerrilla war against South Africa, which was waged in northern Namibia and in southern Angola over the next twenty-three years. Although SWAPO exiles initially numbered only several hundred in the 1960s, conflicts over apartheid policy and the demise of Portuguese colonialism in 1974 spurred thousands more to flee across Namibia's northern border into Angola, Zambia, and Tanzania. There, they received humanitarian aid from the United Nations, the Scandinavian governments, and private solidarity movements, and armaments from the Organization of African Unity and the Eastern Bloc.

With resistance to its policies strengthening inside Namibia and abroad, the South African government's strategies shifted. From 1975 to 1976, it organized the Turnhalle Conference, a series of meetings with Namibian political groups aimed at planning national elections and at achieving an "internal solution" to Namibia's governance. SWAPO, however, boycotted the conference and called for UN-monitored elections, a decision supported by a broad range of Namibians and international observers. In September 1978, the South African regime verbally approved UN Resolution 435, a blueprint for UN-monitored elections in Namibia, but backed out of the resolution before it was passed. The following year, Ronald Reagan was elected as US president, and the US government adopted a new southern Africa policy, which linked the implementation of Resolution 435 to the removal of Cuban troops from Angola. Thereafter, South Africa also adopted this linkage policy, delaying the implementation of Resolution 435 until December 1988. Between April and August 1989, thousands of Namibians returned from exile. In November of that year, the United Nations monitored Namibia's first democratic elections. SWAPO won a majority, and Nujoma was elected as the Republic of Namibia's first president by the members of the first Constituent Assembly.

Since independence, SWAPO has remained Namibia's dominant political party and consolidated its power base. In 2005, the state presidency was transferred from Nujoma to Hifikepunye Pohamba, who also became the SWAPO party president in 2007. In general, Namibia has been praised for creating a relatively stable democracy on the heels of more than 100 years of violent colonial rule. Nonetheless, several policies have been controversial. The national reconciliation policy, adopted at independence, has protected the property rights of colonial (white) society and left perpetrators of human rights abuses on all sides of the liberation struggle unaccountable. The government's decision to enter the civil war in the Democratic Republic of Congo (1998), its response to the attempted secession in the Caprivi region (1999), and its decision to permit the Angolan government to attack the Angolan rebel movement, National Union for the Total Independence of Angola (UNITA), from inside Namibian territory (1999–2000) were each met with criticism. Other contentious issues include authoritarian government practices, the unabated gap between rich and poor, and the HIV/AIDS pandemic.

Bibliography
Diener, Ingolf, and Olivier Graefe, eds. *Contemporary Namibia: The First Landmarks of a Post*

Apartheid Society. Windhoek, Namibia: Gamsberg Macmillan, 2001.
Dobell, Lauren. *SWAPO's Struggle for Namibia, 1960–1991: War by Other Means.* Basel, Switzerland: P. Schlettwein Publishing, 1998.
du Pisani, André, Reinhart Kössler, and William Lindeke, eds. *The Long Aftermath of War—Reconciliation and Transition in Namibia.* Freiburg, Germany: Arnold Bergstraesser Institutet, 2009.
Emmett, Tony. *Popular Resistance and the Roots of Nationalism in Namibia, 1915–1966.* Basel, Switzerland: P. Schlettwein Publishing, 1999.
Hartmann, Wolfram, Patricia Hayes, and Jeremy Silvester, eds. *The Colonising Camera: Photographs in the Making of Namibian History.* Cape Town, South Africa: University of Cape Town Press, 1998.
———, eds. *Namibia Under South African Rule: Mobility and Containment, 1915–1946.* Oxford, UK: James Currey, 1998.
Katjavivi, Peter. *A History of Resistance in Namibia.* London: James Currey, 1988.
Leys, Colin, and John S. Saul. *Namibia's Liberation Struggle: The Two Edged Sword.* London: James Currey, 1995.
Melber, Henning, ed. *Transitions in Namibia: Which Changes for Whom?* Uppsala, Sweden: Nordiska Afrikainstitutet, 2007.
Winterfeldt, Volker, Tom Fox, and Pempelani Mafume, eds. *Namibia, Society, Sociology.* Windhoek, Namibia: University of Namibia Press, 2002.
Zimmerer, Jürgen, and Joachim Zeller, eds. *Genocide in German South-West Africa: The Colonial War of 1904–1908 and Its Aftermath.* Monmouth, Wales: Mirlin Press, 2008.

—Christian Williams

Natal

Located in the southeastern part of the country, Natal was a British colony in the area currently known as KwaZulu-Natal Province. Portuguese explorer Vasco da Gama was the first European to reach the area in 1497 and named it Natal, which means Christmas in Portuguese, because he landed there around Christmastime. From the 1680s onward, Natal, also known as Port Natal because the territory is located along the Indian Ocean, became familiar to both the Dutch and the British, as shipwrecked sailors temporarily settled there. Before it became a British colony in 1843, the BOER settlers established the Boer Republic of Natalia. This republic was organized into three districts: Port Natal, Pietermaritzburg, and Winburg. Although the British settlers in Port Natal had appealed to their home country to annex Natalia, Britain refused to take action until 1841. What prompted the British to annex Natal were the Boer policy toward the indigenous people, the discovery of coal, and other foreign powers' interests in this territory. On May 4, 1843, Natal officially became a British colony after Britain took over the Boer Republic of Natalia. From 1843 to 1910, Natal had one special commissioner, fourteen lieutenant-governors, thirteen governors, and seven prime ministers.

The AFRIKANERS who refused to be under British rule left Natal for other BOER REPUBLICS: namely Orange Free State and Transvaal. By the end of 1843, fewer than five hundred Afrikaner families remained there.

From 1844 to 1856, Natal was administered from the CAPE COLONY due to lack of British settlers and the fragile frontiers around the territory. Natal still faced threats from the Boer republics and the surrounding African kingdoms such as the ZULUS. Additionally, this region was also caught in the conflict between the Boer republics and the British colonies. After defeating the Zulus in the ANGLO-ZULU WAR of 1879, the British annexed Zululand and incorporated it into the Natal colony, which expanded this territory. In 1899, the Boer republics decided to launch a preemptive strike into parts of Cape and Natal colonies and into Bechuanaland in order to avoid being taken over by the British. The territorial conflicts between the Afrikaners and the British eventually led to the formation of the UNION OF SOUTH AFRICA on May 31, 1910, comprising the British Cape and Natal colonies, and the Boer Republics of Transvaal and the Orange Free State. After the Union of South Africa was formed, it became Natal Province. With the introduction of democratic, black majority rule in 1994, the provincial boundaries were once again redrawn, and much of the territory of Natal Province has now been renamed KwaZulu-Natal Province.

National Education Crisis/Coordinating Committee

Around March 1986, the National Education Crisis Committee (NECC) was formed to promote the development of democratic education in the country. The National Education Union of South Africa, the Soweto Parents' Crisis Committee, and numerous student organizations formed the committee under the slogan "People's Education for People's Power" during a conference in DURBAN, in present-day KwaZulu-Natal Province. Instrumental in planning for a postapartheid educational system, the NECC served to complement the struggle against APARTHEID by focusing on the crisis in black education in South Africa as a result of apartheid. NECC's agendas and slogans included destroying the racial segregation of the apartheid system, making education mass-based and accessible to all South Africans, serving the interests of the community instead of the elite class, being based on nonwhite South Africans' actual experiences as opposed to European experiences, uncovering the country's indigenous cultural heritage, unifying the country, and paving the way for people's power, a highly participatory form of black majority rule. These objectives placed it in direct confrontation with the apartheid regime, and the organization was subsequently banned in 1988. Ideally, the NECC wanted to introduce and implement its educational objectives before apartheid's collapse; as one of its members stated, "We do not have to wait for liberation day, we must begin to introduce some of these ideas under the present regime." During the transition period from 1990 to 1994, the NECC changed its name from the National Education Crisis Committee to the National Education Coordinating Committee. The work of the NECC was very influential in the new government's White Paper (policy framework) on Education, and many of its leadership took up senior positions in government.

National Forum

The National Forum was formed by the Azanian People's Organization and other groups sharing similar viewpoints on black consciousness in June 1983 during a meeting at Hammanskraal, near the capital city Pretoria. In many ways, the National Forum's vision of South Africa after APARTHEID was radically different from the UNITED DEMOCRATIC FRONT (UDF), the AFRICAN NATIONAL CONGRESS (ANC), and other political parties. It criticized the UDF for its links with the ANC, as well as the FREEDOM CHARTER for preserving group rights and for recognizing minority rights. The National Forum's belief was that this would only further entrench and institutionalize racial and ethnic divisions in South Africa. The National Forum vehemently disagreed with UDF's perspective of the liberation struggle in South Africa as an antiapartheid and civil rights movement rather than as a revolutionary campaign to restructure society by overthrowing the established racist/capitalist order, which is the underlying foundation of the apartheid system. Neville Alexander, one of the forum's founding members, had stated at the Hammanskraal meeting that white South Africans who wanted to contribute to the antiapartheid struggle had their place, but the country's future leaders must come from the black African working class. The National Forum's Manifesto of the Azanian People called for non-collaboration with "the oppressor and his political instruments." However, the National Forum's black consciousness and radical, left-wing revolutionary ideology had only lukewarm support. This political grouping never managed to mobilize on a mass scale like the UDF, even though it had strong support from some black intellectuals.

National Party

The National Party was South Africa's governing party from June 4, 1948, until May 9, 1994. It was the main creator of the APARTHEID system and a fervent promoter of AFRIKANER NATIONALISM. During the postapartheid era, the National Party experienced dwindling support and decreased popularity despite trying to remake itself into the

New National Party. It eventually dissolved in 2005.

This party was founded in BLOEMFONTEIN in 1914 in what is now the Free State Province by AFRIKANER nationalists after the UNION OF SOUTH AFRICA came into being in 1910. The National Party first came to power in 1924 with JAMES HERTZOG as the country's prime minister. Under his administration, the ideologies and foundations for the apartheid system were established although not systematically implemented until the National Party again came to power in 1948. The party encountered its first split in 1934 when DANIEL FRANCOIS MALAN opposed Hertzog's decision to merge the National Party with JAN SMUTS's South African Party to form the United Party. Malan's opposition to this merger led him to form the Reunited National Party with the Purified Nationalists within the National Party faction that had joined the United Party. In 1948, Malan's National Party successfully defeated Smuts's United Party and retook control of the government.

After becoming the ruling party again in 1948, the National Party began to implement a series of policies to consolidate the apartheid system as well as white economic and political domination of South Africa. It passed the Bantu Self-Government Act in 1951, which created BANTUSTANS, subsequently relabeled as homelands, for the country's black population. Additionally, the government passed the Prohibition of Mixed Marriages Act, the Immorality Act, the Population Registration Act, and the Group Areas Act, the latter prohibiting nonwhite males access to certain areas of the country, especially at night unless they were employed there. Furthermore, to consolidate and expand its power base, the National Party incorporated South West Africa, now called NAMIBIA, which it had occupied since World War I, into South Africa as its fifth province, with seven members elected to represent the Namibian white citizens in the South African Parliament. This move allowed the National Party to increase its parliamentary majority in almost every election between 1948 and 1977, as blacks, COLOUREDS, and INDIANS were excluded from the electoral process. In 1960, the white population (mostly National Party supporters) voted in a national referendum to end South Africa's ties with the British monarchy and to transform the Union of South Africa into the Republic of South Africa, which led to the country's withdrawal from the British Commonwealth. However, in the late 1960s, the National Party softened its Afrikaner nationalist image to attract conservative English-speaking voters and to foster racial solidarity among the white population.

Under P. W. Botha's leadership during the 1980s, the National Party, under tremendous domestic and international pressure, began to reform its racist policies. It attempted to relax the Group Areas Act and grant a measure of political representation to both the coloured and the Indian population by creating separate parliamentary chambers, which allowed them to have control over their own affairs. Despite these reforms, the black majority still remained excluded from political representation because both Botha and his party refused to compromise on the issue of granting political rights to black South Africans. In 1989, Botha resigned as the National Party leader and as the president due to rising political instability, diplomatic isolation, and grave economic problems. He was succeeded by FREDERICK WILLEM DE KLERK. Although de Klerk was a conservative, he was also a political pragmatist and realized that the apartheid system could not be maintained forever. Therefore, de Klerk decided and also persuaded the National Party to enter into negotiations with the black community while the environment would still allow the party to negotiate for a transition to black majority rule on favorable terms.

After winning a bitterly contested election in 1989, the party was persuaded to end the apartheid system, which it had established half a century earlier, by implementing a series of reforms and by entering into several rounds of negotiations with the AFRICAN NATIONAL CONGRESS (ANC). In early 1990, the ANC was legalized, and NELSON MANDELA was released from prison after serving twenty-seven years of a life term. By the end of 1991, multiparty negotiations were launched, leading to the adoption of an interim CONSTITUTION in November 1993. In 1994, the country's first democratic and nonracial nationwide election was held, and the National Party came second after the ANC by winning 82 out of 400 National Assembly seats. After the 1994 ELECTION, de Klerk was named as one of the two executive deputy-presidents under Mandela's ANC-dominated Government of National Unity. In 1997, de Klerk retired from politics, and the National Party's popularity drastically declined. In 1998, it changed its name to the New National Party in order to distance itself from its apartheid past, and in the 1999 legislative elections, it won twenty-eight seats. In the 2004 general elections, the party won only seven parliamentary seats. Subsequently, it merged with the Democratic Party and then with the ANC, and eventually dissolved itself on April 9, 2005.

Natives' Land Act of 1913

Described by the early-twentieth-century writer and politician SOL T. PLAATJE as "the most ruthless law that ever disgraced the white man's rule," the Natives' Land Act (1913) established the legal basis for territorial segregation by institutionalizing the system of "native reserves" throughout South Africa. Similar legislation was first adopted in NATAL in 1846 and was the rural complement to the subsequent Urban Areas Act (1923), which enforced urban segregation and black influx control.

The Land Act divided South Africa into native and nonnative areas. Although Africans made up 67 percent of the population, the act designated only 7.1 percent of the land for the native reserves and prohibited Africans from purchasing or renting land outside of these reserves. The act also required African tenants on European farms to perform at least ninety days of unpaid labor, thereby eliminating sharecropping and cash rentals as options for African tenancy. It thus enabled landowners to expand the production of maize by evicting sharecroppers and herders, enlarged the pool of cheap migrant labor for the mines, satisfied white demands for segregation, and appeased white liberals who wanted to protect African land rights.

Consisting almost entirely of disconnected tracts of land dispersed throughout eastern and northern South Africa, the reserves were characterized by overcrowding, undernourishment, and family breakup due to the MIGRANT LABOR system. The only significant block of territory was the Transkei, located in present-day Eastern Cape Province.

The newly formed AFRICAN NATIONAL CONGRESS (then the South African Natives National Congress) opposed the act and petitioned the British government to prevent its implementation. Plaatje's *Native Life in South Africa* vividly portrays the forced evictions that followed in the wake of the act. JOHN L. DUBE, the first president of the national congress, was ousted from his position in 1917 for insisting that the organization should oppose the details of this act but not the principle of segregation.

In 1936, the Native Trust and Land Act adopted the long-neglected recommendations of the Beaumont Commission (1916) by enabling the government to identify and purchase additional lands for the reserves—eventually expanding their scope to 13 percent of the land. African-owned lands outside of the reserves were labeled "black spots" and targeted for forced removal. This legislation also increased the minimum tenancy requirements from 90 to 180 days of unpaid labor and extended the jurisdiction of the Land Act to the Cape Province, where constitutional protections had prevented its earlier application. In 1951, the APARTHEID regime merged the native reserves into ten homelands (BANTUSTANS) and delegated local administrative authority to African leaders. This formed the basis for the policy of separate development.

The Land Act was finally repealed in 1991 by the Abolition of Racially Based Land Measures Act No. 108. Land restitution for blacks in postapartheid South Africa, which has been slowly and sporadically implemented since 1994, applies only to lands expropriated after the 1913 Natives' Land Act came into effect.

See also APARTHEID

Natives Representative Council

The Natives Representative Council (NRC) was established in 1937 in accordance with the Representation of Natives Act 12 of 1936, which formed part of the South African government's attempt to address and resolve the problem of black South Africans' lack of political representation. The 1936 Natives Act provided for the establishment of a council that consisted of partly nominated and partly elected African council members, whose function would be to advise the government on legislation and on policies affecting black South Africans' welfare. This council purported to be a political body that would serve the black South African population at the national level. When the NRC was first established, black South Africans were optimistic and had high hopes that it might develop into a native parliament or at the very least give them power to shape their own destiny. Some hoped that, with the passage of time, the NRC would be accorded authority and responsibility second to the supreme legislature.

The NRC met once or twice per year on a regular basis. Occasionally, special sessions were held to deal with urgent legislations that were not ready to be presented to the council during its ordinary sessions. The significance of this council was that it allowed both the nominated councilors and the elected representatives to submit recommendations and policies addressing various aspects of the black population's welfare. The NRC's select committees made detailed recommendations on draft legislations referred by the national government or by the provincial councils. NRC members prepared reports on certain aspects of the Native Administration such as the system of political representation for black South Africans, which were outlined in the Natives Act 12. The council also asked the South African Parliament to legislate policies on matters such as the recognition and registration of African trade unions as well as the proper financing and control of African education. The NRC provided a forum for a select group of African intellectuals, eager to compromise with the white South African government, to try to influence government decisions and policymaking.

However, the NRC was not taken seriously by the South African government but was largely confined to engaging and perhaps influencing the Native Affairs Department. The rest of the government took little notice of the council, if aware of its existence at all. The NRC, having become deadlocked with the JAN SMUTS government, ceased to meet after 1946 and was finally abolished by the NATIONAL PARTY government in 1951.

See also AFRICAN NATIONAL CONGRESS; ALL-AFRICAN CONVENTION; JOHN L. DUBE; JAMES HERTZOG

Ndebele

The Ndebele are a Bantu-speaking people, also known as the Matabele or the amaNdebele, primarily of southwestern ZIMBABWE. Historically, the Ndebele were one of the Nguni ethnic groups, which represent approximately two-thirds of South Africa's black population and include other groups such as the ZULU, the XHOSA, and the SWAZI people. Originally, the Ndebele were a branch of the Zulu people who broke away from King SHAKA in the early 1820s under MZILIKAZI's leadership. In the late 1830s, Mzilikazi established the Matabele kingdom in Bulawayo. Under his leadership, many Ndebele became formidable warriors who often conquered the smaller chiefdoms and assimilated them into Ndebele society. With the arrival of the BOER trekkers, they frequently became engaged in territorial disputes with them.

During the APARTHEID regime in South Africa, many Ndebele living in northern Transvaal were assigned to the predominantly seSOTHO-speaking homeland of Lebowa, which comprised several land segments scattered across northern Transvaal. Meanwhile, the southern Ndebele, who had retained elements of their culture and language, were assigned to KwaNdebele, another black homeland created by the apartheid regime.

Culturally, the Ndebele are renowned for their aesthetic talents, especially for their painted houses and colorful beadwork. For over a century, the Ndebele have decorated the exterior of their homes with colorful and multifarious designs. The most frequent theme of their home design is the finger-produced multicolor wall paintings. The dresses worn by Ndebele women and their beautifully decorated homes in South Africa are unique on the African continent.

New Social Movements

In South Africa, the term *new social movements* is employed to designate a diverse set of movements largely formed after THABO MBEKI became president in 1999 and after the effects of the country's neoliberal economic growth policy, GROWTH, EMPLOYMENT, AND REDISTRIBUTION STRATEGY, came to be acutely felt. They opposed key policies of the new black government and were frustrated with the pace of social and economic change in the new democratic dispensation. These movements include the TREATMENT ACTION CAMPAIGN (TAC), established in 1998; Concerned Citizens Forum, 1999; Anti-Eviction Campaign (AEC), Anti-Privatization Forum, and Soweto Electricity Crisis Committee (SECC), all established in 2000; the Landless Peoples Movement (LPM) and Coalition of South Africans for the Basic Income Grant, 2001; the Education Rights Project, 2002; and Abahlali baseMjondolo ("the people who live in shacks"), 2005. In many instances, these movements gained international recognition and attention, as have some of its leaders, most notably ZACKIE ACHMAT of the TAC and Trevor Ngwane of the SECC.

South Africa's new movements are significant for a number of reasons. First, they build upon a legacy of mobilization and organization against the APARTHEID state, but often individuals who struggled together in the past are now on opposite sides of the debate and, many times, protest lines. Second, their rise marked the end of what might be referred to as the honeymoon period for the AFRICAN NATIONAL CONGRESS (ANC)—the first five years of postapartheid government. Third, they call attention to the marginalization of large numbers of South African citizens who, in various ways, have been left behind by the promises of liberation. They have, therefore, raised significant socioeconomic issues that have had a profound impact upon national debates and, at times, also on policymaking. Fourth, as these movements engage in different methods of action and different degrees of competition and cooperation with the government, they demonstrate a range of responses to marginalization. Finally, the interactions between the movements and the government have illustrated both the strengths and weaknesses of South Africa's new democracy.

The antiapartheid struggle mobilized large numbers of ordinary South Africans to work together as workers, women, students, and community residents. The histories and experiences of their organizations have provided a basis for postapartheid social movements by defining successful repertoires of action, organizing and mobilizing strategies, and networks that both younger and older activists have drawn upon. The clearest predecessors to many of the newer movements that organize black township residents to address poor service delivery, housing, and basic living conditions are the civic associations, popularly known as civics. From the first broader civic associations in SOWETO and PORT ELIZABETH launched in 1979, these groups spread to urban townships throughout the country to organize actions from rent boycotts to street cleanups, and they played a significant role in the UNITED DEMOCRATIC FRONT (UDF) and the demise of the apartheid state. In 1992, the majority of civics joined to form the South African National Civics Organization.

With the formal end of apartheid in 1994 and the ANC's election to government, many social movements, including the civics, went into a period of decline. Many either folded or transformed themselves into service-delivery organizations working alongside local government. Though unions remained active and large strikes frequently made headlines, other forms of open protest declined markedly. The end of apartheid also brought many leading activists into the corridors of power and suggested that change would now largely occur through formal institutional processes rather than extra-institutional action such as street protests. However, as the dates of the formation of the movements indicate, by 2000, extra-institutional activism was once again growing.

Many of these new actors have sought to raise awareness of ordinary people's socioeconomic concerns. TAC, for example, seeks to bring greater attention to HIV/AIDS, to eliminate the stigma associated with the disease, and to pressure the government to provide treatment for people living with AIDS regardless of their ability to pay. The AEC and SECC were originally formed to address evictions and electricity disconnections but expanded their mandate over time to more broadly respond to the crisis of service delivery and housing. Finally, the LPM was formed with the support of the National Land Committee, a nonprofit organization born out of apartheid-era anti-eviction campaigns, to address the slow pace of land reform and redistribution to blacks. Together, they have drawn significant attention to the demands of marginalized communities in South Africa. For example, during the August 2002 United Nations World Summit on Sustainable Development, the AEC, SECC, LPM, and other movements marched with an estimated 40,000 people from impoverished Alexandra Township to the wealthy neighborhood of Sandton where the summit was held. This march received prominent coverage in both national and international newspapers such as the *New York Times* (September 1, 2002).

South Africa's movements have sought to find immediate solutions to address urgent material needs while also looking to the longer term by engaging in legal processes. By not only demanding greater access to electricity but also reconnecting individuals disconnected by the electricity supplier, Eskom, the SECC has drawn attention to the electricity crisis in Soweto and beyond, where high rates are being charged for intermittent service. The AEC has helped individuals to resist evictions and supported evicted families in court. The LPM has drawn attention to the lack of land reform and to the lack of access to land through various means, including land invasions, whereby white farms are illegally invaded and taken over by blacks. To effectively force the government to expand its antiretroviral programs, the TAC has employed sit-ins, the illegal importation of a generic form of Flucanazole (an anti-fungal drug used in the treatment of AIDS patients), marches, and court actions. Abahlali baseMjondolo has countered repressive legislation, taking their challenge all the way to the Constitutional Court and winning a significant victory for shack dwellers' rights.

While these movements have effectively drawn attention to the groups' demands, their actions have not usually led to a cooperative relationship with the government nor, with the exception of TAC, significant success in bringing about changes in basic material conditions. In response to the SECC's work, Eskom wrote off 1.39 billion rand (US$190 million) in 2003 in electricity arrears but excluded the SECC from the discussion. It has also refused to change the policies that led to the buildup of arrears, thereby creating an ongoing cycle of disconnections and illegal reconnections of electricity. Government leaders and ANC activists have often adopted part of a movement's demands, such as the need to address land issues or electricity arrears, but often do so without recognizing the underlying problems that the movements seek to address: the inability of poor South Africans to pay for needed services and housing. Activists in the SECC, as well as the LPM and Abahlali, who broadly challenge the government's neoliberal economic program, have also been the target of state harassment, including arrests and extended court proceedings, which work to distract the movements' attention and drain their meager financial resources. In contrast, the TAC maintains a slightly less contentious relationship with the government due to its self-presentation as a government ally in providing access to antiretrovirals, its tendency to favor institutional processes as a means to bring about change, and its high-profile supporters, including former president Nelson Mandela.

Overall, South Africa's new movements have demanded greater accountability from public representatives as well as greater transparency and inclusion in decisionmaking processes. While more marginalized groups, such as the SECC and the AEC, have employed more radical and illegal measures to draw attention to their demands, they have also sought to work within the legal structures whenever possible: by seeking permits for their marches, engaging the courts, working to make ordinary citizens aware of their rights under the new Constitution and subsequent laws, and supporting independent candidates for office in local elections. Although only the TAC has developed a strong formal organizational structure and solid funding support, this does not suggest, however, that its impact has been the greatest. Each of these movements, through its critique of state policies, has broadened public debate concerning the rights of citizens and the duties of the state. While the more radical movements offer a broad challenge to the state's economic policies and therefore are less likely to see their ideas implemented, in the short term their arguments and actions provide an alternative conception of what is necessary and what is possible in defining a new South Africa, not just in the institutional configurations of government but also in the minds of ordinary citizens.

See also ZACKIE ACHMAT; TREATMENT ACTION CAMPAIGN

Bibliography

Ballard, Richard, Adam Habib, and Imraan Valodia, eds. *Voices of Protest: Social Movements in Post-Apartheid South Africa*. Scottsville, South Africa: University of KwaZulu-Natal Press, 2006.

Desai, Ashwin. *We Are the Poors: Community Struggles in Post-Apartheid South Africa*. New York: Monthly Review Press, 2002.

Gibson, Nigel, ed. *Challenging Hegemony: Social Movements and the Quest for a New Humanism in Post-Apartheid South Africa*. Trenton, NJ: Africa World Press, 2006.

Zuern, Elke. *The Politics of Necessity: Community Organizing and Democracy in South Africa*. Madison: University of Wisconsin Press, 2011.

—Elke Zuern

Ngoni

The Ngoni are a broad ethnic category of people living mainly in Malawi, Tanzania, and Zambia, but also in MOZAMBIQUE. They are related to the ZULU who reside in South Africa's KwaZulu-Natal Province. Their original languages are chiTumbuka, chiChewa, and isiZulu. Even though the Ngoni have maintained their identity in their host countries, they have also assimilated into the local societies and adopted local languages as their mother tongues. The Ngoni have a mixed heritage of farming, herding, and cattle raiding, and of extraordinary military tactics and organization, which they brought to southern and eastern Africa. Their history dates back to the early nineteenth century, during the period of political instability in southern Africa known as the MFECANE, when the Zulu Kingdom was established and a number of different ethnic groups were created. The creation and destruction of the various kingdoms led to the mass migration of the Ngoni from South Africa's KwaZulu-Natal region to different venues throughout southern Africa. In addition to the political instability, expanding their cattle herds was one of the main factors motivating them to migrate northward toward current-day Zambia and Mozambique. As they moved northward, the Ngoni also raided and expanded their military power by taking women for marriage and by incorporating men into their armies.

Ngoyi, Lillian (1911–1980)

Lillian Ngoyi was a leading female activist against APARTHEID known as the "mother of black resistance." Born Lillian Masediba in PRETORIA on September 24, 1911, she was educated at the Kilnerton Institution, a theological institution for Methodists that came to include a teacher training college and high school, but she was forced to leave school early to work in order to support her family. She married John Ngoyi in 1934 and they had three children together, but her husband died when the youngest was only three. From 1945 through 1956, Ngoyi worked as a machinist in a clothing factory, became a leading member of the Garment Workers' Union, and actively entered into antiapartheid politics.

Ngoyi joined the AFRICAN NATIONAL CONGRESS (ANC) in 1952, and was elected president of the AFRICAN NATIONAL CONGRESS WOMEN'S LEAGUE within a year. In 1956, she became the first woman ever elected to the ANC National Executive Committee. Ngoyi also held the positions of national vice president and subsequently president of the Federation of South African Women.

On August 9, 1956, Ngoyi (along with HELEN JOSEPH, Sophie Williams, and Rahima Moosa) led 20,000 women on a demonstration against the PASS LAWS at the Union Buildings in Pretoria. After depositing thousands of signed petitions at the doorstep of Prime Minister Johannes Strijdom's office, Ngoyi raised her clenched fist in the liberation salute and led the crowd in a thirty-minute silent protest, followed by the singing of "Nkosi Sikelele y-Afrika," a popular African hymn that is now the country's national anthem. This historic day is now celebrated in South Africa as Women's Day. In December 1956, she was arrested for high treason along with 156 other activists. She stood trial, along with NELSON MANDELA and WALTER SISULU, among others, as one of the thirty accused in the TREASON TRIAL, which lasted from 1956 to 1961. Although the defendants were acquitted, Ngoyi received her banning orders in October 1962 (which lasted until her death eighteen years later). From 1962 to 1972, she was confined to the Orlando Township located outside of JOHANNESBURG and was forbidden to attend meetings or publish. In the mid-1960s, she was jailed under the ninety-day detention act and spent seventy-one days in solitary confinement.

Ma Ngoyi, as she was referred to, was known for her fiery speeches. *DRUM* magazine (1956) described her as "the most talked of woman in politics—she can toss an audience on her little finger, get men grunting with shame and infuse everyone with renewed courage." She often directly challenged men to live up to the example set by the women's resistance movement.

On March 12, 1980, Ngoyi died at the age of sixty-eight, after suffering from an acute heart condition. Two years later, she received the highest award of the liberation movement, the Isitwalandwe/Seaparankoe Medal.

See also WOMEN AND POLITICS

Ngqika (1775–1829)

Ngqika was the paramount chief of the Rharhabe XHOSA. Born in 1775, Ngqika grew up in the Ciskei region of the present-day Eastern Cape Province under his uncle's guardianship after both his father and grandfather died on the battlefield when he was young. As he entered adulthood, Ngqika became enemies with his uncle, Ndlambe, over claims to the chieftainship. When he turned seventeen, Ngqika imprisoned his uncle, but Ndlambe was able to escape from his nephew's captivity and led a revolt against him. In 1818, Ngqika was defeated by Ndlambe and his allies, which included the Gcaleka Xhosa chief Hintsa. Facing defeat, Ngqika appealed to the British authorities in the CAPE COLONY for military assistance. Believing that he was the legitimate Xhosa paramount chief, the British helped him, and Ngqika's forces were able to defeat Ndlambe's army and make them acknowledge his position as the legitimate Rharhabe Xhosa paramount chief.

Despite his victories, Ngqika was not a popular leader due to his greed. He often devised various strategies to exploit his people and to deprive them of their cattle by arbitrarily changing inheritance laws. Additionally, in return for British military assistance, Ngqika had to relinquish a large area of his territory to the British, which weakened his popular support, as the territorial renouncement led to further land encroachments by European settlers. In 1819, Cape governor Lord Charles Somerset forced Ngqika to give up additional territories between the Kei and the Keiskamma rivers, in present-day Eastern Cape Province, to be designated as "neutral territories."

Ngqika died a pariah among the Rharhabe Xhosa people in 1829 and was buried near Burnshill on the Keiskamma River. After his death, his son Fandile succeeded him as the Rharhabe Xhosa paramount chief.

Non-European Unity Movement

The Non-European Unity Movement (NEUM) was short-lived, lasting from 1943 to 1960, and evolving from the All-African and the Anti-Coloured Affairs Department (Anti-CAD) conventions. Launched in BLOEMFONTEIN, in the Free State Province, in December 1943 as an organization for national liberation based on socialist ideologies, NEUM's purpose was to unite all the members of the nonwhite groups in South Africa—blacks, COLOUREDS, and INDIANS—regardless of religion, class, or ethnicity. Its three main objectives were: (1) to eliminate the systematic nationwide oppression of nonwhite South Africans, (2) to acquire guarantees of equal rights and privileges for both the white and nonwhite population in South Africa, and (3) to ultimately incorporate the white population into the formation of a nationwide movement united by its twelve-point democratic demands. To achieve its goals, NEUM aimed to employ nonviolent strategies of boycotts and noncooperation against the APARTHEID regime.

Its democratic demands were:

1. Political rights for every South African man and woman over the age of twenty-one to run and be elected in the parliamentary, provincial, and local elections;
2. Free, compulsory, and equal education for all children up to age sixteen with free meals, textbooks, and school materials for those in need;
3. The right to habeas corpus (protection against unlawful imprisonment) as well as protection from arbitrary arrests and home searches;
4. Freedom of speech, press, meetings, and associations;
5. Freedom of movement and occupation;
6. Equal political and legal rights for all South African citizens regardless of race, sex, and color;
7. Abolition of the poll tax or any other tax specifically geared toward the nonwhite population;
8. Revision of the Industrial Conciliation and Wage Acts by eliminating all restrictions and distinctions between white and nonwhite workers;
9. Equal pay for equal work;
10. Equal access to apprenticeship and skilled labor;
11. Abrogation of all punishments that denigrate a person's basic human dignity (that is, no inequalities in the penalties for crimes committed based on race); and
12. Proportionate land division and distribution for those who work and live on them, so that blacks, who make up more than 77 percent of the population, cannot be allocated only 13 percent of the land.

During its existence, the NEUM gained a strong reputation for its uncompromising stance on nonracism, which became one of the highlights of its political discourse and philosophy. In practice, however, the racial divisions created by decades of apartheid and racial discrimination created tension and a degree of disunity within the movement. To overcome these obstacles and unite the country's three main nonwhite racial groups, the NEUM implemented a federal structure consisting of three branches: ALL-AFRICAN CONVENTION for blacks, the Anti-CAD for the coloured population, and the Indian Congress for the Indians. The hope was that these three branches would eventually merge into one after the ideas of non-European unity were accepted by all. In reality, the NEUM was ahead of its time when it came to its nonracial philosophy. Despite having limited impact at that time, its policies and practices exerted influence on future highly successful anti-apartheid movements and campaigns.

The NEUM responded with boycotts to DANIEL MALAN's election as South Africa's prime minister in 1948 and his implementation of the apartheid system. However, the movement was quickly embroiled in internal feuds and had to contend with splinter groups. When it could not effectively respond to the SHARPVILLE MASSACRE of sixty-nine black protesters on March 21, 1960, the NEUM became marginalized and completely collapsed in 1960. Despite its revival as the New Unity Movement in 1989, it exerts little or no influence on contemporary South African politics or society.

Nongqawuse (ca. 1841–?)

Nongqawuse was a young XHOSA girl whose prophecies prompted the Xhosa Cattle-Killing Movement from 1856 to 1857. The fifteen-year-old niece of the Xhosa prophet Mhlakaza claimed to have received a message from the ancestors instructing people to kill all of their cattle and destroy all of their crops as an act of faith in the ancestors. In return, the ancestors would restore their disease-ridden herds and also drive the white settlers from their lands. For ten months, the Gcaleka and other Xhosa clans killed their cattle and burned their crops almost to the point of self-destruction. Her prophecy turned out to be a hoax but was responsible for the starvation of almost 25,000 Xhosa and the final collapse of Xhosa independence. Nongqawuse survived and was handed over to the custody of a British officer and his wife. In 1858, they took her to CAPE TOWN and placed her in the Paupers' Lodge. It is possible that when the lodge closed the following year she returned to the Eastern Cape. A government official stated in 1905 that she was living on a farm near PORT ELIZABETH.

Bibliography
Peires, J. B. *The Dead Will Arise: Nongqawuse and the Great Xhosa Cattle Killing Movement of 1856–7.* Bloomington: Indiana University Press, 1989.

NP
See NATIONAL PARTY

O

Ohlange Institute

The Ohlange Institute was founded in 1901 by the Reverend JOHN L. DUBE as a ZULU and Christian industrial school. Influenced by his own schooling and experiences in the United States, he modeled the Ohlange Institute after the Tuskegee Institute. This school's aim was to build African self-sufficiency, and it began by teaching the subjects of English and accounting.

The school was renamed Ohlange High School and is a coeducational, public school in the Inanda community outside of DURBAN administered by the KwaZulu-Natal Department of Education. It was at the polling booths set up at Ohlange High School that NELSON MANDELA cast his historic vote on April 27, 1994.

P

PAC
See PAN AFRICANIST CONGRESS

Paleoanthropology

Rivaling the east African countries of Kenya, Tanzania, and Ethiopia, South Africa is endowed with a treasure trove of fossils for paleoanthropologists. Because they confirm the existence of a species between human and ape, the most notable finds are the 1924 Taung Child discovered by Raymond Dart and the 1927 fossil discovery by Robert Broom, dubbed Mrs. Ples. These remains of *Australopithecus africanus* were among the first indications that *Homo sapiens* evolved in Africa.

The Cradle of Humankind, located slightly to the north and west of JOHANNESBURG, is the single most prolific paleoanthropological region in the world, with twelve major fossil sites and dozens of smaller ones, including the world-famous Sterkfontein Cave. Hominin species such as *Australopithecus robustus, Homo habilis, Homo erectus*, and an archaic *Homo sapiens* have been found in the area. These wide-ranging fossil deposits, as well as an apparent validation by modern genetic studies, lead many scholars to believe that the transition from premodern hominins to modern humans occurred in southern Africa.

Because finding a common human family tree was not of interest to South Africa's APARTHEID leaders, paleoanthropological research slowed considerably for about fifty years, from 1948 through 1994. With the 1994 transition to democracy, however, there has been a resurgence in research activity. In 1998, "Little Foot" was the most complete australopithecine early hominin yet to be discovered in South Africa.

The excavations of MAPUNGUBWE, discovered in 1933, and at K2 uncovered previously unsubstantiated information about the political, economic, and social structures of more-recent southern African peoples. Located at the confluence of the Limpopo and Shashe rivers, these Iron Age sites dating from ca. 1050–1270 A.D. document a flourishing, socially differentiated, trading kingdom that was a precursor to Great Zimbabwe, as it had ties with East Africa, Egypt, Persia, India, and China. In particular, these settlements demonstrate the early smithing of gold, iron, and copper for practical, decorative, and trading purposes. Although Mapungubwe was revealed to researchers in 1933, when it became an active site, public knowledge of this ancient African kingdom was squashed because its existence contradicted the "vacant land" and apartheid racial superiority postulates. The vacant land thesis purported that there were no Africans living in South Africa when the Dutch first arrived in 1652 and thus the white settlers had not "taken" anyone's land. Similarly a strong justification for apartheid was the thesis that whites were superior to blacks and that there had not existed African or black civilizations, comparable to white European civilizations, in precolonial Africa.

A. R. Radcliffe Brown, a founder of the structural-functionalist school of social anthropology that views human behavior in its broader social context, started the Department of Social Anthropology at the University of CAPE TOWN in 1921. The Department of Social Anthropology at the University of Witwatersrand began in 1923. The academic standard in social anthropology was intensive field research that led to comprehensive monographs about indigenous societies. These ethnographies typically focused on kinship and or marriage, political organization, and religion.

W. D. Hammond-Tooke describes the 1930s to 1950s as the golden age of South African ethnography. The ethnographers who helped set the discipline's standard were Max Gluckman (*Analysis of a Social Situation in Modern Zululand*), Eileen Krige (*The Social System of the Zulus*), Jack Krige (*The Realm of the Rain Queen*, with E. Krige), Hilda Kuper (*An African Aristocracy: Rank Among the Swazi*), Phillip Mayer (*Townsmen or Tribesmen*), Issac Schapera (*A Handbook of Tswana Law and Custom*), and Monica Wilson (*Reaction to Conquest*). Other important ethnographers of South African peoples in the English-speaking tradition were Hugh Ashton, W. D. Hammond-Tooke, Ellen Hellman, Winifred Hoernlé, and Desmond Reader. Archie Mafeje (*The Theory and Ethnography of African Social Formations*), Harriet Ngubane (*Body and Mind in Zulu Medicine*), and Absolom Vilakazi (*Zulu Transformations*) are among the few successful African anthropologists to emerge from this tradition.

By the 1950s, with Schapera at the London School of Economics, Gluckman at Manchester University, Meyer Fortes (*The Dynamics of Clanship Among the Tallensi*) at Cambridge University, and South African ethnographies firmly established as important sources of anthropological theory, the English-speaking tradition of South African anthropology was at the heart of the discipline.

Anthropology (Volkekunde) in the Afrikaans-speaking tradition took a different trajectory. Though more firmly rooted in language studies, Volkekunde was not in the structural-functionalist school as it looked to US cultural anthropology—in particular to Robert Lowie. Establishing cultural selection as a form of natural selection and relating culture to race were AFRIKANER scholars' major preoccupations, and this view provided much of the intellectual justification and legitimation for apartheid's postulate of racial superiority that emphasized the intellectual and cultural superiority of whites over blacks.

Anthropologists from the Afrikaans-speaking tradition were active members of the BROEDERBOND and formed the NATIONAL PARTY's intellectual brain trust. Some were major architects of apartheid. For instance, although the term *apartheid policy* apparently first appeared in a University of STELLENBOSCH PhD history dissertation in 1937, all members in the anthropology department at the University of Stellenbosch (R. D. Coertze, F. J. Language, and B. I. Van Eeden) advocated the policy of "total apartheid" in their influential 1943 publication, *Die Oplossing van die Naturellevraagstuk in Suid-Afrika: Wenke ooreenkomstig die Afrikanerstandpunt van Apartheid* (The Solution of the Native Problem in South Africa: Suggestions Concerning the Afrikaner Standpoint on Apartheid). After teaching anthropology at the University of Stellenbosch and at the University of Pretoria, W. W. M. Eiselen was appointed secretary for native affairs under H. F. VERWOERD; in 1949, he chaired the commission that recommended the establishment of BANTU EDUCATION. Although Eiselen later repudiated apartheid, P. G. J. Koornhof, a student of Eiselen and Fortes, occupied various ministerial posts in the apartheid governments of B. J. Vorster and P. W. Botha during the 1970s and the 1980s.

The role of anthropologists from the English-speaking tradition with respect to segregation and apartheid is more difficult to determine. This group's defenders argue that the structural-functionalist approach, which viewed human behavior in its broad social context, was an inherent challenge to preapartheid and apartheid social relations, as were the anthropologists who were actually living among Africans. Nonetheless, David Webster, a prominent Marxist who was murdered by a government hit squad in 1989, was among the few activist anthropologists whose work directly engaged the prevailing social paradigms of the time. The social/cultural/political environment seems to have led anthropologists of conscience in the English-speaking tradition to engage with less confrontational issues, such as poverty and underdevelopment, as opposed to tackling issues of race and culture.

Bibliography
Eriksen, Thomas Hylland, and Finn Sivert Nielsen. *A History of Anthropology*. London: Pluto Press, 2001.
Government of South Africa. "Mapungubwe: SA's Lost City of Gold." www.southafrica.info/ess_info/sa_glance/history/mapungubwe.htm.
Hammond-Tooke, W. D. *Imperfect Interpreters: South Africa's Anthropologists, 1920–1990*. Johannesburg, South Africa: University of Witwatersrand Press, 1997.
Hilton-Barber, Brett, and Lee Berger. *Field Guide to the Cradle of Humankind*. Cape Town, South Africa: Struik Publishers, 2004.
Kuper, Adam. *Anthropology and Anthropologists: The Modern British School*. New York: Routledge, 1996.

—Walton Johnson

Pan Africanist Congress

The Pan Africanist Congress (PAC), later renamed the Pan Africanist Congress of Azania, was an important and influential liberation movement founded in 1959 when several members broke away from the AFRICAN NATIONAL CONGRESS (ANC). Today, it exists as a minor party in South Africa's democracy.

ROBERT SOBUKWE is considered PAC's founder and first leader. He and his followers left the ANC because they disagreed with its nonracial approach and advocated a bolder, purely black, African-centered focus to the liberation struggle. These tensions came to a head after the drafting of the FREEDOM CHARTER in 1955, which was co-written by a Congress Alliance of multiracial groups. Sobukwe and his followers were concerned about the influence non-Africans had over the ANC.

Under Sobukwe's leadership, PAC quickly gained prominence and increased its following. It embarked on a number of campaigns against the APARTHEID system, most notably against the PASS LAWS that restricted blacks' movements, which culminated in a series of marches in 1960. One of the antipass marches turned deadly, now referred to as the SHARPEVILLE MASSACRE, and proved to be a key turning point in apartheid and antiapartheid politics.

After the Sharpeville Massacre, the PAC and other liberation movements were banned and forced to operate underground. Many of its leaders, including Sobukwe, were arrested and jailed for many years. In light of the apartheid regime's violent and brutal nature, the PAC decided that armed struggle was now a necessary tactic and formed a military wing named Poqo. It set up operations in exile but suffered greatly from a lack of leadership and never developed the reputation or the organizational infrastructure that the ANC did in exile. After uncovering a number of PAC documents and member mailing lists, the police in 1963 executed a broad sweep of PAC activists, arrested over 2,000 of them, and effectively crippled the organization.

In the mid-1970s, PAC gained a degree of strength and stature, as many young activists fled the country after the SOWETO STUDENT UPRISING and joined the PAC and its armed wing, renamed the Azanian People's Liberation Army, which had camps in Tanzania and Angola. However, especially after Sobukwe's death, leadership problems and weak organization still plagued PAC, tarnishing its image in exile and at home.

In 1990, PAC was unbanned along with other liberation movements but continued to be plagued by infighting. Part of the PAC refused to participate in the multiparty negotiations to draft a new CONSTITUTION, and in the first democratic ELECTIONS in 1994 the party fared poorly as it won only a small percentage of votes. In subsequent elections, its base shrunk even further. However, the party continues to contest national and local government elections, and there are pockets of support for the party around the country.

Parliament
See APPENDIX 3: GOVERNMENT STRUCTURES

Pass Laws

Pass laws provided a powerful and highly adaptable instrument for regulating movement, labor, and settlement in South Africa. Throughout much of South Africa's colonial and APARTHEID history, black Africans were required by law to carry a pass or passbook with them at all times that would indicate their identity, their work status, and their qualifications for being in a particular town or area. Introduced in the 1760s to prevent the desertion of slaves in the CAPE COLONY, pass laws were used to compel the KHOIKHOI and SAN to work for whites after the abolition of the slave trade. By 1827, the Cape also used pass laws to set employment requirements for uprooted, urbanized Africans, and the rural districts used these laws to keep African workers on white farms.

GOLD AND DIAMOND MINING relied on passes to enforce the MIGRANT LABOR system. In KIMBERLEY and the Transvaal, Africans were issued passes by the state only for the duration of their work contracts. This prevented permanent African settlement and enforced a pattern of migrant labor from the African reserves to the mines. It also depressed African wages because mine owners assumed that Africans supported themselves with agricultural production in the reserves.

Pass laws increasingly became an instrument of urban influx control used by the state to prevent overcrowding and social unrest in the white cities. The Native Urban Areas Act (1923) turned passes into tools for policing unemployment—if you didn't already have a job you were not allowed to enter the urban areas. A 1937 amendment empowered municipalities to prevent the entry of Africans into cities with a labor surplus. Also used to break strikes and suppress resistance by expelling or arresting those with illegal pass status, passes became a target of popular resistance—from campaigns by African women in 1913 and 1918–1922 as well as SOUTH AFRICAN COMMUNIST PARTY protests in 1930 and 1943–1944.

Before 1948, pass laws were neither uniformly applicable nor effectively enforced. With growing white fears about *swart gevaar* (black peril), the apartheid legislations tightened the pass laws. The Natives (Abolition of Passes and Co-ordination of Documents) Act (1952) substituted a uniform reference book for eleven provincial pass laws, which required all Africans older than sixteen to carry reference books and gave Africans three days to find work before being "endorsed out" of a white town. The reference book included an African's photo, racial classification, employer's signature, history of tax payments, encounters with the police, and employment status. A large bureaucracy—called the labor bureau—was created to issue passes and allocate labor on the basis of regional demand.

Meanwhile, Section 10 of the Natives Urban Areas Consolidation Act (1945) created pass law exemptions for Africans who had lived in a city since birth or lawfully for fifteen years or had worked for the same employer for ten years. These exemptions helped establish a permanent urban working class while enforcing influx control and perpetuating migrant labor.

In 1956, the Federation of South African Women and the AFRICAN NATIONAL CONGRESS WOMEN'S LEAGUE organized a 20,000-strong march to PRETORIA to protest the extension of pass laws to African women. Prior to 1956 the pass laws had largely only applied to African men. In 1960, an antipass campaign by the PAN AFRICANIST CONGRESS was violently repressed, especially in Sharpeville where police killed at least sixty-nine protesters and injured 180. This wave of protests led to mass arrests and the banning of political organizations.

Pass law violations generated hundreds of thousands of arrests each year, totaling 17.25 million by 1981. Beginning in 1972, pass law offenders were deported to the BANTUSTANS, the reserves created for blacks.

Squatter movements, gray areas, and growing industrial demands for semiskilled rather than unskilled labor led to the pass laws' eventual repeal through the 1986 Identification Act. The apartheid state came to realize that such strict control over the movement of the African population was untenable and economically detrimental. This led to massive urbanization and to severe housing crises in cities throughout South Africa as blacks flocked from the countryside into the cities.

See also APARTHEID; MIGRANT LABOR; SHARPEVILLE MASSACRE

Pedi

The Pedi constitute the major group of the Northern SOTHO, one of South Africa's black, Bantu-speaking, ethnic groups. They comprise nearly 10 percent of South Africa's population, and sePedi is one of the eleven official LANGUAGES enshrined in the CONSTITUTION of the country. The Pedi are found mainly in the Limpopo Province and scattered across the Gauteng Province. SePedi, also known as Bapedi, Marota, and Bamaroteng, diverges from Southern Sotho (colloquially known as Sotho) and includes words derived from the nearby VENDA language as well as the Karanga from ZIMBABWE and Botswana.

The term *Pedi* also denotes a nineteenth-century African kingdom that was defeated in a series of wars by encroaching white BOER settlers and British colonialists. Indeed, historically, throughout the 1800s the Northern Sotho (Pedi) suffered at the hands of other invading southern African forces such as the ZULU and the SWAZI during territorial conflicts. Although several Pedi chiefdoms were able to recover from these clashes, after 1845, they had to deal with a large influx of Boer settlers, some of whom captured their children and forced them to work as slaves. In 1879, the Pedi were conquered by the British, AFRIKANER, and the SWAZI forces. Afterward, they lost their independence and were placed under the European authorities' control. The Northern Sotho territories were subsequently converted into reserves, and the Northern Sotho population was forced to relocate there.

See also LANGUAGE; SOTHO

Plaatje, Solomon (Sol) Thsekisho (1876–1932)

Writer, politician, and journalist, Solomon Thsekisho Plaatje was one of the most skillful and prominent black South Africans of his time. A founding member of the South African Native National Congress in 1912, later renamed the AFRICAN NATIONAL CONGRESS (ANC), Sol Plaatje committed his adult life to the African peoples' struggles against injustice and oppression.

Plaatje was born on October 9, 1876, in the BOER REPUBLIC of the Orange Free State. Early on, he received a mission education and later worked as a student teacher. To give voice to Africans, Plaatje decided to become a journalist and edited a number of African-language journals. He was also an interpreter for a time, having proficiency in at least eight African and European languages. On the eve of the ANGLO-BOER WAR he served as interpreter to the Mafikeng administrator for Native Affairs, but recognized that advancement within the civil service was closed to him. He, therefore, turned to journalism and with the financial backing of the Barolong chief, he established the first seTSWANA-English weekly, *Koranta ea Becoana* (Newspaper of the Tswana) in 1901.

With the UNION OF SOUTH AFRICA's formation in 1910, Plaatje, like many other Africans, saw the need for greater political organization within the black community. He first joined the COLOURED organization and then the African People's Organization led by ABDULLAH ABDURAHMAN. In 1912, he was a founding member of what would later be renamed the ANC and was elected as the organization's first secretary-general. Plaatje took a leading role in organizing black opposition to the 1913 NATIVES' LAND ACT and even led a delegation to Britain to protest this law, which designated over 80 percent of South Africa's arable land to whites and instituted a system of native reserves throughout South Africa for blacks. It was through his political struggles against the Land Act that he found his voice as a writer. His most famous book, *Native Life in South Africa*, was an indictment of the act and of African dispossession. He went on to write several more books that further reaffirmed his native seTswana language and culture. He also translated several Shakespeare works into seTswana.

Plaatje also traveled abroad widely in Europe, Canada, and the United States. In the United States, he met with leaders of the National Association for the Advancement of Colored People (NAACP) and arranged for an American edition of his book *Native Life*.

Plaatje died of pneumonia in 1932 while on a trip to JOHANNESBURG.

Political Cultures and Ideologies

The South African political landscape is laden with multiple ideologies, including liberalism, nationalism, Marxism, and black consciousness. Though claiming distinct ideological labels, they feed off each other, and some are constituted of multiple ideological strands. The predominance of particular political ideologies in South Africa's history has varied over time, with certain ideologies identified with specific historical epochs.

Liberalism

The oldest of the ideologies, liberalism made its initial entry into South African politics in the nineteenth century. Known as Cape liberal tradition, it initially established itself exclusively in the CAPE COLONY through a combination of the British intellectual elite, missionaries, and colonial administrators. This set the Cape apart from the other three colonies, at least until unification in 1910. Liberalism was marked by a free press, an independent judiciary, an elected government, and a nonracial voting franchise.

To be sure, allowing blacks to vote was not unique to the Cape, as it was also exercised in NATAL. However, the Cape was unique in that it was entrenched in the colony's political culture, while in Natal it was a result of political expediency. The British home government had imposed nonracial franchise as a condition for granting settlers in Natal self-government. But Natal's ruling elite did not believe in a nonracial franchise and imposed restrictive measures.

The Cape's liberal convictions also proved short-lived. Before the close of the nineteenth century, liberals supported measures that restricted Africans from qualifying for the franchise, including increasing the value of property qualification from £25 to £75. This drastic turnaround was prompted by a fear of being outnumbered by Africans as they swelled the ranks of voters, particularly in the 1880s, following the annexation of Transkei into the Cape Colony. Their increasing numbers had them constituting more than a majority in five of the Cape's constituencies, making them a decisive vote that swayed the balance of power in parliamentary politics. Steeped in their paternalistic ideas, liberals feared that African votes would eventually elect African representatives to Parliament.

Henceforth, liberals were distrusted by Africans, but the ideology itself held sway with many African elites, revealed in the human rights orientation and the inclusive character of African nationalism that subsequently emerged as a prominent political ideology among Africans. For the English-speaking community, though, liberalism became a cover for their support for illiberal policies. The traditional custodian of liberal values, the United Party, supported the banning of extraparliamentary parties and repressive laws such as detention without trial. However, the new generation of liberal parties that emerged in the 1950s, the Liberal and Progressive parties, vacillated between supporting limited and universal franchise while solidly uniting on the principle of (white) paternalism or tutelage over Africans. They believed that African voters were not fit to provide leadership but needed to defer to white leadership.

Within the black community, skepticism toward liberalism reached a high in the 1970s with the rise of the BLACK CONSCIOUSNESS MOVEMENT (BCM). STEVE BIKO, the founder and eloquent spokesperson for BCM, sarcastically referred to white liberals as "black souls in white skins"; they professed opposition to APARTHEID but were not willing to renounce the privileges accorded them by apartheid. Yet, the liberal influence still remained strong within the African nationalist movement. South Africa's post-apartheid CONSTITUTION, for instance, is hailed as the most liberal in the world. This is because it is partly based on the 1996 BILL OF RIGHTS, which recognizes political, economic, and civil rights and the right of homosexuals to marry with rights similar to heterosexuals.

Afrikaner Nationalism
AFRIKANER nationalism is defined by a myriad of factors, including language, race, ancestry, and religion. Initially articulated in the 1870s by a Dutch-speaking professional elite, Afrikaner nationalism was a response to the economic effects of British cultural imperialism. Language—that is, Afrikaans—was the first thread that tied together the various individuals of European ancestry into what became a cohesive Afrikaner nation by the mid-twentieth century. Afrikaans itself originated as largely a slave language, spoken by slaves, the KHOIKHOI, and by the poor and illiterate Dutch descendants.

From the 1870s onward, however, a group of priests and teachers, who later constituted themselves into a cultural organization called Genootskap van Regte Afrikaners (Fellowship of True Afrikaners), elevated Afrikaans into a respectable spoken and written language. Afrikaners were threatened with economic marginality following the introduction of English as a compulsory language in the Cape Colony's public schools and the severance of ties between church and state, which led to the end of state subsidies for churches. This was a severe blow to the Dutch churches because their congregations, composed of a small Dutch-speaking community, were inadequate to provide sufficient financial resources for the churches' sustenance. By now, most Dutch descendants spoke Afrikaans and were thus alienated from the (Dutch-speaking) churches in South Africa. Therefore, the adoption of Afrikaans as a new language of proselytizing and instruction was meant to expand the church's support base as well as to retain Dutch teachers within the public schools. However, language was not the only criterion for membership into the Afrikaner nation—race too was a defining factor. COLOURED Afrikaans-speakers, for example, were excluded, thus revealing the racist orientation of Afrikaner nationalism.

Post-1880 British military aggression turned the Afrikaner cultural movement into a political one. Rather than submitting to British colonialism, the BOER leaders claimed self-rule on an independent territory for Afrikaners further inland. The 1836 exodus of Dutch-Afrikaners out of the Cape was interpreted as a passion for freedom, and their 1838 military victory over the ZULUS was construed along similar lines and commemorated annually thereafter.

Yet, Afrikaner nationalism was still attractive to the elite, which included the Cape-based wine farmers and financiers dominated by English monopoly capital. They appealed to nationalist sentiments to rally Dutch-speaking voters in order to effect a change in the balance of power between Dutch identity and Afrikaner identity, and to entice them to their budding financial institutions. But, by the close of the nineteenth century, the definition of *Afrikaner* was still contested. The Cape-based Dutch, though somewhat suffocated by British capital, preferred an inclusive definition of the term to include the Uitlanders (foreigners, referring to the English). This was also true of intellectuals in the BOER REPUBLIC of the Orange Free State, who admired the reformist orientation of the English. The schism persisted into the twentieth century, leading to a split in the political leadership between the inclusivist South African Party and the exclusivist NATIONAL PARTY.

It was left to RELIGION to give Afrikaner nationalism cohesion and mass appeal beyond its initial elitist confines. The Nederduits Hervormde Kerk (NHK) (also known as the Doppers) church was particularly central to this expansion, having been formed of nationalist sentiment in 1856. Its founders had broken away from the mother church, Nederduits Gereformeerde Kerk, in protest against the church's insistence on allegiance toward the British Crown—for which they had an enormous enmity arising from its imperial impulses. This nationalist orientation predisposed the NHK toward Calvinism, thereby giving the church a political orientation that was to form the basis of apartheid.

Propounded by a Dutch theologian scholar, Abraham Kuyper, Calvinism resonated with the NHK because of its conviction that the nation existed as a divine creation, the inherent nexus between church and state, and that governments ought to rule in accordance with God's will. Having defined nations (or *volk*) as the basic component of human existence, it thus followed that individualism held little significance. Individuals could only realize their full being within the nation because God had not intended for them to lead an independent existence.

Hitherto justified on the basis of history and culture, now the notion of an Afrikaner *volk* took a religious flavor. To be a God-fearing Afrikaner, one had to submit oneself to the collective will of the *volk*, for it determined an individual's fate. Deviating from the collective norms could also invite divine punishment. All this combined to give Afrikaner nationalism a sense of internal, group cohesion among white Afrikaans speakers. They gave the National Party—the political agent and protector of the *volk*—its historic political victory in 1948 and many more thereafter. Believing in the distinctiveness of nations, Afrikaner nationalism also laid the foundation for the concept of apartheid—that is, separate development not just on the basis of race but also ethnicity in order to divide the numerically dominant African population into multiple ethnic minorities so as to achieve political domination.

However, by the late 1970s, the Afrikaner nationalist government introduced small but significant measures toward building a common society and racial integration, thereby abandoning its long-held principle of separate development and racial supremacy. The separatist and some racist elements of Afrikaner nationalism were increasingly expunged from the National Party. This precipitated a schism within the movement, between the *verligte* (reformers) and *verkramptes* (conservatives). Insisting on the maintenance of apartheid, the latter eventually broke from the National Party in the late 1970s to form the Conservative Party. But the Conservative Party never gained much following within the white populace, as most whites remained with the National Party, which eventually agreed to dismantle apartheid in 1990.

Currently, Afrikaner nationalism no longer holds political potency in the context of post-apartheid, democratic South Africa, where over 77 percent of the electorate is African and only 10 percent is white. The National Party, after a string of poor electoral performances, dissolved and some of its luminaries even joined the AFRICAN NATIONAL CONGRESS (ANC). Many Afrikaans speakers no longer draw a connection between culture and politics; in fact, most of them ditched the National Party for the historically English DEMOCRATIC ALLIANCE.

African Nationalism

African nationalism evolved in the twentieth century. Though sparked by internal circumstances, it was also nudged along by external influences. It comprises different and competing strands, but only one has remained hegemonic and marked it apart from most nationalist movements on the African continent. African nationalism in South Africa has historically been assimilationist at its core, seeking compromise with existing political structures rather than their outright overthrow.

Anglo and Boer COLONIALISM spurred African nationalism. Its intended effect of land dispossession and racial discrimination created a grievance to which Africans sought redress through political agitation. However, they lacked organizational cohesion because of the varying impacts of colonialism and dispersed geographic location. The unification of South Africa in 1910, however, offset these hurdles as it homogenized colonial experience through central administration and residence within the same national boundaries. African franchise became a common rallying point as the unification process got under way after 1905, leading to the formation of the first nationwide political organization around the same time. Early nationalists—for example, Walter Rubusana and Pixley Seme—from the late 1890s to the early 1900s had contact with African-Americans during their international travels who advised them to organize politically. W. E. B. Du Bois was particularly insistent on the necessity and usefulness of direct political agitation through organizations.

Unlike its Afrikaner counterpart, African nationalism was not separatist—territorially, racially, or culturally. It sought inclusion or assimilation into the existing political structures, justified on the basis of social status and acculturation. This testified to the profound liberal and missionary influence among the early nationalists. Products of the British civilizing mission, African nationalists were socialized into believing that rights were earned through social status rather than accorded on the basis of human equality. The Christian teaching also often blinded them to racial prejudice.

Nor was nativism a rallying cry for unity. Rather, African unity was justified on the basis of shared experience of colonial oppression and common interest in securing a nonracial franchise. Thus, the conception of an African nation was constructed out of sociopolitical experience rather than on racial traits or claims to indigenous cultural material. That said, African nationalism was not without challengers from within. In the 1940s–1950s, it faced strong exclusivist and Africanist tendencies, inspired by a continental nationalist wave that culminated in decolonization. Under the rallying cry, "Africa for Africans," it followed the universal adoption of the principle of self-determination to oppressed nations or peoples. However, Africanism was highly resisted within the then lone South African nationalist movement (the ANC), as it came up against a strong tradition of universalism that reaffirmed that "South Africa belongs to all those who live in it, black and white." The result was a breakaway from the ANC that led to the formation of the Africanist-oriented PAN AFRICANIST CONGRESS (PAC) in 1959.

Of the two strands of African nationalism, the inclusivist and universal kind gained wider popularity not only from within but also from without. The (inclusive) nationalist demand for human rights and aspiration toward a nonracial society had a universal appeal that enticed the international community to support the ANC in the antiapartheid struggle. This support has been partly demonstrated by the ANC's electoral dominance of South African politics after 1994.

Marxism/Communism
Marxism counts itself as among the most influential ideologies in South African politics. It fostered the two most dominant and distinct traits of South African politics: nonracialism and trade unionism. Yet, its initial manifestation did not portend such distinction as it seemed fated to follow a racist trajectory.

Marxism was first articulated in the early 1900s, albeit in an embryonic form, by European immigrants working in the growing mining industry. Propounded initially by the Labor Party, Marxism in South Africa had a reformist beginning that sought to secure workers' benefits within the existing capitalist system but proved susceptible to racism. The Labor Party–affiliated trade unions shunned black workers, preferring to remain exclusively white. It was left to the International Socialist League (ISL) to transcend the racial boundaries. The ISL was formed in 1915 by a splinter group from the Labor Party, which disagreed with the Labor Party's support of South African participation in World War I.

The ISL organized black workers, albeit conforming to racial segregation, as they were organized into separate unions. Its predecessor, the Communist Party of South Africa (CPSA, later renamed the SOUTH AFRICAN COMMUNIST PARTY), which was formed in 1921, took multiracial unionism further, even though it too had to pander to the racial prejudice of its majority white workers at times. For example, the party supported the 1922 strike by mine workers where calls were made for white workers' unity for a white South Africa.

It took a historic resolution in 1927 by the Communist International, of which the CPSA was an affiliate, to rid the party of the racial dilemma. Termed the "Black Republic Thesis" or the "Two-Staged Revolutionary Theory," this resolution held that the prospects of success for a Communist cause lay with the numerically dominant black working class. Whites were not only few in numbers but were also reactionary in seeking to retain South Africa's racial hierarchy. A more immediate objective for the black working class, however, was to eliminate racial oppression. Africans were doubly oppressed both as workers and as blacks. If the CPSA wished to gain a popular following among African workers, it could not avoid the issue of racial oppression. Once a democratic and nonracial breakthrough had materialized, the CPSA could proceed to strictly mobilize toward a socialist order.

That historic decision was met with fierce opposition from some quarters within the party. Critics could not be appeased and were eventually expelled out of the party. Following its formal alliance with the ANC in 1927, the CPSA went on to cultivate a nonracial culture within the national liberation movement. It elected its first African general-secretary, Albert Nzula, in 1928, and party officials organized trade unions along nonracial lines. Eventually, through sheer demonstration of commitment to the nationalist cause, Communists were able to persuade the ANC to allow them to serve in the organization in 1967 and were granted full membership in 1985, meaning that they could be elected to the ANC's highest decisionmaking body, the National Executive Committee.

Black Consciousness

A product of the 1970s, black consciousness was a hybrid ideology comprising both Africanist and leftist traits and was most epitomized by the Black Consciousness Movement and the writings of Steve Biko. Essentially a cultural movement, black consciousness predicated black identity as a basis of political action. Oppression, it held, not only rests on sheer brutality but also demands consent or deference from its subjects toward an oppressive authority. This happens at a psychological level through (official) molding of subservient and self-negating perceptions to create an African public image that is synonymous with failure or negativity. Through official manipulation, history tells the story of Africans without precolonial achievements, and their heroes are turned into villains. Historical accounts begin with the settlers' arrival, as if there is nothing to tell of precolonial existence, and anything positive or innovative is ascribed to white agency.

Thus, black consciousness advocated taking ownership of one's identity rather than ascribing to an identity defined by another. Blackness was defined in a positive way, as captured in the slogan "Black is beautiful," and African culture and history were celebrated in ways that instilled pride in black Africans. Once blacks rediscovered their own value, it was believed, they would rise up against apartheid and demand equality.

Though privileging blacks, black consciousness was not prejudiced toward whites. It recognized the positive attributes of European culture and called for the creation of a joint culture—one made up of the best elements from both cultures. Yet, it did not envisage blackness as a cultural identity but as a political one. Black consciousness defined blackness as all those oppressed by the apartheid state on account of race—African, coloured, and INDIAN. This was black consciousness's most unique contribution toward South African politics. It narrowed down the racial distinctions that had been promoted by officialdom and adhered to by African nationalism. Black (referring to coloured, Indian, and African), as opposed to the exclusivist labels of coloured, Indian, and African, is now commonly used in South African lexicon.

On the economic form of society, however, black consciousness was not as lucid, although it showed a preference for a socialist project. It insisted on creating an egalitarian society along the lines of communalist forms of ownership characteristic of a precolonial African society, where public ownership was favored over private ownership. Some black consciousness adherents interpreted this as an endorsement of a socialist project and formed political formations on socialist ideals. Others, however, contested this interpretation, preferring to follow a more centrist ideological project along the ANC's lines.

See also BLACK CONSCIOUSNESS MOVEMENT; POLITICAL PARTIES; POPULAR POLITICS

Bibliography

Biko, Steve. *I Write What I Like*. Johannesburg, South Africa: Ravan Press, 1978.

Bundy, Colin. *The Rise and Fall of the South African Peasantry*. Cape Town, South Africa: David Phillip, 1979.

Gerhart, Gail M. *Black Power in South Africa: The Evolution of an Ideology*. Berkeley, CA: University of California Press, 1978.

Halisi, C. R. D. "From Liberation to Citizenship: Identity and Innovation in Black South African Thought." *Comparative Studies in Society and History* 39, no. 1 (1997): 61–85.

Odendaal, Andre. *Vukani Bantu: The Beginning of Black Protest Politics in South Africa to 1912.* Cape Town, South Africa: David Phillip, 1984.

O'Meara, Dan. *Forty Lost Years.* Athens: Ohio University Press, 1996.

Roux, Edward. *Time Longer than Rope: A History of the Black Man's Struggle for Freedom in South Africa.* Madison: University of Wisconsin Press, 1966.

Trapido, Stanley. "Friends of the Natives: Merchants, Peasants, and the Political and Ideological Structure of Liberalism in the Cape, 1854–1910." In *Economy and Society in Pre-Industrial South Africa.* Edited by Shula Marks. London: Longman Group, 1980.

Walshe, Peter. *The Rise of African Nationalism in South Africa: The African National Congress, 1912–1952.* Berkeley: University of California Press, 1971.

—Mcebisi Ndletyana

Political Economy

Taking a long view of economic and social relations, the various South African traditions of radical political economy were always infused with concern about race, geography, and, increasingly, gender and environment. All came together in the studies of "superexploitative" capital-labor relations that underpinned APARTHEID. While fierce debates between radicals and liberals (whether Weberians or modernizationists) motivated the political economic studies of the 1960s–1970s, these matters go much further back as research problems, as they draw upon longstanding concerns within Marxism about superexploitation.

The Origins of Political Economy

The origins of British capitalism were in "primitive accumulation"—the initial capitalist strategy of dispossessing noncapitalist spheres of social life, most famously in land enclosures, which forced peasants into the proletarianization process. In South Africa, however, the use of political power to dispossess black people of their livelihoods, so as to compel them into wage labor relations, entailed durable extraeconomic, crudely racist methods that were not just a once-off initial condition for primitive accumulation.

For researchers of South African political economy during the twentieth century, the idea of superexploitation was a way to understand an ongoing history of extremely biased accumulation, combining capitalism and noncapitalist sites of work, life, and nature. This process of uneven and combined development can be identified not solely on the basis of exploitation (surplus value extraction) at the point of production—the main point of Karl Marx's *Das Kapital*—but instead in relations between market and nonmarket activities. It is here that an articulation of modes of production, between capitalism and noncapitalist systems, is also of great relevance on the world stage today.

Racial restrictions were initially considered by political economists primarily as power relationships. As an early Trotskyist, Moshe Noah Averbach explained: MIGRANT LABOR would "prevent the formation of a stable, hereditary urban proletariat which would become used to the traditional methods of organization and struggle—trade union and political—of the city working classes." However, the Chamber of Mines also recorded how the "cheap labor" system was crucial to their profitability (in official testimony to a 1944 government commission cited by M. N. Averbach): "the mines are able to obtain unskilled labor at a rate less than ordinarily paid in industry—otherwise the subsidiary means of subsistence would disappear and the laborer would tend to become a permanent resident upon the Witwatersrand, with increased requirements."

Laborers also began generating their own analysis of this kind of political economy. Among urban black African workers and intellectual and political figures were exceptional speakers in the revolutionary tradition—for example, C.B.I. Dladla, Dan Koza, Isaac Bongani Tabata, and T. W. Thibedi—whose arguments have only sporadically been recorded. At the same time, the SOUTH AFRICAN COMMUNIST PARTY (SACP) developed the theory of "colonialism of a special type" (CST). Drafted by leading JOHANNESBURG Communist Mick Harmel, CST was officially adopted during the early 1960s and represents an internal version of dependency theory. According to the most widely circulated analysis, the South

African capitalist state did not emerge as a result of an internal popular antifeudal revolution. It was imposed from above and from without.

Because the CST framework implied that the underlying dynamic of South African political economy was not capitalist, however, it came under repeated questioning from leftist intellectuals. New generations of political economists added several other branches of Marxian analysis: Harold Wolpe's articulations of modes of production argument during the early 1970s; neo-Poulantzian "fractions-of-capital" analysis during the late 1970s; the concept of racial capitalism during the early 1980s; the social history school of the 1980s; French regulation theory during the late 1980s; and the "minerals energy complex" from the mid-1990s.

The central concern remained race/class at the point of production. Although more and more workers began living permanently in cities near manufacturing jobs, there was still a large supply of migrant labor. From 1948 through the 1970s, 3.5 million people were forcibly removed onto the native reserves set aside for black Africans, which simply could not handle the environmental demands placed on them. What Wolpe did not express was how gendered the process became. The migrant "tribal natives" did not, when they were young, live under a system that required companies to pay their parents enough to cover school fees, or pay taxes for government schools to teach the workers' children. When sick or disabled, those workers were often shipped back to their rural homes until they were ready to work again. When the worker was ready to retire, the employer typically left him a pittance, and not a pension that allowed the elderly to survive in dignity. From youth through to illness to old age, the subsidies covering child-rearing, recuperation, and old age were provided by rural African women.

Apartheid's economic functionality was, for Wolpe, a logical and necessary outcome of South African capitalism's postwar development. However, there was ample room for contesting Wolpe's chronology and his understanding of the dynamics of capitalism. Historian Martin Legassick's 1974 work on the increasing capital intensity of manufacturing offered a more fertile direction of inquiry, and a critique of the chronological argument about capitalism and apartheid emerged. In a subsequent book, Wolpe (1988) substantially backtracked from the earlier position that apartheid was necessary to capitalist development and instead agreed with critics that the central aspects of their mutual evolution were contingent.

From the mid-1970s, international trends in historical materialism—especially the success of Althusserian and Poulantzian structuralism—began having a larger impact on South African political economy research, via the University of Sussex. A fascination emerged with "fractions of capital" that controlled the state at particular moments of political change. Although the various fractions became increasingly blurred by the 1960s as South Africa's big mining finance houses diversified into manufacturing, several leading neo-Marxist researchers identified prior distinctions between capitals in terms of their sectors of production (mining, manufacturing, or agricultural); their locations within the circulation of capital (industrial, financial, commercial, landed); or their nationality (AFRIKANER, English-speaking, foreign) (for example, Davies 1979). According to Simon Clarke (1978), however, the Poulantzians' focus on fractions of capital highlighted questions of state power but distracted from the capital accumulation process and the capital-labor conflicts.

With an upsurge in protest beginning with the DURBAN STRIKES in 1973 and with the economic slowdown beginning around 1974, the political economists' attention turned from aspects of apartheid-capitalist stability and control to instability and crisis. The theory of racial capitalism was invoked to link the political and the economic. As explained by John Saul and Stephen Gelb (1981), "From the late 1960s, the growing saturation of the white consumer market limited not only sales but also the ability of the manufacturing industry to benefit from economies of scale." On top of the newfound worker militancy beginning in 1973, Saul and Gelb identified the shortage of skilled labor as a crucial weakness created by the apartheid system's color bar and its

BANTU EDUCATION policies. These shortages became acute by the early 1970s. In addition, as Charles Meth (1991) posited, the overaccumulation of capital also leads to the saturation of both local as well as global consumer and capital goods markets.

The fractions and racial capitalism perspectives were most harshly criticized, starting in the early 1980s, by a Thompsonian school of South African social history, which prided itself on looking at society and economy not from the top (state and capital) but from the lowest levels of the voiceless majority. Charles van Onselen (1996) did the most publicized work in drawing out detailed empirical information, although the social historian's aversion to theory has been criticized. Indeed, no matter how rich and interesting the particularities of the social history case studies proved, they added up to very little of what was generalizable for the purpose of answering the larger questions of capitalist development. The broader theoretical discourse about race and class in South Africa seemed to peak in the 1970s, and with rigorous detailed probing under way in the 1980s in the context of the search for specificity, research into the nature of the mode of production tailed off markedly.

By the late 1980s, the larger questions were again placed on the agenda. It was a time when South Africa's capitalist class demanded, perhaps for the first time, an end to formal apartheid. The reasons for this are closely related to economic stagnation and financial crisis, but what was disconcerting was how dramatically this shook many political economists who had so profoundly rejected earlier the liberal thesis that apartheid and capitalism were incompatible. As Gelb (1987) put it, radicals must "develop a substantial and consistent analysis of capital accumulation which preserves their view of the earlier relationship between apartheid and capitalism, explains the transformation from long run apartheid boom to economic crisis and then analyses the crisis itself." To that end, Gelb introduced the French regulation theory of Lipietz, Aglietta, and Boyer to dissect the relative stability of South African capitalism from 1948 through the early 1970s. In honor of a phrase coined by the Italian Marxist Antonio Gramsci, "Fordism" (signifying the symbiotic relationship between mass production and mass consumption, the product of Henry Ford's assembly line and the US$5/day wages), the French considered this linkage as the basis for a full-fledged "regime of accumulation." South African "Racial Fordism," as Gelb termed it, could not succeed in linking black producers with white consumers. Others used the idea of "peripheral Fordism" to reflect the partial linkages to the world economy.

The task for the regulationists—whether relying upon internal or international causality—then became how to stitch together a new set of post-Fordist institutions and assist in the process of kick-starting capitalist growth. Wage restraint, productivity quid pro quos, social contracts, and even the Taiwanese-style export orientation were advocated by Gelb and other economists connected to the 1993 Economic Trends Group Industrial Strategy Project (for example, Avril Joffe, David Kaplan, Raphael Kaplinsky, and David Lewis). At the same time, however, Regulation Theory lost momentum internationally. After 1991, no further major academic works were published in this tradition.

Ben Fine and Zav Rustomjee (1996, 21) cautioned, "The relationship between abstract theory and empirical application is not unique to the study of South Africa. But the virulent form taken by its racism within the bounds of a predominantly capitalist economy has cast considerable doubt on the simple expedient of examining South Africa's development in terms of hypotheses derived from ready-made analytical frameworks." Their own approach was relatively institutionalist, by identifying the nexus of a minerals-energy complex around which accumulation, state, labor relations, and other economic phenomena could be understood. Within a decade, Fine addressed the postapartheid political economic nexus in terms of financialization, as "macroeconomic policy has been designed to manage the capacity of the South African conglomerates to disinvest."

In contrast, leading AFRICAN NATIONAL CONGRESS (ANC) intellectuals—such as THABO MBEKI (in 2003) and Joel Netshitenzhe—justified the neoliberal economic policies they inherited and amplified, arguing that South Africa was suffering from "two economies." Yet, there remain many structural connections that are still reminiscent of the older labor migration systems.

Bibliography

Averbach, M. N. "A Comment on Trotsky's Letter to South Africa." *Revolutionary History* 4, no. 4 (1993 [1936]).

Clarke, S. "Capital, Fractions of Capital and the State: 'Neo-Marxist' Analysis of the South African State." *Capital and Class* 5 (1978).

Davies, R. *Capital, State and White Labour in South Africa, 1900–1960*. Atlantic Highlands, NJ: Humanities, 1979.

Fine, Ben, and Zavareh Rustomjee. *The Political Economy of South Africa*. Johannesburg, South Africa: University of the Witwatersrand Press, 1996.

Gelb, Stephen. "Making Sense of the Crisis." *Transformation* 5 (1987).

———. *South Africa's Economic Crisis*. Cape Town, South Africa: David Philip, 1991.

Legassick, M. "South Africa: Capital Accumulation and Violence." *Economy and Society* 3 (1974).

Meth, C. "Productivity and the Economic Crisis in South Africa: A Marxist View." Unpublished manuscript, University of Natal, Durban, South Africa, 1991.

Posel, Deborah. *The Making of Apartheid, 1948–1961: Conflict and Compromise*. Oxford, UK: Clarendon Press, 1991.

Saul, John, and Stephen Gelb. *The Crisis in South Africa*. New York: Monthly Review, 1981.

South African Communist Party. *The Path to Power: Programme of the South African Communist Party*. London: Inkululeko Publications, 1989.

Van Onselen, Charles. *The Seed Is Mine: The Life of Kas Maine, a South African Sharecropper, 1894–1985*. Cape Town, South Africa: David Philip, 1996.

Wolpe, Harold. *The Articulations of Modes of Production*. London: Routledge and Kegan Paul, 1980.

———. *Race, Class, and the Apartheid State*. Paris: UNESCO, 1988.

—*Patrick Bond*

Political Parties

See APPENDIX 5: POLITICAL PARTIES IN THE APRIL 2009 NATIONAL ELECTIONS

Political Violence in South Africa

State violence was an important instrument often deployed by the APARTHEID state against the black people of South Africa. The revelations contained in the TRUTH AND RECONCILIATION COMMISSION (TRC) process, established by the postapartheid government in 1995 to uncover the human rights violations in atrocities perpetrated during the apartheid era, go a long way to expose the levels of state violence often committed against those who opposed apartheid. But political violence was also used by black South Africans against the apartheid state and against other members of their community believed to be spies or informants for the apartheid government

In the 1960s, the South African government criminalized the involvement of black people in politics by banning political organizations that represented millions of black people in the country, including the AFRICAN NATIONAL CONGRESS (ANC), the PAN AFRICANIST CONGRESS (PAC), the SOUTH AFRICAN COMMUNIST PARTY (SACP), and many other trade union movements, in the aftermath of the 1956 TREASON TRIAL of NELSON MANDELA and other black leaders accused of plotting to overthrow the government. The government passed a range of statutes making participation in political organizations illegal, such as the Suppression of Communism Act of 1950 and detention without trial for black people. Violence, sanctioned by law, became one of the apartheid state's most lethal weapons in trying to break opposition to its policies. The apartheid government used all forms of intimidation at its disposal in order to destroy the opposition.

Millions of black people responded to the apartheid government's provocation by going underground or by openly defying the state, for example, by supporting PAC's DEFIANCE CAMPAIGNS against the government's PASS LAWS. The defiance campaigns called on blacks to not carry the required pass books and to protest outside of police stations and government offices. They were a nonviolent way of demonstrating to the authorities that black people were dissatisfied with the inhumane treatment meted out to them. Black people all over the country refused to carry their passes or burned them and demanded to be arrested. While political violence became a daily feature of apartheid South Africa beginning in the 1950s, several key instances are worth noting.

In Sharpeville, near JOHANNESBURG, on March 21, 1960, about four thousand protesters marched to the police station and demanded to be arrested for not carrying their pass books. About three hundred police officers responded, and the young officer in charge panicked and ordered his men to open fire on the demonstrators with live ammunition. At least sixty-nine people were killed, and 180 injured, in what is known as the SHARPEVILLE MASSACRE.

The Politically Violent Transition to Democracy

In 1992, in the midst of delicate talks between the apartheid state and the black opposition leaders on the political future of South Africa, the police in the Natal Midlands suppressed political organizations aligned with the ANC by using the rival INKATHA FREEDOM PARTY (IFP) to organize attacks on black communities in the province. At Boipatong, an army of black surrogate forces from the Kwa-Madala hostel, led by police officers, attacked the black Boipatong community in the middle of the night with machetes, hand grenades, AK-47s, and handmade *assagis* (spears), killing forty-two people and injuring eighteen. Eyewitnesses stated they saw white men with balaclavas leading the attack. This event gave rise to a new form of attack where black surrogate forces were used by the apartheid state to attack communities sympathetic to the ANC and the IFP. It was referred to as "black on black" violence by the apartheid state, which wanted to give the impression that the violence was not the responsibility of the state but the result of IFP-ANC or ANC-PAC feuds or vigilantes.

Black on black violence, however, was fueled by a third force made up of members of the apartheid state's military apparatus, including members of the black liberation movement who turned traitors during the capture and subsequent torture by apartheid agents. Known as Askaris, they booby-trapped hand grenades and participated in apartheid paramilitary death squads against ANC and PAC members.

The state also turned to its surrogates in the black homelands, such as Charles Sebe, to prevent marches and to intimidate the opposition. In September 1992, the ANC organized a march to Bisho in the eastern Cape calling for the dismantling of Ciskei, the black homeland established for XHOSA-speaking Africans, and its leader. When the marchers broke through the fence that separated Ciskei from South Africa, the army opened fire and killed twenty-eight demonstrators and injured hundreds of marchers. The escalation of violence during the talks between the apartheid state and the black opposition leaders had a destabilizing effect on the country, with all parties recognizing that the situation could easily deteriorate into civil war.

It was clear that the South African government was losing control of the situation, and by 1992 the country faced a political crisis, as it was unable to stop an uprising on the East Witwatersrand. Areas such as Thokoza near Springs, Vosloorus, and Kwa-Thema faced youth revolts that targeted and attacked community councilors who collaborated with the apartheid government structures.

Black councilors and their families were killed in what became known as necklace killings. After a councilor or a suspected apartheid collaborator was caught and beaten, a tire filled with petrol was placed around his neck and set alight. This practice made the local government system unworkable by spreading fear and terror. Individuals also used the necklace method to settle personal scores with people they did not get along with, often accusing them of being *impimpis* (police informers).

The violence perpetrated by the apartheid state and the challenges mounted against it have had many consequences for the country's current justice system. The stated aim of the antiapartheid political movements was to isolate the apartheid state and not recognize its judicial institutions by, instead, building institutions of people power. The net result of this strategy was to make the country ungovernable, and the unintended consequence was that criminals did not fear the new South African justice system, and hence crime rates increased after 1994.

In many ways, the massacres perpetrated by the apartheid state created an atmosphere of impunity, especially for the perpetrators of violence, which laid the foundation for people seeking to undermine the criminal justice system in the post-1994 period. During apartheid, a strategy of the black opposition was to make the institutions of the criminal justice system unworkable or ineffective. Cracks began to appear in the police force when, in 1985, the internal stability unit of the South African police attacked protesting students in the COLOURED community of Mitchell's Plain in the Western Cape Province after the local station commissioner, Gregory Rockman, had completed negotiations with them to disperse after a march. Rockman was eventually dismissed from the South African police force and led a movement that started the Police, Prisons, and Civil Rights Union, which became a trade union in the policing and criminal justice arena.

As a consequence of the apartheid state institutions' breakdown beginning in the 1980s, and the culture of impunity it had fomented, acts of random and planned violence were a hallmark of the types of criminal terror that plagued the country during and in the immediate aftermath of the DEMOCRATIC TRANSITION. In some cases, criminals committed crimes with impunity because they knew that there would be few consequences for their actions while the criminal justice system came to terms with the new political dispensation.

The formation of the TRC in South Africa assisted some of the victims of state and political violence in finding closure, although the effects of the TRC were not felt by all. Today, South Africa still suffers, as not all victims were recognized by the TRC, and thousands did not receive compensation.

See also SHARPEVILLE MASSACRE; VIGILANTISM

Bibliography

Asmal, Kader, Louise Asmal, and Ronald Suresh Roberts. *Reconciliation Through Truth: A Reckoning of Apartheid's Criminal Governance*. Cape Town, South Africa: David Phillip Publishers, 1997.

Krog, Antjie. *Country of My Skull*. London: Vintage Books, 1999.

Mandela, Nelson. *Long Walk to Freedom: The Autobiography of Nelson Mandela*. Boston, MA: Little, Brown, 1994.

Reed, Daniel. *Beloved Country: South Africa's Silent Wars*. London: BBC Books, 1994.

Sanders, James. *Apartheid's Friends: The Rise and Fall of South Africa's Secret Service*. London: John Murray Publishers, 2006.

—*Irvin Kinnes*

Popular Politics

"Popular politics" in South Africa emerged in the 1980s, and describes the kind of grassroots and broad-based political activities that cut across racial lines and emerged in opposition to APARTHEID at the time. Distinguished from previous forms of politics that were either sectoral-based or political party–driven, "popular politics" describes a variety of activities that were not always political in nature but took on political meaning in the broader context of activities aimed at opposing the apartheid state.

Through the 1970s, collective protest against apartheid was located in two distinct social categories: black workers and black students. Worker and student protests remained an isolated phenomenon rather than a feature of a coordinated rebellion. However, the 1980s witnessed the growth of a broad-based social movement, which mounted a sustained challenge to the apartheid state.

Beginning in DURBAN, in NATAL Province, in early 1973, African workers staged a series of wildcat strikes to protest the rising costs of living. In the first three months of 1973, over 60,000 workers participated in 160 strikes. From 1973 to 1976, Durban remained the center of labor militancy, but the strikes also spread to the eastern Cape and the Witwatersrand. Strikers refused to elect a leadership, thus shielding themselves from the effects of victimization and co-optation. The government's initial reaction was repression, but as a result of the pressure brought to bear by pragmatists and employers, who would rather deal with trade unions than with unwieldy masses of unorganized strikers, the workers' protests finally gained recognition for black trade unions.

Toward the end of the 1970s, radical white students and a young generation of better-educated Africans played a crucial role in the emergence of a new brand of black trade unions. In contrast to the politically aligned mass workers' movement of the 1950s, the new independent unions constituted themselves from the bottom up, factory by factory, forming industry-based unions that initially avoided involvement in popular politics. Union democracy was characterized by regular elections of officials as well as shop stewards and by an emphasis on accountability and reporting back to the membership.

Industrial unrest was followed by protests from increasingly restive black students, who took heart from the independence of Angola and MOZAMBIQUE in 1975. After the banning of the AFRICAN NATIONAL CONGRESS (ANC) in 1960, the BLACK CONSCIOUSNESS MOVEMENT (BCM) emerged as the dominant force in black opposition. Focusing on the need for psychological self-liberation as a precondition for effective resistance to apartheid, the BCM mainly attracted intellectuals, such as students, journalists, teachers, and church ministers. It widened the definition of *black* to include not only Africans but also COLOUREDS and INDIANS as well. Student leader STEVE BIKO became its most eloquent spokesman. Black consciousness was immensely influential in mobilizing, politically educating, and energizing young blacks, but it never developed strong organizational structures or a clear strategy to counter apartheid. Among its main vehicles were the South African Student Organization, formed in 1969 by black university students, and the South African Students' Movement (SASM), founded some years later to organize high school students. The Black People's Convention, an umbrella organization established in 1972, advocated black communalism and community service through literacy and health projects.

1976 Soweto Uprising

In protest against a new ruling that English and Afrikaans had to be used equally as the medium of instruction in secondary schools for Africans, representatives from SASM met at Naledi High School outside of JOHANNESBURG on June 13, 1976, to form a Soweto Students' Representative Council (SSRC). It was this newly constituted SSRC that organized the fateful SOWETO STUDENT UPRISING on June 16. A hastily summoned police detachment fired on a march by some 15,000 schoolchildren, killing two students and triggering a nationwide wave of student riots, with attacks on police patrols and buildings that symbolized apartheid institutions. By the end of the year, the official death toll of the Soweto Uprising and related revolts stood at 575. The photograph of the first casualty, thirteen-year-old Hector Pieterson, became an icon of the youth struggles. For the first time, coloured pupils in the Western Cape joined a protest initiated by African pupils. Before schools were formally reopened on June 26, the government dropped Afrikaans as a medium of instruction. Student protests, however, widened into an all-out protest against the hated system of BANTU EDUCATION, designed to perpetuate black inferiority. Thus, schools remained empty until the end of the year.

In August and September, the SSRC mounted a series of "stay-aways," persuading and at times coercing township residents to stay away from work. One of these stay-aways provoked a violent reaction from migrant workers in SOWETO who were not prepared to take instructions from schoolchildren. The insecure status of migrants in urban areas served as an effective impediment to political mobilization.

Fleeing before the massive crackdown by police, many student leaders left South Africa. Most linked up with the ANC in exile, providing the exiled movement with a fresh supply of eager recruits for its campaigns of "armed propaganda." Although the generation of the Soweto Uprising had been inspired by the black consciousness (BC) ideology, it was the exiled ANC that reaped the benefits. In October 1977, all BC organizations and many of its leaders were banned. Many banned leaders fled the country to join the ranks of the ANC in exile, which already had an established organizational structure and had ties to and received assistance from neighboring countries. In 1978, the Azanian People's Organization (AZAPO) was launched as a successor organization to the banned Black People's Convention (BPC). While the BPC had focused on race, aspiring to give a positive content to black identity as a prerequisite for political liberation, AZAPO moved away from the exclusive focus on race toward a class analysis. This reorientation could presumably have opened the doors for cooperation with the white left, but AZAPO held that in South African conditions, race and class coincided.

The Soweto Uprising also spawned the growth of community organizations, such as the Black Parents' Association and the Committee of Ten, which evolved into the Soweto Civic Association in 1979. Student leaders who remained in the country became seasoned activists who learned the strategic lessons of struggle—notably that it was futile for students to act in isolation.

Revival of Charterist Politics
When mass protests resurfaced from 1979 to 1980, BC was on the decline, while charterist organizations that adhered to the FREEDOM CHARTER and were multiracial in approach were taking the lead. School boycotts, rent and bus boycotts, the anti–Republic Day manifestations of 1981, the Release Mandela Campaign, and the campaign against the imposed "independence" of the black homeland created for XHOSA-speaking Africans, Ciskei, all contributed to a new sense of optimism about the potential for mass mobilization and organization. Protest politics were shifting from uncompromising noncollaborationism with the apartheid state to a more pragmatic result-oriented approach. By taking up the bread-and-butter issues that had occupied local communities, Charterist activists succeeded in broadening popular organizations and in involving ordinary township residents who otherwise were reluctant to become involved in overtly confrontationist politics.

In the Western Cape, a strike over low wages and poor working conditions at the Fatti's and Moni's pasta factory in 1979 became a source of popular legend. African and coloured workers joined forces and linked up with community activists to organize a seven-month nationwide consumer boycott of the factory's products. Students were drawn into workers' struggles, and workers became more politicized. This joint experience laid the basis for the formation of community organizations in the 1980s.

Elsewhere in South Africa, CIVIC ASSOCIATIONS also began emerging around 1980. Civics, as they came to be known, were local neighborhood associations that took up residents' concerns about high rents, high electricity rates, transportation, safety on the streets, and education. From 1981 to 1982, many of these organizations became involved in planning a united front to counter government plans for limited constitutional reforms that would continue to exclude Africans from national politics. In these discussions, disagreements arose over the role of nonracial organizations that included white members, such as the SOUTH AFRICAN COUNCIL OF CHURCHES, the recently formed Federation of South African Trade Unions (FOSATU), and the white student organization the National Union of South African Students (NUSAS). The BC position was that the white activists' role was to politically educate and bring awareness to the white community, while activists upholding the nonracial or multiracial Freedom Charter principles wanted to work toward an all-inclusive broad front against apartheid. At this point, only the churches, the emerging independent trade unions, and the racially segregated student organizations had a nationwide following. Formed in 1979, the Congress of South African Students (COSAS) initially aimed to draw high school students into community issues and wider antiapartheid struggles. After a strategy reappraisal in 1983, COSAS decided to focus on school and student matters. The now-excluded older and more experienced former students were instrumental in forming the broadly inclusive youth congresses that took off in mid-1983. During the 1980s, high school students were in the vanguard of rebellion, while a rainbow coalition of religious leaders, including ALLAN BOESAK, Archbishop DESMOND TUTU, C. F. Beyers Naudé, Frank Chikane, Sister Bernard Ncube, Archbishop Denis Hurley, Smangaliso Mkhatshwa, and Farid Esack, played a prominent role.

Guidance to Charterist traditions was provided by ANC veterans such as ALBERTINA SISULU, Oscar Mpetha, and Archie Gumede, and by progressive South African Indian organizations as well. Unlike the ANC, the Indian congresses had never been banned but had withered away. The revived Transvaal Indian Congress and the Natal Indian Congress played a pivotal role in the UNITED DEMOCRATIC FRONT's (UDF's) early years, contributing dedicated activists as well as material resources.

United Democratic Front

The UDF was formed in 1983 as an ad hoc alliance, with the limited goal of countering constitutional reforms aimed at extending the political franchise (vote) to coloured and Indian people while actually firmly retaining political control in the hands of whites. Initially, its campaigns focused on an elections boycott for the coloured and Indian chambers of the new tricameral Parliament that gave coloureds and Indians representation in Parliament but not enough political power to act against the white majority in Parliament, and for the newly instituted Black Local Authorities in African townships. The boycotts were a resounding success.

In order to maintain the autonomy of workers' organizations, FOSATU decided against affiliation with the UDF. The united front formula posed the risk of workers being swamped by populist politics, as had happened to ANC-aligned unions in the 1950s. The smaller Council of Unions of South Africa (CUSA) was affiliated with both the UDF and the BC-oriented NATIONAL FORUM but ceased active participation in 1985, which gave priority to merger negotiations with FOSATU.

The UDF leadership displayed a keen awareness of the importance of public relations and was able to count on sympathetic coverage in much of the domestic press and in the international media. While the ANC received a mixed reception due to its commitment to armed struggle, the UDF gained near-universal popularity.

Parallel to election boycotts and widespread school protests, a third source of unrest was the locally based community protests against increases in bus fares and rents. The apartheid state made the Black Local Authorities (BLAs) responsible for raising their own revenue, but the resulting increases in rents and service charges proved instrumental in igniting the black township revolts of the mid-1980s. The trigger event was a two-day stay-away from work in the Vaal Triangle townships on September 3 and 4, 1984. In Sharpeville, near Johannesburg, an outburst of popular anger against the BLAs was followed by widespread rioting, which was quelled by massive contingents of police and—for the first time—the army. The Vaal Uprising left twenty-six people dead. By the end of the 1980s, the number of "unrest victims" killed in protests had exceeded 5,000. These disparate strands of protest were joined in a major stay-away from school and work in the Pretoria-Witwatersrand-Vereeniging area on November 5 and 6, 1984. Significantly, both FOSATU and CUSA participated in an overtly political protest action for the first time.

After the successful boycott campaigns against the tricameral elections, the UDF gradually transformed itself from an ad hoc alliance into a movement with a much more ambitious agenda. The UDF's umbrella formula proved eminently suitable for combining a broad range of organizations—from middle-class whites to rural African youth. The front formula enabled people to identify with the banned ANC, without exposing themselves to immediate state repression. It allowed for organizational flexibility and accommodated a wide range of manifestations of protest and rebellion, from prayer services to militant youth actions.

Township protests were mostly led by civic associations. Although most—but by no means all—civics were affiliated with the UDF, the front had little control over local protest actions. In July 1985, the funeral of four assassinated civic leaders—MATTHEW GONIWE, Fort Calata, Sparrow Mkhonto, and Sicelo Mhlawuli—from the small town of Cradock in the Eastern Cape drew a crowd of 40,000, with a massive display of both ANC and SACP flags. On July 21, 1985, the government declared a partial state of emergency that granted the police authority to detain people without charging them, impose curfews, and ban all public gatherings, and that covered the Witwatersrand, the Eastern Cape, and later the Western Cape as well. Thousands of people were detained. In August, COSAS became the first UDF affiliate to be declared an unlawful organization. Two major treason trials ensured that a substantial part of the UDF leadership, including Popo Molefe, Terror Lekota, and Moss Chikane, were taken out of circulation.

From 1985 onward, the UDF's largely reactive strategy was overtaken by a far more ambitious project: the construction of a new, egalitarian, and morally just society. Civics were transformed into "organs of people's power," a term adopted by many UDF-affiliated activists at the time. The first state of emergency (July 1985 to March 1986) did not crush the rebellion but instead inspired new tactics. Consumer boycotts were introduced as a new political weapon. Now that mass gatherings were prohibited, street committees proliferated, after the model of local organization in Cradock. Boycotts were hailed as an essentially peaceful Gandhian tactic of passive resistance, but the enforcement of boycotts frequently entailed the use of physical force and harsh punishments. Successful boycott campaigns conducted by broad-based township organizations relying on the participatory structures of decision-making served to reinforce the civics' political and moral authority. Conversely, coercion, intimidation, and abuse by undisciplined youth often weakened support for the boycott.

With school boycotts becoming a chronic rather than intermittent means of protest, the Soweto Parents Crisis Committee was formed in September 1985 with the aim of getting children back to school. Eventually, in December 1985, the ANC gave its blessing to the parents' initiative, which later widened into a nationwide campaign under the NATIONAL EDUCATION CRISIS COMMITTEE (NECC) banner. The NECC supported the students' demands but transformed the slogan of "No Education Before Liberation" into "People's Education for People's Power." Its efforts were met with only partial success.

People's Power
During the heady days of "people's power," many activists believed that a phase of "dual power" had arrived whereby the grassroots organs of people's power functioned as the embryonic institutions of a new order, and that a revolutionary takeover was imminent. However, the pattern of resistance was uneven and coordination was lacking. Not the UDF itself, but local affiliates and people loosely associated with the UDF wielded power in the townships.

"Liberated areas" no longer under the control of the apartheid state were defined in geographical terms, such as black townships that became no-go areas for the police. But the term could equally apply to the spheres of life where the people were taking over, as in schools, community media, or organs of popular justice. Black South Africans had begun to build alternative social and political institutions in their communities and establish new rules and ways of governing. The people's courts signified perhaps the most fundamental challenge to state authority. In some townships, the people's courts were widely appreciated for their role in curbing crime, disciplining unruly youth, and solving domestic conflicts. But elsewhere these courts were resented for their harsh and arbitrary punishments and were perceived by the older residents as lacking legitimacy, especially when run by the youth.

More durable than the fledgling structures of people's power was the workers' power that manifested itself on December 1, 1985, during the launch of a new giant federation of trade unions, the CONGRESS OF SOUTH AFRICAN TRADE UNIONS (COSATU). In contrast to its predecessor FOSATU, COSATU believed that unions ought to be involved in community struggles and in the wider political arena. The following year, COSATU secretary-general Jay Naidoo and CYRIL RAMAPHOSA, leader of the National Union of Mineworkers, led a trade union delegation to meet with the ANC in Lusaka.

The second state of emergency, prompted by the rash of student protests and worker strikes, was imposed nationwide on June 12, 1986, and lifted only in 1990; it amounted to virtual military rule. Dozens of national and regional UDF leaders were detained, along with some 25,000 other South Africans, many under the age of eighteen. However, rent boycotts continued and provided a key rallying point for township activists. Consumer and bus boycotts flared up intermittently, but township residents began to show signs of exhaustion and started to lose patience with the "rule of the comrades." The UDF's eclipse seemed sealed when it was effectively banned in February 1988. Youth organizations adapted to a semi-underground existence, but most civics ceased to function.

In 1989, mass protests were revived under the Mass Democratic Movement's (MDM's) banner, with the UDF-affiliated organizations, COSATU, and church leaders as its main constituents. In December of 1989, both the MDM and the Black Consciousness Movement's remnants organized the Conference for a Democratic Future, which called for a nonracial constituent assembly to draw up a new constitution.

The UDF not only coordinated and directed internal resistance to apartheid but also provided a cultural framework that gave a wider meaning to a variety of local struggles. The UDF's vision of a new society was egalitarian, with a strong emphasis on grassroots participation. By joining in rent boycotts, stay-aways, boycotts of white-owned businesses, and school protests, people not only addressed their immediate concerns but also played their part in the struggle for a new social, political, economic, and moral order.

See also UNITED DEMOCRATIC FRONT

Bibliography

Baskin, Jeremy. *Striking Back: A History of COSATU*. Johannesburg, South Africa: Ravan Press, 1991.

Bozzoli, Belinda. *Theatres of Struggle and the End of Apartheid*. London: Edinburgh University Press for the International African Institute, 2004.

Brewer, John D. *After Soweto: Unfinished Journey*. Oxford, UK: Clarendon Press, 1986.

Brooks, Alan, and Jeremy Brickhill. *Whirlwind Before the Storm: The Origins and Development of the Uprising in Soweto and the Rest of South Africa, June–December 1976*. London: International Defence and Aid Fund for Southern Africa, 1980.

Cobbett, William, and Robin Cohen, eds. *Popular Struggles in South Africa*. London: Review of African Political Economy in Association with James Currey, 1988.

Cole, Josette. *Crossroads: The Politics of Reform and Repression, 1976–1986*. Johannesburg, South Africa: Ravan Press, 1987.

Friedman, Steven. *Building Tomorrow Today: African Workers in Trade Unions, 1970–1984*. Johannesburg, South Africa: Ravan Press, 1987.

Gerhart, Gail. *Black Power in South Africa: The Evolution of an Ideology*. Berkeley: University of California Press, 1987.

Johnson, Shaun, ed. *South Africa: No Turning Back*. Basingstoke, UK: Macmillan, 1988.

Lelyveld, Joseph. *Move Your Shadow: South Africa Black and White*. London: Michael Joseph, 1986.

Lodge, Tom. *Black Politics in South Africa Since 1945*. Johannesburg, South Africa: Ravan Press, 1983.

Lodge, Tom, and Bill Nasson. *All, Here and Now: Black Politics in South Africa in the 1980s*. Cape Town, South Africa: David Philip, 1991.

Marx, Anthony. *Lessons of Struggle: South African Internal Opposition, 1960–1990*. Cape Town, South Africa: Oxford University Press, 1992.

Mufson, Steven. *Fighting Years: Black Resistance and the Struggle for a New South Africa*. Boston, MA: Beacon Press, 1990.

Saul, John S., and Stephen Gelb. *The Crisis in South Africa*. London: Zed Books, 1986.

Seekings, Jeremy. *The UDF: A History of the United Democratic Front in South Africa, 1983–1991*. Cape Town, South Africa: David Philip, 2000.

Van Kessel, Ineke. *Beyond Our Wildest Dreams: The United Democratic Front and the Transformation of South Africa*. Charlottesville: University Press of Virginia, 2000.

—*Ineke van Kessel*

Port Elizabeth

Located on the southern Indian Ocean coastline of South Africa, Port Elizabeth is a modern metropolis that boasts beaches, sporting amenities (especially for cricket and rugby), proximity to game reserves, and a moderate climate all year round (notwithstanding prevailing westerly winds). As the largest city in the Eastern Cape Province and the sixth largest urban center in the country, the greater Port Elizabeth is home to more than one million residents.

The earliest permanent structure in Algoa Bay where Port Elizabeth is located was Fort Frederick, which was erected during the first

British occupation of the Cape and commanded the landing place from the vantage point of the hill overlooking the mouth of the Baakens River. It was on the shores of Algoa Bay that British settlers arrived in 1820. A military outpost of European wars and small settlements soon developed into a growing town. The settlement was named by the colony's acting governor, Rufane Donkin, in memory of his deceased wife, Elizabeth.

Aside from providing a point of entry for soldiers and settlers in the hinterland, Algoa Bay also became a conduit for trade in wool, ostrich feathers, and agricultural products. By the 1850s, Algoa Bay became the premier port in the CAPE COLONY when its value of trade eclipsed CAPE TOWN's, and Port Elizabeth became known as "the Liverpool of the Cape." In 1860, Port Elizabeth established a town council, dominated by merchants and property speculators, with powers to enact regulations for its administration. Following the discovery of diamonds in the KIMBERLEY area in the 1870s and gold on the Witwatersrand in the following decade, as well as the construction of railway lines to these centers from other harbor towns, Port Elizabeth experienced a slump as investment capital was directed toward the interior.

After Port Elizabeth was upgraded to a city with its own council in 1913, it turned its attention to promoting the establishment of manufacturing industries. Its first success was with leather industries, but it was the erection of automobile assembly plants in the late 1920s by US companies General Motors and Ford that gave the city's economy a substantial boost. Dubbed "the Detroit of the Union," Port Elizabeth became the prime site of the country's automobile industry. Initially, the manufacturing sector was the preserve of poor white labor, but, by the 1950s, the black workforce outnumbered the whites.

Port Elizabeth's growth continued unabated during the 1950s and 1960s. The neighboring town of Uitenhage was bolstered by the establishment of a Volkswagen plant and the subsidiary motor vehicle industries. As with other South African cities, residential segregation was applied fairly rigorously and the imprint of APARTHEID spatial planning is still evident on the urban landscape. The western suburbs have historically been white residential areas, while the black townships are situated to the north in close proximity to the industrial areas. These include COLOURED freehold areas such as Korsten and highly regulated environments for Africans such as New Brighton where ownership was not permitted until the 1980s.

The descendants of British settlers and other English speakers remained the preponderant group in the city's white population and were politically influential until the 1950s. They prided themselves on being liberal toward the local black population and only introduced influx control measures for blacks coming from the rural areas following a riot in New Brighton in 1952. The city council's disposition changed in the early 1950s after the emergence of a new constituency consisting of conservative white Afrikaans speakers who supported NATIONAL PARTY politicians and councilors and endorsed apartheid policies. In response to these developments, local branches of the AFRICAN NATIONAL CONGRESS (ANC) assumed a leading role in protesting unjust apartheid laws during the DEFIANCE CAMPAIGNS. Indeed, Port Elizabeth's townships became an ANC stronghold and many of the organization's national leaders came from this area. This tradition of resistance succored local civic organizations such as the Port Elizabeth Black Civic Organization, which produced a new generation of activists that upped the ante in the struggle against apartheid.

In the 1970s and the 1980s, Port Elizabeth experienced a major economic downturn after disinvestment by multinational companies (following pressure from antiapartheid groups), especially in the automobile industry and as a result of labor action. With the reform of labor legislations, black unions in this and other sectors became sufficiently well organized to halt production. Since the 1990s, there has been greater stability in the labor force, and automobile manufacturers are once again driving economic growth. The establishment of the Coega Industrial Development Zone at the new Ngqura deep-water harbor about twenty miles north of the city has begun to attract investment in heavy industries. Investor confidence has improved, as the city is trying to shed its "Cinderella complex."

Port Elizabeth became the first major urban center to establish a nonracial local government under the new democratic dispensation. Along with the peri-urban areas and towns of Uitenhage and Despatch, it now constitutes the NELSON MANDELA Metropole. The metro has implemented an integrated development plan (IDP) known as Vision 20/20, which has been slow to get off the ground.

The Mandela moniker has been introduced into public discourse by renaming the metro, the bay, and the (recently merged) tertiary institutions. The Mandela Bay Development Agency has appropriated the famous brand name so as to market the city, while local councilors and government officials have given it their imprimatur. The adoption of the name that is synonymous with reconciliation reflects an attempt to create a more inclusive South African identity for a city shaped by its colonial and apartheid past. The change has been incremental, but Nelson Mandela Bay looks set to supplant Port Elizabeth.

Bibliography

Baines, Gary F. *A History of New Brighton, Port Elizabeth, South Africa, 1903–1953: The Detroit of the Union.* Lewiston, NY: Edwin Mellen Press, 2002.

Harradine, Margaret. *Port Elizabeth: A Social Chronicle to the End of 1945.* Port Elizabeth, South Africa: E. H. Walton, 1996.

Kirk, Joyce F. *Making a Voice: African Resistance to Segregation in South Africa.* Boulder, CO: Westview Press, 1998.

Robinson, Jennifer. *The Power of Apartheid: State, Power, and Space in South African Cities.* Oxford, UK: Butterworth-Heinemann, 1996.

—Gary Baines

Precolonial Period

The Later Stone Age is the last of the Stone Age's three main periods in Africa. It began some 40,000 years ago and continued virtually up to the beginning of colonial expansion into South Africa's interior in the seventeenth century. Later Stone Age people were hunters of wild game and foragers of wild plant foods. In this, their legacy can be seen in the aboriginal hunters of southern Africa, the Bushmen or SAN, known as Soaqua in the historical literature.

These hunters occupied every possible ecological niche in South Africa—from Karoo's drier interiors to the Highveld and all around the coast, where shell middens are found at every rocky point, as well as in caves close to the sea. Caves were also desirable lodging in the interior, and Sir John Barrow (1801) described a visit to one such cave in the Drakensberg Mountains in 1797 where he saw rock art and fires that had only recently been extinguished.

The livelihood of the hunter-gatherers required an immense knowledge of the environment, including the animals, which were important not only as a meat source but also as an essential part of their ritual life. This was reflected in the South African rock art, where animals are commonly depicted. This art, widespread throughout the region, comes in two forms: paintings and engravings. It is widely believed to represent deep spiritual meanings in hunter life, which involves healing and rainmaking, among other things. The oldest rock art is a painted slab from the Apollo 11 Cave in present-day southern NAMIBIA, dated to around 26,000 years ago. Other examples in South Africa, such as the Wonderwerk Cave in the Northern Cape, are reckoned to be over 10,000 years old. Such antiquity shows that the ritual use of rock paintings was probably deeply embedded very early on, and depictions showing Europeans with horses and guns indicate that the art continued up to the colonial period, making it the longest-lived rock art tradition anywhere in the world.

Caves have produced some of the best evidence for the hunters' precolonial life, mainly because they often permit the survival of organic material culture and food residues, which disappear on open sites. Caves occupied over long periods also produce chronological sequences that allow archaeologists to see changes over time. These dated sequences can then be compared to produce regional pictures of land use. At De Hangen in the northern Cederberg of the present-day Western Cape Province, forty-one species of plants (many of them food sources) were identified, and mussel shells were found, indicating possible contact with the coast some fifty miles away. Although seasonal transhumance between the coast and the mountains is possible, isotope readings on human skeletons indicate that some individuals probably stayed almost all year at the coast. Thus, the spatial use of resources might have varied considerably over time.

Another example of precolonial life comes from work at Plettenberg Bay in present-day Western Cape, where the occupants of sites on Robberg show an isotope signature firmly based on marine animals, suggesting the precolonial occupants probably ate seals as a primary food source. Not far away, at Matjiesrivier Cave, the signature is more terrestrial. These data suggest contiguous groups that had quite different exploitation territories. Because resources tend to be scattered across large geographical areas, hunter-gatherers would have used much larger territories in the drier interior, where all possible resources were tapped. At Abbot's Cave in the Karoo, forty mammals were identified from their bones.

Two thousand years ago, however, an intrusion came from outside the region: the first shepherds appeared at the Cape. It was initially thought that domestic animals came from the expansion of Iron Age farmers, but dates of 1950 B.C. from several sites in the Cape, such as Spoegrivier Cave, Blombos Cave, Die Kelders Cave, and the open-air Kasteelberg "G," all indicate that sheep arrived several centuries before any Iron Age settlement took place. There is some debate over how shepherds got to the Cape. One theory is that these were the ancestors of people who later became known as the KHOIKHOI (or Hottentots) in the colonial period. Since the Khoikhoi spoke a language closely related to that spoken by hunters in the Caprivi and present-day northeastern Botswana, it was assumed that the shepherds traveled south toward the Vaal and Orange rivers and then westward along the Orange River to the Atlantic Coast, or southward via other drainages, such as the Seacow River to the South Coast.

Another model challenges this idea because it suggests the sheep were passed down the line via internal exchange, and that the aboriginal hunters of the Cape developed into shepherds independently. Underlying this idea was a cyclical model whereby a person with stock was a herder on the upward part of the curve, but if the stock were lost (by theft, disease, drought, etc.), the herder could fall back on hunting. This cycle of fortune would mean that hunters and herders were the same people. Under this model, the Khoikhoi would have been late arrivals at the Cape. The argument against this is that hunters are egalitarian, and all meat has to be equally shared. This makes it difficult for hunters to nurture and sustain a breeding herd, which would need to be at least 100 animals to allow for meat off-take and breeding success. It is also difficult for hunters to become herders without having had a husbandry apprenticeship.

Regardless of the model accepted, hunters and herders appear to have lived side by side after the introduction of sheep and pottery to the Cape. Herder sites at Kasteelberg show a different cultural and economic signature than the hunter site of Witklip, some 5.6 miles to the south. The herder sites of Kasteelberg were basically sealing camps, and the seal oil was probably used as part of ceremonial activities.

Around 200 A.D., the first Early Iron Age, Bantu-speaking farmers arrived in present-day South Africa. The Kwale branch arrived from the north, down the East Coast, as far as present-day MOZAMBIQUE and northern KwaZulu-Natal. By 350 A.D., another group entered the Highveld and was known as the Nkope branch. Shortly thereafter, around 360 A.D., the Kalundu tradition was brought by people thought to have originated in Angola, who crossed the continent via the Kalahari and ultimately reached the southern part of present-day KwaZulu-Natal. These farmers brought with them cattle and African summer rainfall crops—sorghum and millet.

The relationship between hunters and Iron Age farmers most likely was one in which the hunters were gradually subsumed into farming society. This resulted in a one-way gene flow (hypergyny), as Bushmen women were taken as wives by farmers, but hunters rarely would have the bridewealth payments needed for accessing farmer women. Many of the later farmers in the

Later Iron Age of the second millennium, believed to be Nguni speakers of South Africa's southeastern part, have half of their genetic material from the hunters.

In the southeastern part of South Africa, the hunters' encapsulation was virtually completed before the beginning of the colonial era. By contrast, other groups in the west and the interior appear to have continued their foraging lifestyle, although there are indications that most hunters, particularly those close to permanent river systems, were in contact with food producers, from whom they could obtain metal and pottery in exchange for meat and skins. Since the farmers relied heavily on grain crops for their diet, they were unable to move beyond the summer rainfall area of the eastern Cape region. This left the winter rainfall area to the west in the hands of Khoikhoi herders and Soaqua hunters, many of whom seem to have maintained separate lifestyles right up to the colonial period.

Bibliography

Barrow, John. *An Account of Travels into the Interior of Southern Africa in the Years 1797 and 1798.* 2 vols. London: Cadell and Davies, 1801.

Elphick, Richard. *Khoikhoi and the Founding of White South Africa*. Johannesburg, South Africa: Ravan Press, 1985.

Mitchell, Peter. *The Archaeology of Southern Africa*. Cambridge, UK: Cambridge University Press, 2002.

Morris, Alan G. *The Skeletons of Contact*. Johannesburg, South Africa: Witwatersrand University Press, 1992.

Smith, Andrew B. *African Herders: Emergence of Pastoral Traditions*. Walnut Creek, CA: Altamira Press, 2005.

—Andrew B. Smith

Pretoria
See TSHWANE

R

Racial Classification

Most closely identified with the APARTHEID era, the use of racial classifications as part of a system of domination and control in South Africa has its roots in British COLONIALISM and the conceptions of racial and social hierarchy of AFRIKANER settlers at that time. As early as 1911, just after the formation of the UNION OF SOUTH AFRICA, the South African Census classified the population into three racial groups: "European or White," "Bantu," and "Mixed and COLOURED other than Bantu." The 1911 Census further identified twenty-three subcategories for both the "Bantu" and the "Mixed and Coloured other than Bantu" categories. For example, subcategories under "Bantu" included Tongo, Tembu, Fingo, Damara, Basuto, NDEBELE, Xosa (XHOSA), and ZULU. The "Mixed and Coloured" classification was more confounded, incorporating nationalities and African ethnic groups, including Afghan, Chinese, INDIAN, Egyptian, Zanzibari, as well as non-Bantu African groups such as GRIQUA, Hottentot, BUSHMEN, and Namaqua-Hottentot races.

In 1950, a more far-reaching state-imposed system of racial classification was passed into law with the Population Registration Act, which divided South Africans initially into three racial categories: white, Native, and coloured. (Asian/Indian was added in 1959.) The backbone of the apartheid system, the Population Registration Act assigned every person an identity number, part of which was a racial classification that would either improve or diminish one's life chances. For example, 00 meant white, 01 coloured, 02 Malay, 05 Asian, down to 09 for Nama of South West Africa. Two miscellaneous sections, 06 for "Other Asian" and 07 for "Other coloured," provided for those who could not be fit in elsewhere. For Africans, the population registration system was particularly onerous because they had to carry reference books, also known as "passes," to move about the country and to prove that they had a right to live or work in certain areas.

Racial classifications in South Africa have historically been based on physical appearance and social acceptance. The idea of racial purity based on biology or genetics, especially for the white race, was one to which the apartheid state and the white population aspired, but unrealistically so given the interracial and non-European heritage of much of South Africa's white population. During apartheid, the criteria of social acceptance became more important in an attempt to keep white identity separate from that of others, and in a clear effort to keep some of those classified as coloured from passing for white.

During apartheid, the Natives category was changed to include all indigenous Africans, whereas prior to 1950, certain groups of Africans, namely KHOIKHOI and SAN, were excluded from this classification and included in the "Mixed and Coloured" classification. Indians, once categorized as coloured, were subsequently given a separate category. Indeed, the arbitrariness of the racial categories illustrates the social construction of these racial classifications.

Furthermore, the population's self-classifications did not necessarily match the state-imposed classifications. In the 1970s, influenced in part by the BLACK CONSCIOUSNESS MOVEMENT, black became a racial classification embraced by many Africans, and indeed the term was expanded by many to include all nonwhite, oppressed South Africans, including coloureds and Indians. Although in contemporary South Africa the state no longer officially classifies the population according to the apartheid racial categories, most South Africans self-identify as either white, coloured, black/African, or Indian.

Ramaphosa, Matamela Cyril (1952–)

Trade unionist and antiapartheid activist turned businessman Matamela Cyril Ramaphosa is perhaps best known in international circles as the AFRICAN NATIONAL CONGRESS's (ANC's) chief negotiator during the constitutional negotiations with the APARTHEID government and the NATIONAL PARTY, which led to the DEMOCRATIC TRANSITION in 1994.

Born in SOWETO, outside of JOHANNESBURG, on November 17, 1952, Ramaphosa's activism began when he studied law at the University of the North. As a student, he joined the South African Student Organization and the Black People's Convention, as he was especially drawn to the ideology of black consciousness, particularly prevalent in the 1970s. After completing his law studies in 1981, his attention turned to trade union organizing, and in 1982 he was encouraged to form a union for mine workers. The National Union of Mineworkers, which would become the biggest and the most powerful trade union in South Africa under Ramaphosa's leadership as its secretary-general, was formed. Ramaphosa was also instrumental in the formation of the CONGRESS OF SOUTH AFRICAN TRADE UNIONS (COSATU), an umbrella body that now composes part of the ruling tripartite alliance with the African National Congress and the SOUTH AFRICAN COMMUNIST PARTY. In 1985, COSATU formed an alliance with the mass-based, grassroots, and democratic umbrella group the UNITED DEMOCRATIC FRONT (UDF), broadening Ramaphosa's influence across antiapartheid political groupings.

In 1991, when the government lifted the ban on the ANC, Ramaphosa was elected as the ANC's secretary-general. He subsequently played a leading role in the negotiations between the ANC and the National Party, which led to the dismantling of apartheid and the creation of a new democratic dispensation. After the first democratic ELECTIONS in April 1994, Ramaphosa was selected to chair the Constitutional Assembly responsible for drafting the new democratic constitution. He subsequently left the political scene, though he has remained a member of the ANC's Executive Committee. Today, Ramaphosa is a prominent figure in the business community. He founded his own company, Shanduka Holdings, and previously served as the director of New African Investments, both companies participating in a variety of BLACK ECONOMIC EMPOWERMENT opportunities. He is also on the board of a number of national and international companies, including South African Breweries, First Rand Limited, Macsteel Holdings, Alexander Forbes, and Medscheme Limited.

Rand Revolt

The Rand Revolt of 1922, also referred to as the Rand Rebellion, was an armed uprising precipitated by industrial strife among white workers in the mining areas known as the Witwatersrand (or Rand for short) surrounding JOHANNESBURG. It occurred during a period of economic depression and uncertainty, particularly in the mining industry. After World War I, mining costs for the owners had increased, while the price of gold had fallen. This set up a contentious situation between mine owners, who wanted to save on labor costs by employing black workers in positions that were previously reserved for whites, and white workers, who feared their jobs were threatened. The economic slump also fueled a growing number of white, unskilled, and unemployed workers in the urban areas, who were increasingly disgruntled at the government for supporting the mine owners' policies of employing cheap black labor.

As the price of gold fell, the Chamber of Mines implemented policies to remove the color bar in their workforce, opening up previously whites-only positions to blacks who could be paid much less, thereby increasing the ratio of black to white workers. The white workers reacted strongly as they feared their livelihoods were in jeopardy and initiated a series of sporadic strikes in 1921, which became widespread by the end of the year. The trade unions and the Communist Party of South Africa (later renamed the SOUTH AFRICAN COMMUNIST PARTY) were involved in organizing the white workers to action.

In February 1922, negotiations between the owners and the trade unions broke down. Some white workers took up arms, set up barricades, and began bludgeoning innocent African and COLOURED workers and bystanders. In March, a general strike was called, followed by an all-out revolt attempting to seize control of Johannesburg. Many of the white workers acquired arms from white sympathizers in the community, and bloody violence spread throughout the Johannesburg area. It took over a week for the government to put down the rebellion but not before around 200 people were killed and several thousand injured in bloody confrontations with the rebels.

In the aftermath of the revolt, white workers were forced to accept the management's new policies to employ more black laborers. However, the state also began to implement a series of laws that privileged whites for public sector employment and hardened the color line socially and politically.

RDP

See RECONSTRUCTION AND DEVELOPMENT PROGRAM

Reconstruction and Development Program

The Reconstruction and Development Program (RDP) is a socioeconomic policy framework of the AFRICAN NATIONAL CONGRESS (ANC). Developed in the early 1990s in broad consultation with the ANC's alliance partners—the CONGRESS OF SOUTH AFRICAN TRADE UNIONS (COSATU) and the SOUTH AFRICAN COMMUNIST PARTY (SACP)—as well as with grassroots and community-based groups, the RDP was the ANC's policy platform during the first democratic ELECTIONS in 1994. It subsequently became the ANC government's central policy framework during the first few years of President NELSON MANDELA's administration.

The ANC's main objective in developing and in implementing the RDP was to address the immense socioeconomic problems brought about by its predecessors under the APARTHEID regime. Specifically, it aimed to alleviate poverty and address the massive shortfalls in social services across the country. The RDP attempted to combine measures to boost the economy, such as contained fiscal spending, sustained or lowered taxes, reduction of government debt, and trade liberalization, with socially minded social-service provisions and infrastructure projects. Neither entirely socialist nor neoliberal in its prescriptions, the RDP set out a strategy for economic growth through social and economic redistribution and development.

Six core principles guided and gave substance to the RDP:

1. Creation of an integrated, well-coordinated, and sustainable program that would operate in all three spheres of government, civil society, and business;
2. A focus on ending the endemic violence in South Africa by embarking on a national drive for peace and security;
3. Emphasis on nation building;
4. Linking of growth, development, reconstruction, redistribution, and reconciliation into a unified program;
5. A people-driven, bottom-up approach; and
6. Democratization of the decisionmaking processes.

The RDP placed primary emphasis on meeting the population's basic needs and focused the government's efforts on providing housing, clean water, electricity, health care, and land reform as well as other basic infrastructure and social services. In the first few years of democratic rule, significant strides were made in these areas. However, critics argued that the pace of change was too slow and only scratched the surface of what actually needed to be done. Criticism was leveled at the quality of housing and other services provided, and the government and communities were frustrated at the often time-consuming nature of the democratic and consultative processes.

In 1996, the ANC government unveiled the GROWTH, EMPLOYMENT, AND REDISTRIBUTION STRATEGY (GEAR), which it saw as a complement to the RDP. In practice, however, GEAR outlined a different economic growth strategy, one much more in line with the neoliberal principles pushed by Western governments and international donor agencies. In contrast to the highly consultative and open processes that produced the RDP, GEAR was penned by a group of economists behind closed doors. Although the RDP quickly became overshadowed by GEAR, the RDP remains a central program and policy framework of the party's platform, according to the ANC.

See also ECONOMY

Religion

See CHRISTIANITY; ISLAM; JUDAISM

Retief, Pieter (Piet) Mauritz (1780–1838)

Born on November 12, 1780, to French HUGUENOT parents in Wagenmakersvallei, modern-day Wellington located in the western Cape region, Pieter (Piet) Mauritz Retief was a leader of the BOER migration. Because employment opportunities were few for Retief and his nine siblings on his parents' vineyard, he entered into the business world by first working as a store clerk and then becoming involved in the liquor trade. Most of Retief's business ventures were unsuccessful, as he constantly faced lawsuits and financial difficulties. In 1814, Retief married a widow named Lenie Greyling and bought a farm on the Koega River. He and his wife then moved to Grahamstown where he was able to make a fortune and become one of the town's richest men. However, his wealth did not last long as he soon became bankrupt after being swindled by unscrupulous business partners. Retief's bankruptcy forced him to return to farming.

As the Cape region came under British control, the British authorities implemented a series of policies that were unfavorable to the AFRIKANER population. During this time, Piet Retief emerged as one of the Afrikaner community leaders who served as a mediator between the Boer farmers and the British government. However, Retief was unable to negotiate a favorable deal with the British authorities for the Afrikaner population in the CAPE COLONY. Therefore, he decided to organize a mass northward migration of dissatisfied Afrikaner farmers to territories beyond the Orange and the Vaal rivers, which became known as the GREAT TREK. On January 22, 1837, Retief published, in the *Grahamstown Journal*, a manifesto that promulgated the Voortrekker farmers' declaration of independence.

Piet Retief later led the Voortrekker community across the Drakensberg mountain range in hopes of finding more fertile land, but the territories were under ZULU chief Dingane's control. Retief negotiated with Dingane to allow the Afrikaners to settle in NATAL but their agreement was short-lived. On a subsequent visit, Retief and his men were ambushed by Dingane's men during what was supposed to be a friendly celebration. On December 21, 1838, Retief and his delegation's remains were discovered by members of Andries Pretorius's "victory commando" after winning the BATTLE OF BLOOD RIVER with the Zulus.

In 1922, a monument commemorating Retief and his group was built near Retief's grave site. The town of Piet Retief, located in a timber-growing region of the present-day Mpumalanga Province, was named after him, as well as the city of Pietermaritzburg, which was named after Retief and another Voortrekker leader, Gerrit Maritz.

Rhodes, Cecil John (1853–1902)

Cecil John Rhodes is one of colonial southern Africa's most prominent economic and political figures. Not only did he play a major role in expanding British territories in South Africa and across the African continent, he was also the founder of Rhodesia (current-day Zambia and ZIMBABWE) as well as the world-renowned DeBeers Mining Company.

Rhodes was born in Bishop's Stortford, Britain, on July 5, 1853, into a priest's family. He left the United Kingdom for South Africa in 1870 at the age of seventeen to grow cotton with his older brother in NATAL. A year later, in 1871, both he and his brother decided to abandon cotton farming for work in the diamond mines as diamond fever swept across the southern African region at that time. Financed by the Rothschild family, Rhodes began buying up all of the small mining companies in the region. Two years later, in 1873, Rhodes returned to Britain to attend Oxford University. Because he divided his time between the United Kingdom and South Africa while attending Oxford, he did not earn his bachelor's degree until 1881.

Meanwhile, Rhodes became politically active in the politics of the CAPE COLONY. He was elected to the Cape Parliament in 1880. In 1888 Rhodes secured mining grants from Lobengula, the king of the NDEBELE, which led to the founding of Rhodesia. In the same year, he also established the DeBeers Consolidated Mines, by merging his company with that of Barney Barnato, thus controlling all of the diamond operations in southern Africa. In 1889, Rhodes forged an alliance with the London-based Diamond Syndicate to control the production and pricing of the global diamond market, thereby beginning the monopolistic practices Rhodes and DeBeers were so well known for.

That same year, he persuaded the British government to grant a charter for the formation of the BRITISH SOUTH AFRICA COMPANY (BSAC). Rhodes formed the BSAC to undertake economic ventures in southern Africa, and the charter from the British government granted the BSAC certain exclusive rights to economic activities and resources in the region, as well as rights to establish political authority over certain parts of the region. A year later, Rhodesia came into being when the white British settlers who had settled in King Lobengula's territories founded Salisbury (present-day Harare), which became Rhodesia's capital. In the same year, Rhodes became the sixth prime minister of the Cape Colony with support from both the AFRIKANER and the English-speaking populations. However, he had to resign this post six years later, in 1896, after his appointee, Leander Jameson, who was also the administrator of Rhodesia, failed to successfully invade Transvaal, an Afrikaner republic at that time. Moreover, this failed military attempt, intended to take political and economic control of the gold-rich Transvaal region, further sharpened the divisions between the Afrikaners and the English-speaking population, which sowed the seeds for the ANGLO-BOER WAR from 1899 to 1902.

Rhodes died in Muizenberg, in the western Cape region, on March 26, 1902. Even though he never realized his political visions of British territorial expansions on the African continent, such as building a railroad all the way from South Africa's Cape Colony to Egypt's capital of Cairo, he did leave behind an enormous business enterprise as well as a historical legacy in southern Africa. He also left behind £6 million for Oxford University to establish the Rhodes Scholarships (the first large-scale international scholarship program) for students from Germany and from former British colonies (United States, Canada, Jamaica, etc.) to study at Oxford. Furthermore, Rhodes University of South Africa, founded on May 31, 1904, was named after him. In 2004, Cecil Rhodes was voted fifty-sixth among *Great South Africans,* an SABC television series.

Rivonia Trial

The Rivonia Trial, named after the JOHANNESBURG suburb where AFRICAN NATIONAL CONGRESS (ANC) leaders were arrested on Lilliesleaf Farm, began in October 1963. The ten defendants in the trial, including NELSON MANDELA, WALTER SISULU, Ahmed Kathrada, GOVAN MBEKI, and

Prison building on Robben Island.

Raymond Mhlaba, were charged with the following four counts: (1) recruiting persons for training in the preparation and use of explosives and in guerrilla warfare for the purpose of violent revolution and committing acts of sabotage, (2) conspiring to commit the aforementioned acts and to aid foreign military units when they invaded the republic, (3) acting in these ways to further the objects of communism, and (4) soliciting and receiving money for these purposes from sympathizers in Algeria, Ethiopia, Liberia, Nigeria, Tunisia, and elsewhere. They faced the death penalty. Twenty-four co-conspirators were also listed, including OLIVER TAMBO and others who had already fled the country.

The ANC had been banned shortly after the SHARPEVILLE MASSACRE in 1960 and was forced to operate covertly, turning to armed struggle and forming its military wing, Umkhonto we Sizwe. South African security forces seized numerous documents and evidence of the ANC's covert operations at the farm in Rivonia, including information regarding Operation Mayibuye, a plan for a guerrilla insurrection by land and sea.

The trial concluded with the conviction of eight of the defendants, including Mandela, and sentencing to life imprisonment. Ahmed Kathrada was found guilty on one charge of conspiracy and Lionel Bernstein was found not guilty. For the time being, the APARTHEID state had effectively crushed the resistance movement, dealing a hard blow to the antiapartheid struggle.

But the trial's significance also rested on the defendants' abilities to explain their cause to the public and the international community to gain further sympathies for their struggle against the apartheid government. Both Mandela and the ANC had already gained a degree of international recognition around this time. However, Mandela used the opportunity presented by this trial to make a four-hour speech from the dock that was widely reported internationally and served as an inspiration for many young antiapartheid activists at home and abroad. He concluded by saying that the ideal of a free and democratic South Africa was one that he cherished dearly and hoped to see emerge in his lifetime, but, if need be, was one for which he was prepared to die. These would be the last public words he would utter for over two decades.

Robben Island

Robben Island, located 7.5 miles off the coast of CAPE TOWN, has a long, dark history as a place of banishment and imprisonment. Since the Dutch settled at the Cape around the mid-1600s, Robben Island has primarily been used as a prison, first for criminal and military prisoners and then for East Asian exiles. This island has also housed a hospital for lepers and the insane from the late 1800s through 1931. It subsequently served as a military base for both the British and the South Africans.

However, it was its reputation as a prison for political prisoners, most famously NELSON MANDELA, who spent over twenty years on the island during the struggle against APARTHEID, that gained the island its notoriety. During the apartheid years, Robben Island became internationally known for its reputation of institutional brutality. Political prisoners were sent to this island to be isolated and broken psychologically, and some spent over a quarter of a century there.

Remarkably, however, the political prisoners managed to psychologically and politically transform this hellhole into a place of learning and inspiration. The prisoners made demands on the prison administration to allow the prisoners to study and receive degrees while incarcerated. They also pushed for the creation of a prison library. However, much of the education was conducted by the older political prisoners, most notably Mandela and his cohort. They spent many hours a day intellectually unpacking the challenges of revolutionary struggle and debating the merits of socialism, democracy, and nationalism. The young prisoners on the island were schooled in how to channel their anger into constructive strategies and campaigns against the apartheid regime.

After the demise of apartheid, the prison was closed and the island was turned into a museum. In 1999, it was designated by UNESCO as a World Heritage Site and today stands as a symbol of the human spirit's triumph.

S

SACC
See SOUTH AFRICAN COUNCIL OF CHURCHES

SACP
See SOUTH AFRICAN COMMUNIST PARTY

San
The San and the KHOIKHOI are said to be the first inhabitants of southern Africa. They are often considered to be one people but in fact comprise many subgroups. The term *Khoisan*, or *Khoesaan* was developed to denote these aboriginal people of southern Africa who use the "click" language. They are not related to the Bantu-speaking groups of southern Africa, such as the XHOSA, ZULU, TSWANA, etc. They are descendants of Early Stone Age ancestors. The Dutch settlers, who arrived at the Cape in 1652, used the term *Bushmen* to refer to the Khoisan.

However, others saw clear distinctions between the two groups. Khoikhoi is the general name that the Cape's herding people gave to themselves and literally means the "real people" or "men of men." San is the name that the Khoikhoi gave to those who hunted or stole herds from others. While the Khoikhoi owned herds of cattle and sheep and generally lived in large groups, the San were more nomadic and lived in smaller groupings throughout the Cape region of South Africa. Unlike the Khoikhoi, the San lived in small family groups and moved about the land in search of food sources. San men gained a formidable reputation as hunters and trackers.

Unfortunately, many San were decimated by diseases brought by the Europeans. Moreover, COLONIALISM destroyed their migratory way of life. However, small communities continue to exist today in the Northern Cape Province of South Africa and in neighboring NAMIBIA. In addition, San (and Khoikhoi) influence is seen in the development of the Xhosa language, which also has a distinctive clicking sound. Many COLOURED South Africans can trace their roots to the San and the Khoikhoi.

Sangoma
A sangoma is a traditional healer and diviner in the ZULU, XHOSA, NDEBELE, and SWAZI traditions. A sangoma may be male or female. They believe

San rock painting in Zimbabwe.

they are guided by ancestral spirits to provide holistic and symbolic healing to the community. In addition to divination and healing, sangomas play social and political roles by directing rituals, counteracting witches, protecting warriors, and narrating the community's history and myths of their traditions. In South Africa sangomas far outnumber Western-style doctors, and many Africans will visit a sangoma before going to see a doctor. As healers the sangomas are known to use a variety of roots, bark, herbs, flowers, and a wide range of land and animal products in their medicines or *muti* as it is called in Zulu. Training to become a sangoma can be very intense and can take years.

Schreiner, Olive Emile Albertina (1855–1920)

Born on March 24, 1855, in Basutoland (now LESOTHO), Olive Emile Albertina Schreiner emerged as the great South African writer of the late nineteenth century. She is known for her condemnation of imperialism and racism, as well as for her commitment to feminist thinking.

Olive Schreiner was born into an impoverished family of missionaries, although she did not absorb the religious beliefs of her German father and British mother. At fifteen, she left home and worked as a governess. Despite lacking a formal education, she was an avid reader who studied the works of prominent eighteenth- and nineteenth-century thinkers. Barely out of her teens, she wrote her first two novels, *Undine* and *The Story of an African Farm*.

In 1881, Schreiner moved to England to pursue a career in medicine. Though she was not suited for medical training, she found success as a writer. The publication of *African Farm* in 1883, initially under the pseudonym of Ralph Iron, brought Schreiner international notoriety.

After returning to South Africa in 1889, Schreiner continued writing, targeting the racist and imperialist practices of British and South African leaders, as well as gender inequality. She produced a number of short allegories and journalistic pieces that were later published in compilations, such as *Dreams, Dream Life and Real Life* (1893) and *An English South-African's View of the Situation* (1899). In 1893, Schreiner married a like-minded farmer, Samuel Cronwright. She was active in the women's suffrage movement but later resigned from the Cape Women's Enfranchisement League after the organization refused to support black voting rights.

During World War I, Schreiner spent several years living in England, where she suffered from ill health and endured criticisms for her stance against the war. Shortly after returning to South Africa in 1920, she died of a heart attack. A significant amount of Schreiner's work, including her novel *Undine* (1929), was published posthumously.

See also LITERATURE

Shaka Zulu (1787–1828)

Born in 1787 as the illegitimate son of Senzangakona, chief of the ZULU clan, Shaka Zulu was a masterful military strategist and leader who became the king of a powerful Zulu nation. Shaka grew up in Zululand (in present-day KwaZulu-Natal) with neighboring groups and developed his warrior skills in the army of Dingiswayo, the Mthethwa clan's leader. With Dingiswayo's help, Shaka became the Zulu chief in 1816, ousting his senior brother. He consolidated a number of military innovations, including the introduction of a short stabbing spear and the use of a horn formation (or crescent shape) to encircle the enemy, and he developed a powerful standing army. When Dingiswayo was killed, Shaka avenged his death and eventually incorporated the Mthethwa under his rule by establishing a powerful, dominant Zulu state. Some have attributed the MFECANE, a period of political turmoil and social migration in southern Africa, to Shaka's rise as a military leader and the formation of a powerful Zulu state under his leadership.

By the mid-1820s, Shaka ruled a kingdom of more than 100,000 people with a standing army of 40,000 men. By the time of his death, it is estimated that the Zulu Kingdom had grown to 250,000 with 50,000 warriors. He consolidated his power through a series of wars with the neighboring people. Shaka centralized power in the person of the king and his court by collecting tribute from regional chiefs and by placing regiments throughout his state to ensure compliance with his orders. He fostered a Zulu identity by forcing personal allegiance from all subjects of the Zulu state to the king.

Shaka was assassinated in 1828, at the height of his rule, by Dingane and Mhlangana, his half brothers. Dingane succeeded him as Zulu king.

See also MFECANE; ZULU

Sharpeville Massacre

On March 21, 1960, South African police killed sixty-nine black protesters in a community near JOHANNESBURG. The Sharpeville Massacre was a turning point in APARTHEID and antiapartheid politics and signaled the beginning of a particularly brutal and repressive period of the apartheid era. In addition, for many of the black liberation movements and their leaders, it marked the beginning of many years operating in exile or underground, as well as a shift by some organizations to armed struggle.

On the day of the massacre, the PAN AFRICANIST CONGRESS (PAC) organized a series of marches to protest the PASS LAWS, which required all Africans to carry a pass book that contained biographical and employment information and restricted their movement in areas designated for whites only. Because the pass laws had become a particularly sore point for Africans, the turnout to many of the protest marches was significant, topping 70,000 in some places. Twenty thousand angry protesters marched on the police station in Sharpeville, a small, little-known community. The police, fearing they were outnumbered by the crowd, reacted with extreme force after protesters began throwing stones at the armored vehicles. The police opened fire into the crowd, killing 69 people and wounding another 180, by official counts. Philip Frankel, however, has provided compelling evidence to suggest the actual death toll was closer to 200.

This massacre provoked outrage domestically but also internationally. For the first time, South Africa's apartheid system was under scrutiny in the international arena. The United Nations Security Council was forced to take up the issue of apartheid as most foreign governments condemned the apartheid state's heavy-handed action. Domestically, the brutality shown by the apartheid security forces, and the subsequent banning of black liberation movements, compelled the key organizations, the AFRICAN NATIONAL CONGRESS and the PAC, to resort to armed struggle as a means to achieve liberation.

Bibliography
Frankel, Philip. *An Ordinary Atrocity: Sharpeville and Its Massacre*. New Haven, CT: Yale University Press, 2001.

Sisulu, Albertina Nontsikelelo (1918–2011)

A leading activist against APARTHEID and a parliamentarian, Albertina Nontsikelelo Sisulu was born in the Transkei in the eastern Cape region on October 21, 1918. When she moved to JOHANNESBURG to train as a nurse and midwife, she became politically active and also met her husband WALTER SISULU, an eminent leader in the antiapartheid struggle. The couple had five children together.

In 1948 Albertina Sisulu, also affectionately known as Ma Sisulu, joined the AFRICAN NATIONAL CONGRESS (ANC) WOMEN'S LEAGUE and began her long involvement in women's and antiapartheid politics. In 1954, she was a founding member of the Federation of South African Women and became its president in 1981. Sisulu was frequently arrested and jailed for her political activities and suffered numerous banning orders and house arrests. In 1956, she led a demonstration of 20,000 women at the capital, protesting the extension of the PASS LAWS (which restricted travel and movement of African men) to African women. In the early 1980s, she was heavily involved in the newly formed UNITED DEMOCRATIC FRONT (UDF), an umbrella organization that sought to coordinate mass mobilizations against apartheid. She was elected one of three presidents of the UDF. In 1985, she was arrested again with the UDF members and charged with treason, although the charges were later dropped.

When the ANC was unbanned in 1990, Sisulu worked on a committee that reestablished the ANC

Women's League. In 1991, she was elected to serve on the ANC's National Executive Committee. In 1992, as the deputy president of the ANC Women's League, she proposed the drafting of a women's charter that would be included as part of the ANC's election manifesto. During the first democratic ELECTIONS in 1994, Sisulu was elected a member of PARLIAMENT and remained in politics another five years. At the end of 1999 she retired from politics but continued to work for women's rights, justice, and equality for all. At the age of ninety-two, Albertina Sisulu died in June 2011.

Sisulu, Walter Max Ulyate (1912–2003)

A leading activist in the fight against APARTHEID, Walter Max Ulyate Sisulu was born on May 18, 1912, the year the AFRICAN NATIONAL CONGRESS (ANC), the liberation movement that he later helped expand, was founded. He was born in the small village of Qutubeni in the Transkei, now part of the Eastern Cape Province. His mother was a black domestic servant and his father a white civil servant. He grew up with his mother's family and learned much of the XHOSA culture through his uncle and grandparents, who raised him until he was six years old.

Sisulu's formal schooling ended at Standard IV, but he continued to teach himself and took a variety of jobs to make ends meet during his early years. His political awareness began in East London, in the eastern Cape region, where his mother lived. Sisulu became involved in labor organizing and was influenced by union leader CLEMENTS KADALIE. In 1940, he joined the ANC and was one of the group's radicals who founded the AFRICAN NATIONAL CONGRESS YOUTH LEAGUE in 1944. A driving force in the ANC's transformation into a mass-based organization, Sisulu was first elected as treasurer of the Youth League and then became the ANC's first full-time secretary-general in 1949. It was his leadership of the ANC that was largely responsible for many of the successful campaigns launched during the 1950s, including the 1952 DEFIANCE CAMPAIGNS against apartheid laws. Additionally, under Sisulu's leadership, the ANC formed the Congress Alliance with antiapartheid organizations representing other racial groups, which culminated in the drafting and adoption of the FREEDOM CHARTER in 1955.

Sisulu was arrested on numerous occasions and was a frequent target of the apartheid state's repression. In 1956, he stood as one of the principals accused in the TREASON TRIAL of antiapartheid leaders, and in 1963, he was arrested with fellow ANC leaders, who were charged with sabotage aimed at fomenting a violent revolution. During the RIVONIA TRIAL, Sisulu was sentenced to life imprisonment, along with NELSON MANDELA and others. While imprisoned on ROBBEN ISLAND, he completed his bachelor's degrees in art history and anthropology. Sisulu was released from prison in 1989 and was elected as the ANC's deputy secretary-general in 1991, a position he held until ill health forced him to leave active politics in 1994. Sisulu retired to his home in SOWETO, just outside of JOHANNESBURG, with his wife ALBERTINA SISULU, herself a prominent antiapartheid activist and politician. The couple had five children together.

Walter Sisulu died in 2003, just before his ninety-first birthday.

Slavery

Slavery began in the CAPE COLONY in 1658, just a few years after the arrival of Europeans. JAN VAN RIEBEECK, the administrator of the DUTCH EAST INDIA COMPANY, was charged with setting up a refreshment station and a Dutch base for ships traveling to Asia. To build a fort and to plant food crops, he requested slave labor. For the next 176 years, slavery persisted in the Cape until it was abolished in 1834.

Similar to the form of slavery that existed in the United States, slaves in the Cape were chattel slaves, meaning that they were captured from far away and brought to the Cape in captivity. A few of the first slaves came from West Africa (notably Angola and Ghana), but most came from the Indian Ocean Basin, including from MOZAMBIQUE, East Africa, and Madagascar, as well as from farther away, including India, Sumatra, Java, and Timor. The first group of slaves arrived in the Cape on March 28, 1658, aboard the *Amersfoort*. The Dutch had taken the slaves from a Portuguese slave trader who had captured the slaves in Angola. Of the 250 slaves originally captured, only 170 survived the voyage to the Cape.

The slave trade was controlled by the Dutch East India Company, which would send out slavers, primarily to Mozambique and Madagascar; to buy slaves and bring them to the Cape Colony. Another source of slaves was the Dutch East India Company's returning ships from the East en route to Europe. Because slavery was forbidden in the Netherlands, the Dutch officials who had slaves in East Asia had to leave them in the Cape before returning home. They preferred to sell their slaves in the Cape, because they could get a higher price than in the East Indies.

Up until the 1800s, the majority of slaves came from the Indian subcontinent, with nearly 80 percent from India during this period. In 1795, the Cape Colony was briefly taken over by the British, who began importing slaves primarily from southeast Africa. When the Dutch reclaimed the Cape in 1803, this trend continued, with slaves primarily coming from Mozambique during this time period. Slaves in the Cape used many forms to resist their captivity. Several significant uprisings occurred in the 1800s, including the Galant Uprising, named after its leader, as a group of slaves and KHOIKHOI laborers on a rural farm rose up and killed their master. The uprisings were often put down harshly; penalties usually meant death for the instigators.

Once the Cape Colony became part of the British Empire in 1806, movements toward the ending of slavery began, as it was already abolished elsewhere in the British Empire. During this period, some slaves were set free as a reward for hard work while others were able to purchase their freedom. Usually, the slaves had to show that they could speak Dutch and were able to make a living on their own before they were freed. By 1808, slaves were no longer allowed to be imported into the Cape Colony, and laws were passed to improve their living conditions.

All slaves were freed on December 1, 1834. At that time the slave population totaled 38,000. However, approximately 60,000 slaves were imported to South Africa from 1658 until 1807.

Emancipation came with some conditions. All slaves had to work as apprentices for their former masters for four years. In reality, they were doing the same work as when they were slaves and still not paid for their labor.

Many South Africans of all races are descendents of slaves. Slavery had a significant and lasting impact on the Cape Colony's economy and society. Many of the buildings and structures that are still standing today were built with slave labor. The slave society that emerged in the Cape Colony was one that was polarized between slaves and nonslaves, determined along racial lines, and bred a culture of domination by whites over blacks. Such social patterns clearly laid the foundation for the highly polarized racial society that would develop in South Africa in the twentieth century.

Slovo, Joseph (Joe) (1917–1995)

Joseph (Joe) Slovo was a prominent activist against APARTHEID, secretary-general of the SOUTH AFRICAN COMMUNIST PARTY (SACP) in the 1980s, and the first minister of housing in the post-apartheid AFRICAN NATIONAL CONGRESS (ANC)–led government. Born in Lithuania in 1926, his family moved to JOHANNESBURG when he was nine.

His roots in politics and particularly in labor organizing began with his first job as a clerk for a pharmaceutical wholesaler. He joined the union and quickly worked his way up to shop steward. In 1942, Slovo joined the Communist Party of South Africa (later renamed SACP) and served on its central committee from 1953 until his death in 1995.

In 1946, he enrolled at the University of Witwatersrand and graduated with a law degree in 1950. While at the university, he became more politically active and also met his first wife, (HELOISE) RUTH FIRST, a fellow Communist.

Slovo was a founding member of the white political organization the Congress of Democrats, which forged the Congress Alliance with the ANC, the SOUTH AFRICAN INDIAN CONGRESS, and the Coloured People's Congress. He then served on the Congress Alliance's national consultative committee and contributed to the drafting of the FREEDOM CHARTER in 1955. As a result, Slovo, along with many others, was arrested and became one of the accused during the 1956 TREASON TRIAL of antiapartheid leaders.

After the 1960 SHARPEVILLE MASSACRE, in which South African police killed at least sixty-nine black protesters, Slovo helped form Umkhonto we Sizwe, the ANC's armed wing. In 1963, he went into exile and spent the next twenty-seven years outside of South Africa. In 1969, Slovo was appointed to the ANC's Revolutionary Council and was considered as one of the party's main theoreticians. He set up the ANC headquarters in Maputo, MOZAMBIQUE, in 1977 and was appointed to the ANC's Executive Committee in 1985. In 1986, Slovo was elected as the SACP's secretary-general and became Umkhonto we Sizwe's chief of staff in 1987.

He returned to South Africa in 1990, following the unbanning of the ANC and the SACP, and was a key negotiator in the talks over a new dispensation with the apartheid regime. With the April 1994 ELECTIONS that ushered in majority rule, Slovo was appointed the minister of housing in President NELSON MANDELA's cabinet, a post he held until he died of leukemia in January 1995.

Smuts, Jan Christiaan (1870–1950)

General Jan Christiaan Smuts, an influential statesman and soldier, was born in the CAPE COLONY on May 24, 1870. A man of great intellect, Jan Smuts had extremely successful military and political careers, serving as prime minister of the UNION OF SOUTH AFRICA from 1919 to 1924 and again from 1939 to 1948.

Although he only began formal schooling at the age of twelve, Smuts went on to study at STELLENBOSCH University and at Cambridge University in England where he received a law degree. He returned to CAPE TOWN and practiced as an advocate for several years. A republican and an AFRIKANER nationalist, Smuts went into politics at the age of twenty-eight when accepting a position as state attorney under President PAUL KRUGER.

He also distinguished himself as a military strategist early on and became a general in the republican forces. In addition, Smuts attended the 1902 Vereeniging Peace Conference after the ANGLO-BOER WAR had ended between the British and the Afrikaners. He was largely responsible for drafting the Union of South Africa's Constitution, which amalgamated the four British South African colonies.

Smuts became South Africa's prime minister in 1919 after Louis Botha's death. In the next election in 1924, he lost to JAMES HERTZOG and the Afrikaner-led NATIONAL PARTY but remained in politics. In 1933, Smuts was appointed as the deputy prime minister and as the minister of justice under Hertzog's government. Their coalition led to the United Party's formation in 1934. With Hertzog's waning support over whether to remain neutral in World War II, Smuts again took over as South Africa's premier in 1939. He supported entering the war on the British side, which alienated many Afrikaners from his government. At the end of World War II, Smuts was involved in the formation of the United Nations.

In the postwar era, Smuts's government was confronting growing discontent on the part of black South Africans. Unlike the National Party, Smuts did not believe in the idea of separate development or APARTHEID, arguing that it was not practical. However, consensus was growing among Afrikaners that this was an appropriate policy, and in 1948 the National Party won the elections. Smuts resigned, and D. F. MALAN became prime minister.

Smuts died in 1950 on his farm in Doornkloof, located outside of Pretoria.

Sobukwe, Robert Mangaliso (1924–1978)

First president of the PAN AFRICANIST CONGRESS (PAC), Robert Mangaliso Sobukwe was born on December 5, 1924, in Graaff-Reinet, located in the Cape Province. He received his higher education at the UNIVERSITY OF FORT HARE, and joined the AFRICAN NATIONAL CONGRESS (ANC) YOUTH LEAGUE in 1948.

He began his career as a high school teacher in Standerton, in present-day Gauteng Province, and became a lecturer of African Studies at the University of Witwatersrand in 1954. In JOHANNESBURG, Sobukwe was an editor for *The Africanist* and soon began to criticize the ANC for its multiracial views and for being too heavily influenced by white liberals. In contrast, he largely rejected working with whites in the struggle for black liberation.

In 1958, Sobukwe initiated a breakaway from the ANC and formed the PAC, to which he was elected as its first president. He was an intelligent and a charismatic speaker and leader, which helped to boost support for the PAC and position this party as one of the leading liberation movements at the time. In 1960, during the PAC's campaign against PASS LAWS, which restricted blacks' movement, Sobukwe was arrested and initially sentenced to three years but subsequently had his sentence extended for an additional six years. He spent the latter part of his sentence on ROBBEN ISLAND. When released from prison in 1969, he settled in KIMBERLEY, in present-day Northern Cape, with his family, where he remained under a twelve-hour-per-day house arrest and started his own law firm.

In 1978, Sobukwe died after a prolonged battle with lung cancer.

Soga, Tiyo (1829–1871)

Poet and writer Tiyo Soga was the LOVEDALE missionaries' most famous pupil. He was born in Gwali in the eastern CAPE COLONY in 1829. During a visit to Scotland in 1856, he became the first black South African to be ordained in the Presbyterian Church. Soga married a Scot, Janet Burnside, and the two returned to the eastern Cape where Soga worked as a missionary among his own people, the Ngqikas. He was also called upon to set up additional mission stations in neighboring areas. He translated John Bunyan's *Pilgrim's Progress* as well as large parts of the Bible into XHOSA to greatly expand their readership and literary influence in nineteenth century South Africa. Soga was also a prominent writer in the Lovedale newspaper, *Indaba*, which began in 1862. Soga was frequently ill and frail toward the end of his life, and he eventually died of tuberculosis.

Sophiatown

Sophiatown was a vibrant multiracial urban cultural center until its destruction in the mid-1950s, when it became a symbol of forced removals of black residents and resistance to APARTHEID.

In 1897, a white developer named Herman Tobiansky purchased 237 acres of land west of JOHANNESBURG and created a township named Sophiatown in honor of his wife. When the Johannesburg City Council built a sewage disposal facility near Sophiatown, white South Africans lost interest, and Tobiansky began selling freehold plots without regard to race. Since black South Africans were able to purchase land in Sophiatown prior to the 1923 Native Urban Areas Act, it remained exempt from the act's permit requirements and prohibitions on black land ownership.

Sophiatown grew rapidly during the 1920s and the 1930s due to the expansion of manufacturing, which generated demand for black working-class housing. When Johannesburg was proclaimed a "white" area in 1933, many black South Africans who were forced out of the city moved to Sophiatown rather than accept accommodations in the government-controlled native reserves. Sophiatown quickly became an overcrowded suburb with black (African, INDIAN, and COLOURED) landowners and merchants living amid a large and growing black working class.

During the 1940s and the early 1950s, Sophiatown became the heart of an emergent black urban culture, earning the moniker "the Harlem of South Africa." As writer and Sophiatown resident Bloke Modisane explained: "We did not live in it, we were Sophiatown." Known for its cosmopolitan sophistication, Sophiatown featured two movie theaters, countless shebeens (speakeasies), a famous jazz scene, and the latest cars and fashions from around the world. It was home to Can Themba and other writers associated with *DRUM* magazine, as well as politicians such as Dr. Alfred Xuma, musicians such as HUGH MASEKELA, and authors such as Wally Serote and Don Mattera. Working-class community life centered on Sophiatown's numerous schools, civic associations, and churches—including Trevor Huddleston's Anglican Church of Christ. The streets of Sophiatown provided economic opportunities for the poor and unemployed through informal trading, the sale of home-brewed liquor, and the organized activities of gangs such as the Gestapo, the Berliners, the Americans, and the Vultures. After 1948, Sophiatown became a center of resistance to apartheid, with boycotts against increased tram fares, riots against the police, and protests organized by groups such as the AFRICAN NATIONAL CONGRESS (ANC).

To crush the resistance and disrupt the cosmopolitan urban center, the South African government announced in 1953 that Sophiatown would be destroyed in accordance with the 1950 Group Areas Act that divided all residential areas along racial lines, reserving the inner cities and suburbs for whites only. The Western Areas Removal Scheme involved the forced removal of 65,000 residents from Sophiatown, Newclare, Martindale, and the Western Native Township. African residents were moved to Meadowlands (SOWETO), Indian residents to Lenasia, and coloured residents to Noordgesig and the Western Coloured Township. On February 9, 1955, three days before the first removals were scheduled to take place, 2,000 police arrived in Sophiatown and began loading Africans onto trucks and moving them to Meadowlands. Resistance organized by the ANC and the local landowners remained nonviolent but was unable to prevent the forced removals.

Sophiatown's destruction occurred gradually over eight years. In its place, the apartheid government built a segregated white neighborhood called Triomf ("Triumph" in Afrikaans). After the end of apartheid, the ANC government restored the name Sophiatown but not the community or the culture.

Soshangane
See MFECANE; ZULU

Sotho

Sotho, also known as seSotho and Southern Sotho, is a Bantu language, like XHOSA, that is primarily spoken in South Africa, where it is one of eleven official languages; and in LESOTHO, where it is the national language. The Sotho population is divided into two major branches: the Southern Sotho and the Northern Sotho, who are known as the PEDI. Linguistically, the two groups are distinct, as the southern form of Sotho is spoken in Lesotho while the northern one is spoken in South Africa's Limpopo Province. The Southern Sothos compose over 90 percent of Lesotho's population. South Africa has around four million native Sotho speakers, which is about 8 percent of the country's population, and an additional five million people who speak Sotho as their second or third language, most of them residing in the metropolitan areas of JOHANNESBURG, SOWETO, and TSHWANE.

Traditionally, the Sotho society was organized in villages that were ruled by chiefs, and its economy was based on cattle rearing and grain cultivation. In the early nineteenth century, several kingdoms developed due to wars throughout southern Africa. During this period, the Southern Sotho people and other ethnic groups sought refuge in current-day Lesotho. MOSHOESHOE, who had emerged as the Sotho chief, was able to keep Lesotho independent from the invading ZULUS and from the AFRIKANER settlers, but, after his death in 1870, Lesotho's independence became jeopardized as it faced threats from British forces. From 1880 to 1881, in the Gun War, the Southern Sothos attempted to resist British control and were able to fight them off temporarily.

In 1884, Lesotho became a British protectorate, but it was not incorporated into South Africa like the Northern Sotho kingdom and only became an independent nation in 1966. After losing most of their lands by the early twentieth century, the Sotho population in both Lesotho and South Africa turned to mining to make ends meet, as cattle raising had become difficult due to Western economic pressures. By the early 1990s, an estimated 100,000 Sothos were working in South Africa's mines, and many of them also became the country's urban workforce.

Currently, the Sothos in South Africa encounter numerous social problems such as poverty, malnutrition, divided families, and high crime rates as a result of repercussions from policies implemented by the APARTHEID government. For example, the rural territories inhabited by the Northern and the Southern Sothos were severely eroded, overgrazed, and overpopulated as a result of apartheid policies and the allocation of only 13 percent of South Africa's land to black South Africans.

South Africa Act of 1909

The South Africa Act of 1909 was an act of the British Parliament that created the UNION OF SOUTH AFRICA from the British colonies of the Cape, NATAL, Orange River, and the Transvaal.

After the ANGLO-BOER WAR (1899–1902), Britain annexed the South African Republic and the Orange Free State, the two hitherto independent AFRIKANER republics, and renamed them the Transvaal and the Orange River Colony. These new territories were added to Britain's existing South African territories, the CAPE COLONY and Natal. The British government policy also encouraged a closer union among the four colonies, an aspiration increasingly held by the Afrikaner population as well. In 1908, a national convention was hosted to decide the terms and the constitution of a governmental, legislative, and economic union. During the drafting of the proposals, the British yielded to the Afrikaners who thought black South Africans should not have a right to the voting franchise. The result was the South Africa Act, passed by the Parliament on September 20, 1909, and the Union of South Africa, established on May 31, 1910. Although the act brought the independent South African state into being, it took away from the Cape native and COLOURED voters the right of membership to Parliament, as well as denied the franchise to all black South Africans. The act served as the South African Constitution until 1961, when South Africa became a republic and left the British Commonwealth.

See also ANGLO-BOER WAR; BRITISH IMPERIALISM AND SETTLER COLONIALISM (1870–1910); JAN CHRISTIAAN SMUTS

South African Coloured People's Organization

The South African Coloured People's Organization (SACPO), later renamed the Coloured People's Congress, was formed in 1953 and marked a significant shift in the politics of fighting APARTHEID in the COLOURED community. Prior to the 1950s, several organizations served the coloured community's political interests, including the more radical NON-EUROPEAN UNITY MOVEMENT, the more conservative Coloured People's National Union, and the African People's Organization. However, it wasn't until SACPO's formation that the political leadership in the coloured community began to recognize the importance of working with other groups disadvantaged by apartheid.

SACPO quickly joined the Congress Alliance, with the AFRICAN NATIONAL CONGRESS (ANC), the SOUTH AFRICAN INDIAN CONGRESS, and the South African Congress of Democrats, which, in 1955, held the Congress of the People in Kliptown outside of JOHANNESBURG, and drafted the FREEDOM CHARTER, a vision for postapartheid ideologies and principles. Shortly thereafter, a number of SACPO leaders, along with many other liberation movement leaders, were arrested, jailed, and stood as the accused in the 1956 TREASON TRIAL.

After the 1960 SHARPEVILLE MASSACRE, in which South African police killed at least sixty-nine black protesters, and the banning of most of the liberation movements, many antiapartheid leaders, including SACPO members, went into exile. In exile, SACPO members chose to join the better-organized and better-financed ANC or PAN AFRICANIST CONGRESS. In 1966, SACPO was dissolved. Among its most prominent members were ALEX LA GUMA, Barney Desai, and Cardiff Harney.

South African Communist Party

Founded in 1921 as the Communist Party of South Africa, the South African Communist Party (SACP) has since been in the forefront of the struggle against imperialism and racial domination. Today, the SACP is a member of the ruling tripartite alliance, along with the AFRICAN NATIONAL CONGRESS (ANC) and the CONGRESS OF SOUTH AFRICAN TRADE UNIONS.

The SACP first came to prominence in 1922 during the white workers' armed RAND REVOLT.

Despite the party's supposed opposition to racialism, it chose to support the white workers' demands for preferential privileges over black workers. However, when the Rand Revolt failed, in large measure because it lacked black workers' support, the party was forced to change its tune. From then on, the party put its efforts into organizing black workers, who were the overwhelming majority in South Africa. By 1928, the party membership was overwhelmingly black.

In 1950, the Communist Party of South Africa was declared illegal and forced to go underground. In 1953, it reemerged and changed its name to the South African Communist Party. The SACP was a particular target of the APARTHEID government, with the Suppression of Communism Act being a key piece of apartheid legislation used to silence its opponents, especially the SACP members. The SACP's influence in the liberation struggle was greater than its actual size. In the 1950s, it adopted a policy of working with the ANC, as both parties shared many of the same members, and the party was one of the five organizations in the Congress Alliance. The SACP worked on reorienting the ANC's policies from a nationalist position to a nonracial one and was instrumental in the drafting of the FREEDOM CHARTER, which provided a vision for post-apartheid ideologies and principles.

In exile, the SACP helped the ANC establish its military wing, Umkhonto we Sizwe, and SACP's influence within the liberation struggle grew further as Communist states began to provide financial and military support to the ANC. SACP leader JOE SLOVO was Umkhonto we Sizwe's chief of staff, and his wife and fellow Communist RUTH FIRST was a primary theoretician of the revolutionary struggle in which the ANC was engaged. The ANC, however, remained broadly social democratic in its outlook.

With the new democratic government in 1994, the SACP continues to align itself with the ANC. While a number of members of PARLIAMENT and cabinet ministers are SACP members, they were elected on the ANC ticket. The SACP does not contest elections independently. Some prominent SACP members include the late CHRIS HANI, the late Bram Fischer, Jeremy Cronin, Mac Maharaj, and Blade Nzimande.

South African Council of Churches

The South African Council of Churches (SACC) was formed in 1968 as an interdenominational body composed of twenty-six member churches and para-church organizations. It became an important organization in the struggle against APARTHEID because of its willingness to speak out against oppression and discrimination, and because of the prominence of some of its leaders, including DESMOND TUTU, Beyers Naude, and Frank Chikane. As an ecumenical body, it contributed to undermining the claims of apartheid's religious justification. But its opposition to apartheid made it a target of the apartheid state, and in 1988 the SACC's headquarters in JOHANNESBURG was bombed. It was later revealed during the TRUTH AND RECONCILIATION COMMISSION hearings that this was the work of government security forces.

Today, the SACC continues to assist in the nation's reconstruction and development by focusing on issues of justice, reconciliation, poverty eradication, and the empowerment of marginalized groups.

South African Indian Congress

Formed in 1924 to promote the interests of the INDIAN community in South Africa at a time of growing anti-Indian sentiment within the white community, the South African Indian Congress (SAIC) became a prominent organization in the fight against APARTHEID and part of the Congress Alliance with the AFRICAN NATIONAL CONGRESS (ANC), the SOUTH AFRICAN COMMUNIST PARTY, and the SOUTH AFRICAN COLOURED PEOPLE'S ORGANIZATION.

The SAIC started as a relatively conservative organization, relying on petitions and passive negotiations to push its demands. In the 1940s, it was radicalized by a new cohort of leadership, which advocated more militant tactics and greater cooperation with Africans and other disadvantaged groups. Among them were Dr. G. M. Naicker of the Natal Indian Congress and Dr. Yusuf Dadoo of the Transvaal Indian Congress, who were elected to the SAIC leadership in the late 1940s. Under the new leadership, the SAIC entered into a pact of cooperation with the ANC in

1947. In 1952, the SAIC and the ANC jointly launched the DEFIANCE CAMPAIGNS against apartheid laws and forged the Congress Alliance, a multiracial group of antiapartheid organizations, shortly thereafter to draft the FREEDOM CHARTER, a document that outlined a nonracial, democratic vision for a postapartheid South Africa.

South African Jazz
See ABDULLAH IBRAHIM; MIRIAM MAKEBA; HUGH MASEKELA; KIPPIE MOEKETSI; MUSIC

South African War
See ANGLO-BOER WAR

South West Africa
See NAMIBIA

Soweto
Originally an acronym for "South Western Townships," today Soweto is the largest urban black residential area in South Africa and is located just outside of JOHANNESBURG. Soweto was first formed from a cluster of black townships in 1904, which were primarily intended to house black laborers in the mines of Johannesburg. As the black population in Johannesburg grew—a result of economic opportunities as well as displacements and forced removals from the so-called black spots, which were parts of white areas still occupied by blacks—many blacks were relocated to Soweto. Soweto's growth was largely unplanned, which resulted in overcrowding, substandard housing, and poor infrastructure. Its landscape is dotted with informal settlements composed of tin shacks and few parks, trees, or municipal services. With the new democratic government and with Soweto becoming a popular tourist attraction for foreigners, efforts are being made to address many of these issues. However, Soweto is still a place of contrasts. Amid the shacks, where residents suffer high unemployment, are large mansions occupied by prominent black businessmen and the new black elite.

Soweto's history is infused with the history of the struggle against racial oppression and APARTHEID. The SOWETO STUDENT UPRISING OF 1976, led by black schoolchildren, originated in Soweto and spread throughout the country. Soweto was also the starting place for many squatter movements during the 1940s, where homeless blacks would "squat" and establish makeshift homes usually on private or state-owned land, and the DEFIANCE CAMPAIGNS against apartheid laws during the 1970s and the 1980s. Political luminaries such as NELSON MANDELA, WALTER SISULU, and DESMOND TUTU once lived in Soweto, and it's the birthplace of many leading South African social and sporting figures.

Soweto Student Uprising of 1976
On June 16, 1976, close to 15,000 black students from SOWETO gathered for a peaceful protest demonstration against APARTHEID education for blacks, but were met with violence by the apartheid security forces who killed two students and injured hundreds. The protests spread across the country, and the Soweto Student Uprising marked a watershed event in the dismantling of the apartheid system.

At a June 13 meeting of the South African Students' Movement (SASM), pupils at Naledi High School formed the Soweto Students' Representative Council (SSRC). Chairperson Tebello Motopayane led the group, which consisted of two members from each of the secondary schools in the sprawling township south of JOHANNESBURG known as Soweto. An organized march of students protesting the conditions of the inferior BANTU EDUCATION system was planned for June 16.

At this time, government spending for education was an estimated R644 a year per white student and R42 a year per black student. The students' complaints included overcrowding, lack of adequate facilities and resources, and a recent government decree requiring that arithmetic, social studies, geography, and history be taught in Afrikaans. Few teachers were fluent in Afrikaans, which many within the resistance movement regarded as the oppressor's language. In addition, Afrikaans was not helpful to students seeking clerical work, because English was preferred in the business sector.

On the morning of June 16, an estimated 15,000 schoolchildren gathered at Orlando West Junior Secondary School, carrying placards of protest. The police arrived and ordered the crowd to disperse. When the protesting youth stood their ground, the police released attack dogs and fired tear gas into the crowd. Some students threw stones and bottles at the police, who opened fire on the masses. Chaos ensued and the students retreated. By midday, they were launching attacks on the symbols of state oppression by setting alight administration buildings, beer halls, government-run Putco buses, and white businesses and vehicles. While students erected barricades on the streets, the police sealed off the township with roadblocks and attacked crowds of commuters believed to be parents or sympathizers of the students outside railway stations with batons as they returned home from work.

Reports estimated that at least 500 people, many in their teens, were killed that year in the Soweto Uprising and many others like it. The most famous was a thirteen-year-old boy named Hector Pieterson. Popularly regarded as the first victim, his death was captured in six photos by photographer Samuel Nzima. The pictures show another boy carrying the dying Hector as his cousin, Antoinette Sithole, ran beside him with a hand raised in horror. The image of the three youths came to symbolize the apartheid government's brutality and the youth struggle for liberation.

Protests spread across the country from Soweto to other townships in the Rand, East Rand, and at the universities of the Witwatersrand, Turfloop, Ngoye, and NATAL. After three days of rioting, the minister of Bantu education closed the schools and eventually dropped the demand for Afrikaans instruction before reopening them on June 26. Protests continued to spread with youth demonstrations, boycotts, and school burnings in CAPE TOWN and PORT ELIZABETH. The police attacked and raided townships as well as rounded up schoolchildren in mass detentions. The Black Parents' Association (BPA) was formed to help arrange medical, legal, and funerary services for victims of the police action.

As protests by schoolchildren continued to spread, police responded with violence in Cape Town and other cities in the Eastern Cape. In August and September, the SSRC mounted several successful stay-aways from schools, work, and businesses by using a range of persuasion and coercion. The second of these turned into violence when a section of migrant workers in Mzimhlope Hostel, allegedly encouraged by the police, waged an attack on young people on the streets of Soweto. Subsequently, organized youth resistance was geared toward campaigns against shebeens (unlicensed drinking establishments), alcohol, and Christmas celebrations.

In the aftermath of the Soweto Uprising, debates remain unsettled about to what degree the schoolchildren were influenced by the black consciousness ideology, the AFRICAN NATIONAL CONGRESS (ANC), the Students' Representative Councils, intergenerational conflict, changes in the educational system, and labor organization (especially the strikes of 1973 and 1974). Regardless of their roles in planning the revolt, both the ANC and the PAN AFRICANIST CONGRESS received a tremendous boost as young exiles fled to their training camps in neighboring countries. The ANC distributed leaflets calling on young people to continue to resist apartheid policies and further build the constituency of the revolt. Ideas from the BLACK CONSCIOUSNESS MOVEMENT also gained hold as they inspired and incited many youth to action.

Unquestionably, the Soweto Uprising radically transformed both the political landscape and the resistance movement in South Africa and around the world. It galvanized a younger generation, an estimated 12,000 of whom fled the country to join the resistance movement as exiles. The events of June 16 attracted unprecedented national and international attention, scrutiny, and condemnation as the apartheid state became more draconian in its use of violence against the masses. Expressing a greater sense of impatience and urgency, many youth adopted a stance of increasing militancy and became more organized in their attempts to overturn the apartheid state.

In 1994, President NELSON MANDELA declared June 16 Youth Day, which is a national public holiday to remember the massacre and to commemorate the role of youth in the struggles against apartheid and Bantu education. In 2002, the Hector Pieterson Museum was opened in Soweto near the site of the uprising.

Sports

Many South Africans consider themselves citizens of a sporting nation. The International Marketing Council of South Africa describes sport as the "national religion, transcending race, politics or language group. . . . When a South African team wins, a cacophony of hooting, cheering, banging of dustbin lids, trumpeting on cow horns and fireworks reverberates across the largest cities. The national adrenaline goes into overdrive." Evidence of South Africa's status as a sporting nation comes from its hosting of megaevents, including the Rugby World Cup (1995), soccer's African Cup of Nations (1996), World Cup of Athletics (1998), Cricket World Cup (2003), Football World Cup (soccer) (2010), and CAPE TOWN's bid to host the 2004 Olympic games. But if sports ostensibly unites South Africans now, for most of the twentieth century it divided them.

Modern sports arrived in southern Africa in the nineteenth century with British settlers, traders, military personnel, and missionaries who claimed sports as metaphors of their cultural identity. In addition to signifying courage and fair play, cricket, for example, symbolized punctuality, patience, accuracy, and vigilance, while rugby denoted teamwork, earnestness of purpose, and subordination of the self. These were not absolute values or traits but were stereotypes employed by the British to distinguish themselves from AFRIKANERS and Africans with whom they competed for political control of South Africa. Afrikaners dominate South African rugby and Africans dominate South African soccer.

While serving as private secretary to Lord Alfred Milner, John Buchan (1903, 49–50), identified "courage, honour, and self control" as the "'essential' ingredients of sport and measures of 'national character.'" And Buchan, a devotee of British imperialism, found Afrikaners lacking. Sport, he said, captured "the Boer at his worst. . . . Without tradition of fair play, soured and harassed by want and disaster, his sport became a matter of commerce, and he held no device unworthy." Africans fared no better. In *Cricketers of the Veld* (1947), Louis Duffus reduced Africans to disinterested laborers, with nicknames that hid their identities, and whose presence was to minister to the needs of white sportsmen: "out in the centre of the oval Sixpence, the ground boy, is methodically rolling up the mat. As he wheels away the pitch he chants a tune of his kraal-land, a low-toned drawling song that his proud ancestors were wont to sing as night fell over the rolling hills of Zululand."

These images did not pass uncontested. On the contrary, as South Africa increasingly segregated along racial lines, Afrikaners and Africans endowed sports with their own cultural meanings.

Sports in the Era of Segregation

Before the ANGLO-BOER WAR (1899–1902), a handful of Afrikaners played representative cricket. After the war, cricket symbolized widening political divisions between English-speaking whites and Afrikaners; even rapprochement between the two groups in the 1960s did little to generate interest among Afrikaner nationalists. When told that the English had lost three wickets for forty-two runs in a test against South Africa, Prime Minister John Vorster retorted, "their English or our English?"

Rugby was a different matter. In the 1930s and 1940s, Afrikaner nationalists seized it as a cultural icon beside *boeremusiek* (Afrikaner folk music) and *volkspele* (Afrikaner folk dancing). "In symbolic terms" rugby bore "the print of Afrikaner culture—its convictions, aspirations and dreams" (Archer and Bouillon 1982, 73). Sporting relationships between English speakers and Africans also highlighted cultural differences between the two groups.

Nineteenth-century British missionaries to southern Africa subscribed to Enlightenment ideas about human equality and attempted to assimilate indigenous peoples as equals. As part of this process, they introduced Africans to sports, especially cricket and soccer, at schools such as

First match of the International Federation of Association Football (FIFA) World Cup 2010 in Johannesburg.

Healdtown, LOVEDALE, St. Matthews, and Zonnebloem. Mission education helped create an African intelligentsia and middle class that identified closely with nonracialism and played sports to demonstrate their assimilation into European culture and "their fitness as full citizens." Yet, sports offered precious few opportunities for Africans. Declaring that he would "not have a black fellow" in the squad, CAPE COLONY prime minister CECIL RHODES pressured selectors to exclude the internationally respected fast bowler and COLOURED "Krom" Hendricks from the South African team that toured England in 1894.

In the early twentieth century Africans streamed into South Africa's burgeoning cities. The middle class played football and tennis at clubs like the Bantu Men's Social Centre. An initiative of the Johannesburg Joint Council for Bantu and Europeans to supposedly nurture race relations, the center hosted occasional mixed events but few whites were enthusiastic. Criticized in the press for playing with Africans at the social center, the former South African Davis Cup captain G. H. Dodd insisted his visit was "merely an exhibition" without "interracial significance."

Mine owners organized soccer for migrant African workers in the belief that the sport would "detract from work-related grievances" and "entertain" them on weekends. White municipal officials followed suit in the townships. Independent African interests progressively came to the fore, especially in the 1930s, and helped forge an urban sporting culture among working-class Africans.

Apartheid Sports and the Boycott
Beginning in 1948, the APARTHEID government instructed officials to form separate African, coloured, INDIAN, and white associations for sporting competition. Under this arrangement

only whites could play on South Africa's national cricket and rugby teams to earn Springbok honors and represent South Africa in international federations. Some sportspeople refused to racially segregate and formed umbrella nonracial organizations such as the South African Sports Association, the South African Non-Racial Olympic Committee, and the South African Council on Sport (SACOS), which took the lead in challenging apartheid sports. On rare occasions, white sportspeople challenged apartheid policy. In 1961, Springbok cricketer John Waite led a white team, comprising four Springboks and six provincial representatives, against a black team captained by S. A. Haque. In 1971, players participating in a match between Transvaal and the rest of South Africa briefly walked off the ground to hand a statement to the press in which they protested the exclusion of black cricketers from the Springbok team.

South Africa's traditional sporting rivals ignored apartheid policies, believing Pretoria's propaganda that black people showed little interest in Western-style sports. Gradually, however, apartheid practices provoked their moral sensibilities. When Prime Minister Vorster announced that BASIL D'OLIVEIRA, a coloured South African émigré, would not be allowed back into the country as a member of the English cricket team on its proposed tour of the republic in 1968–1969, British prime minister Harold Wilson said the decision placed South Africa "outside the pale of civilized cricket" and the tour was canceled. In the early 1970s, international sporting federations acted en masse expelling or suspending South African affiliates as protests against apartheid South Africa, although rugby officials resisted for another decade. Siege conditions surrounded Springbok rugby tours to Britain (1969–1970), Australia (1971), and New Zealand (1981). Cordons of police kept thousands of protesters at bay, bloody clashes erupted between police and demonstrators, and barbed wire encircled the playing fields. Under these conditions rugby also eventually discarded South Africa.

Sporting isolation concerned the apartheid regime and the white population. As the Minister of Sport Piet Koornhof conceded, "Play and sport are strong enough to cause political and economic relations to flourish or collapse." Vorster offered one concession when he allowed New Zealand to include Maori players in its rugby team that toured South Africa in 1970. The following year the government's policy of multinationalism—a scheme that divided South Africa into ten black "nations," each with its own territory and responsibility for some of their own affairs including sports—allowed black and white sportspeople to compete against each other in open international events such as the Comrades (ultra) Marathon between DURBAN and Pietermaritzburg.

Multinationalism, however, was a token reform. In 1975, for example, 1,500 people ran the Comrades Marathon but the Department of Sport approved the registration of just six blacks from each nation. Yet, even in this crude form, multinational sports marked an ideological turning point. Liberal Afrikaner nationalists increasingly sanctioned mixed sports as a recipe for social stability, and deracialization progressively followed. In 1980, Errol Tobias became the first black Springbok in rugby.

Deracialization did not end sporting isolation. Precisely as the government desegregated sport, the objectives of the sports boycott "moved beyond eradicating racist practices in sport to dismantling apartheid." SACOS's slogan, "no normal sport in an abnormal society," articulated the sentiments of the nonracial sports movement and the international community: black people could not play sports freely and happily while apartheid regulated every aspect of their lives and whites were "just not interested in playing" with blacks. Applied as a form of noncollaboration, the sports boycott gave nonracial sportsmen and -women a psychological escape from helplessness and enabled them to negate the state's policies. But clearly it could not transform the apartheid state. In the late 1980s, elements in the nonracial movement in South Africa and abroad began to question the effectiveness of the boycott. They argued the sports boycott had extracted maximum concessions from the government and that the nonracial movement needed a new strategy. Simultaneously, the black press in South Africa publicly condemned the boycott on the grounds that it failed to distinguish between the victims and beneficiaries of apartheid.

In 1989, a group of dissenters within SACOS, including Reverend Makhenkesi Arnold Stofile, Mluleki George, and Krish Naidoo, launched the National Sports Congress (NSC). Their goal was to renew negotiations with white officials to build a more equitable sporting dispensation based on democratic national governing associations and sports development programs in the black townships. The NSC scored a quick victory. In cooperation with the mass democratic movement against apartheid, the NSC staged large-scale protests against English cricketers touring South Africa in 1989–1990 at the invitation of the government-recognized South African Cricket Union (SACU) and forced SACU to shorten the tour. The NSC achieved immediately what SACOS had threatened for nearly a decade—an end to cricket tours designed to circumvent the official boycott. Moreover, in one action, the NSC seized control of South African sport.

Events overtook the NSC's plans. In February 1990, during the rebel English cricket tour, South African president F. W. DE KLERK unbanned the AFRICAN NATIONAL CONGRESS (ANC), the SOUTH AFRICAN COMMUNIST PARTY, and the PAN AFRICANIST CONGRESS and promised to abolish apartheid legislation. International sporting federations responded by lifting their boycotts. South Africa competed in the 1992 Olympics—its first since 1960—and the following year over ninety South African sports enjoyed international recognition.

Postapartheid Sports

The NSC never realized its plans to lay solid democratic foundations for sports in postapartheid South Africa. Neither the international community nor the ANC were concerned with the details of sporting structures or relationships. After the NATIONAL PARTY repealed the legislative foundations of apartheid, the international sporting community welcomed South African teams—irrespective of their racial composition and administrative structure—onto the playing fields. In its negotiations for a democratic dispensation with the National Party, the ANC ignored sports, focusing on international sports as a vehicle to reassure whites about the reconciliatory intentions of a future black government.

South Africa's postapartheid state is grappling to build a national identity. Like preapartheid and apartheid governments, postapartheid governments have appropriated sports as part of the nationalizing process. They recognize sports' "potency" as a cultural product to "give meaning to life" and "to create and interconnect senses of achievement and identity" (Allison 1993, 4–5). In the wake of national jubilation following South Africa's victory in the 1995 Rugby World Cup—captured by Hollywood in *Invictus* (2009)—many commentators hailed the emergence of a new nonracial rainbow nation. But multicultural rainbow imagery and symbolism quickly evaporated under subsequent government policies of racial nationalism. Unless governments reinforce symbolic sporting successes with material support, national identity achieved in moments of victory will always be ephemeral. Indeed, a chronic shortage of basic infrastructure for human development in South Africa suggests that the optimism around the well-organized 2010 Football World Cup (soccer) will also quickly recede.

Bibliography

Allison, L. *The Changing Politics of Sport*. Manchester, UK: Manchester University Press, 1993.

Archer, R., and A. Bouillon. *The South African Game: Sport and Racism*. London, Zed Books, 1982.

Booth, D. *The Race Game: Sport and Politics in South Africa*. London: Frank Cass, 1998.

Buchan, John. *The African Colony: Studies on Reconstruction*. Edinburgh: William Blackwood, 1903.

Duffus, L. *Cricketers of the Veld*. London: Swinfern, 1947.

International Marketing Council of South Africa. "Sport in South Africa." Online at http://www.southafrica.info/about/sport/sportsa.htm.

Murray, B., and C. Merrett. *Caught Behind: Race and Politics in Springbok Cricket*. Johannesburg, South Africa: Wits University Press, 2004.

Nauright, J. *Sport, Cultures and Identities in South Africa*. London: Leicester University Press, 1997.

Odendaal, A. "South Africa's Black Victorians: Sport and Society in South Africa in the Nineteenth Century." In *Pleasure, Profit, Proselytism: British Culture and Sport at Home and Abroad 1700–1914*, 193–214. Edited by J. A. Mangan. London: Frank Cass, 1988.

Vahed, G. "Cultural Confrontation: Race, Politics and Cricket in South Africa in the 1970s and 1980s." *Culture, Sport, Society* 5, no. 2 (2002): 79–107.

—Douglas Booth

Squatter Settlements

Squatter settlements, or shantytowns, refer to the informal slum settlements that have been established on the outskirts of the major metropolitan areas in South Africa as a consequence both of APARTHEID's racial policies of separate development and of the country's economic development path. Poor, black residents with no land of their own "squat" on vacant land that is either privately or publicly owned. The settlements (also referred to as squatter camps) comprise makeshift shacks of corrugated metal, wood planks, and plastic sheets.

These illegal squatter settlements sprang up as a result of the lack of housing available to blacks in the metropolitan areas (which were designated white areas during apartheid) and the heavy influx of blacks to the cities looking for work beginning in the 1960s. The apartheid police and military would periodically bulldoze entire squatter settlements, compelling black residents to move and start over elsewhere. Also, because they were illegal, the settlements had no facilities, such as running water, toilets, and electricity. By the early 1980s, one of the largest of South Africa's informal settlements, Crossroads, located

Squatter settlement outside of Cape Town.

outside of CAPE TOWN, had a population of over 100,000.

Conditions in the squatter settlements began to change in the mid-1980s when it became apparent that housing for blacks was insufficient and the squatter settlements would have to serve as permanent housing for millions of black South Africans. Post-1994, with the beginning of black majority rule, municipalities have begun providing some facilities to squatter settlements. However, there have also been instances of mass evictions and removals reminiscent of the apartheid era, which has led to violent confrontations between residents and the postapartheid government. Residents have mobilized under banners such as the Anti-Eviction Campaign, and the issue of squatters has become a thorny subject for the ruling AFRICAN NATIONAL CONGRESS government.

Cape Town boasts the largest squatter settlements. This is because the Cape was a COLOURED preference area during apartheid, which meant that blacks were not allowed to work in the city. Thus, no housing was provided for blacks, and those that came had to live illegally in squatter settlements.

It is estimated that around eight million South Africans live in squatter settlements, which represents almost one-fifth of the country's population.

Stellenbosch

The second oldest European settlement in South Africa, after CAPE TOWN, Stellenbosch was founded in 1679 and is situated about twenty miles inland, nestled in what is now the winelands of the Western Cape region. Some of the town's earliest settlers were the Dutch and the French HUGUENOTS, who planted grapes in the fertile valleys surrounding the town.

This town is home to Stellenbosch University, a historically Afrikaans university. In addition to the university activities, the main economy of the town revolves around the wine industry. The town's population, numbering approximately 120,000 in 2008, remains predominantly Afrikaans-speaking with large English- and XHOSA-speaking minorities.

Stokvel(s)

Stokvels are informal savings associations or clubs used by black South Africans, in which members routinely put money into the scheme and are able to take money out on a rotating basis. They have existed in South Africa for many years, perhaps dating back to the early nineteenth century, and have served as an indigenous form of savings and money accumulation for capital-intensive projects in many African communities. Found not only in poorer communities, the more sophisticated versions of stokvels are used by executives as well. Therefore, they have both social and business functions.

Suzman, Helen (1917–2009)

Helen Suzman was one of the few white, liberal members of Parliament during the APARTHEID era. Throughout her political career, she was an outspoken critic of apartheid and often took up the black majority's causes and concerns.

Suzman was born Helen Gavronsky in Germiston in Gauteng Province, on November 7, 1917, to parents of Jewish descent who had emigrated from Eastern Europe. She received her schooling in JOHANNESBURG at Parktown Convent and then at the University of Witwatersrand (Wits). In the 1940s, her interests in politics came to the fore, which were partly influenced by her studies at Wits and partly due to her affiliation with the liberal organization that conducted research on racial issues at the South African Institute of Race Relations.

First elected in 1953 under the United Party's banner to represent the Johannesburg constituency of Houghton, Suzman was one of twelve white liberals who broke away from the United Party to form the Progressive Party when it became clear that the United Party's principles were in line with the AFRIKANER-led NATIONAL PARTY's apartheid policies.

For over a decade, Suzman was the lone white liberal elected to Parliament by somewhat liberal English-speaking whites during one of the apartheid era's most repressive decades—the 1960s. She had served her constituency well, but she also became the advocate for so many South Africans who had no representation. As a member of Parliament, Suzman received hundreds of requests asking for help with housing problems, bannings, detentions, and problems with PASS LAWS, which restricted blacks' movements. She frequently raised unpopular issues and visited political prisoners in jail, among them NELSON MANDELA, which facilitated a wide network of friends and acquaintances in the black community. While many in the black leadership did not agree with all of her views, she was highly respected and regarded for her honesty. Suzman retired from politics in 1989.

She was married to Mosie Suzman, with whom she had two daughters. Helen Suzman died on January 1, 2009.

Swazi

The Swazi are a Bantu-speaking people who reside in southeastern Africa, mostly in the countries of SWAZILAND, South Africa, and MOZAMBIQUE. Presently, there is an estimated total population of 1,173,900 Swazi people. Although their native language is siSwati, they also speak English, Portuguese, and Afrikaans, depending on where they reside. There are presently more Swazis living in South Africa than in Swaziland, although in South Africa they make up approximately 3 percent of the population.

Historically, the Swazi are descendants of the Nguni people who migrated from central Africa many centuries back. Their homeland, Swaziland, is one of the few remaining kingdoms on the African continent, and its origins date back to the fifteenth century. After numerous interethnic conflicts, King Ngwane III led the Swazis out of Mozambique around 1750 and settled in the current area of southeast Swaziland. Over the next few centuries, they integrated many different ethnic groups and clans into their population, despite facing difficult encounters with the ZULUS.

From 1840 to 1868, King Mswati II inherited a kingdom that was twice the current size of Swaziland. During the time of the GREAT TREK beginning in the late 1860s, it subsequently faced pressures and territorial encroachments from the AFRIKANER trekkers who were looking for more land. In 1894, Swaziland came under British control, and, as a result, the kingdom became the British High Commission's territory in 1907. Furthermore, the land was partitioned and the Swazis were given only one-third of their land, which was the least arable portion. During the British colonial era, the European settlers and missionaries exploited, repressed, and culturally isolated the Swazi population. At the same time, CHRISTIANITY was introduced to them. Even though many Swazis are Christians, in reality, they practice syncretism, in which Christianity is mixed with the traditional Swazi religions of animism and ancestor worship.

In 1968, Swaziland gained its independence from Britain. Geographically, this kingdom is surrounded by South Africa and Mozambique. Despite becoming an independent nation, Swaziland faces many of the same problems as its neighboring countries: poverty, poor governance, a high unemployment rate of 45 percent and more, and a high HIV/AIDS prevalence, as around 30 percent of the adult Swazi population are infected with the virus.

Swaziland

Swaziland is a landlocked country surrounded on its eastern border by MOZAMBIQUE and the rest by South Africa. A former British colony, it gained its independence in 1968. Though it harbored resistance fighters from South Africa (former South African president THABO MBEKI operated from Swaziland in the early 1980s), Swaziland also has a more shameful history of collaboration with British and, later, APARTHEID South African authorities. At the late 1990s TRUTH AND RECONCILIATION COMMISSION in South Africa, testimony emerged of official SWAZI collusion of the Royal Swaziland Police with apartheid security forces in the brutal abduction and murder of AFRICAN NATIONAL CONGRESS (ANC) activists in 1986.

Because both colonial and apartheid authorities annexed Swazi land for South Africa, Swaziland has made territorial claims to land in the South African provinces of KwaZulu-Natal and Mpumalanga. The majority of the Swaziland population is ethnic Swazi, mixed with a small number of ZULUS and non-Africans. Swazi government officials refer to Swazis in South Africa as the subjects of their king. Traditionally, Swazis have been subsistence farmers and herders, but some now work in the growing urban formal economy and in government. The Swazi economy, however, is heavily dependent on South Africa. Reportedly 60 percent of Swazi exports, including all its coal production, are sold to South Africa. Swaziland also imports 80 percent of its goods and services from South Africa. There is a long history of migrants traveling across the border to South Africa to work on farms, in the mines, and in the service economy as maids and gardeners.

Though Swaziland is governed by a Constitution (adopted in 2005 after the earlier Constitution was suspended in 1973 by King Sobhuza II), King Mswati III governs as an absolute monarch, and political opposition is not tolerated. The main opposition groups—the People's United Democratic Movement (PUDEMO) and the Swaziland Federation of Trade Unions, whose members are harassed by Swazi security forces—enjoy considerable support from the ruling ANC and its Communist and trade union allies in South Africa.

See also FRONTLINE STATES; SWAZI

T

TAC
See TREATMENT ACTION CAMPAIGN

Tambo, Oliver Reginald (1917–1993)

Born on October 27, 1917, in the rural town of Mbizana located in the eastern Cape Province, Oliver Reginald Tambo spent most of his life in the struggles against racial discrimination and APARTHEID.

Tambo received his early schooling at St. Peter's College in JOHANNESBURG. He then went on to the UNIVERSITY OF FORT HARE in Alice in the eastern Cape Province, where he received a bachelor's of science degree in 1941. He subsequently returned to St. Peter's College to teach science and math. During his time in Johannesburg he became integrally involved in the activities and the leadership of the AFRICAN NATIONAL CONGRESS (ANC). Tambo was a founding member of the AFRICAN NATIONAL CONGRESS YOUTH LEAGUE, along with NELSON MANDELA, WALTER SISULU, ANTON LEMBEDE, and others. He became the Youth League's first national secretary in 1944. In 1946, he was elected to the ANC's Transvaal Executive Committee, and, in 1948, along with Sisulu, was elected to this organization's National Executive Committee. Tambo's leadership was instrumental in reshaping and in revitalizing the ANC during the post–World War II era. He and his peers brought a more youthful and militant outlook to the ANC by transforming it into a more radical, mass-based movement.

Tambo subsequently left teaching and established a legal partnership with Mandela. Their firm quickly gained the reputation of being a champion for the poor and the disadvantaged. He was one of the many volunteers who participated in the 1952 DEFIANCE CAMPAIGNS against apartheid laws and also played a leading role in the 1955 Congress of the People meeting in which the FREEDOM CHARTER, a guiding organizational document for the ANC, was drafted. His high-profile role in anti-apartheid politics at that time led to his arrest and being accused in the 1956 TREASON TRIAL. After the SHARPEVILLE MASSACRE in 1960, in which South African police killed at least sixty-nine black protesters, Tambo was tasked with traveling abroad to set up ANC offices in other countries and to garner international support for the struggle. With the assistance of some African governments, he initially established offices in Ghana, Egypt, Morocco, and London. Under his stewardship, the ANC established twenty-seven missions abroad by 1990.

With Lembede's death, Tambo took over as the ANC's acting president in 1967 and was again elected as president at the next national conference in 1969. In this capacity, he was also the commander-in-chief of Umkhonto we Sizwe, the ANC's military wing. Among black South African leaders, Tambo was probably the most highly respected on the African continent as well as in Europe, Asia, and the Americas. During his ANC stewardship, he raised the organization's international prestige and status to that of an alternative to the Pretoria government. In many parts of the world, he was received with the protocol reserved for heads of state.

In 1989, Tambo suffered a stroke and underwent extensive medical treatment. He returned to South Africa in 1991 and died of a second stroke in 1993. He is survived by his wife Adelaide Tambo, herself a prominent antiapartheid activist within the ANC and currently a member of PARLIAMENT.

Terre Blanche, Eugene (1941–2010)

Eugene Terre Blanche was the founder and leader of the AFRIKANER WEERSTANDSBEWEGING (AWB), a white, right-wing paramilitary group that came to prominence in South Africa during the 1980s. He was born on January 31, 1941, in Ventersdorp, a small town in then Transvaal Province.

In the early 1980s, at the time when President P. W. Botha was considering allowing a limited voting franchise for COLOURED and INDIAN South Africans, Terre Blanche and his followers saw this as a slippery slope to democracy, communism, and black rule. At its height, the AWB claimed a membership of 70,000. Terre Blanche and the AWB gained international attention in the early 1990s when the negotiations for a democratic dispensation were taking place between the APARTHEID government and the black-led liberation movements. He and his followers confirmed the fears for a white, right-wing backlash to the negotiations by setting off bombs throughout the country and even drove an armored vehicle through the glass front wall of the building in which the negotiations were being held. They subsequently launched a failed invasion of the apartheid-designated black homeland of Bophuthatswana, which signaled to many South African observers that their goal of seizing power by force was unrealistic.

In 1997, Terre Blanche was convicted and sentenced to jail for assault on a gas station attendant. He was released in 2004 and lived a rather obscure existence on his farm just outside of Ventersdorp until April 2010 when he was hacked to death allegedly by two of his farmworkers because of a wage dispute.

Theater and Performance

In the centuries before European settlement, there was an active indigenous performance culture in southern Africa, including dramatized songs, rituals, social dances, and enacted ritual narratives. The oldest of these were found with nomadic communities such as the KHOIKHOI and SAN, whose ceremonial and ritualistic dramas and dances are dated by anthropologists at over six thousand years ago. The various Bantu people who would later inhabit the area had similar performance forms, including the well-known XHOSA *intsomi* and the ZULU *inganekwane*, storytelling practices that are still performed today. Of their extensive dance and MUSIC traditions, some forms have survived into the twenty-first century in adapted or hybridized form, especially from the late 1940s onward, by becoming a dominant feature of the theater after 1970. By the 1990s, artists such as storyteller Gcina Mhlope, playwright Matsemela Manaka, the dance company JazzArt, musicians David Kramer and Taliep Peterson, and playmakers Mark Fleishman and Brett Bailey were consciously seeking to revive such traditions in performance by teaching the forms and even making them mainstream.

Theater and Performance After 1652

The European penetration of the Cape region in 1652 introduced new cultural norms and traditions that dominated the area for more than three centuries. Under the Dutch (1652–1799), there was little record of formal theater. But the so-called *rederykerskamers*, social clubs maintained until the 1890s aimed at cultural, moral, and educational uplifting, were an important basis for the later dominant Afrikaans-language theater.

However, formal institutionalized theater only came with the British rule of the region (1799–1910), when some governors encouraged amateur theater in the garrisons and among the civilians, and supported visits by professional companies from the mother country and colonies in the east. The construction of the still extant African Theater (1800) in CAPE TOWN by Sir George Yonge was a landmark event in this regard. This tradition eventually provided the key models for local theater makers—both descendants of European immigrants and aspiring indigenous African thespians. Initially, they performed little locally written work, with most of the materials being standard European texts (English, Dutch, German, and even French for a while), including a great deal of Shakespeare—both in the original and the translated languages. What was original was usually a short topical prologue or epilogue or a musical skit of some sort. An excellent example is the bilingual skit, *Kaatje Kekkelbek*, or *Life Among the Hottentots*, devised in Grahamstown in the Eastern Cape by Andrew Geddes Bain and Frederick Rex in about 1844.

The first substantial body of indigenous plays was written primarily in Dutch (and later in the so-called Kitchen Dutch, or Afrikaans) by descendants of the original white settlers as well as by Dutch-speaking slaves and mixed-race peoples in the Cape. For example, a slave called Majiet wrote protest plays for performance in the slave lodge, while Dutch and French immigrants (for example, Suasso de Lima, Boniface, and Melt Brink) produced short one-act farces and satires for performance by amateurs and schools. A few more-serious writers wrote ponderous nationalistic works on the history and struggles of the AFRIKANER peoples.

Early Twentieth Century
This tradition bore significant fruits in the twentieth century, especially after Louis Leipold's professional production of a one-act tragedy *Die Heks* ("The Witch," 1925), which proved that Afrikaans was a viable dramatic language. Many other Afrikaans literary figures now turned to the theater as a vehicle in their search for the Afrikaner identity, a movement accelerated by the founding of the first two professional Afrikaans touring companies formed by Paul de Groot and Hendrik Hanekom in 1925. By 1940, about thirty were on the road.

In contrast, few indigenously written English plays had been produced in the nineteenth and in the early years of the twentieth century, as the only truly successful British playwright was Stephen Black, whose popular farces (*Helena's Hope*, 1908, and *Love and the Hyphen*, 1910) satirized the multiracial Cape Town society. The global market competition was too strong; a truly local tradition of writing in English would only be established in the 1960s, when the cultural boycott—which barred international artistic productions from traveling to South Africa and prevented South African artistic productions from traveling abroad—deprived the country of access to the best of European and US theater and opened up a market for local work.

As in the previous centuries, black theatrical work was initially limited to the traditional performance forms—dance, songs, and narrative. But gradually, under the tutelage of missionary schools and other European organizations, an interest in formal European play production and playwriting emerged, though the plays were often intended for use as textbooks for schools rather than for production; this is particularly true of the many plays in indigenous African languages published over the century. The Anglo-American influence on playwriting in black communities was evident early on, as shown in the more ambitious works such as the first published Xhosa drama (Guybon Sinxo's *Debeza's Baboons,* 1927) and in Herbert Dhlomo's *The Girl Who Killed to Save: Nongause (*NONGQAWUSE*) the Liberator*, the first play by a black person published in English. Based on a Xhosa legend, it is in the style of English sentimental comedy and melodrama despite its underlying critical stance.

While formal black middle-class theater before the 1960s reflects a taste for European dramatic literature, another popular form was emerging among the black working class, spearheaded by Esau Mtetwa, who founded the first black professional troupe, called Lucky Stars, in NATAL in 1926. This group toured the country, putting on popular sketches and plays based on Zulu legends and customs in the vernacular. When rapid urbanization in the 1930s and the 1940s led to the growth of economically depressed, mixed race areas and slums in the cities, the result was an increasing synthesis of ethnic performance traditions, with the Worker Theater, a vehicle for political agitation and engagement with working-class audiences, and Western forms based especially on US models. Through the creative combinations of ethnic and jazz music with ethnic and international dances, a new and distinctive theatrical form emerged in the country. This is best typified by the hit musical *King Kong* (1959) about the rise and fall of a heavyweight boxer. This collaborative play brought African musicians and actors to the attention of theater establishments at home and abroad and became an inspiring example for black actors and directors who saw the commercial and artistic possibilities for blending both indigenous and imported conventions.

State-Funded and Commercial Theater at Mid-Century

White theater was privileged from the start, since it had a captive local audience in a population trained to value European cultural forms. It was also helped by the Afrikaner-led NATIONAL PARTY government's direct subsidies of theater, initially through the bilingual (Afrikaans and English) state-funded National Theater Organization (1947–1962) and then through four bilingual provincial performing arts councils (1963–1993)—PACT (Performing Arts Council Transvaal), PACOFS (Performing Arts Council of the Orange Free State), NAPAC (Natal Performing Arts Council), and CAPAB (Cape Performing Arts Board)—which evolved from it. These institutions were a home for the cream of the country's white acting and directing talent for many years as they produced fine versions of international classics and hits, both in English and in Afrikaans translation. Most original works produced were by Afrikaans-language playwrights, among which were N. P. Van Wyk Louw, André P. Brink, and P. G. du Plessis (whose urban tragedy *Siener in die Suburbs* ["Seer in the Suburbs," 1971] broke all box-office records and won numerous awards), with a few English playwrights such as Guy Butler and James Ambrose Brown seeing their plays on stage. The new work focused exclusively on South African themes, seeking to develop a distinctively South African idiom, but few writers would achieve the sustained success of key Afrikaans dramatists, until the late 1980s and the 1990s. Thus far, none has achieved Afrikaner ATHOL FUGARD's international stature, who has produced nearly forty plays but is perhaps best known for his novel *Totsi* that was made into an Academy Award–winning film in 2005.

Alongside the state-funded system, a strong commercial theater industry has long existed in the country, from touring companies "playing the Empire" in the late nineteenth and early twentieth centuries and vast conglomerates such as the African Consolidated Theaters, which sponsored theaters and productions throughout the country, to smaller urban companies doing both European and US fare (for example, Leonard Rayne and Brian Brooke) and the local Afrikaans touring companies. In the 1970–1990 period, entrepreneurs such as Taubie Kushlick and Pieter Toerien managed to bypass the international playwrights' boycott and produce primarily US and British hits. After 1990, Toerien and others began to bring large-scale hits from Broadway, the West End, and the European capitals to South Africa, including *Les Miserables, Phantom of the Opera,* and, ironically, *The Lion King.*

A special category of musical—the so-called tribal musical (later, the African musical)—developed after 1945. Rooted in the nineteenth-century tradition of circuses and exhibitions of "authentic" African scenes, this work merged indigenous performance elements with jazz and contemporary dance to produce hybrid musicals such as *King Kong*, Welcome Msomi's *Umabatha* (a Zulu adaptation of *Macbeth*, 1970), and Bertha Egnos's collaborative *Ipi-Tombi* (1974). Later came David Kramer and Taliep Petersen's successful "COLOURED musical" *DISTRICT SIX—The*

Musical (1987); Mbongeni Ngema's popular musicals *Sarafina* (1988), *Magic at 4:00 A.M.* (1993), and *The Zulu* (2000); and Richard Loring's *African Footprint* (2004). Even though criticized as inauthentic and exploitative of indigenous culture, these commercially successful productions created work and training opportunities for many performers excluded from the state system.

An influential side effect of this development was the emergence of the "township musical": a scaled-down, touring version of the big musicals, usually based on melodramatic local stories. The notable catalyst in this was the legendary entrepreneur Gibson Kente (1932–2004), whose musical plays toured the black townships for years during the 1970s and the 1980s. He not only turned black citizens into theatergoers, but also popularized his form to such an extent that it established a vast industry. His template would be snapped up and adapted as an effective medium by the political movements of the time.

Theater and Resistance

By the late 1950s, frustration with the restrictions imposed by politics and the arts system had set in among theater makers and artists across language and cultural divides. Some entrepreneurs produced politically relevant plays from Europe and the United States as well as indigenous antiapartheid plays such as Basil Warner's *Try for White* (Leonard Schach, 1958), Lewis Sowden's KIMBERLEY *Train* (Leon Gluckman, 1959), and Athol Fugard's *The Blood Knot* (1961). However, the tighter censorship and racial laws of the 1960s put a virtual end to the trend for a while, so a search began for alternative ways to continue to resist and also to coordinate and support black and multiracial work. It would lead to what is possibly the most inspiring and fruitful period of theater in the country: 1970–1990.

Within the state system of performing arts councils, Ken Leach, Pieter Fourie, Francois Swart, and others did subversive work in experimental venues, including plays by outspoken critics of APARTHEID such as André P. Brink, Bartho Smit, and Adam Small, though not always without controversy. For example, Smit's *Christine* (written in 1971 and performed by PACT in 1973) and Small's *Kanna hy kù Huistoe* ("Kanna Comes Home," written in 1965 and performed by PACOFS in 1971), both ran afoul of censorship laws.

At the same time, younger white and black activist theater makers were working together, seeking to create important multicultural fringe groups outside the state system. A key early example was Union Artists, whose Dorkay House venue became a focal point for supporting and mentoring many artists. They were also involved in the influential *King Kong* project. Others include Theater Workshop '71 and Junction Avenue Theater Company.

This process was strongly affected by another parallel process: the radical increase in national and international resistance to apartheid and the burgeoning BLACK CONSCIOUSNESS MOVEMENT in the 1970s, which led to a radical change in black resistance politics and a focus on cultural liberation through an alternative, black South African aesthetic. During this time, trade union workers' theater also became an important tool to foster union solidarity and to develop political awareness among black workers. Much of this latter work was linked to Brechtian theories and to Augusto Boal's notions of forum theater or theater of the oppressed, all crucial elements in later political theater. Particularly militant political works emerged from groups such as People's Experimental Theater and the Theater Council of Natal in the mid-1970s, which in turn led to a radical shift toward political theater and what would become known for a while as "black theater."

The most crucial factor, however, was the founding of a number of independent venues in the 1970s—particularly the Space Theater in Cape Town (1972–1979) and the Market Theater in JOHANNESBURG (1976–), venues not controlled through state funding. Focusing on developing theater projects that addressed the cultural contradictions of South African life, they found ways to circumvent the racial laws, such as the mixed marriages act that prohibited marriage between whites and blacks, or the PASS LAWS that required all blacks to carry a valid pass book with them at all times to monitor and restrict their movement. A key achievement was to provide a performance space for significant black theater makers such as Fatima Dike (*The Sacrifice of Kreli*, 1976); Maishe Maponya (*The Hungry Earth*, 1979); Matsemela Manaka (*Pula*, 1986); and ZAKES MDA (*We Shall Sing for the Fatherland*, 1973, and *The Hill*, 1979). Among all these writers, Fugard's steady stream of trenchant plays still dominated much of the period, including his later masterpieces (*Hello and Goodbye*, 1965; *Boesman and Lena*, 1959; *Master Harold and the Boys*, 1982; and *The Road to Mecca*, 1987). His simple but compelling neo-naturalism became the model for young theater makers such as Paul Slabolepszy, Anthony Akerman, Pieter-Dirk Uys, Deon Opperman, Reza de Wet, and others, who began to produce significant new works to add their voices to the clamor for change in the 1980s, beginning with Slabolepszy's *Saturday Night at the Palace* (1982) and leading to de Wet's award-winning Gothic dramas about the Afrikaner psyche. Another phenomenon was the rise of the satirist and stand-up comedian as political activist—the most notable example being the immensely effective Pieter-Dirk Uys and his alter ego, Evita Bezuidenhout, with constantly updated shows like *Adapt or Dye* (1981).

The other immense influence of the resistance period was a distinct shift toward improvised political theater, in which the previously neglected African traditions became dominant. Inspired by the earlier improvised works such as Theater Workshop '71 (*The Women of Crossroads*, 1973); John Kani, Winston Ntshona, and Fugard (*The Island*, 1973, and *Sizwe Bansi Is Dead*, 1972); and Barney Simon (*Cincinnati*, 1979, and *Born in the RSA*, 1985), these plays incorporated aspects of precolonial African genres into their more formal structures and blended these with the new urban cultural experiences of their audiences. This is best epitomized by Barney Simon, Mbongeni Ngema, and Percy Mtwa's seminal *Woza Albert* (1981), Ngema's *Asinamali* (1985), and Junction Avenue Theater's groundbreaking SOPHIATOWN (1986). A distinctive South African form by the 1990s, these hybrid forms continued to develop with haunting works by William Kentridge and the Handspring Puppet Company (*Woyzeck on the Highfeld*, 1992, and *Faustus in Africa*, 1995); Mark Fleishman and the Magnet Theater Company and Jazzart (*Rain in a Dead Man's Footsteps*, 2003); David Kramer and Taliep Petersen (*Ghoema*, 2005); and Brett Bailey and the Third World Bunfight company (*Ipi Zombie*, 1996, *iMumbo Jumbo*, 1997, and *Big Dada*, 2003).

In the mid-1980s, the Afrikaans-speaking youth, inspired by writer Hennie Aucamp, created the Afrikaans political cabaret. Deriving from the controversial and powerful Afrikaans alternative rock music movement, this primarily anarchic and political form expressed abhorrence and resistance to the apartheid regime, culminating in *Piekniek by Dingaan* ("Picnic with Dingane") in 1989—which was another banned play. As a form, cabaret still exists but has lost its edge as the apartheid specter faded and has reverted to the more nostalgic blends of musical presentation, standup comedy, and club theater.

While theater for development, which encompasses live performances and sometimes interactive performances with the audience that are aimed at promoting development aims, has almost become the defining form of African theater, such projects had less prominence in South Africa until recently. Interactive theater processes were sometimes used for educational purposes and as a means of politicizing the youth, especially in the late 1970s. However, the political changes during the 1990s saw the theater-for-development process adapted to focus on social issues such as the AIDS pandemic, violent crime, rape, nation building, and voter education for the formerly disenfranchised masses—and much government funding and private sponsorship has gone into this.

National Arts Council and the Evolution of the South African Festival Circuit

From a structural point of view, the most important facet of the post-1994 period and the beginning of black majority rule has been the radical change in the funding structures, from the selective funding by white-dominated arts councils to the founding of the National Arts Council in 1997 to fund all the arts in theory. However, this has not been matched with adequate funds and has led to a collapse of the state theater system and the inevitable rise of a freelance system by the late 1990s. The consequence has been the rapid development of an alternative freelance system, driven by a vast and aggressive festival culture in southern Africa. The oldest and best known is the annual National Arts Festival in Grahamstown, founded in 1974 to support the embattled English language and culture. Although it was the only national festival for a long time, it soon went beyond its parochial boundaries to encompass all cultures in the country and to showcase emerging trends in the whole subcontinent. Today, it is one of the largest arts festivals in the world. In the 1990s, formerly protected cultures found that they had to look to their own survival and development. This led to the founding of a series of arts festivals, notably the annual Oudtshoorn Festival, dedicated to the now embattled Afrikaans language and culture. Within a few years, this began to rival the Grahamstown festival in size, while ever more festivals catered to a variety of cultures, languages, and economic situations. Growing exponentially, the number of festivals in 2004 was more than 150 local ones, and at least 40 significant arts and cultural festivals were aggressively advertised across South Africa. This included a state-supported Mayibuye Festival of African Arts in BLOEMFONTEIN in Free State Province. These festivals have become the core of the theater industry and, in many ways, constitute the annual theatrical season in which more plays are produced annually than ever in the country's history.

Formally, the style of theater has become immensely eclectic and hybridized, which is strongly influenced by dance and physical theater, as well as by the electronic media. Thematically, the years since 1994 have seen an increasing focus on the struggle for identity and nationhood, the search for peace, and the exploration of notions of memory and forgiveness—issues most notably symbolized by the TRUTH AND RECONCILIATION COMMISSION and endemic to works such as *Ubu and the Truth Commission* (1997) by Jane Taylor and William Kentridge and the Handspring Puppet Company's, *Die Jogger* ("The Jogger," 1997) by André P. Brink; and *Die Toneelstuk* ("The Play," 2001) by BREYTEN BREYTENBACH. Notable too are the many plays focusing on the healing of past wounds, from Fugard's *My Children! My Africa!* (1989) and *Valley Song* (1995) to such festival works as *Peace Shall Prevail, Now Is the Time for Reconciliation, People Like Us, Unity,* and John Kani's thought-provoking *Nothing but the Truth* (2002).

See also ATHOL FUGARD; BREYTEN BREYTENBACH; ZAKES MDA

Bibliography
Bosman, F. C. L. *The Dutch and English Theater in South Africa, 1800 till Today, and the Afrikaans Drama.* Pretoria, South Africa: JH de Bussy, 1951.
Davis, Geoffrey, and Anne Fuchs, eds. *Theater and Change in South Africa.* Amsterdam, Netherlands: Harwood Academic Publishers, 1996.
Fletcher, Jill. *The Story of the African Theater: A Guide to Its History from 1780–1930.* Cape Town, South Africa: Vlaeberg, 1994.
Gunner, Elizabeth, ed. *Politics and Performance: Theater, Poetry, and Song in Southern Africa.* Johannesburg, South Africa: University of Witwatersrand Press, 1994.
Hauptfleisch, Temple. *Theatre and Society in South Africa. Reflections in a Fractured Mirror.* Pretoria, South Africa: J.L.Van Schaik Academic, 1994.
Hauptfleisch, Temple, and Ian Steadman, eds. 1984. *South African Theater: Four Plays and an Introduction.* Pretoria, South Africa: HAUM Educational Publishers, 1994.
International Defence and Aid Fund for Southern Africa. *Black Theater in South Africa.* London: International Defence and Aid Fund for Southern Africa, 1976.
Kavanagh, Robert Mshengu. *Theater and Cultural Struggle in South Africa.* London: Zed Books, 1985.
Kruger, Loren. *The Drama of South Africa. Plays, Pageants, and Publics Since 1910.* London: Routledge, 1999.
Larlham, Peter. *Black Theater, Dance, and Ritual in South Africa.* Ann Arbor: University of Michigan Press, 1985.
Mda, Zakes. "Current Trends in Theater-for-Development in South Africa." *Writing South Africa: Literature, Apartheid, and Democracy, 1970–1975.* Edited by Derrick Attridge and Rosemary Jolly. Cambridge, UK: Cambridge University Press, 1998.

Orkin, Martin. *Drama and the South African State.* Manchester, UK: Manchester University Press, 1991.

Solberg, Rolf, ed. *Alternative Theater in South Africa: Talks with Prime Movers Since the 1970's.* Pietermaritzburg, South Africa: Hadeda Books, 1999.

Tucker, Percy. *Just the Ticket. My 50 Years in Show Business.* Johannesburg, South Africa: Jonathan Ball Publishers, 1997.

Von Kotze, Astrid. *Organise and Act: The Natal Worker's Theater Movement, 1983–1987.* Durban, South Africa: Culture and Working Life, 1988.

—Temple Hauptfleisch

TRC
See TRUTH AND RECONCILIATION COMMISSION

Treason Trial (1956–1961)

The Treason Trial that began in 1956 was the culmination of a series of raids on the offices and private homes of hundreds of APARTHEID opponents by South Africa's Special Branch. On December 5, 1956, policemen across the country descended on the homes of leaders of the Congress Alliance, which included the AFRICAN NATIONAL CONGRESS, the SOUTH AFRICAN INDIAN CONGRESS, the Coloured People's Congress, and the SOUTH AFRICAN COMMUNIST PARTY, and arrested and charged 156 people—104 Africans, 23 whites, 21 Indians, and 8 COLOUREDS—with high treason, which was a capital offense in South Africa. While the case was remanded against most of the accused, thirty of them endured a four-and-a-half-year trial for engaging in activities aimed at overthrowing the government. For the government, this trial was largely a show aimed at intimidating apartheid opponents. Among the accused were, YUSUF DADOO, RUTH FIRST, HELEN JOSEPH, Ahmed Kathrada, ALBERT LUTHULI, NELSON MANDELA, WALTER SISULU, and JOE SLOVO.

In the end, the court acquitted and discharged all the accused. However, as a consequence of the Treason Trial and the banning of the liberation movements in 1960, many leaders fled the country at this time. The Treason Trial also ushered in a period of harsh repression inside the country, as witnessed by the SHARPEVILLE MASSACRE in 1961, in which South African police killed at least sixty-nine black protesters.

Treatment Action Campaign

Founded in December 1998 in CAPE TOWN, the Treatment Action Campaign (TAC) was launched by a consortium of AIDS organizations to advocate for the provision of antiretroviral (ARV) treatments for people living with HIV/AIDS. At the time, South Africans could not access ARVs through the public health system, and the cost of ARVs was exorbitant—as much as US$10,000 per year. Therefore, the targets of early TAC actions were the pharmaceutical industry, to get them to reduce the price of ARVs, and the South African government, to get them to establish a national AIDS treatment program.

It has since established itself as an independent organization and as one of the largest and most prominent AIDS organizations in South Africa and globally. Its leader and founding member, ZACKIE ACHMAT, an HIV-positive gay activist, has also gained international prominence in AIDS and activist circles.

As a membership organization, much of TAC's work is driven by the primarily volunteer-manned local branches. In addition to providing support for those living with HIV and AIDS, TAC has taken up a number of high-profile campaigns against the South African government and the multinational pharmaceutical companies. Its tactics draw from lessons that its activists learned during the struggle against APARTHEID but also from close collaborations with international AIDS organizations such as the AIDS Coalition to Unleash Power (ACT UP). It has held successful public demonstrations, civil disobedience, and defiance campaigns but has also used the courts to wage legal battles against those inhibiting broad access to antiretroviral medicines. TAC first gained notoriety by taking on the pharmaceutical industry in a 1996 legal case that the pharmaceuticals brought against the South African government over the state's attempts to make all medicines more affordable and equally accessible. It then waged its own legal campaign against the South African government over its failure to provide ARV medicines through the public health system. At the time, the government argued that providing ARVs through the public health system was unaffordable and unsustainable given the very high price of the drugs and the large numbers of those who would need them for decades. The health minister at the time, Manto Tshabalala-Msimang, also questioned the safety and effectiveness of ARVs, suggesting they may be toxic. In 2003, the South African government began to roll out a comprehensive national AIDS treatment program. TAC continues to be a vocal advocacy tool both domestically and internationally for those living with HIV and AIDS.

Trekboers
See AFRIKANERS; GREAT TREK

Truth and Reconciliation Commission

The Truth and Reconciliation Commission (TRC) had its origins in debates in the early 1990s in AFRICAN NATIONAL CONGRESS (ANC) circles about how to deal with South Africa's recent past—notably, the human rights abuses that occurred on all sides of the political battle during the APARTHEID era. The TRC was a court-like body created in 1995 by an act of PARLIAMENT to investigate human rights abuses that occurred between 1960 and 1990. The first and main phase of the work of the TRC ended in 1998 when the commission made public its final report.

Dealing with the Injustices of the Past
Prominent ANC legal figures initially favored a series of war crimes trials. The preference of both the AFRIKANER-led NATIONAL PARTY and the ZULU-based INKATHA FREEDOM PARTY (IFP) was to do nothing, emulating the pattern of other southern African states, which had recently undergone transitions to black rule. This was unacceptable to the ANC, which was determined to pursue some form of accountability, though it quickly moved away from the "Nuremberg option." In the context of a negotiated settlement between the old apartheid regime and the major black liberation movements, a war crimes trial was considered to be an impractical and potentially destabilizing approach.

The idea of a truth commission modeled along the lines of processes in Chile and Argentina was mooted by the ANC's national executive in 1993, and a working group under Alex Boraine was established to develop the concept. At that time, the ANC was under pressure from the National Party to agree to a blanket amnesty for all apartheid-era violations from massacres and murders to the inhumanity of the PASS LAWS or Immorality Act, which prohibited sexual intercourse between whites and blacks. The negotiating parties ultimately agreed to a "postamble" to the 1993 interim CONSTITUTION, which made provisions for an amnesty process and left the details to the democratically elected Parliament.

After the May 1994 ELECTION that ushered in black majority rule, the TRC proposal was considered by Parliament. What emerged was a bill combining three instruments of transitional justice—investigations, reparations, and amnesty—in a single process, which was signed into law in July 1995 as the Promotion of National Unity and Reconciliation Act. Two features were unique to the South African process. The first was that no other such commission before or since had combined these different elements into a single process. The second was the "earned" nature of the amnesty. Perpetrators were required to publicly fully disclose their crimes, and demonstrate that they were acting on the orders or policies of a political party or liberation movement. Prior to this (and again since), wherever amnesty had formed part of a transitional political process, it had taken the form of a blanket dispensation without requiring any kind of accountability from the beneficiaries.

The identification of potential commissioners involved a considerable degree of public input. Broadly representative of South Africa's demographic spread, the commissioners consisted of ten men and seven women with a range of political affiliations from the ANC to the far-right Conservative Party. Headed by Archbishop DESMOND TUTU, the commission began work in December 1995. With an initial time mandate of eighteen months, the first phase ended in October 1998 with the release of five volumes of the eventual seven-volume Final Report.

The TRC's mandate was multidimensional and ambitious. It included

- Establishing "as complete a picture as possible of the causes, nature, and extent of the gross violations of human rights committed" in the period from March 1, 1960 (the time of the SHARPEVILLE MASSACRE), to May 10, 1994 (the first democratic election), both inside and outside South Africa, "including the antecedents, circumstances, factors and context of such violations, as well as the perspectives of the victims and the motives and perspectives of the persons responsible";
- "Facilitating the granting of amnesty" to persons who complied with the requirements of the act;
- "Establishing and making known the fate or whereabouts of victims" and restoring the victims' dignity by granting them an opportunity to relate their stories and by recommending reparation measures; and
- Compiling a report of its findings and "recommendations of measures to prevent the future violation of human rights."

The Work of the TRC

The first eighteen months of the TRC were devoted to gathering information on the gross violations of human rights from 1960 to 1990. Gross violations were defined in the act as the violation of human rights through the killing, abduction, torture, or severe ill-treatment of any person; or any attempt, conspiracy, incitement, instigation, command, or procurement to commit such an act. This commission determined that the "severe ill-treatment" category included arson (house burning) and all forms or threats of sexual coercion. It thus focused its work primarily, though not exclusively, on overt and covert political violence directed at individuals at the immediate, experiential level. It was criticized in some quarters for giving inadequate attention to apartheid's other systemic injustices, such as the pass laws, which restricted blacks' movement; the forced removals of blacks from areas designated for whites; and land dispossession.

The TRC pursued its investigative mandate by hearing the statements of some 23,000 individuals who claimed that they or their relatives had been victims of gross violations of human rights. These were supplemented by special institutional hearings examining, among other things, the apartheid-era actions of the armed forces and the roles played by faith groups, the MEDIA, and the medical, legal, and business professions, as well as the prisons service, which focused on the use of capital punishment as a political tool. Special focus hearings were also held on the particular experiences of women, children, and youth, as well as special investigations of the Witdoeke, a state-sponsored vigilante group active on the Cape Flats outside of CAPE TOWN in the 1980s, and of the National Party's chemical and biological warfare program that included the use of anthrax to kill antiapartheid activists. Additionally, the TRC's investigative work was informed and assisted by the information contained in the applications for amnesty.

This commission concluded its investigations with hundreds of findings against individuals (prominent among them were former prime minister P. W. Botha, WINNIE MANDELA, and MANGOSUTHU BUTHELEZI) and political groupings. No party to the conflicts of the mandate period escaped unscathed, a point made by the TRC in its primary findings, which assigned responsibilities for the overwhelming majority of violations to the National Party government and its security forces, aided by two groups from across the racial divide, namely the IFP and the security forces of the black homelands. In reference to the ANC, the TRC made negative findings only in regard to the killing and injuring of civilians in the landmine campaigns of the late 1980s that targeted civilians in an attempt to spread terror, and in some of its attacks directed at "military" targets, such as the 1983 bombing of an air force facility in Pretoria; the torture and execution of suspected informers and mutineers while in exile; and the killing of state witnesses and alleged informers in South Africa.

These findings outraged some in the ANC. While serving as the ANC party chair, THABO MBEKI sought a last-minute injunction to prevent publication of any part of the Final Report that implicated the ANC in human rights abuses. Mbeki argued that the TRC had erred by assigning a moral equivalence to the actions of both those who had supported and those who had opposed apartheid—that they could not be equated, and that motive should be the primary consideration. The commission disagreed, basing its finding on the principle that not even a just cause could justify the use of unjust means. The injunction attempt failed.

The TRC's Reparation and Rehabilitation Committee devised a nuanced and multidimensional reparations policy. It included annual monetary payments over a number of years for those qualifying for financial compensation by specifically rejecting the one-off lottery-type payout. It also proposed community reparations for areas most ravaged by the violence of the 1980s as well as symbolic reparations in the form of monuments and statues and the repatriation of combatants killed and buried outside of South Africa.

About 22,000 victims qualified for reparations. Though the TRC's reparations policy was presented to the government in 1998, it delayed the implementation, rejected the TRC's proposals, and finally began paying victims a one-off grant of R30,000 (approximately US$3,000) in 2003. Ultimately, less was paid out to the victims than the totality of the funds allocated by the treasury and given by donors.

The TRC Amnesty Committee was required by the act to grant amnesty to applicants from all sides of the conflict if satisfied that the application complied with the act's requirements. Principal among these were that the act, omission, or offense for which amnesty was sought was "an act associated with a political objective committed in the course of the conflicts of the past" and that the applicant had "made a full disclosure of all relevant facts." The criteria for whether an act was associated with a political objective included motive, context, superior orders, and "the proportionality of the act, omission, or offense to the objective pursued."

The Amnesty Committee received appeals from 7,115 applicants (for over 14,000 separate violations), of whom about two-thirds were serving as prisoners. The majority of applications were rejected because applicants were unable to establish the required political objective. Applications came from all parties to the conflict, but only a minority of applicants (293) were apartheid-era security force members, and none of the apartheid-era leadership applied for amnesty. In other words, the majority of those who implemented and enacted apartheid laws on a daily basis did not feel compelled to admit to any crimes, and therefore many atrocities and systemic injustices undertaken since 1960 were not revealed.

The TRC legislation did not preclude the prosecution of those who did not seek amnesty from the TRC or those whose applications had failed (although the legislation provided some protection against the use of self-incriminatory evidence given to the TRC). To date, only a handful of minor figures have been prosecuted.

The commission concluded in March 2003 with the release of volumes six and seven of its report.

See also DEMOCRATIC TRANSITION/NEGOTIATIONS; DESMOND TUTU

Bibliography

Bell, Terry, and Dumisa Ntsebeza. *Unfinished Business: South Africa, Apartheid, and Truth.* Cape Town, South Africa: Redworks, 2001.

Boraine, Alex. *A Country Unmasked. Inside South Africa's Truth and Reconciliation Commission.* Oxford, UK: Oxford University Press, 2000.

Daniel, John. "The Truth and Reconciliation Commission in South Africa: A Retrospective." In *Law and Transformation in South Africa.* Edited by Catherine Jenkins and Max du Plessis. Antwerp, Belgium: Intersentia, 2010.

Gibson, James. *Overcoming Apartheid: Can Truth Reconcile a Divided Nation?* Cape Town, South Africa: HSRC Press, 2004.

Graybill, Lyn. *Truth and Reconciliation in South Africa: Miracle or Model?* Boulder, CO: Lynne Rienner Publishers, 2002.

James, Wilmot, and Linda Van De Vijver, eds. *After the TRC: Reflections on Truth and Reconciliation in South Africa*. Athens: Ohio University Press, 2000.
Jenkins, Catherine. "'They Have Built a Legal System Without Punishment': Reflections on the Use of Amnesty in the South African Transition." *Transformation* 64 (2007): 27–65.
Krog, Antjie. *Country of My Skull*. New York: Random House, 1998.
Posel, Deborah, and Graeme Simpson, eds. *Commissioning the Past: Understanding South Africa's Truth and Reconciliation Commission*. Johannesburg, South Africa: Witwatersrand University Press, 2002.
Tutu, Desmond. *No Future Without Forgiveness*. London: Rider Books, 1999.
Villa-Vicencio, Charles, and Wilhelm Verwoerd, eds. *Looking Back, Reaching Forward: Reflections on the Truth and Reconciliation Commission of South Africa*. Cape Town, South Africa: David Philip, 2000.

—John Daniel and
Catherine Jenkins

Tshwane

Tshwane, named Pretoria prior to 2005, is one of three capital cities in South Africa, and the de facto national capital, being the site of the executive branch of government. With a population of approximately 2.5 million inhabitants, Tshwane is the fourth largest city in the country.

The area now known as the Tshwane Metropolitan Municipality was originally inhabited by the NDEBELE. The original city of Pretoria was founded in 1855 by Marthinus Pretorius, a leader of the AFRIKANER GREAT TREK, and was named after him and his father, Andries Pretorius. It became the administrative capital in 1910 when the UNION OF SOUTH AFRICA came into being.

In 2005, over ten years into the new democratic government, the city council voted to officially change the city's name from Pretoria to Tshwane, which means "we are the same." In fact, the Tshwane Metropolitan Municipality incorporates Pretoria as well as its surrounding suburbs and townships. Known also as Jacaranda City, for the many purple-blossomed jacaranda trees that line the city streets, Tshwane is an attractive capital city with many parks and museums.

Tsonga

The Tsonga encompass several culturally similar Bantu-speaking groups, including the Shangaan, Thonga, Tonga, and several other smaller ethnic groups. Together they numbered about 1.5 million in South Africa in the mid-1990s and at least 4.5 million in southern MOZAMBIQUE and ZIMBABWE. In South Africa they reside mainly in the Limpopo Province and in smaller numbers in Gauteng Province. XiTsonga is one of the eleven official LANGUAGES enshrined in the CONSTITUTION.

The APARTHEID-designated Tsonga-Shangaan homeland, Gazankulu, was carved out of northern Transvaal Province during the 1960s and was granted self-governing status in 1973. The homeland economy depended largely on remittances from gold mining and on a small manufacturing sector. Only an estimated 500,000 people—less than half the Tsonga-Shangaan population of South Africa—ever lived there, however. Many others joined the throngs of township residents around urban centers, especially JOHANNESBURG and Pretoria.

See also LANGUAGE

Tsotsi

Tsotsi is a seSOTHO slang word for "thug" but also refers to someone who is cool. In addition, it refers to Tsotsitaal (a slang LANGUAGE; "taal" is Afrikaans for language). Tsotsitaal is also known as *ikasi* (slang for township), and *iscamtho* (in ZULU). Tsotsitaal originated in 1950s JOHANNESBURG and is derived from a mix of seTSWANA, isiZulu, seSotho, and Afrikaans. Today it is mostly spoken in SOWETO outside Johannesburg. Tsotsitaal speakers are usually multilingual—that is, fluent in more than a few African languages. Closely associated with Tsotsitaal is the dance style, Pantsula, as is KWAITO music. In 2005, a South African film titled *Tsotsi* (named for the main character and based on the book by ATHOL

FUGARD), about a young Soweto gangster, was released. It won an Academy Award for best foreign language film in 2006.

See also CINEMA; KWAITO

Tswana

The Tswana, or Batswana, are a black, Bantu-speaking group of South Africa and Botswana. The Tswana originated from the larger SOTHO ethnic group. In South Africa, the Tswana make up just over 8 percent of the total population. Found mainly in the numerous segments of the former APARTHEID-designated homeland Bophuthatswana, North West Province, and in pockets of Gauteng Province, the Tswana number approximately 3 million in South Africa but compose the overwhelming majority of Botswana's population of 1.2 million. There are also approximately 30,000 Setswana speakers in NAMIBIA.

Tswana culture, social organizations, ceremonies, language, and religious beliefs are similar to that of the PEDI and Sotho, although some Tswana chiefdoms were more highly stratified. Tswana culture is often distinguished for its complex legal system, involving a hierarchy of courts and mediators, and harsh punishments for those found guilty of crimes.

SeTswana is one of the eleven official languages enshrined in the CONSTITUTION of South Africa.

See also LANGUAGE

Tutu, Reverend Desmond Mpilo (1931–)

Winner of the 1984 Nobel Peace Prize, Reverend Desmond Mpilo Tutu became a leading figure in the struggle against APARTHEID during the 1970s and the 1980s. He was born in Klerksdorp in the Transvaal Province on October 7, 1931, and was educated in JOHANNESBURG at Bantu High School. Tutu trained to become a teacher at PRETORIA Bantu Normal College and graduated from the University of South Africa in 1954. He taught as a high school teacher for several years before pursuing studies in theology.

In 1960, Tutu was ordained as a priest in the Anglican Church and then continued his theological studies in England until 1966, receiving a master's of theology from Kings College. From 1967 to 1972, he taught theology in South Africa before returning to England for three years to serve as the assistant director of a theological institute in London. In 1975, Tutu was appointed as the dean of St. Mary's Cathedral in Johannesburg, becoming the first black person to hold that position. From 1976 to 1978, he was the bishop of LESOTHO and then became the first black general secretary of the SOUTH AFRICAN COUNCIL OF CHURCHES (SACC) in 1978, a position he held until 1985. It was in this role that he gained national and international notoriety and became particularly vocal in his antiapartheid activism by becoming a visible leader associated with the UNITED DEMOCRATIC FRONT, an umbrella group opposed to apartheid. Tutu used liberation theology and the SACC as a national platform to denounce apartheid as unchristian. He, along with other antiapartheid religious leaders at the time, became the backbone of the antiapartheid movement in the 1980s as religious leaders were less vulnerable to targeting and intimidation by the apartheid state. Tutu's warm and welcoming personality appealed to blacks and whites alike. His sermons and speeches were also less threatening to whites than some speeches of the leading liberation movements at the time, as he called for equality, reconciliation, and retributive justice that emphasized the healing of the victim and the perpetrator. In 1986, Tutu was appointed as the archbishop of CAPE TOWN, a position he held until his retirement in 1996.

With the demise of apartheid and the election of NELSON MANDELA as the country's first democratically elected president, Tutu was asked by Mandela to chair the TRUTH AND RECONCILIATION COMMISSION, tasked with uncovering atrocities committed during the apartheid era and with promoting healing and reconciliation within the nation. Tutu has authored several books, including *No Truth Without Forgiveness*. He has honorary doctorates from a number of leading universities in Great Britain, Germany, and the United States.

U

UDF
See UNITED DEMOCRATIC FRONT

Union of South Africa (1910–1948)

Prior to 1910, the territory now known as South Africa was divided into British colonies (the CAPE COLONY and NATAL), and independent AFRIKANER republics (the Transvaal and the Orange Free State). The independent country with the territorial boundaries that exist today was born with the Union of South Africa at the end of the ANGLO-BOER WAR. The Union of South Africa was the result of a political compromise between the victorious British and the Afrikaners. The Afrikaners were granted political power and control over the new government and over the native population. The British guaranteed their continued economic dominance by maintaining control over the mineral resources (GOLD AND DIAMOND MINING) of the country. Although APARTHEID wasn't established until 1948, racial discrimination and exploitation began to be nationally institutionalized with the founding of the Union of South Africa.

One of the first laws passed by the new Union of South Africa government was the 1913 NATIVES' LAND ACT, a major pillar in the infrastructure of the numerous pieces of segregation legislation in South Africa. Along with other laws, as well as economic and social policies, it formed a web of control that relegated Africans, INDIANS, and COLOUREDS (the South African label for people of mixed ethnic descent), also referred to collectively as "blacks," to subordinated and exploited lives on the margins of South African society. The act itself delimited about 7.1 percent of land for the majority of the African population in the form of "native reserves" and allocated 80 percent of the land for exclusive white ownership. Moreover, it prevented Africans from buying, leasing, or otherwise acquiring land outside of the native reserves.

Although, by 1910, a number of other significant strands of segregation had already been worked out, the consolidation of white supremacy in the new Union of South Africa government still required some considerable work. This was, in part, because a number of internal contradictions remained in the formulation of segregation, and in part because of the uneven effects of the burgeoning industrial economy. Indeed, during much of the period from 1910 until the formal articulation of apartheid by the NATIONAL PARTY government in 1948, the white state had to reconcile contending white interests, ranging from the mining capitalists to the rural farmers and from Afrikaner ethnic ideologues to imperial-minded British financiers. As important, a rising tide of black disaffection with racist politics and exclusivity prompted the state to suppress what it perceived to be radical African nationalist and Communist elements while attempting to reinvigorate "traditionalist" African leadership (chiefs) in a reworked segregated system of indirect rule. This would enable the white minority, which numbered some 1.25 million people in 1910, to dominate the African majority of about 4 million people, as well as half a million coloured and 150,000 Indian people.

White Politics and the Economy

The successes of British and Afrikaners in finding a working relationship in the wake of the bloody and bitter South African or Anglo-Boer War of 1899–1902 set the stage for their long-sought uniform "native" policy. The critical elements were the enhancement of the cheap MIGRANT LABOR system that fed the labor-hungry gold and diamond mining industry and the entrenchment of white control over rural lands for agricultural use. This necessitated the simultaneous forced removal of Africans from lands sought by whites and intensified measures to drive them into wage labor. The first union governments, led by the former Afrikaner generals, Louis Botha and JAN SMUTS (prime ministers, respectively, from 1910 to 1919 and 1919 to 1924), struggled with creating white political unity. They were challenged by determined Afrikaner leaders such as JAMES HERTZOG, who split from Botha and Smuts's South Africa Party to form the National Party. The National Party then forged a new Afrikaner nationalist ideology, which drew upon the common language of Afrikaans and reinvented mythologies from an idealized past based on the GREAT TREK migration into the interior of South Africa in 1836. They resented and resisted Smuts's loyalty to the British Empire and his commitment of South African troops against the Germans in World War I. Their message, moreover, appealed to a wide range of Afrikaners who felt marginalized by the domination of British culture and industrial capital. They sought an ethnic nationalist solidarity in government through an exclusive white electorate and privileges for Afrikaners, especially rural farmers who wanted state support for the control of African labor.

Through the 1910s and the 1920s, the Afrikaners consolidated their political clout in part through the establishment of a secretive political action organization called the BROEDERBOND (Brotherhood), or Bond. The Bond helped consolidate the cultural, intellectual, and economic dimensions of Afrikaner political aspirations through the development of an Afrikaner press, nationalist celebrations of invented traditions, the establishment of Afrikaner education, and especially the support of Afrikaner financial institutions such as banks and insurance companies. Hertzog's Afrikaner-dominated National Party allied with the working-class Labor Party to win the 1924 election, which set the stage for more intensive segregation legislation and a more vigorous AFRIKANER NATIONALISM.

During the global economic depression of the 1930s, the Hertzog government privileged whites—predominantly working-class Afrikaners and farmers—with state support as it sought to boost the economy. The state invested huge sums in white farming and especially in keeping black labor cheap and available. Increased profits from a rebounding gold industry allowed for greater state investment in other industries as well. The government-controlled South African Railways became the largest employer of Afrikaners, many in sinecure positions; and the state-run electricity company (ESCOM) and the South African Iron and Steel Corporation (ISCOR) also became protected havens for white workers. Despite Hertzog's nationalist politics, he could not win over sufficient support from the English capitalists, and, in 1933, he was forced to form a "Fusion" coalition with Smuts in the new United Party. Despite ideological differences, Smuts and Hertzog worked well together, and they managed to generate an economic recovery.

By the end of the 1930s, the Afrikaner nationalist determination and the looming effects of World War II forced white politics away from compromise. In 1934, D. F. MALAN formed the breakaway Gesuiwerdes ("Purified") National Party (which later reformed as a reunified National Party in 1940) in protest over Hertzog's compromises with Smuts. Malan, an Afrikaner ideologue and editor of *Die Burger*, had the Bond's support and attracted many disillusioned Afrikaners to his more openly ethnic nationalist party. Malan nurtured an increasingly inward-looking and insular Afrikaner politics of white domination. It relied upon the cultural icons of LANGUAGE and mythologized history. This cultural politics was particularly evident when, in 1938, the Bond staged a massive celebration of the Great Trek centenary at the site of what would become the imposing Voortrekker monument.

Moreover, both English and Afrikaners began thinking increasingly along the lines of essential biological racial types. Afrikaners sought to define their own race type, and they called on the state to protect their "white purity." They thought of themselves as a special group, the pure *volk*, or people. Malan also championed Afrikaner political and economic power as opposed to the broader international capitalism, which the British dominated. When Smuts once again allied with the British in World War II, many prominent Afrikaners, including two future prime ministers, B. J. Vorster and Botha, openly supported Hitler's fascist cause. Such was Afrikaner hostility to "Smuts's War" that the Ossewabrandwag (Ox-Wagon Brigade), an Afrikaner cultural movement formed in 1939, turned to acts of terror and sabotage. Although Smuts regained power in the 1943 election, increasing numbers of whites perceived him as too moderate in dealing with the Africans and too loyal to the British. By the time of the next election in 1948, rising African opposition would push even more whites into the reactionary National Party fold.

African Opposition Politics

From the late 1910s, African and allied white worker agitation against mining and industrial capital impressed upon the state the urgency of establishing white political unity if it was to retain power over blacks. The government and the powerful Chamber of Mines, which represented predominantly British mine owners, moved to break nonracial labor organization and privileged the smaller number of white workers through labor legislations and wage differentials. The Mines and Works Act (1911), for example, reinforced a white labor aristocracy at the expense of Africans by reserving higher-paid job categories for "skilled"—meaning white—workers only. When white workers felt threatened by the mine owners' efforts to open skilled work to Africans, they went on strike. In the 1922 RAND REVOLT, borrowing from but misrepresenting communism, they called on white workers of the world to unite for a white South Africa. The Smuts government smashed the strike with brutal force, as it had done with an earlier national strike in 1914. The government later passed the Riotous Assemblies Act (1930), which provided the state with sweeping powers to suppress white or black labor and political unrest.

The majority of Africans, however, struggled in the rural areas. Despite the effects of state legislations, environmental challenges, and hostility from fledgling white commercial farmers as well as from traditionalist chiefs, a remarkably productive and resilient African peasantry had emerged. Across the countryside, Africans, especially mission-educated men, managed to stake out land claims largely independent of the strictures of communal African occupation that gave chiefs or white landlords authority to allocate land. By the early twentieth century, however, the white state and farmers began moving against them by closing off market opportunities and, especially through the 1913 Land Act (revised and extended in the 1936 Native Trust and Land Act), access to land or rent tenancy. Henceforth, Africans would be relegated to onerous labor tenancy arrangements on white farms where the landowner could exact excessive demands on the entire family of tenants. Indeed, the state worked assiduously to undermine the once vibrant African peasantry.

African Resistance

From all over the country, Africans sought to challenge and shape the new state. Some brought more conformist liberal ideas about working within the system while others sought to confront it. In the rural areas, Africans fought to retain their independence. In these "reserved areas," designated rural areas for Africans according to ethnic group, compliant conservative chiefs who sought to fend off the threat of proletarianized Africans and a disgruntled youth retained control with government backing. Some of the disaffected men turned to the urban milieu, where they sought to satisfy their bourgeois aspirations through politics. They were joined in their efforts to gain a more equitable situation by tens of thousands of farm and industrial workers.

In 1901, the Reverend JOHN DUBE and other Natal leaders who had worked to realize African aspirations through their own efforts, rather than with white aid, founded the Natal Native Congress and the South African Native Congress in 1902 to fight for voting franchise rights. In 1909, these groups met in BLOEMFONTEIN in the Orange Free State during the South African Native Convention to protest the planned loss of their voting rights. The frustrated leaders heeded a call from African lawyer Pixley KaSeme to meet again in Bloemfontein to form a national African political organization. There, they drafted the Constitution for the new South African Native National Conference, renamed simply the AFRICAN NATIONAL CONGRESS (ANC) in 1925. The ANC asserted a clearly African nationalist message in opposition to the increasingly racist policy of segregation. They reasoned that if whites championed their own race, then blacks, too, should work to fulfill their own aspirations. They sought to be inclusive of a broad range of African political movements, and the Constitution provided for a nominated upper house of chiefs. At the same time, the chiefs were wary of the Western-influenced and democratic tendencies of these men who owed no direct allegiance to them or to the ancestors.

Although African opposition movements remained comparatively restrained in their policies, they had to contend with a groundswell of mass discontent. In 1913, Charlotte Maxeke, who later founded the AFRICAN NATIONAL CONGRESS WOMEN'S LEAGUE, gained some limited support from a wary ANC for her leadership of a women's campaign in Bloemfontein against the PASS LAWS, which restricted Africans' movements. She and some five thousand fellow women signatories employed the standard ANC tactic of sending a deputation with a petition protesting passes to the parliamentary authorities in CAPE TOWN. When they were rebuffed, they tore up their passes in front of the police at a passive resistance demonstration, which invited arrest. Their efforts highlighted the plight of a growing number of African women who were moving to the cities in search of work and independence. For many Africans, of necessity, the focus remained on their day-to-day material concerns. As living costs rose but wages did not, African miners went on strike. They had tried to ally themselves with white miners in strike action, but both the state and the Chamber of Mines intervened to undermine a nonracial class solidarity.

The ANC was eventually drawn into the more radical politics of working-class Africans. Following other strikes from 1918 to 1919, the ANC turned to the related problem of passes. They argued that the pass laws had undermined the workers' rights and called for a mass passive resistance campaign. While the mine owners, with the aid of chiefs whose influence reached from the rural areas to the urban centers, were able to contain the meetings within the mining compounds, the workers' demonstrations exploded outside. Across the city, African workers met in massive groups of up to two thousand and challenged the police. In some cases, reactionary whites formed gangs that moved in to break up the ANC meetings, and this provoked violent riots. The workers sang "Nkosi Sikelele y-Afrika" ("God Bless Africa," now the South African national anthem), as they tried but failed to hold their ground.

By 1920, African workers felt acute economic pressure since their wages had remained stagnant during the war years while costs soared; meanwhile, white wages had risen by about 40 percent. They took up the cause that the ANC had abandoned and demonstrated their capacities to protest with massive strikes. The fearful state acted by sending in troops, arresting leaders, and breaking up the strikes. Resisters were shot and killed. Such violent protests and repression were too much for the ANC moderates, and the organization retreated from the field of strikes, preferring ineffectual petitions to the government instead. This left a vacuum in opposition politics, which would be filled by more radical elements.

The INDUSTRIAL AND COMMERCIAL WORKERS UNION (ICU) and the Communist Party of South Africa (later renamed the SOUTH AFRICAN COMMUNIST PARTY) breathed new life into the African struggle. Although it was beset by internal rankling that led to its collapse, the ICU managed to bridge the divides among major opposition forces in an attempt to create a national movement. CLEMENTS KADALIE, a mission-educated migrant worker from Nyasaland (Malawi), founded the ICU in 1919 among African dockworkers in Cape Town. This movement drew support away from the ANC because it was prepared to organize strike activities, for which the ANC demurred. The ICU promised collective action against the pass laws, fights for higher wages, and even acquisition of land for its members, although this was practically impossible. After some initial success with strike action, however, internal tensions surfaced. The ambitious and charismatic A.W.G. CHAMPION, a leading African organizer from Natal, vied with Kadalie for control. The movement was deeply divided between more moderate elements and a radical group of Communist Party members. Champion formed a splinter branch named the ICU Yase Natal. By 1928, Kadalie had attracted more than 100,000 members, and the organization was far larger than the ANC. Thereafter, however, the movement stalled and fragmented from inactivity and corruption.

Meanwhile, the ANC was infused with a new radical spirit from its young members. In 1927, James Gumede, a radical who favored an alliance with the Communists, was elected as the ANC's president. By this time, the Soviet Union supported an international Communist movement, which appealed to the ANC youth. These radical ideas, however, were too threatening to the ANC moderates, and Gumede was replaced by the more conservative Pixley Seme. For a time, the ANC returned to its moderate politics, but its radical elements had stirred it to broader action. During the 1930s, the ANC linked with other radical opposition organizations and came together at the ALL-AFRICAN CONVENTION (AAC) to consider how to respond to the government's segregationist legislation. Declining to stage protest rallies, the AAC chose instead to rely on the standard ANC tactics of appeals to the government and accepted the racially separate NATIVES REPRESENTATIVE COUNCIL, a body granting Africans some political participation but no real political power. By the end of the 1930s, both the AAC and the ANC were in decline as other more radical groups such as the unions rose in popularity.

By the 1930s, rural Africans also presented a broad but unorganized front of opposition to the state. As drought and depression hit rural South Africa, black Africans in particular were hit hard. The state, fearing a collapse of the rural basis for the cheap migrant labor system, made a vain attempt to shore up the crumbling reserve economy and the authority of compliant chiefs. In the rural areas, opposition to these measures was complicated by the role of chiefs, who had to navigate an ambiguous path between representing their people's interests and following the white state's demands in order to avoid being removed from power. The mythologized ZULU royal family provided a rallying point for some African leaders with the Inkatha movement (not to be confused with the much later established INKATHA FREEDOM PARTY) that promoted the glorification of Zulu identity and culture. Yet, Inkatha fell under the sway of white state segregationists, who sought to adapt it to conform to their own notion of separate development for all ethnic groups in order to prevent rural opposition from spreading. Many Zulu chiefs blended their conservatism with state segregation, leaving rural reserve residents to radical forms of resistance. The residents, who still relied on the tenuous foothold they had in the reserves due to the laws that prevented them from permanently settling in the white urban areas, drew upon a wide range of ideas to confront the economic and political pressures they faced. In many cases, rural protests were also shaped by African CHRISTIANITY derived from adaptations of missionary messages and the new Zionist–Independent African Church Movement.

During the 1940s, the focus of opposition politics shifted to the urban areas, and the ANC became more radical and more national in its outlook. After Gumede had been ousted from the leadership, the ANC retreated to conservative politics for a time, seeking accommodation with the white regime. Meanwhile, World War II stimulated new industries in South Africa, and African workers were drawn into the cities to replace the whites who had enlisted. This industrial growth also meant that employers needed more skilled workers. They started to accept the liberals' arguments that a more stable, skilled African workforce would be more efficient and productive than the costly white skilled workforce. Their pressures on the government resulted in a relaxation of the pass laws, which enabled tens of thousands of Africans to find work in the cities. As they did so, they began to organize unions and fight for better wages and working conditions. By the end of the war, there were over 100 new unions with 150,000 members in the umbrella organization of Non-European Trade Unions, which initiated antipass protests and demands for better wages.

A revived ANC emerged under the leadership of Dr. A. B. Xuma and the newly radicalized AFRICAN NATIONAL CONGRESS YOUTH LEAGUE, led by gifted young men such as lawyer ANTON LEMBEDE and FORT HARE UNIVERSITY graduates NELSON MANDELA and OLIVER TAMBO. These men were inspired by the new postwar global ideals of nonracial democracy and civil rights, but they also embraced an African nationalist political plan. They called for mass action with a passive resistance campaign that would directly confront the state. The more militant ANC then began mass protests and marches in an anti–pass law campaign in 1944.

As the ANC revived, the coloured people in the Cape Province were faced with the challenge of the state's creation of another segregated institution, the Coloured Affairs Department (CAD). In 1944, concerned coloured people formed the Anti-CAD Movement and joined forces with the AAC in the broad NON-EUROPEAN UNITY MOVEMENT, which rivaled the ANC in the Cape. Then, in 1946, African mine workers in JOHANNESBURG who were influenced by Communist Party organizers staged a massive strike. The African Mineworkers Union demanded a living wage and other concessions. When the Chamber of Mines refused and claimed that the union had no legal standing, more than 70,000 men went on a sustained strike. The police violently put down the strike, killed several workers, and arrested the Communist Party leaders involved. Nevertheless, the strike demonstrated the strength of the African trade union movement. By the end of the 1940s, the ANC and the rising trade unions were poised to engage in sustained and effective mass action against the state.

See also SOUTH AFRICA ACT OF 1909

Bibliography

Beinart, William. *Twentieth-Century South Africa.* New York: Oxford University Press, 1994.

Beinart, William, and Saul Dubow, eds. *Segregation and Apartheid in Twentieth-Century South Africa.* London: Routledge, 1995.

Bonner, Philip, Peter Delius, and Deborah Posel, eds. *Apartheid's Genesis.* Johannesburg, South Africa: Ravan Press, 1993.

Dubow, Saul. *Racial Segregation and the Origins of Apartheid in South Africa, 1910–1936.* New York: St. Martin's Press, 1989.

Gerhart, Gail M. *Black Power in South Africa: The Evolution of an Ideology.* Berkeley: University of California Press, 1978.

Jeeves, A., and J. Crush. *White Farms, Black Labor.* Portsmouth, NH: Heinemann Press, 1997.

Karis, Thomas, Gwendolen Carter, and Gail Gerhart. *From Protest to Challenge: A Documentary History of African Politics in South Africa.* 6 vols. Stanford, CA: Hoover Institution Press, 1972–1977; Bloomington: Indiana University Press, 1997 and 2010.

Marks, Shula, and Anthony Atmore, eds. *Economy and Society in Pre-Industrial South Africa.* London: Longman, 1980.

Marks, Shula, and Richard Rathbone, eds. *Industrialisation and Social Change in South Africa: African Class Formation, Culture, and Consciousness, 1870–1930.* New York: Longman, 1982.

Marks, Shula, and Stanley Trapido, eds. *The Politics of Race, Class, and Nationalism in Twentieth-Century South Africa.* New York: Longman, 1982.

Maylam, Paul. *A History of the African People of South Africa: From the Early Iron Age to the 1970s.* New York: St. Martin's Press, 1986.

Meli, Francis. *A History of the ANC: South Africa Belongs to Us.* Bloomington: Indiana University Press, 1988.

Moodie, Dunbar T. *The Rise of Afrikanerdom: Power, Apartheid, and the Afrikaner Civil Religion.* Berkeley: University of California Press, 1975.

O'Meara, Dan. *Volkskapitalisme: Class, Capital, and Ideology in the Development of Afrikaner Nationalism, 1934–1948.* New York: Cambridge University Press, 1983.

Platsky, Laurine, and Cherryl Walker. *The Surplus People: Forced Removals in South Africa.* Johannesburg, South Africa: Ravan Press, 1985.

Roux, Edward. *Time Longer Than Rope: A History of the Black Man's Struggle for Freedom in South Africa.* London: Gollancz, 1948. Reprint. Madison: University of Wisconsin Press, 1964.

Simons, Harold J. *Struggles in Southern Africa for Survival and Equality.* London: Macmillan, 1997.

Thompson, Leonard M. *The Political Mythology of Apartheid.* New Haven, CT: Yale University Press, 1985.

Walshe, Peter. *The Rise of African Nationalism in South Africa: The African National Congress, 1912–1952.* Berkeley: University of California Press, 1971.

Wilson, Francis. *Labor in the South African Gold Mines, 1911–1969.* Cambridge, UK: Cambridge University Press, 1972.

Worden, Nigel. *The Making of Modern South Africa: Conquest, Segregation, and Apartheid,* 2nd ed. Cambridge, MA: Blackwell, 1995.

—Aran McKinnon

United Democratic Front

The United Democratic Front (UDF) was an umbrella body of over 500 organizations that emerged in 1983 in response to the APARTHEID government's attempts to split opposition to apartheid. While offering a token franchise to COLOURED and INDIAN South Africans in a new tricameral Parliament, it continued to exclude Africans, who constituted three-fourths of the population. The call for a United Democratic Front, initially made by Reverend ALLAN BOESAK, later came to include opposition to the government's new influx control laws aimed at regulating the movement of Africans into the urban areas and to local government structures for Africans, known as the Koornhof bills. The UDF's success at organizing a boycott of the new tricameral parliamentary elections established it as a formidable extraparliamentary organization with objectives starkly opposed to those of the apartheid state. Its slogan was "Apartheid Divides, the UDF Unites."

Composed of political, labor, women's, SPORTS, youth, and religious organizations and CIVIC ASSOCIATIONS, the UDF did not compete with other liberation movements but became a galvanizing and unifying force for domestic anti-apartheid groups. Opposition to apartheid became increasingly effective because of the UDF's capacity to provide a national political and ideological center. However, the black township revolts that were instrumental in destabilizing the apartheid regime were not caused by strategies formulated and implemented by the UDF national leadership. With the exception of key national campaigns (for example, the black local authorities' election boycotts of 1983–1984 and the fight against the tricameral Parliament campaigns aimed at placating Africans, coloureds, and Indians by granting them a degree of political participation without any real political power), the driving force of resistance came from below, as communities responded to their terrible living conditions. As these local struggles spread, the UDF played an important role in putting forward common national demands for the dismantling of apartheid. Black communities were drawn into a national movement advocating majority rule as a precondition for the realization of basic economic demands such as decent shelter, cheap transport, proper health care, adequate EDUCATION, the right to occupy land, and the right to a living wage. While youths active in the UDF demonstrated over education issues, the emergence of indigenous liberation theology and the increased state brutality toward people advocating equality and justice brought religious organizations into the UDF, exemplified by the activism of the Reverend Boesak and Archbishop DESMOND TUTU.

Indeed, what was unique about the UDF's organization was its highly decentralized structure, which made it difficult for the repressive state to quell, as this organization's driving engine lay with its hundreds of local affiliates. The UDF also promoted grassroots participatory democracy as a practical example of the kind of national political system to which its members aspired, as well as developed an organizational infrastructure through the organs of people's power, where strong grassroots, community-based organizing could take place. This was evidenced in a number of its campaigns, including one of its first national ones: the Million Signature Campaign opposing the new Constitution and the Koornhof bills granting blacks a degree of political participation but very limited political power. Other successful campaigns included consumer and rent boycotts and DEFIANCE CAMPAIGNS against local governments with the aim of making communities and indeed the country ungovernable. UDF affiliates included the CONGRESS OF SOUTH AFRICAN TRADE UNIONS, the South African National Student Congress, the National Union of South African Students, and the Congress of South African Students. The UDF adopted the FREEDOM CHARTER and the vision for postapartheid ideologies and principles of the AFRICAN NATIONAL CONGRESS (ANC) and others, and increasingly linked itself publicly with the still-banned ANC. With the unbanning of the liberation movements in 1990, the subsequent return of the exiled leadership, and the initiation of negotiations with the apartheid state, the UDF disbanded itself in 1991.

University of Fort Hare

Fort Hare is one of the oldest universities in southern Africa and was the first institution on the African continent to offer a Western-style tertiary education to nonwhite students. It is located on the Tyhume River, in the town of Alice, or eDikeni as it is known in XHOSA, in the current Eastern Cape Province. This university currently has an enrollment of approximately 6,000 students.

Formerly known as the South African Native College and established in 1916, Fort Hare was the second university established in South Africa after the University of CAPE TOWN. It served as an important institution of higher education for black South Africans from 1916 to 1959. Although Fort Hare was racially segregated even before APARTHEID was institutionalized, it embraced the ideals of a diverse and tolerant South Africa, given its origins in an alliance of educated African Christians and liberal white clergies. The university had a mix of black, COLOURED, and INDIAN students, along with both white staff and black academics such as Z. K. MATTHEWS and D.D.T. JABAVU. Both male and female students came from various linguistic backgrounds, including Xhosa, SOTHO, ZULU, and Afrikaans. During these early decades, Fort Hare educated many prominent Africans from throughout the continent, including NELSON MANDELA, DESMOND TUTU, GOVAN MBEKI, ROBERT SOBUKWE, DENNIS BRUTUS, MANGOSUTHU BUTHELEZI, Seretse Khama of Botswana, Julius Nyerere of Tanzania, Kenneth Kaunda of Zambia, and Robert Mugabe of ZIMBABWE.

In 1959, Fort Hare came under the apartheid government's control and, in keeping with this regime's plans of racial separation, was designated as the ethnic university for Xhosa-speaking Africans only. Despite government control of the institution during the apartheid era, Fort Hare remained one of the main centers of antiapartheid activities such as the BLACK CONSCIOUSNESS MOVEMENT led by STEVE BIKO.

In the postapartheid era, the university has experienced numerous financial and administrative challenges, in part due to the opening of formerly all-white institutions that are now attracting many talented black students. As part of an effort to remake itself in the contemporary era, Fort Hare is in the process of merging with the East London campus of Rhodes University, a historically white university also based in the Eastern Cape.

V

Van Riebeeck, Johan Anthoniszoon (Jan) (1619–1677)

Johan Anthoniszoon "Jan" Van Riebeeck, born on April 21, 1619, in the Netherlands, is viewed by many South African AFRIKANERS as the founding father of their nation. A merchant, he started the first European settlement in South Africa in 1652.

Jan Van Riebeeck joined the DUTCH EAST INDIA COMPANY (Vereenigde Oost-Indische Compagnie, or VOC) in 1639 and was commissioned to establish a strong base to provide the company's ships with fresh groceries, mainly meat and vegetables, on the long journey from Europe to Asia. The VOC didn't seek the conquest or the administration of a territory in southern Africa. Their interest was simply to ensure the provision of vital supplies to their shipping fleets on their way to and from the Dutch East Indies. Van Riebeeck's specific instructions were not to colonize the Cape but to build a fort, to erect a flagpole for signaling to passing ships, and to build pilot boats to escort passing ships safely into the bay. His group of settlers, consisting of eighty-two men and eight women, his own wife among them, anchored in CAPE TOWN on April 6. They built the first fort, Fort Duijnhoop.

Van Riebeeck remained administrator of the Cape from 1652 to 1662. He died on January 18, 1677 in Batavia, Dutch East India (now Jakarta, Indonesia).

Venda

The Venda (also VaVenda) population of about one million people presently resides primarily in the Limpopo Province in the north of South Africa and in neighboring ZIMBABWE. The Venda LANGUAGE, tshiVenda or luVenda, emerged as a distinct tongue in the sixteenth century and is now one of South Africa's eleven official languages. The tshiVenda vocabulary is similar to seSOTHO, but the grammar shares similarities with Shona dialects, which are spoken in Zimbabwe.

Venda culture is similarly eclectic, as it appears to have incorporated a variety of east African, central African, Nguni, and Sotho characteristics. For example, the Venda forbid the consumption of pork, a prohibition common along the east African coast. They practice male circumcision, which is common among many Sotho but not among most Nguni peoples.

The so-called homeland of Venda, located in what is now Limpopo Province, became nominally independent in 1979 but was not recognized by any country except South Africa. The APARTHEID regime used the strategy of creating nominally independent black homelands to pursue its policy of separate development and to justify keeping the majority of South African territory for whites only. Unlike other ethnic homelands that in fact were never "home" for the majority of their ethnic group, most of the 700,000 Venda people actually lived in Venda. Its economy depended on agriculture and small industry, and coal mining began in the late 1980s.

See also LANGUAGE

Verwoerd, Hendrik Frensch (H. F.) (1901–1966)

The sixth prime minister of the UNION OF SOUTH AFRICA, Hendrik Frensch (H. F.) Verwoerd is widely regarded as the architect of APARTHEID. He was born in Amsterdam on September 8, 1901, and moved with his family to South Africa at the age of two. A bright student, Verwoerd studied psychology and sociology at the University of STELLENBOSCH, where he received his bachelor's, master's, and doctoral degrees. At twenty-six, he became the first professor of sociology at his alma mater.

In 1934, Verwoerd participated in a national congress of AFRIKANER leaders regarding the problems facing the poor whites, the Afrikaans-speaking peoples of South Africa, that contradicted the notion of white superiority and the development of a racial hierarchy. In 1937, he became editor of *Die Transvaler*, the NATIONAL PARTY's new daily paper, which gave him a vehicle to disseminate his ideas about republicanism. When the National Party was elected to power in 1948, Verwoerd was elected as senator, but quickly rose from backbencher to key minister in two years.

In 1950, Verwoerd became minister of native affairs in D. F. MALAN's cabinet and strongly began promoting the idea of separate development for both white and black South Africans. In 1958, he was elected prime minister and responded to foreign criticisms by reformulating the apartheid policy into a plan of "separate but equal" nations. He argued that contact between different racial groups would hinder their evolution into nationhood. Africans, he argued, could be guided to self-determination once they were ready.

In 1960, Verwoerd led South Africa to become a republic and withdrew the country from the British Commonwealth. Although he was widely criticized by the English press, he had a sizable number of English-speaking followers and succeeded in building the white South African communities into a cohesive unit.

Verwoerd was prime minister during the 1960 SHARPEVILLE MASSACRE, in which South African police killed sixty-nine black protesters; the banning of the AFRICAN NATIONAL CONGRESS and the PAN AFRICANIST CONGRESS; and the RIVONIA TRIAL of apartheid opponents as well. His administration instituted a number of key apartheid acts, including the promotion of the Bantu Self-Government Act, which initiated the process of creating independent black homelands. In 1966, Verwoerd was murdered in Parliament by Dimitri Tsafendas, a COLOURED parliamentary messenger. It is unclear if his murder was politically motivated.

Vigilantism

Recent South African history, dating back to the formation of the UNION OF SOUTH AFRICA in 1910, is replete with incidents of vigilantism. As defined here, *vigilantism* is concerted local action on the part of ordinary citizens involving the application of illegal coercion or violence to others. In practice, vigilantism can be more or less organized in its execution and be informed by different social motivations. Vigilante groups can target their actions to a wide range of social groups that may be considered "deserving" of such reprisals. The diversity in both form and focus notwithstanding, at heart, vigilante actions aim at maintaining, creating, or recreating "order" under conditions where the social order is perceived to be under threat. During periods of dramatic social change or stress, the propensity for vigilante action may increase as the social order itself appears to be under particular threat. An overview of vigilantism in modern South Africa points to its evolution and mutation in response to shifts in power relations and changes in social context. Political constructions and MEDIA depictions of vigilantism—as good or bad, benevolent or sinister, pro- or antistate—tend to vary from one context to another.

As in other contexts, the term *vigilantism* can only be understood as a South African phenomenon in the presence of some form of "duly" constituted political authority, usually associated with a modern state. This proviso is of importance in the case of South Africa, given its turbulent history when borders and authorities were contested or nonexistent. What at the present time might be considered vigilantism could, at earlier points in its history, have been construed as social banditry, group conflict, or communal self-defense.

During the 1940s and the 1950s, vigilante action among black people was widespread and had little overt political content. At a time of rapid African urbanization, crimes by youth and predatory gangs met with little response from the white-dominated state police. The black townships' response to underpolicing was the formation of community guards, as in SOPHIATOWN, usually under the leadership of older members in the black community. The state's reaction was hostile, and organized self-help anticrime groupings in black areas withered as the 1950s gave way to the most severe state repression after 1961.

Effective politicization of vigilantism first occurred during the 1980s, as popular resistance to APARTHEID rule gained momentum and state repression became consolidated in a counterinsurgency strategy. Right-wing vigilante groupings also came to prominence in the mid-1980s. Such vigilante formations were aligned to apartheid-designated, conservative homeland governments (in Ciskei, Kwandebele, and KwaZulu, for example), on the one hand, and to conservative black community councils in urban areas on the other. Operating with the apartheid state's tacit or active support, reactionary vigilante groups focused their action on political groupings aligned to the mass democratic movement. State-sponsored vigilante violence fueled social divisions within black communities, pitting youth against elders, migrant hostel dwellers against township residents, and one political grouping against another. The antagonism between elders and youth, which emerged within New Crossroads and the KTC Squatter Camp outside of CAPE TOWN during 1986, provided proof of the corrosive effects of intracommunity vigilante actions.

On the progressive side, vigilantism also reared its head during the late 1980s. As the struggle between a repressive state and its subjugated people intensified, informal mechanisms of ordering (such as street committees and people's courts in African townships) became mobilized around the political objective of making the townships ungovernable. Over time, the disciplined political activism of such organs of popular justice gave way, in greater or lesser degree, to vigilante-type actions that targeted political opponents. A case in point concerns the tit-for-tat reprisals between politically aligned self-defense formations that emerged among African youths, such as those organized under the rubric of self-defense units and self-protection units. State complicity in fanning vigilante violence within black communities during the 1980s only became clear in later years through the deliberations of the TRUTH AND RECONCILIATION COMMISSION.

By 1994, political negotiations brought a system of constitutional democracy based on human rights and the rule of law to South Africa. The democratic ELECTIONS of 1994 signified the end of an era of internecine political violence. The prospects for peace were, however, dampened by growing public concern with high levels of criminal violence. The centerpiece of the state's crime strategy, the National Crime Prevention Strategy of 1996, endorsed the principle of community involvement in crime prevention. The state made concerted attempts, in partnership with local communities, to channel anticrime energies through various structures (such as community police forums, neighborhood watches, street committees, anticrime forums, and peace committees). Not all anticrime actions were harnessed through structures and in ways supportive of the rule of law. On the contrary, an enduring feature of the new constitutional era has been the eruption of vigilantism, both organized and ad hoc/impulsive, in stated support of controlling crime.

The formations of People Against Gangsterism and Drugs (PAGAD) and Mapogo a Mathamaga provide examples of particular anticrime vigilantism of a more organized kind. PAGAD, formally established in December 1995 in the Western Cape, constituted from the start a predominantly Muslim anticrime formation, targeting especially drug dealers and the gangs that stood behind them. During the course of the next two years, it organized various community meetings and public marches. The organization's impatience with the slow efforts of law enforcement, together with the involvement of radical Islamists, led to extralegal tactics. It became locked in a spiral of vigilante and countervigilante violence, which involved drug lords and, more ominously, the state. By 1998, the initially tolerant stance of the state changed gear as PAGAD was redefined as an urban terror group.

In August 1996, Mapogo a Mathamaga was founded along the lines of a private security firm by a group of businessmen in the Northern Province. At the time of its formation, Mapogo was to act as a bulwark against unprecedented levels of crime in the province's rural areas. Before long, Mapogo also began to deploy violence in the process of apprehending, convicting, and punishing alleged offenders. At first, the leadership defended its use of corporal punishment as rooted in traditional African practices. The state's response to Mapogo was characterized by ambiguity. Early attempts to co-opt Mapogo into obeying state laws failed and thus led to criminal proceedings against senior members of this organization.

Sporadic forms of vigilantism targeted at those suspected of criminal involvement continue to be a feature today, especially in the black townships. In the absence of research, the incidence of such vigilantism is unclear. There is, however, broad agreement about the social factors associated with anticrime vigilantism: high levels of fear of crime and public concern about criminal violence, low levels of confidence in the police, inequalities in access to justice among the poor, public support for tougher action against crime, and low levels of support among South Africans for the rule of law. All of these factors combine to form a potent incentive to self-help policing.

See also POLITICAL VIOLENCE IN SOUTH AFRICA

Bibliography

Africa, C., et al. "Crime and Community Action: Pagad and the Cape Flats. 1996–1997." *Public Opinion Service Reports,* No. 4. Cape Town, South Africa: IDASA, 1998.

Buur, Lars. "Crime and Punishment on the Margins of the Post-Apartheid State." *Anthropology and Humanism* 28, no. 1 (2003): 23–42.

Buur, Lars, and Steffen Jensen. "Introduction: Vigilantism and the Policing of Everyday Life in South Africa." *African Studies* 63, no. 2 (2004): 139–152.

Catholic Institute for International Relations. *Now Everyone Is Afraid: The Changing Face of Policing in South Africa.* London: Catholic Institute for International Relations, 1988.

Dixon, Bill, and Lisa-Marie Johns. "Gangs, Pagad, and the State: Vigilantism and Revenge Violence in the Western Cape." *Violence in Transition Series,* Vol. 2. Braamfontein, South Africa: Centre for the Study of Violence and Reconciliation, 2001.

Harris, Bronwyn. *As for Violent Crime That's Our Daily Bread: Vigilante Violence During South Africa's Period of Transition,* Vol. 1. Johannesburg, South Africa: Centre for the Study of Violence and Reconciliation, 2001.

Haysom, Nicholas. *Mabangalala: The Rise of Right-Wing Vigilantism in South Africa.* Occasional Paper No. 10. Johannesburg, South Africa: University of the Witwatersrand, Centre for Applied Legal Studies, 1986.

Schärf, Wilfried, and Daniel Nina. *The Other Law: Non-State Ordering in South Africa.* Cape Town, South Africa: Juta, 2001.

Schonteich, Martin. *Justice Versus Retribution: Attitudes to Punishment in the Eastern Cape.* ISS Monograph Series No. 45. Pretoria, South Africa: Institute for Security Studies, 2000.

Sekhonyane, Makubetse, and Antoinette Louw. *Violent Justice: Vigilantism and the State's Response.* Monograph Series No. 72. Pretoria, South Africa: Institute for Security Studies, 2002.

Von Schnitzler, Antina, et al. *Guardian or Gangster? Mapogo-a-Mathamaga: A Case Study.* Violence and Transition Series 3. Braamfontein, South Africa: Centre for the Study of Violence and Reconciliation, 2001.

—*Elrena van der Spuy*

Women and Politics

Women's political participation in South Africa has been shaped by their involvement in the struggle against APARTHEID, their role in the transition to democracy, and, since 1994, their participation in civil society organizations and government institutions. Historically, women in South Africa have also faced challenges in terms of gender subordination, but this cannot be separated from the divisions among women along racial classifications and class positions created by COLONIALISM and apartheid. Colonialism brought specific European norms of female domesticity and diminished women's power in public decisionmaking roles within religious societies and governance structures. Yet, there were layers to this subordination along racial lines. For example, white women won the right to vote and stand for office as early as 1930, but their suffrage campaign became a race-based movement, excluding black women. Many of their actions reproduced the nationalistic and racist dogmas of the male-dominated POLITICAL PARTIES of the time and underscored the need to unify the white population in order to diminish black political power.

Black South African women faced not only gender subordination but also suffered under apartheid's race-based policies. During apartheid (1948–1994), black women's main political participation became centered in civil society. They were involved in the women's branches of the male-dominated political parties, in the labor unions, as soldiers in the armed wings of the resistance, and within religious societies. Women were active in opposition politics and used different forms of mass action to challenge white minority rule. Key leaders during this period included RUTH FIRST, WINNIE MANDELA, HELEN SUZMAN, and Adelaide Tambo. Even though there were massive political and class differences among women, during key moments in the struggle, women came together and unified across racial, religious, and class divisions. For example, women of all races united to oppose the PASS LAWS, which strictly governed black women's movements from one area to another. Leaders such as HELEN JOSEPH, LILLIAN NGOYI, and ALBERTINA SISULU and multiracial women's organizations such as the Federation of South African Women brought women together to protest apartheid's educational policies, the pass laws, and racial segregation.

Women's roles in the antiapartheid movement often involved mass action, networking, and mobilization tactics that were not always visible or recognized. Women were labeled the "backbone" of the struggle or the "silent strength" of the antiapartheid movement. The public face of antiapartheid politics remained decidedly, almost universally, male. Therefore, while women developed key skills of networking, collaboration, and mass-based politics, they had not yet ensured a place in formal political life following the end of the struggle.

In the early 1990s, South African women again mobilized for their collective interests during the constitutional negotiations for a new democratic government. Women returning from political exile joined forces with those who had remained in South Africa to form a national umbrella organization, known as the Women's National Coalition (WNC). The WNC brought together women's groups and political party representatives from across various ideological, racial, religious, and class spectrums. They mobilized to gain a voice for gender issues during the transition to a new political system, for example, to make sure women's rights would be enshrined in the new CONSTITUTION and that mechanisms would be implemented to ensure women's representation in all levels of the new government. Certain issues, such as abortion, were tabled because they would create divisions in the coalition and undermine their primary leveraging device: unity. Instead, the WNC created a National Women's Charter that outlined the goals for women's political, economic, and social advancement. The Women's Charter made specific recommendations on women's rights to be included in the new constitution and on new structures of government to be created to promote gender equality. This charter became the initial blueprint for female leaders and activists for the next several years.

Using the pressure and power created by the WNC, women within political parties were able to demand a place for women at the constitutional negotiations and worked to secure protections for gender equality within the Constitution, as well as influence the selection of electoral laws that were likely to advance women in office. Within their individual parties, women were able to point to the WNC's mobilization to demonstrate their effectiveness and power as political leaders. Partly because of these efforts, women within various political parties were successful in their quest to institute party-list quotas for women, such as in the AFRICAN NATIONAL CONGRESS (ANC), or other AFFIRMATIVE ACTION measures, such as the targeted recruitment and mentoring of women candidates. Due to these efforts, South Africa climbed near to the top of international rankings for the number of women in national office. In 1994, following the first democratic ELECTION in South Africa, women occupied approximately 25 percent of the seats in the National Assembly's Lower House of PARLIAMENT. In the 1999 and the 2004 elections, this number increased to 29.8 percent and up to 32.8 percent, respectively. In the 2009 elections, women reached 44.5 percent.

The mass influx of women into national political office had an immediate and visible impact on the institutional culture of Parliament, as well as on the structures of national policies. The place of women as members of Parliament (MPs) is now accepted, and there has been an upward path of women moving from local and provincial legislatures into the national office. Initially, several changes to make the Parliament more parent and woman friendly were made by the first speaker and the deputy speaker of Parliament respectively, FRENE GINWALA and Baleka Mbete. For instance, the parliamentary calendar was changed to match the school calendar, so that MPs are on recess or in their constituency offices when schoolchildren are on holiday. Debates are supposed to end in the early evening rather than going late into the night, reflecting the need for parents to care both for the country and for their own families. Childcare facilities were created for MPs and for staff members with small children, acknowledging the reality that many MPs are also the primary caregivers in their households. Beginning in the first democratically elected Parliament, women were strong leaders in parliamentary life, including PATRICIA DE LILLE and Nozizwe Madlala-Routledge.

South African women leaders recognized that getting women into national office was only the first step toward fulfilling the goals of the Women's Charter and advancing women's status. Through the combined activities of female political leaders, academics, gender activists, and international consultants, women in South Africa designed the National Gender Machinery (NGM) following the end of apartheid in 1994. The NGM was created to mainstream gender issues throughout civil society, Parliament, and governmental agencies. Its structures were designed to institutionalize a focus on the needs of women by creating a diffuse set of institutions throughout the government so women's issues would not be marginalized into one single agency, department, or committee. Gender issues would then become visible, expected, and eventually accepted as part of the government's work.

The national Commission for Gender Equality (CGE), established in 1994, is intended to work as a liaison between civil society and government. With both national and provincial offices, the CGE has programs to promote the status of women and has monitoring functions to evaluate both the government and private sector businesses in terms of their promotion of gender equality.

Based on the idea that governmental policies and legislations mean little if not supported by adequate funding, the Women's Budget Initiative (WBI) is a process that tracked government spending on gender issues. The WBI was started in 1996 through a partnership of Parliament (the Joint Monitoring Committee on the Quality of Life and Status of Women), government (the Department of Finance), and nongovernmental organizations. The first Women's Budget tracked the budget in the sectors of housing, EDUCATION, welfare, and work, and eventually covered all the national departments, revenues, local governments, and job creation. The WBI concluded that gender-biased expenditures existed in many sectors, especially key sectors such as education, for example. Funding for education tends to be allocated toward fields dominated by men, such as science and technology, despite female students outnumbering male students at the university level.

Within Parliament, the Joint Monitoring Committee on Improving the Quality of Life and Status of Women (JMC) was at the forefront of initiating legislations to advance the status of women. Under the leadership of Pregs Govender, who was an ANC member of Parliament, a feminist activist, and independent writer, the JMC became a formidable advocate of gender issues The JMC regularly makes recommendations on other pieces of legislation that potentially have an impact on women. For example, the committee has acted on legislation affecting labor laws, sexual harassment, poverty, domestic violence, parental rights, maintenance, and HIV/AIDS. The committee was renamed the Portfolio Committee on Women, Youth, Children, and People with Disabilities, a controversial move, given the assimilation and coupling of what can be different needs and issues of its representative groups.

The Office of the Status of Women (OSW), established soon after 1994, is in charge of the oversight of gender issues within various government ministries. Each ministry is required to have a gender desk or a gender focal point that assists in the implementation of gendered legislation and/or that deals with gender issues internal to the ministry. The national OSW is located in the Office of the Vice President. Its staff members have conducted evaluations of each ministry's efforts toward gender equality and have organized NGM meetings to strengthen networking and discussion across institutions. The main obstacles facing the work of the OSW and the gender desks include a lack of human resources, program funding, and real oversight power. The recently created Ministry of Women, Youth, Children, and People with Disabilities has taken on many of the implementation functions of the NGM, and there is debate over whether the role of the ministry is in line with the dispersion of gender issues throughout the NGM. In other words, by creating a separate ministry there is concern as to whether gender issues have been sidelined rather than mainstreamed throughout government.

There are distinct disadvantages and advantages to the diffusion of gender issues within the national machinery, as opposed to centralizing the functions within a single ministry or department.

First, the diffusion heightens funding competition in an already resource-poor context. Second, the diffusion model enhances problems of accountability, fractionalization, and viability. Third, some critics have worried that too much emphasis was placed on institution building rather than on directly addressing women's issues or maintaining the fragile national women's movement. Positively, the NGM in South Africa has now made gender equality a fundamental priority throughout government agencies. Women's participation in decisionmaking and government services is not just accepted but expected, and there is evidence that women's visibility has had a demonstrable effect, ensuring that future generations of women will see themselves as part of formal political life.

Women's political participation in civil society was also deeply affected by the transition to democracy. At first, women's groups faced challenges of leadership and agenda setting following the end of apartheid. Due to the massive influx of women into political office, several national and regional women's groups lost their executives to the national or provincial legislatures, which necessitated the development of the next generation of women leaders to step into these positions. Similarly, the agenda of many women's groups has changed from opposing the government, as during apartheid, to working with the government within a cautious partnership for progressive social change. This has created a sense of ambivalence among many civil society organizations, which recognized the benefits of supporting and cooperating with the government but also the limitations of having their organizational missions co-opted by government priorities. Increasingly, the ANC-led government has contracted out service delivery to many civil society groups, relying on them to provide everything from legal services to health and welfare programs to poverty-alleviation projects. Because many groups now depend on the government to financially support their operations, some voice concerns about being too critical of the government due to fears of losing their funding.

Despite these initial challenges, a wealth of women's groups is flourishing in South Africa. Since the apartheid-era suppression of civic action has ended, both nongovernmental and community-based organizations have become a mainstay of political life and social change. Organizations have formed around HIV/AIDS activism, campaigns have been started to combat gender-based violence, unions have regained momentum in supporting women as industrial and domestic laborers, and new dialogues are occurring in competitive SPORTS about the interaction of gender, race, and class identities.

Several women's organizations in South Africa have joined the international 50/50 campaign to attempt to secure 50 percent representation for women at all levels of decisionmaking, either through a legislative quota or through voluntary measures within political parties. Although this movement has yet to reach the 50 percent goal, in South Africa or globally, it is clear that there remains continued faith in the idea that women can make a difference both symbolically and practically. This movement also demonstrates the potential for women within government to work together with their civil society counterparts to secure their political advancement.

See also RUTH FIRST; HELEN JOSEPH; WINNIE MANDELA; LILLIAN NGOYI

Bibliography

Britton, Hannah. *Women in the South African Parliament: From Resistance to Governance*. Champaign: University of Illinois Press, 2005.

Goetz, Anne Marie, and Shireen Hassim. *No Shortcuts to Power: African Women in Politics and Policy Making*. London: Zed Books, 2003.

Gouws, Amanda. "The Politics of State Structures: Citizenship and the National Machinery for Women in South Africa." *Feminist Africa*, no. 3 (2004). www.feministafrica.org/2level.html.

Hassim, Shireen. *Women's Organizations and Democracy in South Africa: Contesting Authority*. Madison: University of Wisconsin Press, 2006.

Liebenberg, Sandra, ed. *The Constitution of South Africa from a Gender Perspective*. Cape Town, South Africa: David Philip, 1995.

Meintjes, Sheila, and Mary Simons. "Why Electoral Systems Matter to Women." In *One Woman, One Vote*. Edited by Glenda Flick, Sheila Meintjes, and Mary Simons. Johannesburg, South

Africa: Electoral Institute of South Africa, 2002.
Russell, Diane. *Lives of Courage: Women for a New South Africa*. Oakland, CA: Basic Books, 1989.

—Hannah Britton

World Council of Churches

The World Council of Churches (WCC) played a visible and controversial role against APARTHEID. Influenced by US civil rights leaders such as Martin Luther King Jr. and southern African liberation leaders such as Z. K. MATTHEWS and Eduardo Mondlane during the 1960s, the WCC began to focus on the global fight against racism and increasingly became involved in southern African politics. Based in Geneva, Switzerland, the WCC is a fellowship of nearly 350 churches, denominations, and Christian groups in over 110 countries. It was established in 1948 to support Christian unity and promote interreligious dialogue.

With the launch of its Program to Combat Racism in 1969, which was attended by AFRICAN NATIONAL CONGRESS leader OLIVER TAMBO and by antiapartheid activist Bishop Trevor Huddleston, the WCC came to play a leading role in directing the global campaign against apartheid. On an ideological level, the WCC was instrumental in countering the South African DUTCH REFORMED CHURCH's efforts to legitimize apartheid ideology through theology. On a practical level, beginning in the 1970s, the WCC's Program to Combat Racism began offering grants to liberation movements in southern Africa, which stirred up a storm of controversy in South African churches and in some Western churches as well. However, it was a move that was strongly affirmed by African churches and by leading US and European denominations.

World Cup

See SPORTS

Xhosa

The Xhosa are one of South Africa's black ethnic groups. IsiXhosa is also one of the Bantu LANGUAGES spoken in South Africa. There are several subgroups of the Xhosa-speaking population: Bhaca, Bomvana, Mfengo (see MFENGU), Mpondo, Mpondomise, Thembu, and Xesibe. Each of these groups has a distinct but related heritage. At present, about six million isiXhosa speakers reside throughout South Africa, the majority in the Eastern and the Western Cape provinces, as well as fewer in Free State and in KwaZulu-Natal. IsiXhosa is South Africa's second most common language among the black population, after isiZULU, to which it is closely related.

Historically, the Xhosa were part of the South African Nguni migration, which moved to the country's southeastern area from the Great Lakes region of present-day Uganda and Rwanda, before the first white settlers' arrival during the 1600s. Due to their cultural, linguistic, economic, and social interactions with other southern African societies and groups, the Xhosa had an open society. For instance, the modern isiXhosa language has large elements of the KHOIKHOI and the SAN languages spoken by the region's original nomadic herders.

The Xhosa first encountered white settlers around Somerset East in present-day Western Cape Province in the early 1700s. During the late 1700s, they clashed with the BOER trekkers who were migrating inward toward the Xhosa territories from the CAPE COLONY. After more than two decades of territorial conflicts, the Xhosa were pushed east by the British colonial forces during the Third Frontier War from 1811 to 1812. Following this, many Xhosa-speaking clans were forced west by the Zulu, who were expanding their territories during the MFECANE, a period of political instability in southern Africa. The Xhosa's unity and abilities to resist colonial expansion were further weakened by famines and political divisions among themselves. Besides losing their lands to both the Zulu and the European settlers, they also faced restrictions on their political autonomy due to the various measures implemented by the British colonial authorities and subsequently by the South African government. Over time, many became impoverished and were forced to become migrant and wage laborers in the urban areas or in neighboring countries.

IsiXhosa speakers made up a large percentage of workers in South Africa's gold mines.

During the APARTHEID era, many Xhosa were forcefully resettled in the BANTUSTANS of Transkei and Ciskei, which were legally designated for them. Furthermore, Xhosa in the bantustans were systematically deprived of basic social services and employment opportunities. In the cities, like other black South Africans, they were subject to raids for failing to obey the PASS LAWS by carrying pass books. These homelands were not dismantled until the apartheid regime ended in 1994, and, since then, their living conditions have improved. For example, the Xhosa literacy rate has increased from 30 percent during the apartheid era to around 50 percent in 1996 as primary schools have instituted Xhosa language curriculums. Currently, isiXhosa is one of South Africa's eleven official languages, and there are two isiXhosa radio stations. At least two of South Africa's three public television stations broadcast partly in isiXhosa. However, many Xhosa are still impoverished because housing and living standards vary among this population. They also face social problems such as high crime rates, broken families, malnutrition, and tensions with other black ethnic groups due to competition for scarce resources. Even though the Xhosa are one of South Africa's poorest populations, a minority of them are also the wealthiest. Prominent Xhosa include former presidents NELSON MANDELA and THABO MBEKI, as well as REVEREND DESMOND TUTU.

Z

Zimbabwe

Zimbabwe lies to the north of South Africa and shares a similar colonial and cultural history. A former British colony, known as Rhodesia (or Southern Rhodesia), Zimbabwe was formed in the 1880s by CECIL JOHN RHODES and the BRITISH SOUTH AFRICA COMPANY.

The minority ethnic group in Zimbabwe, the NDEBELE (also referred to as Matabele), share a language and culture with the ZULU in South Africa, having migrated from South Africa to Zimbabwe during the MFECANE, a period of political instability in southern Africa.

In the early twentieth century, Rhodesia, like South Africa, was exclusively governed by local whites. In the early 1960s, Britain urged Rhodesian whites to end minority rule. The Rhodesian government responded by declaring "unilateral independence" from Britain in 1965. The only government in the world to recognize the rogue Rhodesian regime was APARTHEID South Africa. Black opposition movements in Zimbabwe, thus far peaceful, responded with armed struggle. The full-scale resistance war lasted until 1979, following negotiations mediated by the British government. While the white South African armed forces fought alongside the Rhodesians, the South African resistance movement, the AFRICAN NATIONAL CONGRESS (ANC), maintained strong links with the Zimbabwean opposition groups, especially the Zimbabwe African People's Union (ZAPU). The larger Zimbabwe African People's Front (ZANU) was led by Robert Mugabe, a UNIVERSITY OF FORT HARE graduate and former teacher. At independence, the new government of Prime Minister Robert Mugabe agreed to an official ANC presence in Zimbabwe.

Since 1994, the Zimbabwe–South Africa relationship has been one of both tension and diplomacy. Zimbabwe has experienced an ongoing political crisis since February 2000—when Mugabe and the now ruling ZANU-PF (the result of a 1987 merger between ZANU and ZAPU, with ZANU as the dominating partner) first lost a referendum to extend Mugabe's presidential term and executive powers. In June 2000, the opposition Movement for Democratic Change also defeated ZANU-PF in parliamentary elections. Although Mugabe presumably also lost another election in 2008, he still retained power, refusing to step down. Throughout this time, the Zimbabwe police, army, and ruling party paramilitaries have been implicated in violence and human rights abuses against opposition members and supporters. With regional mediation led by South African president THABO MBEKI, a Global Political Agreement (GPA) was signed in 2008 between ZANU-PF and the opposition Movement for Democratic Change (MDC). The GPA mandated a Government of National Unity (GNU) in which political power would be shared between the two parties. (The Movement for Democratic Change subsequently splintered and there are now two MDC factions represented in the government.) The GPA also called for constitutional and electoral reforms, and established plans for new national elections.

See also FRONTLINE STATES

Zulu

The word *Zulu* has several meanings. It simultaneously designates an ethnic identity, a LANGUAGE, a genealogical lineage, and a surname or clan name (*isibongo*). The terminology preferred by anthropologists, archaeologists, and historians to define Zulu identity and historical development is "Nguni-speaking" and "Bantu-speaking," which denotes a collective name for a group of ethnic groups with common linguistic ties, including Zulu, residing in southern Africa. From the perspective of the Zulu language, *Zulu* is an Anglicized word and an abbreviation of a set of cognates with diverse potential meanings. This set of common but equally ambiguous words includes: *uZulu* ("the Zulu nation"), *amaZulu* ("the people of the Zulu nation"), *abakwaZulu* ("the people of the Zulu country"), *umZulu* ("a Zulu person"), and *isiZulu* ("the Zulu language"). This proliferation of meanings and images is the result of political, historical, social, and linguistic changes as well as contests and debates, which have defined and redefined Zuluness over time. Popular culture in the form of novels, poetry, plays, MUSIC, and movies has also played a role in creating and in sustaining certain images of the Zulu as a people.

Geographically and archaeologically, the area between the Phongolo and Mzimkhulu rivers in present-day KwaZulu-Natal Province is often identified as the main region in which Zulu identity, culture, and political life emerged. The archaeological evidence dates the emergence of a distinct regional communal life, termed the "Late Iron Age," to the period from 800 to 1200 A.D. These communities are characterized as agro-pastoral, iron-smelting, and living in individual family homesteads.

The period that has generated the most intense historical research, analysis, and argumentation is undoubtedly the early nineteenth century. Specifically, the emergence of the Zulu polity as well as the population and cultural turmoils conventionally known as the MFECANE have been the source of debate since the 1960s. At issue is not just the literal meaning of the word *Mfecane* but the historical veracity of ascribing the increase in political conflict to the emergence of a centralized and militarized Zulu state. The Mfecane debate has led to the rewriting of Zulu history in many ways. For one, it has led many historians to distinguish between "pre-Shakan" and "post-Shakan" Zulu identity, referring to the powerful Zulu king, SHAKA. This is in recognition of the fact that the notion of a "Zulu" person does not seem to have had much political currency in the period before SHAKA's ascendancy around 1816. The most common argument offered by historians is that in the precolonial and the pre-Shakan period, the name Zulu was used by a small group of people living between the Mhlathuze and Mfolozi rivers who traced their descent to a common ancestor. These communities were among many groups of Nguni-speaking people living in the region, including the Khumalo, Mchunu, Mthethwa, Ngcobo, and Qwabe. Part legend, part myth, and part enigma, Shaka's life story and the history of the kingdom he created continue to influence the Zulu's contemporary image. Shaka's legacy simultaneously represents the heroism of an African genius and the violent history of the methods he employed.

Whatever agency is attributed to Shaka as the Zulu Kingdom's founder, his assassination in 1828 by his brother Dingane ushered in a different dynamic in the abilities of Zulu leaders to control the direction of political life in the region. This is especially true of the relationship among the Zulu polity, the BOER trekkers, the British colonial state of NATAL, and Christian missionaries. The murder of AFRIKANER PIET RETIEF and his party by Dingane's men and the subsequent BATTLE OF BLOOD RIVER of 1838 have repeatedly figured as the main events that defined the Zulu king's relationship to the threat of colonial intrusion. On closer examination, it appears that Shaka's legacy has left his successors with both internal and external pressures to contend with. Internally, the extensive spread of Zulu power meant that any successor had to continually reinforce a tenuous collective identity while continually bolstering the new social structures and transformations introduced by Shaka's use of the *amabutho* ("regiments") as the basic labor and military resource available to the reigning king. Externally, the European traders' arrival in the 1820s signaled the presence of alternative sources of power, wealth, and influence. These traders did not at first represent pure colonial ambitions but more often brought traded goods: guns, ivory, and, some would argue, slaves. Literacy and writing also entered the equation as written reports of Zulu life and politics began to filter into the CAPE COLONY via these traders.

Dingane's rule ended when Mpande, in an 1840 alliance with the Boer trekkers, overthrew his brother and assumed the throne. Mpande maintained the kingdom's autonomy for thirty years and was succeeded on his death in 1872 by CETSHWAYO, who became the last Zulu king. With the invasion of Zululand by the British in 1879 and the devastation of the ANGLO-ZULU WAR that followed, Zulu autonomy and sovereignty were destroyed, especially through the land partitions in 1883 and 1887 and Zululand's annexation to the British Natal Colony in 1897. Their loss of political independence also meant the loss of economic independence, which, in turn, caused an increase in the region's labor migration mainly to the gold mines around JOHANNESBURG.

In the late nineteenth and the early twentieth centuries, Zulu identity was reshaped by a variety of forces: colonial policy, the intensification of missionary activity, the activities of African Christian communities and leaders, and the consolidation of South Africa into a unitary state in 1910. The rise to prominence of the *amakholwa* (African Christians) intensified the contestation over the Zulu monarchy's symbolic representation. While *kholwa* leaders found new political relevance in allying with the Zulu royal family, the new segregationist state attempted to appropriate the monarchy for its own policies: In 1916, for example, Solomon kaDinuzulu was given recognition as the paramount of *uSuthu*—the term used to identify Zulu royalists since Cetshwayo's time. These *kholwa* cultural entrepreneurs were also instrumental in the growth of isiZulu LITERATURE and its cultural revival during the 1920s and the 1930s. For instance, JOHN DUBE established the bilingual newspaper *Ilanga lase Natal* in 1903, while Magema M. Fuze published the first historical book written in Zulu, *Abantu Abamnyama Lapa Bavela Ngakona*, in 1922. The founding of cultural and self-help organizations such as the Inkatha kaZulu in 1924 is further proof of the growing links between the Zulu elite and the Zulu monarchy, and the desire on the part of the *kholwa* to construct a modern interpretation of Zulu history and culture while also contributing to the emerging nationalist movements and organizations.

The Inkatha of 1924 should not be confused with the Inkatha established in 1975 by MANGOSUTHU BUTHELEZI under different political circumstances. Although Buthelezi's Inkatha claimed to stand for a nonviolent and a gradualist opposition to APARTHEID, the violence of the 1990s and the scandalous revelations of the NATIONAL PARTY's sponsorship of the Inkatha's activities entrenched the image that it was essentially an ethnonationalist movement defined by a federalist political agenda. Its relative success in national and provincial ELECTIONS has meant that the INKATHA FREEDOM PARTY (IFP), as it is now called, has continued to be a recognizable political player in South African politics even though it has not achieved its federalist ambitions.

Today, Zulu constitute just less than 25 percent of South Africa's population and are the largest ethnic and linguistic group in the country. Given their numbers, it is not surprising that many key political and business figures in South Africa are Zulu, including the president of the country, JACOB ZUMA (elected in 2009). The majority of Zulu live in KwaZulu-Natal Province although many have migrated to Johannesburg and the surrounding areas of Gauteng Province. Zulu have also taken up leading positions within the economy.

See also CETSHWAYO; MFECANE; SHAKA

Bibliography

Duminy, Andrew, and Bill Guest. *Natal and Zululand from Earliest Times to 1910: A New History*. Pietermaritzburg, South Africa: University of Natal Press, 1989.

Etherington, Norman. *The Great Treks: The Transformation of Southern Africa, 1815–1854*. Harlow, UK: Pearson Education Limited, 2001.

Fuze, Magema M. *The Black People and Whence They Came: A Zulu View*. Pietermaritzburg, South Africa: University of Natal Press, 1998.

Guy, Jeff. *The Destruction of the Zulu Kingdom: The Civil War in Zululand, 1879–1884*. London: Longman, 1979.

———. *The View Across the River: Harriette Colenso and the Zulu Struggle Against Imperialism*. Cape Town, South Africa: David Philip, 2001.

Hamilton, Carolyn. *Terrific Majesty: The Powers of Shaka Zulu and the Limits of Historical Invention*. Cape Town, South Africa: David Philip, 1998.

La Hausse de Lalouvière, Paul. *Restless Identities: Signatures of Nationalism, Zulu Ethnicity, and History in the Lives of Petros Lamula (c. 1881–1948) and Lymon Maling (c. 1889–1936)*. Pietermaritzburg, South Africa: University of Natal Press, 2000.

Wylie, Dan. *Myth of Iron: Shaka in History*. Scottsville, South Africa: University of KwaZulu-Natal Press, 2006.

—Hlonipha Mokoena

Zuma, Jacob Gedleyihlekisa (1942–)

Jacob Gedleyihlekisa Zuma is the president of South Africa (2009–) and the president of the ruling party, AFRICAN NATIONAL CONGRESS (ANC). He was inaugurated as the country's president on May 9, 2009, after the ANC won the April 2009 ELECTIONS with approximately 65 percent of the votes. Having a long and sometimes controversial history in South African politics, Zuma previously served as deputy president to President THABO MBEKI from 1999 to 2005.

Zuma was born on April 12, 1942, in Inkandla, located in the then NATAL Province. He was raised by his widowed mother, as his father died before he was born. Due to his family's dire economic circumstances, Zuma did not receive any formal education and started working odd jobs to supplement his mother's income when he was fifteen. He joined the ANC in 1959 when he was seventeen years old, influenced by a family member who was an active trade unionist. Three years later, in 1962, Zuma became an active member of the ANC's militant wing, Umkhonto we Sizwe, at the age of twenty. Like many ANC activists, he was eventually convicted in 1963 for attempting to overthrow the APARTHEID government and was sentenced to ten years in prison on ROBBEN ISLAND with NELSON MANDELA, among others.

After serving his prison term, Zuma left South Africa in 1975 to continue the ANC's armed struggles. He first went to SWAZILAND and then to MOZAMBIQUE. In 1977, Zuma became a member of his party's Executive Committee. After the Mozambican government signed the Nkomati Accord with the apartheid South African government in 1984, Zuma became his party's chief representative, as he was one of the few activists who remained in Mozambique to carry out the ANC's activities. The Nkomati Accord prohibited the Mozambican government from providing logistical support to the ANC and other liberation movements fighting the apartheid regime. In return, the apartheid state agreed to withdraw its support from the rebel group Renamo that was fighting a civil war against the Mozambican government. Neither side entirely held up their end of the deal, but it did make it more difficult for the ANC to launch operations from Mozambique. Zuma left Mozambique for Zambia in January 1987 after the apartheid government exerted strong pressures on the Mozambican government to stop providing sanctuaries for ANC activists. When the government lifted the ban on the ANC in 1990, Zuma returned home and took part in the negotiations to end apartheid and establish democratic rule in South Africa.

In the same year, he was elected as the ANC chairperson of the Southern Natal Region at this party's first regional congress. In that position, Zuma took a leading role in stopping the region's political violence and formed peace agreements with the ZULU-based INKATHA FREEDOM PARTY (IFP). In 1991, he became the ANC's deputy secretary-general during the first ANC National Conference, and in 1994 he became a member of the Executive Committee of Economic Affairs and Tourism for the KwaZulu-Natal provincial government after the country's first nationwide democratic ELECTIONS. As a member of this department, his main contribution was establishing the KwaZulu-Natal Reconstruction and Development Project Bursary Fund to help educate the poor population residing in the rural areas. Zuma was also elected as both the ANC national chairperson and as the chairperson of the organization's KwaZulu-Natal regional branch.

Two years later in 1996, he was reelected as the chair of the ANC's KwaZulu-Natal branch, and in December 1997, he became the party's deputy president. After the ANC's victory in the 1999 national elections, Zuma became South Africa's deputy president. In this position, he worked with Yoweri Museveni, the Ugandan president, to help facilitate the peace process in Burundi. Although Zuma became deputy president in 1999, President Mbeki released him of his duties in 2005 after Zuma's financial adviser, Schabir Shaik, was convicted of corruption and fraud. Zuma resigned from his post as a member of PARLIAMENT. Shortly after Shaik's conviction, Zuma himself was formally charged with corruption by the country's National Prosecuting Authority, but the charge was dismissed in September 2006 on the basis of insufficient evidence. A second corruption charge related to the handling of an arms deal between the South African government and a French arms manufacturer was filed against him in 2007. Again the charges were dismissed against him due to lack of evidence.

Zuma continued to remain in the MEDIA spotlight because the daughter of a deceased ANC comrade filed a rape charge against him in 2005. However, like the two corruption charges, this too was subsequently dismissed. Despite being acquitted, Zuma's rape trial generated a storm of controversy in South Africa and across the world because, even though he was the head of the country's National AIDS Council, he admitted to having unprotected sex with his accuser, who was HIV-positive.

Despite serious setbacks, Zuma managed to rebuild his political career after being ousted. Although Zuma's personal and ethical compass has frequently been questioned in both the national and the international media, he maintains a broad popular following among South Africa's electorate. In addition to his strong following of Zulu supporters, Zuma also has strong political support from both the SOUTH AFRICAN COMMUNIST PARTY and from the CONGRESS OF SOUTH AFRICAN TRADE UNIONS. While his government's overall agenda is very much in line with his predecessor's, Zuma began his presidency promising faster progress on key social and economic goals, including housing and job creation. He also promised greater accountability and efficiency within government, and he asked each of his ministers to sign a Service Delivery Agreement that outlined the specific targets and objectives they agreed to meet for the upcoming year.

Zuma has received several awards and honors, including the Nelson Mandela Award for Outstanding Leadership in 1998, an honorary doctorate of literature from the UNIVERSITY OF FORT HARE in 2001, another honorary doctorate of administration from Zululand University in the same year, and a third honorary doctorate of philosophy from the Medical University of Southern Africa, also in the same year.

APPENDIX 1
CHRONOLOGY

3.5 million B.C. It is estimated that the earliest hominids live in southern Africa.

1.95–1.78 million B.C. Early hominids (*Australopithecus sediba*) live on southern African Highveld.

120,000 B.C. Anatomically modern humans (homo sapiens sapiens) leave footprints along the shore of Langebaan Lagoon north of what is now CAPE TOWN.

80,000–70,000 B.C. Early humans create items of personal adornment at Blombos Cave site at tip of South Africa.

2000 B.C. KHOIKHOI herders reach the southern tip of Africa. (By 1300 A.D., Khoikhoi would dominate the southern and southwestern regions of what would be known as the CAPE COLONY.)

200–500 A.D. Early Iron Age people, regarded as ancestors of Bantu-speaking people in southern Africa, settle in what is now Limpopo Province, followed by Bantu-speaking people settling in what are now KwaZulu-Natal, Transkei, and South Africa's Highveld (around JOHANNESBURG).

800–1400 Nguni-speaking people (NDEBELE, SWAZI, XHOSA, and ZULU) establish large farming communities mainly along the southeastern seaboard and the Drakensberg mountain range, between what is now KwaZulu-Natal Province and LESOTHO.

Ca. 1050–1270 The MAPUNGUBWE Kingdom is established, covering parts of what is now South Africa, ZIMBABWE, and Botswana.

1300–1500 SOTHO-TSWANA—a Bantu-speaking group—populate the Highveld.

1488 Portuguese seafarers, aiming to find a sea route to trade in India, round the southern tip of the African continent.

1497 Portuguese set foot on South African soil at St. Helena Bay on the west coast and first see the Khoikhoi, described by the captain of the expedition as "tawny colored." Over the next 100 years, the Portuguese both establish basic trade relations and set off violent clashes with the Khoikhoi.

1652 The DUTCH EAST INDIA COMPANY establishes a small, armed settlement at the Cape of Good Hope.

1653 The first slaves are imported from Batavia (Indonesia) and Angola.

1659 The Dutch defeat the Khoikhoi in the first of a series of wars over land and cattle as well as control of the Khoikhoi labor that last, intermittently, through the end of the eighteenth century.

Ca. 1670 The Zulu royal line is founded.

Ca. 1675 Tshawe founds the Xhosa Kingdom.

1685 To counter growing Dutch-slave unions, marriages between Dutch settlers and female slaves are prohibited.

1779–1781 The first of the FRONTIER WARS between the Xhosa and the Cape Colony initiates a century of intermittent warfare in the eastern Cape Colony.

1794 Tuan Guru, an Indonesian political exile, establishes the first Muslim place of worship in South Africa, in central Cape Town.

1795–1803 The British take over Cape Colony as a result of the Napoleonic Wars in Europe.

1803–1806 Dutch Batavian Republic rules the Cape Colony.

1806 The British take over Cape Colony.

1807 Britain bans the slave trade, but it is still legal to own slaves.

1809 Colonial authorities introduce a pass system that regulates the free movement of the few "free blacks."

1810–1820 Sobhuza founds Swazi state, which is the precursor of today's SWAZILAND.

1816–1828 SHAKA creates the Zulu Kingdom.

1820 Some 5,000 English settlers arrive and settle on land seized from the Xhosa.

1820s MOSHOESHOE founds the Sotho Kingdom, which in time becomes the modern country of Lesotho.

1821 MZILIKAZI breaks with Shaka and forms the Ndebele state, first on the Highveld and then in Zimbabwe.

1834 The English colonial authorities abolish SLAVERY in the Cape Colony.

1835–1840 Approximately 10,000 BOER farmers and their families leave the Cape Colony on the GREAT TREK and encroach on land of African farming communities.

1836 Boer settlers defeat the Zulu army at the BATTLE OF BLOOD RIVER. Their victory bolsters white claims of divine providence.

1839 The first whites-only Boer republic—that of Natalia—is established on Zulu land. (In 1843, the British annex Natalia to form the NATAL Colony.) The Boer Republic of the Orange Free State (in 1854) as well as the South African Republic (1857) follow.

1852, 1854 Britain recognizes the Transvaal and the Orange Free State as independent states.

1856–1857 Xhosa cattle-killing associated with NONGQAWUSE, which effectively ended Xhosa independence.

1860 INDIAN laborers are imported to work on sugar plantations in the Natal Colony.

1867 DIAMONDS are discovered near KIMBERLEY in what is now the Northern Cape Province.

1868 Britain annexes Basutoland (Lesotho).

1877 Britain annexes the Transvaal.

1877–1879 Ninth and last Frontier War between the Xhosa and the Cape Colony.

1878–1879 British defeat PEDI Kingdom, ending its independence.

1879 ANGLO-ZULU WAR ends Zulu independence.

1880 Jews, fleeing persecution from anti-Semitism in Eastern Europe and Tsarist pogroms, arrive in South Africa. By 1930, the Jewish community numbers more than 40,000 people.

1880–1881 Transvaal regains independence in a brief war.

1885 Britain creates the Bechuanaland Protectorate, which today is Botswana.

1886 Gold is discovered near Johannesburg, creating a need for cheap labor on the mines and causing struggles over ownership and control of minerals.

1894–1899 Swaziland is a protectorate of the Transvaal Republic.

1899–1902 The ANGLO-BOER WAR, termed "the white man's war," is fought between British colonial and Boer/AFRIKANER guerrillas. British defeat Afrikaners and hold Boer women and children in concentration camps.

1902 Britain establishes a protectorate over Swaziland.

1904 White city council of Johannesburg begins eviction of black people from the central city.

1910 The UNION OF SOUTH AFRICA is formed out of the existing British territories and the defeated white Afrikaner republics. Blacks have few political and social rights in the new union. Basutoland, Bechuanaland, and Swaziland remain under direct British control as High Commission Territories.

1912 The South African Native National Congress is formed in BLOEMFONTEIN. In 1923 it is renamed the AFRICAN NATIONAL CONGRESS (ANC).

1913 The NATIVES' LAND ACT, expanded in 1936, results in white control of 80 percent of arable land.

1914–1918 South Africa participates in World War I as part of the British Empire.

1914 JAMES BARRY MUNNIK HERTZOG founds the NATIONAL PARTY.

1915 South Africa occupies neighboring German colony, German South West Africa; retains control of the colony as a Trust Territory under auspices of the League of Nations.

1921 The Communist Party of South Africa (later the SOUTH AFRICAN COMMUNIST PARTY) is formed. By 1924, on the insistence of the Soviet Union, the party commits itself to black political liberation.

1922 The RAND REVOLT, involving white workers in Johannesburg region, is suppressed by government troops.

1924 The National Party defeats JAN CHRISTIAAN SMUTS and the South African Party to become ruling party.

1933 In wake of the depression, Hertzog and Smuts unite to form a "fusion government" and ultimately the United Party.

1934 D. F. MALAN leaves the National Party.

1939–1945 South Africa participates in World War II as one of the Allies, which helps foment Afrikaner nationalism.

1944 AFRICAN NATIONAL CONGRESS YOUTH LEAGUE founded.

1946 African miners strike; crushed by the army.

1948 The National Party wins parliamentary elections and institutes APARTHEID policy.

1950 The new government passes a series of laws to make apartheid legal. The main acts prohibit sexual relations and adultery between the different races, codifies racial differences, enforces residential segregation, and strips people of their citizenship.

1952 The ANC and its allies announce the nationwide DEFIANCE CAMPAIGNS to openly defy apartheid laws and campaign for nonviolent disobedience. Some 100,000 people take part in protests, and 8,000 are arrested.

1953 SOPHIATOWN, a black neighborhood in Johannesburg, is declared a white group area. By 1963, all the original black residents are forcibly removed to black townships.

1955 The FREEDOM CHARTER, a blueprint for a postapartheid government and society, is adopted in Johannesburg by the ANC and its allies.

1956 In the TREASON TRIAL the government charges 156 members of the political opposition with treason, leading to a trial lasting until 1961; all defendants are found not guilty.

1958 HENDRIK VERWOERD becomes South African prime minister.

1959 Disaffected ANC members form the PAN AFRICANIST CONGRESS.

1960 In the SHARPEVILLE MASSACRE, outside Johannesburg, police kill 69 demonstrators and wound 150 others protesting against the PASS LAWS, which restrict black movement.

ANC president ALBERT LUTHULI is awarded the Nobel Peace Prize.

1961 Following criticism of its racist policy, South Africa leaves the British Commonwealth and becomes a republic.

The now-banned ANC forms an armed wing, Umkhonto we Sizwe (Spear of the Nation), and attacks government installations.

1963 Looksmart Ngudle, an ANC activist, becomes the first person to die in police detention.

1964 During the RIVONIA TRIAL, NELSON MANDELA, GOVAN MBEKI, WALTER SISULU, and five others are sentenced to life in prison. The black prisoners are transferred to ROBBEN ISLAND, off Cape Town.

1966 A COLOURED parliamentary worker assassinates Prime Minister HENDRIK FRENSCH VERWOERD, who is succeeded by John Vorster.

The government forcibly removes residents of DISTRICT SIX, a mixed area in central Cape Town.

1966–1968 Lesotho, Botswana, and Swaziland gain independence.

1967 Medical student STEVE BIKO forms the University Christian Movement, which becomes the basis for the BLACK CONSCIOUSNESS MOVEMENT.

1973 Black workers in DURBAN hold a major strike over employment conditions.

1975 MOZAMBIQUE and Angola gain independence and declare their support for the ANC.

The Zulu nationalist movement, the INKATHA FREEDOM PARTY, is founded by Chief MANGOSUTHU BUTHELEZI.

1976 In the SOWETO STUDENT UPRISING, black students protest against Afrikaans as the language of instruction in schools in SOWETO, outside of Johannesburg. Police murder over 500 protesters as protests spread countrywide.

1977 Steve Biko is murdered in police custody.

1978 Prime Minister Vorster retires and is succeeded by P. W. Botha, the minister of defense.

1979 The government legalizes black trade unions.

1980 Zimbabwe gains its independence from whites-only rule.

1982 Apartheid death squads murder activist HELOISE RUTH FIRST, who was living in exile in Mozambique. First is a key ANC and Communist Party activist and wife of JOE SLOVO.

A Johannesburg trade unionist, Niel Aggett, is the first white detainee to die in police custody.

1983 The government introduces a new Constitution, which would reform, but not abolish apartheid.

The UNITED DEMOCRATIC FRONT (UDF), a coalition of more than 500 antiapartheid organizations that openly side with the ANC, is formed to oppose the reforms.

1984 REVEREND DESMOND MPILO TUTU, a cleric and UDF activist, is awarded the Nobel Peace Prize.

1985 The CONGRESS OF SOUTH AFRICAN TRADE UNIONS is formed.

The government declares a countrywide state of emergency, resulting in arrests, detentions, and MEDIA restrictions.

1987 The government, under pressure to reform, abolishes the Mixed Marriages Act and pass laws.

A small group of white South African businessmen and intellectuals meet with the ANC outside South Africa, in an effort to see if a power-sharing deal could be negotiated between the black liberation movement and the apartheid regime, and if white economic interests would be protected under an ANC-led government. Most whites, including the apartheid government and media, denounce the meetings. However it contributes to moving both sides toward a negotiated settlement.

1988 Joint military actions by Angolan and Cuban armies defeat the South African army at Cuito Cuanavale in Angola. Subsequently, the South Africans withdraw from Angola and NAMIBIA.

1989 P. W. Botha meets in his office with Nelson Mandela, who is still a prisoner.

Botha has a stroke and is replaced by F. W. DE KLERK as National Party leader and state president.

1990 Namibia becomes independent on New Year's Day.

De Klerk announces the release of ANC leader Mandela and the lifting of the thirty-year ban on the ANC, Communist Party, and twenty-eight other political organizations.

Mandela walks from jail a free man. He had served twenty-seven years in prison.

The ANC and government begin political negotiations for a new government and CONSTITUTION. Political exiles begin to return to South Africa. In late 1990, the ANC announces that it will suspend its armed struggle against the government, and the government frees more than 3,000 political prisoners.

1991 South African writer NADINE GORDIMER is awarded the Nobel Prize for Literature.

1993 Popular ANC leader CHRIS HANI is murdered by white right-wing activists.

Mandela and de Klerk are jointly awarded the Nobel Peace Prize.

1994 South Africa holds its first democratic ELECTIONS. The ANC wins with a clear majority and Mandela becomes president. The ANC forms a Government of National Unity and gives cabinet seats to National Party and Inkatha Freedom Party representatives.

1995 The TRUTH AND RECONCILIATION COMMISSION, with Desmond Tutu as chair, is established to investigate human rights abuses perpetrated during the apartheid era.

The death penalty is declared unconstitutional and is abolished.

1996 The country's new Constitution, which contains a BILL OF RIGHTS, becomes law.

Eugene de Kock, the commander of an apartheid government counterinsurgency unit that had killed scores of antiapartheid activists, is sentenced to 212 years in jail.

1997 Approximately 8,000 amnesty applications, mostly from former ANC or Pan Africanist Congress operatives, are received by the Truth and Reconciliation Commission. As the hearings continue and evidence is gathered, senior government officials, including Botha and de Klerk, face allegations of being involved in unlawful activity.

1998 AIDS activists found the TREATMENT ACTION CAMPAIGN in Cape Town.

1999 Mandela retires from politics. His successor, THABO MBEKI, leads the ANC to a decisive election victory.

2000 At the Thirteenth International AIDS Conference held in Durban, President Mbeki publicly questions conventional science on AIDS. At the time, at least one in ten South Africans are HIV-positive.

2003 Novelist J. M. COETZEE is awarded the Nobel Prize for Literature.

2004 South Africa celebrates its first decade of democratic rule. The ANC wins democratic elections and Mbeki is elected to his second term as president.

2005 President Mbeki fires his deputy president, JACOB ZUMA, over corruption allegations.

Jacob Zuma is charged with raping a woman but, after a court trial, is acquitted of the charges.

2007 Jacob Zuma is elected ANC president.

2008 Xenophobic attacks against non–South African, African migrants in May leave sixty-two dead and thousands homeless.

Thabo Mbeki resigns as South African president, and KGALEMA MOTLANTHE, member of PARLIAMENT and the ANC's general secretary, is installed as interim president until the April 2009 elections.

2009 The ANC wins the April elections. Jacob Zuma is inaugurated as the country's president.

2010 South Africa successfully hosts the WORLD CUP, the first time in its eighty-year history that the World Cup is held on the African continent.

Sources: South African History Online, sahistory.org.za; South African Government Communication and Information System, gcis.gov.za; Nigel Worden, *The Making of Modern South Africa: Conquest, Segregation and Apartheid* (Oxford, UK: Blackwell, 1994).

APPENDIX 2
HEADS OF STATE SINCE 1910

Prime Minister	Years in Office	Party Affiliation
Louis Botha	May 1910–August 1919	South African Party
Jan Christiaan Smuts	September 1919–June 1924	South African Party
James Barry Hertzog	June 1924–September 1939	National/United Party
Jan Christiaan Smuts	September 1939–June 1948	United Party
Daniel Francois Malan	June 1948–November 1954	National Party
Johannes Gerhardus Strijdom	November 1954–August 1958	National Party
Hendrik Frensch Verwoerd	September 1958–September 1966	National Party
Balthazar Johannes Vorster	September 1966–September 1978	National Party
Pieter Willem Botha	September 1978–September 1984	National Party

President	Years in Office	Party Affiliation
Charles Roberts Swart	May 1961– June 1967	National Party
T. E. Donges	May 1967–June 1967	National Party
Jozua Francois Naude	June 1967–April 1968	National Party
Jacobus Johannes Fouchè	April 1968–April 1975	National Party
Johannes de Klerk	April 1975–April 1975	National Party
Nicolaas Johannes Diederichs	April 1975–August 1978	National Party
Marais Viljoen	August 1978–October 1978	National Party
Balthazar Johannes Vorster	October 1978–June 1979	National Party
Marais Viljoen	June 1979–September 1984	National Party
Pieter Willem Botha	September 1984–August 1989	National Party
Frederik Willem de Klerk	September 1989–May 1994	National Party
Nelson Rolihlahla Mandela	May 1994–June 1999	African National Congress
Thabo Mvuyelwa Mbeki	June 1999–September 2008	African National Congress
Kgalema Motlanthe	September 2008–May 2009	African National Congress
Jacob Zuma	May 2009–	African National Congress

APPENDIX 3
GOVERNMENT STRUCTURES

South Africa is a constitutional democracy, meaning that all laws and actions by the government must be in accordance with the 1996 Constitution. The Constitution outlines the powers, functions, and responsibilities of the three branches of government: the executive, the legislature, and the judiciary.

The executive operates at both a national and provincial level. At the national level, the executive consists of the president, deputy president, and cabinet. In the nine provinces, premiers and their executive councils also form part of the executive. The rest of the executive is composed of the various government departments and civil servants. The executive runs the country and makes policy. It cannot make laws but can recommend that the legislature pass laws.

Presidential terms are for five years and are limited to two terms. Presidents can, however, be removed by a vote of the legislature. The president acts as head of state and commander-in-chief of the country's defense forces. Other functions of the president include appointing judges (in consultation with a Judicial Services Commission), appointing and chairing the cabinet, or declaring "a state of national defense" (equal to a state of emergency). The deputy president performs a largely ceremonial role.

The judiciary consists of the Constitutional Court (the country's highest court situated in Johannesburg), the Supreme Court of Appeal (seated in Bloemfontein in the Free State Province), the thirteen high courts distributed among the nine provinces, Magistrate Courts, and various other courts (labor court, electoral court, and small claims court, among others).

At the national level, the legislature consists of a lower house, the National Assembly (currently 400 members), and a National Council of Provinces (NCOP) (consisting of 90 members dividing equally among the nine provinces). The NCOP aims to ensure provincial representation in national affairs. Seats in both houses of parliament are decided proportionally and based on general election results. A Speaker presides over the National Assembly and a Chairperson over the NCOP. Since 1994, the African National Congress has enjoyed comfortable majorities in both houses. There are nine provincial legislatures.

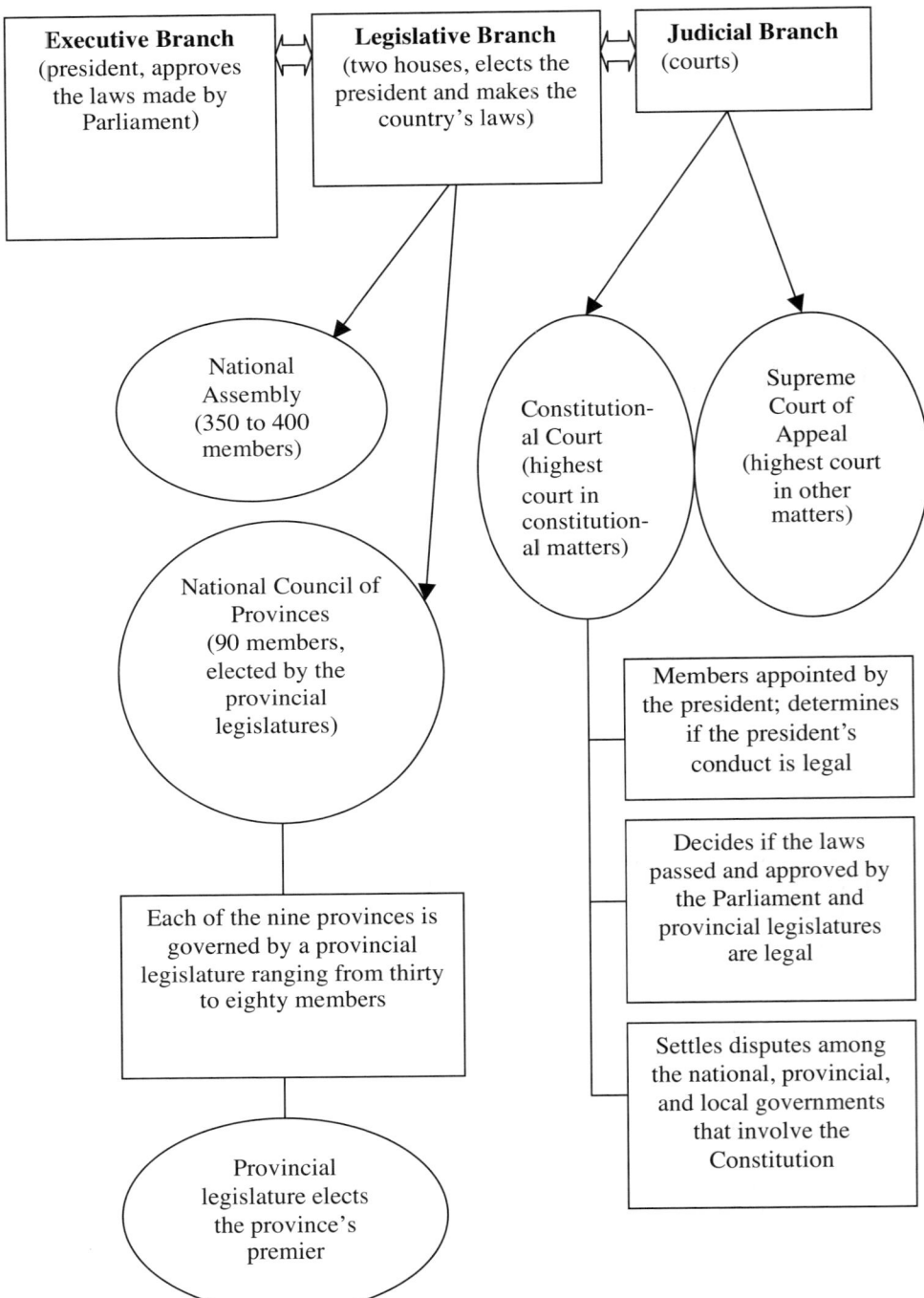

APPENDIX 4
PROVINCES AND MAJOR CITIES

Provinces	Population	Provincial Capitals
Eastern Cape	6,743,800	Bisho
Free State	2,824,500	Bloemfontein
Gauteng	11,191,700	Johannesburg
KwaZulu-Natal	10,645,400	Pietermaritzburg
Limpopo	5,439,600	Polokwane
Mpumalanga	3,617,600	Nelspruit
Northern Cape	1,103,900	Kimberley
North West	3,200,900	Mafikeng
Western Cape	5,223,900	Cape Town
Total Population	49,991,300	

Major Cities (Metropolitan Municipalities)	Population
Cape Town	3,497,097
Durban/eThekwini	3,468,086
Johannesburg	3,888,180
Port Elizabeth/Nelson Mandela Bay	1,050,930
Tshwane	2,345,908

Source: Statistics South Africa, *Mid-year Population Estimates 2010* and *Community Survey 2007*, StatsOnline, www.statssa.gov.za.

APPENDIX 5
POLITICAL PARTIES IN THE APRIL 2009 NATIONAL ELECTIONS

Political Party	Percentage of Votes Received
A Party	0.02
African Christian Democratic Party (ACDP)	0.81
African National Congress (ANC)	65.90
African People's Convention (APC)	0.20
Al Jama-Ah	0.15
Alliance of Free Democrats (AFD)	0.03
Azanian People's Organization (AZAPO)	0.22
Christian Democratic Alliance (CDA)	0.07
Congress of the People (COPE)	7.42
Democratic Alliance (DA)	16.66
Great Kongress of South Africa (GKSA)	0.05
Independent Democrats (ID)	0.92
Inkatha Freedom Party (IFP)	4.55
Keep It Straight and Simple (KISS)	0.03
Minority Front (MF)	0.25
Movement Democratic Party (MDP)	0.17
National Democratic Convention (NADECO)	0.06
New Vision Party (NVP)	0.05
Pan Africanist Congress of Azania (PAC)	0.27
Pan Africanist Movement (PAM)	0.03
South African Democratic Congress (SADECO)	0.03
United Christian Democratic Party (UCDP)	0.37
United Democratic Movement (UDM)	0.85
United Independent Front (UIF)	0.05
Vryheidsfront Plus (Freedom Front Plus)	0.83
Women Forward (WF)	0.03

Source: Independent Electoral Commission (IEC), www.elections.org.za.

APPENDIX 6
KEY RACIAL AND APARTHEID LEGISLATION, 1856–1967

1856–1910 The **Masters and Servants Acts** made breaching of employment contracts, desertion, insolence, drunkenness, negligence, and strikes criminal offenses. Even though these laws on paper applied to everyone, in reality, they were geared toward unskilled employment, which were mostly held by the blacks.

1913 The **Natives' Land Act** proscribed blacks from owning or renting land outside of the designated reserves, which constituted around 7 percent of South Africa's lands.

1923 The **Native Urban Areas Act** made each local authority responsible for the black population in its area as well as divided the country into both urban and nonurban areas. It also strictly controlled movements between these two areas.

1927 The **Immorality Act** prohibited extramarital sexual relations between blacks and whites. This act was amended and expanded in 1950 to include both the coloured and Asian populations.

1927 The **Native Administration Act** stated that all movable property belonging to a black and allotted by him or accruing under black law or custom to any woman with whom he lived in a customary union, or to any house, shall upon his death devolve and be administered under black law and custom.

1936 The **Native Land and Trust Act** expanded the country's black reserves from 7 percent to 13.6 percent of the country's land. It also authorized the Department of Bantu Administration and Development to eliminate black-owned lands that were surrounded by white-owned territories.

1949 The **Prohibition of Mixed Marriages Act** banned marriages between whites and nonwhites.

1950 The **Population Registration Act** required people to be identified and registered from birth as belonging to a distinct racial group: white, Bantu (also referred to as black, Native, and/or African), and coloured (which was further subcategorized into Cape Malay, Griqua, Indian, Chinese, and Cape Coloured). In 1959, Asian was added as a fourth category, referring primarily to those descended from the Indian subcontinent.

1950 The **Group Areas Act** forced all South Africans to live in areas designated for their racial group. It was progressively amended to clarify the plan of geographical, racial planning.

1950 The **Suppression of Communism Amendment Act** dealt with situations where people conspired to overthrow the government, assisted those who intended to overthrow the government, or committed terrorist acts against the government. It was aimed at halting the influence of the South African Communist Party, initially on the Afrikaner working class and later on the African working class. The act further vested the minister of justice with power to restrict or ban any person he viewed to be pursuing Communist activities. A banned person was confined to a particular district and was precluded from occupying an office in any trade union or political organization. He or she was also prohibited from attending political gatherings. The act was progressively amended and made more concise in 1951, 1954, and yearly from 1962 to 1968.

1951 The **Bantu Authorities Act** recognized the country's traditional tribal authorities and established tribal, regional, and territorial authorities in the black reserves.

1953 The **Bantu Education Act** formalized the segregation of education. Specifically pertaining to blacks, it did away with mission education, transferring the responsibilities to the state, and laid the foundation for Bantu education.

1953 The **Bantu Labor Relations Regulation Act** (also referred to as the **Natives Settlement of Disputes Act**) amended the 1937 Industrial Conciliation Act by changing the definition of "employee" to exclude blacks in order to prevent them from registering as union members. Stopping short of outlawing black unions, this act ensured that union organizing would be racially segregated. This law also incorporated the 1942 War Measure, which banned strikes waged by black workers.

1953 The **Public Safety Act** allowed the government to declare a state of emergency and gave both the minister of law and order and the South African police commissioner authority to detain anyone for the reasons of public safety.

1953 The **Reservation of Separate Amenities Act** allowed public facilities and transport to be reserved for particular racial groups.

1954 The **Riotous Assemblies and Criminal Laws Amendment Act** empowered the minister of justice to proscribe blacklisted individuals from becoming members of specific antiapartheid or political organizations, or from attending particular political meetings.

1954 The **Natives Resettlement Act** established a resettlement board that would remove blacks from townships, targeted in particular toward Sophiatown and other black suburbs of Johannesburg that had been designated white areas.

1959 The **Extension of University Education Act** empowered the minister of Bantu education to designate colleges for specified African ethnic groups. It also prohibited black students from attending the University of Cape Town or the University of Witwatersrand without a permit.

1959 The **Promotion of Bantu Self-Government Act** was an extension of the Bantu Authorities Act of 1951. It set up eight distinct "bantu homelands" from the existing native reserves and granted each a degree of self-government. It further created a hierarchy of authority for the black local reserves, incorporating headmen, chiefs, paramount chiefs, and territorial authorities in a progressive chain of power.

1960 The **Unlawful Organizations Act** outlawed organizations perceived as threats to public order and safety. It also immediately banned both the African National Congress and the Pan Africanist Congress.

1964 The **Bantu Labour Act** prohibited Africans from seeking work in urban areas or employers from hiring them unless they were channeled through the state labor bureau.

1967 The **Terrorism Act** prohibited any acts of terrorism, very broadly defined, as well as recruitment for military training, and authorized the indefinite detention of an individual without trial based on a vague definition of terrorism, which included most crimes.

Source: South African History Online, www.sahistory.org.za.

Acronyms

AAC	All-African Convention	CODESA	Convention for a Democratic South Africa
AAM	antiapartheid movement		
ABSA	Amalgamated Banks of South Africa	COPE	Congress of the People
		COSAS	Congress of South African Students
ACT UP	AIDS Coalition to Unleash Power		
AIDS	acquired immune deficiency syndrome	COSATU	Congress of South African Trade Unions
AEC	Anti-Eviction Campaign	CP	Conservative Party
ALP	AIDS Law Project	CPSA	Communist Party of South Africa
ANC	African National Congress	CUSA	Council of Unions of South Africa
ANCWL	African National Congress Women's League	DA	Democratic Alliance
		DoH	Department of Health
ANCYL	African National Congress Youth League	DP	Democratic Party
		DRC	Dutch Reformed Church
APO	African Political Organization	FET	Further Education and Training
ARV	antiretroviral	FOSATU	Federation of South African Trade Unions
AU	African Union		
AWB	Afrikaner Weerstandsbeweging	GDP	gross domestic product
AZAPO	Azanian People's Organization	GEAR	Growth, Employment, and Redistribution Strategy
BCM	Black Consciousness Movement		
BEE	Black Economic Empowerment	GET	General Education and Training
BPA	Black Parents' Association	GNU	Government of National Unity
BPC	Black People's Convention	HIV	human immunodeficiency virus
BSAC	British South Africa Company	ICU	Industrial and Commercial Workers Union
CGE	Commission for Gender Equality		

IDAF	International Defence and Aid Fund
IDASA	Institute for a Democratic South Africa
IEC	Independent Electoral Commission
IFP	Inkatha Freedom Party
ISL	International Socialist League
JMC	Joint Monitoring Committee on Improving the Quality of Life and Status of Women
LPM	Landless Peoples Movement
MAP	Millennium Africa Programme
MDM	Mass Democratic Movement
MK	Umkhonto we Sizwe
MP	member of Parliament
NACOSA	National AIDS Convention of South Africa
NACTU	National Council of Trade Unions
NDR	National Democratic Revolution
NECC	National Education Crisis/ Coordinating Committee
NEPAD	New Partnership for Africa's Development
NEUM	Non-European Unity Movement
NF	National Forum
NIC	Natal Indian Congress
NNP	New National Party
NP	National Party
NRC	Natives Representative Council
NSC	National Sports Congress
NUSAS	National Union of South African Students
OAU	Organization of African Unity
OSW	Office of the Status of Women
PAC	Pan Africanist Congress
PAGAD	People Against Gangsterism and Drugs
PANSALB	Pan South African Language Board
PLWHAs	people living with HIV/AIDS
RDP	Reconstruction and Development Program
SABC	South African Broadcasting Corporation
SACBOC	South African Cricket Board of Control
SACC	South African Council of Churches
SACOS	South African Council on Sport
SACP	South African Communist Party
SACPO	South African Coloured People's Organization
SACU	South African Cricket Union
SAIC	South African Indian Congress
SANCO	South African National Civics Organization
SANEF	South African National Editors' Forum
SANGOCO	South African Non-governmental Organization Coalition
SASM	South African Students' Movement
SASO	South African Student Organization
SECC	Soweto Electricity Crisis Committee
SSRC	Soweto Students' Representative Council
SWA	South West Africa
SWAPO	South West Africa People's Organization
TAC	Treatment Action Campaign
TBVC	Transkei, Bophutatswana, Venda, and Ciskei
TEC	Transitional Executive Committee
TRC	Truth and Reconciliation Commission
UCT	University of Cape Town
UDF	United Democratic Front
UDM	United Democratic Movement
UNISA	University of South Africa
VOC	Vereenigde Oost-Indische Compagnie (Dutch East India Company)
WBI	Women's Budget Initiative
WCC	World Council of Churches
WNC	Women's National Coalition

The Contributors

Adhikari, Mohamed
University of Cape Town

Alexander, Neville
University of Cape Town

Andrews, Penelope
City University of New York

Ansell, Gwen
Author and freelance writer

Baderoon, Gabeba
Penn State University

Baines, Gary
Rhodes University

Barchiesi, Franco
Ohio State University

Bassett, Carolyn
York University

Berger, Jonathan
Section 27/AIDS Law Project, Johannesburg

Bond, Patrick
University of KwaZulu-Natal

Booth, Douglas
University of Otago

Britton, Hannah
University of Kansas

Chen, Jau-Yon
Howard University

Chisholm, Linda
Human Sciences Research Council, Pretoria

Clarno, Andy
University of Illinois at Chicago

Coplan, Steve
Independent researcher

Crush, Jonathan
Queens University and the University of Cape Town

345

Cullinan, Kerry
Health-e News Service

Daniel, John
US study-abroad program, "Social and Political Transformation in South Africa"

Davies, Rebecca
University of Plymouth

Davis, R. Hunt
University of Florida

Decoteau, Claire Laurier
University of Illinois at Chicago

Esrig, Adam
The New School, New York

Friedman, Stephen
Rhodes University/ University of Johannesburg

Gerhart, Gail
Columbia University

Hauptfleisch, Temple
Stellenbosch University

Jeannerat, Caroline
University of Michigan

Jenkins, Catherine
School of Oriental and African Studies, University of London

Johnson, Walton R.
Rutgers University

Kinnes, Irvin
University of Cape Town

Klug, Heinz
University of Wisconsin Law School

Limb, Peter
Michigan State University

MacKinnon, Aran
University of West Georgia

Magubane, Zine
Boston College

Maharaj, Brij
University of KwaZulu-Natal

Marks, Shula
School of Oriental and African Studies, University of London

Mattes, Robert
University of Cape Town

Miller, Kari
Institute of International Education, Washington, DC

Mokoena, Hlonipha
Columbia University

Moyer, Cara
Howard University

Ndletyana, Mcebisi
Human Sciences Research Council, Pretoria

Ntsebeza, Lungisile
University of Cape Town

Patterson, Monica
University of Michigan

Pieterse, Edgar
University of Stellenbosch

Pretorius, Fransjohan
University of Pretoria

Ramsamy, Edward
Rutgers University

Redding, Sean
Amherst College

Reddy, Thiven
University of Cape Town

Ross, Robert
Leiden University

Seidman Makgetla, Neva
Development Bank of Southern Africa

Smith, Andrew B.
University of Cape Town

Van der Spuy, Elrena
University of Cape Town

Van Kessel, Ineke
Leiden University

Wasserman, Herman
Rhodes University

Williams, Christian
University of Michigan

Zuern, Elke
Sarah Lawrence College

INDEX

ABC approach to AIDS prevention, 13
Abdurahman, Abdullah, **1,** 72, 233–234
Abolition of Racially Based Land measures (1991), 219
Abolition of slavery, 268
Abraham, Peter, 180
Abu Bakr Effendi, 180
Academy Awards, 67–68, 297
Accelerated and Shared Growth Initiative for South Africa (AsgiSA), 104–105
Achmat, Abdurazzack (Zackie), **1–2**; new social movements, 221
Act of Union. *See* South Africa Act
Adams, Newton, 2
Adams College, **2**; Dube, John Langalibalele, 91; founding by Lembede, 177; Luthuli, Albert, 182
Adapt or Dye (play), 290
Adapted education, 106
Administrative control: British South Africa Company, 55–56
Affected Organizations Act (1974), 21
Affirmative action, **2**, 84; Afrikaner nationalism, 10; Cape Town coloureds' lack of trust in, 62; Durban addressing inequality, 93–94; Indians' response to, 146; women's political participation, 312
African Association, 29
African Christian Democratic Party, 133
African Cup of Nations (1996), 276
African Economic Community, 8
African Film Productions, 66
African Indian Congress, 79

African National Congress (ANC), **2–6,** 7; Afrikaners' fate under, 8; Afrikaners' tensions with, 10; All-African Convention, 16; antipathy to Biko, 33; apartheid laws, 21; armed struggle against apartheid, 24–26; AWB opposition, 11; Azania, 27; Bantu Education Act, 31; Bill of Rights advocates, 34; black press, 196; Bloemfontein origins, 37; Boesak, Allan, 38; Buthelezi, 57; Champion's presidency, 64; Civic Associations, 68; CODESA, 77; constitution and Bill of Rights, 75–76; COPE's origins in, 74; COSATU alignment, 73; Dadoo, Yusuf, 79; de Klerk and, 80–81; De Lille's criticism, 81; defiance campaigns, 80; democratic transition/negotiations, 87–88; Dube, John Langalibalele, 91; Durban's violence, 92–93; economic policy, 104; Freedom Charter, 121–122; Garveyism, 124; Ginwala's affiliation, 124; Holomisa's leadership and expulsion, 138; Ibrahim's membership, 141; IFP and, 150; Jewish-Muslim friction, 160; Leon's criticism, 178; Luthuli's leadership, 182; Matthews, Z.K., 192–193; Motlanthe's presidency, 206; mutiny, 133; National Forum and, 217; negotiated settlement, 82–83; NIC-ANC-SAIC pact, 145; 1994 elections, 113, 189; PAC split from, 237; political violence during the transition, 243–244; post–1999 politics, 83–84; power sharing, 83; protesting the Natives' Land Act, 219; race and electoral politics, 85; race and voter choice, 116–117; Ramaphosa's leadership, 256; Reconstruction and Development Program,

Note: **Boldface** page numbers indicate main entries.

349

257–258; Rivonia Trial, 259–261; Soweto Student Uprising, 275; Tambo, Oliver, 285–286; Truth and Reconciliation Commission, 293–295; Union constitution, 302; United Democratic Front, 306; voter turnout, 116; Winnie Mandela's politics, 190; Zimbabwe's connections to, 319; Zuma, Jacob, 322–323. *See also* Democratic transition/negotiations; Elections: 1994 to 2009; Reconstruction and Development Program

African National Congress Women's League, 3–4, **6**; Ginwala's contribution to, 125; Ngoyi, Lillian, 223–224; pass laws protest, 232; Sisulu, Albertina, 266; Winnie Mandela, 190

African National Congress Youth League, 4, 6, **7**; Buthelezi, Mangosuthu, 57; formation of, 186–187; Hani, Chris, 133; HIV/AIDS prevention, 12; Lembede, Anton, 177–178; Mbeki, Thabo, 194; Sisulu, Walter, 267; Sobukwe, Robert, 269–270; Tambo, Oliver, 285–286; Union opposition, 304

African nationalism, 236–237; ANC ideology, 3. *See also* Political cultures and ideologies

African Political Organization (APO), 1, 72

African Renaissance, **7–8**; AU creation, 8; Mbeki's support of, 6

African Union, **8**

Afrikaans: Afrikaner nationalism, 235; bilingual theater, 287; language policy, 169–172; origins of, 151; political cabaret, 290; sources of, 179; Soweto Student Uprising, 245, 274–275

Afrikaner Bond, 51–52, 300–301, 300–301

Afrikaner Broederbond. *See* Broederbond

Afrikaner nationalism, 10; Anglo-Boer War, 19; apartheid, 20; Bantu Education Act, 30–31; Battle of Blood River, 32–33; Broederbond, 56; Union of South Africa, 300–301; white press, 197. *See also* Political cultures and ideologies

Afrikaner Weerstandsbeweging, 286; Hani assassination, 134

Afrikanerbond, 56

Afrikaner(s), **8–10**; Anglo-Boer War, 16; Battle of Blood River, 32–33; Broederbond, 56; Cape Town, 61; Carnegie Commission findings on white poverty, 63; citizenship rights, 34; far right politics after 1999, 84; health issues, 134–135; Hertzog promoting culture, 137; Huguenots' assimilation, 139; literary traditions, 179–180; Malan, Daniel Francois, 184; music, 207; in Natal, 216; nationalism, 235–236; opposing Christian conversion of blacks, 65; paleoanthropology, 230; racial classification, 255–256; sports, 276. *See also* Apartheid; Boer(s); Great Trek; National Party

Afrikaner Weerstandsbeweging, **11**

Agriculture: British settlers, 40–41; Dutch colonialism, 97–98; land tenure and dispossession, 167; Milner's reconstruction policy, 54; precolonial period, 252–253; Retief, Piet, 258. *See also* Boer(s)

Agterryers (black henchmen), 18

AIDS, **11–16**; Achmat's activism, 1–2; Constitutional Court, 176; De Lille's criticism of ANC, 81; Durban's population decline, 93; film industry, 67; impact on education, 109; impact on health system, 136; Lesotho, 179; Mandela's involvement, 189; Mbeki questioning HIV-AIDS causal link, 5–6, 83, 195; Muslim groups, 154; Swazi, 282; Treatment Action Campaign, 2, 221, 292–293; tuberculosis and, 134

AIDS Coalition to Unleash Power (ACT UP), 292

Alexander, Neville, 217

Aliens Act (1937), 142

Aliens Control Act, 142–143

All-African Convention (AAC), **16,** 64, 155, 303

Althusserian structuralism, 240

Amabutho (album), 165

Amalgamated Banks of South Africa, 56

amaNdebele. *See* Ndebele

Amandla Cultural Ensemble, 210

Amanzimtoti Institute. *See* Adams College

Amnesty Committee (TRC), 295

ANC. *See* African National Congress

Ancient civilizations. *See* Precolonial period

And They Didn't Die (Ngcobo), 181

Anglican Church, 65; Tutu, Desmond, 297

Anglo-Boer War, **16–19**, 46–47; apartheid education, 106; Broederbund establishment after, 56; film industry, 65; Hertzog's participation, 137; language policy resulting from, 170; origins of, 37; Rhodes's role in, 259; South Africa Act, 272; South African War and, 52–53

Anglo-Zulu War, **19**, 64; Natal expansion, 216; Zulus' loss of autonomy, 321

Angola: armed struggle against apartheid, 25; inspiring student protest, 245; Khoisan languages, 169; slave trade, 267; SWAPO guerrilla war, 215

Anthem. *See* "Nkosi Sikelel' iAfrika"

Anthropology. *See* Paleoanthropology

Antiapartheid movements and activities, 157–158; armed struggle, 24–25; Biko, Steve, 33; Black Consciousness Movement, 35–36; black press, 196–197; Boesak, Allan, 37–38; Breytenbach, Breyten, 38; Buthelezi, Mangosuthu, 57; civil society organizations, 69; coloured political organization, 72; Dadoo, Yusuf, 79–80; De Lille, Patricia, 81; defiance campaigns, 80; Durban strikes, 94–95; First, Heloise Ruth, 120; Fischer, Abraham Louis "Bram," 121; Frontline states, 122; Ginwala, Frene Noshir, 124–125; Global Antiapartheid Movement, 125–128; global antiapartheid movement, 125–128; Goniwe, Matthew, 130; Hani, Chris, 133–134; Holomisa, Bantu, 138; Indian militancy, 145; Jabavu, Davidson Don Tengo, 155; Jewish leaders, 142; Leon, Tony, 178; Lesotho's support of liberation movements, 178–179; Luthuli, Albert, 182;

Mandela, Nelson, 184–190; Masekela, Hugh, 191–192; Mbeki, Govan, 193–194; Mbeki, Thabo, 194–195; migrant labor, 200–201; musical traditions, 208; National Education Crisis/Coordinating Committee, 217; new social movements, 221–223; Ngoyi, Lillian, 223–224; popular politics, 244–249; SACPO resistance, 272; Sisulu, Albertina, 266–267; Sisulu, Walter, 267; Slovo, Joe, 268–269; Sophiatown's black resistance, 270–271; South African Indian Congress, 273–274; Soweto student uprising, 274; Soweto's history of, 274; Tambo, Oliver, 285–286; theater and resistance, 289; Treason Trial, 292; United Democratic Front, 305–306; vigilantism, 309–310; Winnie Mandela's arrest, 190; women and politics, 311–314; World Council of Churches, 315. *See also* Treason Trial
Anti-Coloured Affairs Department, 224–225
Anti-Eviction Campaign (AEC), 221–222, 281
Antiretroviral drugs (ARV), 2, 292–293
Apartheid, 4, **20–24**; abolishing bantustans, 32; affirmative action as reverse racism, 2; Afrikaners, 8; Anglo-Boer War, 18; AWB stance, 11; Baartman symbolizing black experience, 29–30; Battle of Blood River, 32–33; Brutus's advocacy, 56; Carnegie Commission findings on white poverty, 63; chieftancy, 147, 149; Christian support for, 65; civic associations, 68; Coetzee's writings, 70; Coloured Labour Preference Policy, 61; cricket's discriminating practices, 90–91; criminalization of black political participation, 242–244; De Klerk, F. W., 80; democratic transition/negotiations, 87–90; destabilizing Mozambique, 206; discrimination against coloureds, 71–72; Durban's socio-spatial structuring, 92; Dutch Reformed Church, 95; economic functionality, 240; economic status, unemployment and inequality, 101; education, 106–108; end of, 218–219; film industry and portrayal of, 66–67; Hertzog's government promoting, 137; HIV/AIDS response, 12; impact on Indians, 144–145; influence on Gordimer's writing, 131; Jewish ambivalence, 158; Johannesburg's geography, 157; labor migration figures, 142; language policy, 171; law and society, 174; Lesotho exploitation, 271–272; literature, 180–181; Malan, Daniel Francois, 184; Muslims' classification, 153; nationalist roots of, 235–236; Ndebele's homeland assignments, 220; negotiated settlement, 82–83; Port Elizabeth city planning, 250; racial classification, 255–256; religious classification, 60; Republican constitution, 75; Rivonia Trial, 259–261; roots in migrant labor, 202–204; segregation of University of Fort Hare, 306; Sharpeville Massacre, 266; slowing of paleoanthropological research, 229–230; Smuts's criticism of, 269; sports and sports boycotts, 277–279; structure of the economy, 102–103;

suppression of Mapungubwe finding, 191; Suzman's political career, 281–282; Swazi collusion with apartheid forces, 282–283; Union of South Africa, 299–300; Verwoerd's creation, 308. *See also* Antiapartheid movements and activities; National Party; Pass laws
Apprenticeship, 41
Apprenticeship Act (1922), 71
Archaeological excavations, 191
Architecture: Cape Dutch, 59, 100
Armed struggle, **24–26**; ANC-IFP split over, 150; 1870s uprisings, 47; IFP violence during transition, 243–244; Rand Revolt, 256–257; Zuma's role in, 322–323
Armstrong, Louis, 191
ARV therapy, 13
Ashe, Arthur, 127
Ashton, Hugh, 230
Asmal, Kader, 34
Assassinations: ANC members, 5; First, Heloise Ruth, 121; Goniwe, Matthew, 130; Hani, Chris, 12, 89, 134; patrilineal chieftancy, 147; Shaka Zulu, 266, 320–321
Ausbau languages, 171
Australia: global antiapartheid movement, 127; migration, 118, 142
Australopithecus africanus, 229
Authors: Boesak, Allan, 38; Coetzee, John Maxwell, 69–70; *Drum* magazine, 196–197; Dube, John Langalibalele, 91–92; Ginwala, 124–125; Gordimer, Nadine, 131; Head, Bessie, 134; Jabavu, Don Tengo, 155–156; Joseph, Helen, 158; La Guma, Alex, 165–166; Mbeki, Govan, 193; Mda, Zakes, 195–196; Plaatje, Sol, 233–234; Schreiner, Olive, 265; Soga, Tiyo, 270; Tutu, Desmond, 297–298
Auto industry, 103, 250
Averbach, Moshe Noah, 239
Awwal mosque, 151–152
Azania, **27**
Azanian People's Organization (AZAPO), 36, 84, 217, 231, 245–246

Baartman, Sara/Saartjie, **29–30**
Bailey, Jim, 91, 197
BaLemba, 159
Bambatha Rebellion, **30,** 91
Bantu Authorities Act (1951), 23, 31, 75, 149
Bantu education, **30–31**; Adams College, 2; ANC support for, 4; apartheid laws, 21; Hani protesting, 133; labor shortages resulting from, 240–241; language policy, 171–172; purpose of, 106–107
Bantu languages, 169
Bantu racial category, 255
Bantu Self-Government Act, 308
Bantu Women's League, 3
Bantu World newspaper, 196

Bantustan(s), **31–32**; apartheid laws, 23; armed struggled against apartheid, 25; Buthelezi's leadership, 57; constitutions, 75; creation of, 218; economic structure, 102–103; education policy, 107; health system, 135; law and society, 175–176; migrant labor control, 203; pass laws protest, 233; Xhosa relocation, 318
Barnato, Barney, 259
Barrow, John, 251
Bastard communities. *See* Griqua
Basutoland, 205. *See also* Lesotho
Battle at Dithakong (1823), 42
Battle of Blood River, 18, **32–33**, 37, 258, 321
Battle of Isandlwana (1879), 64
Battle of Majuba, 49–50
Battle of Ulundi, 64
Batty, Arthur, 161
BCM. *See* Black Consciousness Movement
Beaumont Commission report, 219
Bechuanaland, 50, 52. *See also* Botswana
BEE. *See* Black Economic Empowerment (BEE)
Belafonte, Harry, 183
Benjamin, Sathima Bea, 141
Bergin, Sean, 210
Bernstein, Lionel, 260
Bezuidenhout, Evita, 290
Biko, Steve Bantu, **33**, 35, 65; Black Consciousness Movement, 238; on liberalism, 234–235; Lovedale, 181; University of Fort Hare, 306
Bill of Rights, **33–35**; customary law, 78; health care, 135; human rights principles, 174–175
Birth of a Nation (film), 66
Black consciousness, 238, 245; Soweto Uprising, 275
Black Consciousness Movement (BCM), **35–36**; ANC exile years, 4; Azania, 27; Biko, Steve, 33; Boesak's activism, 37–38; Civic Associations emerging from, 68; coloured political organization, 72; emergence from student and protest groups, 245; impact on music performance, 210; liberalism, 234–235; racial classification, 256; theater and resistance, 181, 289; University of Fort Hare, 306
Black Economic Empowerment (BEE), **36**; affirmative action, 2; economic policy since 1994, 104–105; language policy, 172; Mbeki's role in, 194; media regulation and ownership, 198; Ramaphosa's participation, 256; transforming the mining industry, 130
Black liberation theology, 65
Black Local Authorities (BLA), 247
Black Nationalist Movement, 177
Black Opinion newspaper, 156
Black Parents' Association (BPA), 275
Black People's Convention (BPC), 33, 245
Black peril, 232
Black press, 196–197
Black Sash, 69

Bloemfontein, **36–37**; Anglo-Boer War, 17; Mayibuye Festival of African Arts, 291; South African Native Convention, 302
Blood River. *See* Battle of Blood River
Boer Republic, **37**; Anglo-Boer War, 16; Boer-British conflict leading to establishment of, 43; constitution, 74–75; Natalia, 216; South African War, 52–53; Union of South Africa, 299
Boerestaat, 11
Boer(s), 157; Anglo-Boer War, 16–19; Cetshwayo's British alliance, 64; defeat of Pedi, 233; the end of African independence, 49–50; Great Trek, 42–44, 131; linguistic policy, 170; Moshoeshoe's diplomatic efforts, 205; Mzilikazi's encounter, 211–212; Retief, Piet, 258; war of Hintsa, 42. *See also* Afrikaner(s); Anglo-Boer War; Dutch colonialism; Great Trek
Boesak, Allan Aubrey, **37–38**, 65, 246, 305
Boipatong Massacre (1992), 5
Booker Prize, 70
Bophuthatswana (homeland), 11, 31–32
Boraine, Alex, 293
Botha, Louis, 17, 54, 137; British collaboration, 54
Botha, P. W., 80, 294; apartheid, 20; Mandela's incarceration, 188; National Party's racist policy reform, 218
Botswana: Frontline states, 122; Head's migration and novels, 134; Khoisan languages, 169; labor migration from, 142; Mapungubwe, 191; mine workers' migration, 130; Tswana, 297
Boycotts: apartheid sports policy, 278; school, 130; tricameral parliament, 305; UDF strategy, 247–248
"Brain drain," 7, 118, 136
Brand, Adolph Johannes. *See* Ibrahim, Abdullah
Breytenbach, Breyten, **38**, 181, 291
Brink, André P., 289
Britain: apartheid regime's break with, 75; Baartman's objectification and exploitation, 29; Cetshwayo and the Anglo-Zulu War, 64; d'Oliveira's cricket career, 90–91; global antiapartheid movement, 125; South Africa's withdrawal from the Commonwealth, 218, 308
British imperialism and settler colonialism (1795–1870), **38–46**, 40–41; Bloemfontein founding, 36; Boers' Great Trek, 37, 42–44; Cape Colony, 59; Cape Franchise, 59; chieftancy under, 148–149; Christian missions, 65; demand for representative institutions, 45–46; Frontier Wars, 122; Great Trek, 131; Islam, 151–152; Jewish migration, 158; Lesotho, 178–179; migrant labor, 201; Natal, 216; Ngqika's claim to the Xhosa chieftancy, 224; Orange River annexation, 44; Port Elizabeth, 250; slavery, 268; sociolinguistic landscape and language policy, 170–171; theater, 287; War of Mlanjeni, 44–45; Zimbabwe, 319
British imperialism and settler colonialism (1870–1910), **46–55,** 48; African nationalism,

236–237; Afrikaner nationalism as a response to, 235–236; ANC activities, 5; Anglo-Boer War, 16–19; Anglo-Zulu War, 19; Bambatha Rebellion, 30; Durban, 92; Hertzog promoting Afrikaner culture, 137; immigration recruitment, 142; Islam, 151–152; Jewish migration, 158; Lesotho, 178–179; literary traditions, 179–180; migrant labor, 201; modern sports, 276; Natal, 216; newspapers, 196; Port Elizabeth, 250; racial classification, 255–256; Rhodes's importance in, 259; Schreiner targeting, 265; sociolinguistic landscape and language policy, 170–171; South African film industry, 65–67; South West Africa, 214; Swaziland's independence, 282; Union of South Africa, 299
British Kaffraria, 42
British protectorates: Lesotho, 271
British South Africa Company (BSAC), 51, **55–56**; Rhodes's creation of, 259; Zimbabwe formation, 319
Broederbond, **56**, 156; apartheid ideology, 20; paleoanthropology, 230
Brown, A. R. Radcliffe, 230
Brutus, Dennis Vincent, **56–57**, 127, 306
Buchan, John, 276
Budd, Zola, 37
Buller, Redvers, 17
Bunyan, John, 270
Burnside, Janet, 270
Burundi, 323
Bush Wars, 133
Bushmen, 162; hypergyny, 252–253; racial classification, 255; VOC confrontation, 99. *See also* San
Buthelezi, Mangosuthu Gatsha, **57**; Adams College, 2; coalition government proposal, 84; IFP, 150–151; Inkatha kaZula and, 321; 1990s negotiations, 88; TRC findings, 294; University of Fort Hare, 306
Butulezi, Wellington, 124

Cabaret, political, 290
Calata, Fort, 130, 247
Calata, James, 3
Call of Islam, 153
Calvinism, 235
Canada: emigration to, 118; film industry, 67
Cape Colony, **59**; administration of Natal, 216; Anglo-Boer War, 16; British oppression of local sovereignty, 49; chieftancy under colonialism, 148; Dutch presence, 97–100; Great Trek, 131; migrant labor, 201; musical traditions, 207; newspapers, 196; Oorlam people, 213–214; origins of coloured identity, 71; political culture and ideology, 234–235; Port Elizabeth, 250; racial hierarchies, 8–9; Rhodes's activity, 259; transfer to British hands, 39; Van Riebeeck's administration, 307
Cape Coloured. *See* Coloured
Cape Dutch, 45
Cape Dutch architecture, **59**, 100
Cape Floral Kingdom, 63
Cape franchise, 45, **59–60**
Cape liberal tradition, 234–235
Cape Malay, 1, **60–61**, 152, 180
Cape of Good Hope Punishment Act (1836), 44
Cape Town, **61–63**; apartheid laws, 21; Cetshwayo's exile, 64; coloured people, 71; Democratic Alliance base, 82; District Six, 90; Dutch founding of, 97–99; economic and social development under the British, 40; Industrial and Commercial Workers Union, 150; introduction of Christianity, 64; Jewish population, 158; Muslims, 152; religion's classification, 60; Soweto Student Uprising, 275; squatter settlements, 280–281; theater and resistance, 289; theater construction, 287
Capital punishment, 294
Capitalism: racial, 240–241
Carmichael, Stokely, 183
Carnarvon, Henry Herbert, Earl of, 47–49
Carnegie Commission, **63**
Catholic Church: Christianity, 64–65; persecution of Huguenots, 138–139
Cattle herding, 45
Cattle theft, 41
Cattle-Killing Movement, 225–226
Caves, 251
Censorship: Gordimer's novels, 131; South African film industry, 65–67; theater and resistance, 289
Central Intelligence Agency (CIA), 206
Centralization of power, 83
Cetshwayo (Zulu king), 19, 49, **64**, 321
Chamber of Mines, 201, 301, 304
Chamberlain, Joseph, 16
Champion, Allison Wessels George, 3, **64**, 150, 303
Charismatic personal leaders, 84
Charterist politics. *See* Freedom Charter
Chattel slavery, 267
Chieftancies: land issues, 168; Luthuli, Albert, 182; Ngqika, 224
Chikane, Frank, 246, 273
Children: Anglo-Boer war, 17; health care system, 135; Hottentot codes, 41; parliamentary calendar accommodating women and children, 312; Truth and Reconciliation Commission, 294
Chinese labor, 54
Christianity, **64–65**; ANC ideology, 3; apartheid ideology, 20; Bantu Education Act, 30–31; Dutch Reformed Church, 95; founding of Kuruman, 163; music, 207; Terre Blanche embracing, 11; three Cs of colonialism, 39; Union opposition, 303; World Council of Churches, 315; Zulu politics, 321
Christine (Smit), 289
Cinema, **65–68**; Fugard's contribution, 122; *Tsotsi*, 296–297
Ciskei (homeland), 31–32, 243, 246

Cities: squatter settlements, 280–281. *See* Appendix 4: Provinces and Major Cities; *specific cities*
Citizenship: Bantu Homelands Citizenship Act, 31; Bill of Rights, 34; Makeba's loss of, 183; results of the South African War, 53
Civic associations, **68,** 246; women's organizations, 313–314
Civil disobedience: apartheid laws, 21
Civil society, **68–69**; ARV AIDS treatment, 13; defiance campaigns, 80; Soweto uprising, 246
Civilized Labor Policy, 71
"Civilized labor" policy, 161
Class. *See* Socioeconomic class
Classical music, 211
Clegg, Johnny, **69,** 210
Clicks, linguistic, 169
Coal, 216
CODESA. *See* Convention for a Democratic South Africa
Coego Industrial Development Zone, 250
Coetsee, Kobie, 188
Coetzee, Basil, 141
Coetzee, John Maxwell, **69–70**
Colonial novels, 180
Colonialism, 38–39; British Imperialism and Settler Colonialism, 38–46; chieftancy under, 148–149; customary law, 78; destruction of the San, 263; the Dutch at the Cape, 97–100; impact on literacy traditions, 179; indirect rule, 75; law and society, 174; migrant labor, 201; sociolinguic landscape, 169–170; three Cs of, 39. *See also* British imperialism and settler colonialism (1795–1870); British imperialism and settler colonialism (1870–1910); Dutch colonialism
Colonialism of a special type (CST), 239–240
Color bar, 55
Coloured Affairs Department (CAD), 304
Coloured Labor Preference Policy, 61
Coloured people, **70–73**; Abdurahman, Abdullah, 1; affirmative action, 2; Afrikaners, 8; All-African Convention, 16; apartheid laws, 23; Black Consciousness Movement, 35; Black Economic Empowerment, 36; Brutus, Dennis Vincent, 56–57; Cape Franchise, 59–60; Cape Town's population, 61; color bar during reconstruction, 54; cricket's discriminating practices, 90–91; DA voter base, 82; defiance campaigns, 80; demand for representative institution, 45–46; education policy, 106; Extension of University Education Act, 31; Griquas, 132; Head, Bessie, 134; health and, 134–135; La Guma, Alex, 165–166; musicians, 207; Non-European Unity Movement, 224–225; political violence by police, 244; Port Elizabeth city planning, 250; racial classification, 255; racist orientation of Afrikaner nationalism, 235; white press targeting, 197. *See also* Racial classification
Coloured People's Congress, 272

Coloured Persons' Representative Council, 23
Come Back Africa (film), 67
Commerce: affirmative action, 2; anti-Indian policies, 145; Black Economic Empowerment, 36; British South Africa Company, 55–56; three Cs of colonialism, 39. *See also* Black Economic Empowerment
Commission for Gender Equality, 35
Commission for Gender Equality (CGE), 313
Commission for Human Rights, 35
Common law, 77–78
Communal Land Rights Act (2004), 149, 168
Communism: black nationalists rejecting, 177; film censorship, 66; political ideology and culture, 237–238; Rivonia Trial, 260; youth movements, 303. *See also* South African Communist Party
Communist Party of South Africa (CPSA), 237, 303; First, Heloise Ruth, 120; Rand Revolt, 257. *See also* South African Communist Party
Community service, 136
Comprehensive Anti-Apartheid Act (1986; US), 126–127
Compulsory education, 105–106
Compulsory national health, 135
Comrades Marathon, 278
Concentration camp, 17
Concerned Citizens Forum, 221
Conflict: anti-VOC activism, 99; Frontier Wars, 122; Mfecane, 41–42; Rand Revolt, 256–257; South African War, 52–53; War at Hintsa, 42; War of Mlanjeni, 44–45. *See also* Antiapartheid movements and activities
Congress Alliance, 272–274
Congress of Democrats, 121, 157; Slovo, Joe, 268–269
Congress of South African Students (COSAS), 31, 246
Congress of South African Trade Unions (COSATU), **73**; ANC-COPE split, 74; Civic Associations, 68; economic policy, 104; GEAR adoption, 86; launching of, 248; Ramaphosa's role in forming, 256; Reconstruction and Development Program, 257–258; SACP and, 272
Congress of the People (COPE), **73–74**; ANC split, 6; Freedom Charter, 121–122; Matthews's role in organizing, 192–193; race and voter choice, 116; SACPO, 272; 2009 elections, 113
Conservative Party, 236; antiapartheid activities, 24; Hani assassination, 134
Constitution, **74–77,** 83, 87, 188–189; Bill of Rights, 33–35; chieftancy provision, 149; CODESA, 77; customary law, 78; education reform, 108–109; Freedom Charter, 121; gender issues, 312; health care, 136; human rights principles, 174–175; land reform, 167–169; language policy, 172–173; liberal nature of, 235; media regulation, 197–198; Million Signature Campaign opposing, 306; multiparty negotiations, 218–219; negotiations over, 89; new social movements, 222; 1994 elections, 113; PAC's

refusal to negotiate over, 232; transforming the mining industry, 130; Transvaal and Orange River Colony, 54
Constitution (Swaziland), 283
Constitution (Union of South Africa), 302; Smuts's role in, 269
Constitutional Court, 35, 176–177
Convention for a Democratic South Africa (CODESA), 5, **77,** 88–89, 188–189; Holomisa's leadership, 138; Leon as adviser to, 178
COPE. *See* Congress of the People
Corruption: African Renaissance, 7; De Lille's criticism of ANC, 81; Motlanthe's stand against, 206; politics after 1999, 84; Sigcau, Stella, 138; Zuma's dismissal, 323
COSATU. *See* Congress of South African Trade Unions
Council of Unions of South Africa (CUSA), 247
Country of My Skull (Krog), 181
Coup attempts, 52
Court system, 37, 175
Cradle of Humankind, 229
Creswell, F.H.P., 137
Cricket, 90–91, 276, 278
Cricket World Cup (2003), 276
Cricketers of the Veld (Duffus), 276
Crime: Durban, 94
Cronje, Hansie, 37
Cronjé, Piet, 17
Cronwright, Samuel, 265
Cry, the Beloved Country (Paton), 67, 180
Cry Freedom (film), 67
Culture: ANC creations, 5; Bantu Education Act, 31; British-Dutch literary clash, 179–180; Cape Malay and South African Indian, 60–61, 153; defining coloured people, 70; *Drum* magazine, 91; Durban's diversity, 92; Dutch culture under British rule, 40; film industry, 66–67; Great Trek, 131; Hertzog promoting, 137; IFP, 150; Krotoa straddling Dutch and Khoikhoi cultures, 162–163; Kwaito, 163–164; literature, 179–181; music, 207–211; Ndebele, 220; Ngoni, 223; political cultures and ideologies, 234–239; resurgence of Afrikaner culture, 10; roots in migrant labor, 202; Sophiatown's black urban culture, 270–271; sports exemplifying, 276; Venda, 307–308. *See also* Authors; Music; Poets/poetry
Currency: AU, 8
Customary law, 46, **77–78,** 148–149
Cuvier, Georges, 29

Dadoo, Yusuf, **79–80,** 273, 292
Dalindyebo, Jongintaba, 184
Dalindyebo, Justice, 184–185
Damara people, 213, 255
Damon, Matt, 68
Davids, Nadia, 153
De Hangen, Western Cape Province, 251–252
De Klerk, F. W. (Frederik Willem), **80,** 139; apartheid, 20; legalizing ANC YL, 7; Mandela's release, 188; 1994 elections, 114; sporting boycotts, 279; transition to black majority rule, 218–219
De la Rey, Koos, 17
De Lange, J. P., 108
De Lille, Patricia, **81,** 82, 312
De Villiers, Pieter, 139
De Wet, Christiaan, 17
DeBeers Consolidated Mines, 51, 162, 259
Defiance campaigns, **80**; ANC development, 4; Dadoo's role in, 79; *Drum* magazine, 91; education reform, 108; global antiapartheid movement, 125; Indian militancy, 145; Luthuli's leadership, 182; Mandela's involvement, 187; nonviolent protest, 242–243; Port Elizabeth as ANC stronghold, 250; SAIC, 274; Sisulu, Walter, 267; Soweto, 274; women's participation, 7
Delagoa Bay, 49
Democracy, institutions promoting, 76. *See also* Elections
Democratic Alliance (DA), **81–82**; De Lille, Patricia, 81; former National Party members, 236; Leon's leadership, 178; post–1999 politics, 83–84; 2000 elections, 116
Democratic Party: 1994 elections, 113. *See also* Democratic Alliance
Democratic politics since 1994, **82–87.** *See also* Government of national unity
Democratic Republic of Congo (DRC), 215
Democratic transition/negotiations (1990-1994), 188–189; addressing inequality, 36; anti-Muslim violence, 153; Bill of Rights advocates, 34; Civic Associations' role, 68; civil society development, 69; constitution as crowning achievement, 74–76; COSATU-ANC alliance, 73; economic structure, 103; Ibrahim's return, 141; land reform, 167–168; law and society, 174–175; literary expression, 181; Meyer's role in, 199; Meyer's role in negotiations, 199; Natal Province, 216–217; political violence, 243–244; Ramaphosa's role as negotiator, 256; redefining migrant labor, 204; SANCO formation, 68; women's involvement in negotiations, 312
Democratic transition/negotiations (1990–1994), **87–90**
Demographics and statistics: AIDS, 134; bantustans, 32; Bloemfontein, 37; Cape Town, 61; Christian population, 65; coloured people, 70–71; Durban, 93; Griquas population, 132; immigrant populations, 142; Jewish population, 158; Johannesburg's population, 157; Muslims, 152; Stellenbosch, 281; Swazi population, 282
Dependency theory, 239–240
Derby-Lewis, Clive, 134
Development: Cape Town's joint process, 63
Dhlomo, H.I.E., 180
Diamonds. *See* Gold and diamond mining
Die Burger (newspaper), 184

Die Heks (play), 287
Difiqane, 41–42. *See also* Mfecane
Dingane (Zulu chief), 258, 320–321
Dinizulu (Zulu King), 30, 50, 91
Discrimination: against coloureds, 71; Jabavu's attempts to unmask, 156; sexual orientation, 2; Union of South Africa institutionalizing, 299. *See also* Apartheid; Racism
Disease: Anglo-Boer war, 17; tetanus, 136; tuberculosis, 13. *See also* AIDS
Disraeli, Benjamin, 47–49
District Six, 21, **90**, 208
District Six–The Musical, 288–289
Dodd, G. H., 277
d'Oliveira, Basil, **90–91**, 278
Domesticated animals, 252
Donkin, Rufane, 250
Doppers church, 235
Dorkay House, 289
DP. *See* Democratic Alliance (DA)
Drug use and trafficking: Cape Town, 63; Fassie, Brenda, 120; vigilantism, 309–310
Drum magazine, **91**, 196–197, 208, 224, 270
Dry White Season (film), 67
Du Plessis, I. D., 153
Du Toit, S. J., 180
Dual power, 248
Dube, John Langalibalele, 3, **91–92**, 219, 227, 302
Dunlop, William, 29
Durban, 22(fig.), **92–94**; Gandhi in, 123; musical traditions, 208; popular politics, 244; rent boycotts, 145
D'Urban, Benjamin, 42, 200
Durban strikes, **94–95**, 108, 203, 240–241
Dutch colonialism: African nationalism, 236–237; British expansion in South Africa, 51–52; Cape Dutch architecture, 59; demand for representative institution, 45; early Dutch at the Cape, 97–100; Frontier Wars, 122; Griqua's origins, 131; introduction of Christianity, 64; Islamic presence, 151–152; Krotoa straddling Dutch and Khoikhoi cultures, 162–163; literary traditions, 179–180; origins of coloured identity, 71; sociolinguial landscape, 169–170; theater, 286–287; Van Riebeeck's orders, 307. *See also* Afrikaner(s); Boer(s)
Dutch East India Company, **95**; Christianity, 65; early Dutch colonialism, 97–99; education for slaves, 105; Huguenot migration, 138–139; language policy, 170; migrant labor, 201; slave trade, 151, 267–268; transfer to British hands, 39–40; Van Riebeeck, Jan, 307
Dutch Reformed Church, **95**; apartheid, 20; Boesak, Allan, 37–38; early Cape colonialism, 64, 98; Malan's ministry, 184; Milner's reconstruction policy, 54; WCC countering theological apartheid defense, 315

Early colonial period: The Dutch at the Cape, **97–100**
Early Iron Age, 252–253
East Timor, 138
Eastern Cape, 138
Economy, **100–105**; Black Economic Empowerment, 36; British development of the Cape Colony, 39–40; Cape Town, 62–63; diamond discovery increasing economic activity, 47; Durban's decline, 93–94; GEAR, 132; global antiapartheid movement, 126–127; key trends, 101; political economy, 239–242; politics since 1994, 104; Port Elizabeth's downturn, 250; racial differentials, 102; Rhodes's role in, 259; structure of, 102–103; Swazi, 283; unemployment and poverty, 101–102; white politics in the Union of South Africa, 300–301
Education, **105–110**; Adams College, 2; adapted, 106; Afrikaans-speaking universities, 10; under apartheid, 106–108; apartheid laws, 21; Bantu education, 30–31; Biko's, 33; bilingual, 137, 184; Brutus's advocacy, 56; Cape Town's struggles, 63; Dube's commitment to, 91; Jabavu, Davidson Don Tengo, 155; Jewish, 159; land reform training, 169; language policy, 171–172; Lovedale, 181; Mambazo Academy, 165; Mandela's, 184–186; music, 208; National Education Crisis/Coordinating Committee, 217; Ohlange Institute, 227; race and economic differentials, 102; racial discrimination against coloureds, 71; school boycotts, 130; University of Fort Hare, 306; women protest movements, 312. *See also* Soweto Student Uprising; Student protest; Teachers
Eiselen, W.W.M., 230
Elections: Zimbabwe, 319–320
Elections: 1994 to 2009, **111–118**, 189; ANC win, 5; democratic institutions, 76; democratic politics, 82; Durban's delay, 92–93; IFP boycott threat, 150–151; Indian voters, 146; Indian-African relations, 146; interim constitution, 77; Mbeki's parliamentary seat, 193; National Party, 218–219; PAC's poor results, 232; race and electoral politics, 84–86; Sisulu's election, 267; TRC proposal, 293; vigilante violence, 309; Winnie Mandela's appointment, 190
Elections: pre-1994, 137; boycott of Malan's, 225; civic associations, 68; Milner's reconstruction, 54; non-whites' exclusion from, 218; tricameral parliament, 305
Electricity company (ESCOM), 300
Ellington, Duke, 141, 191, 209
Emigration, **118**, 136; Ibrahim, Abdullah, 141. *See also* Immigration; Immigration; Labor migration; Labor migration; Migrant labor
Eminent Persons Group, 127
Employment: affirmative action, 2; economic policy since 1994, 104–105; racial discrimination against

coloureds, 71. *See also* Trade unions; Unemployment
Employment Equity Act, 2
English language, 169–173
Entertainment Act (1931), 65–66
Esack, Farid, 153–154, 246
Eskom, 222
Ethnicity: Afrikaner groups affiliations, 10; ANC-COPE split, 74; creation of bantustans, 31–32
Eugenics, 20
European culture: apartheid ideology, 20; Baartman's objectification and exploitation, 29–30; coloured, 70; music, 207; Namibia's isolation from, 213–214; slavery, 267–268; theater, 286–287; theater and resistance, 289. *See also* British imperialism and settler colonialism; Dutch colonialism; German colonialism/Germany; Portuguese colonialism
Eva. *See* Krotoa
Executive, 83
Exile: ANC members, 5; Dadoo, Yusuf, 79–80; Hani, Chris, 133; literary expressions of resistance, 181; Moeketsi rejecting, 205; SACP, 273; SACPO members, 272; Slovo, Joe, 269; from the Soweto Student Uprising, 275
Exploitation of labor: gold mining, 130. *See also* Labor; Migrant labor; Mine workers
Extension of Security of Tenure Act (1997), 168
Extension of University Education Act (1959), 21, 31
Extraordinary rendition, 153

Fairbairn, John, 196
Family: Mandela's, 186
Fanagalo, **119**
Fassie, Brenda, **119–120**
Fatti's and Moni's pasta factory, 246
Federalism: South African unification, 55
Federation of South African Trade Unions (FOSATU), 246
Federation of South African Women, 157, 266, 311–312
Festival culture, 290–291
Fichte, Johann Gottlieb, 20
Film culture. *See* Cinema
Firearms, 47, 53, 323; Namibia, 213. *See also* Armed struggle
First, Heloise Ruth, **120–121**, 158, 201, 292, 311
First Afrikaans Language Movement, 180
Fischer, Abraham Louis "Bram," **121**
Football, 6, 276–277, 279
Ford Motors, 250
Fordism, 241
Foreign investment, 101, 132
Fort Hare University. *See* University of Fort Hare
Fossil discoveries, 229–231, 251–252
Fouché, Leo, 191
Fractions of capital, 240

France: Baartman's repatriation, 30; Huguenots, 138–139
Franchise. *See* Political franchise
Francois, Daniel, 139
Fraser, Malcolm, 127
Fraud: Boesak's conviction for, 38
Free State Province, 37
Free State–Basotho War (1858), 205
Freedom Charter, 68, 120, **121–122**; ANC support for, 4; ANC-PAC tensions over, 231; Indian militancy, 145; Joseph, Helen, 157; land reform, 167–168; Mandela and, 187; Matthews's role in organizing, 192–193; National Forum and, 217; revival of Charterist politics, 246–247; SAIC, 274; Slovo's contribution to, 269; Tambo, Oliver, 285–286; UDF and, 306
Freedom Front, 84, 113
Freedom of the press, 196
Freelance theater, 290–291
Freeman, Morgan, 68
Frere, Henry Bartle, 19, 49
Frontier Wars, **122**
Frontline states, **122**; armed struggle against apartheid, 26; global antiapartheid movement, 127; MK operations, 4. *See also* Zimbabwe
Fugard, Athol, **122**, 181, 288–290, 296–297
Funde, Edwin, 5
Further Education and Training (FET), 109

Galant Uprising, 268
Gandhi, Mohandas (Mahatma), **123**, 125, 144
Gangster films, 67
Garvey, Marcus, 123–124
Garveyism, 3, **123–124**
Gay population: AIDS in, 11–12; gay rights, 1–2
Gazankulu (Tsonga/Shangaan), 31–32, 296
GEAR. *See* Growth, Employment, and Redistribution strategy
Gelb, Stephen, 240–241
General Education and Training (GET), 109
General Motors, 250
Genocide: of Herero people, 214
George, Mluleki, 279
German colonialism/Germany: immigration recruitment, 142; Jewish migration, 158; music, 207; South West Africa, 213–214
Germanic languages, 169
Ghana: slave trade, 267
Ghandi, Mahatma, 79
Gini coefficient, 86
Ginwala, Frene Noshir, 5, **124–125**, 312
The Girl Who Killed to Save: Nonquase the Liberator (Dhlomo), 180, 287
Glasgow University, 182
Glen Grey Act (1894), 166–167
Global antiapartheid movement, **125–128**, 315
Global Political Agreement (GPA), 320

Globalization: African Renaissance, 8
Gluckman, Max, 230
Gold and diamond mining, **129–130,** 163; Anglo-Boer War, 16, 18; Boer Republic, 37; colonial education policy, 105–105k; in Griqualand West, 46–47, 132; increasing economic activity, 47; Johannesburg's roots, 157; Kimberley, 162; land tenure and dispossession, 166; migrant labor, 201; Mozambican labor, 206; pass laws, 232; Port Elizabeth's decline, 250; race and class issues in Kimberley and Witwatersrand, 50–51; Rand Revolt, 256–257; Rhodes's monopoly, 259; Xhosa labor, 318
Goniwe, Matthew, **130,** 247
Gordimer, Nadine, **131,** 180
Gothic dramas, 290
Governance/government: bantustans, 31–32; Boer Republic, 37; Broederbond goals, 56; Cape Malay and, 152–153; Constitution, 74–76; customary law, 77–78; demand for representative institution, 45–46. *See also* Parliament; Political representation
Government of national unity: ANC/INP negotiations over the shape of, 89; Buthelezi's ministry, 57; Cape Town coloureds' lack of trust in, 61–62; education reform, 108; GEAR, 132; health system, 135–136; immigration policy, 143; land reform, 167–168; language policy, 172–173; Muslim figures, 153; new social movements opposing policies of, 221; Reconstruction and Development Program, 257–258. *See also* African National Congress
Government structures. *See* Appendix 3: Government Structures
Gqabi, Joe, 5
Graceland project, 151, 165, 183, 210–211
Grahamstown Arts Festival, 291
Grammy Award, 165, 183
Gramsci, Antonio, 241
The Great Kimberley Diamond Robbery (film), 66
Great Trek, **131;** Boer-British conflict leading to, 42–44; creation of the Boer Republics, 37; film portrayal, 66; Johannesburg's growth, 157; Kruger's family, 163; literary traditions, 180; Retief, Piet, 258; Swaziland, 282; Xhosa clash, 317; Zulu politics, 320–321
Grey, George, 45
Griqua, **131–132;** Bastard communities, 100; Bloemfontein founding, 36; British annexation of land north of Orange River, 44; 1870s uprisings, 47; racial classification, 255; state establishment, 37. *See also* Coloured
Griqualand West, 132, 162
Gross Domestic Product, 100
Gross fixed capital formation, 101
Group Areas Act (1950), 23, 72, 144–145, 153, 218, 271

Growth, Employment, and Redistribution strategy (GEAR), **132;** ANC introduction of, 5; economic policy since 1994, 104; land reform, 168; Mbeki's role in adopting, 194–195; new social movements opposing, 221; race and electoral politics, 86; RDP and, 258
The Guardian, 120
Guerrilla warfare: anti-VOC activism, 99; armed struggle against apartheid, 25; Bambatha Rebellion, 30; Rivonia Trial, 260; South African War, 52; South West Africa, 214
Gumede, Archie, 246
Gumede, J. T., 3, 303
Gumede, Robert, 164
Gunner, Elizabeth, 179
Gwangwa, Jonas, 141, 191, 205, 210

Haggard, Henry Rider, 180
Halachah, 159
Hammond-Tooke, W. D., 230
Hani, Martin Thembisile (Chris), 12, 26, 89, **133–134,** 194
Haque, S. A., 278
Haraware Declaration, 75
Harmel, Mick, 239–240
Haron, Abdullah, 153
HART (Halt All Racist Tours), 127
Head, Bessie, 91, **134**
Head, Harold, 134
Healers, traditional, 137, 263, 265
Health, **134–137;** Treatment Action Campaign, 292–293
Health Act (2003), 136–137
Heemraad (town council), 98
Hellman, Ellen, 230
Hendricks, "Krom," 277
Hendsoppers (having "hands up"), 17
Herero people, 214–215
Hertzog, James Barry Munnik, **137–138;** All-African Convention as response to Native bills, 16; Kadalie and the ICU, 161; National Party, 218; privileging South African whites, 300; racial discrimination against coloureds, 71; Smuts's defeat by, 269
Hertzog Bills, 3
Hierarchy: race in the Cape Colony, 8–9
Higher education. *See* University of Fort Hare
Hintsa, war of, 42
Hip-hop, 163–164
Historical materialism, 240
Historical narratives, 179
HIV/AIDS. *See* AIDS
Hoernle, Winifred, 230
Hogan, Barbara, 14–15
Holloway Commission, 203
Holomisa, Bantubonke Harrington (Bantu), **138,** 199
Homeland, 308. *See also* Bantustan(s)
Homicide, 136

Homo sapiens, 229
Hottentot Codes (1809, 1811, 1819), 41
Hottentot Venus. *See* Baartman, Sara/Saartjie
Hottentots. *See* Khoikhoi
Housing: Cape Town's insufficiency, 62; new social movements addressing, 221–222; Port Elizabeth's segregation, 250; squatter settlements, 280–281
Huddleston, Trevor, 127, 191, 271
Huguenots, 64–65, 98, **138–139**; Retief, Piet, 258
Human rights: Bill of Rights provision, 35; constitutional jurisprudence, 176–177; Hani's involvement in abuse of, 133; Universal Declaration, 174
Hunter-gatherers, 251
Hurley, Denis, 246
Hypergyny, 252–253

Ibrahim, Abdullah, **141**, 183, 191, 205, 209
Identity, 159–160; Afrikaners, 8; BCM and Afrikaner identity, 36; black consciousness, 238; Cape Town's duality, 62; Great Trek, 131; Jewish ambivalence, 158; literary traditions, 179; origins of coloured identity, 71; roots in migrant labor, 202; sports and national identity, 279; Zulu, 320–322. *See also* Afrikaner(s); Coloured people; Indian South Africans
Ideology: African nationalism, 236–237; African Renaissance, 7–8; Afrikaner nationalism, 235–236; ANC, 3; ANC-COPE split, 74; apartheid, 20; black consciousness, 238; Democratic Alliance, 81; Marxism/Communism, 237–238; National Forum, 217; political cultures and ideologies, 234–239. *See also* Freedom Charter
IFP. *See* Inkatha Freedom Party (IFP)
Iintsomi (Xhosa folktale style), 179
Ilange Lase Natal magazine, 91
Immigration, **141–143**; Boers, 258; Cape Town, 62; European Jews, 158–159; Great Trek, 131; sociolingual landscape, 169–170
Immigration Quota Act (1930), 142
Immorality Act, 38, 153
Immorality Amendment Act (1950), 71–72
Immunization, 136
Imperialism, 38; film industry portrayal of, 66. *See also* British Imperialism and Settler Colonialism
Incarceration: Breytenbach, Breyten, 38; Dadoo, Yusuf, 79; de Klerk's liberation of powers, 81; First, Heloise Ruth, 120; Fischer, Abraham, 121; Goniwe, Matthew, 130; Head, Bessie, 134; Joseph, Helen, 157; Krotoa, 163; Mandela, 187–188; Ngoyi, Lillian, 224; 1990s negotiations, 88–89; Robben Island, 261; Sisulu, Walter, 267; Sobukwe, Robert, 270; Terre Blanche, Eugene, 286; Treason Trial, 292
Income inequality, 101
Indaba newspaper, 270
Indentured laborers, 142, **143**, 144, 151–152, 169–170

Independent Democrats, 81
Independent Electoral Commission (IEC), 113–115
India: global antiapartheid movement, 125–126; immigrant populations, 142; indentured labor, 143; 1983 Constitution, 75; slave trade, 267–268
Indian militancy, 144, 255
Indian Muslims, 152
Indian South Africans, **144–147**; affirmative action, 2; All-African Convention, 16; apartheid laws, 21, 23; Black Consciousness Movement, 35; Black Economic Empowerment, 36; Cape Town's population, 61; Charterist politics, 246–247; defiance campaigns, 80; education policy, 106; Extension of University Education Act, 31; Gandhi, 123; Ginwala, Frene Noshir, 124–125; health issues, 134–135; 1983 Constitution, 75; Non-European Unity Movement, 224–225; South African Indian Congress, 273–274. *See also* Racial classification
Indigenous forms of government, **147–150**; constitutional provision for, 175–176
Indigenous people: customary law, 77–78; Griqua, 131–132; Khoikhoi, 162; land tenure and dispossession, 166–169; literacy traditions, 179; Mfecane, 199–200; music, 207; Mzilikazi, 211–212; Ndebele, 220; Ngoni, 223; Pedi, 233; precolonial period, 251–253; San, 263; sociolingual landscape, 169; Tsonga, 296; Tswana, 297; Venda, 307–308; Xhosa, 317–318; Zulu, 320–322. *See also* Traditional culture; *specific groups*
Industrial and Commercial Workers Union (ICU), 3, **150**, 303; Champion's service to, 64; Garveyism, 124; Kadalie's founding, 161–162
Industrial revolution, 39, 46–47
Inequality: BEE policy criticism, 36; Cape Town's duality, 62; Durban addressing, 93–94; economic, 101–102; education policy, 106–108; GEAR and, 132; health and, 134–135; media technology access, 198; poverty and unemployment, 101; race and electoral politics, 85
Influx control of migrant labor, 203–204, 232, 250, 305
Infrastructure: Cape Town, 62–63
Inganekwane (Zulu storytelling), 286
Inkatha Freedom Party (IFP), **150–151**; ANC and, 5, 323; Buthelezi, Mangosuthu Gatsha, 57; Durban's violence, 92–93; 1994 elections, 113; 1990s negotiations, 88–89; political violence during democratic transition, 243–244; politics after 1999, 84; Truth and Reconciliation Commission, 293; Union opposition, 303; Zulu origins, 321
Inkatha kaZulu, 321
Institutions promoting constitutional democracy, 76
Interim Constitution, 89
Internal Security Act, 190
International AIDS Conference, 14
International Defence and Aid Fund (IDAF), 126
International Labour Organization (ILO), 161

International law, 174–175
International Monetary Fund (IMF): GEAR, 132
International Socialist League (ISL), 237
Internet use: media technology access, 198
Intsomi (Xhosa storytelling), 286
Invictus (film), 67–68, 279
Iron Age, 252–253
Irwin, Alec, 73
Isicathamiya, **151**, 165, 193, 207
Islam, **151–154**; Afrikaans literature, 180; Cape Malay, 60; Ibrahim's conversion to, 141; increasing religious diversity, 100; Jewish-Muslim friction, 160; Muslim anticrime groups, 310
The Island (Fugard), 122
Israeli-Palestinian conflict, 152
Ityala Lamawela (Mqhayi), 180

Jabavu, Davidson Don Tengo, 16, **155–156**, 306
Jabavu, John Tengo, 65, 155, **156**; black press, 196; Lovedale, 181
Jameson, Leander Starr, 52, 259
Jameson Raid, 16
Jazz, 208–209, 211. *See also* Ibrahim, Abdullah; Makeba, Miriam; Masekela, Hugh; Moeketsi, Kippie Morolong; Music
Jazz Epistles, 141, 205, 209
Jewish South Africans: First, Heloise Ruth, 120; Gordimer, Nadine, 131; immigration restrictions, 142; Leon, Anthony, 178; Suzman, Helen, 281–282
Johannesburg, **156–157**; AWB violence, 11; Cape Malay's Islam, 60; film censorship, 65–66; Jewish population, 158; Mandela's youth, 186; negotiations over the Constitution, 89; Rand Revolt, 256–257; Rivonia Trial, 259–261; Soweto, 274; theater and resistance, 289; Tsotsi, 296–297
Johnson, Joe, 65
Joint Monitoring Committee on Improving the Quality of Life and Status of Women (JMC), 313
Joint United Nations Programme on HIV and AIDS (UNAIDS), 13
Jordan, A. C., 180
Joseph, Helen, **157–158**, 223, 292, 311–312
Joubert, Christian Johannes, 157
Journalists, 156; First, Heloise Ruth, 120; Mbeki, Govan, 193; Plaatje, Sol, 233–234; Sobukwe, Robert, 269–270; Verwoerd, Hendrik, 308
Judaism, **158–160**. *See also* Jewish South Africans
Judiciary. *See* Law and society

Kadalie, Clements, 64, 150, **161–162**, 267, 303
Kagame, Paul, 8
KaNgwane (Swazi), 31–32
Kani, John, 122
Kanna hy kù Huistoe (Small), 289
KaSeme, Pixley, 3, 177, 236, 302
Kasrils, Ronnie, 158

Kat River, 44–45
Kathrada, Ahmed, 145, 259, 292
Kaunda, Kenneth, 306
Kennedy, Robert, 182
Kente, Gibson, 289
Kenya, 120
Khama, Seretse, 306
Khoikhoi, **162**; Baartman, Sara, 29; Cape Colony, 59; Cape Colony expansion, 39–40; Cape Malay, 60; coloured people classification, 70; Dutch trade, 97–100; Griqua's origins, 131; Hottentot codes, 41; isiXhosa language, 317; Krotoa, 162–163; literary traditions, 179; Muslim slaves, 151; Namibian inhabitants, 213; precolonial period, 252; racial classification, 256; slave resistance, 268; sociolingual landscape, 169; theater and performance, 286
Khoisan, 263. *See also* Khoikhoi; San
Khumalo, Henry (Mr. Drum), 91
Khumalo, Mzilikazi, 210
Kidnapping: Winnie Mandela's arrest for, 190
Kimberley, **162**; Anglo-Boer War, 17; diamond discovery, 47; film industry, 66; pass laws, 232; race and class issues, 50–51. *See also* Gold and diamond mining
King, Martin Luther Jr., 80, 315
King Kong (musical), 183, 208, 288–289
King Solomon's Mines (Haggard), 180
Kitchener, Horatio, 17–18
Kok, Adam, I, 131
Kok, Adam, III, 44, 132
Koornhof, P.G.J., 230, 278
Koornhof bills, 305
Kotane, Moses, 4, 79
Kozain, Rusium, 154
Kramer, David, 288–289
Kriegler, Johann, 114
Krige, Eileen, 230
Krige, Jack, 230
Krog, Antjie, 181
Krotoa, **162–163**
Kruger, Stephanus Johannes Paul, 16, 49–52, **163**
Kuper, Hilda, 230
Kuruman, **163**
Kuyper, Abraham, 20, 236
Kwaito, **163–164**, 211, 296–297
KwaZulu-Natal Province, 151; Adams College, 2; ANC domination, 5; coalition government proposal, 84; COPE support, 6; HIV infection, 11; Indian-African riots, 146; Ngoni, 223; 1994 elections, 113–114; origins of, 216–217; reconstruction and development fund, 323; Zulu, 320–322. *See also* Natal
Kwela, **164**, 193, 208–209

La Guma, Alex, 5, **165–166**
La Guma, James, 150

Labor: apartheid ideology, 20–21; bantustans, 32; Coloured Labour Preference Policy, 61; court system, 175; diamond discovery increasing economic activity, 47; Durban strikes, 94–95; indentured, 143; industrialization of Kimberley and the Witwatersrand, 51; land reform failure, 168; Mozambican, 206; pasta factory boycott, 246; political economy, 239–242; protesting Union rule, 301; Rand Revolt, 256–257; Zulu, 321. *See also* Pass laws

Labor migration: Boers' Great Trek, 37, 42–43; British settlers of the 1820s, 40–41; health care workers, 136; Huguenots, 138–139; Indian South Africans, 144; Mfecane, 42; Natal's labor shortages, 46; racial criteria for immigration, 142–143; reconstruction-era color bar, 54

Labor Party, 237

Labor Tenants Act (1996), 168

Labor unions. *See* Trade unions

Ladysmith Black Mambazo, 151, **165**

Land Act (1913), 166, 301

Land reform, 167–169

Land tenure and dispossession, 60, **166–169**; All-African Convention, 16; Boers, 18; Boers' Great Trek, 42–43; British annexation of land north of Orange River, 44; British South Africa Company, 56; chieftancy, 149; customary law, 78; economic and social development under the British, 39–40; Mfengu, 200; native reserves, 46; Natives' Land Act, 91–92, 219; new social movements, 222; Shepstone's annexation of the Transvaal Republic, 47, 49; Sophiatown, 270; Swazi land claims, 282–283; Union of South Africa, 301; war at Hintsa, 42; Xhosa's loss of land, 317

Landdrost, 98

Landless Peoples Movement (LPM), 221–222

Langalibalele (Hlubi Chief), 47

Langenhoven, C. J., 180

Language: Afrikaners, 8, 151, 235–236; Bantu Education Act, 31; Bantu-language newspapers, 156; bilingual education, 137; bilingual theater, 287; coloured people, 70; Fanagalo, 119; Griquas, 131; home language distribution of the eleven official languages of South Africa, 172(box); Huguenots' assimilation, 139; isiXhosa, 317–318; Jews of South Africa, 159; Khoisan, 162, 263; of Kuruman, 163; literary traditions, 179–180; Lotus Prize for Literature, 166 Malan's campaign for bilingualism, 184; minority cultural rights, 10; multilingual education policy, 109; Ngoni, 223; origins of Afrikaans, 151; precolonial period, 252; religion's classification, 60; resistance to the white media, 197; sePedi, 233; seTswana, 297; Sotho, 271–272; Soweto Student Uprising, 107–108; Venda, 307; Zulu, 320–322

language: Tsotsi, 296–297

Language/language policy, **169–173**

Later Stone Age, 251

Law and society, **173–177**; customary law, 46, 77–78; Gandhi's role, 123; Hertzog's career, 137; HIV/AIDS response, 12; implementing the Constitution, 74; protection under the Hottentot codes, 41

Lawyers: Lembede, Anton Muziwakhe, 177; Leon, Tony, 178; Mandela, Nelson, 186; Matthews, Z. K., 192–193; Smuts, Jan, 269; Tambo, Oliver, 285–286

League of Nations, 214–215

Lebona, Koloi, 119

Legal system. *See* Law and society

Legassick, Martin, 240

Legitimacy, political, 86, 147

Lehore, Jack, 164

Leipold, Louis, 287

Lekota, Mosiuoa, 74

Lembede, Anton Muziwakhe, 4, 7, **177–178**, 186, 286

Leon, Anthony James (Tony), **178**

Leon, Tony, 81

Lesotho, **178–179**; Hani's exile, 133; labor migration, 130, 142, 201; Moshoeshoe, 205; Sotho language, 271–272; Tutu, Desmond, 297

Leutwein, Theodor, 214

Liberal Party (Britain), 54

Liberal Party (South Africa): apartheid laws, 21

Liberalism, 84, 234–235; demand for representative institution, 45; Suzman, Helen, 281–282

Liberated areas, 248

Liberation movement. *See* Pan Africanist Congress

Liberation theology, 38

Life Among the Hottentots (skit), 287

Limpopo Province, 307–308

Linda, Solomon, 208

Literacy, 173

Literature, **179–181**; Zulu, 321. *See also* Authors; Poets/poetry; Theater

Lithuania, 158–159

Livingstone, David, 163

Local government: chieftancy, 149; health care, 137; Port Elizabeth's nonracial government, 251

Long Walk to Freedom (Mandela), 189

Loring, Richard, 289

Lotus Prize for Literature, 166

Lovedale, **181**; Biko's expulsion, 33; cricket and football, 277; establishment of, 65; Hani, Chris, 133; language policy, 171; Soga's studies at, 270

Lowie, Robert, 230

Luthuli, Albert, 2, 4, 177, **182**, 292

The Lying Days (Gordimer), 180

Macbeth, 288

Machel, Graca Simbine, 189

Machel, Samora, 207

Madagascar: slave trade, 267

Madlala-Routledge, Nozizwe, 312

Mafeje, Archie, 230

Mafeking: Anglo-Boer War, 17

Mahlatini, 193
Mahotella Queens, 193
Makatini, Johnny, 5
Makeba, Miriam Zenzi, **183–184**, 191, 208
Malan, Daniel Francois (D. F.), 95, **184**; apartheid, 20; election boycotts, 225; National Party split, 218; Purified National Party, 301; Verwoerd's cabinet position, 308
Malawi: AIDS in mine workers, 12; Ngoni, 223
Malays, 151
Manaka, Matsemela, 181
Mandela, Makaziwe (daughter), 186
Mandela, Makgatho Lewanika (son), 186
Mandela, Nelson, **184–190**; AIDS plan, 12–13; ANC youth league, 4, 7; ANC-COPE split, 74; armed struggle against apartheid, 25; Baartman's repatriation, 30; commemorating Soweto Uprising, 275–276; Fischer as lawyer for, 121; global antiapartheid movement, 128; implementing the Constitution, 74; *Invictus*, 67–68, 279; Islamic celebration, 151; Ladysmith Black Mambazo and, 165; negotiated settlement, 82; 1990s negotiations, 88; Ohlange Institute, 227; release of, 5, 80–81, 218–219; Rivonia Trial, 259–261; Robben Island, 261; Soweto roots, 274; Treason Trial, 120, 292; University of Fort Hare, 306; Winnie Mandela, 190; Xhosa, 318
Mandela, Pumla Mokaziwe (daughter), 186
Mandela, Thembekile Madiba (son), 186
Mandela, Winifred Nomzamo (Winnie) Madikizela, 186, 189, **190**, 294, 311
Mandela, Zenani (daughter), 186, 190
Mandela, Zindziswa (daughter), 186, 190
"Manenberg" (song), 141
Mangope, Lucas, 11
Mantanzuma, Kaizer, 138
Manufacturing industry, 103, 270
Maori: global antiapartheid movement, 125; rugby players, 278
Mapantsula (film), 67
Mapogo a Mathamaga, 309–310
Mapungubwe, **191**, 229–231
Marabi, 193, 208
Market Theater (Johannesburg), 289
Marks, J. B., 4
Marriage: customary law, 78; Mandela's, 186; patrilineal chieftancy, 147. *See also* Miscegenation
Marxism, 133, 237–239
Masekela, Hugh, 141, 164, 183, **191–192**, 205, 208–209, 270
Mashalaba, Ntsiki, 33
Mashiyane, Spokes, 164
Mass Democratic Movement, 80
Mass Democratic Movement (MDM), 249
Masuka, Dorothy, 209
Matabele. *See* Ndebele
Matanzima, Kaiser, 185

Matjiesrivier Cave, 252
Matshikiza, Todd, 208
Mattera, Don, 270
Matthews, Zachariah Keodirelang (Z. K.), 2, **192–193**, 193, 306, 315
Maxeke, Charlotte, 3
Mayekiso, Moses, 68
Mayer, Phillip, 230
Mayibuye Festival of African Arts, 291
Mbaqanga, **193**, 210
Mbeki, Govan Archibald Mvuyelwa, 2, 4, 188, **193–194**, 259–260; University of Fort Hare, 306
Mbeki, Thabo Mvuyelwa, **194–195**; African Renaissance, 7–8; AIDS-HIV stance, 83; AU creation, 8; Baartman's repatriation, 30; Boesak pardon, 38; COPE, 74; denial of HIV/AIDS, 13–14; HIV/AIDS stance, 5–6; Jewish-Muslim friction, 160; Lovedale, 181; neoliberal economic policies, 241–242; TRC findings, 295; 2009 elections, 113; Xhosa, 318; Zimbabwe mediation, 320; Zuma and, 322–323
Mbete, Baleka, 312
Mda, Ashby Peter, 7, 177, 195–196
Mda, Zakes, 181, **195–196**
Mecca, 154
Media, **196–198**; ANC's lack of outlets, 3; Bantu-language newspapers, 156; *Drum* magazine, 91; film industry, 65–68; Islamic radio, 152; language policy, 173; Malan as editor, 184; music radio, 209; Soweto Student Uprising, 275; Truth and Reconciliation Commission, 294; vigilantism, 309; white athletes protesting sports segregation, 278
Mental illness: Head, Bessie, 134
Methamphetamine, 63
Methuen, Paul, 17
Meyer, Roelof (Roelf) Petrus, 77, 89, 138, **199**
Mfecane, 41–42, 157, **199–200**, 223, 317, 319–320
Mfengu, 42, 50, **200**
Mhlaba, Raymond, 188, 260
Mhlawuli, Sicelo, 130, 247
Mhudi (Plaatje), 180
Migrant labor, **200–204**; AIDS in, 12; gold mining, 130; music, 207. *See also* Labor; Labor migration
Military: Anglo-Boer War, 16–19; Anglo-Zulu War, 19; attempt at Transvaal conquest, 259; Cape Dutch resistance to British rule, 40; chieftancies' military legitimacy, 147; Dutch East India Company, 99; global antiapartheid movement, 127; Hani's military service in Zimbabwe, 133; Kruger's service to the Transvaal army, 163; Mfecane, 200; Ngonis' proficiency, 223; Ngqika's claim to the Xhosa chieftancy, 224; political violence during the transition, 243–244; Shaka Zulu, 265–266; Smuts, Jan, 269; TRC findings, 294; Zimbabwe's political turmoil, 319–320. *See also* Umkhonto we Sizwe (Spear of the Nation)
Millennium Africa Programme, 8

Millin, Sarah Gertrude, 180
Million Signature Campaign (UDF), 306
Milner, Alfred, 16, 18, 52–54
Milner's Kindergarten, 53, 55
Mine Boy (Abraham), 180
Mine workers: isicathamiya, 151; migrant labor, 201; origins of Isicathamiya, 165; Ramaphosa's union organization, 256; Rand Revolt, 256–257; soccer games, 277
Mines and Works Act (1911), 301
Mining: British South Africa Company, 56; economic structure, 103; foreign investment, 101; Kimberley and the Witwatersrand, 51; Milner's reconstruction plan, 54; political economy, 239–240. *See also* Gold and diamond mining; Kimberley
Miscegenation: Breytenbach, Breyten, 38; Cape Malay, 60; Griqua, 131; Head, Bessie, 134; Krotoa, 162–163; racial discrimination against coloureds, 71–72
Missionaries, 65; black press, 196–197; cricket and football, 276–277; film industry, 66; founding of Kuruman, 163; Griqua's origins, 131; Kadalie's education, 161; linguistic responsibilities, 170; Lovedale, 181; Schreiner's upbringing, 265; Soga, Tiyo, 270; South West Africa, 214; war at Hintsa, 42; Zulu politics, 320–321
Mitchell's Plain, 62, 244
Mixed Marriages Act, 38, 153
Mixed race. *See* Coloured
Mkhatshwa, Smangaliso, 246
Mkhonto, Sparrow, 130, 247
Mlangeni, Alfred, 188
Modisane, William Bloke, 67, 91
Moeketsi, Kippie Morolong, 141, 183, 191, **205**, 208–209
Moffat, Robert, 163
Mogotlane, Thomas, 67
Mompati, Ruth, 5
Mondlane, Eduardo, 315
Moosa, Ebrahim, 153, 223
Morocco: AU membership, 8
Mortality, impact of HIV/AIDS on, 12
Moshoeshoe, 44, 178, **205**
Mosques, 151–152
Mother-to-child transmission of AIDS, 13–14
Motlanthe, Kgalema Petrus, 6, 14, 195, **206**
Motopayane, Tebello, 274
Motsoaledi, Aaron, 15, 135
Movement for Democratic Change, 319
Mozambique, 51, **206–207**; armed struggle against apartheid, 25; Frontline states, 122; independence inspiring student protest, 245; Mfecane, 200; mine workers' migration, 130; MK operations, 4; Ngoni, 223; precolonial period, 252; slave trade, 98, 267–268; Slovo's exile, 269; Swazi population, 282; Tsonga, 296; Zuma's ANC activities, 322
Mpande (Zulu king), 321

Mpe, Phaswane, 181
Mpetha, Oscar, 246
Mqhayi, S.E.K., 180
Mrs. Ples, 229
Mseleku, Thami, 15
Msimang, Mendi, 5
Msimang, Selby, 150
Mswati II, 282
Mtetwa, Esau, 288
Mugabe, Robert, 306, 319
Multinationalism in sports, 278
Multi-Party Negotiation Process, 188–189
Murder: Biko, Steve, 33; Retief, Piet, 321; Soweto Student Uprising, 275; Verwoerd, Hendrik, 308. *See also* Assassinations
Museveni, Yoweri, 8, 323
Music, 69, **207–211**; AIDS plan, 12–13; Fassie, Brenda, 119–120; global antiapartheid movement, 127; Ibrahim, Abdullah, 141; influencing Mda, 195–196; isicathamiya, 151, 193; kwaito, 163–164, 296–297; kwela, 164, 193; Ladysmith Black Mambazo, 165; Makeba, Miriam Zenzi, 183; Masekela, Hugh, 191–192; Mbaqanga, 193; Moeketsi, Kippie, 205; resurgence of Afrikaner culture, 10; Sophiatown's black urban culture, 270–271; storytelling, 179; theater and performance, 286
Mutwa, Credo, 163
Myths, 179
Mzilikazi, 200, **211–212**, 220

Naicker, G. M., 273
Naidoo, Jay, 73
Naidoo, Krish, 279
Nama people, 214–215
Namibia, **213–216**; global antiapartheid movement, 127; Khoikhoi origins, 162; Khoisan languages, 169; NP incorporation of, 218; racial classifications, 255; rock art, 251; San, 263
Napoleonic Wars, 39
Natal, **216–217**; Anglo-Boer War, 16–17; Anglo-Zulu War, 19; armed skirmishes, 47; Bambatha Rebellion, 30; British annexation of, 44; Buthelezi, Mangosuthu Gatsha, 57; chieftancy under colonialism, 148–149; demand for representative institution, 45–46; Durban, 92; establishment of the Republic, 37; Fanagalo, 119; IFP, 150; Industrial and Commercial Workers Union, 64; migrant labor, 201; Natives' Land Act, 219; nonracial franchise, 234; popular politics, 244; Rhodes's farming, 259; South African unification, 55; theater and performance, 288
Natal Code of Native Law (1891), 148
Natal Indian Congress (NIC), 123, 144–145
Natal Native Congress, 302
National AIDS Convention of South Africa (NACOSA), 12
National Arts Council, 290–291

National Arts Festival (Grahamstown), 291
National Coalition for Gay and Lesbian Equality, 2
National Council of Trade Unions, 81
National Crime Prevention Strategy, 309
National Education Crisis/Coordinating Committee, **217**, 248
National Forum, **217**
National Gender Machinery (NGM), 313
National HIV and AIDS and STI Strategic Plan for South Africa, 14
National Liberation League, 1, 72
National parks, 191
National Party, **217–219**; abolishing the Natives Representative Council, 220; Afrikaner nationalism, 235–236; Afrikaners, 8; ANC's increasing apartheid protest, 4; anti-Indian sentiment, 144; apartheid, 20; apartheid legislative scheme, 75; armed struggle against apartheid, 24, 26; AWB stance, 11; Bantu Education Act, 106–107; bantustans, 31–32; Bill of Rights advocates, 34; Bloemfontein origins, 37; Broederbond goals, 56; CODESA, 77; DA and, 81; democratic transition/negotiations, 87–90; disenfranchisement of coloureds, 72; immigration recruitment, 142; Indian support for, 146; Labor Party alliance, 137–138; Malan's service, 184; Meyer's role in negotiating democratic transition, 199; migrant labor policy, 203; negotiated settlement, 82–83; 1994 elections, 113; paleoanthropology, 230; race and voter choice, 116. *See also* Apartheid
National Policy for General Education Affairs Act of 1984, 108
National Sports Congress (NSC), 279
National Union of Mineworkers, 73, 256
National Union of South African Students (NUSAS), 33, 246
National Women's Charter, 312–313
Nationalism: African, 236–237; apartheid laws dividing cultures, 23; Bambatha Rebellion, 30. *See also* Afrikaner nationalism
Native Administration Act, 149
Native Bills, 16
Native Life in South Africa (Plaatje), 219, 234
Native Recruitment Corporation, 201
Native Trust and Land Act (1936), 167, 301
Native Urban Areas Act (1923), 232, 270
Natives (Abolition of Passes and Co-ordination of Documents) Act, 232
Natives' Land Act (1913), **219;** ANC petitions against, 3; Dube's protest of, 91–92; forced migration of rural Africans, 23; Jabavu's support for, 156; Plaatje on, 166–169, 233–234; Union of South Africa, 299
Natives (racial classification), 256
Natives Representative Council (NRC), 182, **219–220**
Natives Urban Areas Consolidation Act, 232

Nativism, 237
Naudé, C. F. Beyers, 65, 246, 273
Nazism, 20, 301
Ncube, Sister Bernard, 246
Ndebele, **220**, 319; Mzilikazi, 211–212; racial classification, 255; Rhodes's mining grants, 259; sangoma, 263, 265; Tshwane, 296
Nederduits Hervormde Kerk (NHK), 235
Negotiations. *See* Democratic transition/negotiations (1990-1994)
Nehru, Jawaharlal, 125
Nelson Mandela Foundation, 189
Neoliberalism: Indians benefiting from, 146; new social movements, 221–223; political economy, 240–242
Nesbitt, Prexy, 127
Netherlands: global antiapartheid movement, 127; immigration recruitment, 142. *See also* Dutch colonialism
Netshitenzhe, Joel, 241–242
New African Movement, 66
The New Age newspaper, 193
New Growth Path, 104–105
New National Party, 81, 84, 184, 218
New Partnership for Africa's Development (NEPAD), 8, 195
New social movements, **221–223**
New Zealand: emigration to, 118; global antiapartheid movement, 125, 127; labor migration, 142; sporting isolation under apartheid, 278
Newspapers: history of South Africa's, 196. *See also* Media
Ngcobo, Lauretta, 181
Ngo Thi Hoang, Yolande, 38
Ngoni, **223**
Ngoyi, Lillian, 7, 157, **223–224,** 311–312
Ngozi, Winston Mankunku, 209
Ngqika, **224**
Ngubane, Harriet, 230
Ngubane, Jordan, 177, 186
Ngwane, Trevor, 221
Niger-Kordofanian language family, 169
9/11, 151
Nkomati Accord, 322
Nkomo, William, 186
Nkosi, Lewis, 67, 181
"Nkosi Sikelel' iAfrika," 207, 224, 302
Nobel Prize, 2, 4, 69–70, 80, 165, 182, 188, 297
Non-European Unity Movement (NEUM), 16, 72, 79, 155, **224–225,** 304
Nongovernmental organizations, 68–69
Nongqawuse, 45, **225–226,** 287
Nonracism, 225
Nonviolent struggle, 182
Northern Cape Province, 132, 162
Ntoko, Evelyn, 186
Ntshona, Winston, 122
Nujoma, Sam, 215

Nyerere, Julius, 306
Nzima, Samuel, 275
Nzo, Alfred, 5

Obasanjo, Olusegun, 127
Obesity, 134–135
Odinga, Oginga, 120
Office of the Status of Women (OSW), 313
Ohlange Institute, 91, **227**
Oil companies: global antiapartheid movement, 126
Okhela (resistance group), 38
Olympic Games, 56, 91, 278
Omar, Dullah, 34
Omar, Rashid, 153
117 Days (First), 120
Oorlam people, 213–214
Operational Plan for Comprehensive HIV and AIDS Care, Management and Treatment for South Africa, 13
Oral literary traditions, 179
Orange Free State, 17, 37, 43–44, 51–52, 54, 121, 131–132, 216
Orange River Colony, 162, 213, 272
Orangia Unie Party, 137
Order of Luthuli in Silver Award, 130
Organization of African Unity, 8, 75
Orlando West Junior Secondary School, Soweto, 275
Ovambo people, 214–215
Ox-Wagon Brigade, 301

Paleoanthropology, **229–231**
Pan Africanist Congress (PAC), **231–232**; ANC roots, 4; ANC split, 237; ANC Youth League and, 7; apartheid laws, 21; armed struggle against apartheid, 24–25; Azania, 27; de Klerk and, 80–81; De Lille, Patricia, 81; founding of, 186–187; global antiapartheid movement, 127; Head, Bessie, 134; influencing the Soweto Student Uprising, 275; 1994 elections, 113; pass laws protest, 232; post–1999 politics, 84; Sharpeville Massacre, 266; Sobukwe, Robert, 269–270
Pantsula, 296–297
Paramilitaries: Afrikaner Weerstandsbeweging, 11, 286; Zimbabwe's political turmoil, 319–320
Parker, Charlie "Bird," 205
Parliament: Bill of Rights, 34; Cape Town, 61; Constitutional Court, 176; De Lille, Patricia, 81; designing the Constitution, 83; Ginwala's membership, 125; Hani assassination, 134; Holomisa, Bantu, 138; Leon's leadership, 178; media regulation, 198; negotiations over the Constitution, 89; race-based tricameral political systems, 145; Sisulu, Albertina, 266–267; Suzman, Helen, 281–282; SWA annexation, 218; UDM seats, 199; women's representation, 312. *See also* Appendix 3: Government Structures

Pass laws, **232–233**; abolition of, 41; ANC demonstration, 3; apartheid ideology, 21; bantustan strategy of deportation, 32; film portrayal of, 67; Joseph's activism, 157; labor migration regulation, 202; law and society, 174; nonviolent protest, 242–243; PAC's protest of, 187; Sharpeville Massacre, 266; theater and resistance, 289–290; Winnie Mandela's arrest, 190; women and politics, 311–312; women's protest, 223–224. *See also* Defiance campaigns
Paton, Alan, 180
Patrilineal chieftancy, 147
Patriot Movement, 99
Peace of Vereeniging (1961), 18
Peaceful resistance *(satyagraha)* strategy, 24, 80, 123, 274
Pedi, 47, 49–50, **233,** 271
Pegging Act, 145
Pennywhistle, 164, 208
People Against Gangsterism and Drugs (PAGAD), 153, 309–310
People Living with HIV/AIDS (PLWHA), 12
People's army, 4
People's power, 248–249
Performing arts. *See* Music; Theater and performance
Petersen, Taliep, 288–289
Pharmaceutical industry, 14
Phillips, Ray, 66
Physically challenged individuals, 36
Piekniek by Dingaan (play), 290
Pieterson, Hector, 245, 275
Pilgrim's Progress (Bunyan), 270
Plaatje, Solomon (Sol) Thsekisho, **233–234**; ANC leadership, 3; films and newspapers, 66; literature, 180; Lovedale, 181; Natives' Land Act, 166, 219
Playwrights: Fugard, Athol, 122; Mda, Zakes, 195–196
Plettenberg Bay, Western Cape Province, 252
Poets/poetry, 154, 181; Breytenbach, Breyten, 38; Brutus, Dennis Vincent, 56; Soga, Tiyo, 270
Police: A.W.G. Champion, 64; Biko's detention, 33; Sharpeville Massacre, 266; Sophiatown destruction, 271; Soweto Student Uprising, 274–276; vigilantism, 308–310; Zimbabwe's political turmoil, 319–320. *See also* Soweto student uprising
Police, Prisons, and Civil Rights Union, 244
Police Zone, SWA, 214
Polio case, 136
Political autonomy: bantustans, 31–32
Political cabaret, 290
Political cultures and ideologies, **234–239**
Political economy, **239–242**
Political franchise: Afrikaner's aspirations towards native rights, 302; apartheid laws, 21; Cape franchise, 45, 59–60; Cape political culture and ideology, 234–235; coloureds, 71–72; results of the South African War, 53; Schreiner's involvement,

265; South African unification, 55; Terre Blanche's opposition to, 286
Political participation: Muslims, 153
Political parties: Afrikaner Bond, 51–52, 300–301; Congress of the People, 73–74; Democratic Alliance, 81–82; elections of 1994 to 2009, 117–118; global antiapartheid movement, 126; National Forum, 217; National Party, 217–219; 1994 elections, 111–113; Pan Africanist Congress, 231–232; post–1999 politics, 83–84; United Democratic Movement, 138. *See also* African National Congress; Appendix 5: Political Parties in the April 2009 National Elections; National Party
Political representation: coloured identity, 72–73; criminalization of black participation, 242–244; Natives Representative Council, 219–220; Suzman championing black rights, 281–282. *See also* Parliament
Political violence in South Africa, **242–244**; antiapartheid movements, 23; 1994 elections, 111; vigilantism, 308–310. *See also* Apartheid; Violence
Poll tax: Bambatha Rebellion, 30
Pollsmoor Prison, 188
Polygyny, 46
Pop music, 210–211
Popular politics, **244–249**
Population Registration Act (1950), 21, 70–72, 255
Port Elizabeth, **249–251**; Brutus, Dennis Vincent, 56; Civic Associations, 68; Fugard's plays, 122; new social movements, 221; Soweto Student Uprising, 275
Portugal: land struggles, 49
Portuguese colonialism: Mozambique, 206; Natal, 216
Positive Muslims, 154
Poulantzian structuralism, 240
Poverty: Cape Town, 63; Carnegie Commission findings on white poverty, 63; civil society, 69; economic status, 101–102
Power sharing, 83
Praise poems, 179
Prayers, 179
Precolonial period, **251–253**; literary traditions, 179; Mapungubwe, 191; Namibia, 213; paleoanthropology, 229–231; sociolingual landscape, 169; Sotho society, 271
Pregnancy: AIDS and, 13–14; health care system, 135
Presidents: Kruger, Stephanus Johannes Paul, 163; Motlanthe, Kgalema, 206; Zuma, Jacob, 322–323. *See also* Mandela, Nelson
Pretoria: ANC development, 4; pass laws protest, 232. *See also* Tshwane
Pretorius, Andries, 258
Primary health-care (PHC), 135–136
Prime ministers: Hertzog, James Barry Munnik, 137–138, 218; Malan, Daniel Francois, 184; Rhodes, Cecil, 259; Smuts, Jan, 269; Verwoerd, Hendrik, 308

Primitive accumulation, 239
Pringle, Thomas, 196
Private health care, 135
Privatization: steel and heavy chemicals, 103
Program to Combat Racism of the WCC, 315
Progressive party, 178, 234
Prohibition of Mixed Marriages Act of 1949, 71–72
Prohibition of Political Interference Act (1968), 21
Promotion of Bantu Self-Government Act (1959), 31, 75
Propaganda: South African film industry, 65–66
Property Clause, 168
Prophecy, 225–226
Proportional representation, 83
Prostitution, 29–30, 151
Proverbs, 179
Province of Queen Adelaid, 42–43
Public Control Ordinance of 1916, 65
Public Protector, 35
Publications and Entertainments Act (1963), 66
Purified National Party, 218, 301

Qualified majoritarian system, 83

Racial capitalism, 240–241
Racial classification, **255–256**; Afrikaner nationalism, 235–236; black consciousness, 238; District Six segregation, 90; Durban's diversity, 92; economic differentials, 102; electoral politics, 84–86; Head rejecting, 134; HIV infection, 11–12; immigration criteria, 142–143; Indian South Africans, 144–147; Islamic slaves, 151; Kimberley and Witwatersrand, 50–51; Muslims, 153; political economy, 239–242; unionism, 237–238; voter choice, 116–117. *See also* Afrikaner(s); Coloured people; Indian South Africans
Racial Fordism, 241
Racism: Adams College, 2; affirmative action as reverse racism, 2; apartheid ideology, 20; Brutus's activism against, 56; Cape Town's housing shortage, 62; Christian institutions protesting, 65; colonialism *versus*, 38–39; education policy, 107; Mda's plays and writings, 196; Natives' Land Act, 219; Non-European Unity Movement protesting, 224–225; results of the South African War, 53; sports, 277–279; women and politics, 311–314. *See also* Apartheid
Radio Bantu, 209
Railway, 49, 300
Rainbow Nation, 146
Ramaphosa, Matamela Cyril, 73, 77, 89, 194, 199, **256**
Ramphele, Mamphela, 33
Rand. *See* Witwatersrand
Rand Revolt (1922), **256–257**, 301
Rap music, 163–164
Rassool, Ebrahim, 153
Rathebe, Dolly, 91

Reader, Desmond, 230
Reagan, Ronald, 126–127
Reconstruction, 53–54
Reconstruction and Development Program (RDP), 5, 104, **257–258**; GEAR replacing, 132; land reform, 168; Mbeki's abandonment of, 194; race and electoral politics, 86
Record of Understanding, 88
Refugees: Mfengu, 200
Religion: Afrikaner nationalism, 235–236; Cape Malay's Islam, 60; Christianity, 64–65; colonial education policy, 105; Griquas, 132; increasing diversity, 100; Islam, 151–154; Judaism, 158–160; Luthuli, Albert, 182; South African Council of Churches, 273. *See also* Catholic Church; Dutch Reformed Church
Reparation and Rehabilitation Committee (TRC), 295
Reserve, native, 46, 301–302
Resha, Robert, 5
Resistance, 47; Afrikaner Weerstandsbeweging, 11; black press, 196–197; *Drum* magazine, 91; education policy, 106; Gandhi's role, 123; to Germany rule in SWA, 214–215; Indian militancy, 144–145; 1983 Constitution, 75; protest songs and storytelling, 179; slaves' revolts, 268; Sophiatown as symbol of, 270; theater and poetry, 181, 289–290; Union of South Africa, 301–304; to VOC rule, 99–100. *See also* Antiapartheid movements and activities; Armed struggle; Pan Africanist Congress
Retief, Pieter (Piet) Mauritz, **258,** 321
Reunited National Party, 218
Rhenish Mission Society, 214
Rhodes, Cecil John, 51–52, **259**; Anglo-Boer War, 16; British South Africa Company, 55; racism in sports, 277; Zimbabwe formation, 319
Rhodes Scholarships, 259
Rights, 33–35; British settlers' ideology, 41
Riotous Assemblies Act (1930), 301
Rissick, Johannes, 157
Rivonia trial, 25, **259–261**; ANC members, 4; Fischer's role, 121; Mandela at, 187; Mbeki, Govan, 193; Mbeki, Thabo, 194; Sisulu, Walter, 267; Winnie Mandela's house arrest, 190
Roach, Max, 141
Robben Island, 163, **261**; ANC members, 4; Brutus's incarceration, 56; Fugard's play, 122; Langalibalele's incarceration, 47; Mandela's arrest and incarceration, 187–188; Mbeki's incarceration, 193; Motlanthe's arrest and incarceration, 206; Sisulu's incarceration, 267; Sobukwe's incarceration, 270; Zuma's incarceration, 322
Roberts, Frederick, 17
Robeson, Paul, 125
Rock art, 251, 264
Rockman, Gregory, 244
Rogosin, Lionel, 67

Rubusana, W. B., 156
Rugby, 67–68, 276, 278
Rugby World Cup (1995), 276, 279
Rurusana, Walter, 236

Sachs, Albie, 34
Sachs, Solly, 157–158
San, 157, **263**; Cape Colony expansion, 39; Cape Malay, 60; coloured people classification, 70; Dutch colonialism, 97–99; hypergyny, 252–253; isiXhosa language, 317; Khoikhoi and, 162; literary traditions, 179; Muslim slaves, 151; Namibia, 213; precolonial period, 251; racial classification, 256; rock art, 264; sociolingual landscape, 169
Sanctions: global antiapartheid movement, 126–127
Sangoma, 147, **263, 265**
Sarafina (musical), 183
Saturday Night at the Palace (Slabolepszy), 290
Satyagraha (passive resistance), 24–25, 80, 123, 144, 274
Saul, John, 240–241
Savings associations (Stokvels), 281
Scandinavia: global antiapartheid movement, 126
Schapera, Issac, 230
Schlesinger, Isadore William, 66
Schmitz, Oliver, 67
School Board Act (1905), 71
Schreiner, Olive Emile Albertina, 180, **265**
Schreiner, W. P., 55
Science: racialized, 29–30
Scorched earth policy, 17
Scott, Michael, 215
Sebe, Charles, 243
Sechaba publication, 5
Sefularo, Molefi, 15
Segregation, 53; Adams College, 2; Bantu Education Act, 30; Bloemfontein, 37; District Six, 90; Dutch Reformed Church, 95; Port Elizabeth, 250; roots in migrant labor, 202; sports, 276–277; Union of South Africa, 299–300; University of Fort Hare, 306. *See also* Apartheid
Self-determinism, 237
Self-rule: Gandhi's role, 123
Separate Amenities Act (1953), 21, 72
Separation of powers, 83, 176
September, Dulcie, 5
Serote, Wally, 270
Serpant Players, 122
Services: Cape Town, 62–63; new social movements addressing delivery of, 221–222
Settler colonialism. *See* British imperialism and settler colonialism; Colonialism; Dutch colonialism
Sexuality: Baartman's objectification and exploitation, 29
Shabalala, Joseph, 165
Shack settlements: Cape Town, 62
Shaik, Schabir, 323

Shaikh, Sa'diyya, 153
Shaikh, Shamiema, 153–154
Shaka Zulu, 64, 211, **265–266**; defining Zulu identity, 320; Mfecane, 41–42, 199–200; Ndebele's break from, 220
Shaka Zulu album, 165
Shanduka Holdings, 256
Shantytowns. *See* Squatter settlements
Sharecropping system, 167
Sharpeville massacre, 24, **266**; banning of liberation movements, 231; boycott campaigns, 247; coloured political organization, 72; events leading to, 187; film portrayal of racial injustice, 67; Ibrahim's emigration, 141; NEUM's failure to respond to, 225; as protest to pass laws, 243; Verwoerd's role, 308
Shaw, Harold, 66
Sheep farming, 44, 252
Shell Oil, 126
Shepstone, Theophilus, 46–47, 49
Shilowa, Mbhazima Sam, 73–74
Shona people, 191
Siener in die Suburbs (du Plessis), 288
Sigcau, Stella, 138
Simon, Paul, 151, 165, 183, 210–211
Sisulu, Albertina Nontsikelelo, 7, 188, 246, **266–267**, 311–312
Sisulu, Walter Max Ulyate, 266, **267**; ANC youth league, 4, 7; Mandela and, 186; rejecting communism, 177; Rivonia Trial, 259–261; Soweto roots, 274; Treason Trial, 292
Sithole, Antoinette, 275
Sizwe Bansi is Dead (Fugard), 122
Slabolepszy, Paul, 290
Slave Trade Act of 1807, 29
Slaves and slavery, 9, 39, **267–268**; abolition of, 268; Cape Colony, 59; Cape Malay, 60; coloured people classification, 70; constitutional human rights principles, 174–175; early Dutch colony, 98; education, 105; Hottentot Codes and the abolition of slavery, 41; Indian South Africans, 144; Krotoa, 162–163; Muslim presence, 151; origins of coloured identity, 71; sociolingual landscape, 169–170; VOC expansion, 100
Slovo, Joseph (Joe), 4–5, 89, 120, 133, 158, **268–269**, 292
Small, Adam, 289
Smit, Barto, 289
Smith, Harry, 42, 44
Smuts, Jan Christiaan, 54, **269**; Afrikaner nationalism, 301; British collaboration, 54; labor strike, 137–138; Malan's defect of, 184; migrant labor policy, 203; National Party split, 218; Natives Representative Council, 220
Sobukwe, Robert Mangaliso, 186–187, **269–270**; armed struggled against apartheid, 25; PAC founding, 231; University of Fort Hare, 306

Soccer, 6, 276–277, 279
Social acceptance, racial classification and, 255–256
Social Anthropology, Department of, 230
Social grants, 102
Socialism: Brutus's incarceration for, 56. *See also* Communism
Socialist Party of Azania, 84
Socioeconomic class: apartheid legacy, 5; class stratification, 62; HIV infection, 11–12; Jewish population, 159; Kimberley and Witwatersrand, 50–51; new social movements addressing marginalized citizens, 221–223; Reconstruction and Development Program, 257–258; women and politics, 311–312
Soga, Tiyo, **270**
Solidarity trade unions, 10
Sontonga, Enoch, 207
Sophiatown, **270–271**; *Come Back Africa* filming, 67; Fugard's plays, 122; vigilantism, 309
Sotho, **271–272**, 306; Bloemfontein founding, 36; British annexation of land north of Orange River, 44; Moshoeshoe's unification of, 205; Tswana, 297
Soul music style, 209
South Africa Act (1909), 3, 55, 74, **272**
South African Arms Deal, 81
South African Army College, 138
South African Board of Jewish Deputies, 159
South African Broadcasting Corporation (SABC), 197
South African Coloured People's Congress, 121
South African Coloured People's Organization (SACPO), 166, **272**
South African Communist Party (SACP), **272–273**; ANC-COPE split, 74; apartheid laws, 21; armed struggle against apartheid, 25; AWB opposition, 11; Civic Associations, 68; colonialism of a special type, 239–240; COSATU alignment, 73; Dadoo, Yusuf, 79; de Klerk and, 80–81; economic policy, 104; education policy, 106; Fischer's role in, 121; GEAR adoption, 86; Hani, Chris, 133–134; Jewish involvement, 158; Mbeki, Govan, 193; Reconstruction and Development Program, 257–258; Slovo, Joe, 268–269
South African Council of Churches, 246, **273**, 297
South African Council on Sport (SACOS), 278
South African Cricket Board of Control (SACBOC), 90
South African Cricket Union (SACU), 279
South African Indian Congress (SAIC), 4, 80, 121, 145, 272, **273–274**
South African Indian Council, 23
South African Iron and Steel Corporation (ISCOR), 300
South African National Civics Association (Sanco), 68, 221
South African National Editors' Forum (SANEF), 198
South African National Native Congress, 156
South African National NGO Coalition (SANGOCO), 69

South African Native College. *See* University of Fort Hare
South African Native Congress, 302
South African Native National Congress, 3, 233. *See also* African National Congress
South African Non-Racial Olympic Committee, 278
South African Party, 137–138, 218
South African Sports Association, 56
South African Student Organization, 31, 33, 256
South African Students' Movement (SASM), 245, 274
South African War. *See* Anglo-Boer War
South West Africa People's Organization (SWAPO), 215
South West African National Union, 215
Soviet Union, 303
Soweto, **274**; Civic Associations, 68; new social movements, 221; soul music style, 209
Soweto Electricity Crisis Committee (SECC), 221
Soweto Parents Crisis, 31
Soweto Student Uprising (1976), 245–246, **274–276**; ANC exile years, 5; ANC membership, 4; armed struggle against apartheid, 26; BCM role in, 36; Biko's role, 33; causes of, 107–108; coloured political organization, 72; events leading to, 31; impact on music performance, 210; language policy triggering, 171–172; negotiated settlement, 82; questioning apartheid laws, 23; *Sarafina,* 183; Winnie Mandela's activism, 190
Space Theater (Cape Town), 289
Sporting isolation, 278–279
Sports, 56, 90–91, **276–279**
Springboks, 278. *See also* Sports
Squatter settlements, 81, 274, **280–281**
Staggie, Rashaad, 153
Stallard Commission report, 202–203
State of emergency, 11, 88
Statistical information. *See* Demographics and statistics
Stellenbosch, 60(fig.), **281**; Cape Dutch architecture, 59; Dutch colonialism, 97–98; paleoanthropology, 230; Smuts's education, 269; Verwoerd, Hendrik, 308
Stepchildren (Millin), 180
Sterkfontein Cave, 229
Stewart, James, 156
Stofile, Makhenkesi Arnold, 279
Stokvel(s), **281**
Stone Age, 251
The Story of an African Farm (Schreiner), 180, 265
Strijdom, Johannes, 20
Strikes: cost of living protest, 244; Indian militancy, 145; Rand Revolt, 257
Student protest: Biko, Steve, 33; black trade unions, 244–245; ethnically based education, 31; government violence against, 244; Indian militancy, 145; Mandela's involvement, 185; National Education Crisis/Coordinating Committee, 217; pasta factory boycott, 246. *See also* Soweto student uprising

Subsidies, governmental: Cape Town, 62
Suburbanization: Johannesburg, 157
Suffrage. *See* Political franchise
Suicide, 134
Sullivan Principles, 126
"Sunset clauses," 89
Suppression of Communism Act (1950), 21, 56, 130, 133, 187
Supreme Court of Appeal, 37
Suzman, Helen, 82, **281–282**, 311
SWA Police Zone, 214
Swaggart, Jimmy, 152
Swartland, 97–98
Swazi, **282**
Swaziland, 50, **282–283**; Mfecane, 200; migrant labor, 201; music education and growth, 210; sangoma, 263, 265

Tambo, Adelaide, 311
Tambo, Oliver, 4–5, 124, **285–286**; ANC youth league, 4, 7; Mandela and, 186; Mbeki as secretary to, 194; rejecting communism, 177; Rivonia Trial, 260; WCC role, 315
Tanzania: ANC activities, 5; Frontline states, 122; Ngoni, 223
Tatamkhulu Africa, 153
Taung Child, 229
Taxation: Shepstone taxing the white population, 49
Tayob, Abdulkader, 153
Teachers, 156; Goniwe, Matthew, 130; Jabavu, Davidson Don Tengo, 155; Lembede, Anton Muziwakhe, 177; Luthuli, Albert, 182; Sobukwe, Robert, 269–270; Tambo, Oliver, 285–286
Terre Blanche, Eugene, 11, **286**
Terrorism Act, 38, 190, 206
Tetanus, 136
Thaele, James, 3
Thatcher, Margaret, 127
Theater and performance, 181, **286–291**; black music theater, 209; Fugard, Athol, 122; Mda's plays, 195–196
Themba, Can, 91, 270
Theron, Charlize, 67, 139
"Third Force" violence, 210
Tlali, Miriam, 181
Tobiansky, Herman, 270
Tolkien, J.R.R., 37
Tomlinson Commission (1955), 31
Total apartheid, 230
Tourism: Cape Town, 63; Kuruman, 163
Township musicals, 289
Township protests, 247–248, 305. *See also* Sharpeville massacre
Trade: British South Africa Company, 55–56; Dutch East India Company, 95; Dutch founding of Cape Town, 97–99; economic trends, 101; Mapungubwe, 191; Namibia, 214

Trade unions, 4; Afrikaner nationalism, 10; ANC activities, 5; Champion's formation of the policeman's union, 64; Congress of South African Trade Unions, 73; cost of living protest, 244; criminal justice arena, 244; De Lille's presidency, 81; Durban strikes, 94–95; global antiapartheid movement, 125–126; ICU, 150; Jewish involvement, 158; Kadalie's involvement, 161–162; Marxist ideology, 237–238; Motlanthe's activism, 206; Ngoyi, Lillian, 223–224; people's power, 248–249; Ramaphosa, Cyril, 256; Slovo, Joe, 268–269; UDF, 247
Traditional Councils, 168
Traditional culture: customary law, 46, 77–78, 148–149; healers, 137, 263, 265; indigenous forms of government, 147–150; tribal musical theater, 288–289
Traditional Leadership and Governance Framework act (2003), 168
Transforming the mining industry, 130
Transkei, 23, 32, 138
Transvaal Indian Congress, 79, 145
Transvaal Republic, 16–17, 37, 49, 52, 54, 131–132, 216, 272
Treason Trial, 120, **292**; Fischer's role, 121; Freedom Charter, 121; Joseph's incarceration, 157; La Guma's involvement, 166; Mandela, 187; Ngoyi, Lillian, 224; Sisulu, Walter, 267; Slovo's arrest, 269; Tambo, Oliver, 285–286
Treason trial, 4
Treatment Action Campaign (TAC), 2, 14, 221, **292–293**
Treaty of Vereeniging (1902): linguistic policy, 170
Trekboers. *See* Afrikaner(s); Great Trek
Tribal musicals, 288–289
Tricameral political systems, 145, 305
Tripartite alliance, 272
Truth and Reconciliation Commission (TRC), **293–295**; ANC endorsement, 5; apartheid state targeting SACC, 273; Bill of Rights creation, 35; Hani's involvement, 133; Holomisa's ANC expulsion, 138; literary expression, 181; political violence, 242, 244; race and electoral politics, 85; state role in vigilante violence, 309; Swazi collusion with apartheid forces, 282–283; theater and performance, 291; Tutu, Desmond, 297–298; UDF-IFP ties, 150
Tshabalala-Msimang, Manto, 14, 293
Tshwane, **296**
Tsonga, **296**
Tsotsi, **296–297**
Tsotsi (film), 67, 211, 288, 296–297
Tswana, **297**; 1870s uprisings, 47
Tuan Guru, 152
Tuberculosis, 13
Turnhalle Conference (1975–1976), 215
Tuskegee Institute, 227

Tutu, Reverend Desmond Mpilo, 65, 246, **297**; Motlanthe denouncing, 206; South African Council of Churches, 273; Soweto roots, 274; Truth and Reconciliation Commission, 294; University of Fort Hare, 306; Xhosa, 318
Twala, Sello "Chicco," 119

Uitlanders, 52
Umkhonto we Sizwe (Spear of the Nation), 120; ANC criticism, 26; founding of, 4; Hani, Chris, 133–134; Indian nonviolent protest, 145; Mandela's involvement, 187; Rivonia Trial, 260; Slovo's role in, 269; Tambo's leadership, 286
Undine (Schreiner), 265
Unemployment, 101; Cape Town, 62–63; economic status, 101–102; GEAR goals, 132; pass laws policing, 232
Unification, 53–55
Union Artists, 289
Union of South Africa, 1, 81–82, 170–171, **299–304**; chieftancy, 149; creation of, 216; Dube's protest of, 91; education policy, 106; Hertzog's service to, 137; immigrant populations, 141–142; Jabavu's resistance to, 156; labor migration regulation, 202; land tenure and dispossession, 166–167; Plaatje organizing the black community, 233–234; racial classification, 255; South Africa Act, 272; Verwoerd's leadership, 308; vigilantism, 308
Unions. *See* Trade unions
United Democratic Front (UDF), **305–306**; ANC alignment, 4; armed struggle against apartheid, 26; Boesak's role in, 38; Christian roots of, 65; Civic Associations emerging from, 68; coloured political organization against, 72; defiance campaigns, 108; formation and ideology, 247–248; Freedom Charter, 121–122; Goniwe's protest organization, 130; IFP tensions, 150; Indian South Africans, 145; Muslim allies, 153; National Forum and, 217; new social movements, 221; Ramaphosa's role, 256; Sisulu, Albertina, 266–267
United Democratic Movement (UDM), 115; Holomisa, Bantu, 138; Meyer cofounding, 199
United Kingdom. *See* Britain
United Nations: Namibia's trusteeship system, 214–215; Sharpeville Massacre response, 266; World Summit on Sustainable Development, 222
United Nations Charter, 174
United Party, 137–138, 184, 218; apartheid laws, 21; ideology, 234
United States: anti-Muslim policies, 153; defiance campaigns inspiring civil rights movement, 80; destabilizing Mozambique, 206; emigration to, 118; film industry, 66–67; Garveyism, 123–124; global antiapartheid movement, 126; Ladysmith Black Mambazo, 165; Makeba's exile, 183; Mda's life in, 196; musical traditions, 208; Plaatje's travels, 234; theater and resistance, 289

Universal Declaration of Human Rights, 174
Universal Negro Improvement Association, 123–124
University of Fort Hare, 154, 156, **306**; Buthelezi's education, 57; as ethnic university, 193; Goniwe, Matthew, 130; Hani, Chris, 133; Mandela's education, 185; Mbeki, Govan Archibald Mvuyelwa, 193; Mugabe, Robert, 319; Sobukwe, Robert, 269–270; Zuma's honorary doctorate, 323
Unlawful Organizations Act (1960), 21
Urban, Charles, 65
Urban culture, 270
Urbanization: apartheid ideology, 21; bantustan strategy, 32; film portrayal, 67; vigilantism, 309
Uys, Jamie, 67
Uys, Pieter-Dirk, 290

Vaal River, 162
Van de Kaap, Saartje, 152
Van Graan, E.S.J., 191
Van Meerhoff, Pieter, 162–163
Van Onselen, Charles, 241
Van Riebeeck, Johan Anthoniszoon (Jan), 162, 267, **307**
Vehicle accidents, 136
Veldcornet (local government official or military official), 98
Venda, **307–308**; British conquest of, 50; Jewish ancestry, 159; musical traditions, 207; Pedi, 233
Venda (1979), 32
Verloppte (walked away) Afrikaners, 10
Verwoerd, Hendrik Frensch (H. F.), 230, **308**; apartheid, 20, 23; Bantu Education Act, 30; education policy, 107
Victoria East, 42
Vigilantism, 153, **308–310**
Vilakazi, Absolom, 230
Vilakazi, B. W., 180
Violence: ANC-IFP conflict, 5; armed skirmishes in Natal, 47; armed struggle against apartheid, 24–26; AWB, 11; Biko's death, 33; Durban, 92–94; global antiapartheid movement, 127–128; Indian-African riots, 146; Mfecane, 41–42, 199–200; 1994 elections, 115; oppression of music, 210; Ox-Wagon Brigade, 301; political violence in South Africa, 242–244; during 1990s negotiations, 88; Sharpeville Massacre, 266; Soweto Student Uprising, 31, 274; sports boycotts, 278; UDF-IFP ties, 150; vigilantism, 308–310; war at Hintsa, 42; Winnie Mandela's politics, 190. *See also* Armed struggle
Virodene scandal, 13
VOC. *See* Dutch East India Company
Volk (nations), 236
Volkswagen plant, 250
Von Herder, Johann Gottfried, 20
Voortrekkers, 32–33, 43, 131
Vorster, John, 20, 80, 91, 276, 278
Voter choice, 116–117; Indians, 146

Voter Participation, 115–116
Voter registration, 113–115
Voter turnout, 113, 115–116
Voting rights. *See* Political franchise

Wage Act (1925), 71
Waite, John, 278
Walus, Januzs, 134
Walvis Bay, 214
War of Mlanjeni, 44–45
War of the Axe, 42
War on terror, 153
Warwick Trading Company of London, 65
Washington, Booker T., 91
Waterboer, Andries, 42, 131–132
Ways of Dying (Mda), 196
Webster, David, 231
Weekend Special (album), 119
Welcome to Our Hillbrow (Mpe), 181
Western Areas Removal Scheme, 271
Western Sahara, 8
Weyers, Dallie, 2
White press, 197
Wildcat strikes, 244
Williams, Sophie, 223
Wilson, Harold, 278
Wilson, Monica Hunter, 181
Wine industry: Huguenots, 138–139; Stellenbosch, 281
Witbooi, Hendrik, 214
Witbooi, Samuel, 215
Witwatersrand, 50–52, 256–257
Wolpe, Harold, 240
Wolseley, 49–50
Women and politics, 157–158, **311–314**; African National Congress Women's League, 7; AIDS and, 11–14, 136; Anglo-Boer war, 17; Baartman symbolizing black experience under apartheid, 29–30; Black Economic Empowerment, 36; civil society organizations, 69; customary law, 78; De Lille, Patricia, 81; early European immigrants, 98; economic differentials, 102; Ginwala, Frene Noshir, 124–125; health care system, 135; Islamic slaves, 151; literary expressions of resistance, 181; Mandela, Winnie, 190; Milner's reconstruction, 54; Ngoyi, Lillian, 223–224; Nongqawuse, 225–226; oral literary traditions, 179; pass laws protest, 232; Schreiner, Olive, 265; Suzman, Helen, 281–282; Truth and Reconciliation Commission, 294
Women's Budget Initiative (WBI), 313
Women's Charter, 312–313
Women's Day, 7, 224
Women's National Coalition (WNC), 312
Women's suffrage, 55
Wonderwerk Cave, 251
Worker Theater, 288
Workers' power, 248

World Alliance of Reformed Churches, 38
A World Apart (film), 67
World Bank: GEAR, 132
World Council of Churches (WCC), **315**
World Cup (2010), 63, 189, 276, 279
World Cups, 91
World heritage sites, 191, 261
World Trade Organization: AIDS treatment, 14
World War I, 214; Schreiner's criticism of, 265
World War II, 304
Writers. *See* Authors

Xenophobia, 143, 152
Xhosa, 156, **317–318**; Cape Colony, 59; Cape Colony expansion, 39–40; colonial novels, 180; Dutch colonialism, 97–98; folktale traditions, 179; Frontier Wars, 122; kwela, 164; Mfenga, 200; Ngqika, 224; Nongqawuse, 225–226; racial classification, 255; sangoma, 263, 265; segregation of University of Fort Hare, 306; Sisulu, Walter, 267; Soga's biblical translation, 270; Stellenbosch, 281; theater and performance, 286–287; war at Hintsa, 42; War of Mlanjeni, 44–45
Xuma, Alfred Bitini, 3–4, 177, 270, 304

Yesterday (film), 67
Yonge, George, 287
Youth culture: Kwaito, 163–164; Union opposition, 303; vigilantism, 309
Youth Day, 275–276
Youth movements: Democratic Alliance, 82

Zambia, 322–323; Frontline states, 122; Ngoni, 223
Zille, Helen, 82, 116
Zimbabwe, **319–320**; Frontline states, 122; Hani's military service, 133; Mapungubwe, 191; Mfecane, 200; mine workers' migration, 130; Mzilikazi, 211–212; Ndebele, 220; politics after 1999, 84; San rock art, 264; Tsonga, 296; Venda, 307–308
Zimbabwe African People's Front (ZANU), 319
Zimbabwe African People's Union (ZAPU), 319
Zionism, 159–160
Zonk magazine, 208
Zulu, 37, **320–322**; Anglo-Zulu War, 19; Bambatha Rebellion, 30; Battle of Blood River, 32–33; Buthelezi, Mangosuthu Gatsha, 57; Cetshwayo, 64; Champion, A.W.G., 64; 1870s uprisings, 47; the end of African independence, 49; founding by Lembede, 177; IFP, 150; isicathamiya, 151; Ladysmith Black Mambazo, 165; literary traditions, 179; Mfecane, 41–42, 199–200; Moshoeshoe's diplomatic efforts, 205; music, 207; Ndebele, 220, 319; Ngoni, 223; 1990s negotiations, 88; Ohlange Institute, 91; racial classification, 255; Retief's negotiation during the Great Trek, 258; sangoma, 263, 265; Shaka Zulu, 265–266; Swaziland population, 283; theater and performance, 286, 288; threats to Natal, 216; University of Fort Hare, 306; white fears of black uprising, 47
Zuma, Jacob Gedleyihlekisa, 6, 15, **322–323**; chieftancies, 149; COPE, 74; Mbeki firing, 195; Zulu, 321
Zuma, Nkosasana, 2

About the Book

This authoritative, comprehensive reference work covers South Africa's history, government and politics, law, society and culture, economy and infrastructure, demography, environment, and more, from the era of human origins to the present.

Nearly 300 alphabetically arranged entries provide information in a concise yet thorough way. In addition, a series of appendixes present a wealth of data, including a chronology of key events, key racial and apartheid legislation since 1856, heads of state (with party affiliation) since 1910, provinces and major cities, current government structures, and current political parties and representation in Parliament. Photographs enhance the text.

Members of the encyclopedia's international advisory board are R. Hunt Davis Jr., Sandra Klopper, Peter Limb, Zine Magubane, Dominique Malaquais, Shula Marks, and Barney Pityana.

Krista Johnson is assistant professor of African studies at Howard University. **Sean Jacobs** is assistant professor of international affairs at The New School.